Fourth Edition

ECONOMICS

THEORY IN ACTION

Ken Heather

University of Portsmouth

An imprint of Pearson Education

Harlow, England • London • New York • Boston • San Francisco • Toronto
Sydney • Tokyo • Singapore • Hong Kong • Seoul • Taipei • New Delhi
Cape Town • Madrid • Mexico City • Amsterdam • Munich • Paris • Milan

Pearson Education Limited

Edinburgh Gate
Harlow
Essex CM20 2JE
England

and Associated Companies throughout the world

Visit us on the World Wide Web at:
www.pearsoned.co.uk

First published 1994 as *Understanding Economics*
Second edition published 1997 as *Understanding Economics*
Third edition published 2000 as *Understanding Economics*
Fourth edition published 2004

ISBN 0273 67984 8

British Library Cataloguing-in-Publication Data
A catalogue record for this book is available from the British Library

10 9 8 7 6 5 4 3 2 1
09 08 07 06 05 04

Typeset in 9.5/12.5pt Stone Serif by 35
Printed by Ashford Colour Press Ltd, Gosport

The publisher's policy is to use paper manufactured from sustainable forests.

ECONOMICS
THEORY IN ACTION

PEARSON
Education

Contents

20 Exchange rates

List of applications

Economic ideas give us insights into the way people behave and enable us to consider important questions. Below are the issues we shall address in this book. I hope you enjoy thinking about these questions and that, in due course, you will feel fully equipped to come up with some answers!

Preface

If you are coming to the subject of economics for the first time, this book has been written for you. You may be an undergraduate in the first year of a course in business studies, accountancy, economics or any of the social sciences. You may be on a professional course requiring a knowledge of economics. You may be beginning an 'A' level course. This book has been written with you in mind.

Economics is a fascinating area of study. It deals with issues that have a great effect upon all of us. It is also a subject in which you will find considerable controversy. For example, why does the government worry about inflation? Is the euro a good idea? What is a fair wage? It is possible to confront the world of economic principles but lose sight of how those principles can be used to tackle issues that confront society: traffic jams, the state of the National Health Service, economic recessions and so on. As a result, several books have become available in recent years which consider current issues using economic analysis.

However, this book is not simply a list of topics of applied economic analysis. It sets out to address a series of issues of current concern, but in a particular order. The majority of economics courses and textbooks follow a set order in building up an understanding of economic analysis. The choice of applied topics in this text follows that development. It is therefore possible to study economic theory and to find in this book how each of the main areas of theory can be used to shed light on real world issues. In studying this book, then, the student will not learn everything there is to know about economic theory nor about every economic issue facing society. What the student *will* do is gain a good grasp of all the major analytical tools of introductory economic analysis and see how they can be used. It should then be possible to approach other topics of interest and analyse them because the student has begun to think like an economist and has learned to apply economic analysis to real problems.

Inevitably much has happened since the last edition of this book was published three years ago, necessitating this new revised edition. The structure of the book remains unaltered. The topics examined in the previous edition remain stimulating and challenging. However, each chapter has been altered to some degree to reflect current developments. Where appropriate I have added depth and expanded upon concepts without making the book longer.

I hope it will be possible to produce further editions of this text and, as with the earlier editions, I would be glad to receive any written correspondence at the University of Portsmouth (e-mail: Ken.Heather@port.ac.uk) with constructive criticisms or suggestions for improvements.

Ken Heather
University of Portsmouth
June 2003

Approach to the Fourth Edition

Updated material

It is astonishing how quickly the world changes. In the past three years since the third edition of this book we have seen, among other things, the events of 11 September 2001, acceptance of former communist societies into the European Union, a new currency circulating around most of Europe, stock-market upheavals around the world and serious concerns about deflation in a number of key economies. These and other changes are reflected in this new edition. All twenty chapters have been updated

More focus on Europe

As the UK moves ever closer to the rest of Europe, there is a greater focus on the European economy rather than just the UK economy. Whatever one's views about the UK's relationship with Europe, their futures seem to be ever more tightly bound and this edition recognises that.

New chapter on the oil market

The continuing decline of the UK coal industry makes it less useful as part of an illustration of market imperfection. So there is a new chapter using oil in general and OPEC in particular as the focus of monopoly power. Oil also seems more relevant in the wider context of the European economy.

Key websites

I have always been concerned not to overburden students, particularly as many readers are non-specialist students of economics. However, I have included references to a number of useful websites for those wanting to follow up an area of particular interest.

More Questions for discussion

I have expanded the Questions for discussion. At the end of each chapter there are ten questions. Guidance to the answers for the odd numbered questions is available on my website. Guidance to the answers for the even numbered questions is also available on the same website but these are password protected and available only to lecturers adopting the text. The website can be found at **www.booksites.net/heather**.

New Afterword

It is customary to include at the end of each chapter a brief summary of the main points covered. However, I have also included after the last chapter a summary of what the whole book is about. This gives, in just a few pages, an overview of the market mechanism and market failure. It also summarises the key areas of agreement and disagreement over the functioning of the economy at the macro level. I hope you find all these changes to this edition to be of real value.

Ken Heather
University of Portsmouth
June 2003

A word to the student

With this book you can learn a great deal about economic principles by working through economic problems that arise in the world. Before you begin your study here are six suggestions you may find helpful.

1 *Read the chapters in the correct order.* If you try to read just those topics which you find most interesting, you may find them difficult. Each chapter not only introduces ideas in economic theory but also uses concepts already met. You will best be able to build up your understanding by tackling the topics in the set order.

2 *Read each chapter slowly and actively.* No chapter is very long; you should not feel the need to rush. Make brief notes on what you read and draw the diagrams for yourself as you come to them. Doing so will fix things in your mind so much better. When you are referred to tables of data, take time to absorb the information they convey. If there is anything that you do not understand, you need to do something about it in one of two ways. First, you can refer to the Further Reading section given at the end of each chapter. This includes literature on the theoretical topics covered and further reading on the particular issue that the chapter is examining.

   The second way in which you can help yourself is to ask someone else. Try talking to a fellow student or raise the matter with your tutor, but do not leave it unresolved. The next concept will be understandable if you have grasped the previous one. Difficulties will probably arise if you have not made sure of what has gone before.

3 *Give time to the questions for discussion at the end of each chapter.* These questions are a vital part of the learning process. You may be studying on a course where the classes revolve around these questions. You will benefit greatly if you prepare and then take part in the discussion. If your contribution is correct and valid, you will gain confidence. If it is wrong because you have misunderstood something, then that will be put right and you will have gained by improving your understanding. One way or another, if you contribute orally, you must gain.

   If you are on a course where these questions will not be the basis of class discussion, then form your own study group and go through them together. The time will not be wasted. For all odd numbered questions there is guidance to the answers at **www.booksites.net/heather**.

4 *Do not imagine that, when you have studied a topic, you know all there is to know about it.* However much you study, there are always further insights to be gained. In this book you are being introduced to real world problems very early on, so remember that ideas that come later in the course will throw

additional light on topics met previously. It will be valuable if you can apply the ideas you meet not only to the question in hand but also to topics encountered earlier.

5 *Use the glossary at the back of the book.* Sometimes you will come across a term and be unable to remember what it means. Concise definitions of pertinent terms can be found in the glossary.
6 *When you have finished reading a chapter, look very carefully at the Chapter summary box.* You will have learned some key general economic principles: these are summarised in the box and it would be good to check that you have grasped these principles.
7 Finally, when you have studied all the chapters do read carefully the Afterword at the end of the book. It will, in just a few pages, draw together the main themes you have been studying throughout these pages.

Use this book well and by the end of it you will have made a substantial beginning to the process of thinking like an economist.

Outline of contents

Economics is often divided into two: microeconomics and macroeconomics. The first chapter introduces you to some basic concepts in both macro and micro. Microeconomics is the basis of Chapters 2–11. It deals with individual markets. Macroeconomics, the second half of the book (beginning at Chapter 12) deals with the broad aggregates of the economy. So micro will examine the establishment of the price of a particular good or service, for example shares in Chapter 2. Macro deals with the overall economy, for example the general price level in Chapter 15. Micro analyses a particular market, for example the oil industry in Chapter 7; macro will consider a whole sector, for example the manufacturing sector and its relationship to the balance of payments in Chapter 19. Bear in mind that later chapters will pick up and utilise concepts met in earlier chapters: in particular, when dealing with macroeconomic topics, much use is made of the micro principles already analysed.

By the time you come to the end of the book you should know what the major economic problems are and be in a position to engage in intelligent debate about any of them, even if you cannot offer solutions to all of them.

Additional sources of information

The book is self-contained. It will introduce you to the key concepts in economics and illustrate them with problems that are familiar to you. However, you may wish to find out a little more about one or more of the topics covered. So, at the end of each chapter there is a reference to at least one useful website where additional updated material can be found. Most of them will provide a wealth of statistical information that may be of value, especially if you wish to write an essay or engage in further research. These can be used as a launching pad to explore other websites, but the ones I have given are ones that I have found particularly useful.

Self-test questions

Each chapter of this book introduces the student to economic concepts in the context of one or two specific real world problems. However, the ideas have wide applicability. The purpose of the self-test questions are to enable students to test that they have a clear grasp of these principles by tackling multiple choice questions. There are three hundred questions, fifteen to cover the material from each of the twenty chapters of the book. They are designed to help students use the concepts in other contexts. The questions are available to purchasers of the book on the website which accompanies *Economics: Theory in Action* at **www.booksites.net/heather**.

A word to the instructor

This text has been designed to offer maximum flexibility. It can be used in many different ways.

1 The questions for discussion are designed to stimulate student interest. They could form the basis of a seminar programme. Each week the students can read the material, prepare the answers to the questions and bring them to the class. Although much of the discussion will revolve around formal concepts, those concepts will be related to a topic of current interest. The chapter that students have read will have given them ideas on how to apply principles to such topics – the very thing that students find hardest.

   The odd numbered questions are those to which the student can gain help by visiting **www.booksites.net/heather**. The even numbered answers on the website are password protected and available to adopters.

   The even numbered questions for discussion can be covered in around one hour in class. One chapter per week will probably be about right. This may be of particular value on large courses where different people lead different classes. The book will serve as an integrating device ensuring similar coverage for all class groups.

   If classes meet less often than weekly, you could go through some material in formal class groups and encourage the formation of self-help study groups to work through the rest of it.
2 The book is designed to be used as the main textbook for the course, particularly if the instructor wishes to concentrate his/her teaching on theoretical issues. The theory can then be expanded upon as necessary. The main elements of the theory and its relationship to the real world can be left to this book, preferably with discussion groups as suggested above. This may well be a particularly suitable approach to introductory economics courses on professional/business type courses.
3 The book could be used on non-specialist courses over a suitable period. At the end of each section of theoretical analysis a chapter could be used as a point of reference to revise the main elements covered as well as to see its application in the world. A chapter might then be read less often – perhaps every two weeks.
4 In addition to the above, the even numbered questions for discussion can be used as the basis of written assessed work. One could select a question as an essay title: often, the last one will be the best for this purpose. Alternatively, short answers to all of the questions can be requested. It can work well if students bring their answers for submission at the end of class, knowing that they can use what they have written as notes when they are called upon to contribute in the class.

5 Many students will eventually choose a topic for a dissertation. The book provides an initial reference for such work, showing how economic principles can be used to tackle problems and providing some additional references to websites.
6 Whilst the book is designed as a complete introduction to economics, it is possible to use parts of it on shorter courses. For example, an introductory micro course would be Chapters 1–11. A macro course for those having already studied micro would be Chapters 12–20. If the course is a macro one where the student has not studied any micro, then Chapters 1, 2, 5 and 12–20 would be most appropriate. Chapters 16 and 17 are rooted in principles of microeconomics. However, they are helpful for students learning macroeconomics. A crucial part of understanding macro revolves around the extent to which macro policy should utilise private markets.

In whatever way you choose to use it, the theory supporting the topics follows a standard traditional order so it can be used as a stand alone text or in conjunction with other books if required. It can also be used without alteration to your existing economics course.

Solutions to questions

An increasing problem for instructors is shortage of time. To save time needed for working through questions, solutions are available on the web. The solutions give suggested outline answers to the questions raised in the Questions for discussion sections. Go to **www.booksites.net/heather**. The students can access suggested answers to odd numbered questions. Tutors who adopt the text can go to the password protected answers to the even numbered questions. The result is that a complete tutorial package is now available: reading material, discussion material and material for instructors to guide discussion, although some instructors may prefer to work through the questions and prepare their own answers.

Self-test questions

Additional self-test questions are available on the website. They will prove invaluable since they enable the student to work through a set of exercises without recourse to a tutor.

Acknowledgements

I have received much help in writing this book and I wish to record my sincere thanks to those involved.

First, I must thank Dave Bibby and Rob Thomas, each of whom co-authored a chapter with me, and Dr Michael Asteris who shared in the writing of two chapters. Others kindly commented most helpfully on earlier drafts. It is a better book because of this help, but I take full responsibility for any errors and ambiguities that remain.

Since this is an applied text, I have used many sources of data. I would like to offer my thanks to those who gave permission to reproduce material for use in this book. My thanks are also due to the team at Pearson Education and I am particularly grateful to Ellen Morgan. Her insights were invaluable. Her warmth and humour were a great encouragement.

Finally, I wish to record my great gratitude to generations of my ex-students, who helped to sharpen my thinking on many issues. I have fond memories of so many of them, especially the few who still write to me. I recall with particular affection those I have been privileged to teach in other parts of the world especially those in Sofia, whose enthusiasm and kindness I cherish. We discovered that learning economics together can be at the same time both hard work and a lot of fun.

Publisher's acknowledgements

We are grateful to the following for permission to reproduce copyright material:

Figure 2.7 analysis and house price information from Nationwide Building Society; Table 3.1(a) from Department of Transport, Table 3.1(b) from *Road Transport Statistics of Great Britain* and Table 3.2 from *Transport Statistics Great Britain 2002*: Crown copyright material from these three tables is reproduced with the permission of the controller of the HMSO and the Queen's printer for Scotland; Table 3.3 from *The Capital at Risk*, CBI (CBI 1989); Table 3.4 from Land Transport Authority (Singapore); Table 3.5 from *General Household Survey* (Office for National Statistics 1999): Crown copyright material is reproduced with the permission of the controller of the HMSO and the Queen's printer for Scotland; Table 4.1 from the Commission on Macroeconomics on Health, WHO; Tables 5.1 and 14.2 and Figs 4.8, 14.7 and 14.8 from *Economic Trends*, various years (Office for National Statistics): Crown copyright material is reproduced with the permission of the controller of the HMSO and the Queen's printer for Scotland; Table 5.7 extracted from *EU Structural Funds: Commission Decides Financial Allocations*, Press Release IP/99/442, 1 July 1999 (European Commission) © European Communities, 1995–2003. Tables 6.3(a) and 6.3(b) from DTI (SME Statistics Unit 2002); Fig. 6.2 from *OECD Labour Force Statistics 1972–92* (OECD); Table 6.5 from DTI (Small Firms Statistics Unit 2002); Figs 7.1, 7.2, 7.11 and Table 7.1 from *BP Statistical Review of World Energy 2002*, BP plc; Tables 8.2

and 8.4 and Figs 8.3 and 9.9 from *World Air Transport Statistics, 2002*, IATA; Tables 9.5, 14.5 and 20.7 from *Bank of England Quarterly Bulletin*, various years, and Fig. 18.11 *Inflation Report* (2002), Bank of England; Table 10.2 and Figs 10.10 to 10.15 © UK National Audit Office; Table 11.5 from *Labour Market Trends*, Office for National Statistics, Crown copyright material is reproduced with the permission of the Controller of HMSO and the Queen's Printer for Scotland; Table 11.6 from *Labor Economics: A Comparative Text*, McGraw Hill (Elliott, R.F. 1991), by kind permission of Prof. Elliott; Tables 12.3, 12.4, 12.5, 14.1 and Fig. 12.5 from *Blue Book*, Office for National Statistics, Crown copyright material is reproduced with the permission of the Controller of HMSO and the Queen's Printer for Scotland; Tables 12.6 and 12.7 from Norwegian Meteorological Institute/EMEP/MSC-W; Fig. 13.10 adapted from *Economic Outlook* © OECD, (2003); Figs 13.11, 15.2 to 15.5, 15.12, 18.7 and Table 20.3 from *The Economist*, various issues, © The Economist Newspaper Ltd, London; Fig. 15.10 original data from *Monthly Bulletin*, © European Central Bank (Dec. 2002); Table 16.6 from 'Inflation and the UK Labour Market', *Oxford Review of Economic Policy*, Oxford University Press (Nickell, S. 1990); Tables 16.7 and 16.8 from *By Our Own Bootstraps*, Federal Reserve Bank of Dallas; Table 17.4 from 'Economic Deregulation: Days of Reckoning for Microeconomists', *Journal of Economic Literature*, American Economic Association (Winston, C. 1993); Figure 17.7 from 'Slump intervenes in capitalist culture clash', *Financial Times*, 6th November, 2002; Tables 18.2(a) and 18.2(b) from *The European Central Bank: Reshaping Monetary Politics in Europe*, Centre for Economic Policy Research (Alesina, A. and Grilli, V.U. 1991); Fig. 18.10 from 'Central Bank Independence and Macroeconomic Performance: Some Comparative Evidence', *Journal of Money, Credit and Banking*, Ohio State University Press (Alesina, A. and Summers, L.H. 1993); Tables 19.1, 19.2 and Fig. 19.5 from *United Kingdom Balance of Payments*, Office for National Statistics, Crown copyright material is reproduced with the permission of the Controller of HMSO and the Queen's Printer for Scotland; Fig. 19.4 from Wood Mackenzie Consultants Ltd; Table 19.3 from *Economic Bulletin*, Lloyds TSB (April 1999); Fig. 20.5 from *Lloyds Bank Economic Bulletin*, Lloyds Bank (March 1992); Table 20.6 from *Worldwide Benefit and Employment Guidelines*, Mercer Human Resource Consulting.

In some instances we have been unable to trace the owners of copyright material, and we would appreciate any information that would enable us to do so.

Part I

INTRODUCTORY CONCEPTS

Part IV THE INTERNATIONAL ECONOMY
Part III MACROECONOMICS
Part II MICROECONOMICS
Part I INTRODUCTORY CONCEPTS

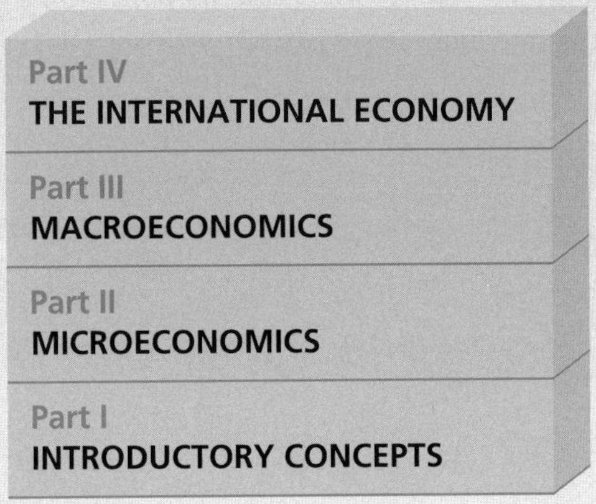

Each part of the book adds a 'building block' in constructing an understanding of how the economic system functions. In this first part we lay a foundation by covering the introductory concepts of economics.

1 Economic models and opportunity cost

East European economic reforms: *the road to freedom?*

CHAPTER OVERVIEW

At the beginning of a new century the old USSR and many of its now independent satellite states are still trying to move their economic system to a western market-based economy – so far with mixed success. The transition is proving costly and difficult.

In this chapter we explain why this is so, introducing the following concepts:

- Economic models
- Resources and opportunity cost
- Market and planned economies

1.1 Introduction

When the old Soviet Union was dismantled in the late 1980s and early 1990s, the way was open for its former communities to form independent governments. Most of the leaders of these newly independent countries wasted no time in declaring that they wished to transform their economic systems into western-style ones. It was clear that the bureaucratic, centralised approach in which they had been obliged to operate had failed. Average incomes were only a fraction of those enjoyed in the West. A western-style market economy would, they hoped, give far greater efficiency in production and lead rapidly to improvements in living standards.

Despite some significant changes in former Soviet-controlled states, this simply has not happened in many countries. Although there have been some places where things have improved substantially, in many of these economies things appear worse now than twenty years ago. Take, for example, Romania. The communist regime of President Ceausescu disappeared in December 1989. The elected government of May 1990 began quickly to change the direction of its economic policies and by the end of that year it had ended price controls on half its products. Table 1.1, though, gives a depressing picture of the state of the economy thereafter.

Table 1.1 Selected economic indicators in Romania (% change)

	1989	*1991*	*1993*	*1995*	*1997*	*1998*	*1999*	*2000*	*2001*	*2002*[a]	*2003*[a]
Real gross domestic product	−5.8	−13.7	1.3	6.9	−6.6	−4.8	−1.1	1.8	5.3	4.0	4.4
Consumer prices	0.9	161.1	256	32.3	154.8	59.3	45.9	45.7	34.5	25.0	21.0
Unemployment rate	0.0	3.0	10.4	9.9	8.8	10.3	11.5	10.5	8.6	na	na

[a] Forecast

Source: adapted from IMF; UN, *Economic Survey of Europe*; Economist Intelligence Unit

Let us make sure that we understand the meaning of the terms given in Table 1.1.[1] *Real gross domestic product* (GDP) means the value of the output of goods and services the country is producing. The change is negative, i.e. output was falling for four years after 1989 and then again in the late 1990s. The change in output has been positive since 2000. However, recent rises have not been sufficient to restore living standards to those of 1989. Consumer prices give us a measure of what is happening to the general level of retail prices. Clearly these prices were rising sharply in the early 1990s: there was rapid inflation. Also, the rate at which those prices were rising increased remarkably for a time. Even though the rises are more modest in recent years, they are still high by West European standards.

In other words, after the period of reforms had started, key indicators of economic activity were moving in the direction opposite to what might have been hoped and improvements are now coming slowly and erratically. Some of the other economies of this kind present a similar picture. Most people expected the gap in living standards between these countries and Western Europe to close rapidly. It has yet to do so. Figure 1.1 shows that most countries had lower levels of output in 2001 than in 1989. The figures are based on index numbers. The level of GDP in 1988 for each economy is set at 100. The numbers for 1999 are given in the figure. Poland, then, was producing 28.1 per cent more output in 2001 than in 1989 whereas some economies, such as Georgia and the Ukraine, were producing less than half of what they produced in 1989.

One explanation of the fall in living standards and output is seen in Table 1.1. Unemployment has been high so that a substantial part of the potential working population is contributing nothing to the economy. You may be surprised by the data relating to unemployment. Why was it so low in 1989? Why did it increase so rapidly after that time? Why has such a depressing picture emerged? By the end of this chapter you should have gained some insights into the reasons. However, it is necessary that you first understand the approach that economists usually take in examining such problems. Indeed, you will find this approach often in this book, so you will need to be clear about it at the outset. Economists deal with problems by constructing economic 'models'. What is meant by this?

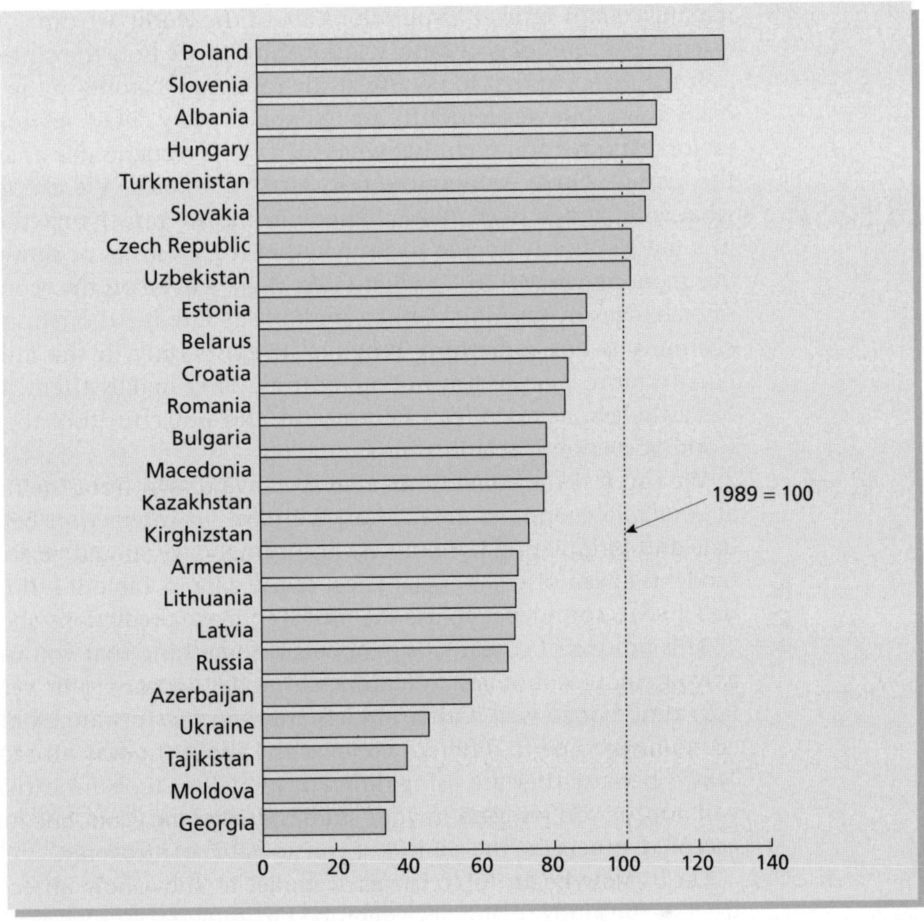

Figure 1.1 Levels of GDP in 1989 and 2001

Source: adapted from UN, *Economic Survey of Europe*

1.2 Use of economic models

When economists wish to examine a problem, they have difficulties not faced by physical scientists. One such difficulty is that they cannot make experiments under controlled laboratory conditions. It is not possible to shake people and prices around in a test tube to see how they react.

It is, however, possible to gain an insight into the main economic relationships that exist by the construction of an economic model. Suppose we make a model railway engine. It may not be the real thing, but it is clearly recognisable as a replica of the original. We can play around with the model, increasing our understanding of how the real one works, and we can experiment by altering certain parts inside and seeing what effect the change produces. This may enable us to discover what would happen without having to experiment on the real thing. The same is true in principle of constructing an *economic* model. By making certain general assumptions about the world, we can concentrate on the essential features of economic relationships to see how they interact.

It may seem at first to be unrealistic to ignore features of the world which are really there, but we are not trying to explain every detail, merely to establish the major relationships, such that what we have is recognisable as an explanation of the way in which economic society can be ordered. We can also then predict what will happen if we make changes. Just as we can change the size of a piston in a model railway engine to see whether it goes faster or slower, so we can use our economic model to see what effect there will be on the economy because of, say, changes in taxation. Unlike the railway engine, though, our model of the economy is not something tangible. It exists only in the mind or on paper. Furthermore people are not machines. This makes them less predictable. Nevertheless, a model can be a useful and powerful tool to analyse the real world of economic relationships.

We can test the conclusions that we have drawn from the model by looking at available economic data. Thus, we have an interaction between observing data and formulating hypotheses. Accordingly, we should be able to construct a model that can offer an explanation of the data in Table 1.1. If the model 'fits' it will give us confidence to use the model to make predictions about the future.

This process of constructing models is something that you will observe often as you study economics. Sometimes a model appears to fit very well, but at a later time not so well. Other models are then put forward. Sometimes different economists come to different conclusions about the way an economy operates. This is because they are using different models as tools for explaining data. You will find, as you progress in your studies, that some economic models are widely accepted; others are the subject of considerable controversy.

Let us now begin to construct a model to show how an economy can find itself in the kinds of difficulty described in Table 1.1.

1.3 Beginning to construct a model

Resources in economics

Microeconomics is all about choice. The essence of choice is that in the selection of one thing we have decided to go without another. This is sometimes called the 'economic problem'. Man's wants are unlimited. There are basic needs of food, clothing, shelter and health; but there are also desires for education, travel, entertainment, books and so on. However, resources necessary for the production of these goods and services are limited. Hence the level of output is necessarily finite, but needs and wants are infinite. Clearly, then, society must make choices about which kinds of output it wants to use its resources to produce. The resources, or factors of production, available to society can conveniently be divided into four main categories.

First, there is *labour*. Some people have the ability to make things; others have the mental ability to work out how to make them. For example, one person may

Table 1.2 Real gross fixed capital formation in selected European economies (indices 1989 = 100 or earliest year available)

	1989	*1990*	*1995*	*2001*
Poland	100	75.2	96.2	157.5
Romania	100	64.4	68.3	73.5
Slovakia	–	100	67.7	100.1
Ukraine	–	100	19.1	18.8

Source: adapted from UN, *Economic Survey of Europe* data

think of how to design a machine for making knitting needles, while another may make the machine itself from instructions. Both are involved in making output. They are therefore a 'resource', and since the population is limited, a finite resource. Over time this resource that we call labour may increase. For example, if the birth rate is sufficiently high and the death rate sufficiently low, or if there is immigration, the labour supply will increase. However, at any moment in time, labour supply is finite. Hence the amount of output that labour can produce for satisfying society's wants is similarly finite.

Second, there is *capital*. Capital is a manufactured resource. Factories, machinery, office buildings are all examples of capital. At first this may not seem to be a finite resource: one could always build more buses or police stations. While this is true, at any moment in time there is a limit to the amount available. Even if a society chooses to have more of such capital goods, it must then have less of something else. If we increase the capital stock over time, we call this act *investment* or *Fixed Capital Formation*. A lack of investment is particularly noticeable in Eastern Europe, where so many machines are antiquated and buildings are in poor condition. The investment picture is mixed. The volume of investment in all Eastern European economies fell after 1989/90 as can be seen from Table 1.2. However, after the turn of the century the picture was very mixed. For example, in Poland investment levels are over 50 per cent higher, in Slovakia they have returned to the levels of the communist era. In Romania they are substantially lower and in the Ukraine investment levels are less than one-fifth of what they were in 1990. These figures are 'gross', meaning that all additions to capital are included, whether they replaced what was worn out, or added to the stock. Since much of the capital was wearing out, the figures suggest that these societies were creating less new capital than is ideal. However, even in western economies, where the capital stock is much higher, the supply of capital is still not infinite.

Third, there is *land*. This is most obviously the resource that is limited. Apart from small land reclamation schemes, notably in Holland, the amount of land available is clearly limited, though for what was previously the USSR the amount of land is vast.

Fourth and finally, there are *other natural resources*. These include, for example, fish stocks, coal seams and oil deposits. Siberia, for example, has enormous oil and mineral wealth, as yet largely unused. Increasingly, media attention has been focused on the view that many of these resources are non-renewable. When oil has been burned for heating, it cannot be used again, although presumably there are, as yet, undiscovered oil reserves. The same is true of other resources. Even though there are resources as yet untapped, such as wave power and deep-sea mineral deposits, there is a limited amount available since we live in a finite world. Furthermore, they are only exploitable with investment. Certainly there is a limited amount of such resources which society can use at any given moment.[2]

Now, whatever the society – whether it is the wealthiest nation on earth, or a relatively poor one such as Romania, or a desperately poor one such as some African economies – each has resources; none has an infinite amount of them. They all have to make choices.

The concept of opportunity cost

Since resources are limited, society has to choose between alternatives. We may desire more accountants and more doctors, but one person cannot be both at the same time. Romania might like more orphanages and more hospitals, but any one building can be used for only one of these purposes. Society must choose how it wishes to use that capital. Similarly we might like more food and more roads but we shall have to choose to which use we wish to put a given piece of land. The same choice confronts us with natural resources. Oil, for example, is something we can use to heat people's homes or to lubricate motor engines but the same barrel of oil cannot do both tasks.

The economist expresses this idea in terms of a concept called *opportunity cost*. Since to make some given output we must commit some limited resources that have an alternative use, the next best alternative that has to be forgone is called the opportunity cost of its production. Suppose a man is an economist and he then changes his job and becomes a policeman. The services of protection of people and property that he produces are only provided at the opportunity cost of the services of an economist. The economist's services must be forgone in order to have the services of the policeman. The principle of opportunity cost applies to all factors of production, not just labour.[3]

An opportunity cost curve

The concept of opportunity cost can be illustrated in a diagram. Figure 1.2 shows the position for the economy of Anyland. We shall use this name as a reminder that although different economies have different resources and different *amounts* of resources, the principles of opportunity cost will apply to *any* economy. Only two goods can be produced each year – here guns and butter.[4] Given that the resources available to the nation are limited, the nation must decide how best to employ its resources. For example, it could decide to use all its resources to produce guns. Society would then have all guns and no butter, a position described by point X. Alternatively, all the economy's resources could be devoted to the production of butter. It would then have a certain output of butter per annum but zero guns; a position described by point Y. Suppose, however, Anyland wanted both guns and butter. By devoting some of its resources to each of these goods, it could produce at, say, point Z, where it could enjoy,

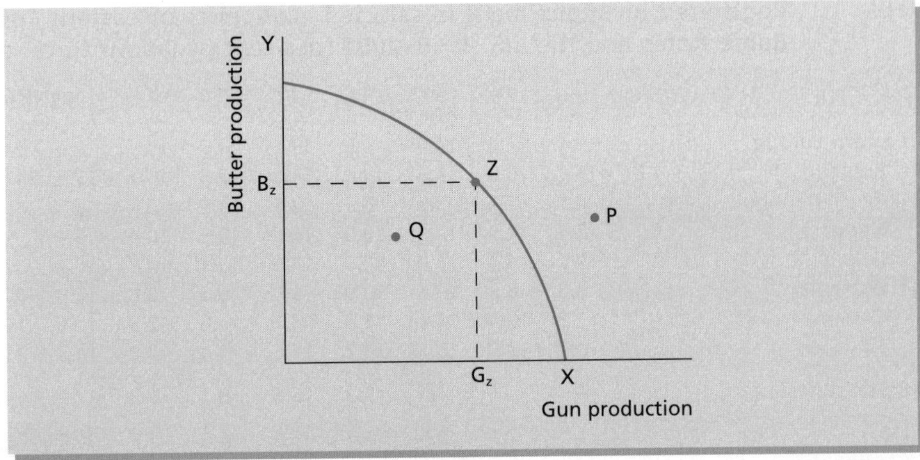

Figure 1.2 Production possibility curve, Anyland

per annum, G_z guns and B_z butter. The curve connecting X and Y would then describe all the different combinations of guns and butter that could be available to Anyland at any given time. Anyland can choose which of these combinations it would prefer. In other words, it decides the point on the curve at which it would most like to be. Since the curve describes the possibilities open to an economy during the course of a year, we sometimes call it a 'production possibility frontier'. A point outside the frontier, such as P, is unavailable to Anyland given its limited volume of resources. It is unable to produce such a level of output. Position Q, on the other hand, would indicate that some resources are not being used efficiently. People would not choose it. They prefer to have more of both goods. The problem for an economy if it *were* at point Q is either one of unemployment or that all resources are being used but some are being used inefficiently. Where this is the case, the opportunity cost of increasing output is nil.

Now look at Table 1.3. You will see how the unemployment situation appeared to worsen markedly as Eastern Europe changed its economic system. Official figures of unemployment rates in the days before Eastern Europe began moving to a market economy were zero. A significant part of the explanation for this is simply that everyone had a job. However, much of it was what we might call disguised unemployment. Several people were employed to do a job which one could do. The shift to a market economy uncovered this 'disguised' unemployment. These societies were inside the opportunity cost curve in 1989, although the data showed virtually no unemployment. Now unemployment in some of these economies is still high by Western European standards but in others it is comparable.

Resources and increasing opportunity cost

Why is the line between X and Y not straight? Why does it curve outwards from the origin? The answer is to be found in the nature of resources. Suppose

Table 1.3 Registered unemployment in selected economies of eastern Europe, the Baltic states and the CIS, 1990–2001 (per cent of labour force, end of period)

	1990	*1991*	*1992*	*1993*	*1994*	*1995*	*1996*	*1997*	*1998*	*1999*	*2000*	*2001*
Eastern Europe	–	9.6	12.4	14.0	13.6	12.5	11.7	11.9	12.6	14.6	15.2	–
Bulgaria	1.8	11.1	15.3	16.4	12.8	11.1	12.5	13.7	12.2	16.0	17.9	17.3
Czech Republic	0.7	4.1	2.6	3.5	3.2	2.9	3.5	5.2	7.5	9.4	8.8	8.9
Hungary	1.7	7.4	12.3	12.1	10.9	10.4	10.5	10.4	9.1	9.6	8.9	8.0
Poland	6.5	12.2	14.3	16.4	16.0	14.9	13.2	10.3	10.4	13.1	15.1	17.4
Romania	1.3	3.0	8.2	10.4	10.9	9.5	6.6	8.8	10.3	11.5	10.5	8.6
Slovakia	1.6	11.8	10.4	14.4	14.8	13.1	12.8	12.5	15.6	19.2	17.9	18.6
Slovenia	–	10.1	13.3	15.5	14.2	14.5	14.4	14.8	14.6	13.0	12.0	11.8
Baltic states	–	–	2.1	4.5	5.3	6.6	6.4	6.3	7.3	9.1	10.0	10.1
CIS	–	–	2.7	3.6	4.4	5.8	6.6	7.6	9.0	8.3	7.0	6.2
Armenia	–	–	3.5	6.3	6.0	8.1	9.7	11.0	8.9	11.5	10.9	9.8
Russian Federation	–	–	5.2	6.1	7.8	9.0	10.0	11.2	13.3	12.2	9.8	9.0
Ukraine	–	–	0.3	0.4	0.3	0.6	1.5	2.8	4.3	4.3	4.2	3.7

Source: adapted from UN, *World Economic Survey* data

Anyland is now producing all guns and no butter – it is at point X. Its citizens then decide they would like some butter for next year. Clearly, there is an opportunity cost involved. Since all its factors of production are already being used, resources must be transferred from gun production to butter production. Therefore the butter output will only be achieved at the sacrifice of some gun output. However, since all Anyland's resources are at present engaged in gun-making, only some resources need to be transferred. Obviously, the best resources to be transferred are resources least suited to producing guns and most suited to producing butter. So, for instance, if we take cows out of gun-making, the loss of gun output to Anyland is likely to be small. But putting them into butter production may well achieve the output of a significant amount of butter. Figure 1.3 serves to show this. Anyland has moved from X to X′. Butter output has risen from nothing to B′ and gun output has declined from its maximum at X only to G′. However, it should be clear that increasing butter output further will be possible only at a higher and higher opportunity cost. This is partly because resources transferred are less and less ideally suited to butter production and partly because those same resources are more and more suitable for gun production.

Suppose Anyland at some stage were to be producing on the curve somewhere near Y, with only a small volume of gun output and a large amount of butter output. Now, a further increase in butter output is possible only through the transference of resources highly suited to gun production, for example, gunsmiths. The curve suggests, then, that increased output of a good is possible only at an increasing opportunity cost.

It should be clear that the curve does not, nor is it supposed to, make any comment on what society's preferences are for various kinds of output. It only indicates what possibilities are open to an economy. Two nations, one butter-loving and the other gun-loving, might well be faced with the same possibilities

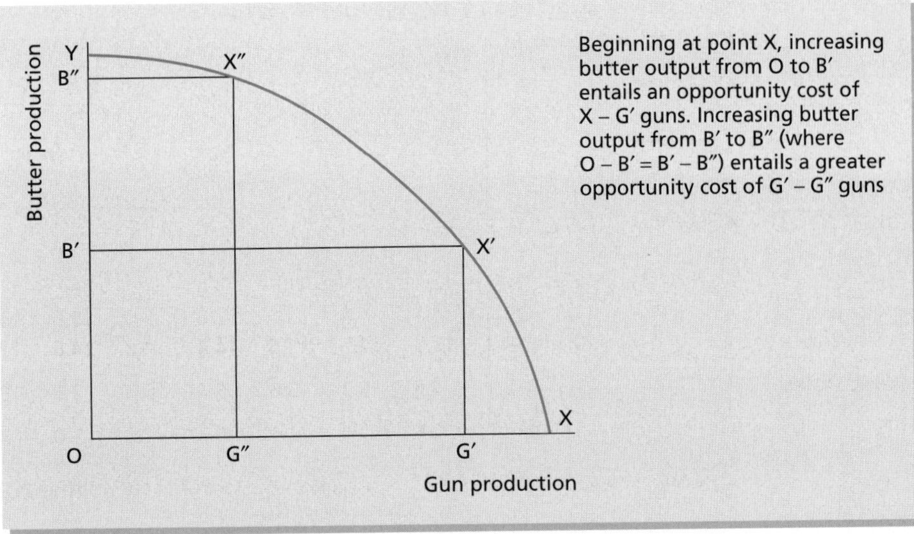

Figure 1.3 Increasing opportunity cost in Anyland

for output if their resources are the same, but their choice of where on the curve they wish to be will be different.

Opportunity cost of investment

The same principle of opportunity cost will apply in choices that the community must make concerning consumption now or in the future. Some resources could be put to either present consumption or future consumption. A piece of steel could be used to make a machine this year to produce something next year or it could be used to make a washing machine for someone to use immediately. Thus, our society faces a choice. How much current consumption do we wish to have? The more we consume the less is available for investment and therefore the less consumption there will be next year. For Anyland the choices would be described by Figure 1.4. Suppose Anyland chose point Z, where its citizens would enjoy OC'_t current consumption. They would be forgoing present consumption of X – C'_t, a volume of goods which they could have enjoyed in addition to the output C'_t. This was forgone so that some resources could be used for investment purposes. This investment in machinery, etc., will enable consumption next year of C'_{t+1}. If the process is to be worthwhile, this year's forgone consumption will generally have to be less than the consumption it will make available for next year. You can see from Figure 1.4 that this is so.

What should be clear is that the 'economic problem' which the opportunity cost curve displays is not a problem faced by some societies because of their particular economic or political systems. It is a problem faced by all societies whatever system they use. Different economic and political systems can be viewed as different ways of attempting to solve the problem. Two such systems are the planned economy, once used in such societies as Romania, and the market economy to which most are trying to move.

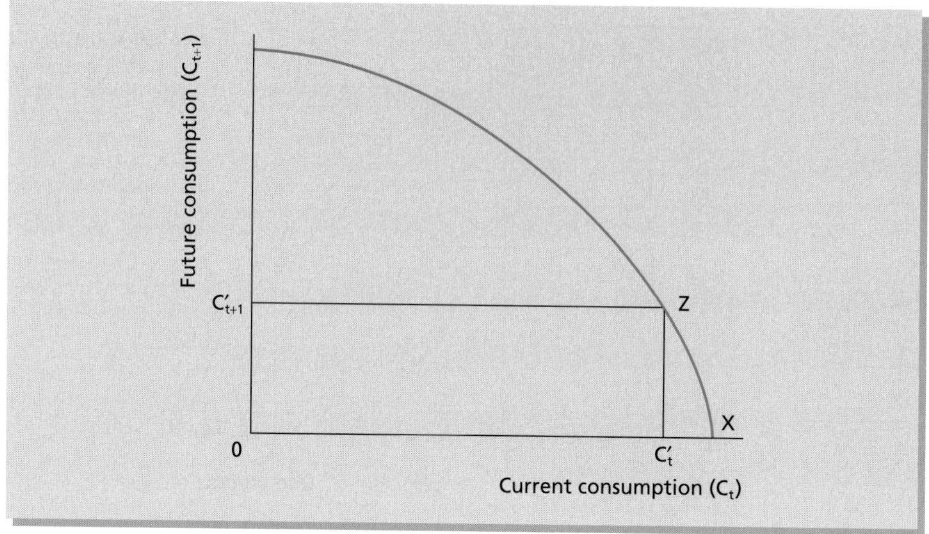

Figure 1.4 Opportunity cost of investment

An idea of the extent of that movement is given in Table 1.4. These countries are referred to as 'transition economies' on the assumption that they are in the process of a movement from a state-planned economy to a market-dominated one. Two things are immediately clear. First, even if the benefits of a market

Table 1.4 Selected transition economies: estimates of the private sector's percentage contribution to GDP

	1990	*1994*	*1998*
Central and Eastern Europe (CEE)			
Bulgaria	9	40	50
Czechoslovakia	5	–	–
Czech Republic	–	65	75
Slovakia	–	55	75
Hungary	16	70	80
Latvia	10	55	60
Lithuania	12	62	70
Poland	31	55	65
Romania	16	35	60
Commonwealth of Independent States			
Belarus	6	15	20
Russian Federation	na	25	70
Ukraine	11	30	55
Uzbekistan	10	20	45

Source: adapted from UN, *World Economic Outlook*; European Bank for Reconstruction and Development; World Bank

economy are not clearly established, progress towards forming such an economy has been made. In some economies the market sector now dominates. Second, some of the transition economies are proceeding much more rapidly towards a market-dominated economy than are others. Later in the chapter an explanation is offered of why this might be so.

1.4 Developing the model: two types of economy

Opportunity cost and planned economies

In section 1.2 above we showed how society must make choices. A key question for any society is: how are society's preferences going to be articulated so that those who control the resources allocate them such that what society wishes is produced? We shall first see how a planned economy answers this question, and in so doing we shall see how this type of economic system earns its name.

In a planned economy, resources are owned by the government. The government decides what society needs and then issues instructions about what output to make. The prices to be charged for the output are also set by government.[5] These prices can be set at a level that is fair and reasonable to purchasers. However, it is this system that has been rejected by many states in recent years. There are four main reasons for this, each of which can be related back to Figure 1.2.

First, if decisions are taken by government for its citizens, there is no reason to suppose that their needs and preferences will be correctly anticipated. People might prefer, for example, more food and less clothing, more cars and less heating than government decides. That is why, by contrast, in market economies decisions are made by households themselves. The communist authorities discovered how strongly people wished to be free to make their own decisions. In terms of Figure 1.2, society might prefer to be on a different point of the opportunity cost curve than that which is selected by government. There is also the distinct possibility that those who make the decisions will reflect their own preferences rather than reflect the preferences of the people. A significant feature of these societies has been the continued mistrust of politicians, though you may not think that is very different in market economies.

Second, the planned system raises enormous coordination problems. The goods that people purchase are called final goods. In order to produce them many intermediate goods are produced, that is goods made by one industry to be used by another. For example, one may buy a car, a final good. To make this possible, rubber, steel and electric wiring have been made by intermediate industries for the car producer. Now, if in a planned economy a decision is taken that one million loaves of bread are needed per day, there is implied in that one decision hundreds of other decisions that must be consistent. This amount of bread requires an adequate amount of wheat to be grown, a sufficient number of combine harvesters, sufficient steel, enough coal, and so on. Now the coordination of these decisions has proved increasingly difficult. If the production of one intermediate good fails, it has enormous knock-on effects for the whole system. Output is lower than it might be. We are inside the opportunity cost curve of Figure 1.2.

Third, the selection of an appropriate price at which to sell the final output creates difficulties. Often the price of a good is one at which the quantity people wish to buy is greater than the amount that is available for sale. The result is long queues for basic commodities. Shortages of this kind are one aspect of inefficiency that puts a society inside the opportunity cost curve.

Fourth, there is the problem of incentive. If wages are also administered, there is no reward for producing beyond a specified target. There is thus no reason to try very hard. The inevitable inefficiency means again that society is inside the opportunity cost curve. But it has a further cost: there is no incentive to learn how to do things better so that, over time, the economy can grow and output can be increased. The opportunity cost curve is not going to move out from the origin over time as far and as fast as it might.

Opportunity cost and prices in market economies

Many East European economies, then, aspire to a western-type market economy. How do these western economies solve the economic problem? The basic means of dealing with the economic problem in a market system is by establishing a link between prices and opportunity cost. Resources are not owned by the state but are privately owned. People are free to use the resources they own in whatever way they wish. You probably have a resource – labour – capable of producing output. When you finish studying economics you may well choose to use it to produce output. You are free to allocate your resource in any way you like. The government will not command you to produce output that it feels others in the community need. How does this lead us to a link between prices and opportunity cost?

Why do you expect to pay more for a new pair of jeans than for an ice cream? In essence the answer is that to produce these goods resources have to be committed to their production. Since more resources are needed to produce the jeans than the ice cream, those people involved in jeans production will not invest the greater resources unless they are persuaded that this is worth doing. The price you pay for a good, then, should reflect the opportunity cost of the resources allocated to its production. Take this book. You would have appreciated the chance to buy it for less. But many people – author, publisher and printer – had to give time to its production, time they could have used for something else. Owners of the capital, printing presses, and so on, could have allocated their resources elsewhere. The price reflected what you had to pay to draw resources into this area of activity – the resources' opportunity cost. Only by the end of the book will you have fully realised what an excellent choice from your limited income you have made.

Now, the publisher would have liked to charge a much higher price than the modest sum for which you were asked. The problem was that you have a limited income. By purchasing the book you denied yourself the opportunity to buy something else: you were not prepared to pay more than the opportunity cost to you of the forgone goods. In a market system, it is this principle of opportunity cost that underlines how the economic problem is dealt with.

Relative price changes in market economies

Armed with this understanding we can see why, over time, prices of goods and services in a market system change dramatically. We illustrate this with some prices taken from an encyclopaedia (Table 1.5), showing price changes over the whole of the last century. First, though, we must be clear what the numbers are that we are looking at. The first column gives the actual price for a selection of goods and services in each year quoted. However, over time, the price level had risen dramatically. The average item was *57 times* more expensive in 1999 than in 1899 (although average incomes had increased by far more than that). So the second column revalues each item to show what the price would have been in each year had the 1899 price level obtained throughout the period. Clearly, what is happening to the general level of prices is of great interest (indeed, it is the subject matter of Chapter 15). But what we are interested in here is *relative* price: how much does one product cost in terms of another? The third column

Table 1.5 Relative prices in Britain over 100 years

Item	*Cost in 1899*	*Equivalent cost in 1999*	*Actual cost in 1999*
Full set of leather *Encyclopaedia Britannica*	£65	£3,741	£49 CD Rom
A copy of *The Times*	3d	£0.72	£0.30
Pair of Levi jeans	£4	£230	£49
$\frac{1}{2}$ lb loaf of Hovis	4d	£0.95	£0.63
Return journey from Crystal Palace to Ludgate Hill	6d	£1.44	Before 9.30am £4.70 + underground After 9.30am £4.60 travel card
Milk powder	11d	£2.63	£1.15
Plain chocolate 1 lb	1s 6d	£4.31	£1.06 (400 grams)
Black glazed rubber Wellington boots	21s	£60.43	£9.99
Standard Raleigh gents bike	£8 10s	£489.21	£400
Pint of beer	1p	£0.24	£1.90
Packet of cigarettes	5s	£14.4	£3.84
Jacobs cream crackers	11d	£2.64	£0.46

enables us to see whether prices had fallen or risen *relative* to other goods over that period. So while almost everything went up in price during the century, the relative price of most items quoted had fallen quite significantly.

Why is information from the encyclopaedia so cheap to acquire now? As technology has improved, the volume of resources needed to produce a copy of it has fallen. A CD Rom uses far less resources than a shelf of books. Fewer resources mean a lower opportunity cost of producing that output. Prices reflect opportunity cost in a market system, so if the opportunity cost is falling over time, one would expect its relative price to be falling.

Why has the price of a rail journey risen relatively as well as absolutely? One possible explanation is a decrease in subsidies so that price now more accurately reflects opportunity cost. You might study Table 1.5 and speculate upon the reason for the significant changes in the relative prices of other goods.

So we now understand a key idea of how a market system uses prices to deal with the problem of resource allocation.

Planned versus market economies

Now let us think through what we saw earlier were the problems of using a planned economy. In doing so we shall see how a market system, which allows changes in relative prices, can overcome these problems.

First, planned economies require a central authority to decide what to produce to meet people's needs. In a market system people express their own preferences by how they use their incomes. When you buy something in the shops because it reflects your preferences, and since the price you pay reflects the resources used in its production, then you are determining how those resources are allocated. Thus resources in a market system follow consumers' wishes, so that we move towards the best spot on the opportunity cost curve.

Second, governments do not need to coordinate decisions between intermediate and final buyers. Markets operate in intermediate industries too. The market determines not only the price of a car but also the price that the car industry pays for the component parts.

Third, governments do not have to administer prices. Prices are determined by the market. They move to a level at which the available output matches people's preferences. It is rare to see people in the West queue for hours to buy food or clothes. The price acts as a rationing device. You may feel that shopping in Sainsbury's on Christmas Eve is an exception to that rule. If so, you are beginning to think like an economist. Before reading on you might ask yourself why Sainsbury's does not raise prices on Christmas Eve.

Fourth, the problem of an absence of incentives is solved by a market system. Since people are paid a price for their output which reflects what buyers are prepared to pay, they have an incentive to produce what society actually wants.

Of course, a market system is not without its problems. It is not perfectly efficient. It has not always produced full employment. Many people feel that it gives an unfair distribution of income – too much for the rich, too little for the poor.[6] These and other problems we shall consider in detail in later chapters, but there are several things we can say about our market model now.

One needs to appreciate that it is only a model. Its conclusions are only as good as its assumptions. We shall see during our studies that, given the right conditions, a market system is the best that can be done with the economic problem. To use the jargon, it represents the optimal solution. However, the assumptions rarely hold in practice. We must also bear in mind that we can increase the validity of the model – and we shall do so. However, the cost is its increasing complexity. So we shall start with something simple and, as confidence grows, make it more realistic.

One can say, furthermore, that the market system must have a great deal to commend it. The enthusiasm of almost the whole of Eastern Europe for rejecting the planned economy and embracing the market is a powerful testimony to its perceived advantages. One must also be aware, though, that no society has ever seen fit to embrace a market system wholly. Some output is always in the hands of government: in Britain that output includes much of health care, much of education, national defence, and more besides.[7] In practice then, western societies are mixed economies, although the mix varies. For example, well over half of what Sweden produces is taken by its government in taxes. This is a measure of the extent to which decisions about spending are made for them by government. In the United States that figure is under one-third.

Although western market-orientated economies have produced much more output per head than planned economies, there is within advanced western economies no close correlation between the extent of government intervention and output per head or growth of output per head. Japan has a relatively small government sector and, until relatively recently, a high growth rate. Sweden has a very large state sector and a very low growth rate. On the other hand, the United States, with a very similar sized government sector to Japan, has, until relatively recently, a much poorer growth rate. Norway, with a substantial state sector, has a growth record which is quite impressive.

1.5 From planned to market economies: some problems

We have seen why East European states have attempted to shift their economic system towards a more market-orientated one. We have also seen that they still have substantial problems. Investment rates are still quite low. Unemployment rates are, in many cases, high. Finally, we use our model to see a number of reasons why East European countries have not met with the kind of economic success that many western countries take for granted.

Immobile resources

Consider Figure 1.5. We might think of, say, the Russian economy in 1990 as represented by point S. There were few consumer goods, and large volumes of resources were committed to military uses, but, given the inefficiencies outlined earlier, point S is inside the opportunity cost curve. Suppose, now, this society

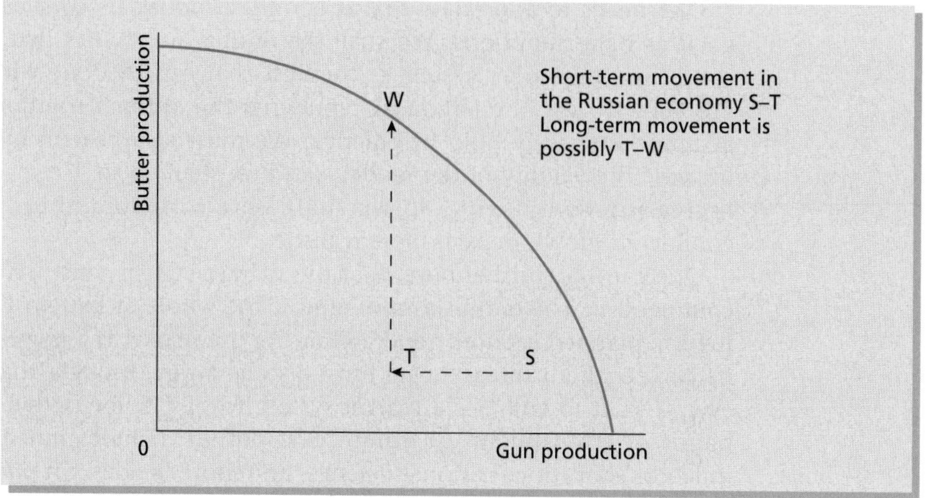

Figure 1.5 Problem of resource immobility

wishes to move to a market economy. People want fewer guns and more butter. They wish to be at point W. This entails a switch of resources. There is an opportunity cost of having more butter, namely having fewer guns. However, this is a sacrifice they are prepared to make. Less output of a military nature is now produced and the labour and capital are supposed to make consumer goods instead. However, the workforce has no training and the machines are not convertible. Given this resource immobility the economy shifts to point T – and there is *less* national output, not more. Perhaps this will be a short-term problem – labour can be retrained, for example. However, it is easier to see the problem in a textbook than for a Russian to accept that his low income is going to get lower before it gets higher.

The problem of the immobility of resources, especially labour, is a real problem faced by some of the transition economies. Consider the data in Table 1.6, which is a forecast made during 1999. As the reforms continue, real output was expected to stop falling and to increase. Inflation was expected to come under some degree of control, while still being high by West European standards. However, forecasts made in the mid-1990s for these economies in the late 1990s proved over-optimistic. It is still easy to underestimate the scale of the problems that remain.

Low capital stock

Inefficient and outdated methods of production have left East European economies with old and worn-out capital equipment that needs replacing. For example, many of their nuclear power stations are unsafe and need rebuilding. This requires large volumes of resources committed to producing new equipment for future power production. In terms of Figure 1.4, C_{t+1} can be increased but only by a reduction in C_t. Again the effect of moving towards a market economy is a reduction in living standards in the short run. Given the immobility

Table 1.6(a) **Growth in transition economies**

	1990–96[a]	*1997*	*1998*	*1999*	*2000*	*2000–04*[a]
Eastern Europe[b]	−1.2	2.6	2.0	1.2	2.5	3.7
FSU[c]	−9.6	0.9	−2.7	−2.5	0.7	2.1
Advanced economies[d]	2.0	2.9	2.3	2.5	2.0	2.4

Table 1.6(b) **Inflation in transition economies**

	1990–96[a]	*1997*	*1998*	*1999*	*2000*	*2000–04*[a]
Eastern Europe	71.9	111.1	18.5	11.7	10.4	9.7
FSU	307.5	17.6	25.4	75.2	25.6	13.9
Advanced economies	3.2	2.0	1.4	1.4	1.8	2.1

Figures to 1998 are actual, 1999 onwards are forecasts

[a] Annual averages

[b] Bulgaria, Czech Republic, Hungary, Romania, Slovakia, Slovenia

[c] Belarus, Estonia, Kazakhstan, Latvia, Lithuania, Russia, Ukraine

[d] US, Canada, Japan, Australia, New Zealand, 15 EU countries, Norway, Switzerland, Iceland

Source: adapted from NatWest, *Economic and Financial Outlook*

of resources problem the short-term effects of improving the capital stock could be severe.

Some East European economies have persuaded western governments to give aid to alleviate the worst effects of this problem. If the aid is in the form of loans rather than outright gifts, then the problem is simply shifted into the future. If things do improve, private investors will be more willing to invest in such countries, and such ventures as a McDonald's in Moscow will seem less remarkable.

Inflation

Our focus in this chapter has been upon relative prices, that is the price of one good compared with the price of others. But societies can find themselves in difficulties if prices in general are rising, in other words, if they are experiencing inflation. In Britain, inflation has been problematic in that the price level has tended to rise every year since the Second World War. At its peak it was rising at over 20 per cent per year. However, for East European countries in recent years, prices have been rising far faster than that.

The reasons why societies experience inflation and the problems created by it will be considered in Chapter 15.

Political resistance

We have seen that the transition to a market economy incurs substantial short-term costs. Many people have found their already low living standards have declined further. In some countries pressure has mounted to slow the pace of reforms or even to reverse the reforms entirely.

It is particularly noticeable that the proportion of GDP in the private sector of the economy is lower in the former Soviet Union countries (FSU) than it is in the states of Central and Eastern Europe. It is also very evident that, whereas some of these countries are on an upward growth path, some other countries continue to see output remain at low levels.

The people of the FSU countries have no experience of market economies, having become communist in 1917. Many of the people of the countries of Eastern Europe have experienced markets, since it was only in the late 1940s that communism was imposed on these communities. It is the latter group which has been more willing to embrace reform. It is clearly easier to have markets in an economy where people are willing to accept it than in economies where those same market reforms are strongly resisted.

1.6 Conclusion

We have seen how difficult it is for a society to enjoy high living standards with a planned economy. We have also seen that former communist countries are finding real problems in their transition to a market economy. We learned that economists usually analyse economic problems by modelling them and we constructed a model of the choices open to an economy. This was represented in a diagram called an opportunity cost curve or production possibility curve. Our model ignored some elements of reality, for example we did not focus on the political elements of the problem. Nevertheless, our model sufficiently reflected reality to enable us to explain and predict certain features of such societies.

We also considered the nature of resources, especially the fact that they have an opportunity cost. We found that one great advantage of market economies is that relative prices can reflect the opportunity cost of resources used in production.

However, the transition from planned to market economies is not an easy one. Resources are often immobile so changes in society's preferences affect resource reallocation slowly. Increasing the capital stock has an opportunity cost in terms of forgone consumption lowering already low living standards in the short run. Furthermore, inflation is a serious difficulty for many of these economies. If the process continues, other problems of market economies will appear, problems which we consider in later chapters. The adjustment process will continue to be painful. But one should not underestimate what has been accomplished. Membership of the EU from the middle of 2004 represents a huge achievement for some of them.

CHAPTER SUMMARY

1. **Economic problems are best analysed by constructing economic models.**
2. **Limited resources imply that societies must make choices.**
3. **Planned economies have generally failed to utilise resources well.**

4 **Market economies have many problems but generally make better use of resources.**

5 **Resources do not always easily shift from one kind of production to another.**

6 **A market economy requires that prices reflect the opportunity costs of production.**

Questions for discussion

Guidance to the answers for the ***asterisked*** *numbered questions is available to students on the website for the book at* **www.booksites.net/heather**.

1* One famous American economist, Milton Friedman, says that the value of an economic model lies in its power to predict, not in the realism of its assumptions. What do you think he means? Is he right?

2 Consider Figure 1.6. Suppose the shape of the opportunity cost curve were to be as in (a), (b) and (c). In each case what would it be telling us about the nature of the resources?

3* Suppose that a government, in its desire for re-election, stimulates economic activity as the end of its term of office approaches. This results in a drop in the unemployment figures and a rise in output. It therefore can claim that the economy is growing: after all, output is now rising. Clearly, the electorate should not miss the opportunity to give the government a chance to continue this good work. But can this growth be sustained? (*Hint*: Where, before the election, was the economy in terms of Figure 1.2?)

4 Why might we be reluctant to compare the Romanians' standards of living on the basis of, say, the number of GPs per head of population or the output of clothing per head? Can you think of more suitable measures of comparison?

5* The data reflect three possible combinations of service goods and manufactured goods that can be produced with a country's resources. If the opportunity cost curve is as in Figure 1.6(a), will the value of X be 100, more than 100 or less than 100?

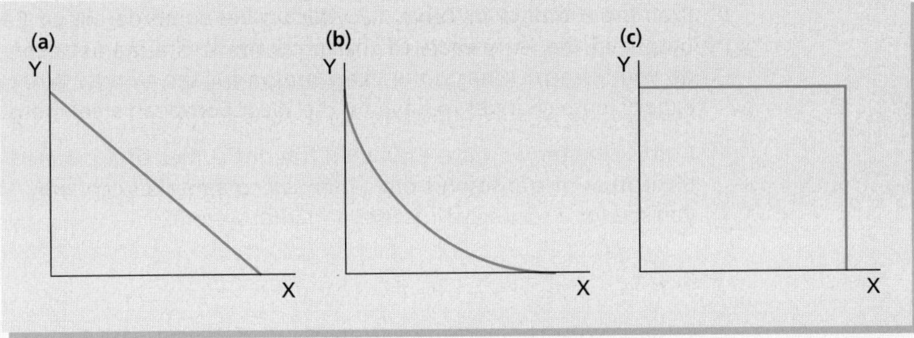

Figure 1.6

Table 1.7 Crude steel consumption and production in Eastern Europe (million tonnes)

	Capacity	*Production*			*Apparent consumption*		*Capacity utilisation*
	1992	*1990*	*1991*	*1992*	*1990*	*1992*	*1992 (%)*
Poland	14.8	13.6	10.3	9.3	10.7	7.3	63
CSFR[a]	16.7	14.9	12.3	10.8	10.3	7.1	65
Romania	19.1	9.8	7.1	5.1	8.1	4.4	27
Hungary	4.3	2.9	1.9	1.4	2.4	1.1	34
Bulgaria	4.7	2.4	1.7	1.3	3.7	2.0	27
Albania	0.4	0.1	0.1	0.1	0.3	0.2	19
Latvia	0.6	0.3	0.3	0.2	0.2	0.1	38
Total Eastern Europe	60.6	44.0	33.7	28.2	35.7	22.2	47
Total CIS	174.0	154.1	133.3	113.3	156.2	117.0	65
Total Eastern Europe and CIS	234.6	198.1	167.0	141.5	191.9	139.2	60

[a] CSFR = Czech and Slovak Federal Republic (the old Czechoslovakia)

Source: adapted from Eurofer data

Manufactured goods	0	50	X
Services	100	50	0

Now suppose the opportunity cost curve is bowed outwards. Will the value of X be 100, more than 100 or less than 100?

6 A point inside an opportunity cost curve is 'inefficient'. What do you understand by the term 'efficiency'?

7* We considered the reasons for significant changes in the relative prices of some of the goods and services in Table 1.5. What explanations would you offer for the price changes in some other goods and services? Particularly consider (a) beer and (b) the bike whose relative price has fallen less than one might have expected.

8 How well does the market system overcome each problem of a planned economy mentioned in section 1.5?

9* Examine the data in Table 1.7 which gives some details of East European steel output in the early years of the move towards a market economy. What trends do you discern? What is the likely reason for the trends? What effects might you expect these changes to have on the West European steel industry?

10 In this chapter we have examined the difficulties of a planned economy and the difficulties of transition from a planned to a market economy. What problems do you see for a society which uses a market system?

Websites

The UN website, Economic Survey of Europe contains up-to-date commentary on the prospects and problems of Eastern Europe including a statistical section:

www.unece.org/ead/ead_h.htm

Notes

1 We have indicated the meaning of the items in Table 1.1. During your studies these concepts will be examined more fully. Gross domestic product (GDP) is explained in Chapter 12. Unemployment is the focus of Chapter 13. Inflation is dealt with particularly in Chapter 15.

2 There are difficulties in defining the term 'non-renewable'. Fish stocks are a good illustration of the point. In one sense a fish is non-renewable. Once it is eaten, it is gone for ever. In another sense it is renewable in that it can have young. The question of oil in this context raises issues discussed in Chapter 12.

3 Some economists draw a distinction between 'relative' and 'absolute' scarcity. An absolutely scarce item is Van Gogh's painting 'Sunflowers'. It is unique. Its supply cannot be increased. Most resources are relatively scarce. They are scarce relative to the demands made upon them, but they can be increased, albeit at an opportunity cost.

4 The choice of these two commodities, as an illustration of a principle, is a deliberate one. 'Guns' will stand for national defence, tanks, soldiers, etc. 'Butter' will represent consumer goods, food, clothing, housing, etc. Therefore in these two headings we have covered all different kinds of output.

5 In principle, the question of ownership of resources is separate from the setting of prices. A state could own resources but set prices that were based on what households were prepared to pay. In practice, in countries where governments have owned resources, government has usually also administered prices.

6 All these and other issues will be considered in later chapters. In particular the question of efficiency is examined in many places, especially Chapter 10. The question of unemployment is the focus of Chapter 13 and the distribution of income is dealt with in Chapter 16.

7 In the first half of the book we shall devote considerable thought to why markets are used for allocating resources. We shall also explore why some output is *not* allocated through markets.

Part II

MICROECONOMICS

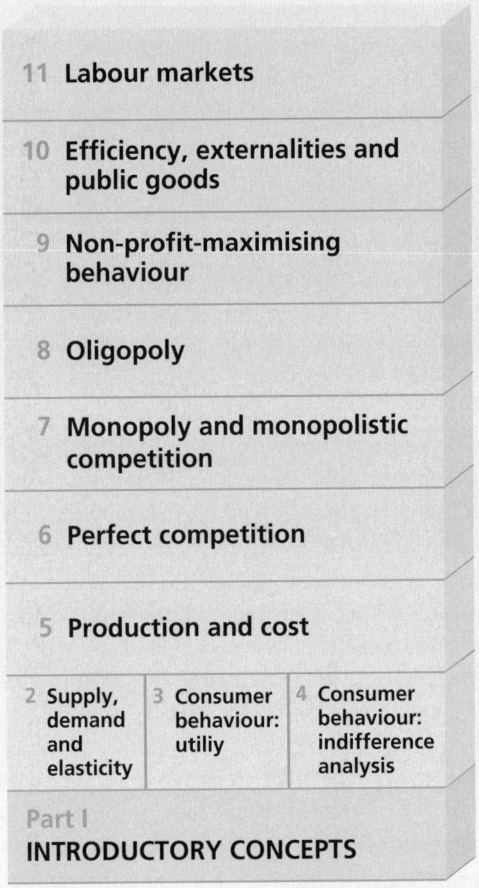

11 **Labour markets**

10 **Efficiency, externalities and public goods**

9 **Non-profit-maximising behaviour**

8 **Oligopoly**

7 **Monopoly and monopolistic competition**

6 **Perfect competition**

5 **Production and cost**

2 **Supply, demand and elasticity**	3 **Consumer behaviour: utiliy**	4 **Consumer behaviour: indifference analysis**

Part I
INTRODUCTORY CONCEPTS

Each chapter adds a 'building block' in constructing an understanding of how the economic system functions. In this part we build on the introductory concepts and understanding of the economy at the micro level.

2 Supply, demand and elasticity

The stock market: *a quick way to riches or poverty?*

CHAPTER OVERVIEW

Why do share prices fluctuate so much? Are large fortunes made and lost as a result? Does it make any difference to the firms concerned? Does it matter for the economy generally?

As we analyse these things, we introduce the concepts of:

- Supply and demand
- Price elasticity of demand
- Speculation

2.1 Introduction: what is the stock market for?

There have been periods in the last ten years when most share prices have been rising sharply. Buying shares during such times seems an easy way to make money. On the other hand there have been periods over which the value of most shares has fallen quite sharply. For example, during 2002 the average price of European shares was falling at a rate not seen since the early 1970s. Buying shares in these periods seems a fairly sure way of *losing* money.

Most newspapers have a financial page on which they list the latest stock market prices for some companies. Many people own shares and are aware of the existence of the Stock Exchange. Fewer people are aware of what actually happens there, why the price of shares fluctuates so much, and what this has to do with the real economy. Do events in the stock market really make any difference to the lives of most people? The answer is that they most certainly do.

Firms need capital, buildings and machinery to produce output; in the case of large firms, many millions of pounds' worth. What sources are available to them if they wish to invest? The main options are, first, internal funds from profits that they have made in the past; second, banks and other financial institutions who will lend at a rate of interest; third, the floating of shares. Shares, or equities, are pieces of paper that show that the holder owns part of the company.

Some people will be willing to hold the shares in the expectation of sharing in the profits that the company hopes to make. The shareholder receives this payment as a *dividend*. This dividend, paid out to all shareholders, will represent only part of the company's profit. Some profit will be retained.

Large companies never concentrate exclusively on just one source but will use a variety of sources to raise funds for investment. At first it might seem that the ideal is to fund all its capital needs out of past profits since it will then not need to pay out interest or dividends. But we must remember two things. First, large companies' capital needs will be too great for this to be possible. Second, even the use of internal funds has costs. There are opportunity costs in terms of the interest forgone by using the funds for capital investment rather than, say, lending to a bank. So large firms use a variety of sources for funds, including equity finance.

When a company wishes to raise finance through a share issue, it usually gets a merchant bank to offer the shares for sale. Often, the merchant bank will be paid a fee by the company to 'underwrite' the issue, that is, to guarantee that all the shares offered will be sold. If people do not offer to buy all the shares, the underwriter has to buy all the excess whether he wishes to or not – taking that risk is part of what he has been paid for. The company then uses the finance raised for investment and those holding the shares will be rewarded according to the degree of success the company has in making profits.

Suppose you bought some new shares in BP so that BP can build a new oil rig, but you then decide that you no longer wish to tie your savings up in BP. It is clearly not possible for BP to sell a leg of an oil rig so that they can pay you your money back. However, they do not need to: the Stock Exchange will enable you to sell your shares to someone else who wishes to buy them. In other words, it acts as a market for the dealing in secondhand shares, which is vital for firms, otherwise they would find it harder to persuade people to buy new issues of their shares. The harder firms find it to float new shares, the less investment society gets. As we saw in Chapter 1, capital is a manufactured resource. Less investment means less capital stock. This results in less growth of output, and therefore lower future living standards. Most Stock Exchange dealings on a day-to-day basis are trades in the 'secondary market', so we shall begin here. Table 2.1 shows a selection of average share price movements for a number of countries in the course of a year. You can see that the movement can be quite substantial. These movements are not at all uncommon. Neither are they the very largest ever known. They are simply representative of a common occurrence.

We are going to see how the share price of such company shares is determined in the secondary market, and, in doing so, see why such fluctuations can occur. We shall do this by using a crucial tool of economists – supply and demand analysis. Supply and demand analysis helps us to see how the price of many things is determined in a market economy. By the end of this chapter you should understand the elements of the analysis. This will help you to understand not only the market for shares, but the determination of many other prices also. We shall begin by looking at the concept of demand, then at the concept of supply. Finally we shall see how demanders and suppliers interact with each other in the marketplace. First we consider demand.

Table 2.1 **Average share price changes for selected countries during 2002**[1]

Country	*Average share price change*
Czech Republic	+44%
Indonesia	+42%
Russia	+17%
UK	−15%
Finland	−30%
Sweden	−35%
Germany	−38%
Argentina	−61%

[1] Figures are subject to currency movements and therefore approximate

Source: Financial press

2.2 Prices in the secondary market: supply and demand

The demand for shares

What factors influence people's plans to buy goods and services? Many things influence the demand for a good: the price of the good, the price of other goods, incomes, sometimes interest rates, sometimes expectation about future prices. For different goods, different things will be important. The demand for apples might be influenced by the price of pears. The price of pears is unlikely, however, to exert much influence on the demand for cars. But we start by considering a crucial influence on the demand for a good – its price. Here we take the example of the demand for Sainsbury's shares and relate it to the price of those shares.

Many individuals would like to buy, but the market demand for Sainsbury's shares is the sum of all individuals' demands at each price. We can graph that relationship, as shown in Figure 2.1. The demand curve, as it is called, represents a set of plans – plans to buy Sainsbury's shares at different possible prices. As with most goods, it is negatively sloped. The lower the price the greater the quantity demanded. The most important reason is that the higher the price, the more that buyers will find it worthwhile to shift their demand into something else, in this case another share. For example, if Sainsbury's share price rises from P_1 to P_2 some who planned to purchase Sainsbury's shares at P_1 will buy another company's share. There would be fewer people planning to buy Sainsbury's shares at the higher price. The change in price from P_1 to P_2 caused *a change in the quantity demanded*.

Of course, determinants of demand, other than the price itself, can change. If this were to happen, it would cause purchasers to demand different quantities at each price. We call such shifts changes in demand, as shown in Figure 2.2. One thing that might shift demand in the way described is the announcement by

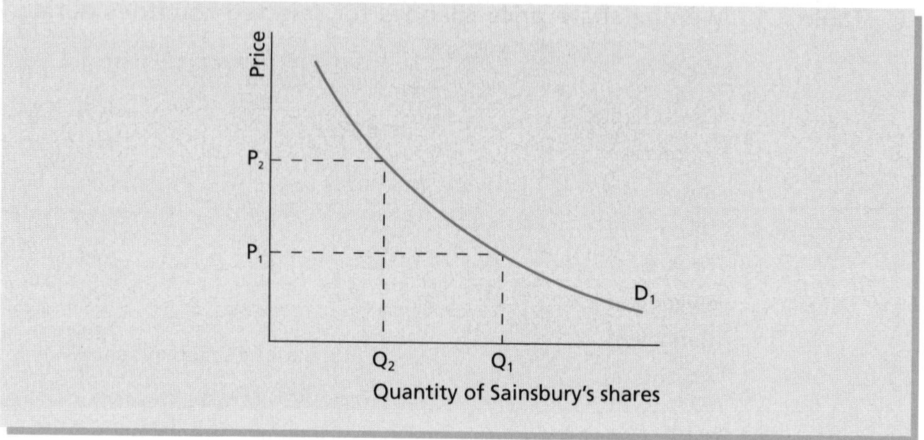

Figure 2.1 **The demand for shares**

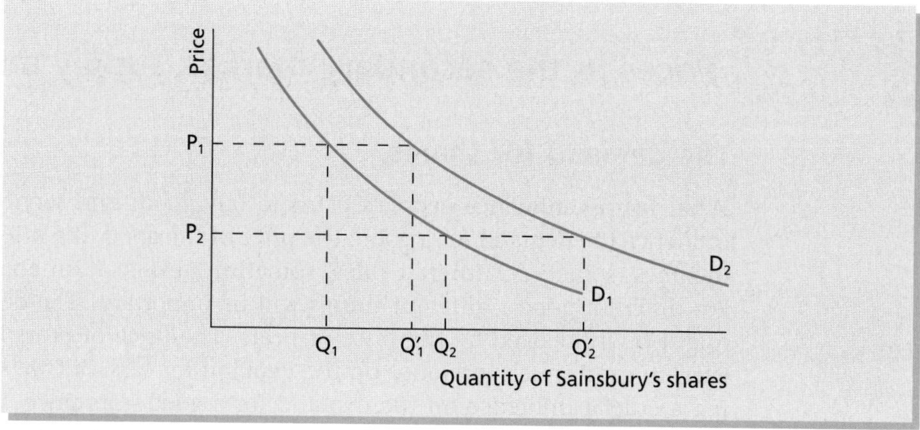

Figure 2.2 **A change in demand**

Sainsbury's of unexpectedly high profits. This is because expectations are one factor influencing demand. Now *at each price* people will wish to hold more shares than they wished to hold before at that price. Now that the demand curve has shifted to the right, plans to buy at P_1 have increased from Q_1 to Q'_1 and plans to buy at P_2 have increased from Q_2 to Q'_2. A similar shift in demand might take place in the market for cars if it was thought that car prices were likely to rise. Perhaps it is anticipated that car taxes are about to be raised. Demand would increase in expectation of the price change.

Many other factors can shift the demand curve. We shall consider some of them shortly.

The supply of shares

The supply of a commodity depends on a variety of things, including its own price. If we hold all things constant except the price of the share we can plot a

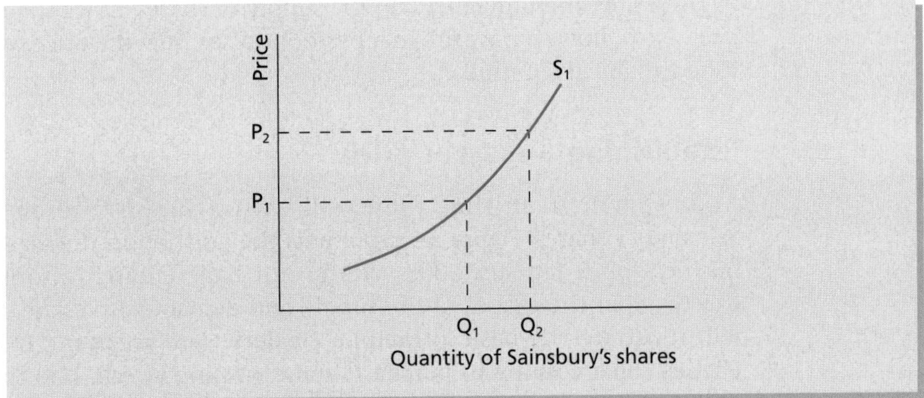

Figure 2.3 A supply curve

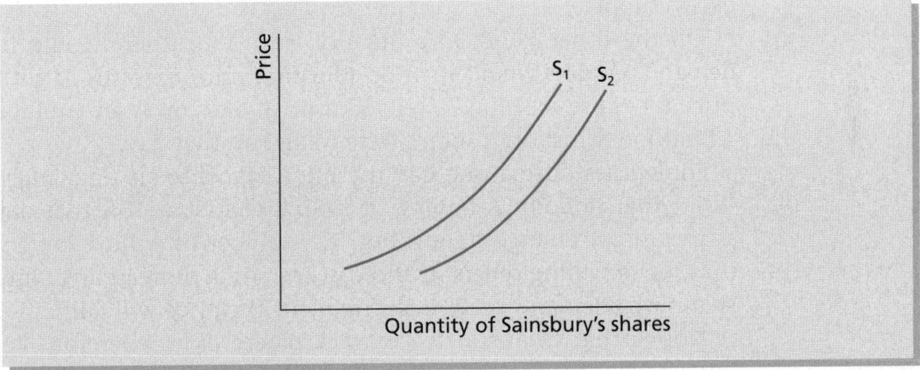

Figure 2.4 A change in supply

supply curve (Figure 2.3). The curve represents a set of plans by those who wish to sell Sainsbury's shares. At higher prices, more shares are offered for sale.

The curve, then, is positively sloped. At first this might seem odd. There is a limited number of Sainsbury's shares which have been issued. Surely people cannot offer more for sale than are available? However, what we are interested in is people's willingness to sell them. At a higher price more people will judge that they would be better off selling these shares and perhaps switching to some other share. A rise in price, then, will cause an increase in the quantity supplied. In Figure 2.3 a change in price from P_1 to P_2 causes a change in quantity supplied from Q_1 to Q_2. The upward sloping supply curve represents the position in most markets, not just shares. If the price rises, more will be offered for sale by suppliers.

However, determinants of supply, other than the price itself, can change. We call such shifts changes in supply. So Figure 2.4 shows a change in supply. Suppose, for example, Sainsbury wishes to raise more funds for expansion and chooses to do it through a new share issue. To the plans of shareholders we must add the plans of the company's board to sell new shares, as we show in Figure 2.4. The supply curve has shifted right from S_1 to S_2.

There are other influences on the supply of shares, as we shall consider a little later. Now, however, we are in a position to see how the price of a share is established at any given time.

Establishing a market price

At any moment in time there will exist a supply and demand curve for Sainsbury's shares. Figure 2.5 represents the position in the market after close of business on 9 January 2003. We do not have enough information to know exactly what the shapes of the supply and demand curves are, but the diagram will illustrate the basic principle. Dealers were receiving instructions from clients, some wishing to purchase, some wishing to sell. Had the price been set at 330p, there would have been more planned sales than planned purchases. Dealers would have adjusted the price downwards in order to find purchasers for their clients wishing to sell – that is to say, at 330p there would have been excess supply.

On the other hand, at a price of, say, 230p there would have been excess demand. Dealers would then be adjusting price upwards to get the best possible price for those wishing to sell. So a price of 276p is an equilibrium price. Over 12 million Sainsbury's shares were traded on that day.

Sometimes during one day the price of a share is unchanged. This does not mean that nobody is buying or selling that share on that day. Thousands of shares might change hands, but the number of willing buyers is equal to the number of willing sellers. If there is, overall, a decreased willingness to hold the shares (the demand curve is shifting left) the price will fall.

Notice that this is a free market. There is no coercion. People are free to buy or sell as they please. What the market does is to establish a price at which suppliers' and demanders' plans are consistent. That is the only price at which this is possible. At a price below equilibrium, suppliers can fulfil their plans. All those who wish to sell at that price can do so, but demanders' plans cannot be fulfilled. That is the nature of excess demand. Similarly, at a price above equilibrium, demanders' plans can be fulfilled but all who would wish to sell at that

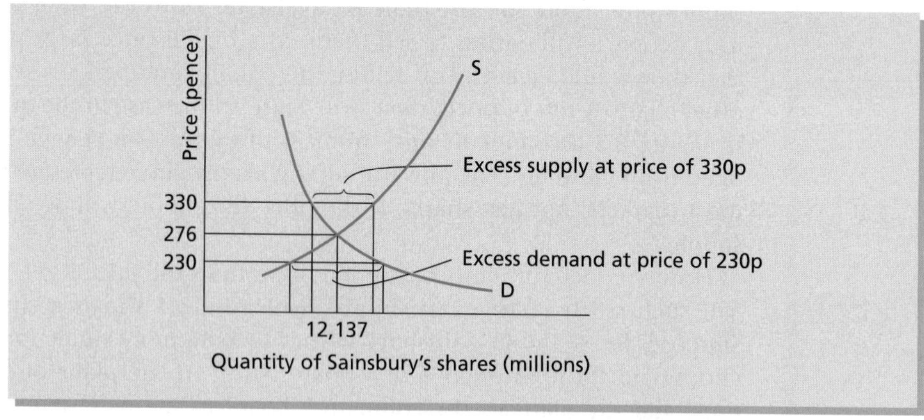

Figure 2.5 Position of market at close of business, 9 January 2003

price cannot do so. This is the nature of excess supply. The market has ensured that both suppliers' and demanders' plans are consistent by the adjustment of price. What is true for shares will be true in the market for most goods and services also.

Market 'clearing' price

There are no queues for shares. They are freely available at the equilibrium price. By contrast, the queues for food that were a feature of the planned economy could occur because prices were administered. If the price were administered at a level at which quantity demanded exceeded quantity supplied, the excess demand needed to be rationed. Queues became that rationing device. In a market system the rationing device is price. The market price is a clearing price. It clears the market of any excess demand or supply.

In the stock market, prices adjust very quickly. Is that true of markets for goods and services? Given that queues for goods are uncommon in market economies, it would appear that they do so.

Do markets for factors such as labour clear quickly? This is a question that we consider later in the book. However, given that some people are unemployed for a considerable time, it would appear that they may not do so. Unemployment can be viewed as an excess supply of labour services. Our model suggests that a fall in the price of labour services would 'clear' the market of unemployment. So, since unemployment often persists for some time, if the price mechanism works for labour services, it would seem that it works much more slowly than for shares.

2.3 Changes in the demand for equities

We have now established that the price of a share, or indeed any good or service, can change because of changes in either demand or supply. We look now at factors most likely to change *demand*.

Expectations

Demand for shares is a derived demand. They are bought not for themselves but for what they represent in the form of an expected income. This contrasts with the demand for most goods where goods are usually demanded for their own sake. The expected income from shares takes two forms. One is the dividend paid out of the company's profits, the other is the prospect of 'capital growth', which is to say an increase in the value of the share. However, the capital value of the share can be seen as representing the future expected stream of earnings of dividends from the shares. Therefore profitability of the company is obviously important because it helps to determine the dividend payment. But profitability is not the main determinant of share price. Eurotunnel shares were floated in 1987 for £3.50 a share, though a dividend would not be paid until into the new century. The key here is *expectation* of profits. The value of the shares is in the anticipated capital growth. The shares become worth more as the time of the expected dividend payments draws near. Expectations can greatly affect share prices through large and sudden shifts in demand. One such example is the announcement by one firm of a takeover bid for another firm. In order for a takeover bid to succeed, the acquiring company has to persuade the owners of over half the target company's shares to accept the price that is offered. This will typically involve offering substantially more than the going market price – a bid premium. Therefore a takeover announcement or even a rumour of one can increase demand, and hence price, considerably. This gives us one reason why companies care about their share prices. A high price may deter other companies from launching a takeover bid.

Expectations may also be important in shifting the *demand* curve for commodities. As we saw earlier, the demand for cars may rise if car price increases are expected. However, for many goods, expectations will be a minor factor. For shares it is of major significance.

Risk

A second important element in determining demand for a company's shares is risk. The future earnings stream is more uncertain than the income from, say, a building society deposit account. Therefore, in the long run, buying shares generally gives a higher return than safer forms of savings. Having said that, not all shares will give higher returns. Some companies will go bankrupt. Some companies' shares are inherently more risky than others because some companies are in riskier markets. In pharmaceuticals, for example, a company can spend millions of pounds on research, and all for nothing. The high risk requires high compensation. Large companies tend to be safer than small companies, and the share price will reflect this. In extreme cases one could be holding shares in a small firm which then goes bankrupt. The shares may then be worthless. Large firms are not immune to bankruptcy but, on average, the risk is somewhat smaller.

Substitutes

Perhaps the other important determinant of the demand for equities is the price of substitutes. As far as the general level of share prices is concerned the substitutes are other forms of saving. So if, for example, building societies were to offer a higher interest rate on savings, some people would decide that the risk of holding shares is unacceptably high. Equity demand might then fall. Equities in other countries are also a substitute. It is perfectly possible to invest in European or Japanese firms. If the return on these financial investments is seen to be rising, demand for British equities might well decline.

What are the substitutes for an individual share? Clearly, the closest substitutes are the shares of other companies, particularly those in the same area of activity. So changes in the prospects of Tesco will not only affect the Tesco share price but Sainsbury's share price also.

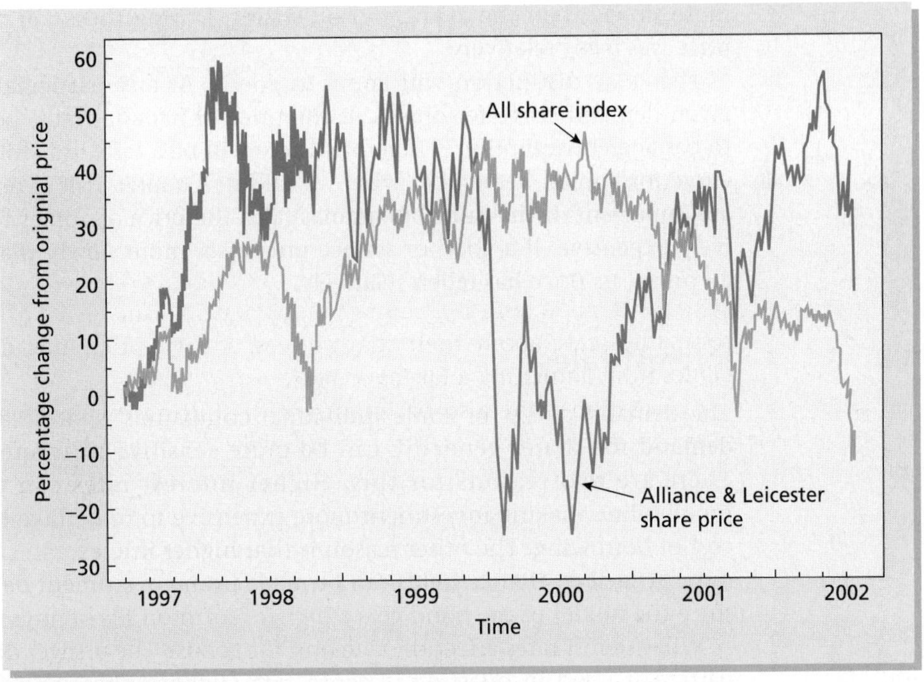

Figure 2.6 Changes in Alliance & Leicester share price
Source: adapted from Stock Exchange data

In recent years the gas, telecommunications, water and electricity utilities have been sold by the government to private shareholders – a process called *privatisation*. This is an issue that we consider in Chapter 17. For now, we concentrate on the price of the shares of the new companies following their transfer to the private sector. All the shares have increased in price. In absolute terms they are more expensive than they were at the time they were sold to the private sector. However, some, particularly the assets of companies formed from the privatisation of gas, have a lower valuation *relative* to the level of UK share prices generally, whilst those of the water companies have risen substantially, absolutely and relatively. It is not hard to understand why this is so. These shares are good substitutes for each other. The gas and telecommunications companies have experienced increased competition and profits have not been as high as might have been expected. In contrast, water companies have experienced relatively little increase in competition. Profits have been high in this sector and the expectation has been for more of the same. The demand for gas industry shares has accordingly fallen relative to the substitute shares, water (and other shares too), where demand has increased sharply. As demand has changed, share prices have adjusted accordingly.

You can see the same point about relative and absolute prices in Figure 2.6 with respect to one share price. Alliance & Leicester's *absolute* share price is shown over a five-year period. By looking at an average of all share prices you can see times, for example 2002, when the Alliance & Leicester share price fell more slowly than the average of all shares. During these periods Lloyds' share price was *rising* relatively.

The same distinction will apply to goods. At any particular time there is a given demand curve for apples. If the price of bananas falls, people will switch to banana consumption. Therefore, there will be a leftward shift in the demand curve for apples. Remember what we said in Chapter 1: it is relative prices that are important. If the price of bananas falls, the price of apples has become relatively expensive. If a good or service price rises more slowly than the average of all prices, its price has fallen relatively.

see pp. 15–16

Interest rates

The demand curve for some individual companies' shares can shift, but the demand for shares generally can be quite sensitive to interest rate changes. There are two reasons for this. Higher interest rates can affect company profitability, making investment more expensive to undertake by increasing the cost of borrowing. The other reason is that higher interest rates make substitutes more attractive. Higher yields can be made from government debt such as bonds since the holder of the bond gets a higher return on his savings.

Will interest rates affect the demand for goods? The answer depends upon the particular good in question. Interest rate changes affect the demand for cars. Since most people borrow money to buy a car, higher interest rates make the purchase of the vehicle more expensive. A rise in interest rates shifts the demand curve for cars leftward. For other goods, interest rates are of small significance. The demand for strawberries will be little affected by interest rate changes.

We can illustrate the effects of interest rates with reference to the housing market. For many people, the purchase of a house represents an alternative way of saving. To some extent, therefore, houses can be seen as a substitute for shares. We would anticipate that a fall in interest rates would result in an increase in house prices. A fall in interest rates will cause the demand curve for houses to move right, *ceteris paribus*, resulting in houses rising in price. Figure 2.7 shows that house prices have tended to rise by over 2 per cent per year in real terms. However, you can see substantial variations from that trend. One explanation for the variations is interest rates. For example, high interest rates in the early 1990s made the demand for houses and thus house prices fall. When interest rates were sharply reduced in the late 1990s house prices began to rise again both absolutely and relatively.

Income

One important determinant of the demand for shares, or indeed of almost any good, is income. If income rises, people will feel able to buy more shares. This increase in demand may happen directly, or indirectly by people increasing their savings in, say, unit trusts or pension funds. So a rise in income will, all other things being equal, move the demand curve to the right.

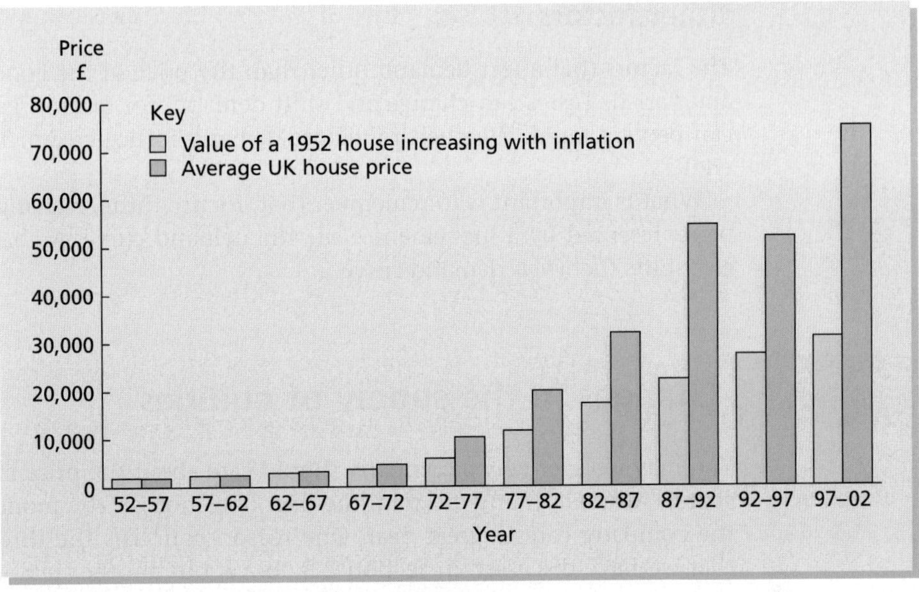

Figure 2.7 **Real house prices over a fifty-year period**

Source: analysis and house price information provided by Nationwide Building Society

This will also be true for most goods. Think of the things that you purchase. You will find that for the great majority of them you would be willing to buy more at any given price, if your income were to be higher.

One exception to this rule is known as an 'inferior' good. This is a good where, as incomes rise, the demand curve moves inwards. An example of such a good is a black-and-white television. As incomes rise, people feel able to afford colour sets. Therefore, as income increases, the demand for black-and-white televisions falls.

Wealth

Wealth can also be an important consideration. Wealth is different from income. Income is a flow of payments received: it is so much per period of time. You may be paid £50 per day for working in Woolworth during the holidays. This is income. Wealth, on the other hand, is a stock; it is an amount that you have. It might be that you have a deposit account at the bank with £1,000 in it. This is not a flow; you are not receiving £1,000 per week. Clearly, an increase in wealth will affect demand for shares. It will also affect the demand for some kinds of good. One thing that was said to exacerbate the recession in Britain during the early years of the 1990s was the fall in house prices which occurred then. A fall in house prices caused house owners to feel less wealthy. They reduced their spending as a result. The fall in demand for goods generally reinforced the recession.

Other factors

The factors that affect demand other than the price of the good itself are many and varied. Tastes can change and shift demand: for fashion goods this change can be very rapid. Weather influences demand for ice cream. The list is almost endless.

What is important is to remember that, for anything, a change in its *price* will be represented by a movement *along* the demand curve. A change in anything else shifts the *whole* demand curve.

2.4 Changes in the supply of equities

You may wonder why a company should care about the price of its secondhand shares. After all, if any are sold, the firm does not get the money. Nevertheless, the company cares a great deal. One reason concerns the threat of a takeover that we have discussed in section 2.3 above, but another reason is the funding of future investment plans. The valuation of the secondhand shares influences the price of any new shares that the company may choose to issue for expansion plans. The higher the price, the more funds that the company can raise for any given dividend payment. In other words, the higher the share price the cheaper it is to borrow money via the issue of new shares. Hence, one might expect more new share issues when stock-market prices are high. This is exactly what happens.

Figure 2.8 describes what usually happens when a new share issue takes place. Supply is increased from S_1 to S_2 so the equilibrium price falls from P_1 to P_2. Fewer people are willing to hold the shares now, since if there are more shares but the same amount of dividends available, the earnings per share will be diluted and the shares will be worth correspondingly less.

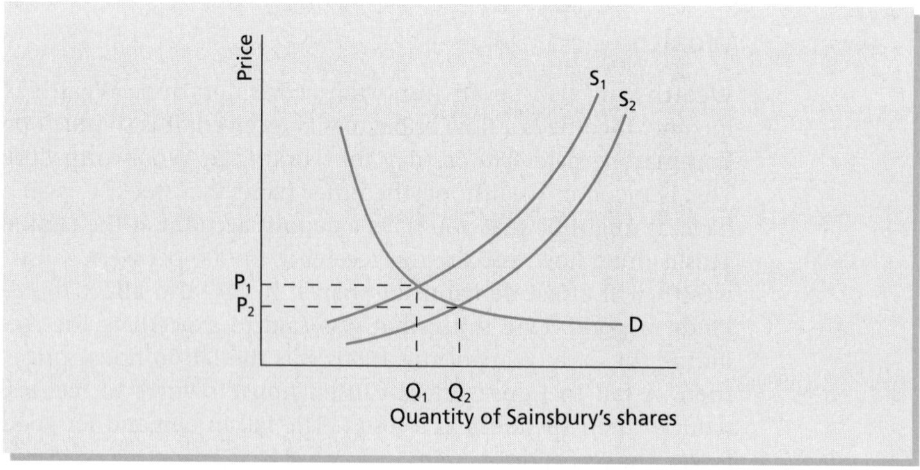

Figure 2.8 **Effects of a new share issue**

2.5 Sensitivity of demand to share price changes: elasticity of demand

By how much will the share price be depressed by an increase in its supply? This is an important question because it decides the price that the company can get for its new share issue. The answer is to be found in the price *elasticity* of demand for the shares.

Price elasticity of demand

Consider Figure 2.9 where we examine assumed supply and demand curves for shares in two companies, Sainsbury and Eurotunnel. Assume now that a new share issue increases supply from S_1 to S_2. If our diagram correctly shows the nature of the demand curve for these companies' shares, it suggests that Sainsbury could float shares much closer to the present market price than could Eurotunnel.

Remembering that these numbers are for illustrative purposes only and may not accurately reflect supply and demand conditions for these companies' shares, let us consider the position as suggested by the diagrams. First, consider Sainsbury, shown in Figure 2.9(a). For a 5 per cent increase in the number of shares demanded, a 1 per cent fall in price will be required. Elasticity of demand is a measure of the sensitivity of demand with respect to price changes. It is given as

$$\frac{\%\ \Delta\ Q_D}{\%\ \Delta\ \text{price}}$$

where Q_D = quantity demanded and Δ = 'change in'.

In this case, given the current price, a 1 per cent *fall* in price was necessary to produce a 5 per cent *increase* in the number of shares that buyers were willing to hold, hence

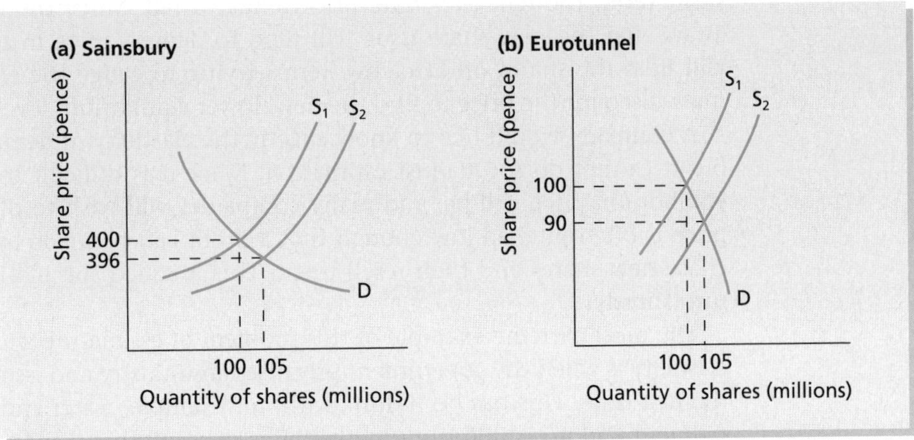

Figure 2.9 **Illustrative changes in share prices in response to new issues**

$$\frac{\%\ \Delta\ Q_D}{\%\ \Delta\ \text{price}} = \frac{5\%}{-1\%} = -5$$

For a 1 per cent fall in price, Sainsbury can issue 5 per cent more shares.

For Eurotunnel the position would be represented by Figure 2.9(b). We can see how elastic is the demand for Eurotunnel shares at that price:

$$\frac{\%\ \Delta\ Q_D}{\%\ \Delta\ \text{price}} = \frac{5\%}{-10\%} = -0.5$$

Notice that the elasticity value is negative. A fall in price yields an increase in quantity demanded. A rise in price yields a fall in quantity demanded. For almost any good, since its demand curve is negatively sloped, price elasticity of demand is negative. Hence for every 1 per cent fall in share price, Eurotunnel could issue only 0.5 per cent more shares. It must be stressed that these are assumed, not known, values. Since Sainsbury's shareholders are assumed to be the more sensitive to price changes, we say that demand for their shares is more price elastic. There are various other ways of measuring price elasticity that the interested reader can examine from the reading recommended at the end of the chapter.

Why would we expect the difference in elasticity of demand for these shares? People are quite willing to hold Sainsbury's shares: it is a profitable company. If Sainsbury is issuing new shares, it will expect to use the money raised to build new stores which will also trade at a profit. The new shares will probably seem like a good deal to potential purchasers. It will not require much of a fall in price to persuade people to purchase in considerable quantities. Demand for Sainsbury's shares is relatively elastic.

Eurotunnel is the company that spent so much money building the Channel Tunnel that it is heavily in debt. It is attempting to raise money from a share issue to help pay the banks the money that it owes them. It cannot put the money into improving services etc. People will therefore be relatively unwilling to take on more shares unless they are very cheap. Demand for these shares is inelastic.

If a company is seen to use the finance raised from a new share issue well and profits are later enhanced, demand may subsequently shift to the right. In the short term, though, the share price tends to fall. Since the company will be aware that the new share issue will tend to depress price in the short term, it will float the shares on attractive terms trying to gauge the extent to which it must discount the price to find the new, lower equilibrium level.

A company would like to know exactly the elasticity of demand for its shares but it cannot do so: it must estimate it. Since it is difficult to gauge what the equilibrium price will be, and many companies will wish to play safe, the offer price is often pitched low enough that a profit can be made by those who purchase new shares and then resell them. This is called speculation, to which we turn shortly.

The most extreme example of this problem of estimating share price demand elasticity is when the government privatises an industry and issues new shares for the first time. This has been done with, for example, water and electricity. Government had no equilibrium market price of secondhand shares by which to be guided. In order to avoid the political embarrassment of a share issue flop the price was generally set rather low. Large profits have been made as people have purchased and then later resold the shares at much higher prices. Sometimes privatisation has been done in parts. So, for example, only about half of British Telecom (BT) was sold in 1984 and immediate profits of about 80 per cent were made. When a further sale of shares was made in 1991 the profits that could be made were much smaller. This was largely because the government then had a market price in BT shares to guide it in pitching the price of the new shares.

In more recent government share issues, the government has invited large institutions to submit bids for some of the shares in order to gain an idea of the value that people place on the shares. This has enabled the government to offer shares at a price closer to the equilibrium price. We return to the privatisation issue in Chapter 17.

see pp. 365–82

Elasticity of demand is an important concept. If the elasticity of demand for its shares is important to a company, the elasticity of demand for its product is important too. If a company raises its price, perhaps in response to a rise in its costs, how much of its sales will it lose? If demand is elastic, it will find that its revenue has decreased as well as its sales volume. Suppose a 1 per cent rise in price causes a 5 per cent fall in quantity sold. Since the proportionate change in price is less than the proportionate change in quantity, a rise in price per unit will not compensate for the loss of sales volume. This will be true of any value of elasticity of (ignoring the minus sign) greater than 1. In this situation we would say the demand for the company's product is elastic.

On the other hand, if demand for the product is relatively price insensitive, a rise in price will raise the firm's revenue even if the volume of its sales falls. Suppose the elasticity of demand for the product is –0.5. A 1 per cent increase in price means a 0.5 per cent fall in the volume of sales. Since the proportionate rise in price is greater than the proportionate decrease in sales volume, company revenue will increase. This is a situation where we would say that demand is price inelastic. This will be the case wherever the value of demand elasticity is (ignoring the minus sign) less than 1.

A word of warning. The link we have developed is between elasticity of demand for the product and the *revenue* that the company receives. The revenue is not the same as profit. Profit is revenue minus costs of production – a matter we explore in Chapter 6.

2.6 Changes in share prices: speculation

People are inclined to think of speculators as people who upset markets and cause damage to the economy. Many economists would take a much more benign view: it can be argued that speculation brings *stability* to markets.

Suppose a company's share price is in equilibrium. This price reflects people's views about the company's performance and is giving correct signals to the market about the company's assets. Now suppose for some reason people begin to sell the shares. This makes them, in some sense, too cheap. This is shown in Figure 2.10(a) as a rightward shift in supply depressing price from P_1 to P_2.

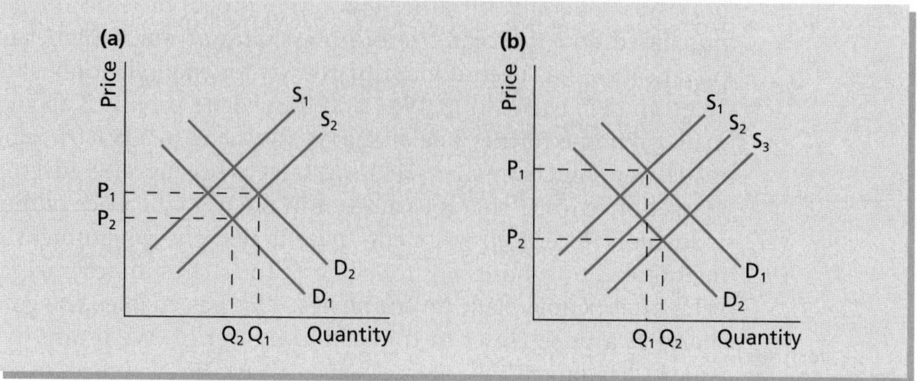

Figure 2.10 Effects of speculation on price

Speculators will anticipate that this temporary low price cannot last and will buy, speculating on the price rise. Demand will shift from D_1 to D_2 and price will return to P_1.

Some argue, however, that what will happen is described by Figure 2.10(b). As price begins to fall, speculators may fear that it will fall further. They sell in anticipation of the fall. The supply curve shifts again to S_3. This may be reinforced by a fall in demand to D_2, further depressing price and destabilising the market.

Which of the above scenarios is more likely to be the case? The answer is that eventually speculation will stabilise the market as in (a). At some point, those who believe that price is set to rise will outweigh those who believe it will fall, but this may take some time to happen. In the meantime the share price may be volatile. Its effects on the real economy may be harmful in making people fear to save via share ownership, thus making it harder for the company to raise funds for investment.

Note that equilibrium is not the same as stability. Equilibrium is a state of rest. A market is in equilibrium where the price is that which causes the plans of those wishing to sell to be equated with the plans of those wishing to buy. If something disturbs that equilibrium, and market reaction causes the equilibrium to be restored, then we have a stable equilibrium. If, when equilibrium is disturbed, forces push the market price further away from equilibrium, the market is unstable. To illustrate this point, imagine a marble in the bottom of a cup: the marble represents a stable equilibrium. If the marble is pushed out of its state of rest, it will nevertheless eventually return to its original equilibrium. A marble resting on an upturned cup is an example of an unstable equilibrium. The marble will stay there if left alone, so it is in equilibrium. However, if it is pushed off the cup, it will not roll back to where it came from. Figure 2.10(a) shows a stable market, Figure 2.10(b) an unstable market.

Fortunately for the market system the vast majority of markets are stable. A market with an upward sloping supply curve and a downward sloping demand curve will, in the long run, find a stable equilibrium. Only in very unusual circumstances, then, will the market for a commodity not be stable in the long run. In the short run, as Figure 2.10(b) demonstrates, speculation might be destabilising. Arguably, this was a significant part of the explanation for the steep fall in share prices around the world in 2002 – the steepest fall for three decades.

Speculation is not unique to stock markets. It happens in the market for foreign currency, as we shall see in Chapter 20. It also happens in markets for agricultural commodities and metals. We have already seen it happening in the housing market. It was the expectation of a continued rise in house prices in the late 1980s that caused people to *speculate* and to increase demand even when interest rates and house prices were rising.

2.7 Share price changes: some illustrations

We turn now to illustrate some of the principles of share price determination via supply and demand analysis by observing the share price movements of a few companies over a period of just twenty-four hours in July 2002. You might find it useful to attempt similar exercise with other share price changes which you can find in the financial press.

Table 2.2 gives the changes in price of four shares during one twenty-four hour period in 2002. In two cases, the price rose, the companies concerned being the brewer, Scottish & Newcastle and the retailer, Marks & Spencer. In two instances (Alliance & Leicester and ICI) it fell. What caused Scottish & Newcastle shares to rise in price? Two obvious possibilities present themselves. One is a rise in demand, the other is a fall in supply. In fact, in this case it would appear to be primarily a rise in demand, shown by a rightward shift in the demand curve from D_1 to D_2 in Figure 2.11(a). On the other hand, the explanation for a rise in the Marks & Spencer share price would seem to be a leftward shift of the supply curve from S_1 to S_2 in Figure 2.11(b). To see why this is the case, refer back to Table 2.2. Notice that for Scottish & Newcastle there was an *increase* in the equilibrium quantity of shares traded from 9 July to 10 July, whereas for Marks & Spencer there was a decrease. A rightward shift in demand increases equilibrium price *and* quantity. A leftward shift in supply causes a rise in equilibrium price but a decrease in the equilibrium quantity.

Table 2.2 Selected share price changes in a twenty-four hour period

Company	*Share price 9 July 2002 (pence)*	*Share price 10 July 2002 (pence)*	*Price change (pence)*	*Quantity of shares traded 9 July 2002 ('000)*	*Quantity of shares traded 10 July 2002 ('000)*	*Quantity change ('000)*
Scottish & Newcastle	597	599	+2	5,491	8,556	+3,065
Marks & Spencer	363	$363\frac{1}{2}$	$+\frac{1}{2}$	25,258	10,827	−14,431
ICI	325	$319\frac{1}{4}$	$-5\frac{3}{4}$	16,783	15,084	−1,699
Alliance & Leicester	845	832	−13	1,893	1,932	+39

Source: adapted from *Financial Times* (July 2002)

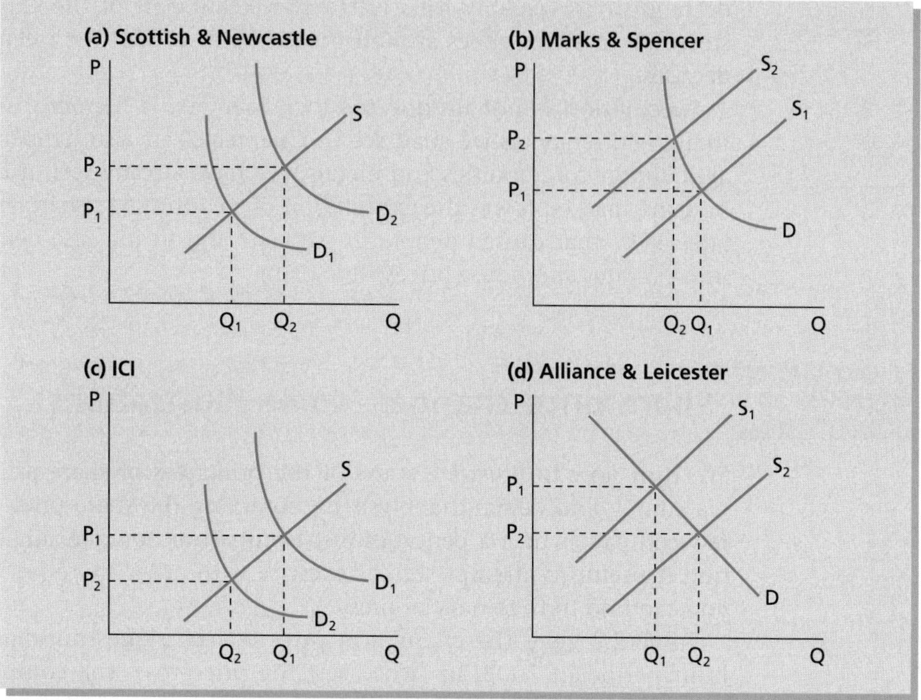

Figure 2.11 Supply and demand changes in the share price of selected companies

Before you read on, check that you have grasped the point with reference to the two share prices in Table 2.2 which show falls at that time. Check the price changes and quantity changes from Table 2.2 and confirm that they are correct.

Supply and demand curves, then, are a valuable tool for explaining changes in share prices. However, they are vital tools to the economist in explaining market price movements in many situations, including the price of many goods and services. We explore some of these other markets in subsequent chapters.

2.8 Conclusion

Is our supply and demand model an accurate model of stock market behaviour? For a *perfect* market, a number of conditions need to hold. There are perhaps three which are particularly important. We look at these next.

Identical product

A supply and demand curve assumes that we are talking about supply and demand for one product. All units of that product must be identical. Shares fit this condition very well. Each share of a given type will have the same rights and benefits attached to it as all the others. In this respect the model very closely resembles reality.

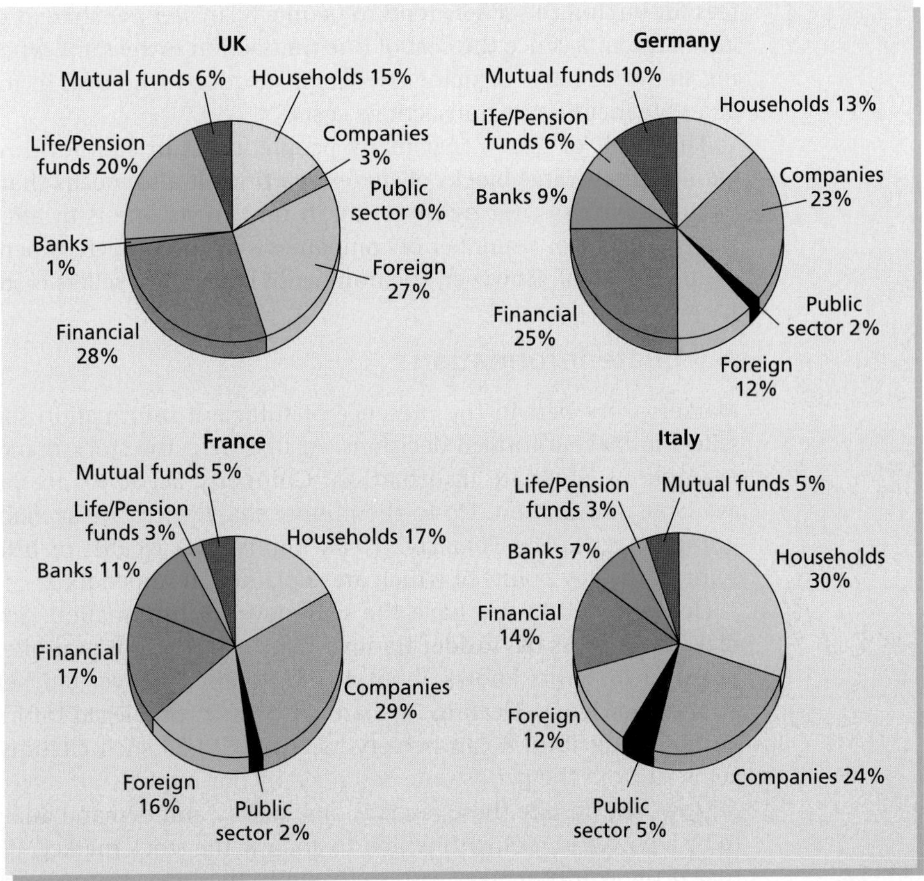

Figure 2.12 **Share ownership in selected European countries at 31 December 2000**
Source: adapted from Stock Exchange data

Many buyers and sellers

The model assumes that no large buyer or seller can dominate the market. Many buyers and sellers meet anonymously through a middleman to buy and sell. The price is derived impersonally. But who are the people who engage in the purchase of shares? The main purchasers are not, in fact, individuals. Indeed, as can be seen from Figure 2.12 the significance of individual buyers of shares is small relative to large institutions, such as insurance companies and unit trusts. Although the degree of ownership of private shares varies throughout Europe, Italy being unusually high, the same pattern of shareholding exists. The reasons for this pattern are not hard to fathom. They can be found largely in terms of what economists call 'transactions costs'. Go back to Figure 2.5, which we used to look at Sainsbury's shares. The implication here is that on that particular day you could buy or sell for that price. In fact this is not so. The dealers require an income which they make by charging a fee for the selling or buying of shares. If a share is quoted at £10.00 they actually sell shares for their clients at, say, £9.70 or buy for the clients at say £10.30, the difference being their own income. The fees for buying the shares tend to be much smaller per share if one is dealing in large amounts, since the cost of one transaction is the same whether one is dealing in a few shares or many. Hence, institutions who deal in millions of shares at a time incur lower transactions costs.

The result of this is that many people invest in equities through unit trusts who purchase large blocks of shares at a time. It also means that individuals can reduce their risks, for by investing in unit trusts one is in effect buying a few shares each from a number of companies – a prohibitively expensive thing to do as an individual. However, the number of buyers and sellers is still quite large.

Adequate information

Markets work best in the presence of sufficient information for all buyers and sellers to make informed decisions. At first sight the stock market seems a good example of adequate information. Company accounts are published giving available information. Up-to-the-minute share prices are available through television screens. The *Financial Times* publishes a wealth of information daily, some of the key points of which are explained in Appendix 2.

However, all do not have the same level of information. Sometimes people make large sums by 'insider trading'. This is where, for example, a member of a board of directors knows about an imminent takeover bid before it becomes public knowledge. Dealing in shares with such privileged information is illegal but tempting since it can be very lucrative. Under such circumstances the market is far from the perfect one described by our model.

However, despite these reservations, supply and demand analysis can be seen to be a powerful tool with which to analyse the stock market. We have seen too that if the equity market works efficiently then it performs a valuable function in allocating resources where they are most needed. If consumers value a product, the price of the product will be high. Profits to the companies producing the product will also be high. The share price will thus be high. These companies will be able to raise funds and therefore to increase investment and output in just those industries where consumers want the resources to go. We have seen that supply and demand can be used to understand many other markets too. Try to think through the value of these tools of analysis for other markets. The questions for discussion will help you begin to do this. Later chapters will further clarify and develop these ideas. Just remember that the extent to which one can use these tools for a given market is the extent to which the assumptions outlined above are valid.

Returning to the question which we posed in the title of the chapter, is the stock market the place to make a fortune? By now you should realise that one key is information. You need to know what others do not. Once the information is known, the market reacts very quickly. You may discover that a company is the target of a takeover bid. If you find this out thirty minutes later than others, the price may already have risen by 20 per cent. The second key is the ability to forecast. If you can correctly foresee changes in key indicators you will quickly make a great deal of money. The third key is luck. Sometimes people buy or sell shares just before the announcement of some economic news and discover they have made a capital gain entirely fortuitously. But be warned: the dealing costs are high. You may easily find that to cover your costs and break even your chosen shares need to rise by 10 per cent. For most people, then, share investment should be thought of as a long-term strategy in which one will probably do better than safer forms of savings. The market will tend to compensate you for the additional risk taken. Short-term buying and selling of shares to make a fortune is like trying to win the pools. Information, ability to forecast and good luck all play their part – but the odds are greatly against success. On the whole, a wiser investment is probably the study of economics.

In the meantime, assuming that you have followed the logic of this chapter, you have done far more than gain an insight into share price determination. You have seen how the prices of many goods and services can be explained by the use of supply and demand curves. This is a very valuable tool of analysis. We shall meet it again and again in our study of economics in the coming chapters.

CHAPTER SUMMARY

1 Price in competitive markets is determined by the interaction of supply and demand. This interaction creates an equilibrium price.

2 The demand curve shows a set of plans in the minds of consumers as to how much they wish to purchase at different possible prices, *ceteris paribus*.

3 Demand curves shift in response to changes in variables such as income, the price of substitutes and expectations.

4 The supply curve shows a set of plans in the minds of suppliers as to how much they wish to sell at different possible prices, *ceteris paribus*.

5 Supply curves shift in response to changes in such variables as the price of substitutes, changes in cost, and expectations.

6 How sensitive consumer demand response is to a change in price is measured by the elasticity of demand. This is defined as the proportionate change in quantity demanded divided by the proportionate change in price.

7 Markets are generally stable. A disequilibrium price, where quantity demanded does not equal quantity supplied, is automatically corrected since excess supply or demand pushes the price back to its equilibrium level.

Questions for discussion

*Guidance to the answers for the **asterisked** numbered questions is available to students on the website for the book at* **www.booksites.net/heather**.

1* (a) Using Figure 2.5, what could you expect to happen to a company's share price under the following circumstances:

(i) A large rights issue?
(ii) A sustained rise in interest rates in the economy?
(iii) A large balance of payments deficit for the British economy?

(b) Consider part (a) again. Which companies' share prices will be *most* affected?

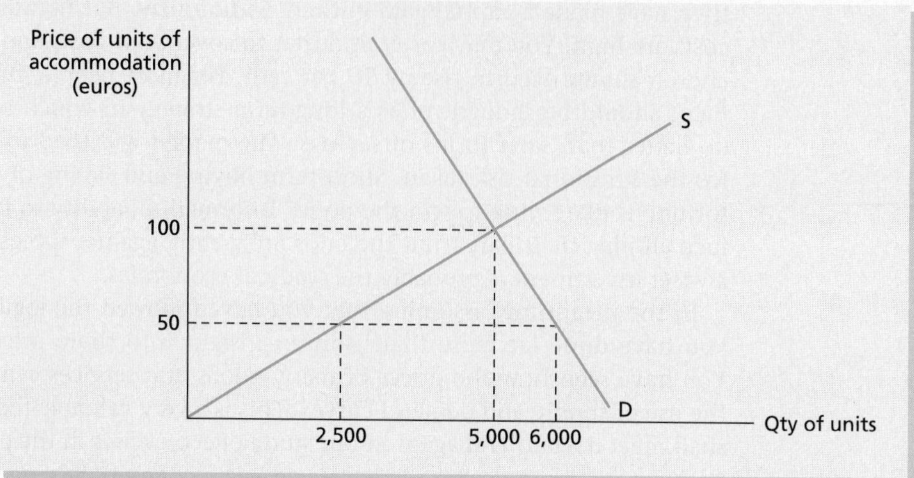

Figure 2.13 **The market for rented accommodation**

2 We have seen that large variations can occur in share prices in a short time. Would price fluctuations be larger or smaller in agricultural markets? Use supply and demand curves to explain your answer.

3* Figure 2.13 shows the market for rented accommodation in a particular university town. (a) What is the equilibrium price of a unit? (b) Suppose the government imposes a 'price ceiling', making it illegal for suppliers to charge more than 50 euros per week. How many units will be supplied? How many will be demanded? (c) What determines who gets the units supplied under the circumstances described in (a)? (d) What determines who gets the units under the circumstances described in (b)?

4 Who are the gainers and who are the losers when governments impose price ceilings? Are price ceilings a good idea?

5* If a company tries to stimulate sales by lowering price, will it be successful if demand is (a) elastic, (b) inelastic?

6 We considered the meaning of the term elasticity of demand. What determines how elastic the demand for a commodity is?

7* (a) Given the present level of prices, rank the following categories of goods from most to least elastic in demand: housing, pork, strawberries, rail travel. Explain your answer.
(b) Why is it difficult for companies issuing new shares to estimate the elasticity of demand for those shares?
(c) Why is it difficult for a company changing the price of its product to estimate its elasticity of demand?

8 If someone successfully speculates in shares and therefore makes a financial *gain*, who makes a loss?

9* The British government offered until recently subsidies to house buyers by granting tax relief on part of the mortgage costs.

(a) Use supply and demand curves to show the effect of this policy on the market for housing.
(b) How might the government's subsidy of house purchases make the task of raising equity finance more difficult?

10 Sketch the supply and demand curves for tickets at a football World Cup final. Is the equilibrium price the one charged in practice? If not, why not? What do you think of the argument that the price of tickets for such events should be low so that the real fans can afford to see them?

Websites

Most countries' stock exchanges will have a website explaining how it works. For example, the London Stock Exchange is:

www.londonstockexchange.com

If you wish to find the website for another country, go to the Google website and type in 'stock exchange'. The list will include the one you seek.

3 Consumer behaviour: utility

Traffic jams: *could European cities import a solution from Singapore?*

CHAPTER OVERVIEW

All over the world, roads, especially in cities, are becoming blocked with too much traffic, causing frustration to people, industry and government. Is there a way out of the problem? One solution is that used by Singapore City.

In this chapter we review the following concepts:

- Opportunity cost
- Supply and demand

We introduce the following:

- Marginal utility
- Consumer surplus
- Income elasticity of demand
- Cross elasticity of demand

3.1 Introduction

There are few of us who have not, at some time or other, sat fuming in a traffic jam. Whenever there is a problem that involves the demand for a scarce resource – in this case road space – we can anticipate that economists will have something to say about it. In this chapter we shall examine part of the theoretical basis for tackling the problem of road congestion. Then we shall look at how one place – Singapore City – has attempted a solution to its rush-hour problems. Their approach is being introduced by more and more governments and urban authorities around the world. We conclude by asking whether one could regard this kind of approach as valid for dealing with road congestion.

Let us first get some idea of the extent of the difficulty regarding transport. We shall be referring to the situation in Britain, but the general picture will be similar for most parts of the world. The volume of road space available in Britain has been growing over time. However, the demand for road space has been increasing more rapidly than its supply, and is forecast to go on doing so.

Table 3.1(a) Forecasts of road traffic and vehicles: 1998–2031

	Actuals, index 1998 = 100			*Central forecasts, 1998 = 100*						
	1988	*1993*	*1998*	*2001*	*2006*	*2011*	*2016*	*2021*	*2026*	*2031*
Vehicle kilometres:										
Cars and taxis	81	90	100	105	114	123	131	138	143	148
Goods vehicles	87	89	100	105	113	121	131	143	154	167
Light goods vehicles	75	86	100	109	122	136	152	169	188	206
Buses and coaches	86	92	100	102	106	109	114	119	124	131
All motor traffic (except two wheelers)	81	90	100	105	115	124	133	141	148	154
Car ownership:										
Cars per person	83	91	100	105	111	118	123	129	133	137
Number of cars	80	89	100	106	113	121	127	133	137	140

Source: Department of Transport

Table 3.1(b) Road length and road area by road class 1955–2001 (thousand kilometres)

	Motorway	*All roads*		*Motorway*	*All roads*
1955	0.0	302.7	1990	3.1	358.0
1960	0.2	312.5	1991	3.1	360.0
1965	0.6	323.6	1992	3.1	362.3
1970	1.1	322.5	1993	3.1	364.2
			1994	3.2	365.0
1975	2.0	330.0	1995	3.2	367.0
1980	2.6	339.6	1996	3.2	368.8
1985	2.8	348.7	1997	3.3	369.9
1988	3.0	354.3	1998	3.3	371.6
1989	3.0	356.6	2001	3.5	392.4

Source: *Road Transport Statistics of Great Britain*

Table 3.1 gives an idea of the size of the problem. The volume of road traffic has doubled in the last twenty years and as Table 3.1(a) indicates the forecast rate of growth is very high. Table 3.1(b) shows the much slower increase in road space supply. This growth rate is unlikely, given current government policy, to change significantly. Such a rapid growth in demand clearly implies an increasing pressure on the more slowly growing supply of road space.

The projections for future demand for road space suggest real difficulties ahead. If incomes continue to grow at the kind of rate we have seen in the past twenty years, the proportion of Britons owning cars will continue to rise. As economists say, the *income elasticity of demand* with respect to cars is positive.

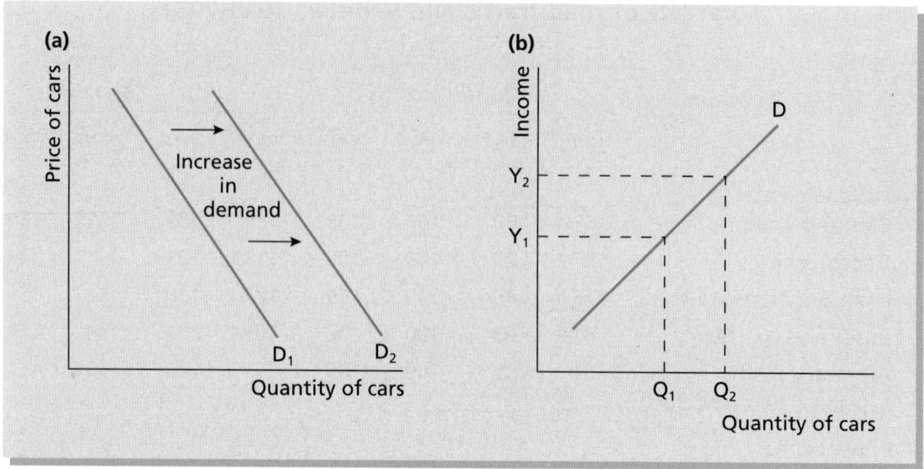

Figure 3.1 **(a) Effect of income increases on the demand for cars; (b) an income demand curve for cars**

You will recall from Chapter 2 that we considered *price* elasticity of demand. We asked how sensitive consumers' demand would be to a change in the price of a good. Looking into the future, car prices are likely to rise as environmental considerations make it necessary to reduce the damage which they do to the atmosphere. However, the demand for cars is also a function of income. If we assume that people's living standards continue to rise, as they have tended to do in most parts of the world in recent decades, what will this do to car demand?

We can use our demand curve analysis of Chapter 2 to see the answer. Look at Figure 3.1(a). The rise in income increases demand. The demand curve moves to the right. At each price more cars are demanded than was the case at the lower level of income.

However, we could show the same effect in terms of an *income demand curve*. An income demand curve depicts the relationship between income and the quality of a good demanded, holding everything constant (including the prices of cars). This is shown in Figure 3.1(b). As we said in Chapter 2, for most goods, a rise in incomes will create an increase in willingness to purchase. Since this seems to apply to cars, we show the income demand curve as upward sloping. So, for example, if incomes increase from Y_1 to Y_2, the quantity of cars demanded will increase from Q_1 to Q_2, assuming that nothing else affecting the demand for cars has altered. Figures 3.1(a) and 3.1(b) thus represent the same information in a different form.

see pp. 36–7

How much will a rise in incomes affect the quantity of cars demanded? How sensitive is demand to income changes? In other words: how income elastic is the demand for cars? Income elasticity of demand for cars is found by the formula

$$\frac{\%\ \Delta\ \text{Quantity of cars demanded}}{\%\ \Delta\ \text{Income}}$$

Table 3.2 Private motoring: households with regular use of cars 1991–2001 (percentage/households)

Year	*No car*	*One car*	*Two cars*	*Three or more cars*	*Great Britain (million)*
1991	32	45	19	4	22.4
1992	32	45	20	4	22.6
1993	31	45	20	4	22.9
1994	32	45	20	4	23.1
1995	30	45	21	4	23.3
1996	30	45	21	4	23.5
1997	30	45	21	4	23.7
1998	28	44	23	5	23.9
1999	28	44	22	5	24.1
2000	27	45	23	5	24.4
2001	26	46	22	5	n/a

Source: Transport Statistics Great Britain 2002

where all other things, including car prices, remain constant. In this case, the proportionate demand change is quite large relative to the proportionate income change: we say that the income elasticity of demand for cars is high. Notice also that it is a positive value. As income increases, the quantity demanded increases. This is typical of most goods.

Not only is the income elasticity of demand for cars high but, surprisingly perhaps, car ownership is still relatively low. Table 3.2 suggests that if incomes across all income groups continue to rise, there is much scope for an increase in the demand for cars and therefore road space. Even among high income professional groups there is much scope for an increase in the number of cars per household. So, given a continued rise in incomes and the limited projected increase in the supply of road space, the problem is set to get worse and worse.

One further indicator of the relationship between income and car ownership in the EU is given by Figure 3.2. The numbers in parentheses represent cars per 1,000 of population, the length of the bars represents average income per head of population. The data cover all countries in the European Union. Many things influence the extent of car ownership, including the price of cars, the cost of running them, availability of public transport, etc. However, it is noticeable that there is a strong correlation between income and car ownership. Luxembourg, for example, with an average income of over double that in Greece, has a degree of car ownership more than twice the Greek level.

If average incomes continue to rise in Europe, governments will face a sharply growing demand for cars. We now reflect on some possible solutions to this problem.

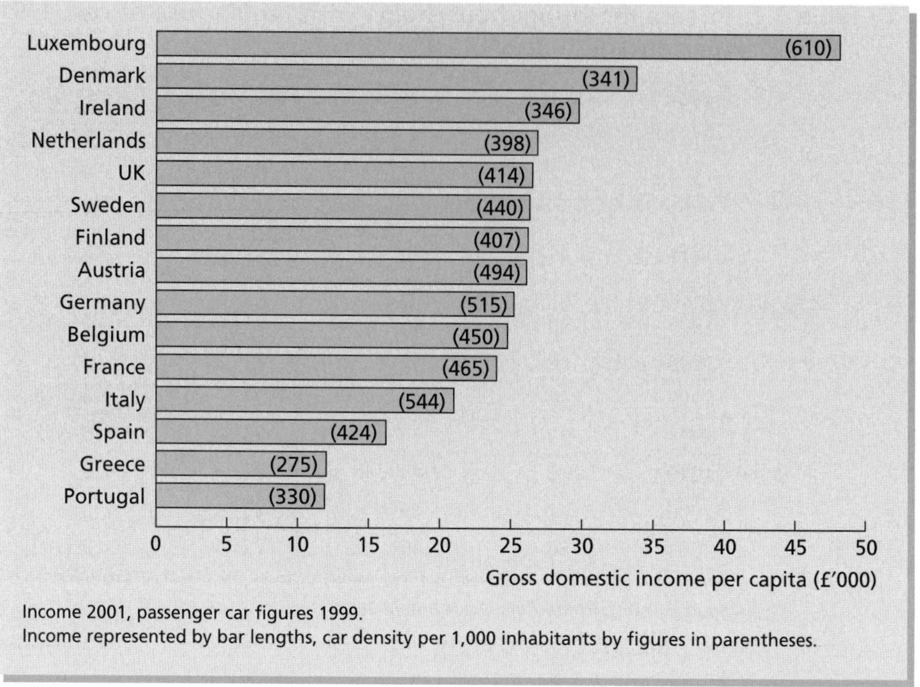

Figure 3.2 Gross domestic income per capita and passenger cars per thousand of population in the EU

Source: adapted from Eurostat data

3.2 The demand for road space

Marginal utility and demand[1]

Why do people wish to consume road space? Clearly, it is because they want to get from A to B. The consumption gives them something they value, or as economists tend to say, it gives them utility. The same principles about the relationship between utility and demand are true for roads as for any other good. The more we consume, the greater our utility up to some point at which additional units of consumption produce no increased satisfaction. However, although utility increases with consumption, it increases at a decreasing rate. Figure 3.3 shows this.

Since total utility rises more slowly as more is consumed, marginal utility, the change in total utility, must be falling. At Q in Figure 3.3, an additional unit consumed adds nothing to the consumer's total utility: his marginal utility is zero, so the total utility curve is flat.

How much will our consumer demand if this is the utility that he derives from road space consumption? The answer is that the consumption of any good also depends upon the price of the good in question, the price of other goods and the level of the consumer's income. Nevertheless he will certainly wish to

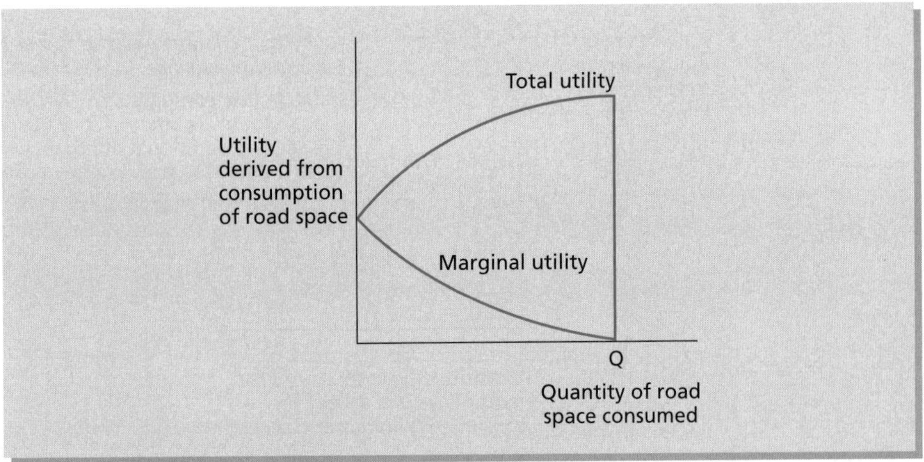

Figure 3.3 Relationship between utility and road space used

arrange his consumption to maximise his welfare. This means consuming goods such that the last pound spent on each good gives him the same utility as the last pound spent on any other good. Formally, this means that the consumer arranges his expenditure such that

$$\frac{MU_A}{P_A} = \frac{MU_B}{P_B} = \ldots \frac{MU_N}{P_N}$$

where MU is marginal utility, P is price and A, B, . . . , N are the various goods that he purchases. This explains why the demand curve slopes downwards: if the price of a good falls, the consumer will no longer be maximising welfare if he continues with the present consumption pattern. He will rearrange his expenditure. If P_A falls, MU must fall to restore his equilibrium. But what brings about a fall in MU? As Figure 3.3 shows, marginal utility will fall when consumption increases. So as price falls, consumption increases. The demand curve has a negative slope because marginal utility declines with increased consumption.

Now, if we know what any individual consumer will demand at different prices, we can sum all consumers' demands at each price to obtain the market demand curve. Suppose that Figure 3.4 shows the market demand for French motorway space. What is the value to consumers of that space? Given that the French set a toll on most motorways, there is a price, P_1. Then we know that Q_1 space is demanded. At present, the price in France is over 4p per kilometre. The price is similar in Italy. In Greece it is far less, in Spain considerably more.

Demand and value

If Q_1 space is being consumed (Figure 3.4), can we now see what that space is worth to consumers? The value in exchange is area A, the number of kilometres demanded, multiplied by its price. Area A in this case represents the revenue received by the government, but it can also be seen as representing the amount that consumers pay in exchange for the space.

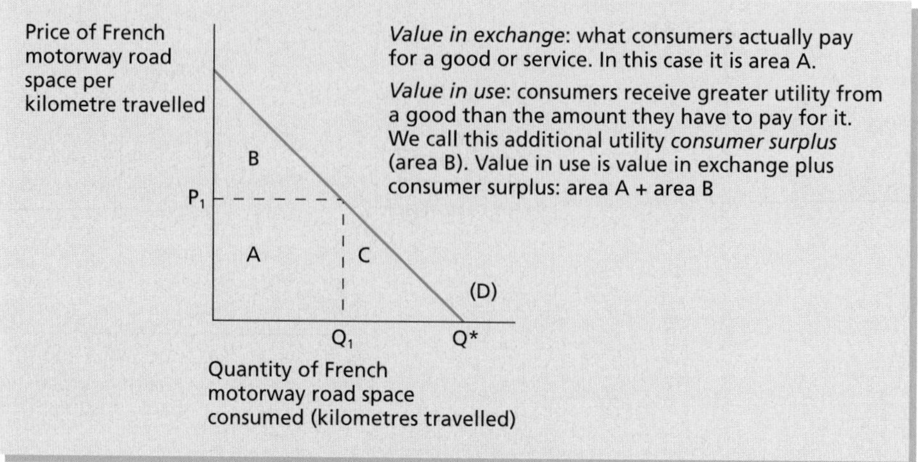

Figure 3.4 The value to consumers of French motorways

Area B represents the utility that consumers receive in excess of what they have to pay for it. Each person except the last marginal consumer at Q thought the utility of the road usage was greater than he or she had to pay for it. This is consumer surplus. If we want to know the value in use of the road space, it will be areas A + B. In other words, value in use is value in exchange plus the consumer surplus, so value in use will, except under very unusual circumstances, be greater than the value in exchange.

Area C represents utility to consumers of road space that they have decided to forgo because the price they are charged is greater than the value they feel they will receive. Since they do not consume the space, either by not travelling or by going on a different, unpriced road, they will not enjoy that utility.

Cross elasticity of demand

One matter to take into account when considering a change in motorway tolls is the burden it imposes on non-toll roads. This question needs to be considered in Britain as the government has put the idea of motorway pricing on the political agenda. An increase in the price of road space will increase the demand for non-motorway (non-toll) roads.

The extent to which the switch to non-toll roads occurs can be examined by elasticity concepts. This time we use the concept of *cross elasticity of demand*. Figure 3.5 shows a cross-price demand curve. It shows the quantity of one good demanded as the price of another good changes, all other things remaining equal. In this case, motorway road space price is changing and we are observing the change in the quantity of other road space demanded. As you might expect, we have a positive relationship. As motorway tolls increase, the quantity demanded of the now relatively cheap substitute rises. Goods that are regarded as substitutes for one another will always exhibit this relationship.

How sensitive will demand for non-motorway roads be to changes in motorway tolls? We can express this in terms of cross elasticity. Formally,

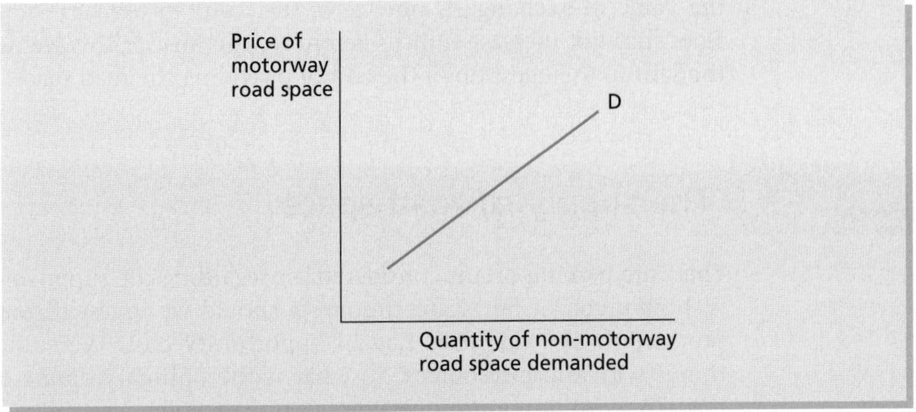

Figure 3.5 **A cross-price demand curve: substitutes**

$$\text{Cross elasticity of demand for X with respect to the price of Y} = \frac{\%\ \Delta\ \text{Q of X demanded}}{\%\ \Delta\ \text{in price of Y}}$$

where X is non-motorway space and Y is motorway space. Notice that the value of this cross-price elasticity will give a positive number. As the price of Y increases, the quantity of X demanded also rises.

Not all pairs of goods exhibit this positive relationship. Figure 3.6 shows a possible negative relationship. As the price of motorway space increases, some may decide not to travel by car at all. Fewer cars will therefore be bought. This is what Figure 3.6 depicts. As motorway space price rises, the quantity of cars demanded will fall. Such pairs of goods are called complements. The two goods complement one another. The cross-price elasticity of demand for such complements will be negative.

By now you should be asking yourself some questions. Have the French got it wrong in charging a price at all? Would it not be better, as is done in Britain, to set a zero price? Consumption would then be Q* in Figure 3.4, so that although

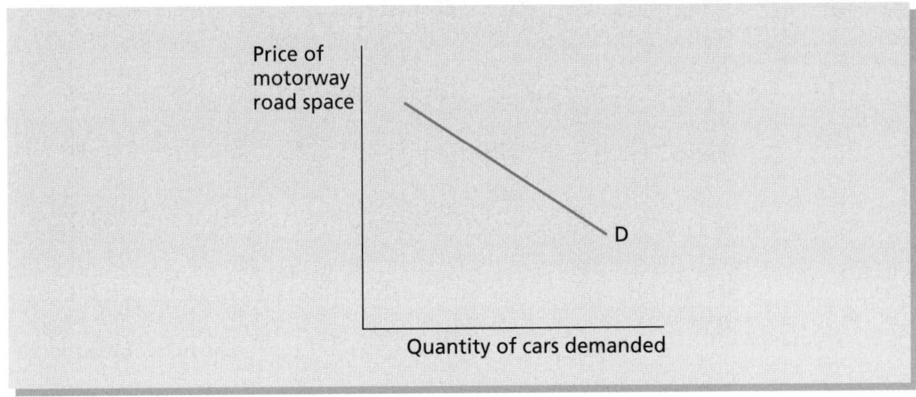

Figure 3.6 **A cross-price demand curve: complements**

the value in exchange is now zero, the value in use has increased by area C. Does that not increase utility? Before we can answer this we need to give some thought to the question of the cost of providing the road space.

3.3 The supply of road space

There are two important considerations regarding the supply of road space. One is, how much of our scarce resources should we invest in road-building? The production of road space has an opportunity cost. We could produce other things with those resources. So what is the optimal volume of investment in roads? It is an important question but one to which we shall give little attention in this chapter. You will be in a better position to think about this question after you have worked through Chapter 10.

The other question that is of direct relevance to us now is: what is the opportunity cost of the road space that we already have? The answer is very little, since the roads have already been built. They are what economists call sunken costs, and are, in that sense, irrecoverable. Hence, if we ignore the wear and tear to the road surface caused by vehicles travelling on it (a question we shall return to later in this chapter) we can represent the position in Figure 3.7. Until the roads have become clogged, say at Q, an increase in the quantity of road space demanded imposes no cost on society. The road is there already. One journey is costless in terms of the use of the road space. Beyond Q this is not so. The supply curve – for that, in essence, is what it is – is vertical. Suppose the demand for that road space is D_1. It is an inefficient use of society's scarce resources to charge consumers for its use. Any price other than zero reduces consumer surplus. Since that surplus is achievable at a zero opportunity cost, there is no logic in taking that surplus away from consumers. Consider Figure 3.4 again. The charge for road space redistributes income from road-space consumers to the government, but at the cost of reducing utility by area C.

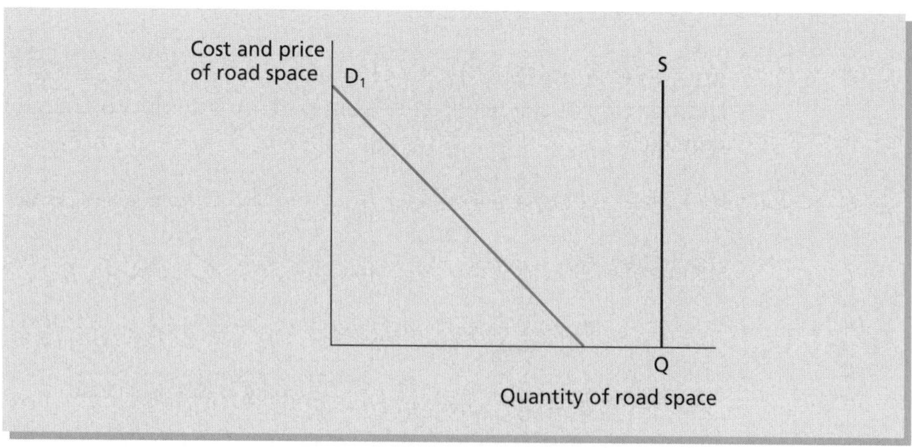

Figure 3.7 Supply and demand for uncongested road space

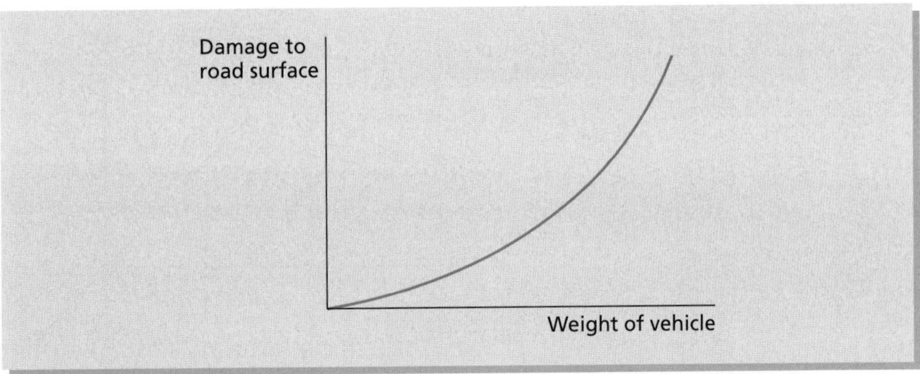

Figure 3.8 Relationship between vehicle weight and road surface damage

Perhaps you feel that those who use roads are the ones who should pay for their provision. If it is felt that road users should contribute to the cost of road-building, a case could be made for saying that there are more efficient ways of doing it. For example, consider a road fund licence in which one makes an annual payment to the government of a given sum *regardless of the demand for road space*. Such a licence will transfer income with fewer effects on efficiency because a rational consumer will still consume road space until marginal utility is zero. However, there will still be some effect. Our proposal will deter marginal consumers of cars from purchasing at all. If the demand for cars is reduced, the whole demand curve for road space will shift inwards, which will itself reduce consumer surplus.

One reason that governments make fixed charges such as the road fund licence is that there are, in reality, costs at the margin. Travelling along a road does impose wear and tear costs, and roads do need repairing. However, collecting it at the point of consumption imposes transaction cost: that is to say, there are costs involved in making the transaction of a payment for the road – toll booths, toll booth operators' wages and so on. These costs would be substantially higher than the cost of issuing an annual licence. Fees for large lorries are often thought of as very high in relation to the car licence. One justification for such large fees is seen in Figure 3.8: the damage done to a road surface does not just increase with the weight of a vehicle but with the square of the weight. The sliding scale of the licence fee is, in part, an attempt to charge for that marginal damage.

3.4 Peak use pricing

Variations in demand

Does the efficiency consideration lead us to suggest that the pricing of road space is a mistaken policy? Not necessarily. Road-space demand varies considerably between different periods, and this variation is the cause of most traffic

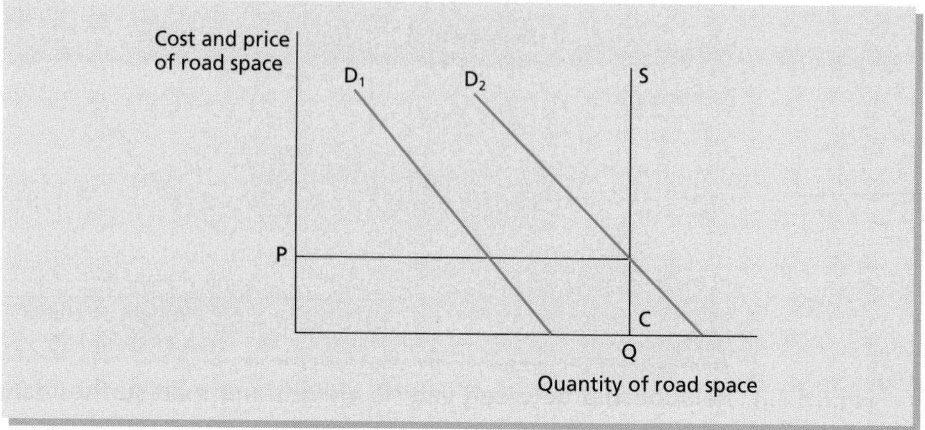

Figure 3.9 Increasing demand for road space

jams. The demand curve will shift to the right considerably during the rush hour or during summer holiday periods in tourist areas.

Figure 3.9 shows the demand for road space in a large city during most of the day (D_1) and demand during the rush-hour period (D_2). Is there a case for pricing on efficiency grounds? There is not during the off-peak period for reasons we have already considered. But look again at the situation during the peak period when D_2 is relevant. There is now a strong case for introducing a pricing scheme on efficiency grounds.

The area C of consumer surplus is simply not available. Road space is not sufficient for that amount to be consumed. A price at P will still enable all of the possible surplus to be gained. Some of it goes to the consumer, and some is transferred from the consumer to the government in revenue that can be used elsewhere.

Pricing at the peak: efficiency considerations

Why the price and the transfer of income? Why not still a zero price? The answer is that now a zero price is not efficient. We want those who gain the greatest utility from consumption to be the ones to use the road.[2] We can be sure that that will be the case only if a price is charged which will act as a rationing device. If price does not ration the output and some other measure is used, then the desired result will almost certainly not be achieved. Some space will be consumed by those who gain little benefit from it. Let us illustrate. Remember, people will attempt to consume any good until its marginal utility is equal to the cost of the alternative. Now, who are the people who will least mind traffic jams? One group is those with little better to do with their time. In other words, those with a low opportunity cost of time. However, some caught in the queues will be those with a high opportunity cost of time. Efficiency considerations dictate that these are the ones who avoid the congestion. They will do so if given the opportunity to buy that avoidance.

Table 3.3 **Averaged additional costs incurred in London and the South East (%)**

Productivity lost due to lateness of staff	1
Delivery time and cost penalties within M25	30
Additional staff/drivers needed to beat congestion	20
Additional vehicles needed	20
Additional vehicle service/repair costs	20
Additional fuel costs	10
Estimated total additional transportation costs in the London area	20

Statistics were compiled from information provided by national organisations that could compare distribution costs in London and the South East with other areas

Source: CBI (1989) *The Capital at Risk*

We have some estimates of the size of inefficiency. Table 3.3 gives the Confederation of British Industry (CBI) estimate of the costs to industry, and ultimately to consumers, of road congestion in south east England. It shows the percentage increase in various kinds of cost over costs outside the South East. The total cost of congestion there is about £15 billion at 1989 prices. More recent studies confirm the size of the problem. The Texas Transport Institute estimate in 1999 was that congestion costs for US drivers was US$72 billion in 1997. This loss of time, increased vehicle operating costs, wasted fuel, etc. represents 3.7% of US GDP.[3]

Clearly, some firms' costs are affected far more than others. A road pricing scheme would cause those firms with most to gain from reduced congestion costs to be willing to pay for congestion avoidance. Even with a peak demand situation as in Figure 3.5 we will need to consider the efficiency gains in the light of the transactions costs. However, if transactions costs are low, the case for road pricing is strong.

The value of the model

You can now see what a powerful tool for analysis is the concept of marginal utility and consumer surplus. Before we turn to look at the way these ideas are used in Singapore, a word of warning. You may be tempted to reject the basis of the case we are constructing on one of two grounds, the first being the realism of the marginal utility assumption. You may feel that consumers simply do not behave in the way we have described. You do not hear someone shopping in Sainsbury's saying to himself or herself 'Is my marginal utility on that pound of sausages divided by its price equal to my marginal utility on that box of cornflakes divided by its price?' In other words, it is tempting to dismiss the arguments about road pricing on the grounds that the theory that underpins it is not true to life.

To argue thus is to show that you have, temporarily we hope, stopped thinking like an economist. Of course, people do not think in terms of the language of the law of diminishing marginal utility. Most people have never heard of consumer surplus. These are formal constructs that help us formulate people's behaviour. Nevertheless, people do behave like this even if they do not think in these terms. Before you started your economics course you still purchased more of a good if the price fell: it is just that now you can describe that behaviour using different terminology.

The second ground on which you might be tempted to reject our analysis is that although consumer surplus is an accurate description of a real world phenomenon, it is of little use because it is not measurable. What is the money value of consumer surplus in the demand for road space? However, as you have now seen, some of these concepts are measurable. We *can* measure congestion costs and we *can* find an equilibrium price, as we are about to see from the illustration of Singapore.

3.5 Example of road pricing

Singapore City's scheme

Singapore is a city state of around three million inhabitants. About 70 per cent of its population live within 8 kilometres of the city centre. Back in 1974 the government looked at the problem of excess demand for road space during the rush hour, forecast that the increase in car demand by 1992 would be over 350 per cent and concluded that something had to be done.

After careful study the government decided that some increase in road space was possible, but the opportunity cost of providing sufficient road space to meet the expected increase in demand was considerable. Thus it was the demand side that would need to be dealt with primarily. However, on the supply side, there was some *reduction* in road space for cars by the provision of bus lanes. The economic rationale is simple. Travelling by car imposes costs on oneself but also on others by increasing congestion. The provision of bus lanes recognises that divergence between private and social benefits.

On the demand side, several possibilities suggested themselves. One was an advertising campaign arguing the advantages of staggered working hours. This shifts the demand curve left at the peak but rightwards off-peak. Provided that the off-peak increase in demand did not create an excess quantity demanded at a zero price, this would result in a net improvement in welfare. There would also be an opportunity cost of the resources allocated to the advertising.

Another measure for shifting the demand curve to the left is to increase the price of complementary goods via increased taxes on cars or petrol. The problem is that it does not control the timing of demand for road space and was therefore rejected. A complete ban on cars fails to recognise that car travel is a benefit and should not be controlled unless the benefit of control exceeds its cost.

The obvious solution, however, was to use the price mechanism for space. This was the option taken. It took two forms: the pricing of road space and the pricing of parking space. Road-space pricing was done via area licences. These required a payment if a car were to be used within a designated restricted zone at peak times. The use of a toll was rejected because it was felt that this would impose too high a transaction cost in terms of collection of payment and in slowing traffic still further.

Not all vehicles paid – commercial vehicles and public transport vehicles were exempt. The other major exception was particularly interesting. A car with at least four occupants was also exempt. This was to encourage pooling of cars since the additional demand for road space is nil if a driver carries extra passengers. Nevertheless, in an attempt to restrain growing demand further, car pooling was no longer exempted after 1989. In fact, all vehicles including motorcycles were included. Only ambulances, fire engines, police vehicles and public buses are now excluded.

A further problem for the authorities was to decide what constituted peak time. The original choice was 7.15–9.30 am. Excess demand was soon apparent immediately after 9.30 am, so the restricted time was extended to 10.15 am.

No restrictions were placed on travel during the evening rush hour. The argument was that the evening is a mirror image of the morning. If morning excess demand is eliminated, the evening problem automatically disappears.

Subsequently an evening peak developed and only vehicles with an area licence were able to travel in the restricted zone. With effect from January 1994 the restrictions apply all day from 7.30 am to 6.30 pm. This reflects the increasing demand for road space in the city centre even at what was once considered off-peak.

The second form of price mechanism was the pricing of parking space. Parking charges in the publicly owned car parks were increased steeply. Since parking space is a close complement of road use, this further shifts demand for road space left. It is not a perfect complement because, for example, it does not affect through traffic. Private car park operators were not able to enjoy a windfall increase in profits because a levy was introduced on them.

A park-and-ride scheme was also introduced but was not judged to be very successful.

Assessing the scheme

The view of the authorities was that, prior to 1974, the excess demand for road space at the peak was 25–30 per cent. That is to say, the estimate was that this was the kind of reduction that would enable traffic to flow freely. The problem was that there was no known study as to how motorists would react to large increases in the price of road space. In other words, it was not known how price elastic demand would be. The equilibrium price was to a large extent guesswork. The area licence was set at S$60 (Singapore dollars) per month or S$3 per day. In fact, with the other measures taken, demand was reduced at the peak by 40 per cent. Diagrammatically it would suggest what we have in Figure 3.10: car parking fees etc. shifted the demand curve left.

Car parking and road space are complementary goods. A rise in the price of car parking fees reduces the quantity of road space demanded. The price that was set moved motorists along the lower demand curve to 10 per cent or so less than road space supply. The authority's decision was to leave the price

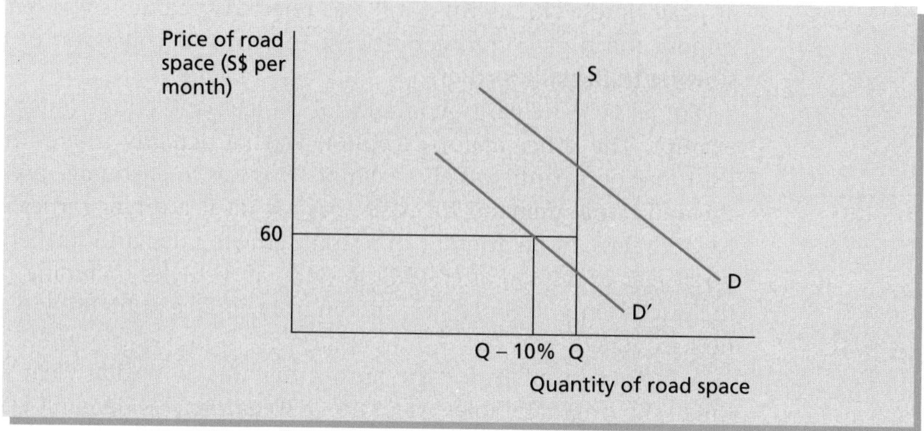

Figure 3.10 Influencing the demand for road space in Singapore

unchanged, anticipating that, over time, increased incomes would move the demand curve back to the right until the optimum was reached.

How has the scheme affected the distribution of benefits within Singapore? There are several things to be thought through. First, the effects of consumption on those walking or using public transport have been reduced – those responsible for creating the effects having to bear the costs. Second, the speed of traffic is now much greater, albeit at considerable expense to those gaining the benefit. Third, government revenue is sufficient to cover all the transaction costs involved so that no cost falls on the general taxpayer.

3.6 Singapore today

Pricing private transport

Improvements in technology have made it possible in recent years to reduce transactions costs and further improve traffic flows. Toll booths which show the flow of traffic are no longer necessary and have been replace by Electronic Road Pricing (ERP). Every new car purchased in Singapore has a unit installed and each journey is read by electronic transponders. This has a number of advantages. It reduces the costs of the system. It allows greater flexibility in charging and therefore speeds up the movement of vehicles. The highest price is now paid for journeys from 8.30–9 am. The system is also sufficiently advanced to distinguish vehicle types. Minibuses, for example are charged a different rate. Table 3.4 gives an idea of the current charges on the Expressways into the centre for passenger cars.

In recent years the price of purchasing a car has also risen significantly. The rise in incomes has shifted the demand curve to the right as the authorities in the 1970s predicted. So in addition to the area licence scheme, demand for road space outside the peak times is being restrained.

Table 3.4 **Charges for passenger cars (with effect from 24 June 2002)**

Monday to Friday	*7.30 am–8.00 am*	*8.00 am–8.30 am*	*8.30 am–9.00 am*	*9.00 am–9.30 am*
AYE between Portsdown Road and Alexandra Road	$0.00	$1.00	$1.50	$1.00
CTE after Braddell Road, Serangoon Road and Balestier slip Road	$1.50	$2.50	$3.00	$1.00
CTE between Ang Mo Kio Ave 1 and Braddell Road	$1.00	$1.00	$0.50	$0.50
ECP after Tanjong Rhu Flyover	$0.50	$1.00	$1.50	$0.50
ECP from Ophir Road	$0.00	$1.00	$1.00	$0.00
PIE after Kallang Bahru exit	$0.50	$1.00	$1.00	$0.00
PIE eastbound after Adam Road and Mount Pleasant slip road into the eastbound PIE	$0.00	$1.00	$1.50	$0.00
PIE slip road into CTE	$2.00	$2.50	$2.50	$1.50

Source: Land Transport Authority (Singapore)

How is this being done? Again it is through price, this time by raising the price of cars – a complementary good to road space. There are two main forms of pricing. One form is the use of taxes and fees on the registration of new cars, the other, introduced in May 1990, is the certificate of entitlement (COE) scheme.

The taxes and fees payable on registration of a car are as follows (amounts are in Singapore dollars):

- Import duty of 41 per cent of market value.
- Registration fee of S$1,000 for a private car, S$5,000 for a company car.
- Additional first registration fee of 150 per cent of market value.
- In addition there is an annual road tax based on engine capacity. A medium-sized saloon would be around S$2,000 for a private vehicle, S$4,000 for a company car.

Certificate of entitlement scheme

The COE scheme is particularly interesting. We have seen how it can be difficult to gauge the appropriate price for restricting demand to a given amount. The authorities have decided that a way of overcoming this difficulty is by a bidding system.

Each month a predetermined number of COEs valid for ten years are issued for various sizes of car, goods vehicles and motorcycles. People are then free to bid for a COE. All successful private bidders pay the lowest single successful bid price for the appropriate category of vehicle, known as the quota premium (QP). Company cars pay double the QP. Notice that some will pay less than they bid. The authorities do not remove all the consumer surplus.

As an illustration of the point, imagine there are five people wishing to purchase a COE. One of them values a COE at S$10,000, one at S$9,000, one at S$8,000, one at S$7,000 and one at S$6,000. This is shown in the demand curve for COEs. Each will bid what he or she is willing to pay. That is what the demand curve tells us.

Assume now that there are only four COEs to be issued at this time. The lowest successful bid will be S$7,000. Government revenue will be 4 × S$7,000 = S$28,000 since all four successful bidders pay the lowest successful bid price.

By charging all bidders the maximum they were prepared to pay, government revenue could have been S$34,000, value in exchange plus value in use. The other S$6,000 is the consumer surplus that the government chose not to take.

The future of traffic management

Reducing the quantity of road space demanded by varying its price is now being copied by other authorities. Some Scandinavian countries are operating such systems. Trondheim, for example, charges the equivalent of about £1 for a journey from 6–10 am and around 50p for a journey outside that time. This modest charge has improved traffic flows. Similar schemes are appearing in the USA. In San Diego tolls are varied every few minutes according to traffic flows so that charges vary between 50 cents and four dollars. Again the evidence is that consumer behaviour reacts to price changes. Central London began to levy a congestion charge in 2003 and several other cities are considering such schemes. General motorway charges in the UK are some way off. There are many political sensitivities to such proposals even though the economic case is overwhelming.

3.7 Conclusion

If incomes continue to grow, the present problems of urban congestion can only become worse. There is still enormous potential for an increase in private vehicle ownership. It is widely recognised that something has to be done. The problems of a low average traffic speed in some British cities are repeated in large towns and cities in many parts of the world. Efficiency considerations suggest that, since road space is a scarce commodity, the supply of which cannot be rapidly expanded, it is demand growth that must be tackled.

To a large extent the problem is one of peak demand. On theoretical grounds, marginal utility analysis suggests that this peak can be controlled via an increase in the relative price of road space from zero to whatever is necessary for equilibrium at those particular times.

Singapore City gives an excellent illustration of an attempt to deal with the problem and provides some idea of the likely size of price increase which this solution to the problem would require. Although every city has its own particular characteristics, the change in relative price needed to achieve equilibrium would, if the example of Singapore were typical, be considerable.

CHAPTER SUMMARY

1 **The total utility that a consumer gains from the consumption of a good is the satisfaction derived from it. Marginal utility is the satisfaction gained from the consumption of one extra unit.**

2 **The demand curve is a reflection of the *marginal* utility (MU) of a good to the consumer.**

3 **An income demand curve shows a set of plans in the minds of consumers as to how much they wish to purchase at different possible income levels, *ceteris paribus*.**

4 **How sensitive consumer demand response is to a change in income is measured by income elasticity of demand: proportionate change in quantity demanded divided by proportionate change in price.**

5 **Cross elasticity of demand measures the sensitivity of consumer demand for one good to a change in the price of another: proportionate change in quantity of X demanded divided by the proportionate change in price of Y.**

6 **A consumer will purchase such that MU/P is the same for all goods (where P is price).**

7 **Consumer surplus is the utility that a consumer receives in excess of the price paid for a commodity.**

Questions for discussion

Guidance to the answers for the ***asterisked*** *numbered questions is available to students on the website for the book at* **www.booksites.net/heather**.

1* If the French government were to raise the toll charged on its motorways, would the value of the consumed road space be higher or lower than before? (*Hint*: What two different ideas did we say that we had for 'value'?)

2 Using the concept of value in exchange and value in use, why is the price of diamonds so high relative to the price of bread, if bread is so much more useful as a commodity?

3* Can you think of other instances where queues are used as a rationing device rather than price? Why, in the instances you have thought of, do you think pricing is rejected as a solution? Is this the correct decision?

4 College canteens are crowded at lunchtime. What would you think of a scheme to solve the problem whereby prices were reduced by, say, 30 per cent from 11.30 am to 12.15 pm and from 1.30 pm to 2.30 pm and increased by 20 per cent from 12.15 pm to 1.30 pm, thus spreading the peak and eliminating the need to queue?

5* Consider Table 3.5. Which goods would appear to be those with the highest income elasticity of demand? Which have the lowest? Are there any which

Table 3.5 Consumer durables by socio-economic group of head of household, Great Britain, 1994[a]

Percentage of households with:	*Economically active heads*								*Economically inactive heads*
	Professional	*Employers and managers*	*Intermediate non-manual*	*Junior non-manual*	*Skilled manual and own account non-professional*	*Semi-skilled manual and personal service*	*Unskilled manual*	*Total*	
Television:									
Colour	98	99	97	96	98	96	98	98	95
Monochrome	1	0	2	2	1	2	2	1	3
Video recorder	89	94	87	87	92	85	82	90	57
CD player	73	70	66	56	59	49	40	61	24
Home computer	54	47	36	25	30	21	16	34	9
Microwave oven	76	82	71	76	78	68	67	76	51
Deep freeze/ fridge freezer	93	95	91	92	94	89	88	93	82
Washing machine	96	97	92	90	95	90	86	93	82
Tumble drier	65	69	54	56	60	53	46	60	35
Dishwasher	48	43	25	17	17	9	7	25	9
Telephone	99	98	95	92	92	85	75	93	89
Central heating	95	92	89	86	86	79	81	88	82
More than one car or van	55	55	29	18	32	14	8	34	7

[a] Excluding members of the Armed Forces, economically active full-time students, and those who were unemployed and had never worked

Source: *General Household Survey* © Crown copyright 1999

appear to be inferior goods? What does the table tell you about the price elasticity of demand for all of these goods?

6 What problems and benefits do you see in introducing a scheme similar to that of Singapore in your own city?

7* Why will all of the costs of purchasing area licences not fall on private commuters? (*Hint*: What happens to businesses if the effect is to reduce the supply of labour to those in the centre?)

8 Why will all of the costs of purchasing area licences for company cars not fall entirely on business profits?

9* What advantages and disadvantages are there in removing all the consumer surplus under the COE scheme?

10 Sketch a diagram of the supply and demand curves for a town car park at 8 am on a Tuesday morning. How does this diagram differ for Saturday morning at 10 am just before Christmas? Does this suggest that the local authority charging policy is rational?

Websites

The UK government's transport department provides information on its policy at:

www.dft.gov.uk/

For further information about Singapore's system consult:

www.lta.gov.sg/

This gives up-to-date information on all aspects of its transport management system.

Notes

1 Some of the concern about the use of cars relates not so much to the problems of congestion but to damage to the environment. There is very little in this chapter on this aspect of the problem of transport. However, the problems raised by such matters are dealt with at various points in later chapters, especially in Chapter 12.

2 You may feel that this is unfair. The rich can afford to consume the road space. In fact there are two factors governing the demand for road space, or indeed for any good. One is willingness to pay; the other is ability to pay. We are concentrating here on willingness to pay. We want those who are most willing to pay to consume the product. In other words, we want, *for any given distribution of income*, those who are most willing to pay to be consumers. The question of ability to pay and the distribution of income is examined in Chapter 16.

3 '1999 Urban Mobility Study', Texas Transport Institute, Texas A and M University, Texas 1999.

4 Consumer behaviour: indifference analysis

The health care system: *is radical treatment needed?*

CHAPTER OVERVIEW

In recent years the provision of many services widely regarded as essential has been moved from the state to the private sector. Would we have a more efficient health care system if we transferred health care entirely to the private sector? Would most people gain? How would it affect the poor? Would we have greater resources devoted to health and a healthier population? We examine this question with particular reference to the UK's National Health Service.

In this chapter we review:
- Supply and demand

We introduce:
- Indifference theory
- Merit goods
- External benefits
- The distribution of income
- Pareto optimality

4.1 Introduction

Most people accept without question the fact that the great majority of things they wish to have are provided on a market basis. Whether it be relatively unimportant items, such as balloons and ice cream, or things essential to survival such as clothing and food, people expect to pay for these things at the point of consumption. One notable exception to the rule is that of health care. The majority of people in the UK favour the provision of 'free' health care through the National Health Service (NHS). Most appreciate, of course, that such treatment cannot be provided at a zero cost, but they believe that those costs should be borne by the government through general taxation so that the care is given free at the point at which it is consumed. To pay to go into hospital for an operation or to pay for a visit to the GP would be regarded as unacceptable.

Let us examine Table 4.1. One striking factor of expenditure on health care is how much importance is attached to it. In established market economies, over

Table 4.1 **Domestic spending and donor assistance on health, 1997–1999**

	Public spending on health (per person, 1997, $US)	*Total spending on health (per person, 1997, $US)*	*Donor assistance for health (per person, average annual 1997–1999)*	*Donor assistance for health annual average ($US millions 1997–1999)*
Least-developed countries	6	11	2.29	1,473
Other low-income countries	13	23	0.94	1,666
Lower-middle-income developing countries	51	93	0.61	1,300
Upper-middle-income developing countries	125	241	1.08	610
High-income countries	1,356	1,907	0.00	2
All countries			0.85	5,052

Note: Unweighted averages for countries in respective categories. Includes only countries with population of 500,000 or more in 1997.

Source: Commission on Macroeconomics and Health, WHO

9 per cent of total output is consumed by health care. Health care appears to be highly income elastic. Per capita, health expenditure in established market economies is about 80 times as great as in Sub-Saharan Africa and 160 times as great as it is in China. Yet even in established market economies, as can be seen from column four, 60 per cent of all this expenditure is incurred by the public sector. The market mechanism plays a fairly small part in Britain, one of the established market economies, since most health care expenditure is undertaken by government. Furthermore, relatively little of it is charged for at the point of use. In Britain the system commands widespread public support. In the course of this chapter, we shall ask whether such a system makes economic sense.

We want to question whether there is any economic rationale in a system where, say, food is not free at the point of consumption and must be purchased from income, whereas health care is distributed on a non-market basis.

What we shall do in this chapter, therefore, is as follows. First, we shall argue the case for treating health care like any other good or service and providing it on a market basis, as is largely the case in the United States. Then we shall consider the main objections to this view, concentrating particularly upon the notion that a free NHS is the only way of ensuring an adequate level of health care to the poor.

4.2 The market case

The demand for health care

The first reason for allocating health care on a market basis is that it gives a solution to the problem of rationing. Allocating health care on a non-market basis tends to assume that the demand for health care is finite even if there is a zero price. One is either 'healthy' or 'ill'. In fact, this is not the case. There are degrees of illness and health. This has become even more obvious with improved medical techniques, which not only cure illness, but also discover it. Body scanners, for example, have the potential to diagnose conditions which twenty years ago would have gone unnoticed. Furthermore, medical technology has created a demand for hip replacements, heart transplants and many other forms of health care. The demand was previously not there because the treatment was, given the state of technology at the time, impossible. The development of Viagra has also brought this problem into focus.

It is, therefore, probably true that health care is capable of absorbing more than the whole of the gross national product. As economists never tire of pointing out, when resources are scarce, choices have to be made. The conclusion is inescapable. Medical care has to be rationed. There has been a significant increase in resources devoted to health care in England in the past 10–15 years – but complaints about hospital waiting lists and overcrowded doctors' surgeries have not abated at all during this period.

Have we reached a point where resources devoted to medical care are now unlikely to grow much? According to the Wanless Report of 2002 substantial increases in spending on health in the UK will be necessary. Figure 4.1(a) shows projected spending on health as a proportion of GDP. It is expected to rise sharply. The government has set targets for improving the nation's health, reducing smoking and obesity for example. The different projections reflect different assumptions about progress in meeting these targets. Figure 4.1(b) shows total NHS spending projections *at constant prices*. That is, if we allow for the effects of inflation we still need large expenditure increases. Figure 4.1(c) appears to show a more optimistic picture of the demand for resources. However, these are for annual *growth* in spending. Because the changes are positive, each year requires more NHS resources even though the rate of increase is projected to slow. The larger increases in the early years are designed to allow NHS spending to move closer to the European average since at present EU economies typically devote greater volumes of resources to health care than the UK does.

All these increases carry a basic assumption that health care will continue to be largely free at the point of use. There will be no significant rationing by price.

The second, closely related, reason for thinking that health care might be better allocated on a market basis is that the market mechanism can offer a means of distinguishing between wants and needs. Medical care *can* mean the difference between life and death; however, a relatively small amount of medical care is for life-threatening conditions. Most trips to hospital or the doctor are for the purpose of improving the state of health: they are 'wants'. How does one distinguish between wants and needs? The economist's answer is: willingness to pay. If something is really *needed*, the consumer will demand it; if it is a *want* he may or may not do so. If one does not use a market system there will be great difficulty making the distinction. An obvious illustration of the difficulty is found in the somewhat arbitrary decisions of government over what aspects of health care should be charged for. Hospitalisation is free, and medication

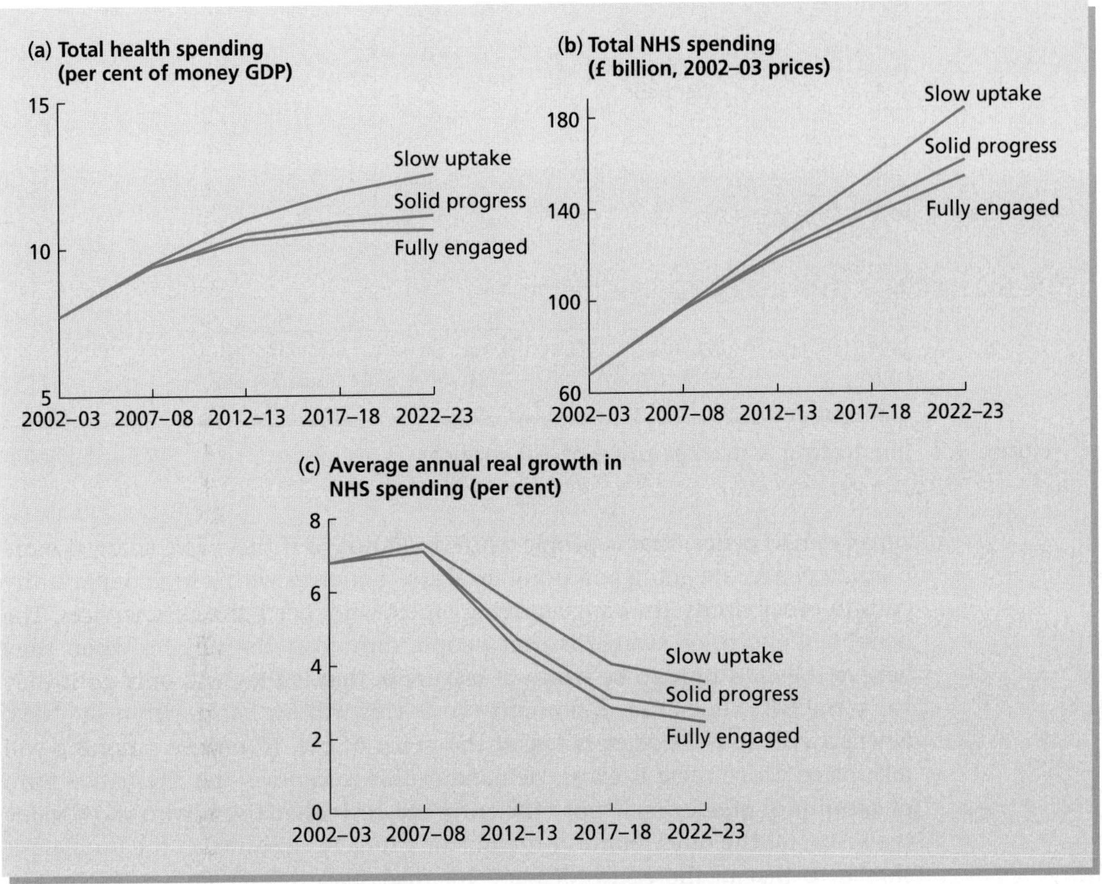

Figure 4.1 Government expenditure on health care in the UK

Source: adapted from *Securing our future health: Taking a long view*, Wanless Report, 2002

provided while in hospital is also free. Medication provided by a GP is, to many, partly paid for in the prescription charge. Suntan lotion to protect from melanoma is not regarded as a need. It is clearly an attractive idea, then, to let the consumer decide which he or she regards as important via the price system.

Rationing health care by price: efficient resource usage

Let us now see how a price system overcomes the disadvantages of an NHS type system. Consider Figure 4.2. We examine one part of the NHS system for illustrative purposes, the GP system. The government determines the number of GPs that it is prepared to fund out of taxation. This gives us a fixed supply of GP services, at least in the short run.

There will be a negatively sloped demand curve for the reasons outlined above. What happens if the price of a visit to the doctor is zero? There is excess demand of $Q_b - Q_a$. This is not simply some textbook problem: it illustrates powerfully what happens all over Britain every day. People who value the visit to the

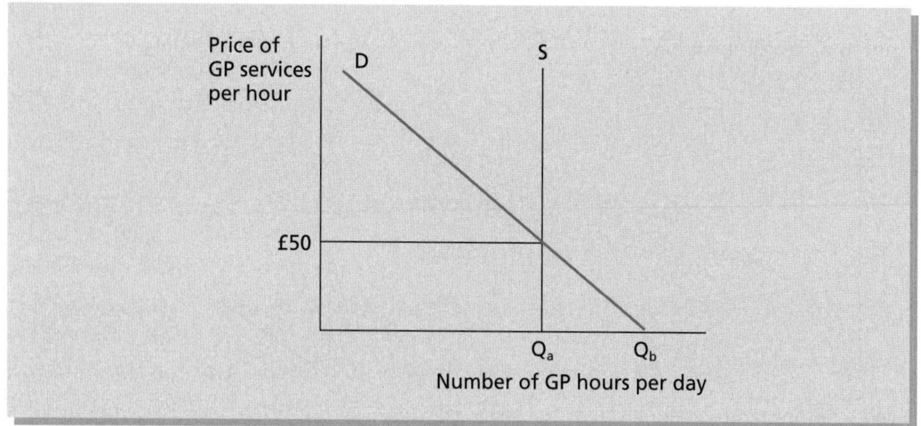

Figure 4.2 Illustrating a market price of GP services

surgery at 20 pence, that is people who would not go if they were charged more than 20 pence, are going and using up scarce resources with a high opportunity cost. In other words, they are depriving others who 'need' the GP's services. The benefit of the price system is that people only visit the surgery when they believe the GP's time to be worth at least £50, that is they will only go if they value the GP's time at its opportunity cost. This will *not* be so within the NHS, where a visit to the doctor is free at the point of use. Non-price rationing will take place. Since there is excess demand at this zero price, the alternative form of rationing, queues, will not efficiently see to it that those who most value the visits are the ones found in the doctor's surgery. In essence, the problem is similar to that of the excess demand for road space which we encountered in Chapter 3.

There are other ways in which this inefficiency displays itself. It is not simply that some who value the doctor's time will not get to see him or her, but the average time spent with the GP is also reduced. Whereas in the United States fifteen minutes is an average consulting time per patient, five minutes or less is typical in the UK. This is probably *not* a reflection of the greater number of GPs per head in the United States than in the UK, but rather of the huge demand for GP services in England owing to the absence of a price mechanism. However, the nature of medical care in the United States tends to mean more specialists and fewer general practitioners than in the UK, so that comparisons are difficult to make.

Non-price rationing also reduces the array of services provided by a GP. Except for the elderly and chronically sick, it is not always easy to get a check-up on the NHS. Tests to detect breast cancer, for example, are also less common than in the United States. There is simply not time to provide such services if price does not ration output. GPs now have to meet targets in terms of numbers given check-ups etc. These have been introduced in recent years specifically to try to deal with the excess demand situation.

Another inefficiency which non-price rationing creates is, alas, by its nature virtually impossible to measure. Excess demand where there is an effective price ceiling usually results in the creation of some form of discrimination. Doctors and surgeons can, on occasion, allow someone to 'jump the queue'.

Finally, one must not underestimate the degree of inefficiency associated with transferring decisions about health care from the economic sphere to the political one. Most people who have a relatively minor complaint can get treatment quickly. A throat infection requiring a GP to prescribe antibiotics can usually be treated within a few days. More serious conditions will be treated far more slowly. Waiting times for surgical treatment of a heart condition may take months or even years. In a market system this would not be so likely to happen. Since the heart condition treatment would be valued more, it will be treated relatively quickly. So why in an NHS-type system is the reverse the case? One explanation is that when resources are allocated by politicians, they are primarily interested in buying votes. There are more votes in providing resources to treat large numbers of people for minor complaints than there are in allocating large volumes of resources to treat relatively few. This may or may not be the best way to use limited health care resources.

4.3 Private medical care using indifference theory

So far the discussion has been conducted as though there were no private health care market in Britain. Such is not, in fact, the case. Although it is prohibitively expensive for almost everyone to purchase medical care whenever it becomes necessary, it is possible to insure through organisations such as BUPA against the need for many kinds of such care. Growing numbers of people have chosen to do so. The proportion of people so insured in the UK has been strongly increasing. In 1985 it was less than 6 per cent. By 2000 it was well over 9 per cent.

One advantage of having a state health care service *plus* a private service would appear to be that *more* resources are thus devoted to health care. Careful thought, however, will lead us to the conclusion that this may not be so. In order to follow the argument we need to acquaint ourselves with the elements of *indifference theory*, or what is sometimes called indifference curve analysis.

When we looked at consumer behaviour in Chapter 3 we used the concept of marginal utility analysis. An alternative approach to explaining how consumers behave is indifference theory. There is more to indifference theory than we shall consider now,[1] but understanding the elements of this approach will shed light on choices that people make with respect to consuming many goods and services, including health care.

Consider, first, people's preferences for health care and all other goods (Figure 4.3). We are particularly interested in people's health care preferences, but the principles we are developing apply for most consumers with any good or service.

Figure 4.3 shows Jessica's preferences. Each spot represents a level of utility she receives from consuming the given quantities. So spot X gives some level of utility, or satisfaction, received by consuming O–H_1 of health care and O–O_1 of other services. Other combinations which lie along IC_1 (indifference curve 1) are assumed to give the same level of satisfaction. She would regard herself as

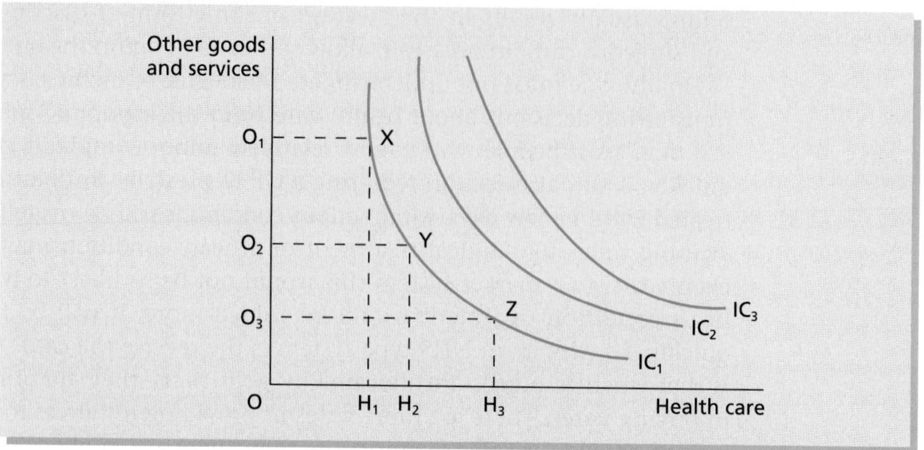

Figure 4.3 Indifference curves for health care and other goods and services

'indifferent' between any such combinations, including spots Y and Z. Notice the slope of the curve: it is negative. This shows that in order to retain a given level of utility, Jessica requires more health care in order to compensate for a reduction in the amount of other goods and services she consumes. The shape of the curve is also significant. It is what one would expect for most consumers and most goods and services. She is indifferent between X and Y, yet she gets only a little more health care at Y for a large sacrifice of other goods and services. This is reasonable. The loss of some goods of which Jessica has a great deal is not too serious. The gain of a little more health care when she has so little is worth quite a lot to her. But the less of other goods she has and the more health care she has, the less enthusiasm she has for switching into even more health care. So moving from Y to Z will keep her equally happy, but she will need greater amounts of health care to compensate for the loss of other goods. This is the principle which underlies the shape of the indifference curve as being convex to the origin.

We assume that consumers would prefer more of both goods if it were possible. So combinations along IC_2 are preferred to combinations along IC_1 since these show greater combinations of both goods and hence greater welfare. Can our consumer afford all these combinations? Clearly that depends upon her income and upon the prices of the goods and services in question. We can use Figure 4.4 to show the constraint income places on the ability to meet preferences.

Assume her income is £1,000 per month. She could consume at point A, spend all her income on other goods and none of it on health care. She could be at point B, spending her entire income on health care. It is much more likely that she will choose one of the combinations of health care and other goods and services which her £1,000 income will purchase. These combinations are represented by the straight line AB called a *budget line*. Which combination will she actually choose? Figure 4.5 shows both her preferences and the budget line. The solution is simple: she chooses the combination which gets her on the

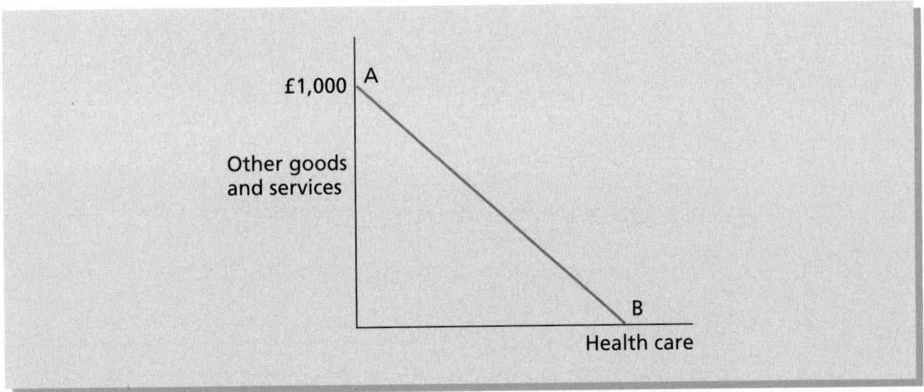

Figure 4.4 **Price of health care relative to other goods and services**

indifference curve furthest from the origin. This is because the further from the origin the curve lies the higher the combinations of all goods she is able to enjoy. For Jessica this is at point W, which for this consumer with her particular preferences means she buys £400 worth of health care and £600 of other goods.

All this assumes that there is no NHS and that any health care she consumed must be purchased. We turn now to see the effects on consumer preferences towards health if we introduce an NHS service giving a free but limited amount of health care.

There is one interesting thing which may surprise you about a system of private health care existing alongside state provision of a free statutory amount of health care. If a statutory amount is offered free in the hope of increasing the amount of health care that everyone receives, it is unlikely to achieve its goal for all. In fact, it may actually reduce the amount that some receive. If you find this surprising look at Figure 4.6.

The budget line AB represents the options open to a consumer with a given income with respect to health care where there is no state scheme. The consumer can choose any combination of health and other goods and services

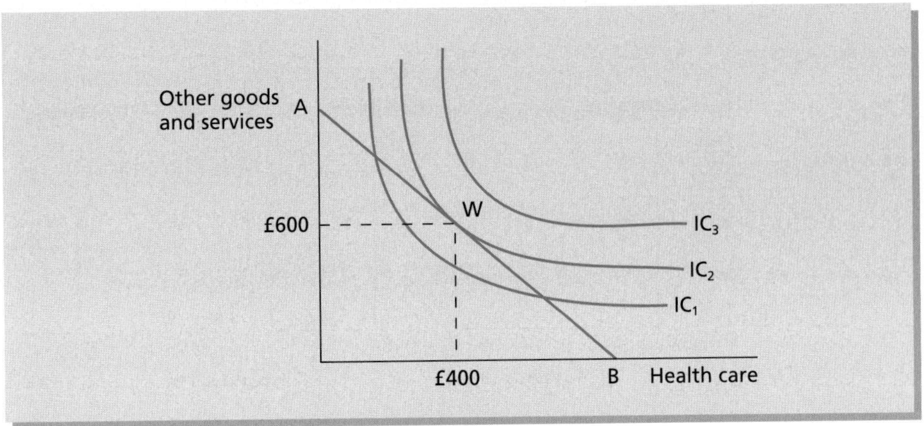

Figure 4.5 **Consumer equilibrium in health care preference**

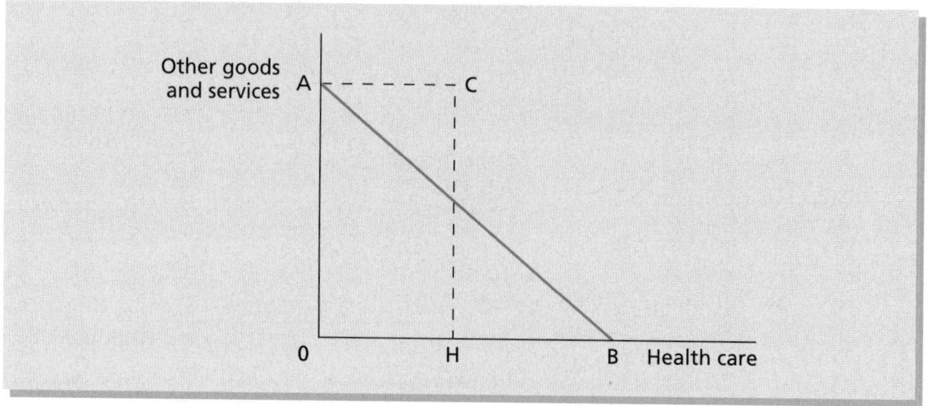

Figure 4.6 **Free government provision of health care: effects on consumer choice**

along that budget line. Now, though, the government introduces an NHS scheme. There is a limited amount of health care offered, OH. However, since it is free at the point of consumption, the consumer is being offered the combination at point C in addition to all combinations along AB. Note that if this consumer chooses point C, he or she can have OA of all other goods because he or she does not have to pay for the volume of health care OH offered by the government. Now, suppose that one could either choose NHS provision or private care, but not a combination of both. Will a rational consumer always choose point C? Indeed not. It will depend upon his or her preferences. The volume of health care that one may wish to consume may exceed what is on offer free from the NHS. Let us look at three different consumers and impose their preferences on the budget line from Figure 4.6. We do this in Figure 4.7(a), (b) and (c).

Catherine, the consumer in (a), does not value health care very highly and would choose little of it in the absence of an NHS. Point C is on a higher indifference curve for this particular consumer. So, given an NHS system, Catherine will choose point C and be healthier. The consumer in Figure 4.7(b), Simon, is much more health-conscious: he is willing to devote a high proportion of his income to health care. How does NHS provision affect him? Not at all. Point C

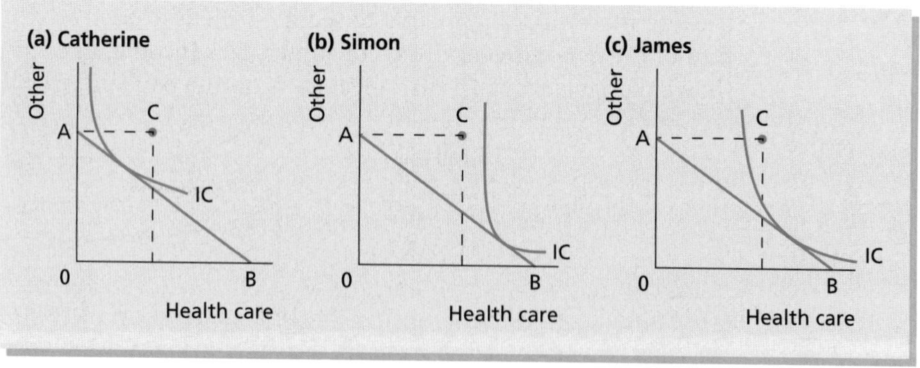

Figure 4.7 **Possible consumer reactions to government free health care provision**

puts him on a lower level of welfare because he values so highly the additional health care which he will continue to purchase from the private sector.

Now consider James, whose preferences are shown in (c). He has some concern for health care but not a passionate one. Does such a person seem most typical? Now look again at his preferences. Point C puts him on a higher indifference curve. When the NHS is provided he will opt out of private health care into the state provision of the statutory amount. Notice that this means he is consuming less health care than he would have done without that provision. It is distinctly possible that the government's provision of health care of the kind offered by the NHS would reduce the volume of health care which society consumes, if those choosing private health care were excluded from the consumption of free state care.

4.4 The case for publicly provided health care

The NHS system is politically popular. During the early 1990s in Britain it was rumoured that the Conservative government was considering abandonment of the NHS. The government was left in no doubt that it would be highly unpopular for doing so. The present Labour administration is adamant that although it will seek to reform the NHS by making it more efficient, it will not seek to abandon the principle of universal health care free for all at the point of consumption. On what grounds might one seek to justify the present system? There are four areas where a case can be made. We shall briefly examine each one in turn.

Merit goods

First, health care is a merit good. Unfortunately the textbooks do not agree as to what a merit good is. Some say that they are goods or services provided on the basis of need such that those with a particularly low level of income are able to consume them. Defined thus, health care is often seen as a merit good since some would not be able to afford health care without government subsidy. This is clearly a matter of some importance to which we return shortly.

Others see merit goods as those which people will choose to under-consume because they will fail correctly to see the benefit to themselves of the consumption of the good. It is not that consumers lack income, or even information, but they are unable to make the judgements on the basis of that information which would maximise their welfare. If we accept this as a definition of a merit good, we can illustrate the merit good case for an NHS via the debate about payment for eye tests. Eye tests were provided free in Britain until the late 1980s when it was decided that most recipients should pay a contribution towards the cost of providing them. Those unhappy with the charge protest on three grounds. First, some cannot afford it even though they need it. By some definitions, this makes it a merit good. We shall not examine the point here since we return to it below.

Second, some feel that the eye test charge is wrong since people will be put off taking it even though it is worthwhile given the potential benefit of early treatment for eye conditions. Again, this is a point we shall examine below but it does not constitute a 'merit good' case: it is simply a problem of inadequate information.

Some argue that the charge for the eye test is wrong because some will not be capable of evaluating the information even if it is available and will therefore make a free choice which will reduce their own welfare. By some definitions of a merit good this is the key point: merit goods should be provided free to protect people from themselves. Let us stay specifically with this argument for government provision of health care. Several points should be thought through as you consider the strength of this view. Clearly, it is essentially paternalistic. Perhaps the British are more enthusiastic about such an argument than the Americans. It is interesting to note that virtually all British introductory economics textbooks make reference to the question of merit goods – and virtually no American text does so.

One other thing needs to be thought through with respect to merit goods. There is no obvious distinction between what is and what is not a merit good. Health care certainly has a strong claim to be one, however one defines a merit good. Other goods have a less strong claim. It will not be easy to decide which things people should decide for themselves and which things should be decided for them. The use of the market mechanism is built on the belief that people can act in their own interests better than others can act for them.

External benefits

The second area where a case can be made for the provision of state health care centres around the concept of external benefits. An external benefit occurs where an action confers benefits on parties not directly involved in an exchange. If you purchase a good or service you will gain some benefit from it. This benefit is internal to you. Sometimes, however, your purchase brings benefits to others as well. This is an external benefit. One illustration of such an external benefit in the context of health care is inoculations against communicable diseases. If you choose to be inoculated against diphtheria it increases the chances of your not catching it. That is a private, internal benefit. However, your inoculation also decreases the risk of someone else catching the disease. Clearly, this presents a powerful case for government intervention, in that the benefits to society as a whole, the external benefits plus the internal ones, are greater than the benefits accruing to those purchasing the benefits in a market.[2]

However, we must be careful in our thinking at this point. The consumption of most health care has no such external effects. If you break your leg, whether or not it is mended properly does not affect the chances of my 'catching' your broken leg. Most health care confers private benefits only. Powerful though the externalities argument is, then, its power embraces only a limited amount of health care provision.

Imperfect information

The third area of thought in which NHS provision is often justified is in relation to the lack of information on which decisions by consumers are taken. The argument is as follows. When consumers make decisions to purchase any commodity it is because they believe the purchase will improve their welfare. Markets are efficient, therefore, only if consumers have sufficient information to make informed choices. This is not the case in the doctor/patient relationship. The patient has come to the doctor because he lacks knowledge. Markets, therefore, are not efficient because the necessary conditions for efficient exchange are not present. This justifies the removal of a price mechanism such that the doctor or surgeon has no incentive to cheat on the basis of his superior knowledge, undertaking expensive medical treatment of little value to his patient.

As you think through your own views on this matter, let us see how a market economist might argue when faced with this point of view. He would probably say something like this. We are inclined to think that information is something costless to acquire, but it is not. If we want to buy a car which represents the best value for money, we need to spend time acquiring information about fuel consumption, prices, etc. Each of us decides how much information we think it is worth acquiring before taking a decision. In other words, as with any other area of life, we proceed until the expected marginal benefit of acquiring more information equals its additional cost. Since information is not costless, there is an optimal volume of information, which the market will itself provide at a price which reflects its cost. For example, in the case of cars, one does not have perfect information, but it can be bought from such sources as the Consumers' Association magazine *Which?* Such a journal is, in essence, part of the market in information.

In the case of health there is nothing to stop us asking for advice from a number of qualified people. We do not have to put ourselves at the mercy of one doctor only, unless the extra cost of acquiring the additional information from others is high relative to the benefits. The 'inadequate information' argument then may not be very strong. It does not matter that consumers do not have perfect information; they need only be aware that the information they have is not perfect.

Even if the above argument is thought to be unconvincing it would still not be clear that NHS provision is a good use of resources. In other areas of essential services, food for example, there are laws requiring producers to give some kind of information on the content of packets, and so on. It is not felt that imperfect information provides an argument for government provision of food on a non-market basis, but merely for some control of the market.

We have still not examined the major concern of most people about leaving health care to market forces. The major concern is surely this. Could the poor afford to buy health care? In other words, we should think not only about questions of efficiency but also about equity. It is to this important matter that we now turn.

Equity

If we want to know how many people in Britain are poor, we have an obvious problem. What constitutes poverty? One definition is to say that someone is poor if he or she lives at or below the level of income support set by the

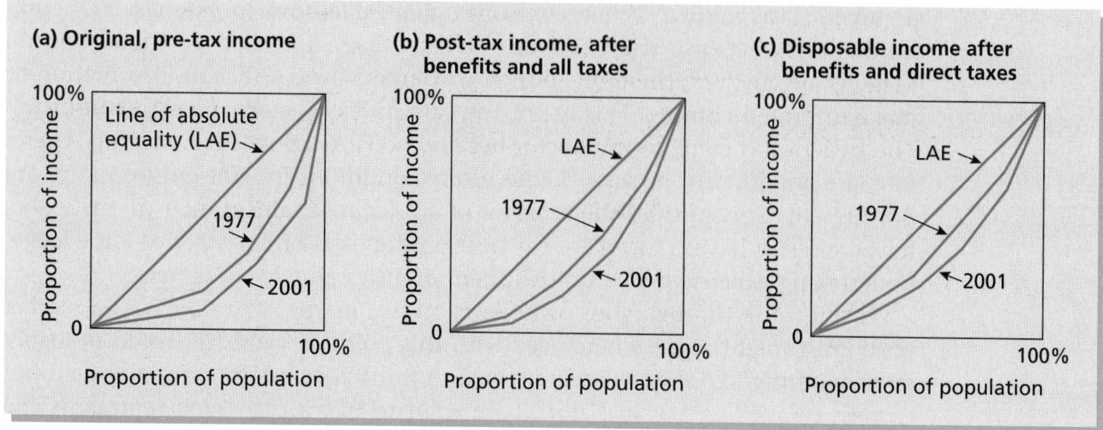

Figure 4.8 Shares of UK household income

Source: adapted from *Economic Trends*, April 2002

government. For a married couple with two children this is around £100 per week. On that basis about 9 million people in the UK are poor. It is obvious why it is so difficult to find an unambiguous definition of poverty. However, if the government were significantly to raise income support so that lower income groups were made substantially better off, just as many people would still be poor by the above definition.

Another aspect of the problem of measurement is that we may not agree whether poverty is an absolute or a relative concept. An income of £90–£100 per week is large compared with that received by a family in Bangladesh. It is pretty minimal compared with average incomes in the UK.

Before we look at the question of health care provision in the light of the problem of poverty, it is worth gaining some idea of the distribution of income in Britain and how it has changed in recent years. Consider first Figure 4.8(a). The device we are using to represent the distribution of income is known as a Lorenz curve. It shows on the vertical axes the proportion of income available to UK citizens, and on the horizontal axes the proportion of the population cumulated from the poorest. Consider first what this means in terms of the line of absolute equality. Suppose that everyone in society had the same level of income. Then 10 per cent of the population would have 10 per cent of the income, and 80 per cent of the population would have 80 per cent of the income and so on. The line representing this distribution is indeed the line of absolute equality. Any other distribution can be represented by a Lorenz curve. So, considering the 'original' distribution of income, the income before tax for the year 1977, it can be seen that the poorest 20 per cent of the population had only 2 per cent of income before tax and social security payments were taken into account. Since the next poorest 20 per cent had 7 per cent of the income, the poorest 40 per cent had 9 per cent. Notice how the top 20 per cent had 50 per cent of income before tax.[3]

The numbers on which Figure 4.8 are based have been 'equivalised', that is to say, allowance has been made for the number of people in each household.

Table 4.2 **Households with private health insurance, UK 1997**

Group	%
Professionals, employers and managers	17.2
Intermediate non-manual	15.1
Junior non-manual	7.7
Skilled manual	6.7
Semi-skilled and unskilled manual	4.8
Self-employed	13.6
Retired[a]	7.0
Unoccupied[b]	4.8

[a] Males aged 65 and over and females aged 60 and over who are not economically inactive
[b] Males aged under 65 and females aged under 60 who are not working, nor actively seeking work
Source: adapted from Association of British Insurers data

Clearly, a larger household with more children needs more income to support it. These figures take account of this.

The above statistics show a number of important things. First, the distribution of income before tax has widened over the last twenty-five years. Clearly, the more even the distribution of income, the closer to the line of absolute equality the Lorenz curve would be. The curve bulges further from the origin for 2001 than for 1977. The post-tax distribution of income has also widened. Figure 4.8(b) largely reflects the cuts in higher rate taxes made during the 1980s. Cuts in higher rates of tax paid by higher income groups have moved the 2001 Lorenz curve further from the line of absolute equality. Whether it should be more even we consider in due course. The current UK government appears to think so. The post-tax Lorenz curve moved slightly inwards in 2001 for the first time in many years.

Finally, remember that when comparing the distribution of income over time, the total income is, over the long run, tending to rise. A constant proportion of increasing national income will still mean that a group is, on average, getting absolutely better off. The diagrams do not take account of this, and they therefore disguise the fact that some, even at the lower end of the scale, have become better off absolutely while becoming worse off relatively. Others are worse off both relatively and absolutely.

It is this equity consideration which presents the problem of using a market for health care. It is felt by many that the distribution of income is simply too uneven for such a policy. Notice how closely the proportion of people having private medical insurance is related to social grade (Table 4.2). Given the uneven distribution of income in society, one could argue that it is more just to distribute health care on a non-market basis, even if efficiency considerations suggest otherwise. A market for health care would bear heavily on lower income groups.

As we think through this key issue there are some areas of thought of which we need, as economists, to be aware. The first area concerns what is usually referred to as Pareto optimality.

4.5 Developing the equity argument: Pareto optimality

Pareto optimality is a state in which it is not possible to improve one person's welfare without reducing someone else's. It follows, therefore, that freely negotiated trades are regarded as good because they offer a Pareto improvement. If you buy my CD player, presumably you regard yourself as benefiting from the trade, or you would not have bought it from me. Similarly, I will also have improved my welfare or I would not have sold it. As a result of the exchange we are both better off and nobody is worse off (assuming you do not produce an external effect by the noise). If, however, the government taxes me and increases your student grant, then your welfare has increased but mine has reduced. This is not considered a Pareto improvement because it is not a voluntary exchange.

This is the main reason why economists tend to approve of the free market: it maximises the number of mutually beneficial exchanges. But then how do they regard enforced exchanges, as for example when higher income groups are made to pay taxes which are used for income support for lower income groups or for the provision of more medical care than lower income groups would choose to buy? Are these bad? The answer is that most economists feel that, as economists, they cannot pronounce upon such matters. Since one cannot measure the extent to which one person has lost welfare and the extent to which another has gained, there is no objective way of deciding whether the enforced exchange improves community welfare. It is not, therefore, Pareto-optimal. It is a subjective matter to which we are all entitled to a view: but economists, as economists, are not able to make such value judgements.

Does this leave us in a position where economists as economists have nothing to say about equity considerations? Indeed it does not. Economists have much to say, particularly about the form of redistribution.

If you are impressed by the view that the NHS is a good system on equity grounds, you might return to Figure 4.2 and think it through a little further. An argument for an NHS system could be made along the following lines. Given the NHS, what will determine who visits the GP? One factor is clearly the assessment that one has of the benefit of receiving medical care; the other is the opportunity cost of receiving it. In a market system, when the price of £50 per hour is payable, that would be largely the alternative goods and services one had to sacrifice in order to pay the GP. In an NHS system there is no price, so the opportunity cost is largely in terms of the time spent waiting. During that time one could, for example, have been working and earning an income.

Now who are the people with the lowest opportunity cost? The answer is those with lower incomes who foresake fewer pounds of income to queue. Hence lower income groups will receive more of the scarce resources available. On equity grounds this is what we are looking for.

Not everyone is an enthusiastic supporter of this view. Some who are concerned about the equity issue fear that in practice those with high incomes from high socio-economic groups are better able to overcome the administrative hurdles imposed by a rationing system. For example, many GPs use an

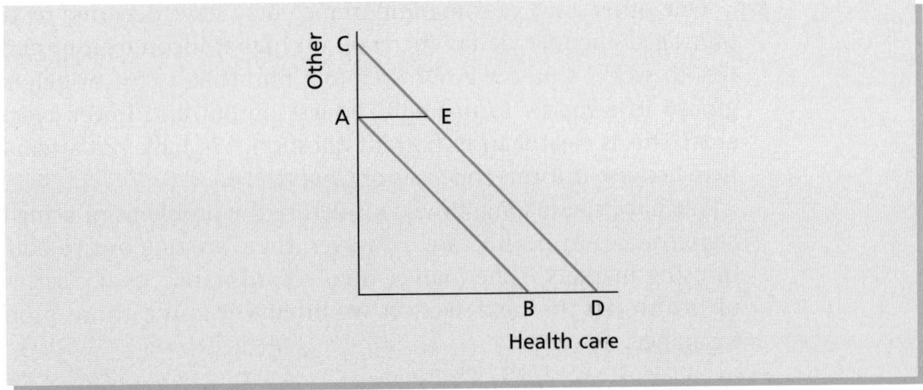

Figure 4.9 Free health care provision or income transfers to the poor?

appointments system which may mean several days' wait for an appointment. Those from higher income groups may be more persuasive in arguing that their own case is urgent.

Thus, of those who believe that low income people need free health care, many would still prefer to see some kind of market system in which only low income groups are exempted from payment.

One other interesting aspect of the equity argument concerns the question of whether lower income groups would benefit more from free health care provision or from an equivalent increase in income via a direct transfer while still having to pay the market price for health care. There is an argument that says that such groups would gain more from an income increase than from free health care provision. We use Figure 4.9 to demonstrate this view.

The budget line AB shows the combinations of medical care and other goods which our low income consumer can choose if no redistribution of income and no free provision of health care is offered. Suppose now this consumer is offered free health care. The budget line becomes AED. He can have more care but not more of other goods. This improves his welfare and enables him to be on a higher indifference curve. Suppose now this consumer is offered additional income instead, equivalent in value to the health care. What options are open now?

His budget line is now CD. Notice that by offering free health care the low income consumer cannot choose greater levels of other goods and services. The options in triangle ACE are denied him. This may or may not lead him to increase his demand for health care but it can further improve his utility by offering combinations of health care and other goods which the subsidy did not make possible. Hence, there is a case for saying that an increase in disposable income is a better policy than a distorted relative price of health care, if one wishes to help lower income groups. There is, however, an important qualification to this. If one feels that the externalities or merit goods argument is valid, one may not *want* the low income consumer to choose combinations of health care and other goods which leads him or her to higher utility but lower health care consumption. In this case the restricted options offered by free health care provision may be a better option.

One other issue of some importance may have occurred to you. Couldn't the transfer of income via tax increases on higher income groups affect their incentives to work? Could we not therefore find that a cost of helping lower income groups in *whatever* form might be less output and lower average living standards? This is clearly an important question. We have not attempted to analyse it here because it forms the basis of Chapter 16.

We have spent some time considering the problems of using markets to allocate resources in health care. However, there are one or two additional problems in using markets if the market involves insurance, as it clearly does in the case of health. In the next section we briefly examine those problems specific to insurance.

4.6 Inefficiency in the market for insurance

A free market in health care inevitably involves private insurance. Insurance itself creates the risk of inefficiency owing to two particular problems. One of these problems is known as *moral hazard*, the other is called *adverse selection*.

Moral hazard

The very fact that you have taken out insurance can change your behaviour. As a student, for example, you may well take less care about locking your bike before going to a lecture if you have theft insurance. That change in your behaviour which results from being insured is called moral hazard. It is easy to see how this problem relates to medical insurance. People may choose to live a less healthy lifestyle knowing that if they fall ill they do not have to pay directly for any treatment which may then be necessary. They may also demand operations for minor ailments which they would not have done had they been paying directly. The existence of such health insurance, then, may lead to overconsumption of medical resources. The problem may be exacerbated if doctors in such markets 'over-treat', performing unnecessary operations or prescribing unnecessary drugs, knowing that their patients are unlikely to object since they have no financial incentive to do so.

Americans spend over 14 per cent of national output on health care and over 60 per cent of that is private health care expenditure. Britons spend around 7 per cent of national output on health care, and only around 15 per cent of that is private health care. One interpretation of such figures is that American health care is inefficient because of its reliance on private health insurance.

Adverse selection

How does a company such as BUPA estimate the risk of insuring someone for health care? It cannot do so accurately because it does not have sufficient information to do so. It will then have to work out an average level of risk for everyone and set a common premium accordingly. This makes the policy a good deal for high risk people and a bad deal for healthy, low risk people. Many low risk people may therefore choose not to insure, increasing to the insurance company the average risk of those who *are* insured. This is the problem of adverse selection.

Insurance companies seek to overcome the problem by screening out high risks such as the old and obviously weak, who will be uninsured. Alternatively, if there is a state sector as well as a private sector, as there is in the UK, the state will tend to be looking after all of the old and chronically sick, and private companies will concentrate on the healthy.

Such problems, which apply in principle to any insurance market, may well lead to inefficiency in resource allocation generally, but in health care resources in particular.

4.7 Conclusion

Overall, how good is the UK health care system? One way of answering this is to try to make international comparisons. This is fraught with difficulties but a few figures might be instructive. Look at Table 4.3.

The first thing which is immediately apparent is that, despite the increases in demand over time for private health insurance, the UK spends a lower proportion of national income than most other EU countries. Its private health spending as a proportion of total health care expenditure is among the lowest in Europe. The second thing is that public expenditure as a proportion of the total is relatively high in the UK. In other words, the UK makes relatively little use of the private sector. It could be argued that it is a measure of how efficient the NHS is that we need so few resources to achieve health care for British consumers. Alternatively, it could be argued that it shows how, in the absence of market mechanism, a fixed amount of medical care means that people are unable to get the amount of health care resources they wish for.

One can also look at figures for the level of some specific health inputs. One such measure is the number of physicians per thousand inhabitants. On this measure also, the UK is seen to put relatively little into health care compared with most other EU countries.

Perhaps, therefore, we need to look not so much at inputs as at outputs. In other words, what is achieved by the volume of resources going to health care? Are Britons as healthy as the citizens of other countries which do not have an NHS-type system? Clearly this is difficult to measure. We consider two rather crude measures: namely life expectancy and infant mortality rates. Take the data given in Table 4.4 which gives figures for a much wider range of countries than just those in the European Union. As incomes rise from very low levels, life expectancy tends to increase. For example, in developing countries, life expectancy is much less than in high income EU countries where much more is spent on health care. However, it is not possible to tell from these figures whether the higher life expectancy is a function of higher amounts of health care expenditure or whether it is a function of income itself. Higher income

Table 4.3 Health care inputs in selected European countries

	Income per head, 2001 (1000 euros)	*Health spending as percentage of GDP, 2000*	*Public expenditure as percentage of total health care spending, 2000*	*Practising physicians density per 1000 population*
Germany	25.2	10.6	75.1	3.6
France	24.0	9.5	76.0	3.0[1]
Belgium	24.7	8.7	71.2	3.9
Greece	12.0	8.3	55.5	4.4[2]
Denmark	33.7	8.3	82.1	3.4
Portugal	11.9	8.2	71.2	3.2
Italy	21.0	8.1	73.7	6.0
Netherlands	26.8	8.1	67.5	3.2
Austria	26.1	8.0	69.7	3.0[2]
Sweden	26.3	7.9[1]	83.8[1]	2.9[2]
UK	26.5	7.3	81.0	1.8
Ireland	29.7	6.7	75.8	2.3[2]
Finland	26.2	6.6	75.1	3.1
USA	39.4	13.0	44.3	2.8[2]

[1] = 1998
[2] = 1999

Source: adapted from OECD health data, Eurostat data

people live in better accommodation, stay warmer and eat better, for example. It is noticeable, though, that a correlation between life expectancy and health expenditure is absent among those within higher income societies. The average Mexican female, for example, lives longer than the average US female despite a lower income and relatively little spent on health care.

Much the same picture emerges with regard to infant mortality rates. Higher incomes and greater health care resources are closely correlated as income rises from low levels. Developing countries have an infant mortality rate fifty times greater than that of the EU. Again, the relationship is much less noticeable within high income societies. Again, it may well be that any relationship which does exist is with income rather than with health care expenditure. Such is the case in the UK, where there is a strong relationship. Infant mortality rates decline as the social class of the father rises, and there is a close correlation between income and social class.

However, these output measures are only indicators. It is not a summary of all output measures. We do not know, for example, whether people in the UK are generally in more pain and discomfort compared with countries which devote more resources to health care.

In the past few years the British government has attempted to make the NHS more efficient with the introduction of an 'internal market' where, for example,

Table 4.4 Selected health care outputs

	Life expectancy at birth[1]		*Infant mortality: deaths per 1000 live births*
	Females	*Males*	
Australia	81.8	76.2	5.2
Denmark	79.0	74.2	5.3
Czech Republic	78.1	71.4	4.1
France	82.5	75.0	4.5
Germany	80.7	74.7	4.4
Hungary	75.1	66.3	9.2
Mexico	77.3	72.8	24.9
Poland	77.5	68.8	8.1
Sweden	81.9	77.0	3.4
Switzerland	82.5	76.8	4.9
Turkey	70.7	66.1	39.7
UK	79.2	74.0	5.6
USA	71.8	78.9	7.1

[1] Data is for 1999
[2] Data is for 2000, except USA is 1999
Source: adapted from OECD health data

many NHS doctors are given budgets from the government but then have to 'buy' operations etc. from hospitals, forcing them to make choices in order to maximise patient welfare from limited funds. The move is designed to make health care resource usage more efficient. One possible problem is that costs associated with markets – advertising, distribution costs, etc. – are bound to rise. The allocation of resources within the NHS must improve sufficiently to outweigh these costs. It remains to be seen whether this will be so.

One possible benefit of trying to bring market considerations into the NHS is that it forces those involved to consider the resource allocation questions we have been examining in this chapter. In order to examine the problem, we considered health care as one good. One can also see it as a group of products meeting a great variety of needs. The scarcity of resources forces society to face unpleasant choices. We have to decide whether to have more health care and fewer television sets. But should we have more dialysis machines and less maternity care? How do we decide between the competing requirements of lung cancer patients and road accident victims? It is rather too early to judge how successful or otherwise the internal market will prove, but the issues the internal market was devised to address will not go away.

We have not resolved the question of whether an NHS scheme improves welfare in Britain, but the most important areas of debate should now be in sharper focus.

CHAPTER SUMMARY

1 **Consumer preference can be expressed by indifference curves which, for most goods, will be drawn convex to (bowed outwards from) the origin.**

2 **Consumption patterns are constrained by a budget line, showing income and the prices of goods.**

3 **Consumer equilibrium is on the highest indifference curve possible within the budget constraint.**

4 **Consumers may not be able or willing to purchase an optimum amount of merit goods.**

5 **If the benefit to society exceeds the benefit to the individual resulting from consumption, this excess is called an external benefit.**

6 **If a market works efficiently all mutually beneficial exchanges are undertaken. Such a situation is called a Pareto-optimal state.**

7 **Economists cannot say that a given distribution of income is superior to any other.**

Questions for discussion

Guidance to the answers for the ***asterisked*** *numbered questions is available to students on the website for the book at* **www.booksites.net/heather**.

1* Consider Figure 4.10. What is implied about the nature of a consumer's preferences for the goods described in each of (a), (b) and (c)?

2 Consider Figure 4.1 again. What does this figure suggest about the extent to which this would represent a real increase in resources allocated to health care in Britain?

3* In the United States many people pay insurance to cover unforeseen medical care needs. To what extent can one argue that it is virtually the same in Britain with the NHS? Is not the only difference the fact that the insurance payment in Britain is compulsory?

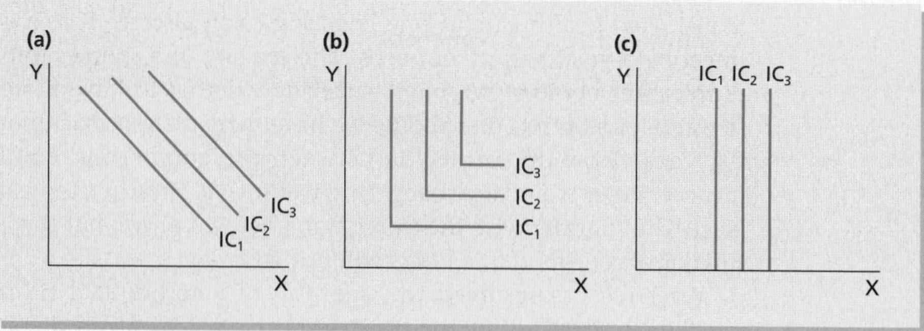

Figure 4.10 **Shapes of indifference curves**

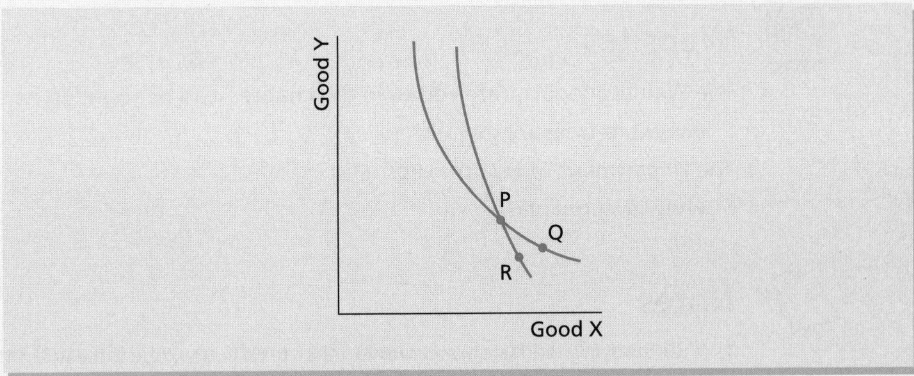

Figure 4.11

4 Examine Figure 4.11. This is an indifference curve map which is of the kind described in Figure 4.3, but this time two of the curves cross. What would such a picture say about the consumer's preference? (*Hint*: Think about how contented you would be at points P, Q and R.)

5* On the definitions of merit good used in the text, would you rate the following as merit goods? Vaccinations against tropical diseases for those travelling overseas? Education? Fluoride? Cornflakes?

6 Suppose Fred goes to a private doctor with stomach pains and is provided with pills costing him £200 with a guarantee that Fred's stomach pains will disappear in three days if he takes all the tablets. Three days and £200 later Fred's pains have gone. As it happens he had indigestion. The pain would have gone anyway as the doctor knew very well but Fred did not. Does this not represent a Pareto improvement in welfare? No? Really? Fred is happy: £200 was well spent to be rid of quite horrid pains. The doctor is happy too. Both parties are better off. No one is worse off. Does that not define Pareto-efficient welfare improvement?

7* Should people be made to wear seat belts in cars? (*Hint*: Who pays if they do not and they have an accident?) Do compulsory MOT certificates raise the same issues?

8 Should the provision of all private health care be made illegal?

9* In a Gallup opinion poll survey, 77 per cent of those interviewed agreed with the statement that 'everyone should have all the health care they need no matter how much it costs'. Comment.

10 To what extent are the health reforms in Britain of the past few years a smokescreen for the refusal by the government to commit adequate resources to the NHS?

Websites

The Wanless Report, referred to in the chapter, can be found in its entirety at:

www.hm-treasury.gov.uk/

The Department of Health website is:

www.doh.gov.uk/

Notes

1 When studying indifference curves in other texts you will be introduced to what are referred to as 'income effects' and 'substitution effects'. This distinction is a useful one but we shall use these concepts a little later in the book (see Chapter 16) rather than stop to examine them now.

2 Frequently, actions taken by one person or group can impose *costs* on others not party to an exchange. A factory may emit pollutants which damage forests. This is an external cost. We consider the problem of external costs in Chapters 10 and 12.

3 An explanation of how the distribution of income can be calculated is given in Appendix 3.

5 Production and cost

Europe's regional problems: *why so depressing?*

CHAPTER OVERVIEW

In this chapter we examine the problem of regional imbalance. Can market forces deal with it? If not, what is the most appropriate action for government to take? We look first at the regional problem within a country, then at the problem from a wider, European perspective.

In order to do this we review the following concepts:

- Opportunity cost
- Supply and demand

We introduce the following concepts:

- Arbitrage
- Short and long run
- Diminishing returns
- Isoquants and isocosts

5.1 Introduction

In most economies we find that there are significant differences in living standards amongst different geographical areas. For example, in the UK it is well known that, generally speaking, people in Northern Ireland and parts of the North have a lower living standard than people in the South East. This is an average. The South East has its poor and Northern Ireland its rich. It is also well known that some areas of Europe are much better off than others. What is true of living standards is also true of levels of unemployment. Northern Italy is much more prosperous than the South. The East of Germany has, on average, a lower standard of living than the West. The Stockholm area is much more prosperous than the rural parts of Sweden. Areas of relatively low living standards are generally areas with a high level of unemployment. As we shall see, these two measures of regional disparities are not unconnected. In this chapter we consider the size of these regional disparities within the UK and examine government views on what is the appropriate action to deal with the problem. We then consider the problem from a wider, EU perspective and ask what the future holds for Europe with respect to this regional problem.

This is a topic that is dealt with rather later in most introductory courses. However, there is a great advantage in thinking through this problem now. It is a problem that we can look at within a framework of supply and demand analysis which makes for good revision and extension of ground already covered. We then develop some ideas of how firms make decisions about employing people, which will throw further light on this problem. After that we shall be in a good position to understand the microeconomic aspects of the regional problem. There are certain macroeconomic aspects of this matter, to which we return in a later chapter.

see pp. 449–50

5.2 Illustrating the size of the problem: the UK and Germany

The most commonly used indicator of the problem of uneven regional development is unemployment of labour. The level of unemployment in the UK has varied considerably over time, including the level in the more prosperous regions, so we usually consider the level of unemployment in relation to the national average. Table 5.1 shows unemployment for the different regions of the UK at two very different periods in its recent history. Look first at the data for January 1993. The economy was in a deep recession and output was flat.

Table 5.1 Regional unemployment in the UK (% unemployed)

	1993 (annual average)	*2002 Q1 (seasonally adjusted)*
North East	13	7.3
North West	9.5	5.5[1]
Merseyside	15.2	–
Yorkshire and Humberside	10.4	5.0
East Midlands	9.6	4.7
West Midlands	10.9	5.6
Eastern	9.4	3.8
London	11.6	6.8
South East	8.7	3.5
South West	9.5	3.5
Wales	10.4	5.7
Scotland	9.9	6.7
Northern Ireland	14.1	6.1

[1] Includes Merseyside

Source: *Economic Trends*, various issues © Crown copyright

However, firms had not sufficient confidence that a recovery was imminent so unemployment remained substantial. This explains the high level of average UK unemployment.

Now examine the unemployment data during the first quarter of 2002. There is a particular reason for choosing this time: the UK had been experiencing growth for some years. Demand for goods and services was strong and so the demand for labour to produce that output was also strong, so unemployment was comparatively low. However, at both periods, unemployment rates in certain parts of the country, though lower during this time, were still well above the national average.

These figures are clearly a cause for concern. Unemployment represents a considerable cost to society, socially and economically. Unemployment is a social problem in that people feel a loss of self-worth and, over a longer period, despair. The economic cost is also high. It represents an enormous waste of resources in terms of output forgone. You will recall from Chapter 1 that if an economy is producing a level of output that is inside its opportunity cost curve, then the opportunity cost of increased output is zero. Yet, as we shall see later, the problem viewed from a European perspective is much worse. We shall see that if one thinks of each EU country as a European 'region', regional disparities within the UK are comparatively minor.

We must also recognise that the delineating of a geographical area as a 'region' is to some extent arbitrary and the figures quoted in Table 5.1 can to that extent be misleading. For example, in some areas of the Lake District average unemployment can be lower and average disposable incomes higher than in the South East. Since property is cheaper there, and mortgage burdens are smaller, some of these subregions can be highly prosperous. That said, there is clearly a problem for large areas of the country.

The UK is just one example of regional disparities in Europe. Let us now look at Germany. Table 5.2 is a snapshot of the German economy in the depths of

Table 5.2 Regional unemployment in Germany, January 2001

Western Germany	%	*Eastern Germany*	%
Schleswig Holstein	9.2	Mecklenburg-Vorpommern	19.6
Hamburg	8.6	Berlin[a]	16.4
Bremen	12.8	Brandenburg	18.1
Lower Saxony	10.0	Saxony	18.5
North Rhine-Westphalia	9.1	Saxony-Anhalt	21.3
Hesse	7.1	Thuringia	16.8
Rhineland Palatinate	7.4		
Saarland	9.6	East Germany, average	18.7
Bavaria	6.2	West Germany, average	8.0
Baden Württemberg	5.2	Germany, average	10.0

[a] Part of Berlin was controlled by West Germany before unification in 1989

Source: adapted from *Bundesanstalt für Arbeit*

its most recent recession. A number of things can be seen. First, there is a significant regional problem. The unemployment rate in Saxony Anhalt was well over three times as great as it was in Bavaria, for example. However, we must remember that until the advent of German reunification in 1989, East Germany was part of the communist bloc. It was always going to be a huge task for the West German government, after reunification of the two parts of the nation, to reconstruct the East German economy. Some of the problems we considered in Chapter 1 still remain.

However, even if we concentrate only upon West Germany, the regional disparities are considerable. The unemployment rate for Bremen was over twice that of Bavaria, a greater disparity than for the 'best' and 'worst' regions of the UK.

We now turn to some possible solutions to the problem of regional imbalance. In what follows we shall *not* be considering ways of reducing average unemployment for an economy: that must wait until Chapter 13. Here we consider only possible means of reducing the gap between the regions.

5.3 A possible solution: the market case

One approach to the regional disparity problem needs to be thought about carefully. Some economists believe that the appropriate response to the problem is to do nothing. The case is based on the view that market forces will do a better job of correcting regional imbalance than governments will do with interventionist policies. The case needs to be examined with care, because, to a considerable extent, it reflects the thinking of the UK governments for many years. The government was much less interventionist until recently than in the 1960s, 1970s and early 1980s. The amount of government expenditure aimed at promoting regional development was cut back sharply in the belief that markets deal with regional difficulties better than governments do. Expenditure provided by the EU's regional funds was, to some extent, making up that reduction for some time as we shall see later in the chapter. Nevertheless, it is clear that the regional problem was lower down the government's list of priorities. The present government in the UK, however, seems less convinced by the market case that we are about to examine.

see pp. 111–12

Market disequilibrium

So what is the market case for non-intervention in regional unemployment? In essence it amounts to the view that firms and individuals will make better decisions than governments. There are two main strands to the argument. The first revolves around the concept of market disequilibrium, the second around the concept of arbitrage. Let us first examine the idea of equilibrium.

We have already seen that goods are traded in a market where a clearing price will tend to be established, if the market is free. That is, a price will be found at which plans to supply a good are consistent with plans to consume. In most

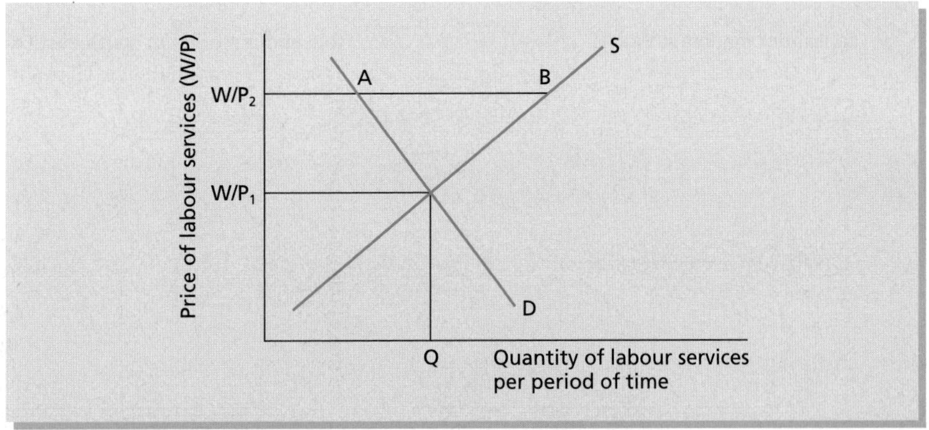

Figure 5.1 **Market supply and demand for labour services**

markets this equilibrium price is a stable equilibrium. If the price moves from equilibrium, excess supply or excess demand will develop. Plans will be adjusted and the equilibrium price will be restored. Now, one model of the labour market suggests that what is true of goods and services will be true of resources such as labour. Resources in a free market will also have a price which will be established in much the same way. Consider the diagram, Figure 5.1. It shows the market for labour services, let us say in Wales, with the usual variables – quantity and price – on the axes. The vertical axis requires a word of explanation. The price of labour services is, of course, the wage rate. This is expressed as W/P in Figure 5.1 to show real wages, that is to say the money value of the wage rate divided by the price level. In other words it shows what the price of the labour services will buy for the one who receives the wages.

If the wage rate is W/P_1, all those who wish to work will have a job – supply plans are equal to demand plans. So how can Wales have unemployment? Clearly, if the wage rate is too high, say at W/P_2, not all those wanting a job can find one. AB represents that excess supply of labour we call unemployment. You can see now how some economists argue that the problem of unemployment will solve itself. In a free market the price will fall – employers can get all the labour they wish to employ at the lower wage rate. Therefore equilibrium will be found at W/P_1 and there will be no unemployment except for those who choose *not* to work. We have found an equilibrium wage rate for Welsh workers and an equilibrium quantity of labour.

Arbitrage

It could be argued that we still have a problem. Consider Figure 5.2. We may feel that it is unfair that Welsh workers receive lower wage rates than those in the South East of the UK. Market economists argue that even this problem will be dealt with in a free market via a process called arbitrage. If significant wage differentials exist, two things are likely to happen. One is that employers, those who demand labour and who are always seeking to minimise production costs,

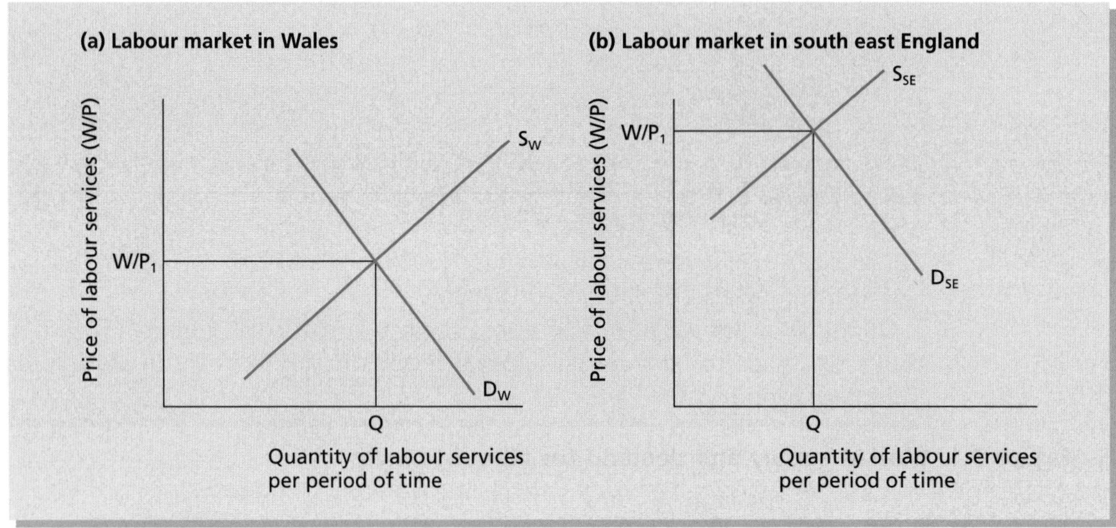

Figure 5.2 Equilibrium wage rates in different parts of the country

will wish to take advantage of the relatively low wage rates in Wales. It will be worth their relocating. How will this affect the markets? As firms leave the South East and move to Wales, demand in the South East, D_{SE}, moves left and demand in Wales, D_W, moves right. Note how in Figure 5.3 this begins to reduce differential wage rates. At the same time, though, Welsh workers will have an incentive to move to the South East to take advantage of the higher wage rates there. We can see from Figure 5.3 how this also reduces wage differentials, since the supply in Wales, S_W, will shift left, reflecting the willingness of fewer people to supply labour in Wales. S_{SE} shifts to the right, reflecting the increase in the

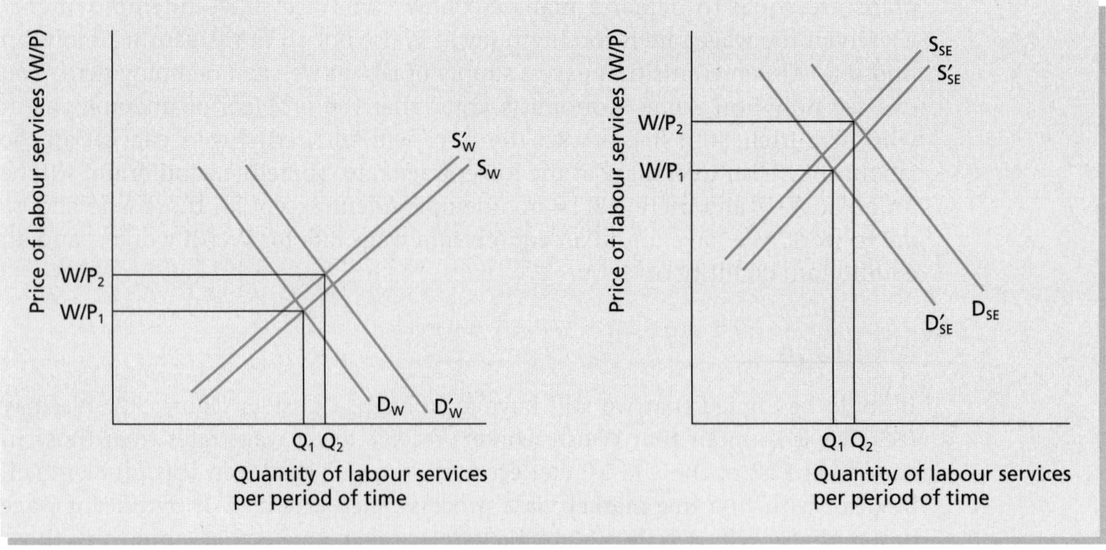

Figure 5.3 Arbitrage in the market for labour services

number of willing workers in the South East. The process of arbitrage evens out wage differentials in different parts of the country.

So why does Figure 5.3 not show this process of arbitrage continuing until all labour receives the same wage rate? The answer is that there are costs in moving, but Welsh workers will move if they think the gains exceed the benefits. Since some will choose not to move, the remaining difference in the wage rate reflects the non-pecuniary value they place on staying where they are. In other words, there are non-wage benefits of remaining near one's family for example. Welsh and English workers finish with wage rates reflecting an equal net advantage, although the pecuniary rewards are higher in the South East.

Of course, what we have said about these two particular regions of the UK could be argued to be true for any two regions in any country in Europe, or indeed the world.

5.4 The interventionist case

Needless to say, not everyone would agree with the above reasoning. Some of the questions for discussion will encourage you to think through some of the objections. We now concentrate on objections to the strand of argument we have considered which deals with arbitrage. We mention three areas of thought very briefly and a fourth one that we will examine with more leisure. In essence, the arguments are based on the view that the model of the labour market presented above is incorrect or that it is incomplete. Other considerations alter substantially what happens in practice.

Some argue that the above model is invalid because it assumes that knowledge is readily available to workers and firms. This may well be untrue. For example, firms may be unaware of potential cost savings of relocation. Again, people may not be aware of wage rates or potential job opportunities in other areas. In other words, the first objection to the market forces case is that markets require adequate information. In this case, that information is not available.

Others argue that firms will not move because they need to be near their main markets to minimise transport costs. If these markets are mostly in the more prosperous regions where the greatest purchasing power is located, they may not be willing to move for lower wage rates even if they are aware of them. This argument has to be approached with care. One is not looking for all firms to move, only those with the greatest advantage in doing so. Some firms are far too market orientated but others are relatively footloose and may be able to reduce costs by a relocation decision. For example, modern information technology makes it possible for firms to move away from high wage areas because communication costs with input suppliers, who may choose to remain, are much lower.

Others argue that, given time, market forces may work but that the process is too slow. If intervention can reduce unemployment more quickly, the benefits of higher output may exceed the costs of money spent on a proactive regional policy.

The fourth interventionist argument that we will examine in more detail is based on the law of diminishing returns. This argument is particularly interesting, because it suggests that government intervention is a benefit not only to the regions of high unemployment but also to areas of relatively high prosperity too. First we examine the law of diminishing returns, then we relate it specifically to the problem of uneven regional development.

5.5 The law of diminishing returns

The law of diminishing returns says that if we go on adding more of one factor such as labour on to a fixed quantity of another factor, say land or capital, the additional output received from each additional unit of the variable factor must eventually diminish.

Let us take an example of a farmer who wants to vary the output of his parsnips, for which he requires labour and land. He has one field which he rents and he has a contract to rent the field for a year. Alternatively, if he owns the field, the cost of the capital is the opportunity cost of the funds tied up in the field, and we assume he would take a year to negotiate the sale of it. The farmer therefore has to work with a fixed volume of land, but he can change parsnip output by changing the number of people he employs to work the field. Table 5.3 shows how many parsnips per week he can get from the field with different amounts of man-days of labour. Note how if at present he is only employing a few man-days, adding a few extra men seems a good idea. For example, they may cooperate and do jobs better when there are few men, so the extra man-day produces a lot of extra parsnips. That is to say, there are increasing returns to labour. If the farmer goes on employing more men, however, the inevitable

Table 5.3 **Short-run product**

Number of man-days	*TP*	*MP*	*AP*
0	0	–	–
1	10	10	10
2	24	14	12
3	42	18	14
4	56	14	14
5	65	11	13
6	72	7	12
7	77	5	11
8	80	3	10.1
9	81	1	9
10	81	0	8.1
11	77	–4	7

TP = Total product MP = Marginal product AP = Average product (TP/no. of man-days)

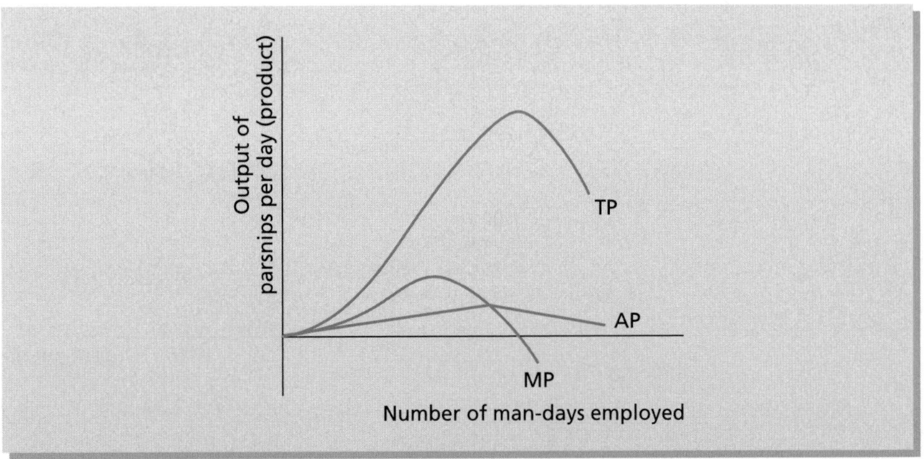

Figure 5.4 **Relationship between total, average and marginal product**

occurs. Additions to parsnip output get less since each extra man employed has less land to work on. That is, there are *diminishing returns* to each additional man employed. Indeed, there comes a point where an additional man-day employed would result in a fall in total production. That is, the extra men will add a negative amount of output (though no rational farmer would employ that much labour). The *additional* output from one more man-day is called marginal product (MP) (or sometimes marginal physical product (MPP) to emphasise that without knowing the *price* of parsnips we do not know what the value of the parsnips is worth to the farmer). We can also work out average product (AP) and find out how many parsnips per man-day the farmer gets at differing levels of labour employment. To find this, simply divide the total parsnip output by the number of man-days employed.

Now we can plot a graph of the information (Figure 5.4). Keep it firmly in your mind that all the time we have kept the farmer with the same amount of land – the size of the field is a fixed factor. He cannot invest in the short run; he can simply make optimal use of previous investment decisions.

What does this suggest about (short-run) production costs? If we ignore the fixed costs associated with the rent of the field and assume that the farmer can employ labour at some given wage rate, we can see the following. While total product (TP) is rising rapidly, total variable costs will be rising relatively slowly, since, for the cost of one extra unit of labour, large numbers of extra parsnips are being produced. At some point, though, diminishing returns must set in. Extra units of labour can produce only small additions to output, so variable costs rise rapidly.

The principle can easily be extended to average variable and marginal cost, as shown in Figure 5.5. Average variable cost (AVC) is the variable cost per parsnip, or whatever unit of output we are considering. It is found by dividing total variable cost (TVC) by the number of units of output. Short-run marginal cost (SMC) is simply the extra cost of producing one more unit of output. We plot these relationships on the lower diagram of Figure 5.5.

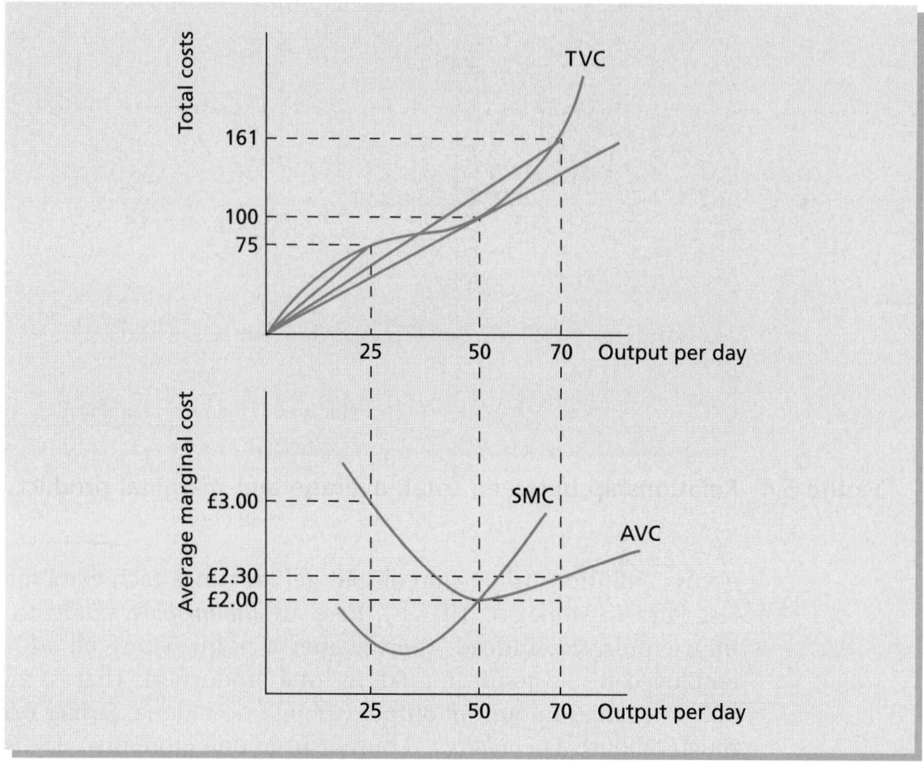

Figure 5.5 **Short-run production and cost**

Consider first AVC. Suppose 25 parsnips per day are being produced. TVC is, we shall assume, £75. AVC is then £75/25 = £3. This can also be seen by referring to the ray that emanates from the origin to the appropriate point on the TVC curve: it is the third side of a right-angled triangle, the other two sides being output and TVC.

At 50 units of output per day TVC is £100. AVC is thus only £2. The fall in AVC as output is increased can be seen drawn on the lower diagram. It can also be observed from the fact that the ray from the origin to that point on TVC is less steep than it is at 25 units. If output were to be any higher than 50, however, say at 70 parsnips per day, the ray from the origin would steepen again. TVC is £161 here and AVC has risen to £2.30.

Now look at the marginal cost curve (SMC). For any level of output, how much extra would it cost to increase output by a further unit? To put this another way, how fast does total variable cost rise when output rises by one unit? The rate at which TVC rises is given by the slope of TVC at any point. At low levels of output the slope becomes less steep as output increases. SMC falls. At higher levels of output the law of diminishing returns causes SMC to rise. Thus we have explained the shape of SMC.

Notice that we have drawn SMC such that it equals AVC when AVC is at its minimum. This is bound to be true. Take this case where AVC is at 50 units. This is the level of output where the ray from the origin (AVC) is least steep. But

MC is given by the slope of TVC. At this level of output the slope of TVC is the same as the slope of the ray from the origin. In our case, at 50 units of output, SMC and AVC are both £2.

In order to check that you have understood what has gone on so far, you might work out how to add fixed costs to the top diagram to give total costs and how to add average fixed costs to the lower diagram to give average total costs, but you will not need to do this to follow the argument developed below.

5.6 Diminishing returns and the optimum population

Now let us see how the above relates to the problem of the regional imbalance. Consider Figure 5.6. As population increases, income per head rises. There are increasing returns as more of the variable resource is added to the fixed resource, land. However, this income per head will rise at a diminishing rate as the proportion of labour to land changes.

Now what of costs per head? At first, if population expands, costs per head will decrease. The provision of schools, hospitals and roads – what we refer to as social capital – becomes more economical in areas of higher population. A village school of ten children may seem to some to be idyllic, but costs per head are very high. So a larger population reduces costs per head. Beyond a certain point, though, land becomes relatively scarce and costs per head rise. Transport costs increase significantly, for example, as we saw in Chapter 3. Hence the socially optimum population is at P_{opt}.

However, the increased social capital costs fall on government, not on private producers. There is, therefore, no reason why private citizens will, left to themselves, produce a socially optimal level of population. For example, suppose there is a strong movement of population from Wales to the South East. This might have social costs for Wales in that social capital is under-utilised, and for the South East where congestion costs are increasing rapidly. It can, therefore, be argued that it is of benefit to the whole country for the government to intervene in location decisions.

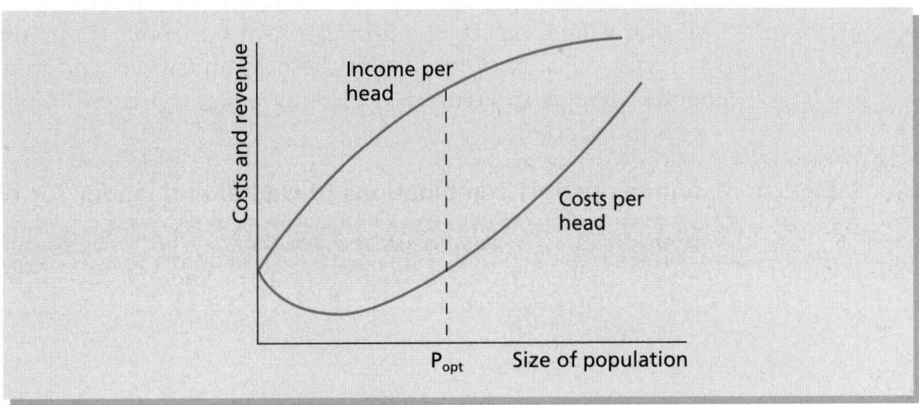

Figure 5.6 Optimum population for a region

5.7 The form of state intervention

Recent government policy

Most governments are not convinced by the market-based arguments we considered earlier. In most economies intervention on a large scale is typical, although, as we have seen, it has been less so in recent years in the UK. However, one basic principle stands out. For most countries the basic form of intervention is to try to influence the location of firms by inducements to them to locate in areas of high unemployment. The inducement is usually in the form of an offer to subsidise the costs of building or of capital equipment.

This is the principle employed throughout Europe. A few examples will illustrate the point. In parts of Belgium, 25–30 per cent of investment costs are recoverable by firms locating in depressed areas. In Holland, total expenditure on regional assistance is smaller than in most European countries but is again on investment. France has a large regional scheme. Some areas have a range of incentives for firms, including 25 per cent subsidies on new buildings, and low interest rates on loans. In the UK, automatic investment subsidies for depressed regions have been replaced since 1988 with selective assistance. Since this recent form of assistance is discretionary, it is harder to say definitively that it amounts to an investment subsidy.

Firms' investment decisions – isoquants and isocosts

Let us examine the principles governing long-run production and cost. We shall see whether this kind of subsidy, widely available throughout Europe, is likely to be a successful policy in terms of reducing unemployment in disadvantaged regions.

We shall build a model of how companies make decisions to minimise costs. How does a producer choose the best combination of capital and labour when he has the freedom to change his capital as well as labour in the long run? Table 5.4 shows several possible technically efficient ways of making 100 blips, each one involving a different combination of labour and capital.

As you would expect, the firm can save on labour (L) by using more capital (K) or vice versa. Now let us plot these combinations and join them to form a smooth curve as in Figure 5.7. Plotting a smooth curve implies that there are

Table 5.4 Assumed possible combinations of capital and labour for blip production

Process	*Number of labour-hours*	*Number of machine-hours*
P	5	10
Q	10	7
R	15	5
S	20	4

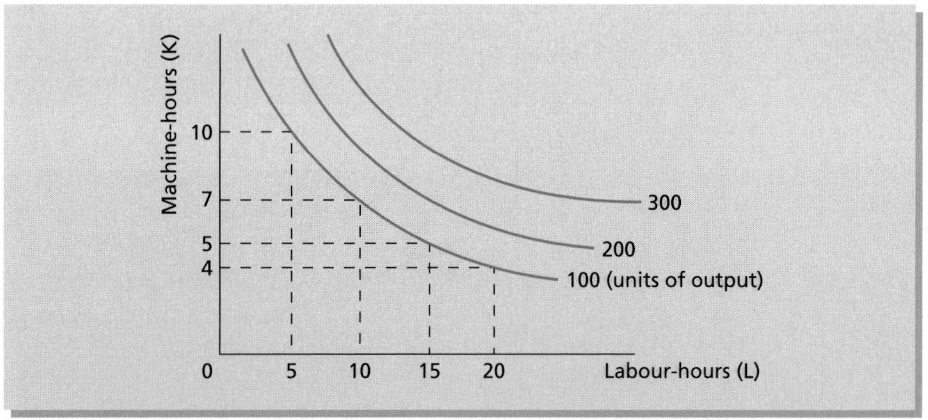

Figure 5.7 Isoquants showing the outputs for varying combinations of inputs

other processes available which we have not specified. What we have drawn is called an *isoquant*. We have also drawn other isoquants showing combinations of capital and labour needed to produce larger levels of output.

Now suppose you are going to produce 100 units of output using one of the above four combinations of K and L. Which will you choose? That is, what is the optimal volume of investment in K?

The answer is that you cannot decide unless you know how much capital costs and how much labour costs. In other words, you have to know the relative prices of K and L. Consider the line K_1L_1 in Figure 5.8. It is called an *isocost* curve and tells you all the combinations of K and L that you could purchase for some given amount of expenditure. If you choose all investment expenditure you can buy OK_1 capital. If you choose no capital and all labour, you can buy OL_1 labour services. Different combinations costing say £1,000 can be represented by points on a straight line between K_1 and L_1. So the isocost curve tells you how expensive capital is relative to labour (like the budget line for consumers).

Now look at Figure 5.9 where the isoquant and isocost curves are together. Which production process minimises costs to the producer of producing 100 blips?

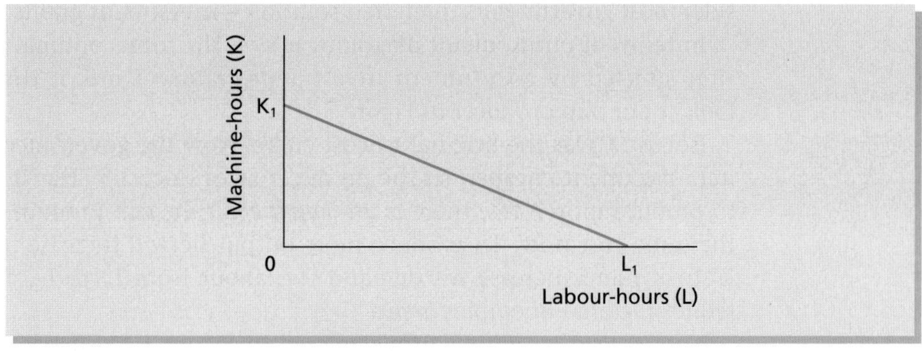

Figure 5.8 Relative price of capital and labour services

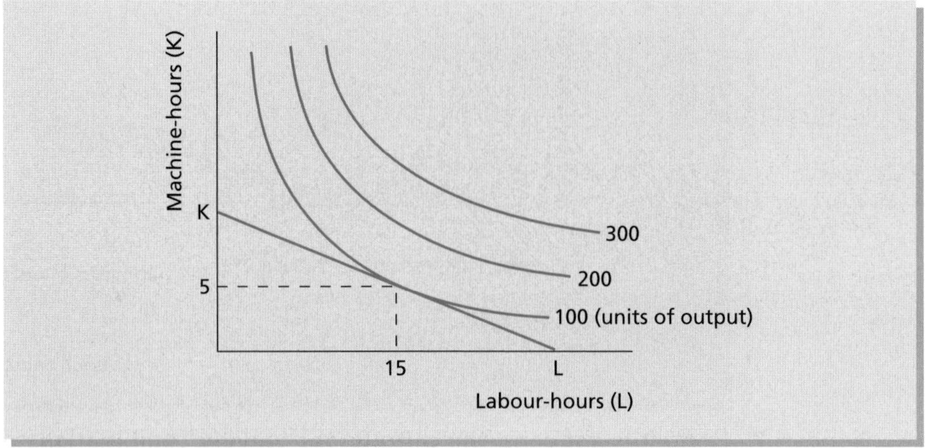

Figure 5.9 **Equilibrium combination of capital and labour services**

Only the combination of 5 machine-hours and 15 man-hours keeps costs down to £100. You have found the optimal volume of investment for a blip producer wishing to produce 100 blips per hour. If the producer were to pick any other combination of K and L that could produce 100 units per week, the isocost curve going through that point on the diagram would be further from the origin, implying a higher cost.

It should not be difficult to see that the minimum cost of producing 200 units of output will be found by an isocost curve drawn parallel to the one drawn in Figure 5.9 touching the 200 unit isocost curve. Given the relative price of capital and labour we can now find the minimum cost of producing any level of output for the long run. From that information the firms's long-run cost curve could be found.

Effect of investment grants

Let us now see whether we can use the concepts we have studied to examine this problem faced by successive United Kingdom post-war governments – the high level of unemployment in certain regions of the country. We can also consider most governments' preferred solution – investment grants.

In terms of our isoquant diagrams, how is the firm's optimal investment decision affected by government investment grants? Think it through first, then look at our blip producer in Figure 5.10.

Isocost X was the original isocost curve. Now the government has made capital investment cheaper, so the producer faces isocost Y. Has it encouraged him to produce more? Yes, there is an *output effect*: he can produce more output for the same cost now. To produce more output he will increase investment (from K_1 to K_2) and increase his demand for labour from L_1 to L_2. This should help reduce regional unemployment.

Now consider another firm depicted in Figure 5.11. It has the same isocost curves but slightly differently sloped isoquants. Compare the firm's output

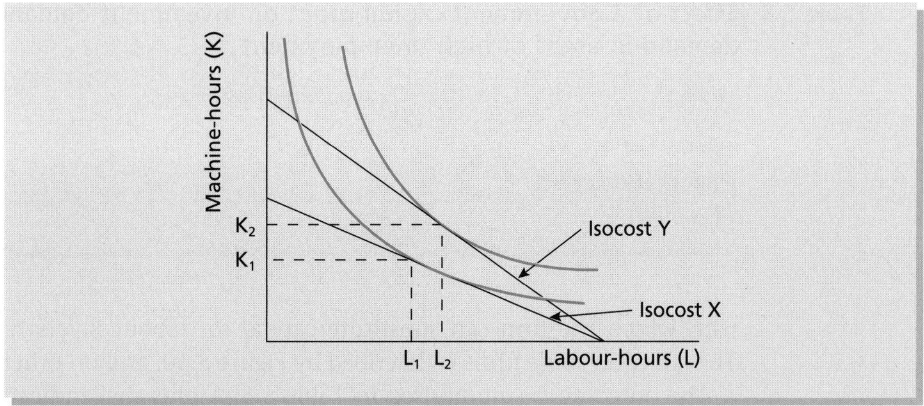

Figure 5.10 Lower capital prices may increase demand for labour services

levels before and after the subsidy. Now compare its investment plans, and look at the amount of labour it wishes to employ. Can you suggest any reasons for what may seem a curious result? The firm is using *less* labour because of the government's subsidy. There is more output and more investment but less demand for labour.

The answer to the problem lies in the fact that the investment grant has two effects on the firm. First, there is an output effect – the lower costs of production encourage the firm to expand output, which requires more investment *and* more labour. However, since the grant makes capital cheaper, there is also a second effect, a substitution effect. That is, the grant on capital encourages the firm to substitute what is now relatively cheap capital for what has become relatively dear labour, thus reducing the demand for labour. So one effect, the output effect, is encouraging the firm in the area of high unemployment to *increase* its demand for labour. The other effect, the substitution effect, is encouraging it to *reduce* its demand for labour. Which of these two effects is stronger decides whether the grant increases or decreases the demand for labour in the area of high unemployment. Which is the stronger effect will depend upon the ease

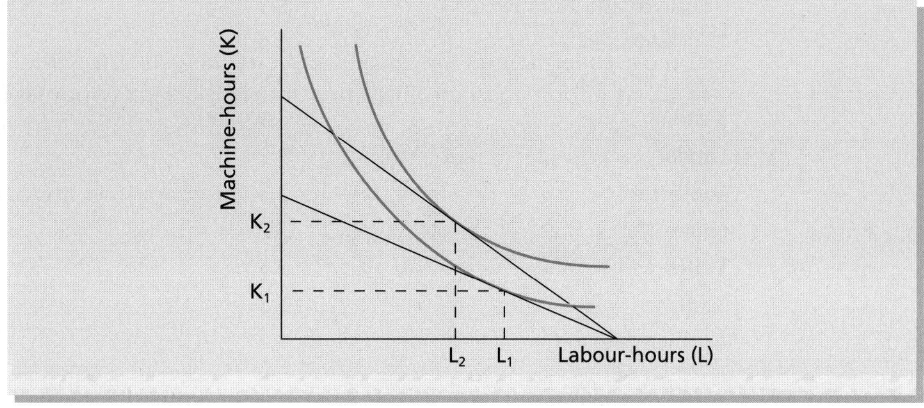

Figure 5.11 Lower capital prices may decrease demand for labour services

Table 5.5 Effect of a government capital grant on investment demand and labour demand in areas of high unemployment

Effect	*Change in investment*	*Change in labour*
Output effect	+	+
Substitution effect	+	–
Total effect	+	?

with which the firm can substitute capital for labour if relative prices change. The effect on some firms is described by Figure 5.10, and on others by Figure 5.11.

The outcome is summarised in Table 5.5. A plus sign indicates more demand for the factor, a minus sign a reduced demand and a question mark that its change is indeterminate. We would predict, then, that most governments' policy towards the regions – that of investment grants – will, at best, narrow output differentials more than it will narrow differences in unemployment rates. It seems strange, then, that most governments are reluctant to subsidise labour in order that output and substitution effects should increase the demand for labour. At worst, capital subsidies could exacerbate the problem of high regional unemployment.

There is one piece of evidence which suggests that our predictions may be correct. Consider Table 5.6. GDP per head measures the output of the region divided by its population. Observe that there is a high correlation between unemployment rates and GDP per head; but observe also that the variations

Table 5.6 Variations in income and employment in UK regions[1]

	Average unemployment rate (%)	*Index of GDP per capita (UK = 100)*
North East	7.5	86.3
North West	4.2	90.7
Merseyside	8.8	90.7
Yorkshire and Humberside	5.3	90.7
East Midlands	3.9	98.6
West Midlands	4.8	94.5
Eastern	3.1	107.8
London	4.9	123.3
South East	2.5	110.4
South West	3.2	96.3
Wales	5.5	84.0
Scotland	5.5	97.8
Northern Ireland	7.2	82.1

[1] Figures are for 1999

Source: adapted from NatWest, *Market Intelligence Report*

between regions are greater for unemployment than for output. For example, unemployment in Northern Ireland is several times greater than the 'best' regions. By contrast, the proportional differences in GDP per head between Northern Ireland and the 'best' regions are much smaller. Average output per head in the UK's 'best' region, London, is only 40–50 per cent higher than Northern Ireland's.

As we said earlier the present UK government is more proactive in the regions than its predecessor. It has established in recent years Regional Development Agencies charged with furthering regeneration, economic development, investment, competitiveness and business efficiency.

As yet there is little evidence that they achieve much. The reasons are not difficult to find. It is not clear how they are to meet these goals, particularly because they have little direct influence in decisions affecting regional development. Furthermore, the funds at their disposal are small. For the nine agencies in total it amounts to around £1.5 bn. The annual output of each of the regions, on the other hand, varies from around £20 bn to upwards of £120 bn.

5.8 The problem at the wider level

Regional policy is increasingly being seen in the EU as a problem of the Union rather than as a series of individual problems faced by its members. There are, perhaps, three important reasons why this should be so.

Existing disparities

First, there are enormous differences in regional incomes that are regarded as socially and politically unacceptable. With the accession of more countries into the EU during the 1980s and 1990s, some relatively poor, the disparities between countries are so great as to make those between regions within Britain seem minor. With the further accession of countries considered in Chapter 1 these disparities will seem much larger still.

Let us think of each country of the EU as a region. How uneven is such regional development? Figure 5.12 shows output per head in the fifteen member states of the EU, the length of the bars indicating that the richest country (Luxembourg) is over twice as rich as the poorest country (Greece). This represents a greater disparity than exists between regions within the UK. Notice also that the spread of 'regional' unemployment rates is far greater than the spread within, say, the UK or Germany.

European integration: widening disparities?

Second, the removal of barriers to trade between countries within the EU which has taken place in recent years is generally thought to accentuate the differences in average incomes. As a rule, incomes per head are higher close to the centre of the EU and lower towards the fringes. The countries at the bottom of the

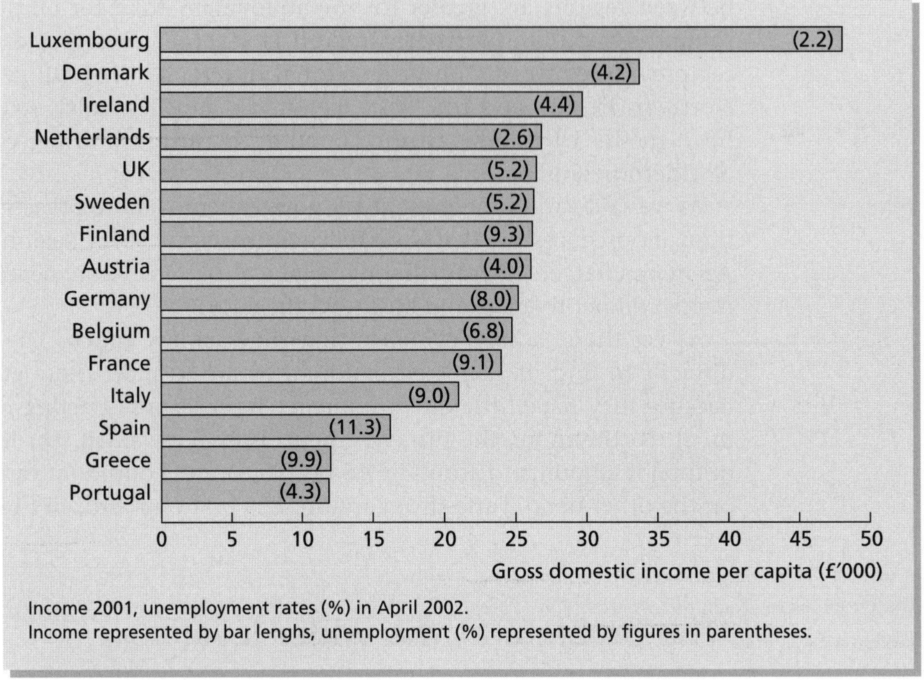

Figure 5.12 Unemployment rates in the EU
Source: adapted from Eurostat data

'income league' of Figure 5.12 tend to be situated around the edge of the EU. This is partly because firms locating at the centre have an advantage in that their market is potentially nearer to them. Transport costs limit the area over which firms can hope to sell. The area they can cover reaching out from the centre is obviously greater than if they are reaching inwards from the fringe. The fewer the barriers to trade, the more this is so. Hence, although greater trade in Europe may raise output, it probably widens relative incomes.

Market economists would argue that regional unemployment would still not result in the long run, since wage rates would fall until some firms found it worthwhile to relocate to the fringes and some workers relocated to the centre. In other words, the process described in section 5.3 in the context of the UK would work equally well on a Europe-wide basis if barriers to resource movements are eliminated. Others believe that the relative wages that would make this possible are too low on the fringes to be politically and socially acceptable.

Labour immobility

Third, there are great problems with labour mobility. It is often thought that labour immobility makes reductions in regional wage rates and unemployment levels difficult for areas within a country. Significant language and cultural barriers would be much greater between countries. If people are reluctant to move from Saxony-Anhalt to Baden Württemberg to get a job, how much less likely are they to move from Greece to Luxembourg? Therefore, however effective the market mechanism we described earlier, it is likely to be less effective across countries in the EU. It must be said, though, that some economists feel that labour immobility may be lessened over time through, for example, mutual recognition of diplomas, degrees and other qualifications.

5.9 European regional policy

Since 1975 The EU has had a European Regional Development Fund (ERDF). Funds are allocated to member countries for assistance in addition to those provided by the member states themselves. The allocations to each country for the years 2000–2006 are given in Table 5.7. Objective 1 funds refer to allocations for regions where average income is less than 75 per cent of the EU average. Objective 2 funds cover a range of area types. They are those undergoing rapid socio-economic change, rural areas of high unemployment, deprived urban areas and finally fishing regions suffering change as a result of attempts to reduce fishing in order to conserve stocks. Objective 3 funds are to support education, training and employment. FIFG funds are further funds to support fisheries areas. The phasing out columns refer to funds yet to be allocated under the previous allocations to 2000. In addition to these structural funds are the

Table 5.7 EU structural fund allocations, 2000–2006 (million euros, 1999 prices)

Country	*Objective 1*	*Phasing out Objective 1*	*Objective 2*	*Phasing out Objective 2*	*Objective 3*	*FIFG (outside Objective 1)*	*Total*
Belgium	0	625	368	65	737	34	1,829
Denmark	0	0	156	27	365	197	745
Germany	19,229	729	2,984	526	4,581	107	28,156
Greece	20,961	0	0	0	0	0	20,961
Spain	37,744	352	2,553	98	2,140	200	43,087
France	3,254	551	5,437	613	4,540	225	14,620
Ireland	1,315	1,773	0	0	0	0	3,088
Italy	21,935	187	2,145	377	3,744	96	28,484
Luxembourg	0	0	34	6	38	0	78
Netherlands	0	123	676	119	1,686	31	2,635
Austria	261	0	578	102	528	4	1,473
Portugal	16,124	2,905	0	0	0	0	19,029
Finland	913	0	459	30	403	31	1,836
Sweden	722	0	354	52	720	60	1,908
UK	5,085	1,166	3,989	706	4,568	121	15,635
Total	127,543	8,411	19,733	2,721	24,050	1,106	183,564

Source: Adapted from *EU Structural Funds: Commission Decides Financial Allocations*, Press Release IP/99/442, 1 July 1999 (European Commission)

Cohesion Funds aimed at reducing income and employment differences. Total annual receipts from Structural and Cohesion Funds combined must not exceed 4 per cent of GDP for any member state.

All the member states pay into the EU budget from which the structural funds are taken. Since the money paid in is to some extent directly proportional to national income per head, and the money paid out is to some extent inversely correlated with national income per head, there is a transference of resources from rich to poor countries within the EU as there is from rich to poor regions in a country with its own active regional policy. The correlations are far from perfect: Germany receives more from the structural fund than does Greece overall, for example. However, one must remember that this would not be true on a per capita basis. The German economy contributes vastly more to the EU budget than does Greece.

Given the scale of regional support, the probability must be that EU regional policy reduces regional income differentials to less than they would otherwise have been. It is doubtful, however, whether the capital bias so prevalent in regional policy in recent decades will do so much for the reduction of regional unemployment differentials.

Agreement between EU members on the size of regional aid and on its distribution will not become easier. One reason for this is the probable widening of the EU to include some of the East European countries discussed in Chapter 1. As we have seen, their GDP per head is substantially lower than that of current members. They will feel that they have a strong claim for a large degree of support to reduce differentials.

5.10 Conclusion

Disparities within regions, whether measured by income per head or by unemployment rates, are significant within the UK and even more so between member countries of the EU.

Supply and demand analysis suggests that over time these differences will narrow, but the model makes several assumptions that may be unrealistic. For example, significant unemployment levels over a long period in the UK and much of Europe suggest that markets may not clear quickly. This is an issue to which we return in later chapters. The law of diminishing returns can be argued to show that government intervention would be worthwhile, either on a country basis or at a European level.

Given that firms make investment decisions based on profit maximisation there is a strong case for suggesting that regional subsidies are misdirected and should be altered.

Increased emphasis on European regional policy can be argued to be worthwhile, but the form it takes will need to be thought through carefully, especially with the accession of many new members from Eastern Europe from 2004.

Finally, we must add a word of warning. We have said some important things about regional policy but we have been using microeconomic analysis to say them. We shall discover later in the book that we can gain further insight into the problem with a knowledge of macroeconomics. Hence there will be more on regional problems, especially in Chapter 20.

CHAPTER SUMMARY

1 **The price of factors of production such as labour can be explained by supply and demand, the price of labour services being the wage rate.**

2 **If the price of a product or factor is different in different parts of the country, the difference will be reduced over time through the process of arbitrage.**

3 **Short-run average and marginal costs tend to increase as output increases.**

4 **The shape of firms' short-run cost curves is explained by the law of diminishing returns.**

5 **In the long run, firms can substitute capital for labour, the optimum amount of each factor being determined by isocosts and isoquants.**

6 **There may well be significant resource immobility in labour markets which may justify some intervention in the form of regional policy.**

Questions for discussion

Guidance to the answers for the ***asterisked*** *numbered questions is available to students on the website for the book at* **www.booksites.net/heather**.

1* The size of the regional problem was examined in the text by considering regional unemployment figures and output per head. What other indications of regional welfare might be used? What problems arise with using your suggested variables?

2 If total product is rising, what is happening to (a) average product and (b) marginal product? Is it (1) rising (2) falling or (3) it is not possible to tell?

3* The European economy since 1945 has gone through periods of relatively rapid growth followed by periods of slowdown. What would you expect would happen to regional disparities during these 'trade cycles'? Why?

4 How impressive do you find the case for intervention in regional location decisions? Consider especially the arguments mentioned in the text based on knowledge, the nature of firms' location decisions, the speed of adjustment arguments and the optimum population argument.

5* The UK government once attempted to influence regional location by insisting that all firms undertaking large development schemes in heavily populated areas obtain an Industrial Development Certificate from the government. It could then refuse a certificate in the hope that the firm would expand in the areas of high unemployment. The scheme was abandoned in 1982. What do you think were its main advantages and disadvantages?

6 Suppose that you were producing 100 blips at point P (refer back to Table 5.4) and you decided to use a *more labour-intensive* method it would require 5 extra man-hours to replace 3 machines. However, if you were at Q and you decided to be more labour intensive still, another extra 5 man-hours would enable you to save on the investment of only 2 machine-hours. Why? What does this suggest about a government policy to subsidise labour in order to stimulate regional employment?

7* At the end of the eighteenth century Thomas Malthus argued that the vast majority of people would always be desperately poor. As the population increased and land resources remained constant, the marginal product of labour would continue to fall. So incomes would fall as the population rose. Was he right?

8 What counter arguments might be made to defend regional policy's capital bias?

9* How would transport improvements within Europe affect regional location?

10 On balance, should regional policy be more or less interventionist?

Websites

The European Commission maintains a regional policy website at:

http//europa.eu.int/comm/regional_policy/

For the UK, information about government policy towards the regions can be found on the Department of Trade and Industry website at:

www.dti.gov.uk/regions/

6 Perfect competition

Small firms: *is small beautiful?*

CHAPTER OVERVIEW

Every year, whether the economy is in recession or not, many small firms go out of business. Is this a reflection of the market allocating resources efficiently? Or are the large and powerful ruthlessly exploiting the small and weak? Is it true that small is beautiful and that, therefore, governments must protect small firms? If so, how should they do it?

In this chapter we review the following concepts:

- Supply and demand
- Long- and short-run costs

We introduce the following:

- Perfect competition
- Normal profits
- Minimum efficient scale

6.1 Introduction

Many people have a desire to run their own business. Some hope that it will grow into a large organisation, but most want it to remain small. At present there are over 19 million firms employing less than ten people each in Europe. What that figure does not show is that many who begin their own business are rapidly disappointed. Some of them do not survive for more than six months.

In some industries the disappearance of small businesses is readily apparent. Small grocers have not survived the growth of the large supermarket chains. Many independent estate agents have disappeared so that now most estate agencies are part of a large national organisation. Does such a trend matter very much? If Tesco provides cheaper food, is there any reason for bewailing the loss of the grocery outlets whose costs are too high? This is an important question that we shall examine in this chapter. We shall also offer explanations about why many firms *do* survive and consider why the government provides encouragement to them through various schemes.

6.2 The presence of small firms in Britain

Defining the small firm

Defining the small firm is no easy matter. We might think of it as one that has no market power. The small firm in the model of perfect competition, which we shall examine shortly, has to be small enough so as to have no control over its prices. Furthermore, it is assumed to produce a product identical to that of all other firms in the market. Why can we not find examples of exactly this in the real world? One reason is that if a firm is too small to have much control over price, it probably survives by differentiating its product – providing a better or more personal service or whatever. So, although we can find many firms whose market power is very limited, we cannot have a precise measure of that limit. Thus, the size of firm which we call small is somewhat arbitrary.

If we choose to define the small firm in terms of size, we can avoid the arbitrary nature of what constitutes power, but the choice of size variable is also arbitrary. Should we define size in terms of the number of employees? An alternative possibility is to use turnover or the value of sales. A further possibility is to look at the value of the firm's capital, but this is especially arbitrary since it creates problems with respect to the valuation of capital. How much is a firm's two-year-old machinery really worth? Finally, one might use value-added, the difference between the value of a firm's output and its purchases from firms in other industries. This gives a good idea of the importance of the firm in terms of its contribution to the economy's output. In practice, turnover and employment size are the two most commonly used criteria. Eurostat categorises by employment, all firms being either micro, small, medium or large (see Table 6.1). As we shall see shortly the vast majority of European firms are micro in size. By any definition, we can say that while there is no perfectly competitive firm, there are many tiny firms that survive in an atmosphere of intense competition. Their position, we can argue, can usefully be analysed in terms of the perfectly competitive model that we shortly consider.

Table 6.1 Eurostat definitions of firm size

Category		*Number of employees*
SME's	Micro	0–9
	Small	10–99
	Medium	100–499
LSE's	Large	500+

The importance of small firms

It is clear that small firms play a major part in the economy of Europe. Using the definitions in Table 6.1 we can consider the importance of firms or enterprises by the number of employees. By Eurostat's definition over 93 per cent of private, non-primary enterprises are micro.

To some extent this figure can be said to *overstate* the importance of small firms. Although over 93 per cent of firms are micro, they do not account for 93 per cent of European employment. In fact, according to Eurostat, micro firms account for about 34 per cent of non-government employment. The proportion of the labour force working in different sized firms is given in Figure 6.1. However, micro and small firms are still of great significance in the economic structure of Europe.

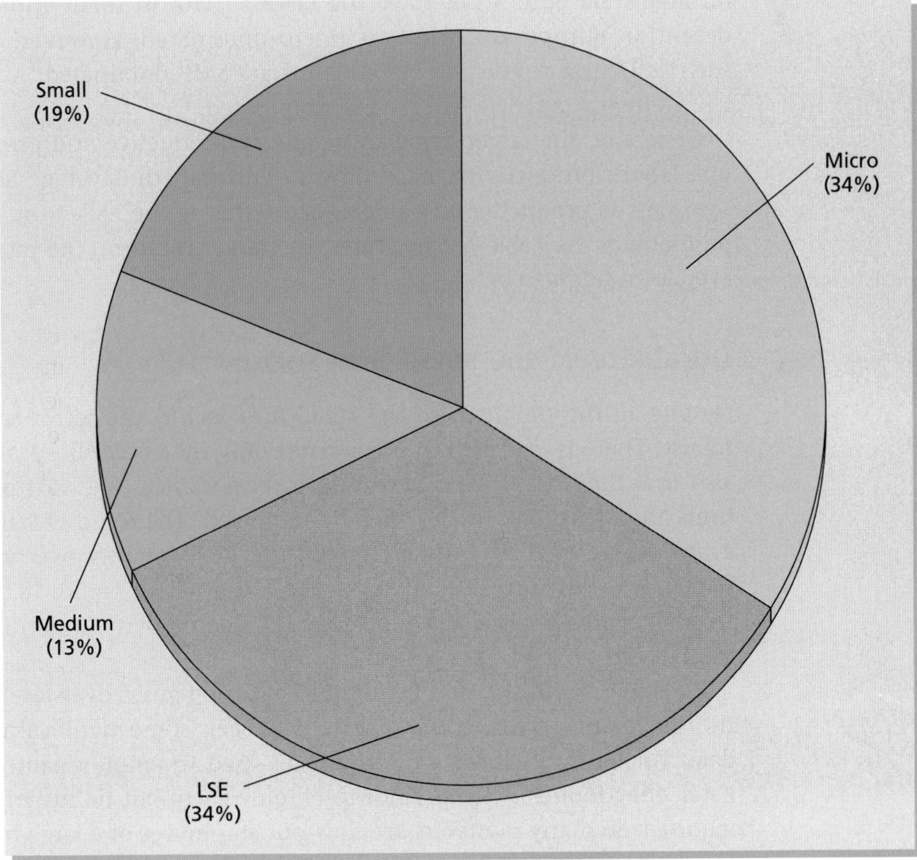

Figure 6.1 **Employment in non-primary private enterprise, Europe-19, 2000**
Source: Adapted from Eurostat data

Table 6.2 Profitability as a percentage of value added by firm size class, Europe-19, 2000

Size category	*Percentage added*
All	39
Micro	14
Small	31
Medium	41
Large	51

Source: Adapted from Eurostat data

In most countries industry is 'dominated' by the smaller organisations. A country or sector of industry is said by Eurostat to be micro, small and medium-sized or LSE dominated, if either micro, small or medium-sized (taken together), or large-scale enterprises have the largest share in total employment. By this definition Europe as a whole is micro dominated. However, a few countries, such as Denmark and the Netherlands are SME dominated. A few, such as the UK, Germany and Sweden, are LSE dominated.

Generally, the larger firms are relatively productive and profitable. Consider first labour productivity. According to Eurostat, the average SME is not much over half as productive in value added terms as the LSE. Now consider relative profitability. As Table 6.2 indicates, the larger the firm, the more profitable, on average, it tends to be.

Durability of the small firm sector

Despite all the problems of the small firm sector, the sector seems to be quite robust. There is evidence to suggest not only that small firms are important but also that they have been increasing in importance. The vast majority of small firms are owned and run by the self-employed. The trend of self-employment as a proportion of total employment of the UK economy over a period of more than thirty years exhibits a clear long-run upwards trend. It may be that this trend has now peaked although female self-employment continues to grow in significance.

To some extent it could be argued that the figures overstate the resilience of the small firm sector in that there have been some significant changes to the data. For example, many building firms used to employ painters or plasterers. Later, they found it cheaper not to employ them but to buy in their services as required. So many plasterers are now not employees of a large firm but are small firms selling their services to the building industry.

Distribution of small firms between sectors

We have seen that the importance of small firms varies considerably from country to country. It also varies from sector to sector. This can be seen from Tables 6.3(a) and (b). Table 6.3(a) shows the distribution of employment by size of enterprise for the major areas of economic activity of the UK economy. So the table shows, for example, that 40.3 per cent of people working in agriculture, forestry and fishing are working in micro enterprises, whereas for mining, quarrying, energy and water, the proportion in such micro organisations is just over 2 per cent.

Variations between sectors of the economy are equally significant if one considers the distribution of turnover. Whereas 92 per cent of the turnover of agriculture, forestry and fishing is from enterprises employing fewer than 50 people, only 10 per cent of the turnover from mining, quarrying, energy and water comes from firms of that size. Note two things about Tables 6.3(a) and 6.3(b). First the definitions of small firms is different in each case. Second, the asterisks indicate that the data is not being disclosed. This is to give a measure of confidentiality to the firms concerned.

The recent growth of the small firm sector has been faster in the UK than in most other European countries. In the past, self-employment as a percentage of total employment was much less in the UK than the average for the rest of the European Union. Now, as Figure 6.2 indicates, the UK is very close to the European average.

Table 6.3(a) Employment by size of enterprise in the private sector, 2001, UK

Employment ('000)	*= 100%*	*Size (number of employees)*			
		None[1]	*Small (1–49)*	*Medium (50–249)*	*Large (250+)*
All industries	22,622	12.8	30.6	12.0	44.6
A,B Agriculture, forestry and fishing	452	40.3	53.8	*	*
C,E Mining, quarrying, energy, water	221	2.2	5.1	*	*
D Manufacturing	4,103	4.7	24.3	21.8	49.2
F Construction	1,666	36.1	38.7	9.7	15.5
G Wholesale, retail and repairs	4,652	7.0	33.6	9.5	49.9
H Hotels and restaurants	1,560	1.6	41.8	10.4	46.2
I Transport, storage, communication	1,657	12.6	17.9	8.6	60.9
J Financial intermediation	1,076	4.7	10.3	*	*
K Real estate, business activities	3,491	18.5	38.4	13.4	29.8
M Education	289	38.2	30.2	16.0	15.6
N Health and social work	2,253	9.4	24.1	8.5	58.0
O Other social/personal services	1,200	27.3	35.9	9.9	26.9

[1] Sole proprietorships and partnerships comprising only the self-employed owner-managers and companies comprising only an employee director

Source: DTI, SME Statistics Unit, 2002

Table 6.3(b) **Turnover by size of enterprise in the private sector, 2001, UK**

Turnover (£million)	*= 100%*	*Size (number of employees)*			
		None[1]	*Small (1–49)*	*Medium (50–249)*	*Large (250+)*
All industries	2,112,013	7.2	29.0	15.1	48.6
A,B Agriculture, forestry and fishing	26,250	24.6	67.4	*	*
C,E Mining, quarrying, energy, water	95,418	6.6	3.4	*	*
D Manufacturing	457,239	1.7	16.4	18.3	63.6
F Construction	136,927	18.7	40.0	16.0	25.3
G Wholesale, retail and repairs	725,436	4.9	32.9	15.0	47.2
H Hotels and restaurants	49,359	3.1	43.9	11.4	41.5
I Transport, storage, communication	168,449	5.3	20.2	12.6	61.9
J Financial intermediation[2]	–	–	–	–	–
K Real estate, business activities	292,203	13.9	41.0	17.1	28.1
M Education	9,912	26.1	42.5	17.5	14.0
N Health and social work	74,911	5.5	23.9	7.4	63.2
O Other social/personal services	75,909	17.2	34.2	12.0	36.5

[1] Sole proprietorships and partnerships comprising only the self-employed owner-manager(s) and companies comprising only an employee director

Source: DTI, SME Statistics Unit, 2002

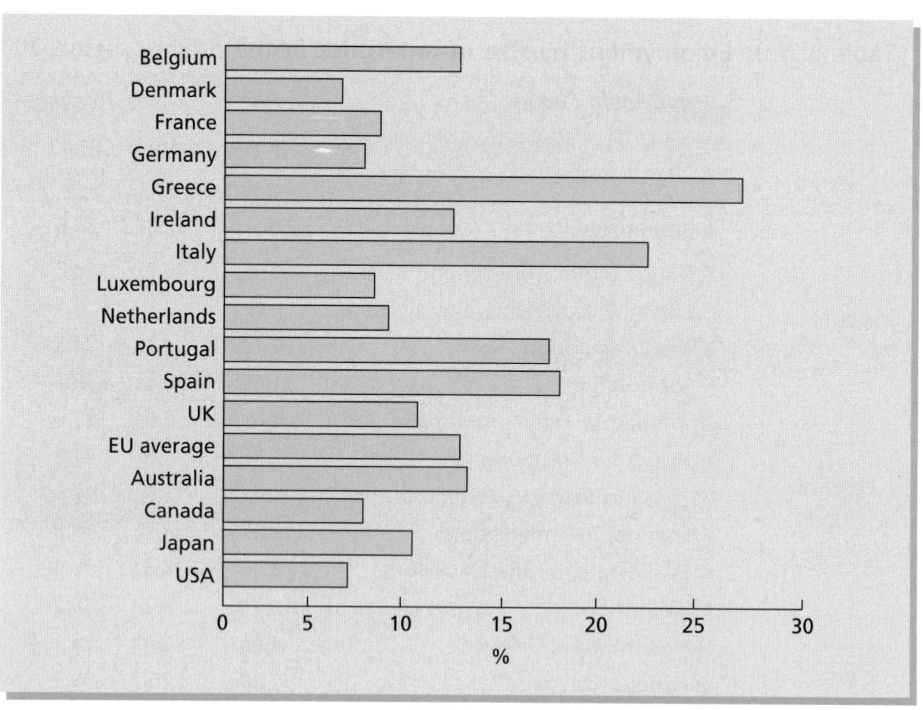

Figure 6.2 **Self-employment (non-agricultural) as a percentage of total employment in the EU, 1992**

Source: adapted from OECD labour force statistics 1972–92

Having seen something of the significance of the small firm sector in Europe we now consider an important question. Do small firms need government help or are they best left to help themselves? There is a case for saying that they should *not* be given assistance. It is to this argument that we turn first.

6.3 The case for non-protection

Perfect competition: a model for analysing small firms

In Chapter 1 we explained the value of an economic model. Our model of perfect competition will throw much light on the behaviour of small firms. The essence of perfect competition is that firms in the market are too small to have any control over price. Price is determined by supply and demand. The small firm has to accept that price in order to sell its output. It will not be able to sell if it tries to charge more. It has no need to charge less since it can sell all the output it chooses at the ruling market price. Notice that smallness in this sense is not an absolute concept: firms must be small in relation to the total size of the market. (For further elaboration of the assumptions of perfect competition, refer back to section 2.8 of Chapter 2. Note, though, that we did not use the term 'perfect competition' there.)

see pp. 44–7

What does the model suggest about firm behaviour and the need for government assistance? Recall from Chapter 5 that we make a distinction between the long run and the short run. The long run is the time in which all factors of production are variable. The short run is the period in which one factor of production, usually capital, is fixed and other factors are variable.

see pp. 100–1

We look first to see the case for saying that no government protection of firms is needed in the short run. We first see what our model predicts about short-run behaviour and then consider why we can argue that no government intervention is needed.

Small firms: the short run

You will recall from Chapter 5 that the short-run cost conditions of the firm are determined by the law of diminishing returns. Figure 6.3 shows the position. Section 5.5 of Chapter 5 derived the short-run marginal cost (SMC) curve and the average variable cost curve (AVC).

see pp. 100–1

see pp. 100–3

However, variable costs are not the only short-run costs which a firm must meet. There are also fixed costs. In terms of our example of the farmer in Chapter 5, he had to pay the rent on the field. This is a fixed cost – fixed in the sense that it is a charge to be met whatever the amount of output he chooses to make. Let us suppose that rent per week is £48. This is the fixed cost. What is the average fixed cost (AFC)? This will depend on the chosen level of output. If the farmer chooses to produce 1 unit of output per week, the AFC will be £48. The total fixed cost (TFC) will be spread over just the 1 unit. Formally,

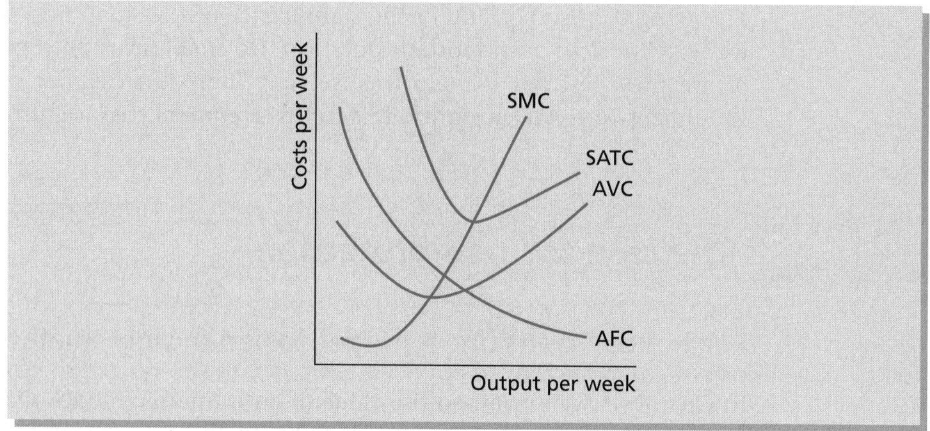

Figure 6.3 Short-run costs of production

AFC = TFC/Q, where Q is the level of output. At this output AFC = £48/1 = £48. Suppose he makes 2 units per week. AFC = £48/2 = £24. Fixed costs remain the same, but as output increases average fixed costs will fall. If he makes 48 units, then AFC = £48/48 = £1 per week. Figure 6.3 shows an AFC at all levels of output.

Now let us consider short-run average total cost (SATC). SATC is simply AFC + AVC. This is shown in Figure 6.3. To AVC at each level of output is added the vertical distance of AFC.

We have figured out the short-run cost structure. What of the price that the firm can get for its output? Since this is a perfectly competitive market the price is decided by supply and demand. Figure 6.4 shows that the firm can sell as much output as it chooses, but only if it is prepared to charge that price, assumed to be £100. The reason for this is contained in the assumptions. The firm is one of many, all of which are selling an identical product, so it has no control over price. If it were to raise its price, people would go to one of the other firms to purchase. A firm can only have control over its price if it can differentiate its product.

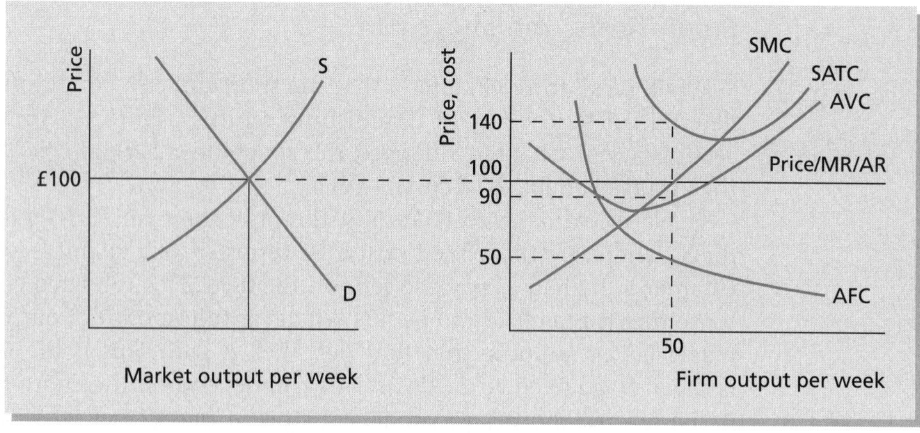

Figure 6.4 The short run in a perfectly competitive industry

How much output would it choose to make if it wanted to do as well as possible? The answer is to produce 50 units per week since that is the level of output at which marginal cost = marginal revenue (SMC = MR). Why is that the best? Recall that SMC is the extra cost of producing one more unit. MR is the extra revenue received for making an additional unit. Since, for each unit made, the firm receives £100, the extra revenue achieved by expanding output by 1 unit must be £100. In other words, MR is the same as price. Now if making an extra unit adds more to revenue than to cost, it is clearly worth making, but, at 50 units, addition to revenue (MR) is as high as addition to cost (SMC). There is no logic in expanding output beyond this level.

Whether this level of output will result in a profit depends upon whether price is high enough to cover all the costs. In the case of the firm in Figure 6.4 price is obviously not sufficiently high. The revenue received per week is the output multiplied by price: 50 × £100 = £5,000. Now consider its costs, though. It has fixed costs of £2,500 (at 50 units of output AFC is £2,500/50 = £50). It also has to cover variable costs. Average variable costs are £90 so total variable costs are 50 × £90 = £4,500. Total weekly costs (output × SATC) are the sum of the variable and fixed costs, which means £7,000 per week. The firm is losing £2,000 per week since revenue is £5,000 per week and total costs £7,000.

Is there anything the firm could do to improve its position? Could it increase its revenue by raising price? No, it has no control over price. It could not find a market for its product at more than £100 per unit. Could it lower its costs? No, the assumption we have made about the cost structure is that the cost curve represents the minimum possible costs associated with each level of output.

Could it shut down operations entirely? Indeed it could. It could decide to produce nothing at all. It would then receive no revenue but it would incur costs in the short run – fixed costs. So fixed costs would represent the size of the loss. In this case the costs having shut down are the £2,500 per week of fixed costs. However, continuing in production would be a better option, and since this more than covers the variable costs, the firm can make a £500 per week contribution to the fixed costs. This reduces the losses from £2,500 to £2,000 per week. In general, if a firm is making a loss but can more than cover variable costs, it will be worthwhile continuing in production in the short run.

An illustration of the point could be made from the holiday industry. Figure 6.4 might represent someone letting out holiday flats on the coast of Cornwall. Although not perfectly competitive, no-one else has exactly the same facilities and view, and there is sufficient competition for us to use our model of perfect competition. The situation described in Figure 6.4 might represent the firm in February. Demand, and therefore price, is low and profit cannot be made. The only option open to the firm is the one we have explored above. It can either let the flats for £100 per week each or close down for the winter if, as in the figure, it cannot cover the wear and tear on the carpet, and the lighting and heating. At least if the £100 per week more than covers such variable costs, it will make a contribution to the fixed costs of rates and insurance, and so on. This explains why some holiday cottages are available all year, though at much higher rents in the summer, whilst others are not offered for let at all during the off-season – their variable costs in winter are too high relative to the price that can be charged.

It should now be clear that there is a case for saying that no government assistance is required for firms making short-run losses. In the longer run, demand may increase, prices will rise and losses will be eliminated. This might be true, for example, of seasonal industries, including large firms such as British Gas which makes losses in the summer months. The summer's revenue covers variable costs but is not sufficient to cover all the substantial fixed costs. The same thing would also apply to industries during a recession – in the long run prices will rise. If there is a case for help from government, then, it would have to be found in the long run. It is to that we now turn.

Small firms in the long run

Free market economists would argue that the small firm does not need government intervention in the long run because the market sees to it that price will be high enough to cover all the firms' costs. To see why this is so, we need to understand the nature of long-run production costs. The long run, remember, is the period long enough for a firm to adjust the amount of its capital as well as its labour.

What happens if a firm increases its output in the long run? It takes on more capital and more labour to produce this output. Clearly this will cost more. But what happens to costs per unit? There is a concept called *economies of scale* which suggests that, as output increases, unit costs fall. What might these scale economies be?

Some economies are financial. Small firms can appear risky to lenders of money such as banks, who therefore charge higher interest rates to compensate for that risk. Larger, apparently safer, firms get financial economies. They get lower interest rates for borrowing, so that a larger output will tend to lower their unit costs. Some economies are technical. Larger firms can utilise capital which is impractical for small firms. Robots for operations on a car factory lower unit costs. Such technology is not possible for small producers. These and other scale economies cause average costs to fall as output increases.

There is also an argument to say that at very large output levels long-run average costs rise. This is the result of *diseconomies of scale*. Diseconomies can occur since very large firms need a large management structure. A large structure of this kind creates coordination problems. The firm becomes difficult to manage, causing unit costs to increase. Figure 6.5 shows an assumed long-run average cost curve (LRAC) falling as output rises and economies of scale are obtained, then rising beyond some point because of diseconomies.[1]

Figure 6.5 also shows the position with respect to costs and revenue. Notice now how the equilibrium price determined by market forces is at a level at which a firm can break even. The firm picks its profit-maximising output where marginal cost = marginal revenue, Q_{pm} on the diagram. Total revenue, that is output × price, the shaded area on the diagram, is the same as total cost, i.e. output × average cost.

Why should price tend towards P_1? The reason is that in the long run firms can leave or join the industry. If price were higher, new firms would be attracted

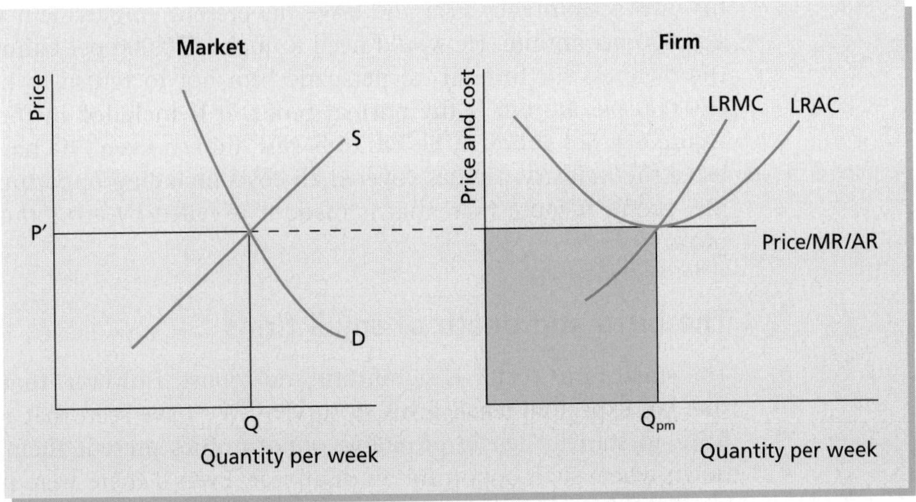

Figure 6.5 **Long-run equilibrium in a perfectly competitive industry**

by the profits available. As they entered, supply would increase, the supply curve would shift right, causing the price to fall. Similarly, if price were lower than P_1 and firms were making losses, some firms would leave the industry. This would shift the supply curve left and the price would rise until firms were covering costs. Therefore, help for such firms can be argued to be unnecessary. The market mechanism protects them by ensuring a long-run price high enough to cover costs.

Normal profit

At this point, however, one might ask why people who can only just break even would stay in an industry. Would they not leave for another industry where profit prospects were better? The answer is no, because of the key concept of *normal profit*. Normal profit is the income an entrepreneur needs to persuade him not to move his resources elsewhere. It is an income representing the opportunity cost of the resources. He must receive this or he will by definition go elsewhere. Economists regard this income as a cost, which is included in the cost of the business (see Table 6.4). For example, suppose a person were to set up

Table 6.4 **Illustrating the concept of normal profit**

(a) Accounting profits

Total revenue (£100,000) less total costs (£70,000) = total profit (£30,000)

(b) Economic profits

Total revenue (£100,000) less total costs including opportunity cost (£100,000) = total normal profit (£0)

his own accountancy firm and leave his present employment where he is paid £30,000 per annum. He would need to make £30,000 per annum to take out of the business for himself, to persuade him not to return to his old job. That £30,000 per annum is the normal profit. It is included in the shaded area of Figure 6.4. So, although he has only just 'broken even', he has no incentive to leave the industry. He has covered all costs including opportunity cost, or normal profit. If more than that is made it is called by economists 'supernormal profit'.

The birth and death of small firms

The small firms sector is significant and robust. However, that does not mean that we expect all small firms to survive. We have seen that we would expect firms to start up where profitable opportunities present themselves and close down where such opportunities disappear. Even if there were no change in the number of small firms over a given period, they would not be the *same* ones at the end of the period as at the beginning. This is exactly what does happen. Many new firms enter markets, but not all firms survive. Of those businesses starting up and registering for value added tax, almost all of them small firms, only about 30 per cent are still surviving ten years later. This is not necessarily a bad thing for the economy, as resources need to move in response to changes in consumer demand.

Table 6.5 gives an indication of the process for the UK economy. The best official guide to the pattern of business start-ups and closures is VAT registrations and deregistrations. It is not perfect. For example, some firms are too small to need to register for VAT. However, it is a good indicator. In 2001, with the UK economy growing, there was an increase in the total number of VAT registered businesses. In years when the economy is in recession, such as 1994, there will be a decrease.

Table 6.5 VAT registrations and de-registrations, 1994–2001[1]

	Registrations		*Deregistrations*		*Stock at end year*
	'000	*rate*	*'000*	*rate*	
1994	168.2	36	188.1	40	1,609.3
1995	164.0	35	173.2	37	1,600.1
1996	168.2	36	165.1	35	1,603.2
1997	182.6	39	164.5	35	1,621.3
1998	186.3	40	155.9	33	1,651.6
1999	178.5	38	172.0	37	1,658.1
2000	183.3	39	177.1	37	1,664.4
2001	175.5	37	162.7	34	1,677.1

[1] UK, thousands and rate per 10,000 resident adults

Source: DTI, Small Firms Statistics Unit, 2002

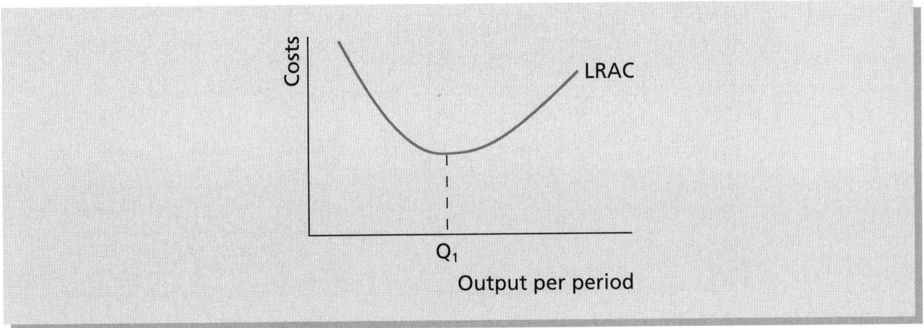

Figure 6.6 A U-shaped long-run average cost curve

6.4 Competing against large firms: long-run cost curves in practice

Cost curves in practice

We have now seen how, in perfectly competitive markets, the small firm produces its profit-maximising output where marginal cost is equal to marginal revenue. In the long run this is also a level of output at which average cost is minimised for such firms. The assumption is that the firm must produce a large enough level of output to take advantage of all the economies of scale available. If it does not do so, it will be disciplined by the market's competitive pressure and it will die. If it attempts to go beyond the level of output at which average cost (AC) is minimised, it will suffer diseconomies of scale. Again it will be disciplined by the market and will either go out of business or return to its optimum size.

One assumption that we have been making is that the long-run average cost curve is U-shaped. We have also been assuming that the level of output needed to be at the bottom of the LRAC curve is quite small. Neither of these assumptions is necessarily valid.

Consider Figure 6.6. The firm must produce Q_1 output in order to minimise unit costs, but it may well be that Q_1 represents a large part of the market for the product. For example, estimates are that for some industries a firm would need to produce about 10 per cent of all European output to reach Q_1. The small firm, then, is going to experience higher unit costs at an output significantly less than Q_1. If it produces at Q_1 it is not going to be a small firm.

In other markets, a different shape of long-run average cost curve is possible. It may be as in Figure 6.7. The market may be one in which there is no significant diseconomy of scale at large levels of output. Smaller firms are inevitably going to have trouble surviving in such markets. This explains why there are no small firms in, for example, aircraft production.

In yet other markets, the LRAC may be as in Figure 6.8. Here Q_{mes} represents minimum efficient scale. It is the lowest level of output that a firm can produce

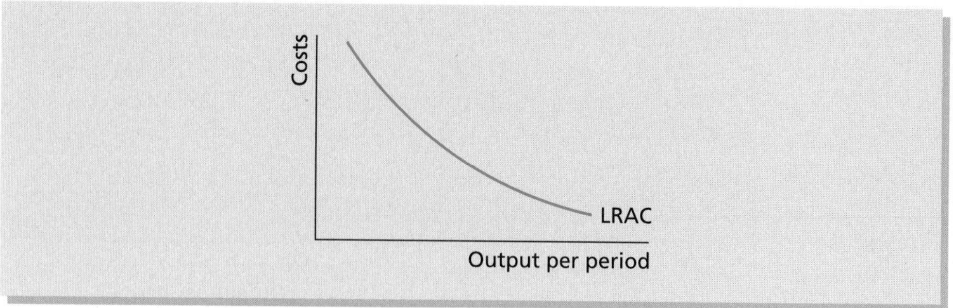

Figure 6.7 **A falling long-run average cost curve**

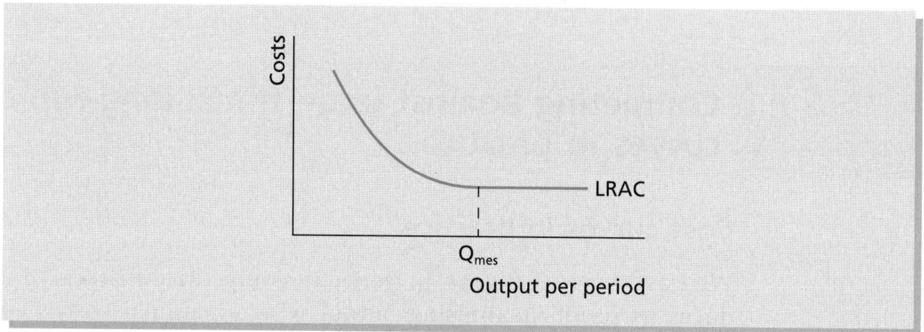

Figure 6.8 **An L-shaped long-run average cost curve**

and still obtain all the available economies of scale. There are two potential difficulties for the small firm in this kind of market. One is that Q_{mes} might represent a substantial part of the market. The small firm is therefore at a much lower output than Q_{mes}. The other potential difficulty is that the LRAC may fall sharply from zero output to Q_{mes}. If so, the cost disadvantage of being at a sub-optimal output level can be crippling. It is easy, then, to see why small firms may find it hard to survive.

Table 6.6 gives some estimates for several industries to show how this might work in practice. A washing machine producer needs to have a plant big enough to produce 57 per cent of all UK machines or 10 per cent of EU output or his unit costs will be higher than optimally sized competitors. That will not be a very small firm.[2]

On the other hand, a firm producing bricks will need to produce only 1 per cent of UK output to be at minimum efficient scale (MES). However, suppose that the firm is smaller than that, say half that size. Then one can see from the right-hand column of Table 6.6 that such a firm's unit costs will be 25 per cent higher.

Government assistance

Clearly, then, in many markets small firms will not survive without government assistance. They will die because they are uneconomic, will grow into larger

Table 6.6 **Some estimates of scale economies in selected industries**

Industry	*MES[a] as % of EU output*	*MES as % of UK output*	*% increase in costs as fraction of half MES*
Beer	3	12	5
Bricks	0.2	1	25
Cement	1	10	26
Cigarettes	6	24	2.2
Oil refining	2.6	14	4
Paint	2	7	4.4
Washing machines	10	57	7.5

[a] MES = minimum efficient scale

Source: adapted from C. F. Pratten (1989) *Costs of Non-Europe*, Vol. 2, European Commission

units or will be taken over by larger firms. The forms of possible assistance can be many and varied. The several different kinds of assistance that many small firms can apply for in the UK are considered in section 6.7.

However, government assistance does not, by itself, present a case for saying that *it is in society's interest that small firms should survive.* After all, if large firms have lower unit costs, they will produce output for fewer resources. To put it another way, large firms' output will be at a lower opportunity cost and society's scarce resources will be better used. Indeed, many small firms will continue to survive without government help. It is to the reasons for their continuing survival that we now turn.

6.5 The survival of small firms

Despite significant scale economies in most markets many small firms continue to survive. Let us look at the major reasons for their survival.

Market dynamics

First, there is the dynamics of the economy. We must not think of the economy as being in equilibrium. The market is always changing in response to changes in technology, changes in demand, changes in international competition and so on. Thus, at any time, there are new young firms who are in the process of developing into much larger ones. Also, there are industries where low set-up costs have induced would-be new entries who simply will not survive in the longer run either because they will die or because they will be taken over by larger, more cost-efficient firms. Then again, a rapidly expanding economy can lead to short-term disequilibrium, since larger firms cannot take advantage immediately of all the possible profitable opportunities for expansion. So even if the large firms have a cost advantage over the smaller ones, smaller firms will, at least for some time, have a significant presence. We have argued in earlier chapters that markets tend to have a stable equilibrium. What we are saying here does not contradict this. What is at issue is the speed at which markets move to equilibrium. It may not be rapid.

Size of market

Second, there is the size of the market. It may be so small that there is only room for one or two firms. This may seem unlikely at first sight. However, to follow the argument, we need to understand the problem that arises in defining a market. Take the example of food. Food retailing is an enormous market. If a consumer in Birmingham wants a loaf of bread, however, he will not buy it from a Sainsbury's store in Plymouth, even if the bread there is cheaper than anywhere in Birmingham. The relevant market to him is much smaller. If he does not have a car, then even a large supermarket a mile away may be of no relevance to him. The small corner store, insignificant in the food retailing sector, is the relevant market. In general terms, some kinds of activity are not suited to large firms. Those requiring personal attention or the ability to meet individual customer needs may survive by having a local monopoly of a tiny market.

In other words, the perfect competition model assumes that firms have no control over price because they all produce an identical product. In many markets firms can have some control by differentiating their products.

Transport costs

Third, there is the question of transport costs. These can be high for certain industries and this makes the presence of small firms highly likely. If transport costs are high, relative to the advantage of production economies, many small local plants will be required rather than a few large ones. If there are high costs to a large firm of coordinating those many small plants, small individual firms will be the more efficient.

Large firm behaviour

Fourth, the presence of small firms may benefit large firms. One may have an industry where there is one large producer, but many smaller ones too even though the large firm may have lower costs and thus be capable of driving the smaller firms out of the industry. However, to preserve an aura of competition, perhaps to keep government anti-monopoly bodies happy, the large firm becomes a price leader, dictating whatever price it chooses. Small firms must take this as the going price. The large firm deliberately chooses a price high enough to enable some small firms to survive. In this way the large firm has not eliminated all the apparent competition.

Changing technology

Fifth, the reduction in information costs associated with modern technology can encourage the existence of small firms. Until a few years ago, the conventional wisdom said that increases in technological development encouraged large-scale production and therefore large firms at the expense of small business. This is now open to question. One reason that firms felt the need to be bigger was the need to integrate vertically, that is to control as much as possible of the manufacturing process from raw material production to the point of sale to the final consumer. One major advantage of vertical integration is that it avoids the costs of acquiring information on which to negotiate prices from input suppliers. The advance of computer technology has reduced those costs and has made more realistic a decision to stay small. The small firm can purchase from a specialist input supplier, who can gain economies of scale in the production of the input.

For all these reasons, even without government aid many small firms do survive.

6.6 The case for small firm protection

Is there, therefore, no case for government intervention to help the small firm sector? Indeed, there is a case which we shall develop more fully in the next two chapters. Let us first briefly pick out five areas in which one can now see how state assistance might be justified.

Market power of large firms

First, there is the fear that large firms, despite their lower unit costs, might have the power to raise prices to consumers in a way in which smaller firms could not. In other words, there is no guarantee that the benefit of lower unit costs will be passed on to consumers in the form of lower prices. On the other hand, it is one attraction for social welfare of small firms that they cannot control prices. The price is impersonally determined by market forces.

Barriers to entry

Second, the barriers to market entry of new firms may be substantial. The most obvious example of an entry barrier is size. Referring back to Table 6.6, there may be significant profits in washing machine production, suggesting that consumers wish to see more resources allocated to this area. A new firm will not be able to survive if it sets up in a small way, yet it is unlikely to be able to find the finance to start up at a size representing 57 per cent of UK output. There may, therefore, be a case for helping small firms to set up in the market.

'Unfair competition'

Third, large firms in a market may attempt to use their power to drive smaller competing firms out. For example, large firms may sell their output at prices below cost in the short term, subsidising their operations by past profits or profits from other markets. Then they can raise prices again when the smaller firms have been driven out. This may not be a case for helping small firms financially; it may be that they should be protected by law. In fact, in 1991 the EU enacted just such laws against unfair competition.

Government behaviour

One loud complaint heard from small firms is the burden that they carry which government itself has imposed. Many laws and regulations bear unfairly on small firms. Preparing accounts for value added tax (VAT) and dealing with planning regulations, for example, create proportionately more problems for a small business than for a large enterprise.

Changes in macroeconomic policy during the past ten or fifteen years have had their effects on the small firm sector. Control of the economy has been more through interest rate policy leading to higher real interest rates than in earlier years. This has probably had a detrimental effect on small firms since they are often more heavily reliant upon bank borrowing than larger firms. We consider the reasons for such a change in macroeconomic policy in later chapters.

There is, therefore, a case for government helping firms financially to overcome the burden that it has imposed upon those businesses itself.

Job creation

The UK government has frequently argued that small firms are a better potential source of job creation than larger firms. Encouragement to such small firms is then justified as a means of reducing unemployment. The figures in Table 6.7 appear to give some support to this. For the period from 1993–98 size class and employment growth are negatively correlated. However, two things should be

Table 6.7 Employment growth by size-class, Europe-19 and USA (1993–1998)

	Europe-19	*USA*
SMEs		
Micro	0.6	1.1
Small	0.4	1.9
Medium-sized	0.3	2.2
Total	0.5	1.8
LSEs	0.3	3.5
All enterprises	0.4	2.7

Source: adapted from Eurostat data

noted. By comparison with the USA Europe's record for job generation has been very poor. Much greater regulation and government burdens on all firms have discouraged job growth. Note also that in the USA where the job generation record is so much better, size-class and employment growth are positively correlated.

The figures for Europe should, however, be treated with caution. It could be argued that it is not small firms that are good at generating employment, rather it is government support of them that has produced such results. Could it be that if the government help given to small firms had been given to larger firms instead, the table would have looked somewhat different?

6.7 Government aid for small firms

Despite having had successive governments in Britain during the last 30 years claiming to be strongly committed to market forces, the case for intervention in the small firm sector has not gone unheard. The government has introduced changes specifically to assist small firms. The following are probably the most important. The principles which lie behind such assistance are used by governments all over Europe.

VAT exemption

Firms in most sectors of the economy have to pay VAT – a tax on the difference between their purchases and the value of the output that they produce. Small firms in all sectors are exempt from the payment of the tax. The size of turnover that is the benchmark for qualification for exemption has increased by more than the rate of inflation at most budgets in recent years. Small firms also pay a lower rate of corporation (profits) tax.

Subsidies on training and research

Small firms can get grants from government to offset costs of training in marketing and management. They can also get help for developing new technologies. This is because small firms have an excellent record for innovation but a poor record for taking ideas through to selling the product. This is often because of the high development costs which the small firm finds itself unable to afford.

Enterprise Investment Scheme

The Enterprise Investment Scheme is designed to help small businesses find investment funds. Individuals can invest in new and unquoted companies and receive generous tax incentives on both their income from the shares and from the capital gains if held for a long enough period.

Loan Guarantee Scheme

Small firms are often seen as high-risk by potential financial investors, and this can be a source of difficulty for them. In recent years, the government has been willing to underwrite part of the original loans made by some institutions. The government thus acts as a kind of cheap insurance company easing the burdens that small firms face in raising finance.

Enterprise Allowance Scheme

The Enterprise Allowance Scheme is designed specifically to encourage the creation of small firms. An individual who has been unemployed for a qualifying period can receive a weekly allowance in the first year of his setting up a business. In effect, then, it is a scheme that subsidises high set-up costs.

Support from the European Union

The Regional Development funds and the social funds of the EU both spend part of their budget on small firm assistance. There are also various EU funds specifically earmarked for small firms.

How successful have all these and many other initiatives been in terms of increasing output and generating employment? Clearly, there have been successes, but the number of new businesses that grow rapidly is quite small. Some will be unsuccessful and die, many will stay small simply because the owners do not wish to grow beyond a size with which they feel comfortable. As a result, much government expenditure is committed for a small number of successes. This leaves the government with two choices if it wishes to improve its use of expenditure. One is to say that it is too expensive to subsidise small businesses and to allow market forces to decide which firms start up and which firms grow. The alternative is to try to identify which factors make small firms successful, so that policy can be better targeted. This would require research to see whether certain sectors have a higher success rate, whether certain regions are more successful, or whether certain forms of intervention prove more cost effective than others.

Finally, we turn to one area that has proved of particular concern to small businesses in recent years, their relationship with the commercial banks.

6.8 Small firms and the banking sector

One example of an economy of scale is in finance. Larger firms can typically borrow from banks at a lower interest rate than smaller ones. Smaller firms are regarded as more risky and therefore banks require an 'insurance premium' to cover the additional risk. Typically, the difference in borrowing costs between large and small firms has been of the order of 2–2.5 per cent. During the recession in the British economy of the late 1980s and early 1990s, interest rates had risen to very high levels and costs of borrowing had risen accordingly. From 1991 onwards, interest rates fell sharply and larger firms found that their borrowing cost fell accordingly. Many small firms claimed that *their* borrowing costs did not fall at all. Thus, it was claimed, the disadvantage of smallness was magnified to around 5 per cent by the middle to late 1990s.

The banks themselves were under pressure. Increased competition from the building societies in the mid to late 1980s had reduced their profits. A long and deep recession had hit them hard, particularly since their bad debts had increased as many firms to whom they had lent went out of business, so banking profits fell sharply. Nevertheless it was the small firms that felt that they were bearing the brunt of the banks' problems.

There were at least three areas of disquiet. One was the belief by some that the similarity of charges between the banks reflected the fact that the banks were not in competition but in collusion. The establishment of such a cartel is illegal. The banks denied any such collusion, arguing that the similarity in charges reflected fierce competition and that the higher charges for smaller businesses simply reflected the increased risk of lending to small businesses during a recession. The Treasury examined the banks' lending practices and passed their findings to the Office of Fair Trading (OFT), which made a formal investigation into the matter during the early 1990s. No evidence of collusion was found, although the OFT was critical of the banks' lack of sympathy towards the problems of small firms.

A second area of concern was the belief by some that banks had panicked. During a recession, trading conditions for even the most efficient firms are difficult, but house prices were falling and houses are the collateral for many small business loans. With house prices falling as well as firms' profits, the banks, panicking, closed down businesses with viable long-term futures. In essence the banks failed to understand the mechanism that we described in section 6.3.

The third area of disquiet is the process by which some small businesses go into liquidation. If a bank is concerned about its customer's ability to repay its debt it can send in a team of accountants to examine the firm's books. On the basis of their findings, the bank may foreclose on the business. The source of disquiet is that the receivers generally appointed by the bank will be the same accountants as originally looked at the viability of the business. Since the income received by the accountants for acting as receivers is around ten times the fee for doing the original audit, questions are raised about the impartiality of the accountants' advice.

The banks have little to lose. If the business is wound up and there are not enough assets to pay off the creditors, the banks will still receive loan repayment since they have a higher priority than almost anyone other than the Inland Revenue.

This whole issue certainly caused a loss of goodwill towards banks, but that is not the same as saying that the banks have behaved unreasonably towards small firms.

In recent years much lower interest rates have reduced the scale of complaints. However, it is still an important issue for two reasons. First, although lower interest rates do reduce small firms' costs, the *relative* disadvantage *vis-à-vis* large firms remains. Second, there is no guarantee that the period of relatively low interest rates will continue indefinitely.

6.9 Conclusion

Does small mean beautiful with respect to firms? The economic theory of perfect competition says that it does, and that small firms can survive. Where they cannot do so is in markets where large economies of scale are available. In such markets it is not best that they survive for it would require an inefficient use of scarce resources.

Nevertheless, market imperfections can offer grounds for government assistance to encourage and protect smaller firms. It must be remembered, though, that wherever such assistance is provided, there are not only potential benefits but costs too. Resources provided for small firm assistance are not available for use elsewhere. Opportunity cost applies even when considering government assistance.

In the UK, government assistance for small firms has been substantial but controversial. Small may mean beautiful – but it may not always be beneficial to society.

CHAPTER SUMMARY

1. **Markets with many small firms can be analysed in terms of perfect competition.**
2. **Short-run profits are maximised at an output at which SMC = MR.**
3. **In the short run, firms may make profits, break even or make losses, depending upon demand conditions.**
4. **In the long run, new firms may enter or established firms may leave a market so that firms tend to make only normal profit, i.e. cover opportunity cost.**
5. **In practice, firms' long-run cost curves may be U-shaped or L-shaped.**
6. **Some economists believe that small firms should receive government assistance; others believe that they should be left open to market forces.**

Questions for discussion

Guidance to the answers for the ***asterisked*** *numbered questions is available to students on the website for the book at* **www.booksites.net/heather**.

1* Right-wing political parties are committed to the operation of free markets. Why, then, do you think that they tend actively to seek to support small firms?

2 Suppose a perfectly competitive industry is in long-run equilibrium. Now suppose that there is an increase in demand for its output. Outline the steps that lead to the industry producing the additional output that consumers demand.

3* Evidence suggests that for much of the post-war period in Britain the share of output of the largest 100 manufacturing enterprises was increasing but that the share of output of the largest 100 manufacturing plants was not. What does this suggest:

(a) about the significance of economies of scale?
(b) about the climate in which small firms operate?

4 Do you see any disadvantages in laws which prevent large firms from eliminating small firm competition by setting prices below average cost?

5* When economists wish to illustrate the workings of the perfectly competitive system and the place of small firms in an industry, agriculture is the most commonly chosen example. How closely does this industry relate to the perfectly competitive model? Why is it an industry in which government intervention is massive in most countries?

6 Many small firms find it difficult to change their bank and reduce their borrowing costs if they feel that interest charged for their borrowing is too high. Does this suggest the banks are operating a restrictive practice?

7* In the UK, the building societies have provided very effective competition for the banks in providing banking services for private customers. Could they do the same for small businesses?

8 What economic case might be made for government action against banks charging high interest rates to small firms? What problems do you see with such action?

9* One claimed diseconomy of large-scale production is disaffection of the workforce. What do you understand by this? How could you measure it?

10 To what extent should governments be willing to aid small firms?

Websites

All information from the DTI's Small Firms Statistics Unit is available at:

www.sbs.gov.uk

Notes

1 You will observe that long-run marginal cost is the same as long-run average cost when long-run average cost is at its minimum. This is inevitable for the long run, as it was for the short run.

2 Over time there has been a tendency for this figure to fall as the size of the EU has increased.

7 Monopoly and monopolistic competition

The price of oil: *does OPEC hold the West to ransom?*

CHAPTER OVERVIEW

Western economies depend heavily on oil. For example running our cars depends upon it and many people use it to heat their homes. Yet easily the largest amounts of oil are to be found in the Middle East so we rely upon that region for much of our supplies. Do these countries charge exorbitant prices for their oil? Are the European and US economies being held to ransom?

In this chapter we review
- Perfect competition
- External benefits

We introduce
- Taxes and market supply
- External costs
- Monopoly power
- Monopolistic competition

7.1 Introduction

In this chapter we consider a commodity that is a vital one to European economies – oil. Europe, amongst other economies, is heavily dependent upon this commodity. Many people feel uncomfortable about this because we are largely dependent upon economies outside of Europe for our supplies. The region of the world that heavily dominates production is the Middle East. This situation is unlikely to change in the near future. Figure 7.1 shows the sources of proven reserves of oil in the world. Europe has less than 2 per cent of such reserves, the Middle East has two thirds of it.

In this chapter we shall begin with a brief history of the oil industry and the movement of oil prices in recent years. Then we shall explain the view that says that Europe should not worry about oil prices. The market system is the best way of dealing with energy prices in general and oil prices in particular. After this we shall be in a clearer position to see why others feel that governments

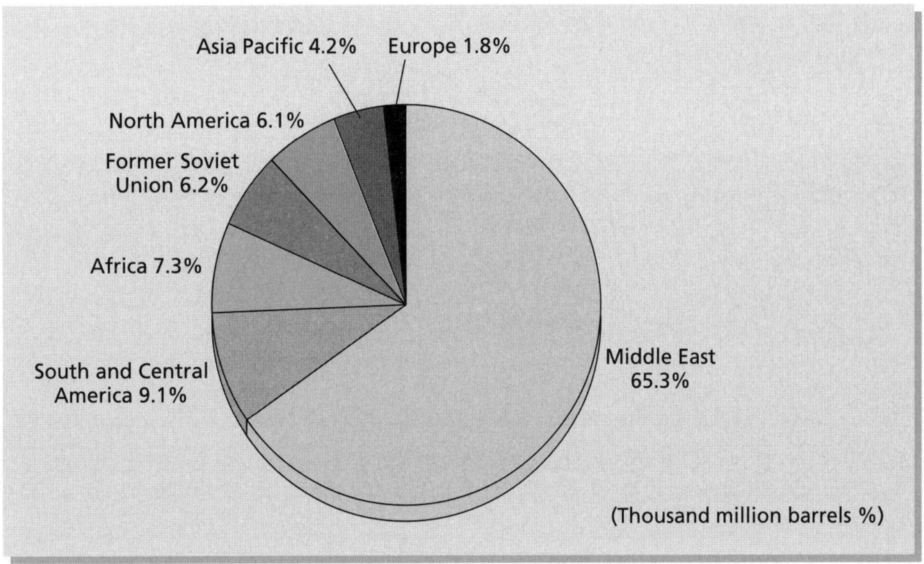

Figure 7.1 Share of proven oil reserves in 2001
Source: *BP Statistical Review of World Energy*, 2002, BP plc

should be actively involved in the determination of oil prices and in encouraging other sources of energy.

7.2 Oil: a brief history of the industry

Oil prices from 1948 until well into the 1960s were about $2.50–$3.00 per barrel. Since prices in the world generally were rising throughout that period the 'real' price was slowly declining. Middle East suppliers felt they were not getting a fair deal for their oil and in 1960 the governments of some of them, Saudi Arabia, Iran, Iraq and Kuwait together with Venezuela formed the Organisation of Petroleum Exporting Countries (OPEC). By 1971 the United Arab Emirates, Algeria, Qatar, Indonesia, Libya and Nigeria had also joined. From around this time OPEC agreed that Saudi Arabia, the largest producer, would set the price and all the other members would follow their lead. This did not give huge power to raise price except when either demand was buoyant or there was some interruption in production, reducing supplies.

If you refer to Figure 7.2 you can see that the first sharp rise in oil prices occurred in 1973–74 in the Yom Kippur War when Syria and Egypt attacked Israel. When the USA and other countries in the western world supported the Israelis, Arab countries placed an embargo on them. Arab production was reduced by about 5 million barrels per day (MMBPD). Production from other countries increased by around 1 MMBPD. The net reduction of 4 MMBPD led to a fourfold increase in the oil price. OPEC has learned that cuts in production when demand is inelastic raise prices and increase revenue.

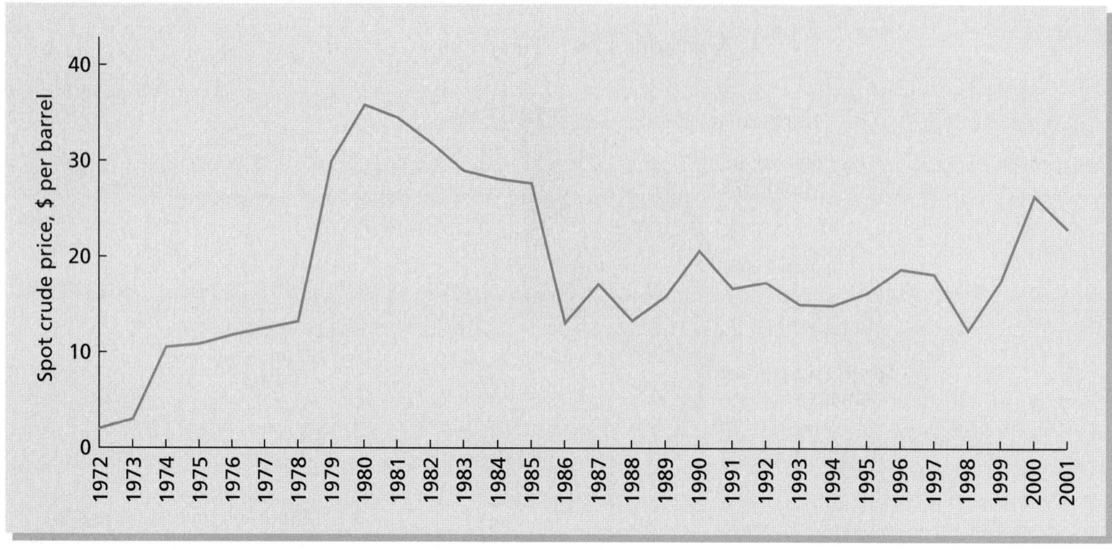

Figure 7.2 Oil prices 1972–2001

Source: *BP Statistical Review of World Energy*, 2002, BP plc

An Iranian revolution and a war between Iran and Iraq at the end of the 1970s and the beginning of the 1980s reduced output again and, as Figure 7.2 indicates, caused another sharp rise in oil prices. Prices reached $35 per barrel in 1981. It was at about this time that OPEC changed its pricing to one of targeting supply directly. Members agreed to stick to agreed quotas of output in order to restrict supply and keep prices up. However, except when events outside of OPEC's control caused sharp falls in production, these high price levels proved unsustainable.

The difficulties in persuading members to stick to agreed quotas has dogged OPEC in recent years. Although a strong world economy in the mid-1990s saw an increase in the demand for oil and hence some increases in prices, a recession in the Far East in the late 1990s reduced demand and prices.

However, since the turn of the century political uncertainty in the Middle East, including the political situation in Iraq has seen oil prices rise quite sharply again, reviving concern that it is not good for Europe to be dependent for its oil supplies on the OPEC economies.

7.3 Oil prices: 'market forces at work'

Understanding the supply curve

In this section we will assume that there are many, many owners of oil wells each behaving independently of the others. Later we will drop this assumption and see what happens when owners begin to work together and make joint decisions.

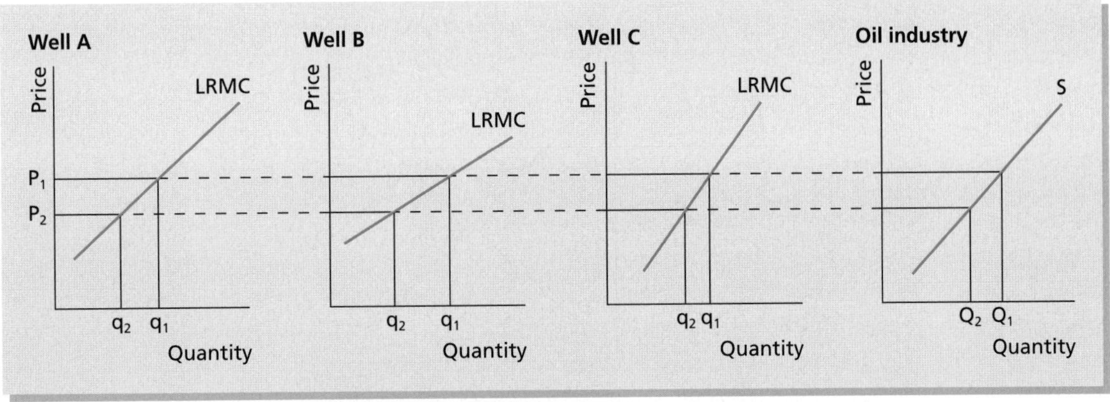

Figure 7.3 Obtaining a long-run oil supply curve

We have already seen in Chapter 2 that, left to itself, a market will bring about a situation where supply and demand are equal. Let us look a little more closely at the supply curve to see why that equilibrium can be argued to be an optimum state for society.

see pp. 124–6

In Chapter 6 we saw that economies and diseconomies of scale can produce a U-shaped long-run average cost curve and an upwards-sloping long-run marginal cost curve. We also saw that in the long run a firm produces output where marginal production costs equal price. One might see this as being an oil well such as well A in Figure 7.3. If the price of oil is P_1 the well will produce output q_1. If oil prices are lower, for example, at P_2 output will be less at q_2. This assumes that prices are high enough to cover unit costs, as we saw in Chapter 6. There are many such wells: Figure 7.3 shows a sample of three of them.

If we sum the output of each well at price P_1 we have output Q_1 from the oil industry. This is one spot on the industry supply curve given in Figure 7.3. At a lower price P_2, each well will produce less output. The industry output is given as Q_2. In other words, the industry (long-run) supply curve is given as the sum of the individual wells (long-run) marginal cost curves (above long-run average total cost[2]).

We can go one step further. The long-run supply curve not only shows marginal production costs, it also shows the opportunity cost to society of resources used in producing output. If one well's marginal production costs are $15 per barrel at some level of output we can ask *why* is it $15 and not $5 or $100? The answer is that it needs resources to produce the output. The $15 is being spent on land, labour and capital. These resources have an opportunity cost. Other firms in other forms of production are willing to pay something for these resources to make the output they could produce. Thus the oil supplier will have to pay $15 to bid these resources away from that use. In other words, the $15 represents the value of output forgone elsewhere. The supply curve therefore shows not only marginal production costs but also marginal opportunity costs.

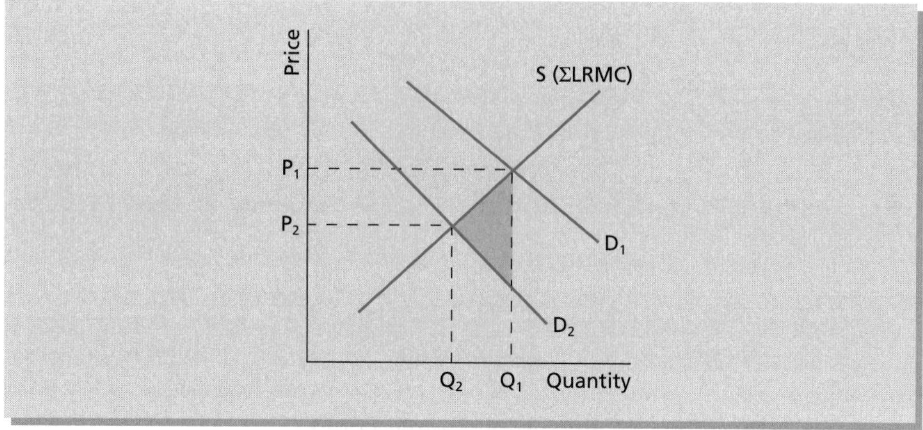

Figure 7.4 **Demand for and supply of oil**

Now let us consider Figure 7.4. The demand curve for oil is at D_1, the supply curve is at S. Equilibrium price is at P_1. Market output is at Q_1. Is the output that the industry produces optimal for society? There is a strong case for saying yes. The demand curve shows us the value that society places on the output, the supply curve shows us the opportunity cost of its production. Hence, if Q_1 is produced, all the oil is being produced which society values at its opportunity cost. Society would rather have those resources in oil production than in any other industry. Output Q_1 is socially optimal while demand remains at D_1. Notice that we have concentrated the argument on long-run rather than short-run costs. The significance of this will become apparent later in the chapter.

Responding to demand changes

The demand for oil depends not only on its price but also on other variables. One of the most crucial of these is alternative energy sources. As gas has become relatively cheap in recent years the market demand for oil has reduced. Another variable is income. During a recession when people's incomes fall their demand for energy also falls. This is shown in Figure 7.4. Demand for oil shifts from D_1 to D_2. Marginal oil wells are no longer profitable at the lower price and must be closed as output contracts to Q_2 at the lower price P_2. This makes sense from society's viewpoint because each unit between Q_2 and Q_1 is valued by society at less than its opportunity cost. The measure of society's welfare loss if the wells are kept open is the shaded triangle in Figure 7.4. The socially optimal output is, given the lower demand, Q_2.

The market for oil in an open economy

So far we have assumed that whatever demand for oil exists in Europe will be met from European production. This is not so. Foreign oil is often cheaper than

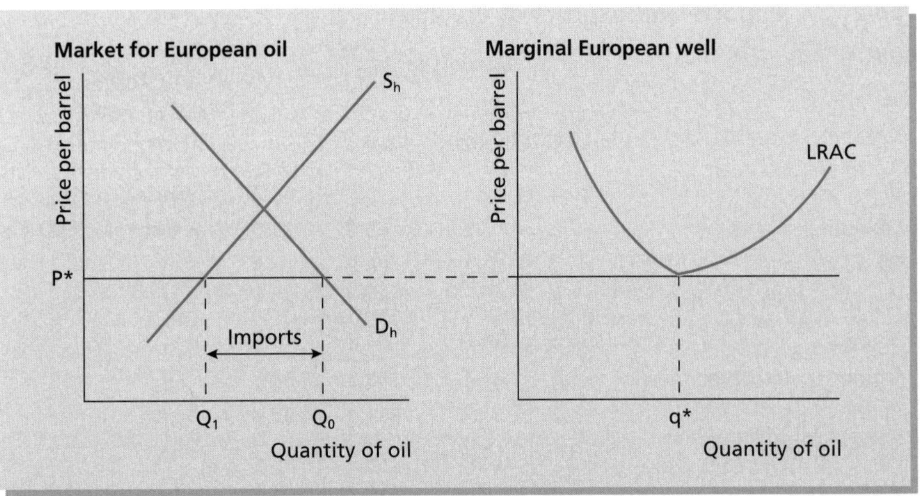

Figure 7.5 Equilibrium in the market for oil in an open economy

oil from within Europe. Given this situation, equilibrium in the oil market can be described by Figure 7.5.

At any one time the world price of oil is, say, P* per barrel. Demand in Europe is represented by home demand curve D_h and home supply S_h. At P* per barrel European suppliers competing against such a price can sell only Q_1 oil; European oil demand is Q_0. The gap is filled by imports.

The amount of European imports at present can be seen from Table 7.1. Europe imports around 570 million tonnes per annum, or ten million barrels daily. Most of this is from the Middle Eastern countries that, as one would expect, are easily the biggest exporters. It may seem strange at first sight that Europe both imports and exports oil and that even the Middle East imports a little crude oil. This is because not all oil is exactly the same. Some kinds of oil are not found at all in the Middle East but are found in the North Sea. Again Saudi Arabia has light low-sulphur oil, Venezuela's is largely low quality high-sulphur oil.

Now return to Figure 7.5. This also shows the marginal European well that is able to survive against competition from imports. Given that we have a price of imports equal to P*, then costs, including opportunity costs are just covered if q* output is produced. The reason for the relatively small level of European output is not hard to see. Costs in Europe are much higher. Much oil has to be extracted from the North Sea under hostile circumstances. The costs of sinking a well and extracting oil in the Middle East from flat sandy deserts are much lower. This applies to both average and marginal costs.

Allowing markets to determine freely the price and quantity of oil produced and consumed can be argued to be in the best interests of consumers. As we shall see more fully in Chapter 19, there is a strong case for saying that it is best for Europe to import products that are relatively cheap and to concentrate on products that we can produce better. We can then export these goods and services to pay for the imports.

Table 7.1 **Imports and exports of oil, 2001**

	Million tonnes				*Thousand barrels daily*			
	Crude imports	*Product imports*	*Crude exports*	*Product exports*	*Crude imports*	*Product imports*	*Crude exports*	*Product exports*
USA	455.4	118.3	1.9	41.7	9,145	2,473	38	872
Canada	47.0	9.8	65.9	23.0	944	205	1,323	481
Mexico	–	16.0	90.8	2.8	–	334	1,823	59
S. and Central America	44.6	9.7	105.2	49.3	896	203	2,113	1,031
Europe	464.6	105.3	54.8	40.5	9,330	2,201	1,101	847
Former Soviet Union	–	5.5	159.5	70.6	–	115	3,203	1,476
Middle East	4.2	4.4	838.7	107.9	84	92	16,843	2,256
North Africa	8.1	5.1	98.7	35.5	163	107	1,982	742
West Africa	2.6	8.1	154.7	3.6	52	168	3,107	75
East and Southern Africa	26.5	5.1	7.1	0.2	532	107	143	4
Australasia	26.1	4.4	16.2	5.0	524	92	325	105
China	60.3	28.0	6.6	7.9	1,211	585	133	165
Japan	212.0	45.2	–	4.5	4,257	945	–	94
Other Asia Pacific	332.6	90.4	48.4	56.4	6,679	1,890	972	1,179
Unidentified[1]	–	20.0	35.5	26.4	–	418	713	552
Total world	1,684.0	475.3	1,684.0	475.3	33,818	9,936	33,818	9,936

[1] Includes changes in the quantity of oil in transit, movements not otherwise shown, unidentified military use etc.
Note: Bunkers are not included as exports. Intra-area movements (for example, between countries in Europe) are excluded
Source: *BP Statistical Review of World Energy*, 2002, BP plc

7.4 Objections to the 'market forces' view

Although it is possible to object to the market forces argument outlined above, not all the arguments that one hears are equally strong. For example, it is sometimes said that the government should protect an industry from market forces 'to preserve jobs'. There is little logic in taxing people to pay workers a wage to produce output which nobody wishes to buy. A case for protecting an industry must be made on other grounds. There are five grounds upon which one *can* make a case for not leaving the oil industry to market forces. They are the problem of resource mobility, the question of a 'level playing field', the problem of externalities, the uncertainty of future energy supplies and finally the problem of 'monopoly power'.

Resource mobility

It is often claimed that if people are put out of work, perhaps because of a fall in the price of the good they produce, they do not go into other industries and

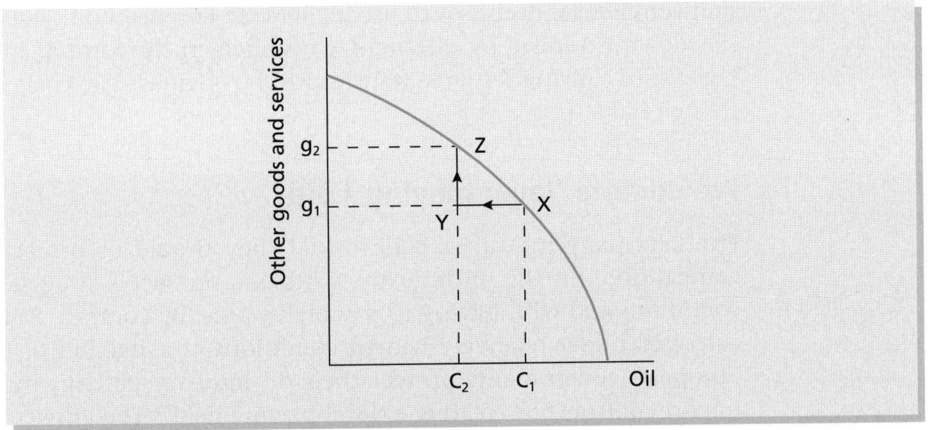

Figure 7.6 **Resource immobility in an economy**

produce output but remain unemployed. For example, when all prices fall for a period, North Sea oil workers are laid off and unemployment in such towns as Aberdeen in Scotland increases substantially. In terms of Figure 7.6 we can express the view like this. If demand for oil falls, society wishes resources to be shifted out of oil into other goods. As demand falls, the price of oil falls relative to other goods, and the relative price change is a signal to resource owners to relocate resources to other forms of production. Society has signalled that it wants a move from C_1g_1 to C_2g_2, but in a way similar to what we saw in Chapter 1 in planned economies, resources may be unemployed in oil. This moves us from point X to point Y but then the resources may stay unemployed. Then we shall not get the shift from Y to Z, at least not in the short term. The argument can be made, then, that the opportunity cost of producing the oil is zero. Not only this, but government is also saved the unemployment benefit it would otherwise pay.

see pp. 17–20

How does one evaluate such an argument? First, a clear difference of view exists over the question of the timescale. If the market forces case is a legitimate one, it is based on the idea of a long-run optimum. The objection is, in essence, that one should be concerned with the short run also. One way of looking at the debate, then, is to see it as a disagreement over the relative importance of the short-run costs and the long-run benefits of the market forces solution.

Second, there is a powerful case for saying that some resources, including labour, are highly immobile. Most redundant oil workers do not get other jobs. The problem is that in a dynamic economy resources must move in response to demand and technological change or output will not grow quickly. However, there is a strong case for saying that government can help with that transition by ensuring that the rate of decline is only as fast as the mobility of resources will allow. Furthermore, considerable resources for retraining should be made available in areas such as Aberdeen when oil prices remain low.

Third, however, there are costs to society in slowing down the decline of an industry. Either general taxpayers must provide subsidies or government must oblige consumers of oil such as the power generators to take what they regard as non-commercial decisions to use higher cost European oil. The result is that the slowdown is funded by electricity consumers in the form of higher prices. The benefits of slowing resource transfer will be obvious. The costs may well be real though hidden.

Providing a 'level playing field'

Firms in many industries believe that they should be protected from 'unfair competition'. In the oil industry North Sea producers struggle with hazardous conditions and with having to pay high wages. By contrast, Saudi Arabian oil is extracted under relatively benign conditions at a fraction of the cost. Should European governments protect their oil industry perhaps by subsidies or by import control thus creating a 'level playing field'? The answer is no. The benefit of international trade is to be found in cost differences. It is to our advantage to import relatively cheaper goods and services – goods and services that are cheaper because foreign costs are lower. We can pay for such products by exporting those things that we can produce relatively cheaply but which are relatively dear to foreigners. Government interference in this area simply makes people worse off by denying them the benefits of lower-priced goods.

An apparently more credible form of the level playing field argument comes when foreign governments are themselves interfering with free trade by offering subsidies to their own producers. Perhaps this argument is advanced most strongly in a related energy market, the coal industry.

Coal producers have often argued that they are able to compete in a genuinely free market, but the market is not in fact free. One way in which this can be seen is that the competition receives subsidies. For example, there are subsidies offered by European governments to their coal producers enabling them to undercut British coal, notably Germany whose production costs are over twice the average of British coal's costs.

Let us consider the question from the German perspective. The market price of an unsubsidised tonne of German coal might be around £120. Thus £120 of resources are used to produce one tonne of coal, resources that have an opportunity cost. When the exported coal sells for £30 because the German government has subsidised it, Germany obtains the right to import £30 worth of goods from Britain. It makes no sense for Germany. The remaining £90 is a grant from the German government to British consumers. It is not at all clear that the appropriate response of the British should be to deny ourselves such largesse or to return the compliment by subsidising our goods.

Logically, the only objection to the above reasoning is that coal miners in Britain will produce nothing if we take German coal. This leads us to an important conclusion. The objection to subsidised imports has no validity except in so far as resources are immobile. The 'level playing field' argument cannot stand on its own. It is the resource immobility argument that is really being used.

Not much coal is now imported into the UK from Germany. Only 2 per cent of coal imports come from the whole of the EU. This reflects the extent to which German coal subsidies are being reduced, partly at the wish of the German government and partly as a result of pressure from the EU which has a policy forbidding such industrial subsidies to continue unless circumstances are exceptional.

The problem of externalities

A further argument for intervening in the market for oil concerns the environmental damage done by its consumption in transport and heating. Economists analyse such problems using the concept of externalities. In Chapter 4 we introduced the idea of an external benefit in the context of inoculations against infectious diseases. An externality can give rise to either an external benefit or an external cost. Furthermore, the externality can be caused by production or, as in the case of inoculations, by consumption. Let us look first at externalities in production. Consider an external cost of production. We have seen that to produce output requires resources. In a market system the amount of resources used in production is equal to the cost that a supplier has to bear. Sometimes, however, a supplier has to bear less than the full costs to society of his or her actions. He or she may, by producing output, impose costs on the rest of society. An example of such an action would be a firm producing chemicals that have an unwanted by-product. The firm then tips the by-product into the nearest river. The firm pays some of the costs of producing output but not all of them. It does not pay the external costs of cleaning up the river, or the loss of fish stocks resulting from its actions. Figure 7.7(a) shows how there is a breakdown in the identity between private costs (costs to the firm) and social costs (costs to society). The difference between the two is the external cost imposed by the externality. The most obvious way to deal with this problem is for a government to assess the size of external cost and impose it on producers as a tax. The effect is to raise the firm's marginal private cost upwards to coincide with society's social cost.

Figure 7.7(b) shows an example of how production can lead to benefits to society that the firm itself does not gain. Social costs are lower than private costs. Probably the most significant example of such a situation is where a firm

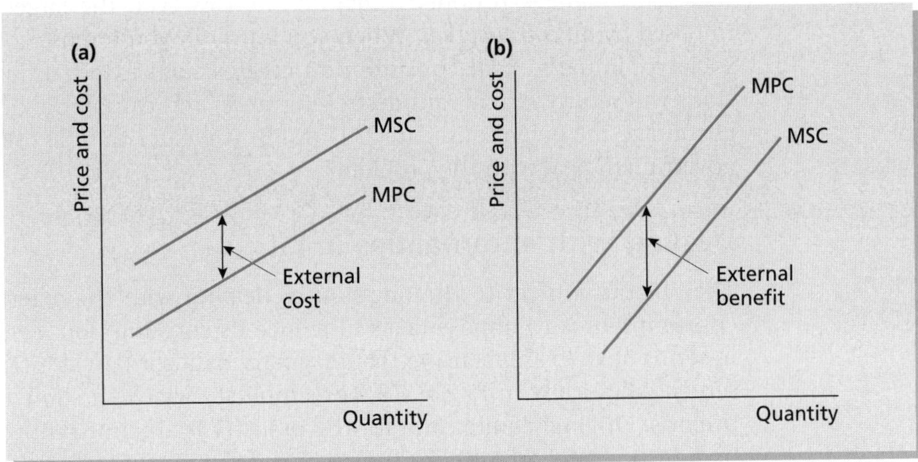

Figure 7.7 **(a) External costs and (b) benefits in production**

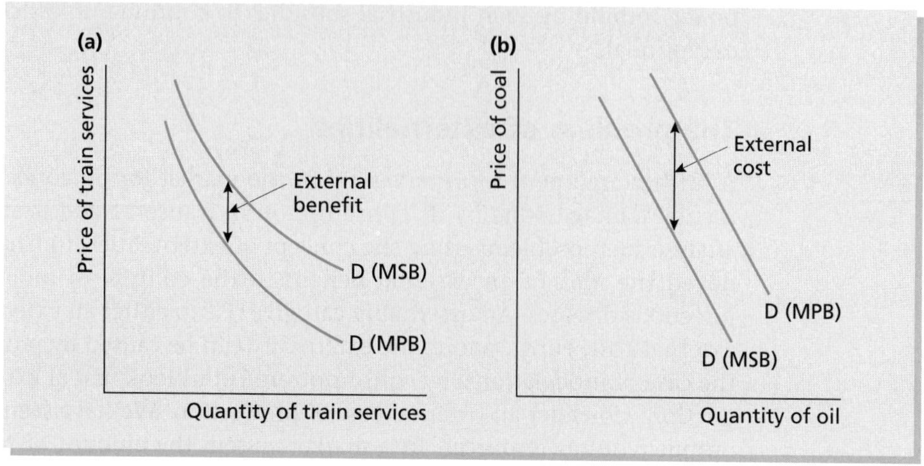

Figure 7.8 **(a) External costs and (b) benefits in consumption**

trains its workforce, some of whom then change jobs. The benefit of the training then accrues to the rest of society but not to the firm that paid the training costs. Such a situation suggests a subsidy to reduce marginal private costs to coincide with marginal social costs. Many economists feel that the gap between private and social costs in this area is much greater in Britain than the level of government training subsidy implies.

Sometimes it is not the act of production that creates such external effects but the act of consumption. Consumption can impose external benefits or external costs on society. Consider Figure 7.8(a). The demand for train services D (MPB) reflects the marginal private benefits derived privately from consumption. It could be argued, though, that marginal social benefits are greater in that trains free up road space and create less atmospheric pollution. On that basis the demand curve for train services should be shifted outwards until MPB coincides with MSB. In contrast, Figure 7.8(b) describes externality effects with oil consumption. One can argue that there are external effects in production of oil in that some damage is done to marine life. However, the larger problem is that imposed by oil *consumption*. When you burn oil, you impose costs on the rest of society. Similarly, coal consumption creates such externalities. Sulphur emissions will return as acid rain destroying trees, and carbon dioxide emissions will encourage the greenhouse effect. D (MPB) is greater than D (MSB). How should government deal with the problem?

Dealing with externalities in oil

The obvious answer to the question of dealing with the external effects of oil consumption is to impose taxes to reduce its consumption. Let us see its effects in terms of an example using the imaginary data contained in Table 7.2 and presented graphically in Figure 7.9. For simplicity we will assume that there are no imports. Original equilibrium for the industry is an annual output of 25 million barrels at a price of $40 per barrel. This assumes that the government ignores the external consumption effects.

Table 7.2 Illustrating the effect of a tax by shifting the supply curve

Price of oil ($ per barrel)	*Quantity demanded (D_1) (million barrels)*	*Quantity supplied (S_1) (million barrels)*	*Quantity supplied after tax of $10 per barrel ($S_2$) (million barrels)*
50	20	50	25
45	22	40	22
40	25	25	18
35	30	22	14
30	40	18	–
25	45	14	–

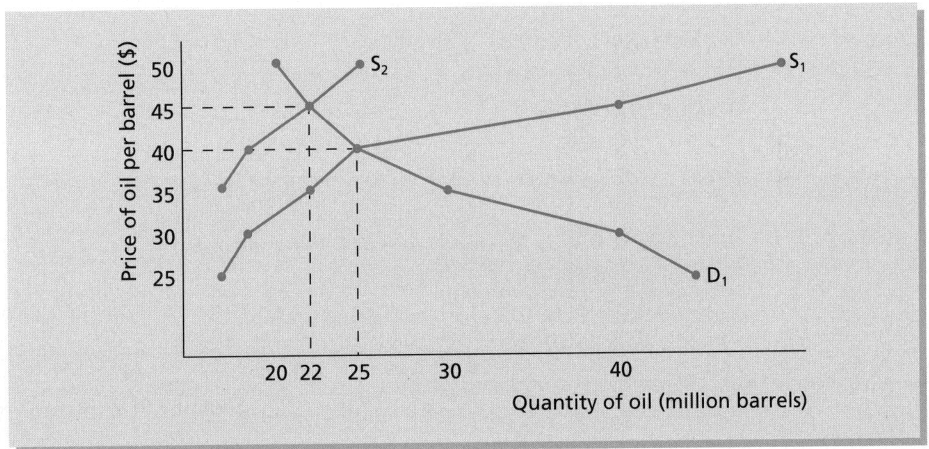

Figure 7.9 Effect of a per unit tax on oil

The effect of a $10 per barrel tax is shown in Table 7.2, column 4. At a price of $50 per tonne and no tax, suppliers were willing to supply 50 million barrels to the market. If the price is $50 per tonne and there is a $10 per barrel tax, how much will the quantity supplied be now? Since the suppliers are left with $40 for themselves we know they will supply 25 million barrels. By similar reasoning we can find other spots on the new supply curve. When we plot this as S_2 in Figure 7.9 we can see that we have a higher oil price and less output, so fewer resources are needed in the oil industry.

It is possible, however, to see the tax, not as an addition to the cost of suppliers but as a reduction in the demand curve for oil by consumers. We do this in Table 7.3 and Figure 7.10. Beginning from the original data, consider the effect of a tax on the demand for oil. When the price to the supplier was $25 per tonne consumers of coal were willing to purchase 30 million barrels. What happens now that there is a $10 per barrel tax? With a price to the supplier of $25 per barrel, the consumer must pay the $25 to the supplier plus the $10 tax to the government. Given the total of $35 consumers are prepared to buy 30 million barrels. This is plotted on Figure 7.10 as a spot on demand curve D_2. We

Table 7.3 **Illustrating the effect of a tax by shifting the demand curve**

Price of oil ($ per barrel)	*Quantity demanded (D_1) (million barrels)*	*Quantity supplied (S_1) (million barrels)*	*Quantity demanded after tax of $10 per barrel ($S_2$) (million barrels)*
50	20	50	–
45	22	40	–
40	25	25	20
35	30	22	22
30	40	18	25
25	45	14	30

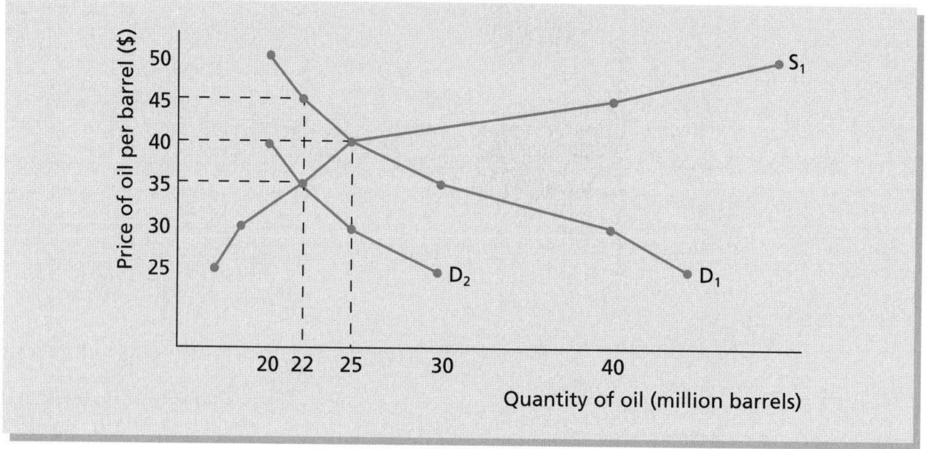

Figure 7.10 **Alternative presentation of the effect of a tax on oil**

can work out other spots on the demand curve in the same way, giving column 4 in Table 7.3 and demand curve D_2 in Figure 7.10. This gives an equilibrium price to the supplier and consumer net of tax of $35 and a price *with* tax of $45. The effect is the same as before. The equilibrium quantity of oil falls to 22 million barrels. In principle, then, it does not matter whether a tax is placed on the supplier or the consumer, the outcome in the market on price, output and resources will be the same.

The *form* which government policy takes is unimportant. A tax on suppliers or a tax on consumers will achieve the same end with respect to the effect on oil consumption. It restores the identity between social and private cost. 'Going green' is not cheap. We pay for our greenery in higher energy prices.

Uncertainty in future energy supplies

The view that the government should intervene in the market for oil because of the uncertainty about future supplies has two aspects to it, an economic and a political one. We deal with the economic issue first.

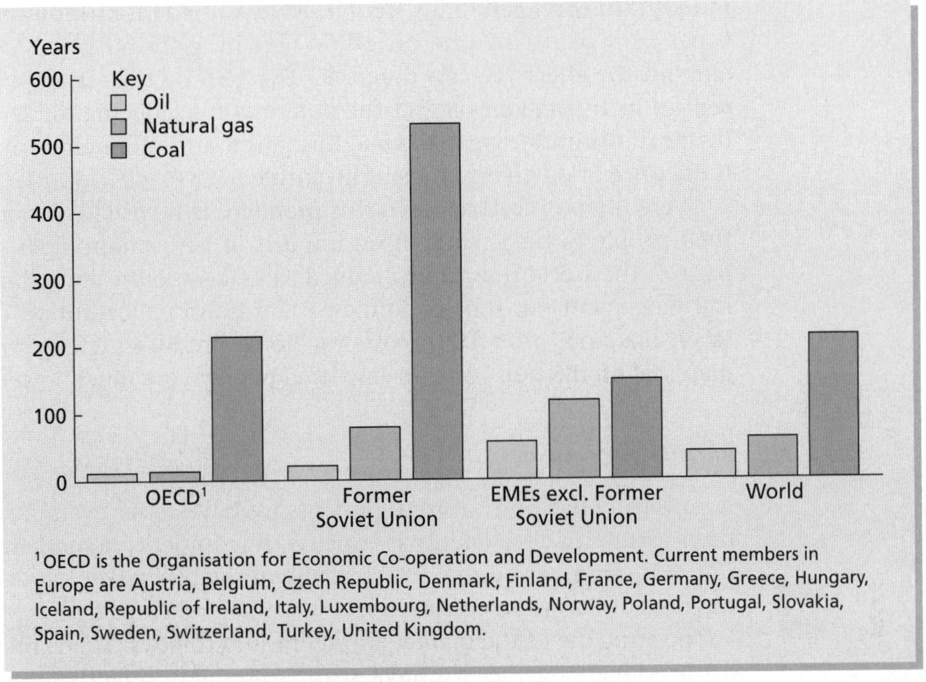

Figure 7.11 Fossil fuel R/P ratios at end 2001

Source: adapted from BP Statistical Review of Energy, 2002, BP plc

There is an argument that goes along the following lines. Oil is a finite commodity. There is only a limited stock of it in the world. So if governments do not restrain current demand there will come a time when future generations will have no oil to use. Clearly this kind of argument can be extended to many other commodities also. The case, however, is greatly overstated. First it ignores the fact that over time technology is continually improving so that supply increases. The higher the price the greater the quantity supplied but over time, as technology improves quantity supplied will be greater for any given price. In the 1970s global reserves were less than two-thirds of what they are today. Increasingly advanced search and recovery techniques make possible the recovery of oil that was not possible 30 years ago. At present day rates of consumption oil would have been expected in 1970 to be exhausted by 2003. On the same basis now the forecast is that this will happen in 2046. Similar improvements in technology have occurred for other commodities. Of course, this still implies that European countries will continue to import oil. Figure 7.11 shows the current reserves to production ratio (R/P) which tells us the number of years supplies are expected to last using current consumption patterns and known reserves. Without imports OECD countries could survive only a few years on oil and natural gas although their R/P ratio for coal is much greater.

There is a second fact that the pessimistic scenario ignores. Market prices change and this changes consumption patterns. If oil reserves begin to run out oil prices will rise and consumption will decline as consumers switch to alternative sources of energy or reduce overall energy consumption. One can see this in recent history. Before the Iran–Iraq war caused oil prices to rise the USA spent 8 per cent of its income on oil. When in 1999 oil prices rose by a similar amount the effect was less dramatic. The USA by then was spending only 3 per cent of its income on oil. Yet the potential for reducing oil dependency further by oil substitution, greater home insulation and more efficient cars is immense if the price of oil gives sufficient incentive.

There is a political aspect to this problem. Is it wise for governments to allow their people to be dependent on imports of key commodities particularly from parts of the world that can be argued to be less politically stable? This is a political judgement but the economic cost of import substitution can be very high when marginal production costs for home-produced energy are very high and marginal production costs for imported energy very much lower.

Monopoly power

A powerful objection to the arguments we have so far examined is that we have been assuming that energy is a perfectly competitive market. Manifestly it is not. It is often argued that the structure of the oil market has worked against the interests of European consumers.

The structure of the market at present is as follows. There are many individual oil producers but, as we have seen, some act collectively as OPEC. Perfect competition requires, among other things, a large number of producers acting independently. The oil market, then, is not perfectly competitive. If a market structure is not perfectly competitive there exists a degree of *monopoly power*. How much monopoly power depends upon the number of competing firms. If there are just a few, we call this *oligopoly*. If there is only one producer we say that producer is a *monopolist*. In the case of the oil market the OPEC producers are oligopolists attempting to act together as a monopoly. Accordingly we shall analyse the oil market with a model of monopoly. In the next chapter we analyse a different market using an oligopoly model.

Why does this monopoly arrangement adversely affect European consumers? To answer this question we need to examine what economic theory suggests is the effect of private monopoly. We develop these ideas in the next section and then relate them to the question of oil.

7.5 Developing the concept of monopoly power

Monopoly price and output decisions

A monopoly is a single supplier of a good or service. In consequence, the industry demand curve is the firm's demand curve. If the firm is a monopolist, the firm is the industry. So a regional electricity company is faced with a downwards sloping demand curve as in Figure 7.12. This has important consequences for the revenue situation of the firm.[2]

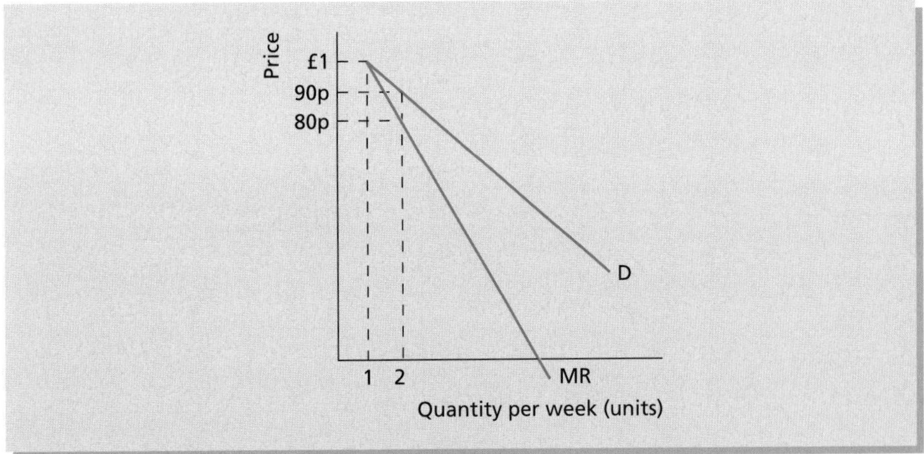

Figure 7.12 **Revenue conditions with monopoly power**

These consequences can be seen with reference to Table 7.4 and Figure 7.12 where we use some illustrative data for a representative monopolistic firm. Columns 1 and 2 in Table 7.4 give us the monopolist's assumed demand curve. The total revenue received at each different level of output, column 3, is found by multiplying output by price. As we saw in Chapter 6, marginal revenue is the additional revenue received for selling one more unit of output. Notice how, for a monopolist, this falls with increased output. So, for example, if the firm were making two units of output each week and it then decided to increase output to three units, what would happen to its revenue? To sell three units per week it must drop the price to 80p. If it cannot price-discriminate and charge different prices to different customers for the same good or service, it must sell all three units at 80p. Thus to gain the 80p from the extra customer it must forgo 10p on

Table 7.4 **Illustrative revenue and cost conditions of a monopolist**

Quantity demanded per week	*Price*	*TR*	*MR*	*LRAC*	*LRMC*
1	100p	£1.00	100p	60p	60p
2	90p	£1.80	80p	60p	60p
3	80p	£2.40	60p	60p	60p
4	70p	£2.80	40p	60p	60p
5	60p	£3.00	20p	60p	60p
6	50p	£3.00	0p	60p	60p
7	40p	£2.80	−20p	60p	60p
8	30p	£2.40	−40p	60p	60p

TR = Total revenue MR = Marginal revenue LRAC = Long-run average cost
LRMC = Long-run marginal cost

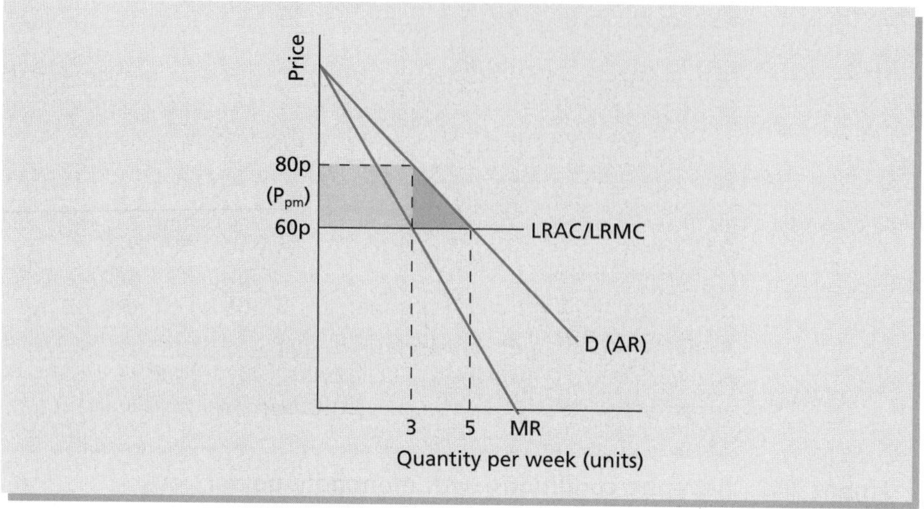

Figure 7.13 Social cost of monopoly power

each of the two units for which it could have charged 90p. Hence marginal revenue is only 60p. The marginal revenue curve is plotted in Figure 7.12. Notice how this contrasts with the perfectly competitive firm's demand and marginal revenue curves that we examined in Chapter 6.

Before we can see how the monopolist arrives at a price/output decision, we need to consider his or her cost situation. We shall assume that in the long run his or her unit costs are constant. Given what we saw in Chapter 6, this is probably true for some but not all monopolistic firms. If long-run average costs (LRACs) are constant so that each unit costs 60p on average then each additional unit must cost 60p to produce. If LRAC is constant, LRMC is equal to it. In the context of Middle Eastern oil production the assumption of a low and constant marginal cost seems reasonable.

So how will a profit-maximising monopolist price? Clearly, he or she will want to produce any unit of output that adds less to cost than to revenue. So he or she will want to produce three units of output per week where marginal cost – addition to total cost – is equal to marginal revenue – addition to revenue. This is shown in Figure 7.13.

We now have the monopolist's profit-maximising level of output. What price would he or she charge for these units? The answer is the most he or she can get for them. The demand curve tells us that this is 80p per unit, shown on the diagram as P_{pm}. The shaded square shows his or her profit, namely the difference between LRAC and average revenue multiplied by output. In this case that means 20p × 3 units of output, or 60p. Remember that, since normal profit is included in the cost structure, this 60p represents a profit above the normal. Moreover, competition will not erode this over time since there are substantial barriers to the entry of new firms in monopolistic industries, which prevent this process from taking place. If there is a single monopolist the profit is his or hers. If a group is acting as a monopolist the profit is shared among the group members.

The social costs of monopoly power

We are now in a position to see that such behaviour is not socially efficient. It is in society's interests that the monopolist in Figure 7.13 makes five units of output since his or her marginal cost, and therefore the opportunity cost of the resources used, is less than the value of output to society. Consider the two units per week that he or she will not make. The opportunity cost of the resources is given by the rectangle under the marginal cost curve. The value of the output if the monopolist were to make those two units is given by the area under the demand curve between three and five units. So the loss of consumer welfare through the monopolist's behaviour is the shaded triangle. In terms of the oil industry, the case is as follows. Oil producers charge too high prices to consumers. This will reduce the quantity demanded. The quantity of oil consumed is less than that which is socially optimal.

Is this less than socially optimal demand a sufficient problem to make much impact on consumer welfare? The probable answer is no. There are several reasons for thinking this.

First, there are alternatives to oil. The degree of monopoly power in an industry is determined by a number of factors but most critically by the closeness of *substitutes*. What gives a firm power to raise price is that there is nobody else supplying the same good. In reality there are always substitutes available, even if they are not close substitutes. Nobody else supplies Coca-Cola but Pepsi is a reasonably close substitute. Only Ford can sell Mondeos – they have a monopoly – but that monopoly power is limited by other car firms producing similar models of their own.

In the case of the oil industry these include natural gas and coal for heating. For transport fuel there are other forms of power beginning to appear, including hydrogen. These are not perfect substitutes but they are close enough substitutes to limit the ability of oil producers to control price.

A further limit on the power of OPEC is other oil producers. If OPEC prices rise non-OPEC oil producers can increase production. The extent to which they can do so depends upon rivals' marginal production costs. Indeed, the competition to OPEC has partly come as a result of OPEC's own price behaviour. Had they set price near marginal production costs North Sea oil would not have become profitable. The attempt, then, of a monopolist to exploit its position is limited by the extent to which new entrants can appear in the market.

A final limitation on the monopoly power of OPEC is the discipline of its own members. To maximise profits requires a level of output that is optimal for the group. They must then agree who produces how much of this output. However, it is often easy for group members to cheat on the agreement and produce more. This increases quantity and forces price down below the group's private optimum output. This has frequently been OPEC's experience. Sometimes Saudi Arabia, the biggest producer, has been willing to reduce its own output to compensate for the increased output of other members. However, when output increases are large, the discipline of the group cannot be sustained. This further limits the monopoly power of OPEC.

All this competition reduces the degree to which oil producers can exploit consumers. Their monopoly power is real, but limited.

7.6 The market for petrol: monopolistic competition

One of the most important products from crude oil is petrol for our cars. At first sight the market for petrol might be thought to be an oligopolistic market. One sees a limited number of large companies' petrol for sale. However, many of the petrol stations are owned not by the petrol companies but by independent retailers. So there are many providers of petrol. They produce a similar but differentiated product. The differences are small but significant to consumers. There are differences in location – some are easier to get to. Some are self-service but some offer the service of filling the car for you. Some offer a range of products in a shop to purchase with the petrol. A market with many suppliers producing a similar but differentiated product is one we refer to as *monopolistic competition*. Other such markets would include chemists and hairdressers.

Monopolistic competition in the short run

We can analyse the price and output decisions of firms in such an industry. First consider the short run. The cost structure of a firm will be the same as for a competitive firm. The shapes of the short-run cost curves will look like those given in Figure 7.14. These shapes are determined by the law of diminishing returns. We have already met and explained this law and the way it determines short-run costs in Chapter 6.

The demand curve for an individual firm is downward sloping. This is because the product it sells is differentiated from its competitors. This gives the firm some control over price. If the petrol station raises its price a little, quantity demanded will not fall to zero. Some customers will continue to buy even though many will go to alternative providers. So demand is downward sloping. This is true, you will recall, for a monopolist also, although the monopolistic competitor's demand curve tends to be relatively elastic because of the closeness of substitutes. For reasons we explained earlier in the chapter, a firm with a downward sloping demand curve will have a marginal revenue curve that falls faster than the demand curve. These demand conditions are also drawn in Figure 7.14.

We can now see what output the firm will produce and what price it will charge. Profit maximisation requires the firm to set marginal revenue equal to marginal cost. For this representative firm it is at Q_{pm}. What price will it charge? As with the monopolist earlier in the chapter it will wish to charge the highest price it can. This is given by the demand curve. So the price is P_{pm}. Competition between producers sees to it that petrol prices are very similar. Small differences in the nature of the product result in small variations of price between petrol stations.

The profit for the producer can easily be established. Total revenue is the number of units sold multiplied by the price per unit. This gives the area

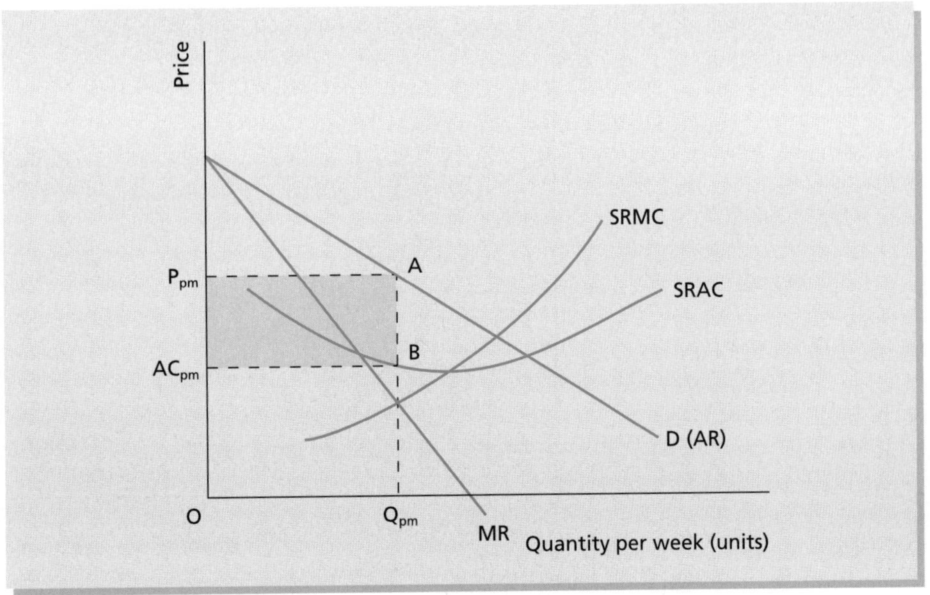

Figure 7.14 Monopolistic competition: short-run equilibrium

$OQ_{pm}AP_{pm}$. Total costs are the number of units sold multiplied by the average cost of each unit. The area $OQ_{pm}BAC_{pm}$ gives this. Profit is the difference between revenue and cost. This is shown in Figure 7.14 as the shaded area $AC_{pm}BAP_{pm}$. Note that we have shown this firm making a profit. How much profit it makes, indeed whether it makes any profit at all, will be determined by the level of costs and the strength of demand.

Monopolistic competition in the long run

One reason why there are many firms in markets of this type is that there are no significant barriers to the entry of new firms. This is an important consideration for firms in the long run. Where short-run profits are made new firms will be attracted to the industry. Whereas oil extraction requires enormous amounts of resources and therefore high entry barriers, setting up a new petrol station requires comparatively little investment. If, therefore, there are profits in the short run, what will be the effect on existing firms of new entries into the industry in the long run?

You can see the answer in Figure 7.15. New entries take some of the existing trade from established firms. The established firm's demand curve shifts inwards. In the long run all its profit above normal will be eroded. When firms are making only a normal profit there is no incentive for new firms to enter. Accordingly Figure 7.15 shows long-run equilibrium for a monopolistically competitive firm.

This time we have the long-run structure of costs based on economies and diseconomies of scale. We have said that not all firms experience diseconomies at high levels of output. However, in monopolistic competition they tend to do

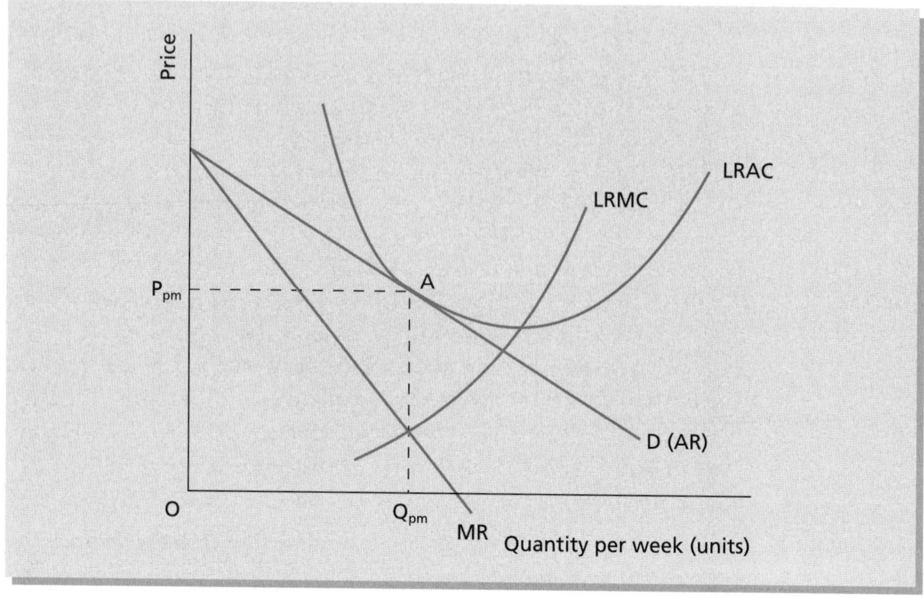

Figure 7.15 **Monopolistic competition: long-run equilibrium**

so. This is what keeps the structure of the industry to one where there are many small firms. The demand curve of a typical firm is only just far enough to the right to enable the firm to make a normal profit. Any further right and the abnormal profit it could make would have attracted new firms reducing its own demand.

Once more we have a profit maximising output where MC = MR at Q_{pm}. Price is at P_{pm}. The area $OQ_{pm}AP_{pm}$ represents revenue and cost. Since costs include a normal profit the firm stays in the industry in the long run.

You may feel that petrol stations charge a price many times the cost of producing the petrol they sell. You would be right. However, they make only a normal profit. Most of the price you pay for a tank of petrol goes to the government in tax. The typical petrol station makes just enough in the long run to keep it in the industry.

Problems with monopolistically competitive markets

Since the petrol station makes only a normal profit it cannot be seen as exploiting its monopoly power against the interests of consumers. Yet economists have pointed out that monopolistic competition is not an ideal market structure from society's point of view. We briefly mention two reasons for thinking this. First, the output produced by a firm is not that at which MC = D, the output we showed earlier to be socially optimal. Output is less than this. Furthermore, government could not make firms produce where MC = D. As you can see from Figure 7.15 this would be a level of output at which average revenue is less than average cost. The firm would be making a loss. It would rather go out of business and use its resources to produce some other output.

Second, the level of output it produces is less than that which is at the bottom of the average cost curve. The firm is too small to take advantage of all the economies of scale. One could argue that society would be better served with fewer, larger petrol stations where all economies of scale were being exploited. These arguments can apply to any industry that is in monopolistic competition.

7.7 Conclusion

Governments do worry about the oil market. The economic case for concern depends upon the extent of confidence one has in the market as a means of allocating resources. Economic models can be a valuable means of analysing these issues. This applies not only to the market for oil but to many other markets also.

CHAPTER SUMMARY

1. **An industry's (long-run) supply curve is the summation of its firms' LRMC curves (above LRAC).**
2. **Where benefits (costs) accrue to a society not borne by the individual consumer (producer) these are known as external benefits (costs).**
3. **A per-unit tax on an industry's firms increases marginal costs, and this reduces industry supply.**
4. **Reduced supply will raise price to the consumer but not necessarily by as much as the tax. The incidence of the tax is determined by market conditions.**
5. **A monopolist produces at an output where LRMC = MR and may well make long-run profits in excess of normal.**
6. **The monopolist's output is less than the socially efficient level of output which is where LRMC = demand (AR).**
7. **Firms in monopolistic competition may make short-run profits above normal but they are eroded by new extracts in the long run.**
8. **Monopolistic competition is not a socially optimal market structure.**

Questions for discussion

*Guidance to the answers for the **asterisked** numbered questions is available to students on the website for the book at **www.booksites.net/heather**.*

1* Firms in a perfectly competitive industry have a constant marginal cost of 20 euros. There are external costs in production amounting to 5 euros per unit. What is the market price? What is the socially efficient price? If the industry structure changes so that there are fewer firms colluding on price, will the market price tend to rise, fall or stay the same?

2 In Table 7.2 a $10 tax on oil production led to a $5 increase in market price. Why wasn't it $10? What determines the extent to which prices rise when taxes are imposed?

3* How would an import tax help the European oil industry? Is such a policy desirable?

4 It is often claimed that although a community, heavily dependent upon one declining form of production, suffers when not protected from market forces, in the long run things do improve. The town of Corby was once heavily dependent on a steel plant which was closed. Unemployment rose significantly. Now its unemployment rate is about the same as the national average. Clearly in the long run resources do shift. Assess this argument.

5* Why is the marginal revenue curve faced by a perfect competitor so different from that which is faced by a firm with monopoly power?

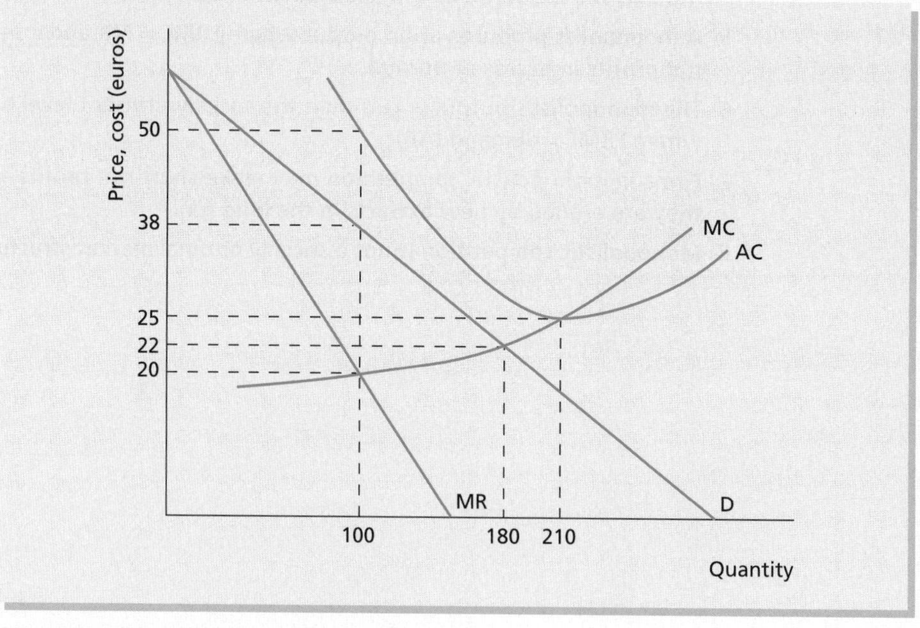

Figure 7.16 A monopolist's costs and revenue

6 Why will a profit-maximising monopolist wish to set a price at which demand is elastic? (*Hint*: What does elastic demand suggest about marginal revenue? How does the profit-maximising monopolist's price and output decision relate to marginal revenue?)

7* Consider Figure 7.16. Calculate (a) the profit-maximising level of output, (b) the profit-maximising price, (c) total costs of production, (d) total revenue and (e) profit or loss in excess of normal. Is this a short- or long-run situation?

8 Consider Figure 7.13. Now redraw it assuming increasing LRMC. Suppose a ceiling of a socially optimum price is set. What price/output results? Will profits be made? What problems will there be in determining a socially optimal price in practice?

9* 'OPEC producers have so much power they can set prices at whatever level they like.' Do you agree?

10 To what extent should the government intervene in the market for oil?

Websites

The very useful *BP Statistical Review of World Energy* is published annually. It contains a wealth of information about the oil industry but also often energy sources as well. It can be accessed at:

www.bp.com

Notes

1 Currently the list of OPEC members is as follows: Middle East: Iran, Iraq, Kuwait, Qatar, Saudi Arabia, United Arab Emirates. North Africa: Algeria, Libya. West Africa: Nigeria. Asia Pacific: Indonesia. South America: Venezuela.

2 Suppose LRMC is below LRAC. If a firm produces an output at which LRMC equals price it will make a loss, because average revenue is less than average cost. Although it may be willing to make a loss in the short run it will not produce anything if it cannot cover all of its costs in the long run. Hence, the LRMC below LRAC does not show the long-run supply of the industry.

3 Notice that our concern here is not that of the have country *vis-à-vis* the foreign country but with the consumer *vis-à-vis* the producer.

8 Oligopoly

Europe's airline prices: *the sky's the limit?*

(with Dr Michael Asteris)

CHAPTER OVERVIEW

Europe's airline passengers frequently complain about the price they pay for the service they receive. Why are prices so much higher on some routes than others? Can't governments in Europe *do* something? In this chapter we consider government attitudes to airline fares.

We review:

- Economies of scale
- Pareto optimality

We introduce:

- Oligopoly
- Cartels
- Mergers
- Contestable markets
- Price discrimination

8.1 Introduction

Europe's airline passengers frequently complain about the price of the services provided. Prices vary enormously between routes. They are, however, now much lower on some routes than a decade ago. Table 8.1 shows a selection of fares available on routes within Europe and the wide variations that exist. These fares do not include the very lowest that are available as 'special offers' where some flights can be purchased for just a few pounds.

How does the situation compare with the USA? Are markets there different?

These questions are addressed in this chapter. It begins by examining the structure of the European airline industry and what such a structure suggests about the likely level of prices that will obtain in the marketplace.

Table 8.1 Selected return air fares in Europe (£), 2003[a]

Route	*Standard fare*	*Lowest available price*
Southampton–Jersey	240	89
East Midlands–Venice	62	62
Bristol–Paris	463	101
London–Toronto	1,013	276
Birmingham–Turin	470	118

[a] Lowest prices available subject to certain restrictions.

8.2 The European airline industry: an oligopolistic market

Defining oligopoly

A market structure is one characterised by oligopoly when there is only a small number of firms in the market. Normally one would expect it to be an industry where there were significant economies of scale available such that, as we saw in Chapter 5, small firms would not survive. However, competition may still remain among the few, indeed it may be very fierce.

How few firms would be needed for an industry to be classified as oligopolistic? There is no specific number. The principle is that there should be few enough for there to be interdependence. In other words, decisions taken by one firm have a direct effect on other firms in that market. If you were a farmer and your neighbour decided to double his output of wheat, his decision would have no direct effect on you, since the effect on total wheat output, and hence prices, would be essentially nil. However, if Shell were to double its output of petrol, the effect on other firms in the oil market would, in terms of price and output, clearly be direct and significant.

It is this feature of interdependence which makes the economic analysis of any oligopolistic market a tricky one. With interdependence comes uncertainty. If British Airways (BA) decides to cut its prices to increase market share, how will other airlines respond? Will they follow its lead? Leave their fares unchanged? Increase their advertising? Different models of oligopoly make different assumptions as to how firms react to one another in the presence of uncertainty. In this chapter we examine two such models. In Chapter 9 we shall examine some other ideas which may throw light on large firms' behaviour.

However, oligopoly is not defined simply by the number of firms but also by the nature of the product. In an oligopolistic market, what is produced by the various firms is not identical but differentiated. One farmer's wheat is much like another but, by contrast, one journey on an aircraft is not identical with another. Companies may compete not only on price but also on comfort, friendliness of cabin crew, quality of food, timing and frequency of flights and so on. In other words, since oligopolistic products are not perfect substitutes for one another, oligopoly is characterised by what is often referred to as non-price competition.

see pp. 127–9

One other feature which characterises oligopoly is that, as with monopoly, there exist substantial barriers to the entry of new firms. It is useful to mention briefly a few. Economies of scale can be a barrier as we saw in Chapter 6. A firm cannot effectively compete unless it is very large, but it is not easy to begin business as a large organisation.

Product differentiation can be a barrier. An existing firm may have established such strong brand loyalty that it is difficult for a newcomer to attract sales. Part of the logic of advertising is to build up a group of consumers who are committed to the product. In that way advertising also acts as a barrier to entry in that it is advertising which helps to differentiate the product in the mind of consumers.

Finally, governments can create entry barriers. In the case of the airline industry a government may refuse to allow a foreign-owned airline the landing rights necessary for it to operate a service. This is important since if existing firms are making substantial profits, new firms cannot easily provide increased competition to push prices downwards. The competition must be largely between the existing firms.

Structure of the airline industry

Is the airline industry sufficiently concentrated for us legitimately to regard it as an oligopolistic industry? At first sight, one might come to the conclusion that the answer is no. Table 8.2 lists the top 20 airlines in the world by passenger kilometres flown, but even these represent a relatively small proportion of the total number of airlines worldwide. However, the existence of many airlines tells us less than we might at first think about the degree of competition that each company faces, since clearly not all airlines compete on all routes.

A more realistic idea of the degree of competition might be given by looking at the European market, but even here the picture that the data would present would be somewhat misleading. Often on any particular route a passenger's choice is limited to perhaps just one or two airlines. Although BA has very limited UK competition on international routes, it has more competition on domestic routes, especially from the newer 'low-cost' airlines such as Ryanair and easyJet. Nevertheless there are probably few enough 'firms' to describe the UK market as oligopolistic. This is a point to which we return briefly later in the chapter.

Market shares are another example of how the statistics may mislead regarding the degree of competition. The smaller the segment of the market, the more market power that firms have. On some routes there is only one carrier. On many routes there is a choice of only two.

One crucial way in which large companies keep competition at bay is by creating barriers to the entry of new firms. Barriers to entry can be high in the UK airline industry since the main airports at Heathrow and Gatwick have a limited number of landing slots. These slots are not open to bidding. They are allocated. At Heathrow, in particular, BA dominates the ownership of landing slots.

Table 8.2 **Scheduled tonne–kilometres flown**

International			*Domestic*			*Total*		
Rank	*Airline*	*Millions*	*Rank*	*Airline*	*Millions*	*Rank*	*Airline*	*Millions*
1	Lufthansa (1)	7,160	1	Federal Express (1)	6,407	1	Federal Express (1)	10,809
2	Singapore Airlines (3)	5,848	2	United Parcel Service (2)	3,661	2	Lufthansa (2)	7,176
3	Korean Air Lines Co. Ltd. (2)	5,331	3	Northwest Airlines (4)	768	3	United Parcel Service (4)	5,955
4	Air France (4)	4,622	4	American Airlines (5)	590	4	Singapore Airlines (5)	5,848
5	Federal Express (6)	4,402	5	United Airlines (3)	570	5	Korean Air Lines Co. Ltd. (3)	5,424
6	British Airways (5)	3,929	6	Delta Air Lines (6)	505	6	Air France (6)	4,633
7	Cathay Pacific (8)	3,887	7	China Southern Airlines (7)	478	7	Japan Airlines (7)	4,116
8	KLM (9)	3,878	8	All Nippon Airways (8)	370	8	British Airways (8)	3,936
9	Japan Airlines (7)	3,855	9	Japan Airlines (9)	261	9	Cathay Pacific (9)	3,887
10	Cargolux (10)	3,768	10	Varig (10)	241	10	KLM (10)	3,878
11	United Parcel Service (14)	2,294	11	Air Canada (11)	235	11	Cargolux (12)	3,768
12	United Airlines (11)	2,231	12	Air China (12)	219	12	American Airlines (14)	2,810
13	American Airlines (15)	2,219	13	China Eastern Airlines (-)	216	13	United Airlines (11)	2,802
14	Northwest Airlines (12)	2,022	14	Japan Air System (13)	134	14	Northwest Airlines (13)	2,790
15	Nippon Cargo (13)	1,962	15	Shanghai Airlines (16)	121	15	Nippon Cargo (15)	1,962
16	Swissair (16)	1,636	16	Qantas (20)	117	16	Delta Air Lines (16)	1,853
17	Thai Airways (19)	1,634	17	Continental (15)	109	17	Thai Airways (20)	1,669
18	Alitalia (18)	1,524	18	Korean Air Lines Co. Ltd. (17)	93	18	Swissair (17)	1,636
19	Emirates (23)	1,496	19	China Yunnan Airlines (-)	89	19	Air China (22)	1,600
20	Malaysia Airline System (17)	1,477	20	Iberia (22)	88	20	Qantas (21)	1,570

Source: IATA, *World Air Transport Statistics 2002*

The low-cost carriers

Although oligopolistic markets are by definition dominated by a few large producers, there are many markets where much smaller firms exist alongside the larger players. In the case of the airline industry new no-frills firms such as easyJet have entered the market in recent years. Indeed they have increased their market share partly at the expense of the more established operators. Because entry barriers are so significant it is difficult for new entrants to establish themselves in such markets but two factors usually play a crucial part in making this possible. One is product differentiation.

Differentiating a product from that which is supplied by others enables the building of brand loyalty. In the case of the low-cost carriers they supply what is in some ways a lower quality product. There are no in-flight meals, fewer cabin staff and sometimes more tightly packed seating. Also journeys may be taken to and from lower cost airports further from the city centres. However, these and other cost savings enable such carriers to offer much lower prices. The result is that they have gained market share, both leisure and business, and forced established operators to cut costs and reduce their prices to the benefit of consumers.

The other key factor in gaining entry to a market is diversification. It is often extremely difficult for a firm to raise sufficient capital to enter. Economies of scale are considerable. As a result new competition often comes from established firms 'diversifying', that is moving into other products from an already existing market. The founder of easyJet, Stelios Haji-Ioannou, is the heir to a Greek shipping fortune. After setting up his own shipping line he diversified into the airline business. On the other hand, Ryanair was a full service airline that successfully switched its strategy to target the low-cost sector of the market.

In general, the number of rivals – an important element in oligopoly – is difficult to determine in practice. However, the dominant players will be few in number and there may or may not be other smaller firms in the market.

Pricing in oligopoly – kinked demand

In some markets, oligopolistic structures are virtually inevitable. If firms find that there are significant economies of scale, they will merge to take advantage of them. Arguably BA's acquisition of other smaller airlines in recent years is an example of the point. Small firms are too small to gain economies of scale. It is thus more efficient for society if those resources are in the hands of a large airline.

Society may benefit from such mergers in that lower unit costs mean fewer resources used to produce a given volume of output. The problem pointed out by BA's competitors is that increased firm size means, *ceteris paribus*, increased market power and a potentially non-optimal price/output decision for society. One way of seeing this is via the 'kinked demand model'.

Let us assume that two airlines, A and B, have a given segment of the airline market between them and they face no other competition on that route. If A is charging £180 for the journey, then A's demand schedule might be as described in Table 8.3 and its demand curve will be as drawn in Figure 8.1. Why? The argument is that the shape of the curve depends upon the reaction of its rival. In our case the rival is firm B.

The demand curve is kinked in this way because the model assumes something about the nature of a rival's reactions to a price change. If company A lowers its price in order to increase quantity demanded of its service, company B is assumed to cut its price also out of a fear that it might lose its market share. In consequence it is relatively difficult for company A to increase its output by lowering its price. Demand is relatively price inelastic when price is cut.

Table 8.3 Assumed demand and revenue conditions faced by an oligopolist, firm A

Output of airline journeys	*Price firm A can charge £*	*Total revenue £*	*Marginal revenue £*	*Short-run marginal production costs £*
1	260	260	260	20
2	240	480	220	20
3	220	660	180	20
4	200	800	140	20
5	180	900	100	20
6	140	840	−60	20
7	100	700	−140	20
8	60	480	−220	20
9	20	180	−300	20

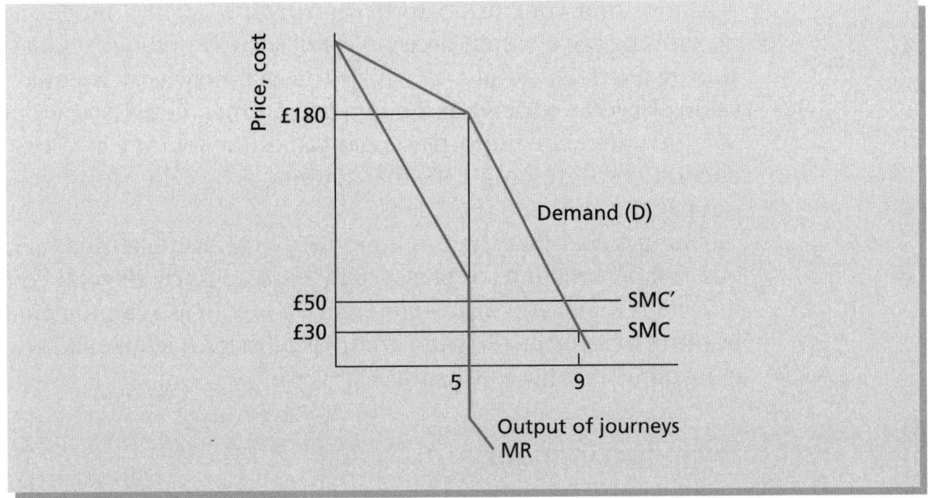

Figure 8.1 Oligopoly with kinked demand conditions

What happens if company A attempts to increase its price? The assumption of the model is that the rival is likely to leave its price unchanged in the hope of increasing its market share. Hence, the effect of a price increase by company A is a significant reduction in the quantity demanded. So A's demand curve is relatively elastic for a price increase. This is shown in Figure 8.1 as demand curve D.

Notice the implications of such a kinked demand curve for firm A's revenue. Table 8.3 shows how marginal revenue falls steeply if firm A tries to stimulate quantity demanded for its product via a price cut from the present price of £180. The marginal revenue curve is plotted in Figure 8.1 as MR.

see pp. 100–3 To determine the profit-maximising price/output decisions of firm A we also need to know about its cost conditions. For reasons we established in Chapter 5, a firm's marginal cost curve may well slope up in the short run as a result of diminishing returns. In the case of an airline, though, it would be more reasonable to assume a low and constant marginal cost – at least until the plane is full. An extra passenger entails some extra cost – the provision of a ticket, a meal and perhaps a little extra fuel – but most of the costs in the short run are fixed. Once the plane is full, the marginal cost of the next passenger is very high. The low, constant SMC is shown in Figure 8.1. Profit maximisation, as always, requires the firm to choose an output at which marginal cost equals marginal revenue. The price is £180 per ticket.

Two important points follow from the above argument. First, an oligopolist's prices are going to tend to be 'sticky', even in the face of shifts in marginal costs. That is to say, the firm has no wish to change price even if there are changes in marginal cost. For example, if fuel costs rise and marginal costs shift from a constant £30 to a constant £50 per unit of output, the profit-maximising price (and output) remains the same. This can be seen in Figure 8.1. SMC has risen to SMC′; profit maximisation is where SMC = MR. This is still at an output level of 5. It needs a substantial increase in marginal costs before SMC = MR at a lower level of output and a higher price.

The second conclusion to be drawn from such a model is that the profit-maximising price/output decision is not socially optimal. Recall that social optimality requires an output at which the marginal cost is equal to the marginal value placed by society on the output. In other words, social optimality is where MC = D. Since the ninth passenger values the journey at £30 and marginal production costs are only £30, that journey is socially worthwhile even if it does not pay the airline to provide it.

You may feel that there is a problem here. If the airline had to charge everyone £30 per seat and so set a socially optimal price, its total costs may not cover its total revenue and so it would make a loss. This is a problem for governments wanting to intervene in industries where there is some market power. This issue is examined further in Chapter 17.

see p. 374

Price discrimination

A feature of pricing in some markets where monopoly power exists is *price discrimination*. This is where a company charges different prices to customers for the same product. Charging more for a first-class seat is *not* price discrimination. You are paying more because you are receiving a better product, wider seat and so on. However, when two passengers board the same plane and have the same quality of seat and service but pay different prices the airline is price discriminating.

One condition necessary for an airline to do this is that some passengers are willing to pay more. For example, business passengers may have to go for an important conference whereas leisure passengers can simply not go on holiday at all if they feel the price is too high. In other words one group, in this case business passengers, has a more inelastic demand than the other and airlines will charge more to such a group.

At first you may feel this is not possible. When you book a ticket, you do not have to declare the purpose of your journey. However, there *are* ways of price discriminating. One of the most common is to charge lower prices for return air fares where a stay on a Saturday night is involved. Business people will often fly during the week but want to be home at the weekend. Leisure passengers will want to be away on a Saturday night. This makes a significant degree of price discrimination possible and enables airlines to increase profitability.

Oligopolistic markets: takeovers and cartels

Both price and non-price competition can be fierce in oligopolistic markets. Clearly there is an attraction to firms in such markets to try to reduce that competition. One way to do so is by takeover. In most countries, governments have laws to prevent such an occurrence until they are sure that it is in the public interest to allow the increase in market power which the takeover creates. A further complication for government policy towards takeovers occurs when there is a proposal for a merger between two relatively small firms. Such a merger could be seen as increasing market power by reducing the number of firms in the market. Alternatively, it can be seen as making competition more effective by

		B's strategy	
		Low price	High price
A's strategy	Low price	A. small profit B. small profit	A. very large profit B. loss
	High price	A. loss B. very large profit	A. large profit B. large profit

Figure 8.2 **Possible pricing strategies for two oligopolists**

creating a large company that will reap economies of scale, and thus be better able to compete with other large companies in that market.

Even mergers which clearly increase concentration can sometimes be argued to be in the public interest. One case in point arose when BA bought Dan Air in 1992. Dan Air's financial position did not allow it to continue trading and BA was allowed to purchase the company for a nominal sum. Some of Dan Air's employees were able to keep their jobs now working for BA. It was argued that without the merger the unemployment situation for the former Dan Air employees would have been even worse. The competition authorities therefore allowed the takeover on employment grounds, despite the reduction in competition which would result.

An alternative means of reducing competition is by the operation of a cartel. A cartel is an agreement between two or more producers to restrict the degree of competition amongst them, often by reducing output, raising price and agreeing not to compete on the higher price. One way of seeing how this might benefit the companies is via *games theory*.

Suppose again that there are just two airlines on a particular route. (When there are just two companies involved in a market, the companies are often referred to as duopolistic.) Suppose also that market demand is fairly price inelastic at the present price. It is still likely to be the case that the demand curve faced by either company is very price elastic in that there is a close substitute available – a flight on the rival's airline. Company A might see itself facing the choices outlined in Figure 8.2 which represent a pay-off matrix. Each square shows the pay-off for the two companies, the players in the 'game', given the strategies adopted and given that there is no collusion between the players. Taking firm A, then, the firm knows the size of its profits given each of its strategies. Which strategy will it adopt? It may decide that the worst it can do if it chooses a low price is make a small profit. The worst it can do if it chooses a high price is make a loss. It will therefore choose a low price, and this will be its dominant strategy. By the same reasoning company B will, if it adopts the same strategy, choose a low price. Both airlines finish up making small profits. If both were to collude and to agree a high price, both could do better and make large profits. A cartel is therefore an attractive option for an oligopolist.

Under the laws of most countries such agreements are illegal, though it is not always easy for a government to know that companies are using such cartels.

Companies can make secret deals, agreeing not to compete on price, but argue publicly that the similar prices are a reflection of fierce competitive pressures. It would be difficult for the authorities to prove otherwise.

In the case of the European airline industry, some elements of a cartel are present with government approval. The reasons for this and the pressure for change are examined in the next section. It is not intended to suggest that European airlines operate *illegal* cartels, but to show that such arrangements can be profitable for the participants.

Cartels are not always very stable. Although two companies may agree to raise prices, there is now an incentive for one of them to lower prices a little. Even though its price will now be high, it is low relative to its erstwhile rival. If the other company becomes aware that this is happening it will lower its price also and the cartel agreement will have collapsed. On the other hand, knowledge that this is a possible outcome may prevent 'cheating' on their cartel partners by the companies concerned.

Alliances

Most national airlines are immune from takeover. Governments protect them, seeing the airline as a national virility symbol. Airlines are getting around such restrictions by forming alliances. Airlines in an alliance will cooperate on marketing. They also operate code sharing where you may book a flight with

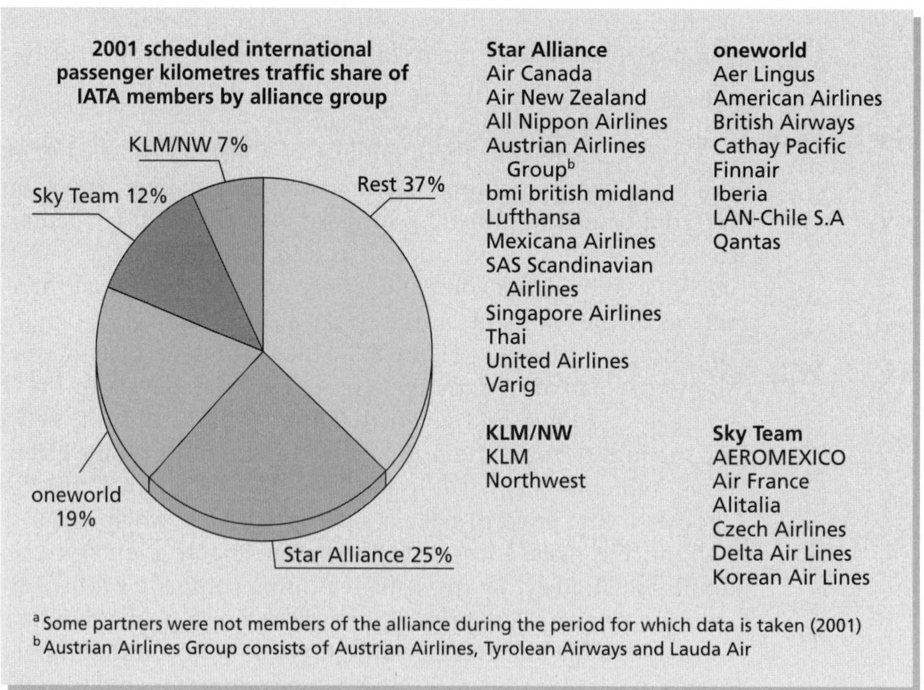

Figure 8.3 **IATA major world alliance group members, May 2002**[a]

Source: IATA, *World Air Transport Statistics*, 2002

Table 8.4 IATA market shares of Alliances, 2001

Ranking by international scheduled revenue passenger-kilometres (millions)		*IATA market share (%)*	*Ranking by domestic scheduled revenue passenger-kilometres (millions)*		*IATA market share (%)*	*Ranking by total system scheduled revenue passenger-kilometres (millions)*		*IATA market share (%)*
1 Star Alliance	412,894	25	1 Star Alliance	199,727	20	1 Star Alliance	612,622	23
2 oneworld	309,531	19	2 oneworld	146,649	15	2 oneworld	456,180	17
3 Sky Team	198,221	12	3 Sky Team	145,727	15	3 Sky Team	343,948	13
4 KLM/Northwest	110,109	7	4 KLM/Northwest	65,116	7	4 KLM/Northwest	175,225	7
5 Japan Airlines	65,013	4	5 US Airways	61,075	6	5 Continental	92,702	4
6 Continental	32,256	2	6 Continental	60,446	6	6 Japan Airlines	81,700	3
7 Swissair	30,889	2	7 America West Airlines	29,705	3	7 US Airways	73,944	3
8 Malaysia Airline System	30,666	2	8 TWA (Trans World Airlines)	29,320	3	8 Malaysia Airline System	35,869	1
9 Virgin Atlantic Airways	28,411	2	9 China Southern Airlines	20,013	2	9 TWA (Trans World Airlines)	33,411	1
10 Emirates	23,126	1	10 Alaska Airlines	16,707	1	10 Swissair	30,889	1
Total Top Ten	1,241,117	75	Total Top Ten	774,485	79	Total Top Ten	1,936,491	73
Total IATA	1,665,397		Total IATA	976,525		Total IATA	2,641,922	

Source: IATA, *World Air Transport Statistics 2002*

one airline only to find that you are flying with a different airline altogether, with the price of your ticket being shared out between the members. Some are now sharing facilities such as catering, training, maintenance and aircraft buying. Such economies can lower costs and therefore prices to passengers. The main groupings can be seen in Figure 8.3. The extent to which these alliances dominate international air travel can be seen in Table 8.4. This reveals that 60 per cent of passager kilometres by IATA members is in the hands of the four main alliances.

Despite the potential for scale economies, there are fears that such groupings can raise prices by operating like a cartel. A cartel usually aims to act as if it were a single company setting a monopoly price. An alliance could be seen as acting like a cartel also.

The balance of evidence seems to suggest that alliances may well bring benefits to consumers and to airlines themselves. Consumers gain non-price benefits, especially in terms of an increase in the number of flights available on any given route. They may also gain in terms of lower prices. However, the lower prices of recent years may be the result of increased competition rather than the formation of alliances. Economies in shared facilities probably allow the airlines themselves to improve their financial performance.

8.3 Government attitudes towards the airline industry: state regulation

So far we have assumed that airlines take account of other airlines' pricing and non-price behaviour, but that governments do very little by way of controlling the industry. For some oligopolistic markets, government intervention is relatively limited, but with airlines its intervention is substantial.

Form of airline regulation

Regulation of air transport constitutes a situation where the state tightly controls entry to the industry, services offered, fares to be charged, routes to be flown and the capacity to be provided. For example, it has been the norm for air service agreements between two countries to share out capacity on a 50/50 basis, to grant each nation the power of veto over fare levels, and to specify the number of carriers allowed to operate. Indeed, the American and UK governments' agreement of 1977, known as Bermuda II, went so far as to name the individual carriers allowed to fly between Britain and the United States.

Motives for airline regulation

Why have nations felt it necessary to regulate air transport so closely? To answer this question we need to refer back to the early years of the industry. During the 1920s passenger aircraft were characterised by relatively poor performance and high costs. At the same time, intense competition resulted in financial instability and difficulties in establishing route networks. Consequently, governments curbed competition via regulatory bodies such as the Civil Aeronautics Board (CAB) in the United States and the Air Transport Licensing Authority in the UK. These bodies controlled market entry, fares, service frequencies and capacity on routes.

Moreover, nations were anxious to maximise the political and military benefits of civil aviation. Generous subsidies were, therefore, given to selected carriers so that they could operate scheduled services. Ever since, governments have sought to protect the market position of their national airlines. These are often perceived as more than simply a means of conveying passengers and freight; instead they are treated as though they reflect the strength of a nation. In short, national airlines (often state owned) tend to be looked at almost as virility symbols. This view is reflected in the term 'flag carriers' to describe major operators such as British Airways, Air France and KLM. Hence, governments normally adopt a partisan attitude towards the airline industry, seeking to ensure a 'fair' market share for their champions rather than the most efficient service for consumers.

Tight state control has, therefore, continued to be a dominant feature of air transport.

The problem of safety

Perhaps the greatest concern about unfettered competition in the airline industry is the question of safety. Figure 8.4 demonstrates just how safe airline travel is despite the tragic events of 11 September 2001. Could it be that one reason for this is government policy to limit competition? Would less government regulation lead to such intense price competition that safety considerations were ignored in an attempt to cut costs?

An alternative view might be that people are better able to make their own judgements about such matters. Those who wish for greater safety will pay higher

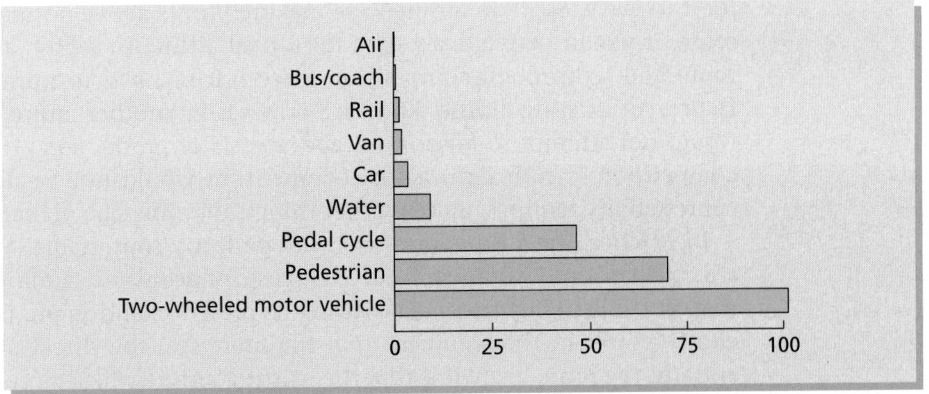

Figure 8.4 Average number of deaths in Britain per billion passenger kilometres (data is for 1990–2000)

Source: adapted from *Transport Statistics of Great Britain*

fares on airlines which provide the higher standards. We said that oligopoly is characterised by product differentitation, and this could be argued to be an example. Companies could compete on airline safety. If passengers value such safety highly, airlines will find it profitable to provide this, even though it means charging higher fares. On this view, government setting of safety standards would not be needed.

see pp. 70–92

A counter argument could be made following the same line of thought as we saw in the context of health care in Chapter 4. We could reason that the argument above will only be correct if passengers have adequate knowledge of the degree of safety offered. If they do not, they will not be able to make informed choices.

A third view which deserves consideration is that airlines should be free to engage in competition on all matters such as price, routes flown, and so on, but that government will lay down minimum safety standards with which all airlines will comply. This is an attractive option, but is one not free of difficulty. How stringent should safety standards be? Increasing safety standards will impose higher costs and, in the long run, increased prices. Society does not believe that safety costs are paramount – if it did no one would fly at all. A government will not find it easy to determine the point at which the costs of increased safety standards become greater than the value of the benefits. This is what makes the idea of allowing passengers to decide for themselves an attractive one to some economists.

'Open skies' a way forward

As part of the move towards a single market, certain members of the EU sought to liberalise Europe's airline industry. Progress is incomplete, however, for the reasons examined above. One reason why many economists believe that greater competition and more open skies would be beneficial is that the airline industry comes close to being what, arguably, is called a contestable market. A contestable market is one in which it is costless for a firm to enter and costless for it to leave. So, if an airline were making profits above normal on a particular route, it would be relatively easy for a rival airline to switch aircraft onto that route and so through competition force prices down to normal profit levels. Hence, an existing airline, knowing how easily another airline could compete, would not attempt to raise prices above costs of production. The very threat of competition is sufficient; actual competition would not be necessary. Perfect contestability requires, among other things, that there be no barriers to entry.

In practice, the airline industry is not perfectly contestable. A new entrant on a particular route would still have the costs of acquiring landing slots, even if it were possible to buy them, advertising its presence, and so on. However, there is clearly power in the argument that the more real the threat of a possible new entrant, the more likely it is that the existing airline will set a competitive price.

A further reason for believing that more open skies would be beneficial is the US experience of deregulation. It is to that experience that we now turn.

8.4 US experience of airline deregulation

History of US deregulation

By the 1970s, regulation was being called into question by mounting evidence of the relative efficiency of airlines operating in the least controlled sectors of civil aviation. In particular, US studies revealed that intrastate operations, which were not subject to Civil Aeronautics Board (CAB) regulation, could offer fares of about half those of CAB regulated carriers and still show a profit. It is not surprising, therefore, that the pressure for change was great.

Following a series of Congressional hearings in the early 1970s, the Airline Deregulation Act was passed in 1978. This removed the framework of economic controls and the industry became competitive for the first time in forty years. New carriers entered the market: the number providing scheduled services tripled by 1984. However, the domination of the industry by a limited number of firms continued because the new entrants were small. Hence, while in 1976 the top twelve carriers accounted for about 96 per cent of overall passenger miles, by 1984 they still accounted for 91 per cent.

Nevertheless, faced with the challenge of new, efficient companies, the main carriers were compelled to reduce costs and make themselves more competitive or risk the loss of a much larger market share. Consequently, fares were reduced, service frequency improved and traffic rose rapidly – by almost 50 per cent between 1978 and 1985. At that time deregulation appeared to be an unqualified success. Since then, however, competition has diminished.

Problems for new entrants

see pp. 127–8

Firms faced with increased competition tend to seek to be more cost efficient. They also prefer that potential competition faces high entry barriers. Sometimes these barriers are natural ones. For example, if there are substantial economies of scale in a market, it will be difficult for a new firm to enter the market at a sufficient size to compete. Some barriers can be raised by the existing firms themselves. For example, in the United States some airlines were able to replace their linear (point-to-point) route systems with hub-and-spoke networks. This has proved particularly effective in this respect.

The latter arrangement allows an airline to concentrate its operations at a central airport to which passengers are flown from surrounding cities so as to connect conveniently with outbound flights. During the early stages of deregulation this type of scheduling involved coordinating deals with local 'feeder' operators, which were later consolidated by means of takeovers. As a result, many of the hub-and-spoke systems are now dominated by a single airline. This is able to feed traffic along one spoke into its hub airport and then out along other spokes. Passengers are thereby encouraged to fly with the same carrier for their entire journey, so reducing interline traffic. It is thus more than coincidental that the most powerful and most profitable airlines, such as United and American, are also those with the strongest hub-and-spoke networks. By contrast, airlines such as Pan Am, which lacked dominant positions at major hubs, have failed to survive as major firms.

This system is now being widely used by the alliances of which we spoke earlier in the chapter.

Existing carriers also had the advantage that where airports were congested, new firms were often unable to obtain access. The reason for this was that take-off and landing slots were awarded by scheduling committees of incumbent carriers. The allocations were based on 'grandfather' rights, whereby carriers owned capacity at an airport merely as a result of having been there at an early stage in its development. Consequently, while there was no formal restriction on an airline flying a particular route, its ability to do so could be jeopardised by an allocation of slots favouring incumbents. Shortage of airport capacity was also a powerful motive for agreed mergers and takeovers involving scarce take-off and landing options.

Control of an efficient computer reservation system is second only to a dominant position at a major hub as a source of market power because travel agents tend to favour the airline supplying the reservation system. It is, therefore, noteworthy that the reservation systems of two giant airlines – United and American – account for over two-thirds of the terminals used by travel agents in the United States. More broadly, information technology constitutes an important management tool since it provides instant market information. Consequently, those firms which can afford sophisticated systems are able to fine-tune their pricing policy, for example by varying the availability of discount tickets. Large US carriers were able to harness these systems so as to maximise the profit of each aircraft seat in a manner denied to smaller firms. Major airlines were also able to obtain economies of scale of the kind mentioned earlier in the chapter.

Outcome of US deregulation

The advantages enjoyed by large carriers in the US airline market are such that their share of it is now marginally greater than it was under regulation. In 1977 the five largest airlines accounted for 63 per cent of traffic; by the turn of the century they accounted for over 70 per cent. To a considerable degree this outcome reflects a highly sympathetic attitude towards takeovers on the part of the Department of Transportation, which scrutinised airline mergers following the abolition of the CAB. The refusal to allow foreign airlines 'cabotage rights' – the ability to fly internal US routes – also played a part, by excluding an important potential source of competition. That said, the failure to permit freer access to the US market was understandable bearing in mind the reluctance of most governments to deregulate international flights.

Whilst the United States' deregulation of its internal airline industry has been flawed in some respects, it has, nevertheless, proved highly successful. Domestic airlines now have lower real costs than in the mid-1970s, partly as a result of more efficient use of labour. Overall, after allowing for inflation, fares are now, on average, some 20 per cent lower. Moreover, there are far more flights and the number of passenger-kilometres travelled has more than doubled. Consumers have thus gained a great deal without the adverse effects on air safety which some critics of liberalisation had predicted.

The financially fragile carriers have, however, found the more liberal environment extremely uncomfortable with a consequent division of the industry between the strong and the weak. The most successful airlines are those which have consolidated their position in the market. Those at the other extreme experienced severe financial problems. A number of middle-ranking carriers, have been sandwiched between the strong and the weak. Overall the trend since deregulation is towards a comparatively small number of strong firms – in the language of economists, a more concentrated industrial structure.

Mergers and takeovers, then, can come about in an oligopolistic industry whatever the level of profitability of the firms concerned. For example, BA has, for the most part, remained profitable and has gained a dominant position in the airline industry, but, as Table 8.5 shows, it has realigned its position via a whole series of acquisitions and disposals.

Table 8.5 British Airways ownership

Airline	*Stake held*	*Details*
CitiExpress	100%	Formed in 2002. Includes what was formerly BRAL, Brymon Airways, British Airways Regional and Manx Airlines
Comair	100%	Operates as one of many franchise agreements around the world
Go	100%	Sold to easyJet, 2001
Deutsche BA	100%	Selling to easyJet, 2003
Iberia	9%	Acquired in 2000
Qantas	21.4%	Diluted in 2001 from 25% when BA did not take up an allocation of new shares to institutions and shareholders

Source: adapted from Air Transport Intelligence, BA company reports

On the other hand, loss making firms may well wish to merge if they feel that the resulting economies of scale, or the resulting increase in market power, will lead to improved financial performance.

8.5 Applying North American lessons to European airlines

Two crucial lessons

The US experience thus suggested two crucial lessons for Europe. First, that there were huge potential gains from deregulation in the form of increased efficiency, lower fares, improved service frequency and a substantial increase in air travel. By 1985, at 1977 prices, US consumers and producers probably enjoyed total gains of around $8 billion a year as a result of an open skies approach to air travel.

The second lesson was that deregulation does not automatically prevent the acquisition of a high degree of monopoly power by certain airlines. Measures directed towards encouraging and sustaining competitive forces are thus highly desirable. In this context, freer access to take-off and landing slots for new entrants at major airports is particularly important. It is also important to use anti-cartel legislation to avoid reductions in competition. Anti-merger legislation is more problematic in that preventing mergers may keep up competition, but at the expense of preventing the gaining of scale economies.

Differences in the two airline markets

By far the most significant intercontinental difference, however, is the fact that the United States constitutes a single economic entity, while air transport in Europe is still organised as a set of national markets. The political obstacles to change are, therefore, substantial because some governments are fearful of even limited competition.

In attempting to learn from US experience it is essential to take account of certain important differences between Europe and America. To begin with, the US civil aviation industry is more than four times larger than its European counterpart, thereby presenting more opportunities for scale economies. For example, the larger US market permits more extensive use of wide-bodied jets. Second, unlike the situation in the United States, the various computer reservation systems in Europe are owned by a number of airlines and present information in an unbiased manner. The danger that these systems will become sources of monopoly power is thus minimised. Third, holiday travel in Europe has tended to be mainly the preserve of charter airlines, which during the past two decades have accounted for more than 50 per cent of the total market. The relative cheapness of air charter travel goes some way to explaining why there has been less pressure for reform of scheduled services than in the United States.

Changing European policy

There are, however, considerable benefits to be reaped from freer skies. It is, therefore, encouraging that for some years the EU has followed a liberalisation strategy which includes freeing carriers to compete in each others' markets, permitting more competition on fares and the ending of bilateral agreements for sharing revenue and capacity in the case of airlines flying the same routes.

The achievement of a single market in civil aviation was approached in three stages. The first, agreed in 1987, was mainly symbolic. While providing for some relaxation of controls on fares, capacity and market access, its effect was comparatively modest because the main flag carriers remained largely undisturbed. The second stage came into force in November 1990 and has had greater impact. In essence, the package of measures included the relaxation of existing capacity rules so that one country can take up to a 75 per cent share, greater freedom in fare-setting, and route access for more airlines.

The third and last stage provided for the ending of capacity sharing, multiple designation of carriers on all routes, freedom for airlines to set fare levels, unless there are objections from the governments of both countries at each end of the route, and uniform licensing. This final measure was particularly significant because it implied that any EU airline would ultimately be able to fly any route within the Union. Hence, since January 1993 the area within the EU's boundaries has been increasingly perceived as a single 'domestic' market. Because of the reluctance of some nations wholeheartedly to support liberalisation, however, the full benefits of the final stage have yet to be reaped.

Nevertheless, there is evidence that the change has taken place. To begin with, an increasing number of flag carriers, such as Austrian Airlines, KLM of Holland and Lufthansa of Germany are now operating, like BA, as private businesses rather than as state-owned bureaucracies. Indeed, Kleinwort Benson has estimated that such quoted European airlines are, on average, about 40 per cent more cost efficient than their state-owned counterparts. Second, a freer market with lower entry barriers is permitting the emergence of a large number of low-cost 'niche' airlines in France and Spain as well as in the UK. The competition is forcing the established airlines to become more price-conscious.

Third, largely in response to increased competition, airline fares are falling in real terms. This is not at first obvious, in that quoted air fares have been rising somewhat. However, around 70 per cent of passengers actually pay less than the full quoted price. The effect of low-cost UK airlines such as Ryanair has been significant for the dominant producer, BA. Part of its response to the challenge was to introduce its own no-frills service, Go. Subsequently, however, this new airline was subject to a management buy-out and was eventually acquired by easyJet. More recently, BA's response to the challenge of the low-cost airlines on short-haul routes has been to reduce many fares substantially and alter the conditions attached to them.

Problems for European deregulation

It is clear that the liberalisation measures have produced substantial change in European air transport. Even so, US experience suggests that the attempt to

Table 8.6 Selected subsidies to European airlines in 1990–2002

Airline	*Country*	*Size of subsidy US$ billion*
Air France	France	3.70
Olympic	Greece	2.30
Aer Lingus	Ireland	0.25
TAP	Portugal	1.10
Iberia	Spain	1.89

Source: adapted from Financial press

generate a far more competitive environment could prove futile unless two threats are dealt with vigorously.

The first is the method by which take-off and landing slots are awarded at airports, especially at peak periods. As in the United States, allocation within the EU is decided by committees of incumbent airlines largely on the grandfather principle. In the presence of capacity constraints at most leading European airports, newcomers find it very difficult to acquire slots. A better allocation mechanism is required. In a market economy, scarce capacity has a price. Slot auctions could, therefore, be used to solve the congestion problem, with airlines bidding for access to runways. Those wanting peak-time slots at congested airports would have to pay a high price for them: conversely, space at less popular airports could be obtained relatively cheaply. A pricing system of this kind would have substantial advantages.

The second impediment is that inefficient national flag carriers, albeit to a diminishing extent, are still allowed by the European Commission to receive subsidies from their governments as an alternative to substantial downsizing or exit from the market. Table 8.6 gives some examples of subsidies received by major flag carriers even as liberalisation was underway. In theory, the subsidies were given to allow the airlines time to restructure their operations; in practice, they simply enabled the airlines to survive with minimal response to changing market circumstances. Subsidies in various forms were also granted by many governments to their flag carriers following the tragic events of 11 September 2001. These were justified on the grounds that insurance costs became prohibitive and in some cases insurance was unobtainable. It was argued that without government underwriting many of the world's airlines would have ceased to operate.

The second obstacle to a freer market is concentration in the European aviation industry. To the extent that Europe is allowing freer markets to develop, the inefficient will be supplanted or taken over by the more efficient. Unless entry barriers are kept low, enabling new airlines to continue to enter, further increases in concentration are likely.

Major European airlines are following the example of their US counterparts in seeking to protect themselves from competition by means of mergers, cross-shareholding agreements and various kinds of commercial pacts. The European Commission is rightly concerned that deals of this kind will stifle competition at birth. It has, therefore, examined proposed mergers very closely. On the other hand, in a global context, there is a danger that a highly fragmented EU aviation industry, consisting of small- and medium-sized carriers, might not be able to compete with the very large airlines of the United States and Asia. In addition, the possibility exists that, in an attempt to ensure a competitive environment, the EU could end up introducing a new range of tight regulatory devices.

In an ideal world, the dilemma of size versus competition could be solved by opening the European market to international competition. However, such a liberal policy is unlikely to be adopted unless the rest of the world reciprocates by abandoning a protectionist stance. Unfortunately, at present there appears to be little chance of such a fundamental change in attitude. Now that the EU has substantially liberalised its air transport industry, it would be possible to achieve many of the benefits of openness if Europe and the United States were to grant each others' airlines reciprocal access, thereby creating a trans-Atlantic Common Aviation Area.

8.6 Conclusion

We began by seeing that the European airline industry has an oligopolistic structure. That leads us to draw certain conclusions about the type and degree of competition one might expect. Government attitudes in Europe have tended to restrict that competition, whereas within the United States a more open skies policy prevails. Europe is under pressure to deregulate too.

US experiences suggested that the deregulation of civil aviation would prove to be an extremely uncomfortable experience for many of Europe's traditional airlines while presenting new opportunities for the more efficient. This is indeed proving to be the case. As we saw earlier in the chapter low-cost carriers have entered the market. It was also clear from the course of events in the United States that passengers in Europe would benefit greatly from a freer air-travel market: they would enjoy improved service, lower fares and more choice. Evidence to date suggests that this is happening.

However, in order to extract the maximum benefit, Europe must be careful not to reproduce two major flaws in the US deregulation process. The first was the failure to ensure that entry barriers were as low as consistent with scale economies. In particular, there was a failure to ensure that an airline wishing to start operating on a popular route had a high probability of gaining access to a busy airport. Britain's opening up of Heathrow, the home base of BA, to greater competition earlier in this decade set an example to the rest of Europe in this respect. More specifically, the move demonstrated a willingness to discomfort the national carrier in the interests of an ideology.

With hindsight, the second flaw in the US deregulation process was too relaxed an approach to anti-trust and merger controls. The European Commission is determined not to repeat this error and has made it clear that activities which could pose a threat to competition will not be tolerated. It has also scrutinised proposed airline mergers very closely.

Unfortunately, not to sanction mergers runs the risk of leaving the EU airline industry too fragmented to compete with the world's mega carriers. However, the scale versus competition dilemma could be neatly solved if an open skies policy in the EU proves to be the prelude to a North Atlantic free market in air travel embracing both Europe and America.

CHAPTER SUMMARY

1 **A market dominated by a few large firms is an oligopoly.**

2 **Oligopoly is characterised by firm interdependence, competition being not only on price but on non-price variables too.**

3 **In some oligopoly markets each firm may face a kinked demand curve.**

4 **In such cases, changes in marginal costs do not always lead to price changes.**

5 **Competition is sometimes lessened by takeovers, mergers and the formation of cartels.**

6 **Governments sometimes regulate behaviour in oligopolistic markets.**

Questions for discussion

Guidance to the answers for the ***asterisked*** *numbered questions is available to students on the website for the book at* **www.booksites.net/heather**.

1* Another oligopolistic market is the market for cigarettes. In Chapter 7, question 6, we saw that profit maximisers operate on the elastic section of the demand curve. However, it would appear that cigarette manufacturers are on the inelastic section of their demand curve. Consider what happens to cigarette prices when the Chancellor increases tobacco duty in the Budget. Usually prices rise by the full extent of the tax. Hence at the current price demand is inelastic. Can this be profit-maximising behaviour?

2 How realistic are the assumptions of the kinked demand model? How far does it aid our understanding of oligopolistic price determination in general, and the European airlines in particular?

3* Construct a pay-off matrix similar to Figure 8.2. In doing so, assume (a) that the variable which the duopolists are considering is high or low volumes of advertising and (b) that advertising is much more effective in shifting demand between brands than in increasing demand for the product.

4 Why might a cartel agreement between firms be unstable? Would it be easier to stabilise for price or non-price variables?

5* How much government intervention in the airline industry is appropriate to ensure adequate safety standards?

6 The market for cross-Channel journeys constitutes another oligopolistic market. Eurotunnel is a relatively new entrant. Since their arrival P&O European Ferries and Stena Sealink are allowed to run a joint service in competition with Eurotunnel. Is this beneficial or harmful to consumers?

7* The small low-cost airlines have increased market share in recent years. What factors will determine their future success?

8 What are the main differences between oligopoly and monopolistic competition?

9* Which of the following industries would you classsify as oligopolistically and which monopolistically competitive? (a) washing powder, (b) butchers, (c) aircraft, (d) pharmaceutical drugs and (e) chemists.

10 How much does oligopoly theory add to our understanding of how prices are determined in a market system?

Websites

Useful data for the airline industry can be found at IATA's website, which is:

www.iata.org/index.htm/

However, some information is only available on payment of a subscription.

9 Non-profit-maximising behaviour

Business behaviour: *are profits everything?*

CHAPTER OVERVIEW

What is the business community really trying to achieve? Making as much profit as possible? Enjoying a quiet life? Increasing the size of their businesses as quickly as they can? Do the shareholders know what the firms are doing and can they do anything about it? In previous chapters we have assumed that the overriding aim is profit maximisation – but are profits everything?

In this chapter we review:

- Monopoly
- Oligopoly
- Normal profit

We introduce:

- Full cost pricing
- Sales revenue maximisation
- Growth maximisation
- Managerial utility

9.1 Introduction

An assumption commonly made by economists when they analyse business behaviour is that firms, in whatever market structure they operate, attempt to maximise profits. For example, in Chapter 6 we assumed small firms aimed to maximise profits. In Chapter 8 we assumed that airline companies do likewise although they may have sufficient market power to pursue other goals. Whether this is a legitimate assumption or not is an important question. There are, perhaps, two things that make it so important. One is that it is at the heart of the market economist's claim that, given certain conditions, society maximises its welfare by allowing resources to be used by their owners in whichever way they choose. After all, part of profit maximisation is the minimisation of costs for whatever is the firm's chosen level of output. Now, if the firm minimises costs, see p. 155 it keeps to a minimum the amount of resources needed to produce that output and so resources are not wasted. We have already seen in Chapter 7 that a monopolist's chosen level of output may well not be that which maximises welfare for society. However, the presumption of profit maximisation is that, having chosen a level of output, the monopolist will seek to minimise the cost of producing that output.

This leads us on to a second, related reason. Where markets do not produce an optimum use of resources, for example, in the view of most economists, where there is monopoly power, governments will wish to intervene. The appropriate form of intervention may depend upon the way in which firms are choosing price/output decisions. For example, the logic of price controls in monopolistic industries such as gas, electricity distribution and water depends, among other things, upon an assumption that managers of these industries will behave by attempting to maximise profits, and thus dividends for the shareholders.

Profit maximisation, then, is an important assumption often made by economists. What does the evidence suggest? Are profits everything?

9.2 The profit maximisation view

Let us briefly remind ourselves of the normal assumptions made about firm behaviour. In competitive markets there are no barriers to the free movement of resources. Therefore if firms make more than a normal profit, new firms will enter the market thus increasing supply and depressing price until only normal profit is made. Since, in the long run, firms can only make normal profit, that is, just cover all costs including opportunity costs, they *have* to be profit maximisers to survive. We saw this in Chapter 6.

see pp. 124–6

In markets where there are barriers to entry, firms may be able to make profits above the normal even in the long run. For example, a profit-maximising monopolist's price/output decision would be as shown in Figure 9.1. We first

see pp. 152–4

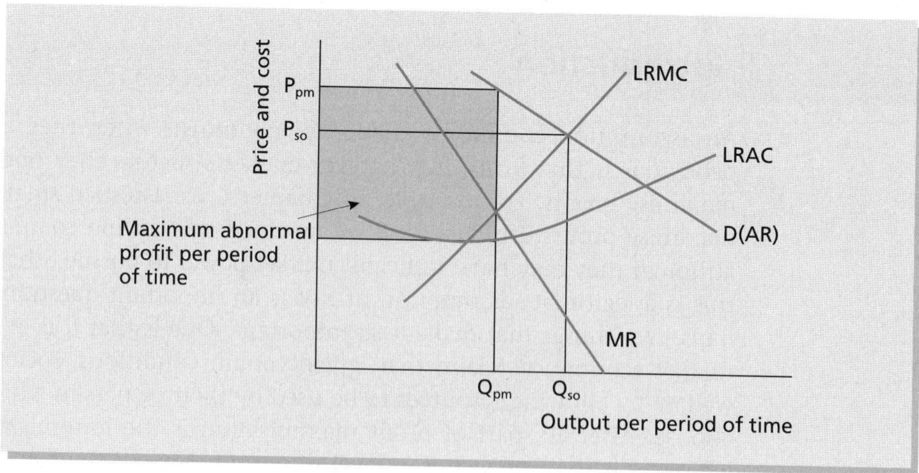

Figure 9.1 Profit-maximising monopoly

met this in Chapter 7, although here we are assuming that unit costs increase with increased output.

Since the firm has some market power, it is shown as having a downward sloping demand curve. If the demand curve is downward sloping, the marginal revenue curve will be as described in Figure 9.1. The relationship of these curves to one another was examined in Chapter 7.

see pp. 152–4

The profit maximiser chooses an output level Q_{pm}, at which marginal cost = marginal revenue. He or she sells that output for the highest price he or she can get. This is P_{pm}. The total profit is then given as Q × AR (TR) minus Q × LRAC (TC). If he or she were to make any more output, and therefore be obliged to lower price, addition to cost, LRMC, would be greater than addition to revenue, MR. He or she would therefore make a marginal loss on such units thereby reducing his or her overall level of profit. Accordingly Q_{pm} is his or her optimum output.

Management is assumed to produce Q_{pm} output at a price of P_{pm}. Notice, though, two important points. First, costs are still assumed to be at a minimum. By this we do *not* mean that the firm produces at the bottom of LRAC, but that at whatever level of output it chooses to produce, here Q_{pm}, it will produce that output as cheaply as it can. Although the firm could make some profit if it failed to do so, it will not wish to forgo the lost profit that would result. Therefore it will still strive to minimise the costs of producing Q_{pm}.

Second, notice that it is assumed that management under these conditions will seek to restrict output to below the social optimum. The socially optimal output is where addition to opportunity cost, LRMC, is equal to the value that society places upon that marginal output (D). So management is assumed to produce less output than the level which would maximise social welfare in its drive to maximise profits.

Some economists, notably those of what are generally known as the Austrian school, would not see this as a reason for government intervention in firm behaviour. To them, the profit above normal is a reward for efficiently meeting society's needs. If it is really in excess of a fair return that is being made, others will, in a free society, use their resources to compete.

We saw in Chapter 7 that profit maximisation is an assumed goal in oligopolistic markets too. Firms will have to think carefully about rivals' reactions. There is much greater uncertainty but the goal is still the same.

Although many economists would regard profit maximisation as a legitimate assumption for analysing firm behaviour, others have real doubts about these assumptions. In general, the models that do *not* assume profit maximisation relate to oligopolistic markets.

9.3 Full cost pricing

One interesting criticism of the profit maximisation assumption is that firms may indeed wish to maximise profits, but they cannot do so because they do not have all the information that the textbooks assume they do. So how do they choose their price and output decision according to this view?

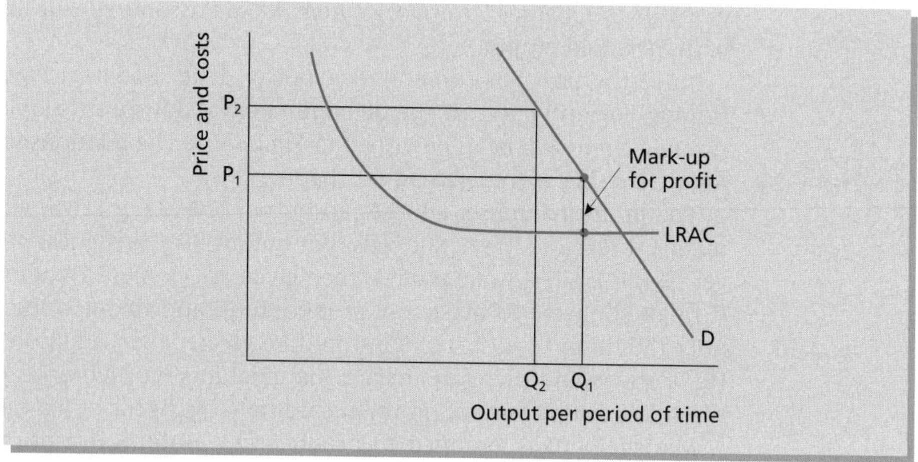

Figure 9.2 Full cost pricing

The problem of inadequate information

We start with the information available to a firm. First look at costs. The firm can get a good idea of its cost structure. Typically, it will have a good idea of what it would cost to produce any level of output it chooses. This model assumes that the typical production process gives it a long-run average cost curve of the shape described in Figure 9.2. As output increases from low levels, economies of scale become available. At some output these are exhausted, but the firm can avoid diseconomies of scale by decentralising its operations and running a number of largely separate plants. Some support for this assumption was presented in Chapter 6.

see pp. 227–9

Now consider the firm's demand conditions. Its demand curve is given in Figure 9.2 as D. The problem is that the firm does not know where its demand curve is. It knows one spot on its demand curve, it knows the output it is selling at the present price, but it does not know what output it would sell at other prices.

You may feel that if the firm wishes to know this then it is not too difficult to find out. One way of getting the information would be to raise price for a period and see how much of an effect the rise had on sales. It could set a price of, say, P_2 and observe the extent of fall in sales to Q_2. Alas this will not do. It may find that it loses a lot of sales and the goodwill of its customers in the experiment that could do lasting damage. In other words, the cost of acquiring the information it needs to establish its demand curve is simply too high. There is another problem, too. Recall that demand is a function of price, incomes, the price of other goods and perhaps of other things too. However, when we draw a demand curve we are assuming that all things affecting demand other than price are held constant. If the firm raises its price to P_2 and observes a fall in its sales to Q_2, it must be sure that the only thing that has changed is price. If something else has changed, consumer tastes or other prices, for example, the whole demand curve will have shifted. It will not have found two spots on one demand curve at all: it will have found one spot on one demand curve and one spot on the new one.

The argument, then, is that the firm must make a price/output decision knowing only its cost and very little about the nature of demand for its product. Its decision will then be a simple one. It will take its full average costs, including overheads, add a mark-up for a profit margin to establish its price, and sell whatever it can at its chosen price.

Predictions of the full cost pricing model

If the firm's mark-up is as in Figure 9.2, it sets a price equal to P_1 and finds that it can sell Q_1 output. Suppose now that demand increases. The firm will not raise the price, but will simply sell more at its chosen price. Suppose the firm's costs increase. It will, of course, increase price in order to restore its profit mark-up. What is the prediction of the model if demand is falling? Provided that it falls over a range where unit costs are constant, there will be no change in price. If demand falls back to the range where the firm begins to lose its scale economies, the price may even rise.

Table 9.1 compares these predictions with those we would make using the traditional profit-maximising model where information is perfect. (Check back to Figure 9.1 to make sure that you understand the predictions of the traditional model.) Notice also that we show in the table the choice of variable. Our full cost pricing model recognises, as does the traditional model, that a firm cannot choose price *and* output. It can choose any output it wishes but the demand curve then constrains it with regard to the price it can set. Alternatively, it can choose any price it wishes and the demand curve will constrain the output it can make at that price. The traditional model predicts that the firm will decide its output by establishing the point at which LRMC = MR, and then selling at the highest price it can get for its chosen output level. On the other hand, the full cost pricing model predicts that it will select its price. In fact, most businesspeople in fact say that they choose price rather than output.

You may like to give some thought to what decides the *size* of the mark-up that the full cost pricing model predicts that the businessperson will choose. We shall not deal with that question now but you will be asked to think about it as part of the questions for discussion at the end of the chapter.

Table 9.1 Profit maximisation and full cost pricing predictions

Model	*Set price or output?*	*Rise in demand*	*Fall in demand*
Profit maximisation with perfect information	Output	Raise price and output	Cut price and output
Full cost pricing model	Price	Raise output	Cut output; possibly raise price

9.4 Sales revenue maximisation

Doubts about the profit maximisation assumption

In the full cost pricing model, firms wish to maximise profit. Their ability to do so is constrained by imperfect information. We turn now to consider several models of business behaviour where the assumption is that management is not even trying to maximise profits. Although these models are very different in what they believe is important to management, they all have one feature in common: they all assume that in the great majority of markets there is significant market power. In other words, they believe that monopolistic or oligopolistic structures are prevalent. They also believe that in these markets there is a separation of ownership from control. This is a very important idea and we need to be clear about what it means. In small firms the owners are the ones who take the decisions. Since their income is determined by the profit they make, they may well attempt to maximise profit in the way in which the perfectly competitive model suggests. Large firms, however, are owned by shareholders. They wish firms to maximise profit since their incomes, in the form of dividends, depend largely on those profits. However, the ones who take the decisions, the managers of the companies, do not usually find a close correlation between company profits and their incomes. If managers are given incentives, they are often in the form of rewards for increasing sales rather than profit. Salespeople, in particular, are often paid a commission not on the profits of the company, but on the level of sales achieved. Management has less incentive, therefore, to maximise profits and may well pursue other goals, such as growth or sales revenue.

If shareholders had perfect knowledge they would know if management were not maximising profit and would seek to replace the managers. They do not have that knowledge. Further, the distribution of a company's shareholding is so wide that any individual shareholder has little influence over how the company is run. If large numbers of shareholders were disenchanted with profit performance, they would sell their shares, with the effect of depressing the share price of the company, leaving it in danger of a takeover bid. Clearly, this is something management will wish to avoid, so profit is not irrelevant. An adequate level of profit to keep the shareholders happy is a constraint upon management behaviour. Thus managers are seen as seeking to achieve other goals subject to an adequate level of profit rather than as profit maximisers.

The Baumol model

One example of a model not assuming profit maximisation is that associated with William J. Baumol. Baumol suggested that firms seek not to maximise profit but to maximise sales revenue subject to a profit constraint. The size of the profit constraint is, as explained above, whatever is necessary to keep the shareholder happy. Let us see from Figure 9.3 what that will mean for the firm's behaviour.

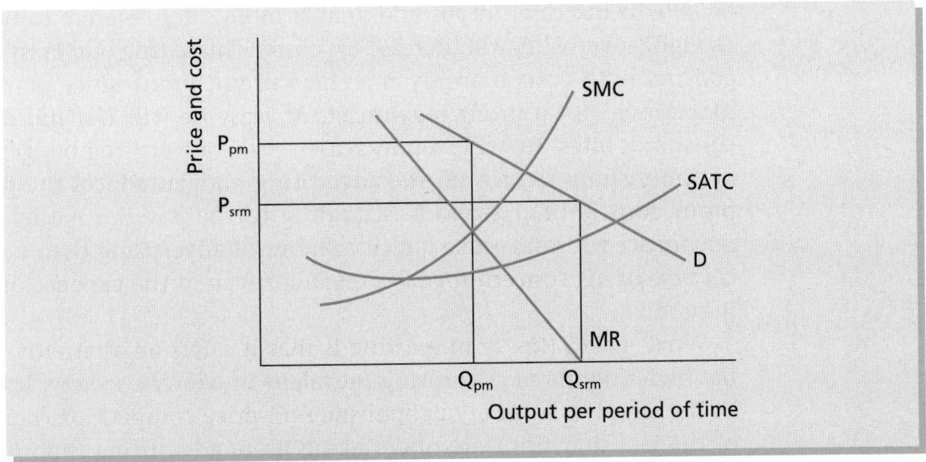

Figure 9.3 Sales revenue maximisation

The model, in its most commonly discussed form, concentrates upon short-run management goals. Accordingly, Figure 9.3 shows a firm's short-run cost and revenue conditions.

The short-run cost curves are those which we have met before. Their shapes, you will recall, are determined by diminishing returns. However, we need show only SATC. The profit maximiser produces where SMC = MR at Q_{pm} and price P_{pm}.

On the other hand, the sales revenue maximiser is not trying to achieve maximum profits but maximum sales revenue. What output and price is appropriate for him? He will always increase output provided that the increased output causes his total revenue to rise. In other words, it is worth making more if marginal revenue (addition to total revenue) is positive. The appropriate level of output is therefore Q_{srm}, where marginal revenue is zero. The appropriate price is P_{srm}.

The sales revenue maximiser wants to produce more output than the profit maximiser, since although it reduces profits if output is increased beyond Q_{pm}, it raises sales revenue. His ideal is Q_{srm} where sales revenue maximisation is achieved. The problem for him, though, is whether the smaller level of profit that he will then make is sufficient to keep the shareholders happy. If the minimum profit felt to be necessary is greater than his profit constraint, he would not be able to achieve his goal. Interestingly, Baumol argued that the profit constraint is *always* effective. That is to say, he will never be in a position where he can ignore the profit constraint when trying to maximise total revenue. Baumol's argument goes as follows.

Suppose the profit constraint were to be quite low. In other words, suppose at Q_{srm}, in Figure 9.3, the level of profit being made is sufficient to keep shareholders happy. Would he not just produce Q_{srm} output and be able to forget the profit constraint? The argument is that since he is a sales revenue maximiser he would simply advertise more if he were faced with this situation. This will shift the demand curve to the right, and cause MR to shift right too. He would then be able to increase output and enable more sales revenue to be earned. Surely, though, advertising will increase his costs? This is true but, even if the advertising adds more to costs than revenue, he will not mind, since he is a sales revenue maximiser, not a profit maximiser. At least he will not mind until the profit constraint bites. He will stop increases in the advertising budget when the effect of diminishing returns on the advertising budget reduces the profit level to the profit constraint. Therefore, according to the Baumol model, a sales revenue maximiser will undertake larger volumes of advertising than a profit maximiser because of his concern for sales revenue, even at the expense of some reduction in profit.

What makes this so interesting is that it offers an alternative explanation for the high volume of advertising prevalent in western society. It can be argued to be not simply a form of oligopolistic non-price competition, but also a reflection of the fact that firms are undertaking more advertising than is consistent with profit maximising behaviour. You may have wondered whether the enormous costs to the advertiser are justified by the increased sales. One view is that they are justified. We could use the games theory idea developed in Chapter 8 to show that, while it would be better for these companies if they all decreased advertising, one company alone cannot afford to do so because of the devastating effects on its profits.

see pp. 168–71

We now have an alternative explanation: perhaps the motive is sales revenue maximisation. Provided that the advertising increases sales a little, it will not matter if the increased costs are greater than the increased revenue, subject to the proviso that the advertising costs do not push profits below the profit constraint.

9.5 Growth maximisation

Growth versus security

An alternative view of business behaviour is given by Professor Robin Marris. His view of firms is that their managers concentrate on the *growth* of the company. However, they discover that pursuing growth creates problems for themselves in terms of their security. They, therefore, have to trade growth against security. Figures 9.4 and 9.5 explain the Marris view.

Consider Figure 9.4. Security is in essence security from the fear of being taken over and hence possibly losing position, status and salary. How do we measure security? We cannot do so directly, but we can do it indirectly. The likelihood of a takeover is much reduced if management can gain a high valuation ratio (V). This we figure out by taking the value of the company as measured by the stock market (number of shares issued × price of shares) and dividing it by the book value of the company, that is, the assets as valued by the accountants in the company's balance sheet. So, for example, if the book value of the company is £1 million and the stock market values the company at, say, £½ million, it becomes an attractive takeover target. On the other hand, a

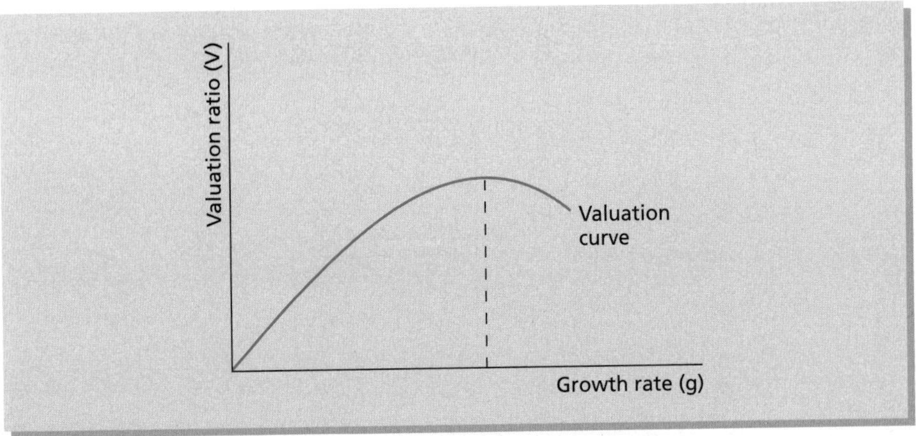

Figure 9.4 **Relationship between growth rate and valuation ratio**

potential takeover may well be deterred if, in order to acquire £1 million worth of assets, the price to be paid via a takeover bid is around £2 million. So, *ceteris paribus*, the higher is V, the happier is management.

However, management also wants growth. Greater growth may mean enhanced status and salary. So what will happen if management decides to undertake more investment and go for a greater rate of growth? As g rises, V rises also. Management is undertaking profitable projects. Even if shareholders receive lower dividend payments they will not sell their shares and depress the valuation ratio. They expect to be compensated by enhanced profits in later periods. At some point, however, increased growth can only be achieved with poorer investment projects. Shareholders do not feel that they are likely to be compensated later for lower dividend payments. The valuation ratio will fall as the growth rate gets beyond g. Clearly, profit maximisation requires a growth rate of g, maximising the worth of the company to its shareholders.

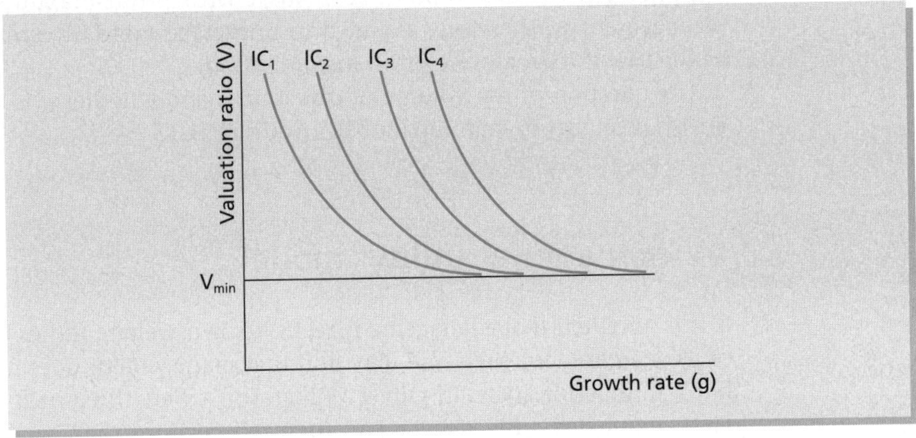

Figure 9.5 **Management preferences between growth rate and valuation ratio**

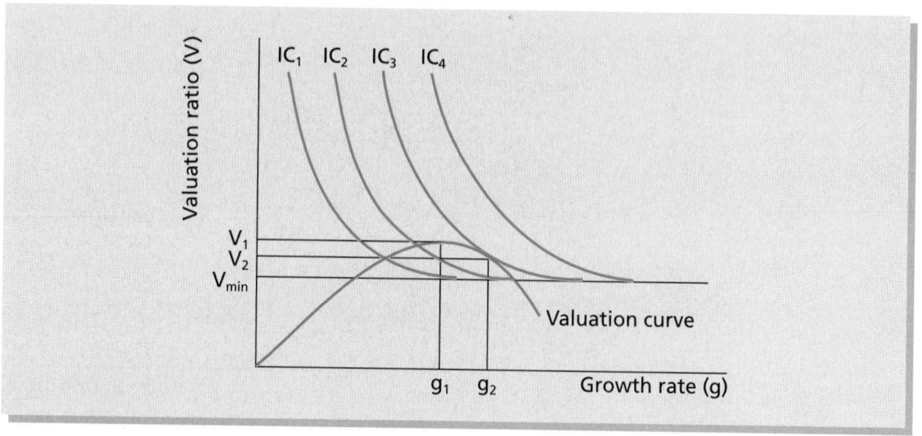

Figure 9.6 **Maximising welfare for management**

Optimising the trade-off

Given that management has a desire for growth and security, what will management choose? Management preferences are found in the indifference curves in Figure 9.5. Just as for a consumer there is a diminishing marginal rate of substitution between goods, so for management there is a diminishing marginal rate of substitution of growth for security. Just as a consumer would always prefer to be on a higher indifference curve where he can obtain more of both goods, so management would prefer more security *and* more growth. However, fear of being taken over is so strong at V_{min} that when the valuation ratio has fallen to this level, no amount of extra growth compensates for the increased feeling of insecurity.

see pp. 75–7

We can now see what management will actually choose if we combine Figures 9.4 and 9.5 in one diagram. Clearly, given the constraint of the valuation curve management will choose g_2 and V_2, the highest possible indifference curve it can reach, as shown in Figure 9.6. Notice that this means that there is a higher growth rate than is consistent with profit-maximising behaviour. Management is, therefore, assumed to undertake more investment than would be the case if its goal were profit maximisation.

The question of the volume of investment and whether it is adequate for the British economy is examined further in Chapter 13.

9.6 A 'managerial utility' model

If it is accepted that management seeks its own welfare rather than the welfare of its shareholders, then one may find that management does not have *one* goal but a number of goals. In Oliver Williamson's view three such goals stand out. First, managers will wish to pay themselves more than would be necessary

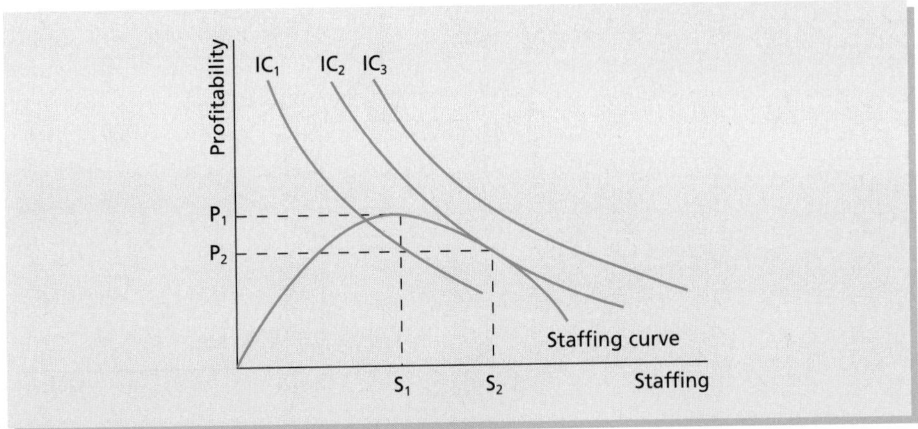

Figure 9.7 Trading off profitability with staffing levels

to cover the opportunity cost of their services. In recent years there have been frequent complaints that top pay is out of all proportion to the value that management contributes to company profitability. This pay may include staff perks such as company cars and expensive offices. Second, managers will wish to have more staff than is necessary, since a greater staff enhances their status and prestige. Third, they will wish to undertake 'discretionary investment'. Discretionary investment covers projects which may not add to company profitability but give managers utility in other ways. It may be that buying a newspaper company or a football club gives management utility while not adding to profit.

In the Williamson view, profit is of some importance: it is not only a constraint to keep shareholders content but also provides funds which enable such things as discretionary investment to be pursued. However, profit will not be maximised for it is not the only thing that gives managerial utility. Consider the trade-off between staffing and profitability in Figure 9.7. The staffing curve shows the relationship between the number of staff and profits. If no staff are employed no profits are made. As more staff are employed, profits rise until S_1. Beyond that level the usefulness of additional staff as measured by their marginal output is less than the wage paid. Profit, therefore, falls. A profit maximiser employs S_1 staff and makes P_1 profit. Williamson suggests that managers will, given their indifference curves as between profit and staffing, maximise their utility as S_2 P_2.

One interesting possibility is that this sheds light upon the behaviour of companies during a recession. Companies frequently say that conditions are such that they have to become more efficient, which often means laying off staff. If they were profit maximisers, they would already be cost efficient. One could argue that during a recession a reasonable level of profit is harder to earn. Thus, at such times, scope is reduced for employing additional staff beyond the optimum level for profit maximisation. Hence, while the need to be more efficient during a recession is meaningless for a profit maximiser, such statements fit very well with the Williamson view.

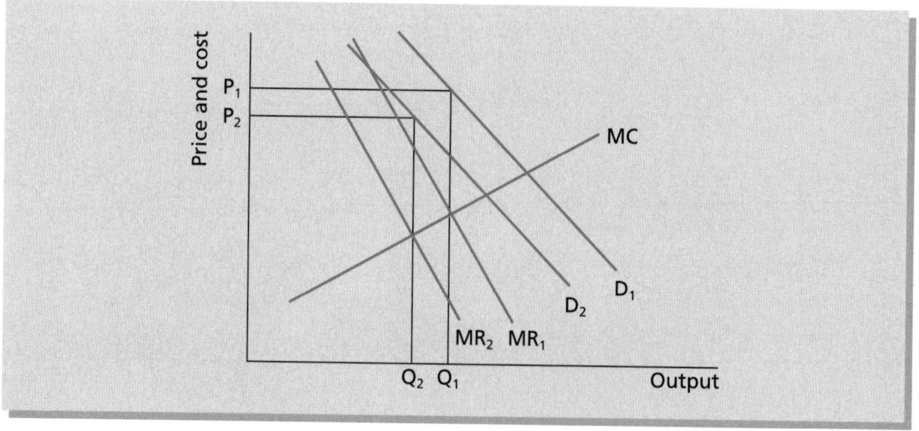

Figure 9.8 **Response of profit maximiser to a fall in demand**

The argument needs to be stated with some care. At first sight it may not seem to lead to a different result from a traditional profit maximising assumption. Consider Figure 9.8. The original position is represented by demand curve D_1 and marginal revenue curve MR_1. Profit maximisation requires an output level of Q_1 where $MC = MR_1$. Suppose a recession causes demand to fall to D_2. The marginal revenue curve will shift to MR_2. Then the profit maximising response is to reduce output to Q_2 (and price to P_2). Less output requires less input, so some staff are laid off.

Reducing staff in a recession, then, is not inconsistent with the traditional model. What *is* inconsistent is to say that the reason for the reduction in staff levels is the need to become more efficient. The traditional model assumes that whatever level of output is chosen, the profit maximiser will seek to minimise the cost of producing that output.

9.7 Other models

There are other attempts to explain managerial behaviour, an analysis of which goes beyond the scope of this chapter but which are worth mentioning. Some view management behaviour not as an attempt to maximise *anything at all*, be it profits, sales, revenue or whatever. They believe that management is essentially satisfying: that managers have a variety of interests and goals, and that they have an idea of what is a satisfactory performance rather than what constitutes maximisation. Frequently, these models examine the process by which management achieves its goals. Unfortunately, it is difficult, using this approach, to get a general model of firm behaviour which we can use for the purposes of prediction, as the goals of management may vary from firm to firm.

A different view of management behaviour is presented by the well-known US economist Professor J. K. Galbraith. In essence, Galbraith's view is that managerial decisions are taken primarily to reduce risk. Firms seek, therefore, to control the environment within which they operate. They do so largely by advertising and manipulating people's preferences. In the western world the problems of scarcity have generally been overcome, and incomes are more than adequate to provide for people's basic needs. People therefore need to be persuaded to buy all kinds of things for which they have no real use, in order to ensure the continuous flow of production necessary for the survival of the firm. Markets can therefore be seen not in terms of consumer sovereignty but of producer sovereignty. The teaching of profit-maximising models of behaviour in colleges and universities serves business well in that it diverts attention from an analysis of how large businesses really operate and suggests that, apart from a few small problems associated with monopoly power, the market system is a benign one. In reality the resources consumed go into producing largely unwanted products. This means that resources do not flow to those areas of the economy where they are really needed – social services, public goods, and so on. Private oligopolists produce far too much output. Galbraith would therefore regard as ridiculous the idea that large firms do not produce enough output for the social optimum.

9.8 Some strands of evidence

It is not easy to test which of these differing views best explains firm behaviour. One reason for this is that it is difficult to test for *motives* directly. One is looking for things that one can measure, which will suggest what management motives are. We look briefly at four strands of evidence which will help you to decide whether you think management seeks profit maximisation as its goal.

Ownership and control

First, let us consider the question of the divorce of ownership and control. Remember that a key idea behind some profit maximising models is that owners – shareholders – have neither enough information about whether management is profit maximising, nor enough power to oblige management to change its behaviour.

One can argue that this divorce is now less marked than in the past. Concentration of shareholder power has moved increasingly into the hands of groups large enough to force changes in management behaviour. This is exactly what the rise of the institutional investors has been causing. As Table 9.2 shows, fewer shares are owned directly by individuals and more are held indirectly by individuals in their pension funds, unit trusts, and so on, although the decline in the proportion of individual shareholding seems to have slowed in recent years. You will remember that in Chapter 2 we looked at the question of share ownership. What we are emphasising here, however, is not so much the present structure of share ownership but its dramatic change over time.

see pp. 45–6

Table 9.2 **Structure of UK shareholders, 1963–2000**

Share of beneficial owner[a]	*1963 (%)*	*1981 (%)*	*1990 (%)*	*1997 (%)*	*2000 (%)*
Individual investors	54.0	28.2	20.5	16.5	15
Pension funds	6.4	26.7	31.4	22.1	20
Other UK	32.6	41.5	36.3	37.4	38
Overseas	7.0	3.6	11.8	24.0	27

[a] This series is affected by sampling errors and by the varying methods of identification of nominee holdings

Source: adapted from Stock Exchange; ONS data

It has also become more common for these institutions to hold larger blocks of shares in fewer companies than was once the case. This further increases institutional power. Moreover, company management is increasingly aware of the decisiveness of the institutions' voting behaviour in takeover battles. This makes management far more receptive to institutional pressure. It can therefore be argued that it is becoming more difficult for the management of large companies to pursue goals other than profit maximisation.

Owner- and manager-controlled firms

A second strand of evidence could be found by looking at owner-controlled firms to see if they do better, in terms of profitability, than manager-controlled firms. The difficulty here is deciding what constitutes an owner-controlled firm. Since many shareholders are passive, never voting or attending shareholder meetings, it has been argued that an owner can be an individual or family which has only perhaps 15–20 per cent of the shares as this gives sufficient power to exercise effective control. Studies made over the past twenty years or so, using this idea of active shareholder control, have found that manager-controlled firms in both the UK and United States are less profitable.

Profits: are they inevitable in oligopoly?

Some models suggest that decision-takers in oligopolistic markets have considerable control over their economic environment. Galbraith, in particular, feels that firms can control prices and production, so that while profit is not the dominant motive, a reasonable level can virtually be guaranteed. The occurrences of recessions and unexpected events make this difficult to believe: some companies in oligopolistic markets have made large losses. The airline industry, which we studied in Chapter 8, is just one industry amongst many where this is so. Figure 9.9 shows the dramatic turnaround in the fortunes of the International Air Transport Association (IATA) members in a short space of time. A recession in the early 1990s caused air traffic demand to fall. This led to significant losses. There followed a period of relative prosperity followed by

see pp. 162–82

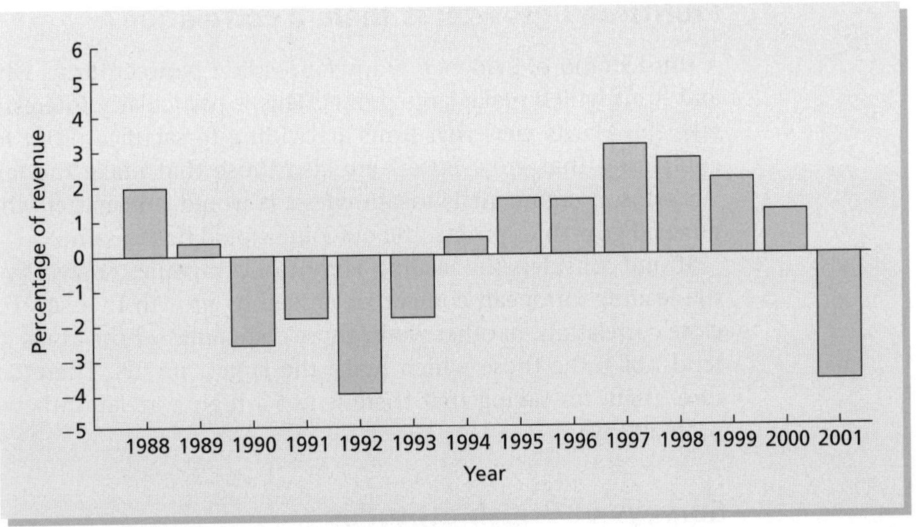

Figure 9.9 **Profit figures for IATA airlines (1988–2001)**

Source: IATA, *World Air Transport Statistics*, 2002

a milder recession around the turn of the century plus the events of 11 September 2001. The overall picture, then, is still one of an oligopolistic industry unable to control its economic environment in a way which guarantees a reasonable return to its shareholders. The airline industry is by no means unique in this respect. Even when the market recovered and most airlines were profitable again, there were large variations between companies in performance. In recent years some large companies' performance has been so disastrous that they have had to file for bankruptcy. Table 9.3 shows some of the largest of recent years from a wide range of industries.

Table 9.3 **Largest bankruptcies, 1987–2002**

Company	*Bankruptcy date*	*Total assets pre-bankruptcy*
Worldcom, Inc.	21 July 2002	$103,914,000,000
Enron Corp.	12 February 2001	$63,392,000,000
Texaco, Inc.	12 April 1987	$35,892,000,000
Financial Corp. of America	9 September 1988	$33,864,000,000
Global Crossing Ltd	28 January 2002	$25,511,000,000
UAL Corp.	9 December 2002	$25,197,000,000
Adelphia Communications	25 June 2002	$24,409,662,000
Pacific Gas and Electric Co.	6 April 2001	$21,470,000,000
MCorp	31 March 1989	$20,228,000,000
Kmart Corp.	22 January 2002	$17,007,000,000

Source: New Generation Research, Inc.

Profits and growth: is there a correlation?

A third strand of evidence is any correlation between firms which grow rapidly and firms which make large profits. This is particularly interesting to those who take the Marris view that firms are willing to sacrifice profit for growth. If the companies that grow fastest are also those that make the largest profits, the Williamson argument is meaningless. It would not matter whether companies pursued growth or profits, the outcome would be the same.

If one considers the leading European companies ranked by profitability and the leading European companies ranked by growth in assets there is rarely any close correlation. In other words those companies whose assets grow most rapidly tend not to be those which make the largest profits. There does seem to be a case, then, for saying that there is not a high correlation between growth and profitability.

Surveys of British attitudes

Another possible source for discovering the attitudes of senior management to profit maximisation is surveys. One such survey was published in 1993, under the title *How ethical is British business?* Of those sent the questionnaire, about 16 per cent responded, representing 645 replies. Table 9.4 refers to the 480 replies which came from senior managers and professionals. It records the responses to only three of many statements. What do these responses suggest about attitudes to profit maximisation?

The results are mixed. The first statement shows that few wanted to place environmental friendliness so high that profits were sacrificed. This is consistent

Table 9.4 Percentage of senior managers' and professionals' responses to statements on business attitudes

1 Environmental procedures should always be followed, even if profits are reduced.					
Score	1	2	3	4	5
%	1	14	20	53	12
2 There is only one rule for business behaviour – make as much money as you can.					
Score	1	2	3	4	5
%	37	40	11	9	2
3 Products which use scarce resources should be banned.					
Score	1	2	3	4	5
%	7	31	30	23	9

1 = strongly disagree; 2 = disagree; 3 = neutral; 4 = agree; 5 = strongly agree

Source: adapted from T. Burke, S. Maddock and A. Rose (1993) *How Ethical is British Business?*, University of Westminster, Research Working Paper, Series 2, No. 1

Table 9.5 Percentage of firms who would change prices in response to a shock

	Number of firms	*Reduce price in response to a fall in demand*	*Raise price in response to an increase in demand*	*Reduce price in response to a reduction in costs*	*Raise price in response to an increase in costs*
All firms	355	62.3	47.2	54.5	88.3
No of competitors:					
1–5	117	56.8	48.3	50.0	89.8
6–10	130	65.4	42.3	54.6	91.5
11–30	61	77.1	49.2	55.7	88.5
More than 30	47	82.3	55.1	63.3	75.5
Own market share:					
1–10%	140	66.0	50.7	59.7	86.1
11–20%	47	61.7	42.6	42.6	85.1
21–30%	52	65.4	50.0	53.9	86.5
> 30%	116	56.5	43.5	53.0	93.0

Source: Bank of England, *Quarterly Bulletin*, August 1999

with the attitude that profits must be maximised. On the other hand, only 11 per cent of senior managers and professionals were prepared to agree with the view that the only rule for business is to make as much money as possible, that is maximise profits.

One must recognise that there are drawbacks to a questionnaire approach to attitudes. One difficulty is that people may be reluctant to be honest despite guaranteed anonymity. A further major drawback is that attitudes may not be consistent. Look at the third statement. All resources are scarce. If such products were banned, there would be no output and these managers would not have a job at all. Yet only 7 per cent of the respondents strongly disagreed. Surveys may be useful, but they must be interpreted with care.

One rather different survey is also worth mentioning. The *Bank of England Quarterly Bulletin*[1] reports the results of a study of the reactions of firms to shocks, changes in demand or changes in costs (Table 9.5).

There are several things worthy of note. First, in a large number of cases prices do not appear to be sticky. In over half the cases firms *do* respond to demand changes by changing prices. Second, prices respond differently according to whether firms felt that shocks warranted price increases or decreases. Sixty-two per cent said they would reduce price if demand were to fall; only 47 per cent said they would raise price in response to a demand increase. Similarly, differences can be seen with regard to cost shocks. Finally, it is worthy of note that the degree of monopoly power, as measured by the number of competitors or by the firm's market share, is important in determining reactions to shocks. For example, 82 per cent of firms with over thirty competitors say they will cut price when demand falls. Only 56 per cent say they will do so if they have between one and five competitors.

9.9 Conclusion

By no means all economists are convinced that management, in whatever market structure it operates, aims to maximise the welfare of its shareholders. Some economists believe that only the divorce of ownership and control makes such an argument a possibility. They feel that one gains much greater insight into the working of large companies if one focuses on other goals. They do not all agree, however, on what those other goals are. Some economists are still convinced that the profit maximisation models are the most useful. Some argue that even if they are less descriptive, profit maximisation models are still valuable because they yield predictions about firm behaviour.

see pp. 166–71

You might help your own thinking about these issues by considering again what we learned in Chapter 8. Do the models we have examined in this chapter cast light on firms' behaviour in the European airline industry?

CHAPTER SUMMARY

1 **Many economists believe that firms do not have a single goal of profit maximisation.**
2 **Because of inadequate information, firms may price on the basis of average cost plus a mark-up for profit.**
3 **The divorce of ownership and control may allow management to pursue goals other than profit maximisation for the shareholders.**
4 **Some believe that managers aim to maximise sales revenue. This gives a higher output and lower price than that which maximises profit.**
5 **An alternative view is that management concentrates upon growth maximisation whilst also being concerned about being taken over.**
6 **Other possible goals include risk minimisation and managerial utility (covering a variety of aims).**
7 **Evidence is not conclusive, but some of it supports non-profit-maximising approaches to explaining firm behaviour.**

Questions for discussion

Guidance to the answers for the ***asterisked*** *numbered questions is available to students on the website for the book at* **www.booksites.net/heather**.

1* Consider Figure 9.10. What level of output corresponds to the following business goals? (a) Maximise profits. (b) Maximise sales subject to covering costs. (c) Minimise costs per unit. (d) Maximise sales revenue. (e) Produce a socially efficient level of output.

2 What factors would you expect to determine the size of the mark-up in the full cost pricing model of business behaviour?

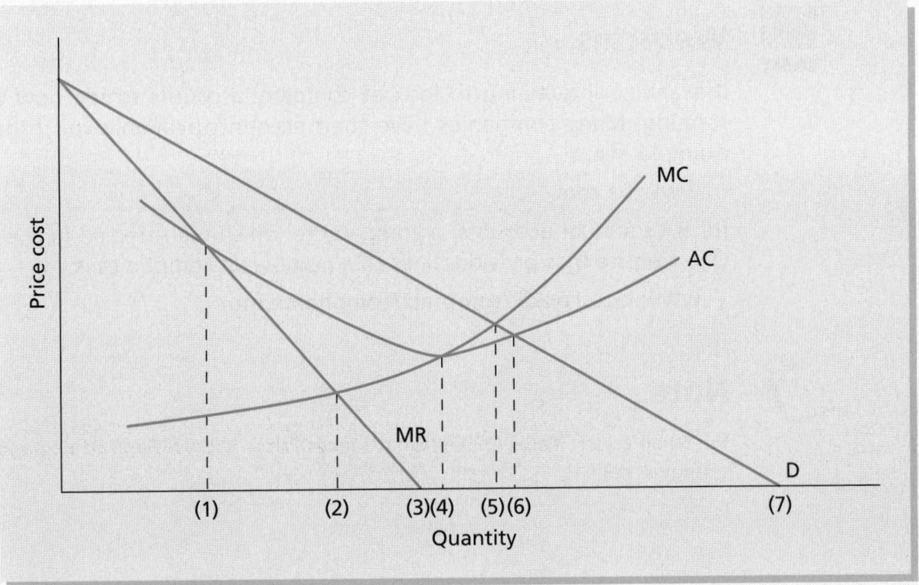

Figure 9.10 Output decisions of a firm

3* A profit maximising firm has a constant average cost and a downward sloping demand curve but it does not know exactly where the demand curve is. How will it react to the following? (a) Its average cost curve shifts up. (b) Demand falls.

see pp. 162–82

4 Check back to Chapter 8. Now explain the criticism of the Baumol model that says it does not matter whether firms maximise profit or sales revenue, their price/output decision is the same.

5* In the sales revenue maximisation model we saw that firms make a higher output at a lower price than if management were seeking to maximise profits. Since the socially optimal price/output decision is a greater output at a lower price, does it follow that sales revenue maximisers come nearer to social optimum pricing than profit maximisers?

6 Not all studies have found that the companies who get taken over are those with a low valuation ratio. Why do you think this might be?

7* How can Galbraith sustain the view that people do not really want some of the things they buy? If there is a demand, must this not be because people gain utility from the goods they purchase?

8 If one is interested in the motives of firms' managers, what are the problems associated with asking them what their goals are?

9* How easily can firms in oligopolistic markets increase demand for their products?

10 Which of the models of pricing that you have studied seem to be the most valuable for understanding business behaviour?

Websites

It is always interesting to look at company accounts to see how well they are performing. Many companies have their accounts available for inspection online. For example, see:

www.ba.com

for BA's annual accounts, a company to which we referred in the previous chapter. One website that provides links to a number of companies is:

www.bized.ac.uk/compfact/comphome.htm

Note

1 I. Small and T. Yates (1999) 'What Makes Prices Sticky?' *Bank of England Quarterly Bulletin*, August 1999.

10 Efficiency, externalities and public goods

Government expenditure: *is the money efficiently spent?*

(with David Bibby)

CHAPTER OVERVIEW

The government takes away much of our income in taxes, which it spends on roads, health, education, defence, and so on. Does it spend wisely? Or is much of it wasted? When we spend our own income on things we wish to buy we try to get value for money. How can we be sure that our government's spending is equally efficient?

In this chapter we review:

- Isoquants and isocosts
- Monopoly

We introduce:

- Efficiency
- Public goods

10.1 Introduction

A significant proportion of people's earnings is taken in taxation and spent by governments. As Figure 10.1 shows, some of what is taken in tax is redistributed to the poor and the unemployed in social security benefits. Large sums are also spent on goods and services which are provided on a non-market basis. Is it well spent, or is much of it wasted? Is there any way of testing for the efficiency of government spending?

It is the task of the National Audit Office (NAO) to raise and answer such questions. The NAO describes its role as 'to provide information and advice to parliament on the way government departments and many other public bodies account for and use the taxpayers' money'.[1] The NAO, headed by the Comptroller and Auditor General, is completely independent of government and the executive and works closely with the Public Accounts Committee. There are two facets to the NAO's work: financial audit and value for money audit. It is the latter task that interests us here.

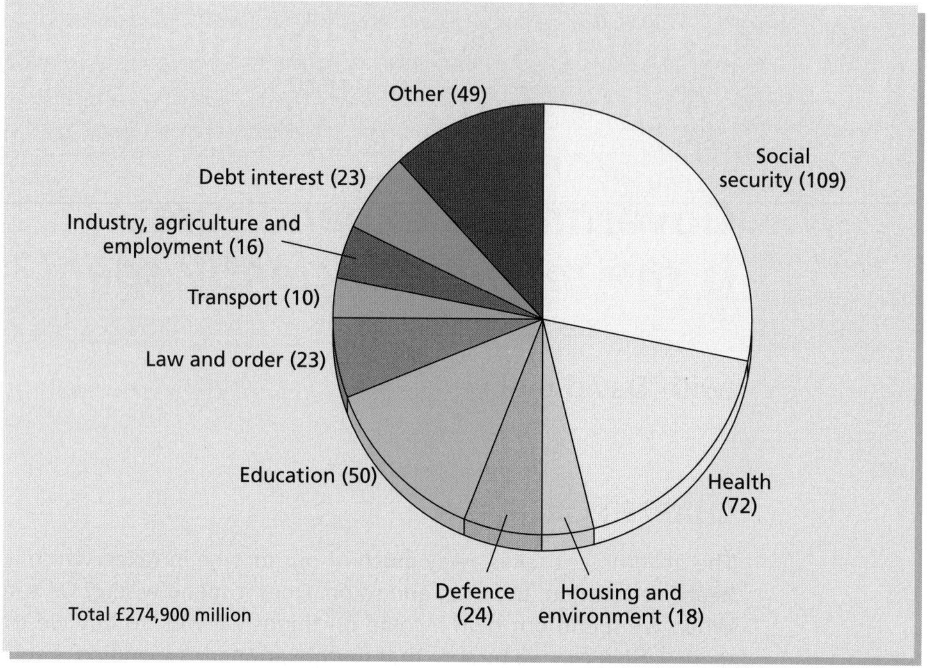

Figure 10.1 **Government expenditure by major spending departments, 2001–2 (£bn)**
Source: adapted from HM Treasury data

In order to understand how the NAO operates we first examine how efficiency might be achieved in the private sector. In doing this we review some of the concepts raised in earlier chapters. We then see how the NAO attempts to see that these aspects of efficiency are achieved for the taxpayer in the state sector.

10.2 Understanding efficiency

We have already defined economics as the study of how scarce resources are allocated between competing ends. An economy is endowed with a certain amount of resources which can be transformed into a certain quantity of goods and services. How do we know that we have produced as much as we possibly can? Even if we are satisfied that we have maximised production quantities, how do we know that we have produced all the different goods and services in amounts that are appropriate for the consumers?

There are, in fact, three separable elements to the efficiency question here. We may refer to them as technical efficiency, cost efficiency and allocative efficiency. Let us examine each of these in turn, asking whether such efficiency will be obtained in the *private* sector. Later, we shall use those concepts to examine the work of the NAO in its attempts to check for efficiency in the public sector.

Table 10.1 Maximum possible output with combination of inputs

Units of capital (K)	Units of labour (L) 2	4	6	8	10
10	19	29	37	44	50
8	17	26	34	40	46
6	16	24	30	36	41
4	13	20	26	30	34
2	10	15	19	23	26

Technical efficiency

Technical efficiency means producing a particular quantity of output using as few inputs as possible, or, equivalently, producing the maximum output from a particular quantity of inputs. This means minimising waste. Garments are made with the minimum amount of fabric on the cutting-room floor, furniture is manufactured with as little sawdust and wood shavings as possible. The labour force should not be making unnecessary journeys and stocks of raw material and finished goods must not be gathering dust in warehouses. These are just a few of the things that affect technical efficiency, but there are many other factors that will have been taken into account before operations began, from the design of the buildings to the type of machinery used.

It is not easy to be technically efficient, and the ability to keep such matters under continual review and to recommend improvements is an important part of what managers are paid to do.

How does technical efficiency fit in with what we have already learned about production and cost? How do firms make long-run decisions about the right combination of capital and labour needed for producing output? (You will remember that we introduced this question in Chapter 5.)

see pp. 104–9

Table 10.1 shows the maximum output of some good per period of time that we assume can be produced when a certain quantity of labour and capital is used. In other words, it is a list of technically efficient outcomes. For example, if the firm uses 10 units of capital and 2 units of labour it can produce 19 units of output per period but no more.

If we focus on 26 units of output we can see that there are a number of different input combinations that can be used to produce this output. Figure 10.2 shows that it can be done with, for example, 8K + 4L, 4K + 6L or 2K + 10L.

Figure 10.2 has been drawn with the assumption that inputs can be divided up into small amounts so that the curve linking all the points representing 26 units is a smooth one. The curve shown is what we referred to in Chapter 5 as an isoquant, a line or contour of constant output. We could have selected any output we wished: in each case we would have obtained an isoquant that had a similar shape but was located closer to, or further away from, the origin

see pp. 104–5

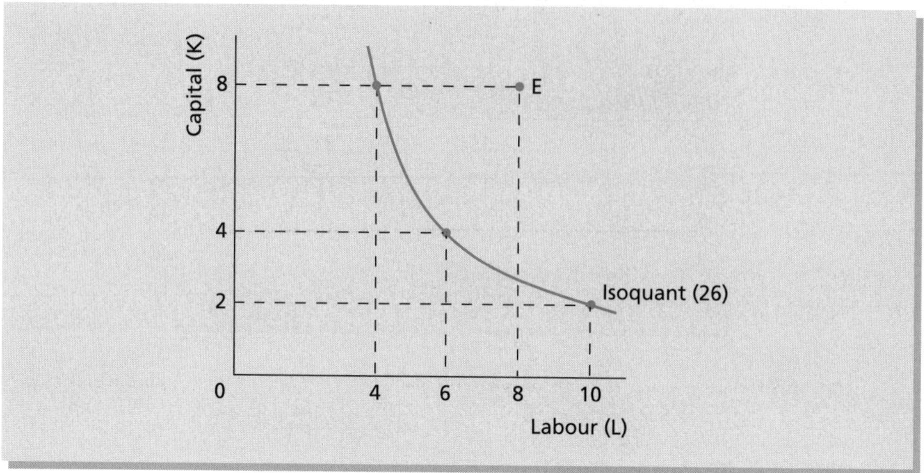

Figure 10.2 **Maximum possible output with combination of inputs**

depending on whether the selected output was higher or lower than 26 units, as Figure 10.3 shows.

If we take point E in Figure 10.2 which represents input quantities of 8 units of both labour and capital we would expect to be able to produce 40 units of output as shown in Table 10.1. However, this is only true if the firm is technically efficient; if it is not so, it is quite possible that 8 units of capital and labour will together produce less than 40 units of output.

To be technically efficient, then, means to avoid waste. It means that for any given usage of one factor we are using the minimum of another factor to produce a particular output. Figure 10.3 shows a series of isoquants. Each one represents the technically efficient combinations of capital and labour for a given level of output. Notice that technical efficiency says nothing about the prices which must be paid by the firm to purchase those factors.

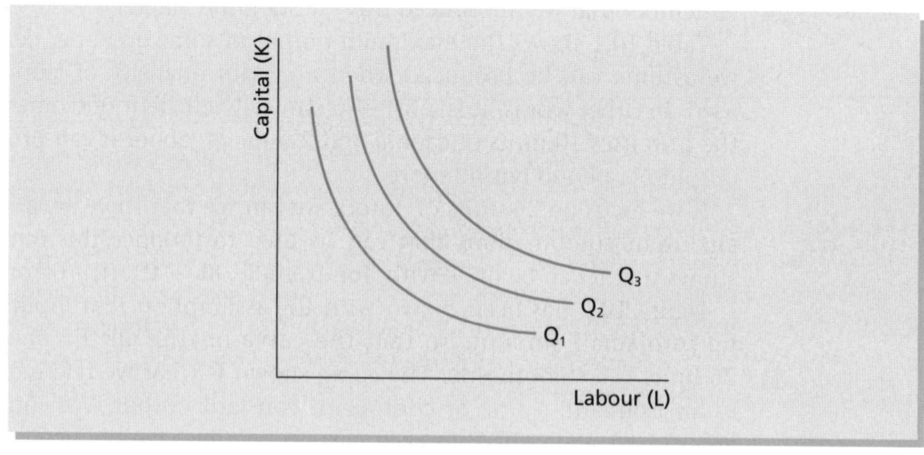

Figure 10.3 **Isoquants for successive levels of outputs**

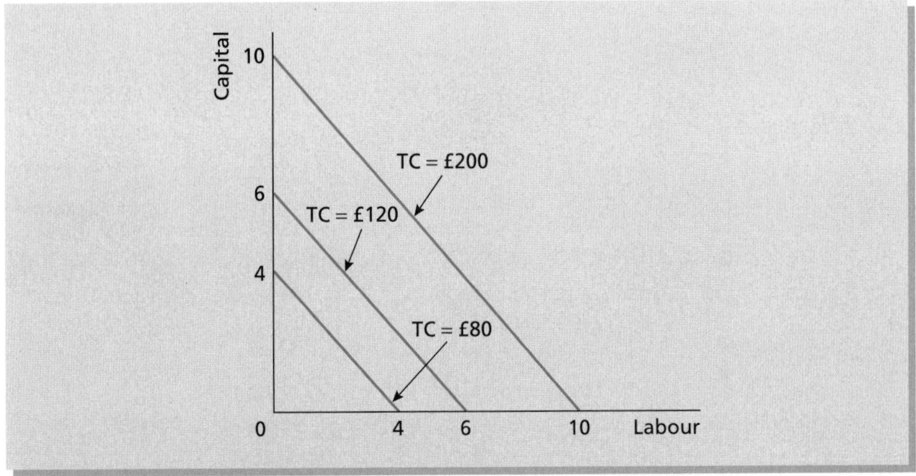

Figure 10.4 **Isocost curves: the relative price of inputs**

Cost efficiency

We have shown that any output level can be produced in a technically efficient way if the point is 'on' the relevant isoquant. The isoquant in Figure 10.2 gives us a number of possible combinations of capital and labour which can be used to produce our 26 units of output. Which particular input combination should be used? To decide this we need information on the money available to buy inputs and the prices of those inputs. Figure 10.4 illustrates three isocost lines. As their name implies, they are simply lines of constant cost; their slope is determined by the relative price of capital and labour. (If you have forgotten how to construct an isocost curve, refer back to Chapter 5.)

see pp. 104–5

The next task is to put the information in Figures 10.3 and 10.4 together. This gives us Figure 10.5 which shows the maximum output that can be produced for a given cost outlay at points A, B and C. Looked at the other way around, these points also show the minimum cost of producing a given level of output.

It will be useful now to examine the link between isoquants and isocosts and long-run costs. The line that links points A, B and C in Figure 10.5(a) is called an *expansion path*. When we move from input space in Figure 10.5(a) to cost space in 10.5(b) it can be seen that this enables us to construct a long-run total cost curve.

Long-run total cost curves do not have to be this particular shape as we have seen in earlier chapters; we have chosen this one for illustrative purposes. Figure 10.5 exhibits constant returns to scale: doubling inputs doubles output. Then total costs increase at a particular rate. If returns to scale are not constant, other shapes for the long-run total cost curve will obtain.

Given the total cost curve of Figure 10.5(b), what would this suggest for the firm's average and marginal cost curve? If total costs increase at a constant rate, average costs – costs per unit of output – must be constant. What of marginal costs? Remember, marginal costs are those which tell us the speed at which the total costs are changing. It is clear that total costs are increasing at a constant

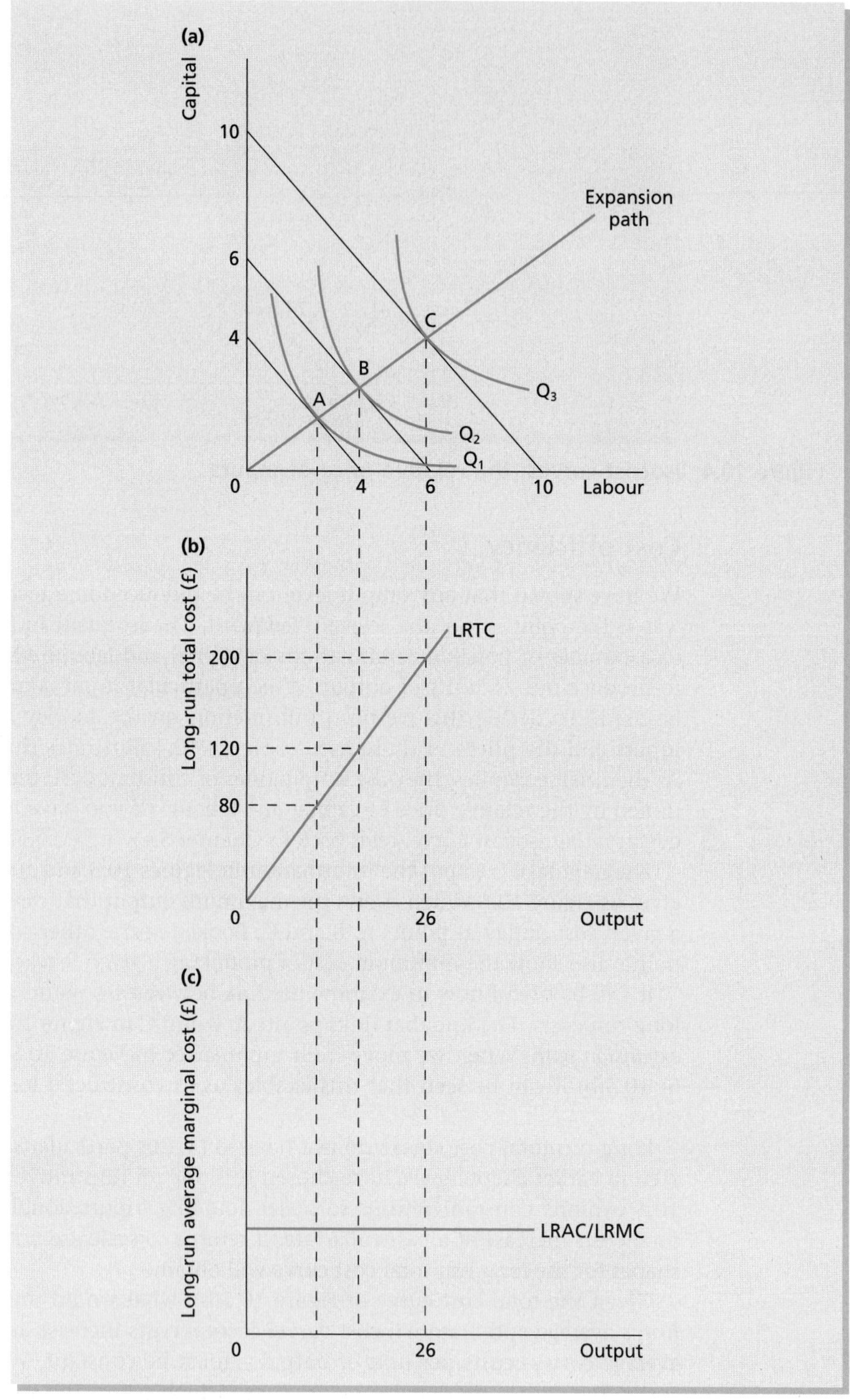

Figure 10.5 **Developing the cost curves**

rate; in other words, marginal cost is constant. What may not be so obvious is that average costs and marginal costs will be the same at all levels of output, as one can see in Figure 10.5(c).

see pp. 101–3

Perhaps the best way of seeing why this must be the case is to remember what we learned in Chapter 5 about graphical techniques for deriving the average cost and the marginal cost from the total. Recall that the slope of the ray from the origin to any point on the total curve gives the average. Average cost is constant at all levels of output. Remember that the slope of the total curve at any point gives the marginal. Marginal cost is not only constant, but at any point on the total cost curve the ray from the origin has the same slope as the slope of the total cost curve. This is what is plotted in Figure 10.5(c).

see pp. 127–8

We could think through what set of isoquants could produce the shapes of long-run average cost curves given in Chapter 6. In particular, what isoquants give rise to the U-shaped long-run average cost curve? We explained the shape of this curve in terms of economies and diseconomies of scale. We can express the same thing in terms of isoquants. If doubling inputs causes output to increase by more than double, average total costs must fall. If doubling inputs causes output to increase by less than double, average costs must rise. Hence the isoquants will come closer together as output increases for low levels. At higher levels of output the isoquants will become progressively further apart.

Now let us return to our efficiency considerations. Points A, B and C are 'least cost' points. In terms of our theme of efficiency they can be defined as cost efficient. Technical efficiency means minimising waste, and cost efficiency means minimising money cost. Note that in Figure 10.5(a) all points on a given isoquant are technically efficient but only one point is also cost efficient. Thus technical efficiency is a necessary but not a sufficient condition for cost efficiency.

We have seen the least cost points form a long-run total cost curve, so it should now be clear that such cost curves presuppose the existence of both technical and cost efficiency. What you should also remember is that this applies not only to the long-run total cost curve but to all the cost curves that you encounter.

All cost curves are in fact boundaries between cost levels that are attainable and those that are not. When looked at in this way we see that it is quite possible for firms to be cost inefficient, that is, to operate above their cost curve. Relatively little attention is paid to such behaviour because economists often assume that where output is produced in a market, firms will wish to maximise their total profits, and cost minimisation is an important precondition for this. You will, however, remember that we questioned the validity of this assumption in Chapter 9.

see pp. 183–202

10.3 Allocative efficiency

The two dimensions of economic efficiency that have been examined so far relate to how goods are produced or, as businesspeople sometimes say, 'doing things right'. Our third and final dimension is rather different. It refers to what

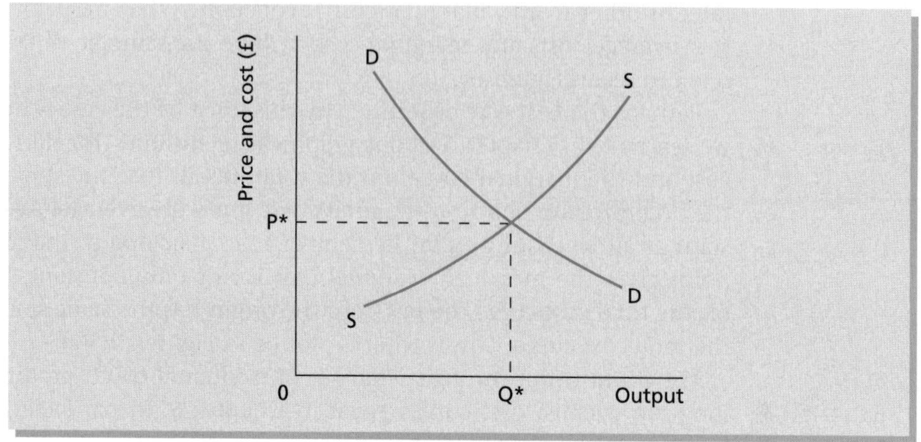

Figure 10.6 An allocatively efficient price and quantity

goods are produced and in what relative quantities, that is, 'doing the right things': there is little point in producing goods in a technically and cost efficient way if nobody wants the goods in question. Even if consumers do want some of the goods, we must still produce them in the right quantities otherwise we will not be making the best use of our scarce inputs. This last dimension is called allocative efficiency.

The 'right' quantities are those that exactly match the tastes of consumers. When does such an exact match occur? Consumers' tastes and preferences lie behind the derivation of individual and market demand curves for commodities. Allocative efficiency will therefore have to involve bringing together cost and demand considerations. Although it was not described at the time in efficiency terms, the equality between demand and supply curves in earlier chapters did exactly this.

The equality between demand and supply will only occur in competitive markets, and so it follows that only competitive markets can achieve allocative efficiency. To see how this is accomplished consider Figure 10.6. The market demand curve DD summarises the maximum prices that consumers are prepared to pay for the different quantities produced. The supply curve SS summarises the minimum prices that producers are prepared to accept for the same quantities. The equilibrium price P* clears the market and satisfies the wishes of both consumers and producers.

see pp. 140–1

What has the equilibrium price P* to do with efficiency? You may recall from Chapter 7 that the supply curve is simply all of the marginal cost curves of the firms added together. Remember, too, that these marginal costs are the same thing as opportunity cost. We also know from this chapter that these costs are the lowest possible because of the existence of technical and cost efficiency. Thus the market clearing price has ensured that the value of the good to consumers is exactly equal to the minimum opportunity cost of producing that particular output. If less were produced then there would be allocative inefficiency because consumers would value additional units of the good above the cost to society of producing the extra units; if there were more being produced then the cost to society would exceed the value to society of the extra output, and once again we would have allocative inefficiency. The argument we have developed makes assumptions which may not be realistic. We consider some of these next.

10.4 Market imperfections

Markets do not always ensure efficiency. We consider three possible circumstances where such efficiency is not likely to be achieved.

Producing too little: monopoly power

see pp. 152–5

If an individual firm faces a downward sloping demand curve for its product then it has a degree of monopoly power. Unlike the competitive firm, it will not lose all its sales if it raises its price, and so it is a price-maker rather than a price-taker. As we saw in Chapter 7, the downward sloping demand curve means that marginal revenue is less than average revenue for any given output, and since all profit-maximising firms will wish to equate marginal revenue with marginal cost, it follows that marginal cost will be below price at the optimum point. This situation is shown in Figure 10.7.

The monopolist's profit maximising price and output (P_m and Q_m) are different from the competitive market's price and output (P_c and Q_c). For reasons we gave in Chapter 7, the value of the underproduction is represented by the shaded area in Figure 10.7, which is often used in economic analysis as a measure of welfare loss. Since the argument which underlies this point is so important for an understanding of efficiency, let us remind ourselves why this is so. The marginal cost curve represents the cost to the firm of producing an extra unit of output, but since it is using up scarce resources, and those resources have an

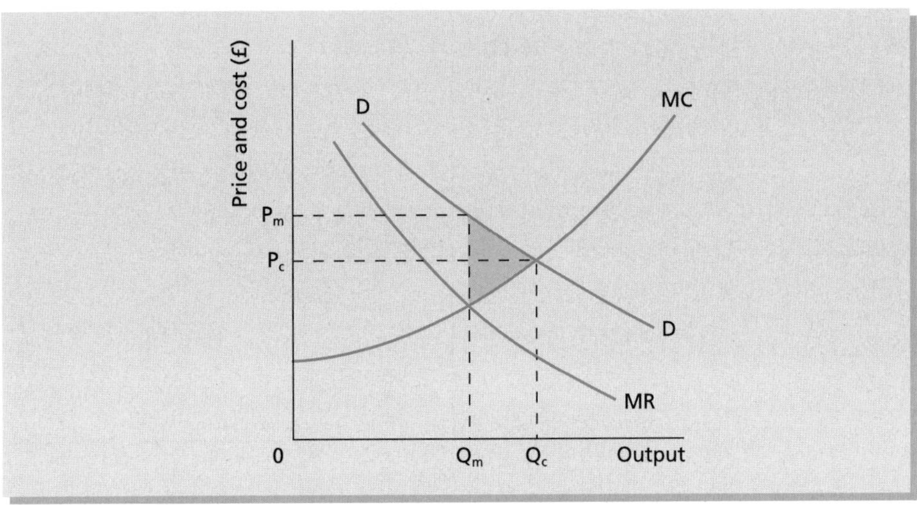

Figure 10.7 **Allocative inefficiency and monopoly power**

opportunity cost, the marginal cost curve also shown is the value of the output which we could have if those resources were used elsewhere. The demand curve you will recall tells us the value we place on the output, so those units between Q_m and Q_c, which the monopolist will not produce, are valued by society at more than their opportunity cost. The value in excess of opportunity cost on this output, a value which society will not be able to enjoy, is given by the shaded area.

The allocative inefficiency has occurred because the price of the good is not the same as the marginal cost or opportunity cost of producing the last unit.

Producing too much: external costs of production

Our second case of market failure and allocative inefficiency has the opposite effect to monopoly power and results in overproduction. Figure 10.8 illustrates the case of a competitive market which generates equilibrium at price P and output Q. However, unlike the situation in Figure 10.7 this does not result in an allocatively efficient outcome because there are external costs of production.

External costs are costs that are external to the firms but internal to society, as exemplified by such things as pollution or congestion. If external costs are a consequence of production then they pose a problem precisely because the firms will only calculate their private marginal costs and ignore the additional external cost when deciding how much to produce.

see pp. 147–8

If the external cost were added to the private marginal cost we would get what is called the social marginal cost of production, the true full cost to society. In Figure 10.8 this true cost to society is given by SMC, the sum of the social marginal cost curves of all firms in the industry. The cost of the overproduction is given by the shaded area. Once again we can see that the allocative inefficiency follows directly from the fact that price and marginal social cost are not the same.

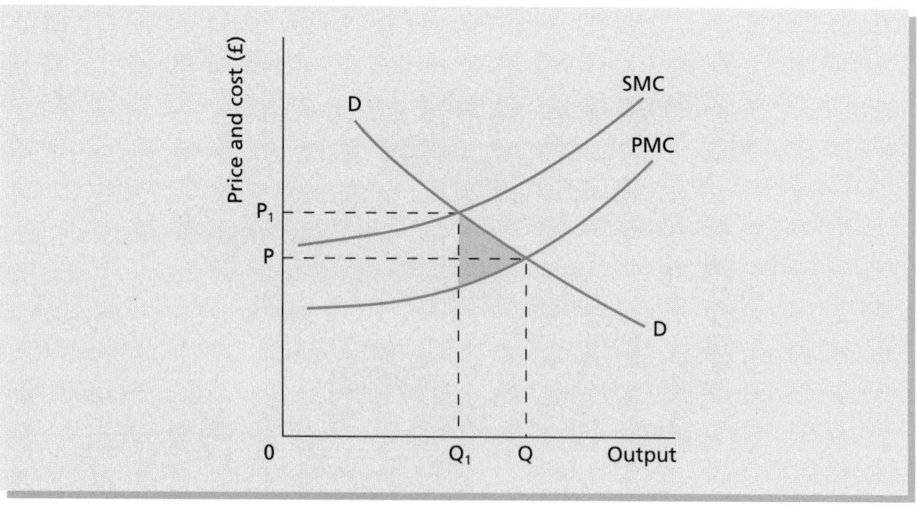

Figure 10.8 **Allocative inefficiency and externalities**

No production at all: public goods

Our final case of allocative inefficiency is provided by what we call public goods. Pure public goods have two very interesting characteristics: they are not depleted by additional users (non-depletion), and it is not possible to exclude anyone from their consumption (non-excludability).

Consider first the characteristic of non-depletion. If *you* use some street-lighting, you do not use it up such that *I* cannot consume it. This contrasts with, say, an apple. If *I* eat it then *you* cannot. The apple is a private good; streetlighting has this characteristic of public goodness which is called non-depletion. Your use of streetlight does not deplete the amount available to the rest of society.

Consider also the characteristic of non-excludability. Most goods are excludable. This enables me to say that I will not allow you to consume the apple, unless you pay me. I can exclude you from its consumption. On the other hand, street lighting is non-excludable: it is wholly impracticable to exclude from its consumption those unwilling to pay for its usage.

Not all goods and services fall neatly into the category of public or private. For example, an uncrowded swimming pool has the characteristic of non-depletion. It is, however, clearly excludable. Such goods and services are called impure public goods. Pure public goods are rare and the 'deterrence' effect of defence expenditure is one of the few examples of a pure public good. However, there is an extensive list of goods which have significant public goods characteristics such as flood control schemes, police services, street lighting and investment in basic research.

The central question that now has to be addressed is, what is the most efficient level of output of the public goods? If we were considering a private good produced under competitive conditions then the benefits would be measured by adding up all the amounts that consumers are prepared to demand at different prices. Similarly, the amounts that producers are prepared to supply would be added up and the point where the market demand and supply curves coincide gives us our optimum level of production.

In the case of a public good we are again involved with balancing the benefits and costs but the procedure is different in some important respects. Figure 10.9 represents the benefits and cost of providing a public good. The MV curves are the marginal valuation of the good for three consumers A, B and C. The MV curves are not quite the same as demand curves. They do represent the value that consumers place on different quantities of the public good but this valuation is not measured by the price that they are prepared to pay. Since nobody can be excluded from enjoying the benefits of the good it follows that they do not and cannot pay a price at 'the point of delivery'.

Obviously, there is no market for the public good and for this reason it is difficult to measure the benefits even though they exist. There is an additional reason why benefits are difficult to measure: even if all consumers were asked, they would have an interest in understating their true desire for the public good. This understatement is called the free-rider problem. Free-riders exist because of non-excludability, that is, if everyone can enjoy the good regardless

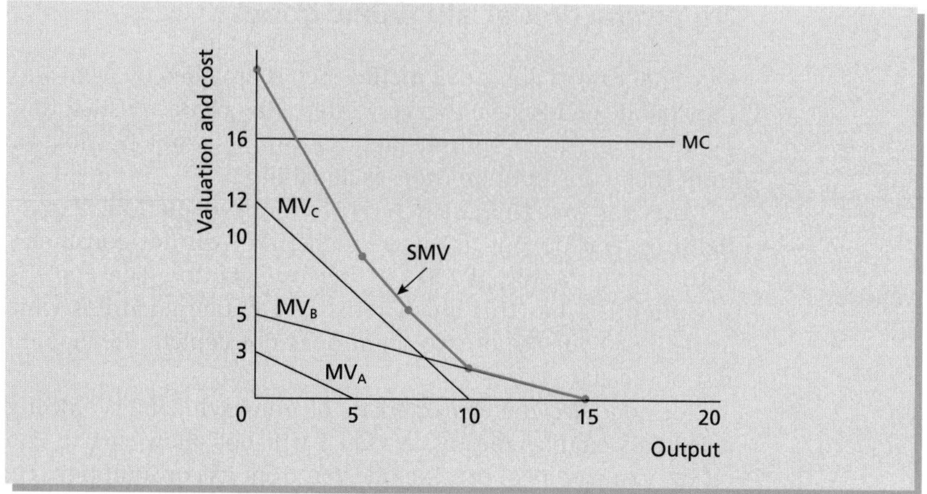

Figure 10.9 **An allocatively efficient level of flood control provision**

of whether they pay for it then there is a strong incentive either to avoid paying altogether or to understate the true amount that you are prepared to pay.

Let us assume that the public good in Figure 10.9 is flood control provision. Our three consumers live in a low-lying area in East Anglia that is prone to flooding by the sea. We assume that the MV curves represent their true valuation of protection from flooding, and the MC curve represents the cost of erecting the sea wall that would ensure protection (for simplicity the marginal cost of building it is assumed to be constant).

We are now in a position to define the efficient level of provision of flood control. In Figure 10.9, we sum each consumer's valuation *vertically* to get the curve SMV (social marginal valuation). Allocative efficiency occurs at the optimal point E and quantity Q* where social marginal benefits equate with marginal cost of provision. You may be puzzled by the fact that the SMV curve was obtained by vertical rather than horizontal summation. We sum vertically because the consumers are not getting different units of the public good at a given value (horizontal summation), but have simultaneously a collective value for the same non-rival public good (vertical summation).

Additional consumers could enjoy the flood control service at no extra cost. In other words, the marginal or opportunity cost of supplying additional users is zero, and since we know that, for any good, allocative efficiency is maximised when price is equated with opportunity cost, it follows that price should be zero.

The above analysis has shown us that we can define allocative efficiency for public goods but it does not explain whether or how they will be produced. Figure 10.9 shows the valuation curves for each consumer well below the cost that would be incurred if the sea wall were actually constructed. This means that the wall may not be constructed even though the social marginal valuation indicates that it would be allocatively efficient to do so.

The production of public goods depends, not surprisingly, upon consumers acting collectively. Getting people together and obtaining sound agreements on these matters is both costly and time consuming. Although it may not always be necessary for provision to be undertaken by local or national governments, it is easy to see why it usually is done in this way.

10.5 Government policy on efficiency

We have seen that, under perfect competition, both cost and allocative efficiency are realised. Moreover, even under monopoly the drive to maximise total profits was assumed to promote cost efficiency. This represents the intellectual basis for those governments that advocate the market mechanism as an integral part of what is known as industrial policy.

Since 1979 successive Conservative governments in the UK have had a fairly consistent approach to the promotion of efficiency in the production of goods and services. The main focus of attention has been on the market mechanism. Privatisation and deregulation have simply transferred publicly owned resources to the private sector, while initiatives such as hospital trusts and locally managed schools have been created in the belief that economic efficiency is enhanced if decision-takers have the discretion to manage funds themselves.

Our analysis of the causes of allocative inefficiency focused on those areas characterised by market failure. It is reasonable to expect that such areas will be of interest to governments, especially Conservative governments that have the market mechanism as the centrepiece of their industrial policy.

Market failure because of monopoly power has traditionally been dealt with by competition policy which covers restrictive trade practices, dominant firm monopolies and mergers that might result in a dominant firm monopoly. Such policy is administered by the Office of Fair Trading whose director-general has the power independent of government to examine restrictive practices and dominant firm monopolies. Mergers are the exceptions to this procedure and have to be referred to the Office of Fair Trading by the Secretary for Trade and Industry.

Like monopolies, mergers and restrictive practices, our second and third categories of market failure, externalities and public goods will also be the focus of government policy and ultimately of government expenditure. How is economic efficiency assessed and promoted in these areas? Central to this question is the work of the National Audit Office (NAO).

10.6 National Audit Office: getting value for money

As we said earlier there are two facets to the NAO's work: financial audit and value for money audit. It is value for money audit that concerns us here.

Value for money (VFM) has three elements: economy, effectiveness and efficiency.

Table 10.2 **Value for money of a hospital building programme**

Economy	The tendering, contract and project control procedures to establish how far the hospital and associated facilities had been built to specification, on time and at lowest achievable cost or within approved cost limits.
Efficiency	Utilisation of wards, beds, theatres and equipment; medical and administrative staff allocations and mix; integration of services; management and resource allocation systems, etc.
Effectiveness	Results in terms of, for example, reductions in patient waiting lists, increases in operations performed, improved diagnostic and treatment rates and (ultimately) improvements in health and quality of life, reduced mortality rates, etc.

Source: © National Audit Office

Each of these elements is defined by the NAO in the following way:[2]

- *Economy* is concerned with minimising the cost of resource acquired or used, having regard to appropriate quality.
- *Efficiency* is concerned with the relationship between the output of goods and the resources used to produce them. How far is maximum output achieved for a given input, or minimum input used for a given output?
- *Effectiveness* is concerned with the relationship between the intended results and the actual results of projects. How successfully do outputs of goods and services or other results achieve policy objectives?

Although the NAO only uses the word 'efficiency' once, it should be clear from the detailed definitions that the '3Es' are nothing other than cost efficiency (economy), technical efficiency (efficiency) and allocative efficiency (effectiveness). In other words, the NAO is attempting to achieve for the public sector's spending what markets are supposed to achieve for the private sector.

Table 10.2 summarises the NAO's own explanation of how these concepts might relate to a particular project. Notice again how these areas are ones in which, if a market were operative, the market itself might be able to achieve these goals.

In order to understand better how the NAO operates we now look at three areas of expenditure to see how their assessment work is done.

10.7 Purchasing defence equipment

An important area of expenditure for the National Audit Office is that of defence expenditure. The *Report of the Ministry Initiatives in Defence Procurement* (1991) examines the procedures for purchasing equipment, stores and services for the Armed Forces. In the five years prior to this report, over £40 billion had been spent on defence equipment and the NAO was evaluating the more commercial approach that had been adopted by the Ministry of Defence and the private firms that supply the equipment.

Figure 10.10 defines the four ways for placing a contract. The essence of the commercial approach is the introduction of an element of competition as a mechanism for ensuring cost efficiency. This is in marked contrast to the cost-plus-percentage system (cost-plus) which had inadequate incentives for cost minimisation and led to some waste of taxpayers' money.

The NAO assessed how far the commercial system had been introduced, what cost savings had been made, and what might be done in the future.

Figure 10.10 shows the rising trend of contracts placed competitively: a rise from 36 per cent in 1982/83 to 67 per cent by value in 1990/91. In the same period, cost-plus contracts had fallen from 16 per cent to 4 per cent by value.

The evaluation of cost savings was made by examining the figures from the government's *Statement of the Defence Estimates*, 1988. Six projects valued at £2 billion yielded savings of £0.25 billion when put to competition. Net savings of £0.35 billion were made from post-tender negotiation and net savings of £0.25 billion were estimated over the following twenty years through improved reliability and maintainability.

An interesting by-product of the commercial approach was said to be the sharpening of the competitive edge of the UK defence industry which had improved its position in the world league of defence equipment manufacturers.

The report concluded that, for the future, efficiency could be enhanced by the extension of competitive principles into non-competitive tendering. What this means is that, as far as is practicable, procurement arrangements for non-competitive contracts should determine the price before the contract is placed. Rather surprisingly this was often not the case for existing contracts, and in 10 per cent of cases contracts were still unpriced when all work had been completed. Calculating an appropriate price is often difficult because of the nature of the non-competitive environment. The NAO stressed the importance of obtaining 'external yardsticks of cost' wherever possible.

Since 1998 the Ministry of Defence has been working under a process known as 'Smart Acquisition' intended to enable the department to buy military equipment more cheaply, and faster. By 2000 the NAO was still critical. All but two of the most expensive projects are an average of four years late and then cost overruns were substantial. Two years later, however, the NAO reported that performance on time and cost had improved and the rate of time slippage was lower. However, there were problems measuring the extent of the benefits that Smart Acquisition had brought. (See the annual Ministry of Defence: *Major Projects Report*.)

The relevance of these reports to our discussion of efficiency is that although government expenditure relates to goods which are not produced by private firms competing with one another, arrangements can be found to mimic the efficiency-enhancing effect of the market by a partial introduction of market forces.

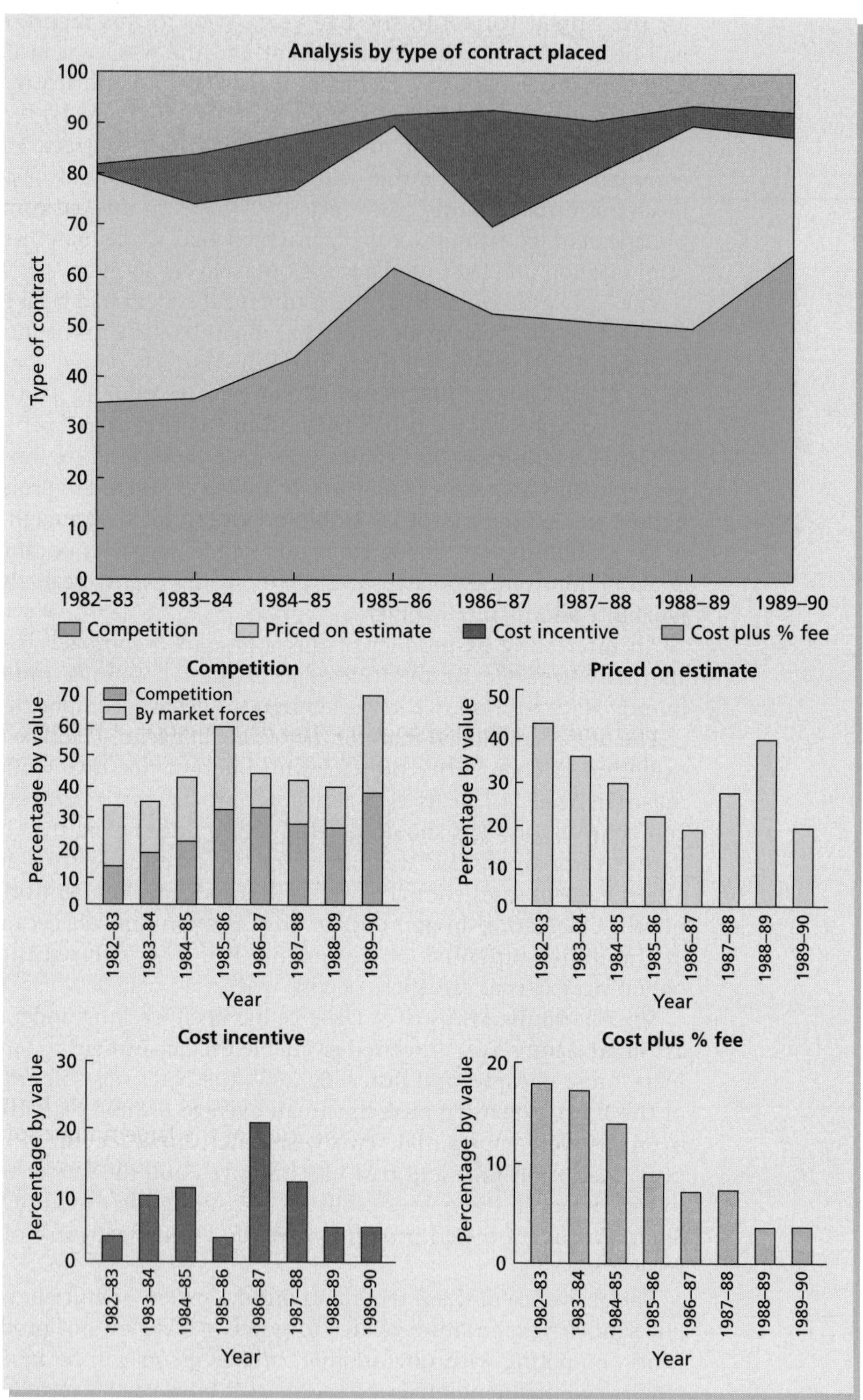

Figure 10.10 **Proportion of contracts awarded by type, 1982–91**

Source: © National Audit Office

10.8 Coastal and inland defences in England

We look here at defences against coastal erosion and also defences against the flooding of rivers inland. The report relates directly to our earlier analysis of flood control as a public good.

The 1992 NAO report on coastal defences in England covered both of the categories of work to protect the English coastline, namely:

- Sea defences (including tidal defences) to protect against the flooding of low-lying areas. These are usually built by the nine English regional offices of the National Rivers Authority (NRA).
- Coast protection works to prevent the erosion of land and encroachment by the sea. These are usually carried out by 89 maritime district councils.

You may remember that the principles underlying the optimum provision of flood control were straightforward, namely to equate social marginal valuation with the marginal cost of providing the good. This case study is an excellent illustration of the practical problems of applying the theory to the real world.

The NAO employed a team of economists and engineering and environmental consultants to assist them in examining three dimensions of the good:

1 *The performance of coastal defences and the storm tide warning service.* The NAO found that at the three NRA regions they visited there was no system of post-project appraisal to assess the performance of schemes against intended standards of protection and the severity of events experienced.

   In addition to physical defences against the sea, coastal defence also involves national and local flood warnings so that suitable precautions can be taken to minimise damage. Coordinating the various agencies responsible poses operational problems and there was scope for improvements via the introduction of performance indicators.

2 *Planning coordination and financing of coastal defences.* Coastal defence relies on sound planning to ensure that the more urgent works have priority and that the funds are available to carry out the work. (Economic theory does not spend much time on these matters, which are usually studied in such disciplines as social and public administration. Real world problems often involve a number of disciplines which is why teams of experts are frequently assembled to deal with them.) The coordination of the large number of agencies administering coastal defence gives rise to what economists call transactions costs. Transactions costs are often reduced if the transactions in question occur within rather than between agencies. Not surprisingly, therefore, the NAO recommended a reduction in the number of agencies involved with sea defences. It also advocated reducing transactions costs by more effective transmission of information about financial arrangements.

3 *Engineering, economic and environmental appraisal of coastal defence schemes.* Of the three dimensions considered in this report, this is without doubt the one that is of most interest and relevance to the economist. Coastal defence is a public good that involves questions of technical efficiency, which is why

engineers need to advise on such important matters as water levels, erosion damage and project control. The reader may remember that the production isoquant in Figure 10.2 was derived on the assumption that we were not wasting scarce resources by combining resources in ways that engineers would not approve.

After the engineers have considered the practicable options, the NAO was concerned that relevant costs and benefits should be identified and correctly valued. Our model of optimal public good provision in Figure 10.9 depicted marginal valuation curves for each consumer and the marginal cost curve of providing the good. In reality there are many reasons why the data necessary to measure accurately these benefits and costs are difficult and costly to obtain. Some of the main reasons are:

- The free-rider problem may result in consumers understating their true willingness to pay for the good.
- There are physical and logistical difficulties in obtaining direct information on preferences.
- Many costs and benefits are intangible, for example environmental or amenity impacts, risk to life, health and social effects of stress resulting from flooding. It is difficult to estimate what people feel those benefits are worth.
- The calculation of benefits and costs of coastal defence has to take account of the passage of time. The costs occur immediately. The benefits accrue over a period of many years. Estimating benefits accruing many years into the future raises additional difficulties. We examine this problem in Chapter 14.

see pp. 301–4

Allowing for the difficulty of measurement, the government requires that schemes demonstrate a predicted benefit/cost ratio of 1 or greater to qualify for grant aid; in other words, expected benefits must exceed the costs. Figure 10.11 provides data on these ratios.

What does such a benefit/cost ratio imply? To the extent that the number is greater than unity, the benefit to society outweighs the scheme's opportunity cost. Almost all schemes, according to NAO, were very worthwhile, even though a market would not have provided them.

However, NAO clearly felt that government failure also constitutes a problem. The conclusions of the NAO consultants regarding the eight schemes examined included the following:

- Maintenance costs were wrongly excluded for three schemes.
- Property damage was generally well addressed but recreational, traffic or services benefits were not adequately assessed in any of the schemes.
- There was confusion over the treatment of benefits to local tourism and caravan sites.
- Significant problems arose with double-counting of benefits for one scheme.
- Agricultural benefits featured in three of the schemes but were properly assessed in only one case.

In the early years of this century there has been an alarming increase in the amount of damage done by the flooding of rivers across Europe. As with coastal defences there are elements of the public good problem here. Individuals may

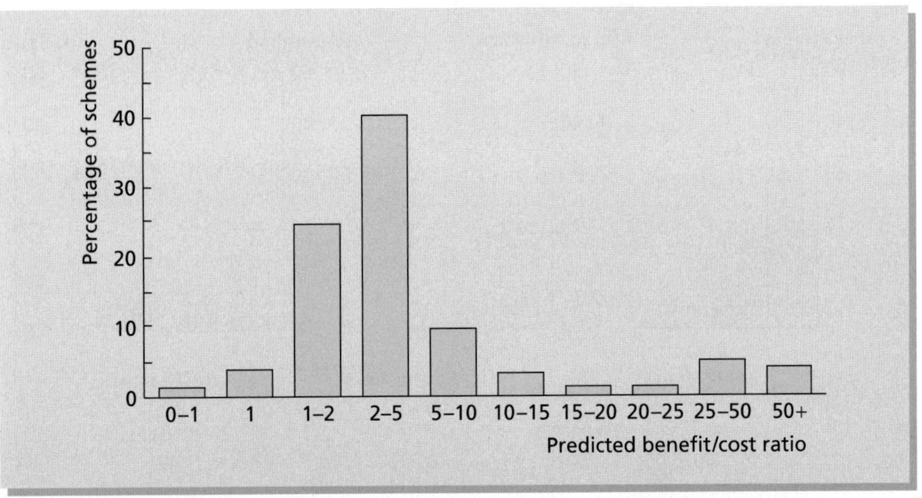

Figure 10.11 Range of predicted benefit/cost ratios for coastal defence schemes, 1986/87 to 1990/91

Source: © National Audit Office

be able to insure against the damage done to their own property but the market will not efficiently handle the provision of flood control measures. In 2001 the NAO reported on such defences.

It estimated that currently there is an investment of around £400 million annually on inland and coastal defences. This expenditure reduces damage annually by around £2 billion and thus represents good value. However, a survey of the Environment Agency's flood defences showed that around 40 per cent of structures are in a poor or very poor state and, as Figure 10.12 shows, there are substantial regional variations. This suggests that although an underprovision of such defences would occur if left to the market, this also tends to happen when left to the state. Marginal increases in investment by the state would yield high returns in terms of flood damage reduction.

10.9 Innovation

For our final example we turn to the NAO's 1995 value for money report on the government's support for innovation.[3] Innovation has, perhaps, less obvious public good characteristics than defence or flood control, and is interesting because the new products and processes that it might generate seem at first to be ideally suited to private sector provision (the reportedly large profits to be obtained by such things as genetic engineering come readily to mind).

Although there are many successful innovation and research-based firms in the private sector, there is nonetheless a strong case to be made for government intervention to rectify instances of market failure. The Department for Trade and Industry's 'design process' for evaluating whether or not to support a given

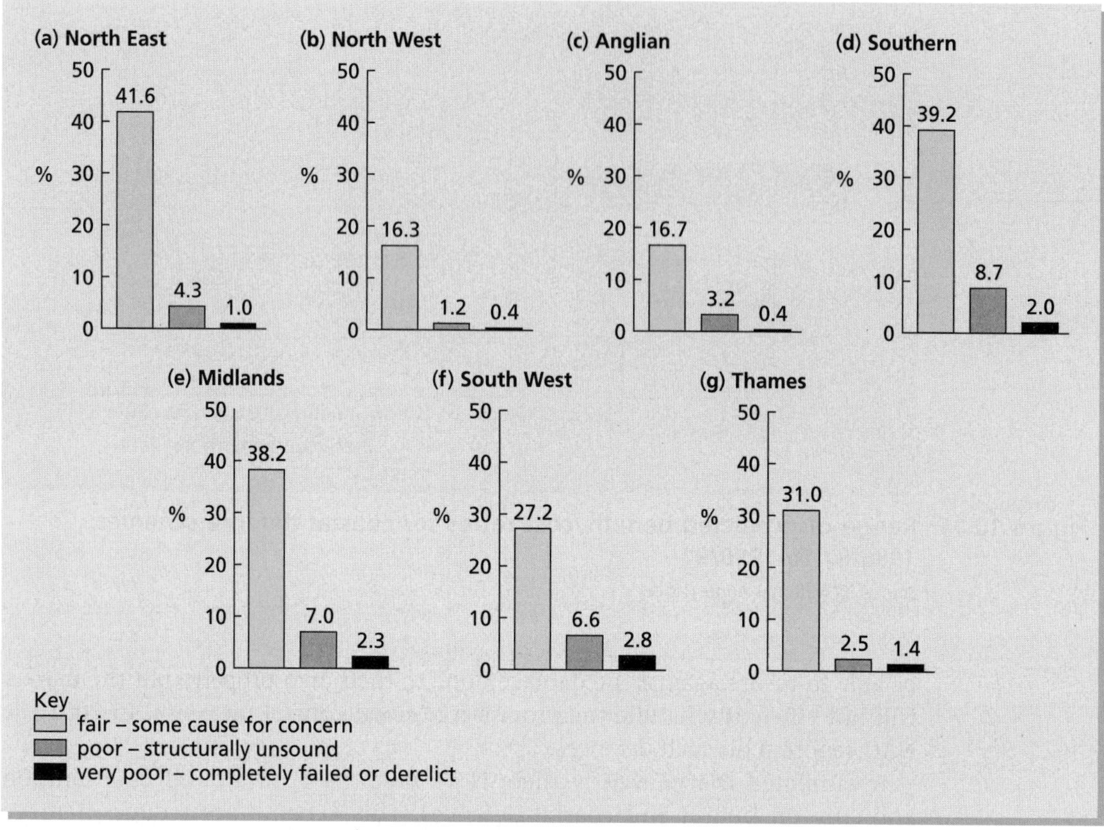

Figure 10.12 **NAO assessment of UK flood defences 2001, showing percentage of structures in a given condition**

Source: © National Audit Office

scheme has, as its first stage, the requirement to 'demonstrate existence of significant market failure'.

On closer inspection, innovation can be seen to have significant public good characteristics because once a new discovery has been made, its use by one firm does not reduce its availability to another (non-depletion). Further, it is difficult to prevent other firms from taking advantage of your successful but costly innovation once it becomes known (non-excludability). Therefore, while much innovation will undoubtedly take place through private investment, society will not get as much as would be socially beneficial because firms know that they may not be able to appropriate all of the benefits of their efforts. The DTI tries to combat this allocative inefficiency by providing direct financial support for selected schemes. Figure 10.13 summarises these schemes.

Note that this case is different from defence and flood control in that the NAO is not examining the direct provision of something by a publicly owned agency. Instead it is examining the way in which the taxpayer's money is being spent on support for private firms to develop new products and processes that we will want to buy.

Technology development	**LINK**	A multidepartmental scheme which supports industrially relevant collaborative research between industry and academia
	SMART	A single small company grant scheme which aims to stimulate innovative and marketable products, run on the basis of an annual competition (Small Firms Merit Award for Research and Technology)
	SPUR	A single small and medium-sized company grant scheme designed to help firms to develop new products and processes (Support for Products Under Research)
	RIN	A single small company grant scheme for firms in designated geographical areas to develop commercially viable innovative products (Regional Innovation Grants)
Technology access	**Biotechnology Means Business**	A scheme which disseminates information to potential industrial users about the commercial potential offered
	Manufacturing Intelligence	A scheme which disseminates information about the application and operational benefits of knowledge-based computer systems
	Teaching Company Scheme	A multidepartmental scheme which facilitates the transfer of technology and skills from academia to business
	Managing in the 90s	A scheme which disseminates information on management best practice, particularly on the need to innovate and manage change effectively

Figure 10.13 **Summary of schemes examined by the National Audit Office**
Source: © National Audit Office

Evaluating the value for money of the eight different schemes in Figure 10.13 is obviously difficult. In principle, the technology development schemes were a little easier because the NAO could focus specifically on the firms receiving the grants. Two rather ingenious measures were derived for these four schemes: 'additionality' and 'dead weight', which are shown in Figure 10.14. An activity is additional if it would not have taken place in the absence of DTI support. Dead weight is the difference between the actual funding received and the minimum necessary to encourage firms to proceed with the project. Thus, as the words tend to suggest, greater additionality for any given scheme is a positive measure, while greater dead weight is negative.

So far we have shown that the NAO has derived information on half of the schemes in which it tried to measure the number of projects encouraged and their relative cost. The final assessment of the value for money of all eight schemes was a complex process which combined an assessment not only of whether costs had been minimised but also whether innovation had been maximised. The results are given in Figure 10.15. The higher the score, the better the scheme, so that the Teaching Company Scheme ranks as most successful, with LINK the least successful.

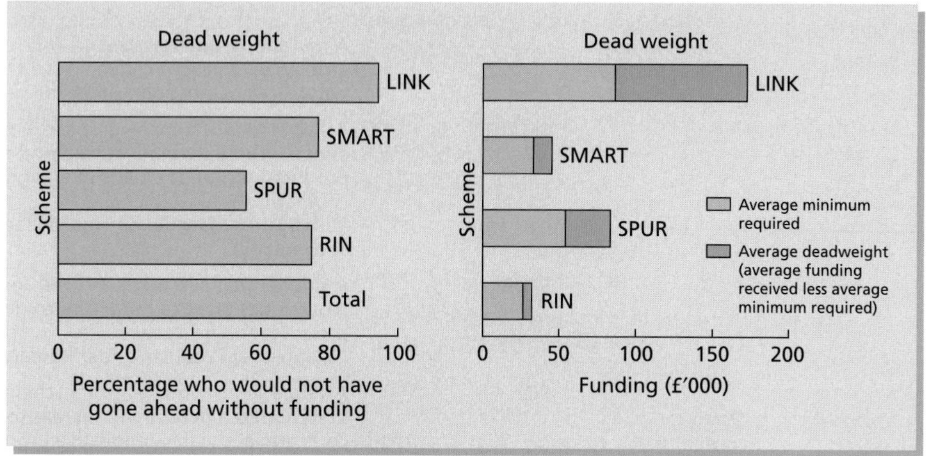

Figure 10.14 Additionality and dead weight in the technology development schemes

Source: © National Audit Office

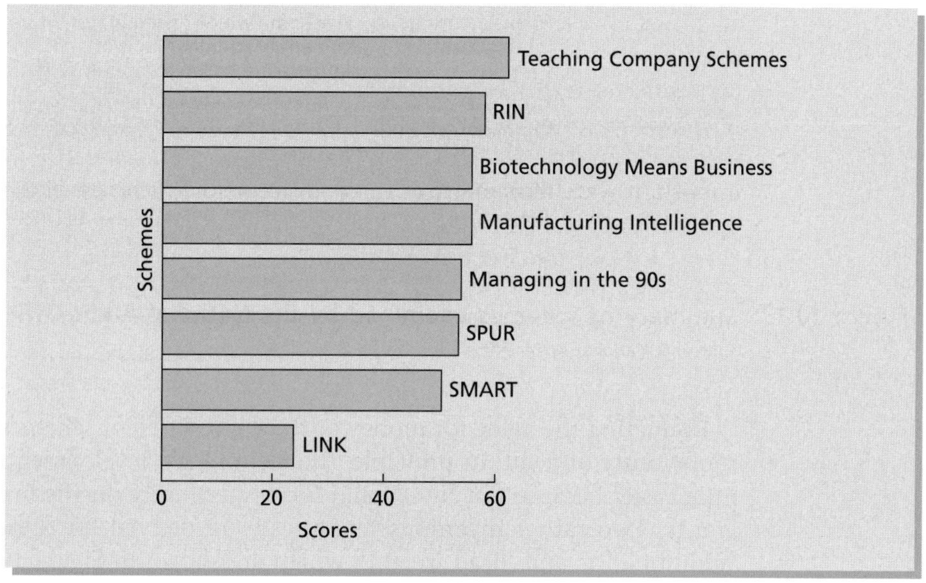

Figure 10.15 Comparative scores of the eight schemes

Source: © National Audit Office

10.10 Conclusion

This chapter has identified three dimensions that underlie the concept of economic efficiency. When firms operate in the private sector the assumption of self-interest in the form of profit maximisation is the mechanism for encouraging efficient operation. We have seen how, under certain conditions, such efficiency is unlikely to be achieved in the private sector without government intervention.

Since 1979, government policy has attempted to promote efficiency either by privatising previously publicly controlled enterprises, or, where this was not feasible, as in the case of defence, by the partial introduction of market competition. Some public goods, such as coastal defence, are not even amenable to partial influence of the market, and under these circumstances institutional arrangements have to be kept under constant review to ensure value for taxpayers' money. It would appear that the NAO has had some success here. The costs to the UK taxpayer of running the NAO in the early years of the new century are around £50bn each year. In their recent annual reports, they show savings of over eight times that amount. We have considered just three areas in which there are reports but each year there are many reports covering many areas. The range covers, among others, central government, national defence, education, employment, health and the environment. The savings made as a result of the activities of the NAO are probably greater than the figures above suggest. This is partly because their work improves the quality of service on occasion as well as reducing costs. It is also partly because the identification of poor practice in one area can be applied to other areas. For example, following a recent examination of the efficiency of hospital catering, a letter was issued by the National Health Service executive endorsing the NAO report and asking all hospitals to review their services. This would probably have resulted in further cost savings. The concept of value for money employed by this increasingly important watchdog matches those concepts of efficiency which we have developed throughout the book and forms the basis of its attempts to see that we do get good value for government expenditure.

It should now be clear that markets are not a guarantee of efficient resource usage and allocation – but neither are governments.

CHAPTER SUMMARY

1. **Efficiency is a multidimensional concept embracing technical, cost and allocative efficiency.**
2. **A business is technically efficient if it is producing on its isoquant.**
3. **Cost efficiency requires producing some given output at the least possible cost where the isoquant is tangential to the isocost curve.**
4. **Allocative efficiency means optimising consumer welfare where MC = D.**
5. **Public goods are those which are non-rival, non-excludable and consumed equally by all.**
6. **Without government intervention, monopoly power tends to lead to less than optimum output, and external costs to more than optimum output.**
7. **In the absence of government intervention the level of a public good produced may well be zero.**
8. **If society's welfare is to be maximised, efficiency is required for the public sector as well as the private sector.**

Questions for discussion

*Guidance to the answers for the **asterisked** numbered questions is available to students on the website for the book at **www.booksites.net/heather**.*

1* Distinguish carefully between 'non-rival' and 'non-excludable'.

2 In terms of Figure 10.7, why is the argument about allocative efficiency expressed as an argument about marginal output rather than the degree of abnormal profit?

3* Does the level of profit not matter when discussing allocative efficiency?

4 What problems will services such as street-lighting create for a market system?

5* Public goods provide a strong argument for state ownership of assets. Would you categorise the following as public goods?
(a) Art galleries.
(b) Police services.
(c) The weather forecast on TV.

6 Is there any point in analysing whether resources such as flood control have been used efficiently? Should we not be deciding whether to invest in flood control at all? How could we do that?

7* Can a market system ever produce public goods?

8 In recent years the government has experimented with an 'internal market' in health care. What do you think this means? Are the reforms beneficial?

9* The market demand for a private good is simply the horizontal sum of the individual demand curves for that good. Why is this not a legitimate procedure for finding the market demand curve of a public good?

10 Should a higher or lower proportion of society's output be allocated on a market basis?

Websites

The National Audit Office has a website listing all of its reports. One can look at a summary at a full version of any of them at:

www.nao.gov.uk

Notes

1 NAO Annual Report, 1991, p. 4.

2 *A Framework for Value for Money Audits*, National Audit Office, 1984, p. 4.

3 *The Department of Trade and Industry's Support for Innovation*, HMSO, 1995.

11 Labour markets

Trade unions: *labour market manipulators?*

(with Rob Thomas)

CHAPTER OVERVIEW

To some people, trade unions are crucial protectors of the weak. To others, they force up wage rates to unrealistic levels and contribute to unemployment. What role do trade unions have in a modern economy? How successful are they in raising the real wages of their members? To what extent do they manipulate labour markets?

In this chapter we review

- Indifference curves
- Cartels

We introduce

- Demand for labour
- Wage rate determination

11.1 Introduction

As we have already seen, market forces play a crucial role in determining the prices of products. Where a large number of suppliers and consumers operate, supply and demand determines an equilibrium price. However, we saw in Chapter 7 how suppliers, given certain conditions, might be able to cooperate in order to raise price above that equilibrium.

see pp. 152–4

In this chapter we consider the determination by market forces of the price of labour services. We also consider the extent to which labour can combine into trade unions to raise wages above the level that would be determined by uncoordinated market forces.

Trade unions are often seen as institutions designed to correct or reverse the unequal relationship between the asset-poor employee and the asset-rich employer. The Conservative governments in the UK after 1979 viewed unions as a distortion (or friction, as economists often call it) in the working of market forces. These administrations passed a large amount of legislation to curb the power of unions, directly via their activities in the marketplace, and indirectly by changing the democratic processes within unions. Much of this legislation remains in force to the present day.

In this chapter we investigate the nature and role of unions and then develop an analysis using economic principles in order to assess their impact on market pricing, known in this case as pay or wages. These two terms can be used interchangeably to indicate the financial remuneration received by an employee, be this in the form of a wage or salary, with or without fringe benefits such as a company car, company health insurance or employer's pension contributions. The conclusions we reach can help us to understand how wages are determined. It will also help us later to consider some key macroeconomic concepts such as unemployment and inflation.

11.2 Trade unions and industrial relations in the UK

A widely quoted definition of a trade union is 'a continuous association of wage-earners for the purpose of maintaining or improving the conditions of their working lives'.[1] It is not always a *voluntary* relationship because there are circumstances where there is coercion by fellow workers to join. The term 'wage-earner' is no longer strictly correct, as unions recruit employers, particularly the self-employed. It can be argued that the aim stated in the definition is too restrictive because unions pursue other causes: full employment (not just of union members) and social issues both domestically and internationally. However, as our focus is on unions in labour markets, the definition can be accepted as a first step.

Types of trade unions

Unions differ in many respects, including structure, rules of membership and recruitment policies. This last aspect has in the past been used as the basis for classifying unions: craft unions recruit only from a particular skilled occupation; industrial unions from an industry, whilst towards the end of the nineteenth century, there developed general unions ready to recruit from a range of occupations and industries.

Unionism in the UK, as indicated in Table 11.1, has continuously declined since 1979. Factors ranging from the economic environment and changing structure of employment, to government policy and cultural attitudes have been proposed as causes of the fall in union membership. Union membership 'density', the proportion of the labour force who are members of unions, varies markedly between countries, with the UK having by no means the highest union density in the EU (see Table 11.2). Faced with the decline in membership in the UK, unions have merged so that average union size has increased and the large unions have not suffered a reduction in their relative importance (Table 11.3).

Table 11.1 Number of trade unions and trade union membership in the UK, 1979–2000[a]

Year	*Number of unions at end of year*	*Total membership at end of year ('000)*	*Percentage change in union membership since previous year*
1979	453	13,289	+1.3
1980–84[b]	405	11,775	–3.8
1985–89[b]	332	10,474	–1.6
1990–94[b]	265	9,112	–4.0
1995–98	234	7,907	–1.5
1999	218	7,843	+0.5
2000	206	7,640	–2.5

[a] Compiled from returns to the Certification Officer for Trade Unions and Employers' Associations
[b] Annual average

Source: adapted from *Employment Gazette*, various editions

Table 11.2 Trade union density in selected EU member states

	% among wage and salary earners	
	Density (%)	*Year*
Sweden	91.1	1994
Denmark	80.4	1994
Belgium	51.9	1995
Ireland	48.9	1993
Italy	44.1	1994
UK	32.9	1995
Germany	28.9	1995
Netherlands	25.6	1995
Spain	18.6	1994
France	9.1	1995

Source: adapted from International Labour Organisation, *World Labour Report 1997–98*, Table 1.2

Trade union structure

In the union merger process unions have tended to look beyond their traditional craft/industry/white collar recruitment. The general union, with sections for particular groups of members, has come to dominate.

This structure can be important. First, the sections or divisions in large unions help to retain a sense of loyalty via a unity of purpose within the subgroup. Second, the structure helps to continue the long-held principle of democracy in unions. This has been an important factor in shaping union structure so that members' views are heard and acted upon. Most unions have some form of local organisation based around the role of the shop steward who represents

Table 11.3 **Relative size of UK trade unions in 1979 and 2000**[a]

Number of members	*Percentage of unions*		*Percentage of membership of all unions*	
	1979	*2000*	*1979*	*2000*
Under 1,000	53.7	49.6	0.5	0.4
1,000–9,999	27.6	26.9	3.0	2.6
10,000–49,999	9.5	13.8	8.0	10.1
50,000–99,999	3.3	2.6	6.9	4.6
100,000 and more	5.9	7.1	81.6	82.2

[a] Compiled from returns to the Certification Officer for Trade Unions and Employers' Associations
Source: adapted from *Employment Gazette*, various editions

a group of members working for the same employer. There is also likely to be a local branch with meetings attended by members from different local employers. In the case of larger firms, the branch may only be for members in that company. From this local level, information and views are passed up and down a regional hierarchy, which stretches to the national executive of the union, its general secretary and the ultimate rule-making body, which is usually the annual conference. A generalised structure such as this does not apply to all unions, but it clearly displays the political nature of unions, a topic to which we will return.

Structure of collective bargaining

The different levels in the structure of unions tend to be mirrored by the levels at which collective bargaining occurs in the UK. National, or multi-employer, agreements negotiated between the union leadership and an employers' association representing employers in an industry are largely concerned with setting basic pay rates and standard weekly hours; bargaining at the individual company level will supplement the national agreement or, in the case of large companies which do not belong to an employers' association, will replace national bargaining.

However, multi-employer bargaining has decreased in importance over the last two decades in the UK, in part because it cannot always take into account the particular circumstances of a plant/office or even of a part (known as the 'shopfloor') of the local operation. Bargaining at these levels can focus on working practices and incentive payments to meet local needs. Exactly what is negotiated at which level in this decentralised bargaining structure is a matter of historical precedent, though surveys carried out during the 1980s indicate a tendency to formalise industrial relations. Written procedures for dealing with grievances have become more prevalent and these have sought to move bargaining away from the shopfloor level.

11.3 Economic analysis of trade unions

The economic nature of trade unions

Embarking on the economic nature of trade unions immediately brings us to their dual identity. On the one hand, a union operates to supply services which are demanded by members; the services range from bargaining to legal advice and representation, and in recent years have included discount cards and favourable credit terms. Unions compete both with each other to get members to 'buy' via subscription (competition amongst member unions of the Trades Union Congress (TUC) was limited by the Bridlington Rules until legislation in 1993 made them unenforceable) and with other providers of the services in the public and private sectors. In this respect, the union is like a product market firm, except that it would be difficult to justify the assumption that unions seek to maximise profits.

On the other hand, while a union's behaviour in labour markets is often portrayed as being similar to that of a monopoly firm supplying, in this case, labour, the analogy is difficult to sustain. A union does not supply labour services in the same way as a product market firm; the individual member owns and supplies his/her labour services. Therefore, when combining with others in a union, individuals are doing so in order to exploit their combined market power. This is not so much a monopoly as a cartel.[2]

see pp. 168–70

The problem of a cartel, as we saw in Chapter 8, is that while all the participants gain by agreeing to limit supply, it is in the interests of one participant to break the agreement and increase supply, as long as the others continue to abide by the rules. Let us take an example in the context of a union. Suppose an overtime ban to support a pay claim is in force but one union member breaks the ban: he would get paid overtime and the rise in pay if the ban produces the pay increase. Of course, the one member working overtime could reduce the effectiveness of the ban, and thereby decrease the cohesion of the union. Therefore, union rules aim to prevent this breaking of ranks, though recent changes in the law make it illegal for a union to discipline a member who breaks a strike. However, the individual's fellow workers are likely to have far more effective sanctions (for example, refusing to speak to a strike-breaker).

Union objectives

see pp. 75–9

In order to analyse the objectives of a union, we turn to utility analysis which was introduced in Chapter 4 to examine consumer behaviour. A utility function can be specified for each member of the union and these can be aggregated to give the union's utility function. The aggregation is not straightforward if, as seems reasonable to assume, particularly in respect of a general union, the individual members' utility functions differ or even conflict. For example, unskilled members may want to narrow the pay differential between themselves and skilled workers while the skilled members oppose such a lowering of their status. Then there are the objectives of the union leaders who will be concerned with the survival and

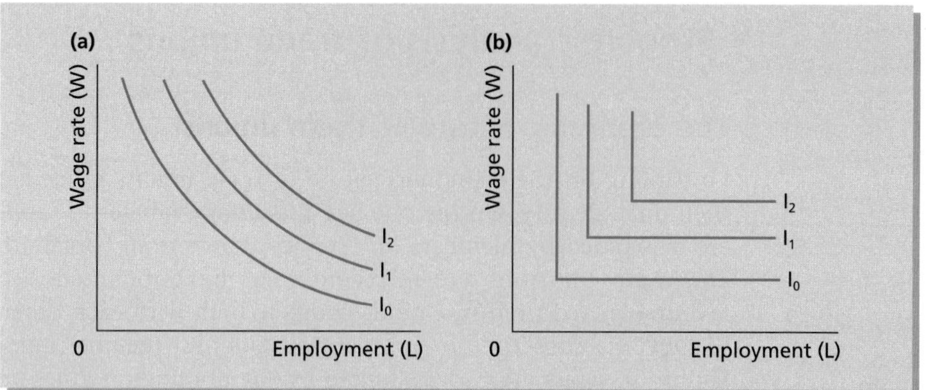

Figure 11.1 Indifference curves showing preferences between wages and employment

growth of the union in financial and membership terms. Despite these problems, economists wish to concentrate on the wage (W) and employment (L) aspects, specifying the union utility function as follows. Union utility (U) depends in some systematic way upon wage rates and upon the level of employment of members. The idea of a systematic relationship of this kind may be expressed as:

$$U = f(W, L, \ldots)$$

where f( ) indicates that the variables in the parentheses influence union utility, although the exact relationship is not being specified. The terms in the parentheses are the wage and employment levels, plus other, unspecified variables that affect union utility. The analysis requires that all the unspecified influences be held constant during the period of study. Some dispute this assumption, arguing that a union is a political organisation with the leadership reconciling the various internal pressure groups by continually changing the emphasis given to the objectives.

Holding the assumption allows a union's indifference curve map between wages and employment to be derived as shown in Figure 11.1. Each indifference curve is drawn to show how different combinations of wages and employment give rise to the same level of union utility; different curves represent different levels of utility, with higher utility shown by curves lying further to the right. The view taken in Figure 11.1(a) is that a union will experience the same level of utility if a fall in wages is compensated by an increase in employment and vice versa. Figure 11.1(a) reflects the usual assumptions about indifference curves and indicates a smooth trade-off between wages and employment. Not so in Figure 11.1(b), where the indifference curve map depicts the limiting case: no increase in the wage rate can compensate for a fall in the employment level and vice versa.

Demand for union labour

Orthodox economic theory does not see the union as being able to move to higher and higher indifference curves and thereby greater and greater levels of

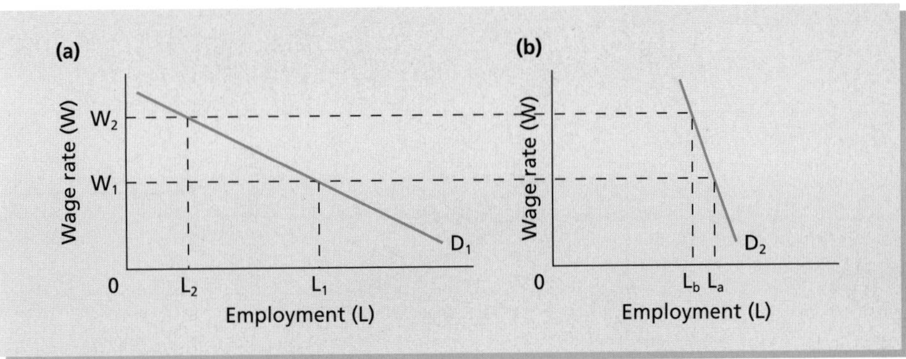

Figure 11.2 **Possible labour demand curves**

utility. There is a constraint on its actions in the form of the demand curve for labour, the derivation of which is explained in Appendix 4. What is important to note at this stage is that the labour demand curve shows the employer's profit maximising employment level for each wage rate: the lower the wage, the more labour the firm will find it worthwhile to employ. The position and slope of the demand curve are dependent on conditions in the firm's product market and its method(s) of production. Changes in the degree of competition in the product market or in consumer tastes for the product will alter the position and/or slope; as will alterations in the method of production whereby the method becomes more or less labour intensive.

Figure 11.2 illustrates two possible labour demand curves. If a union manages to increase the wage from W_1 to W_2, the union will prefer to face the relatively inelastic[3] (more steeply sloped) labour demand curve shown in Figure 11.2(b) because the consequent reduction in employment (OL_a to OL_b) is much less than when the curve is relatively elastic as in Figure 11.2(a) and the employment decrease is OL_1 to OL_2.

Pay determination in unionised labour markets

We can now bring the various threads of analysis together and begin considering the impact of a union on pay.

Figure 11.3(a) illustrates both the orthodox economic theory of market forces and the way in which a union is perceived to intrude and alter the outcome. The labour demand (D) and supply (S) curves intersect at A to give the market equilibrium wage (OW_e) and employment (OL_e); without the presence of a union, the market would be expected to settle at A. If a union is then formed it will use its cartel power to maximise its utility subject to the labour demand curve constraint; it will force the market to point B, where the highest indifference curve that can be attained just touches (is tangential to) the demand curve, resulting in a higher wage (OW_u) but lower employment (OL_u). Point B is assumed to lie above A on the labour demand curve because it is believed that the union will wish to obtain a higher wage than is set by market forces in order to encourage workers to remain in/join the union. Figure 11.3(b) gives an

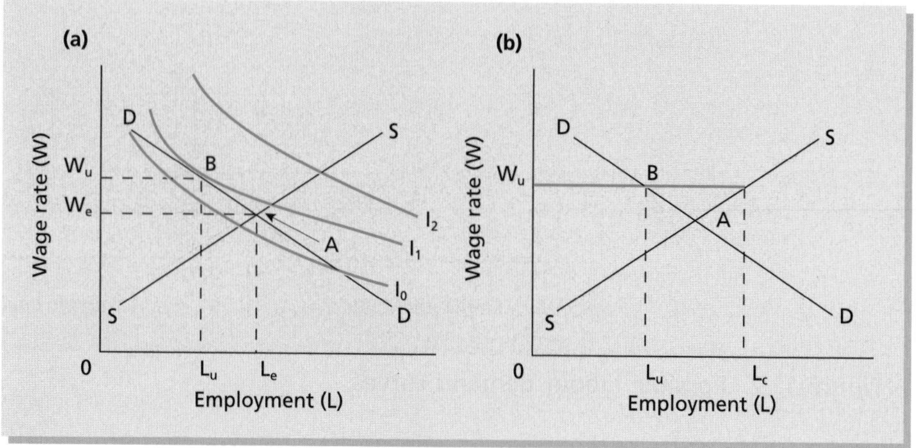

Figure 11.3 **Union preferences and the market for labour**

alternative picture of the situation with the union controlling the going wage (OW_u) so that the labour supply curve is horizontal at this wage until it intersects with the original supply curve when it takes on its usual positive (bottom left to top right) slope. What Figure 11.3(b) illustrates is how the union's action is believed to increase unemployment with L_uL_c the amount of labour being willing to work at wage OW_u but unable to get a job.

Point B arguably lies above A on the labour demand curve, but how far above? What determines exactly where the union aims to be on the demand curve? Can it attain its goal? A significant part of the answer is to be found in the constraints upon union activity.

Figure 11.3(b) also illustrates another way in which pay may be kept above the equilibrium level, namely a national minimum wage. Legislation is necessary to underpin the minimum. This was introduced in the UK in 1999. However, unions have been very vocal in their support of its introduction (and are represented on the Low Pay Commission which recommends the level at which the minimum wage should be set) because they see it as a way of setting pay levels in sectors of the economy where unions are weak or non-existent. The debate centres, as with the determination of pay in unionised sectors, on whether it results in higher unemployment. Whilst Figure 11.3(b) suggests that it does, this is based on the assumption of competition existing in the marketplace. If, instead, some employers have the power to determine the level of pay, it is argued that a minimum wage corrects the 'exploitation'.

11.4 Constraints on union action in labour markets

To examine the constraints upon union action we must delve a little further into both the demand and supply sides of unionised labour markets. The aim is to take the analysis beyond the simple, somewhat mechanical application of market forces. We need to consider the institutional structure of the wage bargaining process in order to understand how the two sides of the market interact to produce an outcome.

Demand for union labour

The most obvious constraint on a union's ability to use its cartel potential is the demand curve for labour. It summarises the profit-maximising employer's position and implies that the employer will not be shifted off the demand curve. The reason for this is that with perfect competition in the product market, the employer will earn less than maximum profit. As maximum profit equals normal profit, the firm will go out of business if its profits are reduced. However, this is not the end of the analysis.

First, union action can, theoretically at least, alter the labour demand relationship. Figures 11.2(a) and (b) show that the union will prefer to face an inelastic demand curve, and it can increase the degree of inelasticity by bargaining over workforce levels. If unions can obtain agreements or legislation which stipulates minimum crew numbers then this will reduce the ability of employers to decrease employment when the wage increases. Also, if the union can organise the whole of the industry then all the employers will incur the same union-induced wage cost increase and so no single firm need suffer a fall in product demand relative to other firms.

Second, a pay increase obtained by a union for its members may have a positive effect on productivity in the firm or industry (depending on the coverage of the agreement). An inefficient employer may be 'shocked' into introducing more efficient methods of production in order to keep costs down and restore competitiveness. Higher pay may also boost morale amongst employees so that they work harder and are less likely to leave, thus providing the employer with a more stable labour force. This 'efficiency wage' theory implies that the wage rise leads to a shift of the labour demand curve to the right (as each extra unit of labour generates more revenue than before) and, partially or completely, offsets the expected reduction in employment. The process can be seen in Figure 11.4.

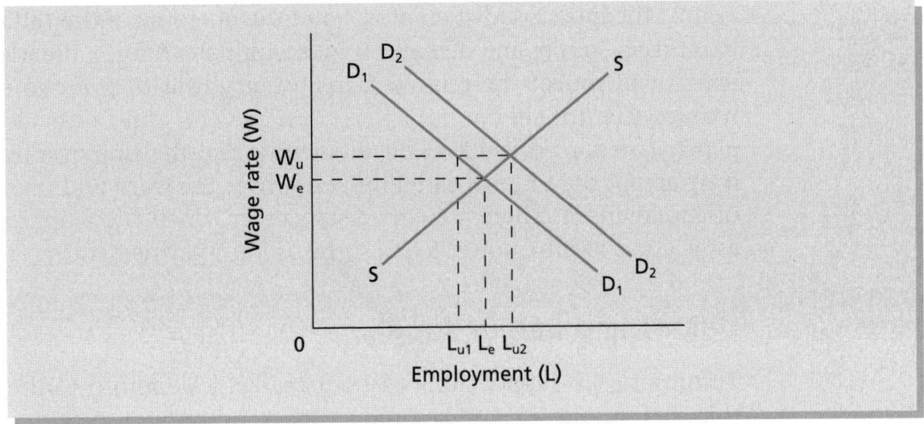

Figure 11.4 **Efficiency wage rise leads to a shift of the first labour demand curve to the right**

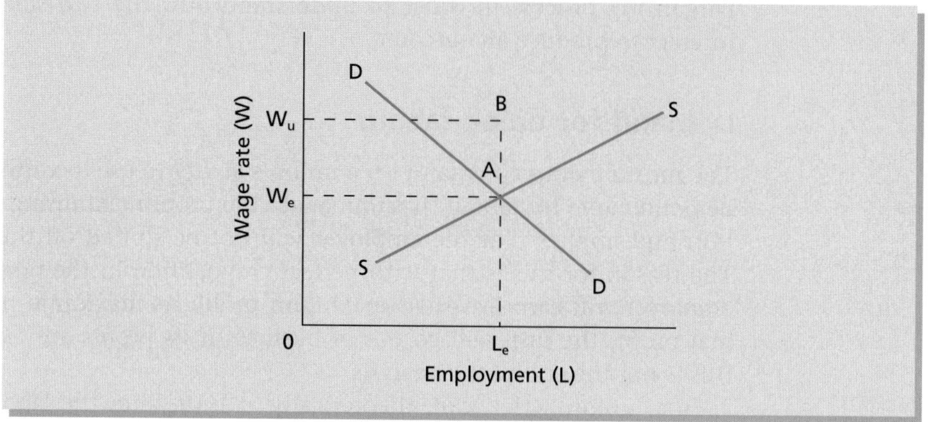

Figure 11.5 Wage rates in the absence of perfect competition in the product market

The increased productivity shifts the labour demand curve from D_1 to D_2 and leads to a new equilibrium level of employment, L_{u2}.

Third, if there is not perfect competition in the product market, the firm may be able to continue trading even if it earns less than maximum profit. An employer could then pay a wage above the perfectly competitive wage and maintain the level of employment, such as at point B in Figure 11.5. Obviously there is a limit to this in that eventually the firm's costs of production would cause the product price to rise to an uncompetitive level; but the limit could lie well to the right of the labour demand curve.

Fourth, the firm may have labour market power itself. Economists refer to such power as monopsony power. Thus a firm which has product market power or is the major employer in a particular locality can use its position to exert influence in its labour market(s). Employers can also group together for bargaining purposes, forming an employers' association. Monopsonistic firms will be able to increase profits by paying a wage below the competitive wage and employing less labour. In these circumstances, the monopoly union comes up against the monopsonist employer and the outcome of this 'bilateral monopoly' in terms of supply and demand is indeterminate. Rather, the wage (and employment) will reflect the relative bargaining power of the two sides, a topic to which we return later.

What we can conclude at the moment is that the employer need not just passively accept the union's cartel influence over the wage and then adjust the level of employment. There are circumstances in which the employer or employers' association has the power to resist the union's pay demand.

Unions and labour supply

Turning to the supply side of labour markets, we return to the line of thought that sees unions acting like product market monopolists with complete control of the supply of a product. A union as a cartel, however, only possesses this power if all the members of the labour force are members of the union and they abide by the cartel's decision to alter the labour supply. Difficulties arise for the union in its attempt to achieve this total control because of the multidimensional nature of labour supply, which comprises:

- the person
- the number of hours supplied
- the amount of effort supplied
- the amount of skill supplied
- the amount of ability supplied

where the distinction between skill and ability is that skill is expertise obtained from some form of training while ability is expertise that is inherent in the individual.

As already noted, individual members of the union do not necessarily hand over control of their labour supply to the union executive. At best, the member agrees to abide by the decisions of the majority following a vote on a particular issue. Even then, the individual member can increase his/her labour supply by accepting the decision of the majority over one dimension (say, number of hours supplied) but altering the supply of another dimension (say, amount of effort supplied). In fact, unions normally do not seek to control all the dimensions of labour supply and much depends on the type of union and the work context of the rank and file members. A craft union will seek to control the number of workers with the appropriate skill via control over an apprenticeship scheme such that only by successfully completing a minimum number of years of training can an individual obtain work as a skilled operative. Alternatively, the union negotiates the number of hours that comprise the standard working week but leaves it to the employer and employee to agree on the number of overtime hours. Rarely do unions formally attempt to control the amount of effort supplied, although groups of members may take it upon themselves to limit informally the pace of work.

What the union wishes to achieve can be interpreted as a shift of the labour supply curve to the left, thus raising the wage set in the labour market, though it is at the expense of employment below the competitive level. In doing so, the most obvious aim for the union is to organise all the workforce via a 'closed shop' agreement. Under this, the firm agrees either to recruit only union members (a pre-entry closed shop) or to make it a condition of employment that the new recruit becomes a union member (a post-entry closed shop). Unions argue that closed shops are justified because they overcome the free-rider problem, that is, non-union workers who benefit from union-obtained improvements in pay and working conditions but do not pay subscriptions or take part in industrial action. Conservative governments since 1979, however, have legislated to remove closed shops on the grounds that they are the basis of a major form of labour market monopoly.

Industrial action

So far, we have seen that unions have the potential to exercise monopoly-like power in labour markets because they act as a cartel. This enables them to raise wage rates above the competitive equilibrium level: but by how much? In other words, we are concerned with the circumstances under which unions can realise some or all of their cartel potential in raising wages above the level that would be set by the unimpeded forces of demand and supply.

Power lies at the heart of the issue in that power is the ability to force somebody to do something against their will. In this case we are considering the ability of the union to obtain agreement to its demands. Union power comes mainly from the degree of control it can exercise over labour supply, aspects of which have already been discussed. Now we focus on the power that comes from taking industrial action. This can involve the union members in a go-slow, work to rule, or withdrawal of cooperation, all aimed at reducing the pace of work and volume of output. Alternatively, it can call for an overtime ban or a strike, with strikes being not just 'all out' confrontations but also taking the form of regular one-day stoppages or a process of short stoppages by subgroups of the employees involved in the dispute. Industrial action seeks to impose costs on the firm in order to obtain a satisfactory (from the union point of view) agreement, but the outcome is determined by a wide range of factors that make up the circumstances of the bargaining.

The threat of industrial action hangs over each negotiation between union representatives and those of the firm, even when the negotiations are informal. How potent a threat it is depends first on the proportion of the labour force which is unionised or, if the proportion is low, whether the union members have a crucial position in the production process. These form the basis of the threat but, even if a large proportion of the workforce is in the union, it is the individual union members who must be willing to take action. They must therefore believe in the importance of the issue and must agree on the action to be taken. In other words, there needs to be membership cohesion and unity. Cohesion, some may use the term militancy, is again a matter of degree which can be related back to the economic concept of the cartel and the ability of the cartel to use its potential power.

The final part in the jigsaw of factors determining the potency of the threat of industrial action are the costs incurred by both sides. As Table 11.4 shows, the level of strike activity can be substantial, although it has been less in recent years. Table 11.5 shows the situation across the EU and also gives data for the USA and Japan for comparison. A strike is the most obvious form of industrial action in which the rank and file lose pay, but the other forms of industrial action listed above can also involve a reduction in earnings (they are sometimes called 'cut-price' actions because the costs to union members are likely to be less). The potency of the threat will depend on the willingness of the members to put up with the hardship of having no or lower income for the duration of the dispute. On the other hand, the employer will also be suffering lost output which will lead to lost profit, although the size of the costs to the firm will be lower if it has stockpiled the product and can continue trading by selling from stock or if the product market is depressed so that the firm would not have sold much anyway. Furthermore, the costs to both sides are reduced if the output can be made up by extra overtime working after the dispute is resolved: the

Table 11.4 Stoppages of work due to industrial disputes in the UK, 1970–2001

	Number of stoppages	Number of working days lost ('000)	Percentage of stoppages	
			caused by pay disputes	lasting less than 3 days
1970–74[a]	2,885	13,990	58.2	49.2
1975–79[a]	2,310	11,364	55.8	42.6
1980–84[a]	1,351	10,392	44.6	54.9
1985–89[a]	895	3,940	39.0	65.2
1990–94[a]	334	824	37.3	72.1
1995–98	215	559	40.0	74.2
1999	205	242	69.0	76.0
2000	212	499	39.0	71
2001	194	525	36.0	68

[a] Annual average

Source: adapted from *Employment Gazette*, various editions; *Labour Market Trends*, various editions

Table 11.5 Labour disputes: working days not worked per 1000 employees, all industries and services

	Annual average 1991–95	Annual average 1996–00	2000
UK	24	21	20
Belgium	33	21	8
Denmark	45	296	51
Finland	215	56	126
France	95	68	114
Germany	17	2	0
Ireland	108	91	72
Italy	183	76	59
Netherlands	33	4	1
Spain	451	182	296
Sweden	50	9	0
EU average (excluding Greece)	90	48	60
USA	42	61	163
Japan	2	1	1

Source: *Labour Market Trends*, Vol. III, No. 1

union members receive extra pay to compensate for that lost during the dispute and the firm can sell the extra output (profits may not be fully restored in that the extra overtime would usually be paid at a premium wage rate above the standard rate).

During the negotiations, the representatives of the union and of the employer will attempt to gauge the potency of the threat. As both sides will incur costs if industrial action takes place, the negotiations can be portrayed as attempting to avoid an industrial dispute with the weaker side giving ground to the other until a settlement is reached. However, should either side fail to recognise its true relative power position, then the threat of industrial action will be tested and its potency measured by how long the action lasts. The resulting settlement will reflect the true relative positions of the sides before the action occurred.

Some tentative conclusions

What is obvious from this discussion is that the ability of the union to capitalise on its potential cartel power and to force the employer to pay above the free market wage is circumvented by factors ranging from the cohesion of the union to the general economic climate. The number of 'ifs' and 'buts' makes it difficult to apply economic theory but some generalised inferences can be drawn about the impact of the union on pay.

1. Unions can have different objectives: while some may seek high pay increases others may be more concerned with employment prospects for members. There may be other objectives that the union wishes to pursue (status of the union and its leaders, survival of the union) which also mean the union does not focus only on pay.
2. The cohesion or unity of the members will be important in determining whether the union can achieve its objective(s). No satisfactory measures of this factor exist.
3. The degree of unionisation will be a factor in determining the union's ability to achieve its goal(s). If the union can recruit the whole workforce in an industry then it will be easier for it to push for higher pay, as all the firms in the industry will be affected and their relative competitiveness in the product market will remain unaltered by the pay rise.
4. Large firms with product market power offer unions the double prospect of (a) being able to organise employees in the industry at lower cost (not so many employers with which to negotiate bargaining rights) and (b) the firms having the ability to pass on pay increases in the form of price increases so making them less resistant to union demands. This will not be the case, however, if there is product market competition from abroad.
5. Economic conditions can influence the ability of unions to obtain pay increases in several ways. In times of economic prosperity, strikes will be more costly for firms in terms of lost business while it will be easier for the strikers to find part-time work to offset the lost pay. If there is inflation, the firm may be able to pass on the pay rise in higher prices without a marked effect on demand for the product.

11.5 The empirical evidence

Sources of data

At first glance there seem to be plenty of data available by which to judge the impact of unions on pay in the UK. The Office of National Statistics publishes monthly figures for earnings, employment and stoppages of work caused by industrial disputes and there are three main sources of statistics on union membership: the TUC; the Certification Officer for Trade Unions and Employers' Associations; the *Labour Force Survey* provides annual, and more recently quarterly, survey data. In the main, these are accepted as accurate measures though there are some problems associated with their use. 'Stoppages of work due to industrial disputes' does not include non-strike actions and in fact does not include all strikes, deliberately omitting stoppages where less than 100 working days are lost. The TUC union membership figures only relate to those unions which are affiliated to the TUC, while the Certification Officer includes as trade unions some organisations which are not unions in the strict sense of being independent of the employer(s). Therefore, the statistics that relate to the basis of union power need to be interpreted carefully.

Interpreting the data

It seems such a simple task to complete: we obtain the data on the pay of union members and then compare it with the pay of non-union members; assume non-union pay is equal to the wage that would be set if the forces of demand and supply operate freely; then the difference in pay is the measure of the impact of the union on pay. Matters, though, are not so straightforward.

First, there are various reasons, other than the influence of unions, why pay will differ between two people (for example, between males and females, between skilled and unskilled, between different industries and between different geographical areas). The influence of these other causes of pay differentials must be removed so that the data compare like with like.

Second, in the UK, many collective agreements on pay are applied to union and non-union members alike. So, for the purposes of empirical work, do we include those non-union members who are covered by the collective agreement as being union members even though they are not? Or, do we place them in the non-union category when they are paid the union pay rate?

Third, as is obvious from the previous point, non-union pay need not be equal to the competitive market wage. Figure 11.6 illustrates how the emergence of a union in a labour market affects non-union wages. Omitting the supply curves in order to make the diagrams clearer, Figure 11.6(a) represents the unionised part of the market and Figure 11.6(b) the non-unionised part. Initially, there is no union and the competitive wage is set at OW_e in both sectors and resulting employment of OL_a and OL_b respectively. Then the union is formed in sector (a) and it uses its cartel power to raise the wage to OW_u and employment in the sector decreases by L_aL_u. This unemployed labour seeks work

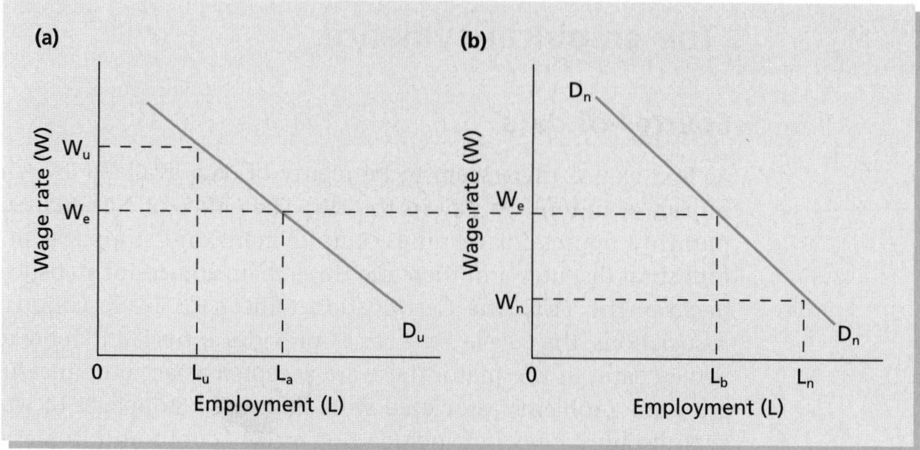

Figure 11.6 (a) Unionised and (b) non-unionised labour markets

in the non-unionised sector, bidding down the wage to OW_n (note that all the unemployed labour seeks work in the non-unionised sector so that L_aL_u equals L_bL_n). Obviously in these circumstances the non-union wage does not equal the competitive wage.

That, however, need not be the end of the story. Non-union employers may wish to ensure that their workforces do not become unionised. Therefore, they may be willing to 'buy off' their workforces by paying a wage just about equal to the union wage (maybe even higher than the union wage) in order to persuade their employees that a union is not necessary.

These so-called spillover effects muddy the empirical waters and certainly it is not possible to hold that the non-union wage is the wage that would prevail if unions did not exist. The union pay gap is thus to be interpreted as a measure of how much union members gain in pay over non-union workers.

Assessing the data

A large number of studies have been carried out to discover whether, and by how much, union pay differs from that of non-union employees in the UK. The results are much in line with our previous analysis: the differential varies. However, certain patterns do emerge.

First, it is by no means always the case that union pay exceeds non-union pay when comparing similar types of labour in the same broad industry. However, most of the evidence points to a positive wage gap in favour of unions (see Table 11.6).

Second, the union/non-union pay differential tends to be larger when union pay has been at least partially determined by bargaining at the company, plant or shopfloor level. Conversely, where the union pay is set by national bargaining, the pay gap tends to be smaller.

Third, skill level, company size and establishment size appear to influence the size of the pay differential, with unions able to gain greater advantage for the

Table 11.6 **Estimates of the percentage overall union pay gap in Britain, 1970–87**

Year	*Percentage union pay gap*	*Year*	*Percentage union pay gap*	*Year*	*Percentage union pay gap*
1970	26	1976	29	1982	34
1971	28	1977	26	1983	31
1972	31	1978	28	1984	32
1973	30	1979	19	1985	24
1974	22	1980	28	1986	19
1975	33	1981	34	1987	22

Source: R. F. Elliott (1991) *Labor Economics: A Comparative Text*, McGraw-Hill, Maidenhead, p. 437. Reproduced with the kind permission of McGraw-Hill Publishing Company

semi-skilled than for the skilled and for those members who work in large companies, especially if those companies have a significant degree of product market power.

Fourth, the size of the overall union wage gap varies over time and the variation seems to be related to the business cycle. This can be seen from the data in Table 11.6, where the estimates for Britain measure the gap as fluctuating between 19 and 34 per cent over the period 1970–87. The percentage gap tends to get smaller during times of economic prosperity but becomes larger during downturns in economic activity.

In general these findings are in line with our theoretical expectations; the exception might seem to be the last one about the influence of economic conditions. The explanation normally given is that the union gap widens in the downturn of the business cycle because, while pay falls (or does not rise as rapidly) in the non-union sector, unions will have some success in resisting pay cuts (or maintaining the rate of pay rise) in the unionised sector.

11.6 Conclusion

Our analysis and consideration of the empirical results have given few definitive answers to the questions of how and to what extent unions affect relative pay. However, we have built a framework for understanding the role of unions; a framework which seeks to combine the economic analysis with the political nature of unions in order to analyse union behaviour. It is not a rigorous, technical analysis because unions are not susceptible to such an approach.

In respect of the impact of unions on relative pay, the theoretical analysis and the empirical evidence lead to the conclusion that, overall, unions push up wages above the non-union level of pay. 'Overall' should not be taken to mean in every situation because both theoretically and empirically this is not the case.

CHAPTER SUMMARY

1. **The demand for a resource such as labour is derived from the demand for the product.**
2. **The demand curve for labour can be affected by institutional factors.**
3. **Indifference analysis can be used to analyse institutional behaviour as well as that of households.**
4. **Trade unions may prefer higher wage rates for members even if this involves some unemployment in the industry.**
5. **Efficiency wage theory suggests that increased wages may *not* cause an increase in unemployment.**
6. **It can be difficult to obtain, interpret and assess economic data.**

Questions for discussion

Guidance to the answers for the **asterisked** *numbered questions is available to students on the website for the book at* **www.booksites.net/heather**.

1* Suppose the labour market in the building trade is competitive. How do you think the demand and supply of labour, and the wage rate will change under the following circumstances? (a) A sharp and unexpected rise in interest rates. (b) A relaxation of planning laws on residential housing. (c) A lowering of the age of retirement in the industry.

2 How do you think unions will react to a leftward shift of the demand curve for its labour (due, for example, to a fall in demand in the product market)? (*Hint*: What is happening to the union in terms of Figure 11.1?)

3* Doctors are paid more than gardeners. Now suppose that there is perfect mobility of labour. Would this situation continue? Why or why not?

4 Why do some employees decide to join trade unions? Why do others decide not to do so?

5* Suppose that an employer takes on an extra employee. Why might the marginal cost of doing so be greater than the wage the employer must pay the extra employee?

6 Recent legislation in the UK has made it possible for an employer to be taken to court if an applicant is rejected for a job because she/he will not join a trade union. In this way the government is seeking to remove closed shop agreements. But is a closed shop necessarily a bad thing?

7* A union in a particular industry is considering making a wage demand of a 20 per cent rise for all. It fears that if it is successful some employees may be laid off. The estimate is that the demand for this kind of labour has an elasticity of –1. How many employees will be made redundant if the claim is accepted in full? What will happen to the employer's wage bill?

8 Under what circumstances can a strike be said to be successful or unsuccessful?

9* The wages received by employees are made up of transfer earnings and economic rent. Find out what these terms mean from the glossary. Suppose the labour supply is totally inelastic. How much of the wages received is transfer earnings and how much is economic rent?

10 What can be concluded about the determination of pay in the absence of unions (a) in non-unionised labour markets or (b) where the union is not recognised for bargaining purposes?

Websites

The ILO is useful for information on labour markets. Their website can be accessed at:

www.ilo.org

Notes

1 S. and B. Webb (1965) *The History of Trade Unionism*, reprinted by Augustus Kelly, New York, p. 1.

2 You will recall that we discussed cartels in the product market in the context of airline prices in Chapter 8.

3 Both of the demand curves in Figure 11.2 have an elasticity ranging in value from infinity to zero. However, one can say that at any given wage rate, the value of elasticity for the steeper curve is less elastic at that point. In that sense (a) is elastic compared with (b).

Part III

MACROECONOMICS

18 Money and banking

16 Supply side behaviour: taxation

17 Supply side behaviour: privatisation

15 Inflation, aggregate demand and supply

13 Keynesianism and unemployment

14 Investment

12 National income

Part II
MICROECONOMICS

Part I
INTRODUCTORY CONCEPTS

Microeconomics gives us a basic foundation for understanding how markets operate. We use this knowledge as a building block for seeing how the economy functions at the macro level.

12 National income

Damaging the Earth: *how much does it really matter?*

CHAPTER OVERVIEW

Pollution and the depletion of the Earth's resources affect us all. How serious is the problem? To what extent do such activities reduce our well-being? How much does it really matter?

As we analyse these questions we review

- External costs

We introduce

- Circular flow of income
- National income accounts

12.1 Introduction

Most people know, at least in general terms, what constitutes pollution, and most people do not like it and would prefer less of it to be produced. Yet people, industry and governments all over the world have tolerated the increase in pollution levels over a substantial period. The quality of the physical environment is diminished by pollution, and since people have votes in many societies, governments view pollution as a matter of concern: more effective and wide-ranging action to combat rising pollution levels is possible, and is being actively considered or implemented. But are pollution and the quality of the physical environment genuinely related to the functioning of national economies? As we aim to show in this chapter, the answer is yes. The pollution problem is one of genuine concern to economists, and economists are actively involved in examining this whole issue.

Pollution is generated as a result of both household and industry activity in fuel combustion and as by-products of manufacturing processes. There are many different types of pollutants, and their impacts, whether they be on air, water or land, vary in geographical distribution as well as the time period over which they may be seen to be causing damage. The timing of the damage ranges from the almost instantaneous (for some highly toxic dangerous pollutants), to decades and centuries (for example, the expected damages via climate changes caused by global warming gases).

Damage to the physical environment has real effects that can reduce household welfare and may directly or indirectly increase production costs to industry. For example, river pollution caused by one factory's discharges may necessitate the installation of special water purification devices for a factory using water further downstream. Alternatively, it may lead to increased water purification charges for all water consumers.

see pp. 147–8

Since this damage generates real costs, why do most emitters of pollution not take adequate account of these costs when they are engaged in the production activities that generate the pollution? The key reason relates to the nature of the pollution damage costs. We have already seen that such costs are known in economic terms as external costs or negative externalities. They can be said to exist when an economic activity by one party causes a loss to another group. When an externality is present, the loss of welfare for one party is not compensated in any way. This describes the nature of most polluting activity. The right to pollute the environment is still typically not traded in a market. This is sometimes said to be the problem of missing markets. If there are no established market rights to pollute the environment then pollution emitters perceive that the effective 'market price' is zero. We saw from our understanding of demand curves that if the price of some good or service is free, then usually more of it will be wanted than if its price is higher. So a perceived zero price encourages overconsumption of the services of the physical environment.

In this chapter we focus on the extent of welfare loss implied in such overconsumption. Our attention will be at the macroeconomic level. We examine the problem by considering the extent to which we overstate our level of welfare *as a society* when we ignore the effects of polluting activity. However, we also consider the effects on our welfare of running down the stock of the world's resources, through the consumption of oil, minerals and so on. This is a separate problem but it is still a concern to environmentalists in that it can be argued to be damaging the Earth on which human life ultimately depends.

We begin by seeing how economists usually measure the extent of the welfare that we enjoy from the output produced. We shall see that this form of measurement ignores the problems of pollution. Subsequently, we consider how we might modify the traditional measures to take account of environmental concerns.

12.2 The circular flow of incomes

The interdependence of firms and households

The link between welfare and production of goods and services can best be seen in the context of what economists call the circular flow of income (Figure 12.1). The diagram shows a simplified economy in which is depicted the relationship between household (consumers) and firms. It is in fact a double relationship.

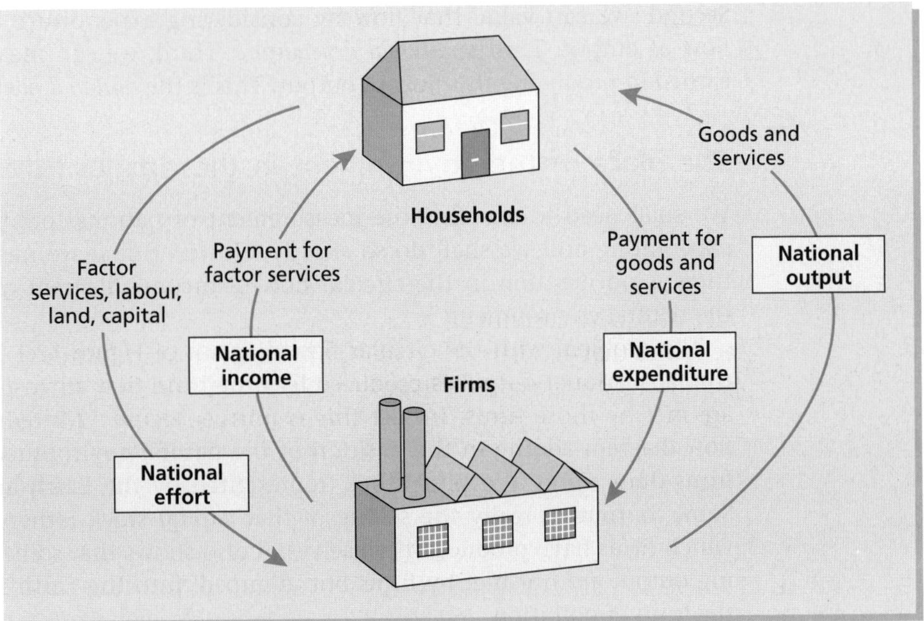

Figure 12.1 **The circular flow of income**

The first relationship is depicted on the right-hand side of the figure. It shows that households purchase a flow of goods and services from firms. Firms provide the products in return for a flow of payments from households.

How are firms able to produce the output? The left-hand side of the figure gives us the answer. The second relationship is that households provide firms with factor services. For most households this will mean that people will be supplying labour. For others it means supplying capital, through, for example, the purchase of shares. For others it means supplying land. For yet other households it may mean the provision of a combination of different factors. In return for these services firms provide payment as wages and salaries, dividends and rent. These payments provide the income which enables households to purchase goods and services. The relationship is a circular one.[1]

Measuring the circular flow of income

These exchange relationships are made easier to organise because of money. Money functions as a medium of exchange. Its value is that it represents a claim on output: it can be used to purchase goods and services which you require. It is the existence of these money flows which has enabled economists to measure the value of goods and services produced and, more controversially, to make a link between such output and consumers' welfare. Let us concentrate first on the measurement of the output. The circular flow of income diagram of Figure 12.1 enables us to see that there are three points at which we can measure this flow of output. First we can measure in money terms the flow of goods and services to households during the year. We refer to this flow of goods as *national product*.

Second, we can value that flow by considering expenditure upon that year's flow of output. This is *national expenditure*. Third, we can measure the income earned in producing this flow of output. This is the *national income*.

The place of the environment in the circular flow

We shall need to examine the measurement of national product, income and expenditure and we shall do so shortly. However, first we need to notice that there is no mention in the circular flow of income diagram of the position of the natural environment.

The problem with the circular flow diagram of Figure 12.1 is that it implies that all national output is produced by firms, and that all costs of producing it are met by those firms. In fact this is untrue. Figure 12.2 redraws the circular flow diagram adding in the position of the natural environment. It shows that firms draw upon a 'capital stock' represented by the Earth and its resources. Some 'output' is really the selling of that capital stock rather than something which firms have produced themselves. It also shows that some costs of producing output are not met by firms but 'dumped' into the Earth's capital stock in the form of pollution.

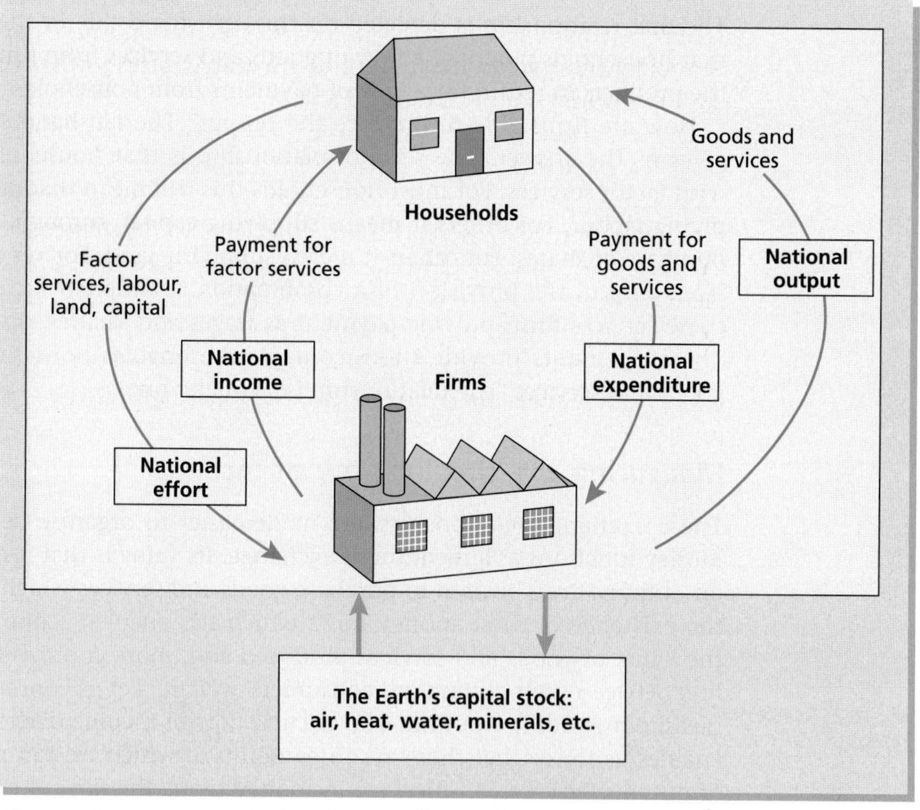

Figure 12.2 **The environment and the circular flow of income**

We turn, in the next section, to how the national output, income and expenditure accounts are measured. Having done that we shall be in a position to see how such a procedure might be modified in order to capture the damage done to the environment during the production and consumption of output.

12.3 The traditional measurement of national output flows

In this section we explain how the size of national product is measured, paying attention to its claim as a measure of welfare. We shall not be interested in the problems of detail that arise in compiling these accounts, but we will concentrate on the major problems that are at issue in producing these data.

Measuring the flow of output

The basic method of establishing an economy's output is to take each kind of output in physical volume terms and to multiply this quantity by its price. This gives a figure for output in money terms. We are thus assuming that the value of output to society is represented by what consumers are prepared to pay for it. As a first approximation this seems reasonable. To purchase a good from limited income involves a sacrifice of an alternative, its opportunity cost. So a member of society *must* value the output at least at its price, otherwise the output in question would not be purchased at all.[2]

There is one immediate problem with this assumption. In terms of Figure 12.3, we value each industry's output at P_1Q_1. In fact, as you will recall from Chapter 3, all except the marginal consumer value the output more than that price. This additional value we called *consumer surplus*, shown as the shaded area. The value of the consumer surplus is ignored for the purpose of national income measurement. To that extent the level of national output understates its value to society in terms of its power to satisfy wants.

One way of measuring the value of national output is to consider only output sold to households. Such output is called final output. However, if we listed all

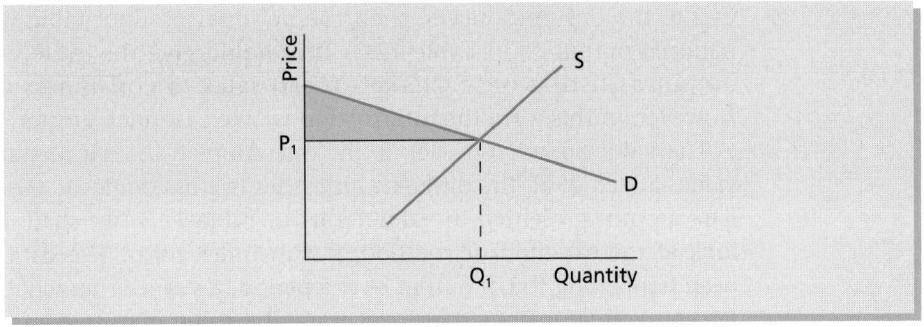

Figure 12.3 **Valuing output by price**

Table 12.1 **Illustrative measure of national output**

Industry	*Output*	*Value of output (£m)*	*Value-added (£m)*
Farming	Wheat	10	10
Milling	Flour	25	15
Baking	Bread	55	30

Table 12.2 **Illustrative national product table**

	£m
Farming	10
Milling	15
Baking	30
National product	55

final output, we could not observe contributions made by intermediate industries, that is, output sold not to households but to other firms. For example, virtually no steel is bought by households. Most is sold to industries such as the car industry, which in turn sells much to households. So measuring all final output and ignoring intermediate output would imply that the steel industry produces almost nothing whereas the car industry's output is substantial. Both industries contribute to consumer want satisfaction, although the steel industry does so indirectly. It might, therefore, be informative to present national output in a way which made it clear that this is the case.

An equivalent approach to measuring national output is to list the value-added of each industry. This, as the following simple example shows, will give the same value for national output as measuring all final output.

In our example in Table 12.1 farmer Copas grows wheat which sells to millers for £10 million. Miller MacMillan turns the £10 million of wheat into £25 million worth of flour, thus adding £15 million of value. This £25 million of flour is then sold to baker Clarke, who adds £30 million in value and sells it as £55 million of bread. If this were the economy's only output and Copas, MacMillan and Clarke the only producers, then the national product table would show this national output as in Table 12.2. This would give the same value of national output as listing only Clarke's bread sales to consumers as £55 million. However, in this form the information we have is much greater.

The value-added approach is the one adopted in official statistics. The total values-added of all the different industries is gross domestic product (GDP). The data are not presented in value terms in Table 12.3 (we shall do this when we look at the expenditure method) but in index form. The data show what has been happening to UK output over a period of years. From what we have said so far you will appreciate that, over time, the value of output can change for two reasons: either because the quantity of outputs has changed or because the general

Table 12.3 **National accounts: output measure**

Year	At current prices	At constant (1995) prices
1988	65.2	89.0
1989	71.5	90.9
1990	77.5	91.6
1991	81.5	90.4
1992	84.9	90.6
1993	89.3	92.9
1994	94.8	97.2
1995	100	100
1996	106.0	102.6
1997	112.8	106.2
1998	119.5	109.3
1999	125.5	111.9
2000	132.1	115.3
2001	137.4	117.6

Source: adapted from ONS, 'Blue Book' (2002) © Crown copyright

level of prices of the outputs has altered. Table 12.3 shows the data measured at 'current prices'. The changes are attributable both to physical output changes and to changes in the price level. The 'constant price' column has removed the effect of inflation and shows changes only if they are the result of changes in the level of output. This we call real output. We say that we are measuring the output at constant prices. The value of the output in 1995 was given the number 100. What has happened over time to real output changes can then be easily established. In 1995 the index was 100. By 2001 it was 117.6. So output, value-added in real terms, rose by 17.6 per cent over the course of those six years.

Notice that real output does not always increase. In the recession of the late 1980s and early 1990s output declined. What is true of total output can also be true of any particular sector. For construction, for example, the index for 1990 was 111.3. Real output from that sector declined in the recession of the early 1990s and by 1995 had fallen by 11.3 per cent. By 1998, it was rising again.

Another thing to note from Table 12.3 concerns a problem of using market prices to establish values for output. Not all products and services are sold through a market. For example, one of the items included in the output of services is public administration and national defence. However, we cannot measure this item at market prices since it is not distributed on such a basis. How, then, can we place a value on this output? In the accounts it is valued at the cost of its provision. If a soldier is paid £20,000 per annum as a wage, the assumption is made that he provides £20,000 worth of national security for society during that year.

Gross domestic product represents the value of the output produced within the borders of the UK during a given year. However, some output produced by

UK resources is produced overseas. Some oil extraction, for example, takes place in other countries with UK capital. As a result there is an inflow into this country of profit dividends and interest which represents the volume of UK output produced outside UK borders.

Similarly, some output produced in the UK is produced with foreign-owned resources. For example, Japanese car companies produce cars in Britain. Part of this output is British – British workers contributed to its production. The part of this car output which is Japanese is represented by the flow of profit, dividends and interest *out* of Britain to Japan. So for Britain, as for other countries, there is both an inflow and an outflow of profits, dividends and interest. The net flow we call net property income from abroad (NPIA) or, as it is referred to in the UK accounts, 'real current transfers from the rest of the world (receipts less payments)'.

Gross domestic product plus NPIA is called gross *national* product (GNP). This figure is not shown in Table 12.3 but the figure for the UK is usually positive – Britain earns more from its overseas assets than it pays to foreigners as a reward for owning UK assets.

We need to consider one other item in this measure of output, which will form a particularly important part of our thoughts about the damage to the environment shortly. The measure of the output that we have considered takes no account of the wear and tear of machinery in producing output. This is the meaning of the term 'gross'. It means that no allowance has been made for the reduction in value of capital in all industries during the year. If an estimate of the value is made, it can then be subtracted from the gross figure to get net domestic product. Again, this is not shown in Table 12.3, but we will discuss its value later in the chapter.

Measuring the flow of income

An alternative way of valuing output is to value the income derived in producing it. Since we are measuring the same flow at a different point on the circular flow diagram of Figure 12.1, we may expect to arrive at the same total value. Income is income earned in producing output.

Let us illustrate, with a particular example, why this must be so. Consider again miller MacMillan who, as you will remember from Table 12.2, produced flour as her contribution to national output. She received £25 million for the sale of the flour and spent £10 million of it buying wheat from Farmer Copas. We recorded her national output contributions as a value-added of £15 million. What did she do with this £15 million? She will have spent some of it on the wages of those she employed. Some will have paid for the rent of the land. Some will be left over for profit to distribute to shareholders. In other words, all of the £15 million must be an income to some factor of production involved in the production of the output. Therefore national output will equal national income. There is one important proviso: when calculating national income we must be sure only to count income earned in producing the national product. Incomes to groups such as pensioners and students will *not* be counted because they are not factor incomes. They have been transferred from other factors of production

Table 12.4 **National accounts: income measure**

	Approximate percentage of GDP in any year
Compensation of employees (wages and salaries)	64
Rental income	9
Profits of private companies	15
Surpluses of public corporations and government enterprises[a]	–
Income from self-employment	12
Gross domestic product (at factor cost)	100

[a] Less than 0.1 per cent

Source: adapted from ONS, 'Blue Book', various editions © Crown copyright

whose incomes have been taxed. Such 'transfer incomes' are therefore excluded from the accounts.

Table 12.4 lists the major sources of incomes earned in producing the output. Any statistical discrepancy apart, the sum of all these factor incomes, gross domestic income, must be the same as gross domestic product. As you can see from the table, easily the largest income is to labour, in the form of wages and salaries, typically around two-thirds of national income.

Gross *national* income can be found by adding the net property income from abroad. Net national income can then be found by subtracting capital consumption.

Measuring the flow of expenditure

The final method of calculating the value of output produced is to examine *expenditure* on that output. Since all output is purchased by some person or agent, the value of national output will be equal to the value of national expenditure.

We can see the items of national expenditure with reference to Table 12.5. Who purchases the output which Britain produces? Most of it is purchased by households, listed in the table as household expenditure. This item covers a vast array of expenditures on food, clothing, travel, entertainment, and so on. Some output is purchased by government, some of it by central government, the rest by local authorities. Some is purchased by firms as capital equipment – buildings, machinery and so on. This is called gross domestic fixed capital formation. It is 'gross' in that it makes no distinction between the replacement of worn out capital stock and new additions to capital – both are included. It is 'domestic' in that it is for firms in this country. It is 'fixed' in that it is the purchase of plant and machinery as distinct from investing in stocks of finished goods.

All these items taken together – consumption, government expenditure and investment – represent *domestic* expenditure. However, some of our output is purchased by foreigners. So foreign demand exports are also included as national

Table 12.5 **National accounts: expenditure measure, current prices (£m)**

	1990	*2001*
Household expenditure[1]	349,047	655,265
Central government	66,434	114,718
Local government	43,816	75,945
Gross fixed capital formation	114,173	162,607
Changes in stocks	−1,800	1,441
Exports of goods and services	133,887	268,451
Less imports of goods and services	−148,257	−290,912
Statistical discrepancy	–	499
Gross domestic product at market prices	557,300	988,014

[1] Includes non-profit institutions serving households
[2] Includes acquisitions less disposals of valuables
Source: adapted from ONS, 'Blue Book' (2002) © Crown copyright

expenditure. The sum of all these items gives total 'final' expenditure. It is expenditure on final output. It does *not* include expenditure by firms on the purchase of intermediate goods (goods bought by one firm from another).[3]

Some consumers' expenditure, government expenditure and investment expenditure have been made on foreign goods and services. These are *not* items of expenditure on British output. To the extent that we import, we have overstated the amount of such expenditures on British firms' output. Hence the table shows a subtraction of import expenditure. If this seems odd at first, remember that we are not measuring expenditure by British citizens but expenditure on British output.

So the sum of expenditure by consumers, investment, government and exports minus import expenditure gives us gross domestic expenditure. If we wished we could subtract NPIA to give gross national expenditure, where all these expenditures are at appropriate market prices, i.e. the prices actually paid by those who purchase.

We have argued in earlier chapters that the logic of a market system is that prices should reflect opportunity cost. We have shown that opportunity cost will be the opportunity cost of the factor incomes used in producing output. However, governments distort that relationship when taxing certain goods and subsidising others. For national income accounting purposes we wish to value expenditure as the expenditure at the factor cost of producing, say, a packet of cigarettes. This might be about £1 for a packet of 20, but the tax means that the market price is £4. The expenditure items in Table 12.5 are valued at market prices, which includes the tax. There is a 'factor cost' adjustment that removes these indirect taxes, valuing the output at the resource cost.

The mirror image of this problem is government subsidies. The effect of such subsidies is to reduce prices to below factor cost. Since expenditure items have been at the 'distorted' price, we have to add subsidies to produce expenditure at factor cost. The adjustment of subtracting indirect taxes and adding subsidies gives us gross domestic expenditure which will be equal to gross domestic income and product, or as it is called in the official UK accounts, 'Gross Value Added'.

There is one other thing to notice about Table 12.5. The data given are at current prices. No attempt has been made to remove the effects of inflation on the numbers. So expenditure in real terms has risen more slowly than is suggested by the table. The 'Blue Book' also produces figures for national expenditure at *constant prices*. By removing the effects of inflation this will show national expenditure increasing rather more slowly. You can see this in Table 12.3 where National Output is given (in index form) at both current and constant prices.

Using national output estimates as a guide to welfare

We have now seen how economists attempt to measure the size of national output. Many economists believe that this measure is the best guide we have on which to base estimates of welfare. Since prices reflect people's willingness to pay, we can value the output produced. All other things being equal, the more output we produce, the more welfare society has.

The usefulness of this measure is limited. We need to know what size of population this output supports. In other words, we need to look at income *per head*. Nevertheless, that figure would still not tell us how income is distributed. Furthermore, it is a measure which ignores other non-monetary sources of welfare. There is no perfect correlation between income and contentment. Nevertheless, it is this measure which is widely used as a link to welfare. Thus if we could improve it in some way, it would be most helpful. It is to that which we now turn.

12.4 Environmental pollution and the national income accounts

One seemingly obvious way of improving the measuring of welfare is to take into account the depletion of the Earth's resources and the degradation of the environment which economic activity causes. Much thought has been given in recent years to doing just that. It is a procedure fraught with difficulty, yet in principle the procedure would appear to be simple. We already measure 'capital consumption'. To the extent that resources have to be committed to the replacement of worn out capital stock, economic welfare is reduced. Why do we not simply extend this analysis? We could count environmental degradation as a depletion of society's capital stock and show net national product as net of such degradation.

There are substantial problems associated with this seemingly simple idea. We shall consider the main ones. In this section we deal with the problems of building estimates of pollution damage into the accounts. Later we briefly consider the problems associated with the depletion of mineral deposits, and so on. First, then, let us look at problems associated with measuring the reduction in welfare caused by pollution activities.

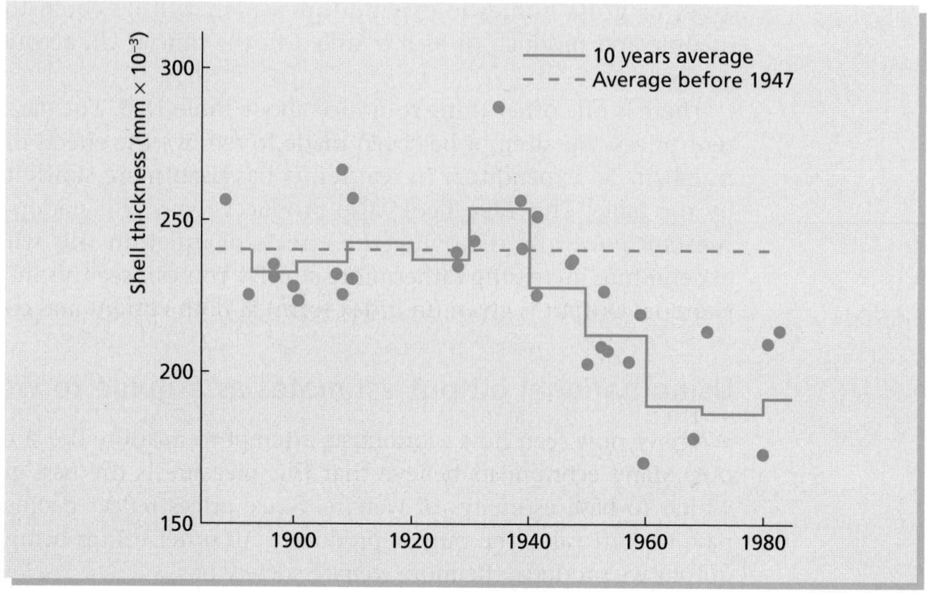

Figure 12.4 **Eggshell thickness of the merlin, 1885–1993**

Source: adapted from OEDC (1993) *Economic Survey of Europe*

The non-linearity of pollution damage

Machines wear out. When more output is produced from them, the value of that capital stock declines proportionately. Much environmental pollution damage is unlike that. In terms of Figure 12.2, the Earth's capital stock can absorb some output waste at minimal cost, but beyond a critical point serious depletion sets in. Two examples will illustrate the point.

Environmental pollution has reduced the thickness of the eggshells of birds of prey. Figure 12.4 shows, in particular, the post-war effects of the pesticide DDT usage on the shell thickness for one bird, the merlin. The effect of the DDT was to reduce thickness by around 15 per cent. Merlins, however, continued to breed, so there appears to be no problem. In fact there is a real difficulty. Such a reduction has brought the shell's thickness close to the point where further deterioration will cause the shell to break when the parents sit on the egg during incubation. Should this happen the chicks will not hatch and the merlin population would be decimated. If the pollution problem were to become a little worse, we could move from apparently minimal effects to catastrophic effects in this instance.

A second, though controversial, example may prove to be global warming. A rise in the ocean's temperature of a fraction of one degree may be apparently irrelevant. Just a small increase in warming might, at some critical point, cause a rise in the sea level sufficient to engulf a whole island. Again the damage to the environment is non-linear.

Here is our first problem of measuring environmental damage: it is not a linear function of output. Placing a value on the reduction of the Earth's capital stock is therefore extremely difficult.

Avoiding a mess or clearing it up?

There is a second problem in measuring environmental pollution damage. It involves one aspect of the problem of *damage valuation*. The statistical office of the United Nations has suggested a measure of welfare called 'green domestic product'. This is arrived at in the following way:

GDP – capital consumption (conventionally valued) = NDP

NDP – natural capital depreciation = green domestic product

The United Nations Statistical Office (UNSO) then goes on to suggest a method of calculating natural capital depreciation based upon the cost of avoiding a reduction in the Earth's capital stock. At first this seems unambiguous. That is far from the case. Suppose an industry discharges a poisonous chemical into the river, causing damage to fish and making the water unsuitable for alternative uses such as drinking. The UNSO suggestion is in effect that we reduce the value of the natural capital stock by the cost involved in not incurring the pollution. In other words, the degradation of the capital stock equals the loss of the output from the resources needed in using a more expensive, less environmentally destructive way of producing the output.

It is possible that the cost of avoiding the pollution would have been quite small. It might have involved rendering the poison harmless by adding some additional chemical. Measured in this way, the amount of capital depreciation is small. However, since the firm did not have to incur the clean-up costs – the cost was an external cost – it chose not to be environmentally friendly. The cost of cleaning up the mess was far higher than the cost of prevention.

An alternative approach, then, to the measurement of environmental damage, would be to reduce the green capital stock by an amount equal to the cost of clearing up the mess. This could be argued to be a more realistic alternative if the damage has already been done. This gives a much higher figure than UNSO's.

International pollution

When governments consider the level of welfare enjoyed by their citizens, they may well want to know how much that welfare is reduced by the capital stock depletion costs we have been considering. Knowing what these costs are enables appropriate action to deal with the problems. Sometimes, however, governments are virtually powerless to act because the pollution is created by production processes in other countries. The problem is particularly severe in Scandinavia.

Consider Tables 12.6 and 12.7. They give estimates of the production of some key pollutants, oxides of sulphur, SO_x, and oxidants of nitrogen, NO_x, which react with water to create acid rain. These acids are responsible for, among other things, damage to forests – a matter of particular concern to Scandinavian countries. Norway emitted, in 1990, 21,000 tons of SO_x and received 159,000 tons, mostly borne from Europe on the prevailing winds. The EU was a net 'exporter' of such pollutants, emitting 6.3 million tons of SO_x and 2.44 million tons of

Table 12.6 Sources of emissions and deposits of SO*x* in Europe ('000 tons, 1990)

	Norway	*Other Nordic*	*EU*	*UK*	*West Germany*	*East Germany*	*Emitters Other EU*	*USSR*	*Eastern Europe*	*Poland*	*CSFR*	*Other Eastern*	*Others*	*Total*
Receivers														
Norway	8	4	70	36	14	4	15	11	12	7	4	2	54	159
Other Nordic[a]	3	76	120	36	45	11	29	66	53	35	13	5	104	422
EU	0	2	3,092	653	856	244	1,339	15	294	80	126	88	396	3,799
UK	0	0	508	478	7	3	20	1	3	2	2	0	37	548
West Germany	0	0	710	16	643	28	23	2	73	19	52	2	19	804
East Germany	0	0	436	49	120	161	105	3	62	23	35	4	40	551
Others	0	1	1,438	111	86	52	1,190	9	156	37	37	82	291	1,895
USSR	1	32	375	52	228	32	63	1,924	727	404	128	196	557	3,617
Eastern Europe	0	3	777	42	537	55	144	68	2,628	895	580	1,153	223	3,700
Poland	0	2	416	26	328	28	34	20	910	741	130	40	60	1,409
Czech and Slovak Federal Republics	0	0	171	8	130	15	19	3	474	68	357	50	26	675
Others[b]	0	1	190	8	80	12	90	44	1,244	87	93	1,064	137	1,616
Others	8	45	1,882	619	266	82	917	241	560	183	120	258	1,560	4,295
Total	21	162	6,316	1,438	1,945	428	2,506	2,325	4,274	1,603	970	1,701	2,893	15,992

[a] Finland, Iceland, Sweden [b] Bulgaria, Hungary, Romania, Yugoslavia

Source: Norwegian Meteorological Institute /EMEP /MSC-W

Table 12.7 Sources of emissions and deposits of NOx in Europe ('000 tons, 1990)

	Norway	*Other Nordic*	*EU*	*UK*	*West Germany*	*East Germany*	*Emitters Other EU*	*USSR*	*Eastern Europe*	*Poland*	*CSFR*	*Other Eastern*	*Others*	*Total*
Receivers														
Norway	6	5	60	26	3	12	18	2	5	3	2	1	21	98
Other Nordic[a]	7	38	95	28	11	27	29	17	18	12	5	1	39	213
EU	2	3	897	155	47	229	466	5	64	21	28	15	163	1,134
UK	0	0	78	56	2	6	14	0	1	1	1	0	14	94
West Germany	0	1	91	10	17	42	22	1	11	4	7	0	9	113
East Germany	1	1	225	30	14	103	78	1	15	6	9	1	25	267
Others	1	1	503	60	14	78	352	3	35	10	11	14	116	660
USSR	4	38	241	37	46	86	72	332	185	112	40	33	168	968
Eastern Europe	1	6	344	29	67	124	123	19	267	99	73	95	85	722
Poland	1	4	156	18	40	62	37	6	95	61	27	7	26	287
Czech and Slovak Federal Republics	0	1	71	5	14	33	19	1	42	13	22	7	12	128
Others[b]	0	1	117	6	14	30	68	12	130	25	25	81	47	307
Others	13	30	807	236	40	150	380	49	102	39	30	33	413	1,414
Total	33	119	2,443	512	214	629	1,088	425	640	286	177	178	890	4,550

[a] Finland, Iceland, Sweden [b] Bulgaria, Hungary, Romania, Yugoslavia

Source: Norwegian Meteorological Institute /EMEP /MSC-W

NO_x in 1990. It received less at 3.8 million tons of SO_x and 1.13 million tons of NO_x.

In one sense it does not matter much where such pollution was created. Its presence in Norway still reduces the country's net welfare. In another sense it matters a great deal. If the purpose of constructing green accounts is a first step towards a national decision-making process of *doing* something about the problem, it matters greatly if governments are unwilling importers of other people's pollution.

It seems, then, that pollution damage can have serious effects on welfare. Clearly, some acknowledgement of those effects in estimates of national output would be of benefit to policy-makers. Alas, the problems of incorporating such estimates into the tables are formidable.

12.5 Resource depletion and the national income accounts

A related but separate problem is that raised by our extraction and use of the Earth's stock of oil and mineral deposits. Are we not depleting the Earth's capital stock while pretending that we are not doing so if our national income accounts make no mention of such activities?

The case for doing nothing

The argument for taking a relaxed view of the decline in natural resource stocks is based on a confidence in the market system to deal with scarcity. Suppose oil stocks are run down rapidly. The reduction in the available supply will drive up the relative price of the product. A higher relative price will draw forth alternative sources of energy not previously profitable at the lower price. For example, the United States has vast resources of shale oil, which is not at present worth exploiting because the costs are too great relative to the price. However, if oil prices rise sufficiently, the output from such sources will become profitable. One could widen the argument to include wind, wave and solar power. At present they are used very little, since energy prices are lower than the opportunity costs of the resources involved in enhancing such power. If other, cheaper, energy sources are nearing exhaustion, relative price changes will bring forth these alternative supplies.

Pessimists have for years concerned themselves over a future 'energy gap'. This concern is based on estimates that the demands for energy will grow faster than its supply. Some might argue that this will only happen if relative prices do not alter. However, such an energy gap will alter energy prices sufficiently to eliminate the gap. Shortages are simply a reflection of disequilibrium in relative prices. By this view, the problem of resource depletion can be ignored.

Others remain unconvinced. Sir John Hicks argued that income should be considered as whatever one can consume while remaining as well off at the end of the period as at the beginning. In other words, capital depletion does matter to society. The problem is that, even for those who *do* believe that resource depletion is a serious problem, there is little consensus about how to measure it.

Measuring changes in environmental degradation

If we are going to count resource depletion as part of capital depreciation to help produce a 'green GDP', how we are going to measure the change in the value of such stocks? There are many possibilities but we focus on the approach of the Office for National Statistics given in the 'environmental accounts' section of the National Income 'Blue Book' (2002).

Here estimates are given for the change in the value of oil and gas reserves over time. First, an estimate is made of the physical amounts remaining at any time. This requires some guess as to what future discoveries might be made and also the extent to which these stocks are recoverable. This depends, among other things, on technical know-how since some stocks are known to exist but difficult to extract.

Second, an estimate is made concerning the rate of extraction of reserves and also the future price per unit less the costs of extraction. Using these estimates we get the data presented in Figure 12.5. Extraction reduces the physical stock of reserves but since prices over the period have tended to rise the value of the reserves has generally risen over the period. At the end of 2001 UK oil reserves were valued at £52 billion and gas reserves at £39 billion.

The degree of concern about the effect of production and consumption on the environment varies between economists. Even within the increasingly large group expressing concern about these effects, there is no unanimity about how all this should be represented in the national accounts. The differences of outlook produce very different estimates. For example, over the last 25 years welfare

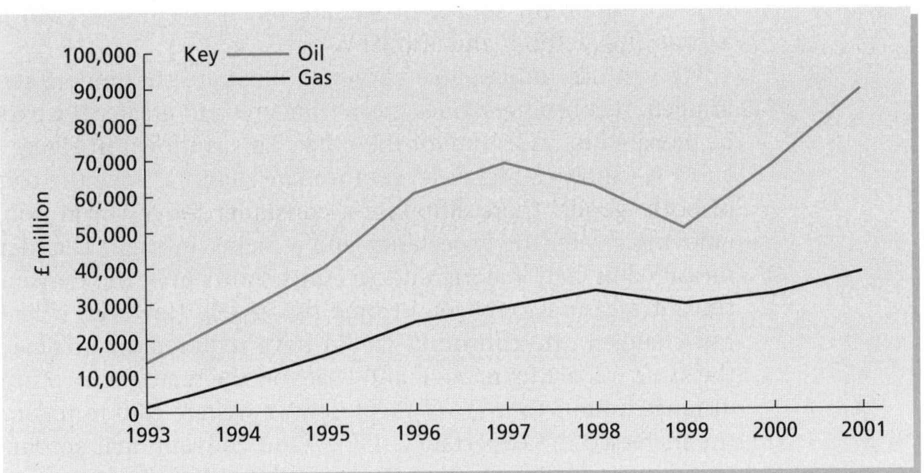

Figure 12.5 **Value of UK oil and gas reserves 1993–2001**

Source: ONS, 'Blue Book' (2000) © Crown copyright

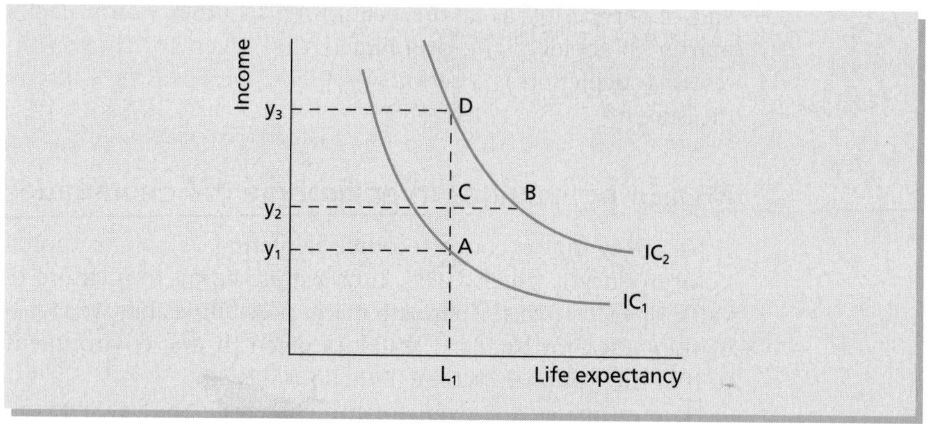

Figure 12.6 A trade-off between income and life expectancy

measured by GNP per head rose by an annual average of around two per cent in the UK. The New Economics Foundation, a green economics think-tank, measures welfare by its Index of Social Welfare (ISEW)which is based on a variety of measures of welfare, including environmental degradation, noise, pollution levels and the cost of commuting. This index suggests that welfare has *declined* over the same period.

However, it should not be assumed that the pessimistic conclusions of ISEW are necessarily correct. Nicholas Crafts[4] has argued that ISEW as currently conceived fails in two important respects. First, it substantially overstates the valuation of environmental degradation. His attempts to estimate national welfare by modifying the ISEW procedures give a much more positive picture of increasing real national income. Second, Crafts argues that ISEW, and indeed the conventional accounts, importantly understate welfare in a key area. No allowance is made for increasing life expectancy. Since this presumably has value for people it is an important source of welfare but it is ignored both by conventional accounting methods and also ISEW.

We can use indifference curves to illustrate the understatement of welfare implied. A consumer values greater income and greater life expectancy and will be prepared to trade one for the other. This is shown in Figure 12.6. The higher curve IC_2 shows a higher level of welfare than IC_1 since the consumer has more of both 'goods' there. Suppose a consumer moves from point A to point B, enjoying greater life expectancy and a higher income. The increased welfare as measured by national income accounts shows only the movement from A to C since it measures only the income rise, Y_1–Y_2. However, if life expectancy had not changed, the consumer would have required an income of Y_3 to achieve the same welfare increase. B and D are on the same indifference curve. Thus the distance from C to D (Y_2–Y_3) represents a welfare gain in income terms equal to the increased life expectancy. ISEW (and conventional accounting procedures) ignore such a gain. Crafts makes an attempt to value increased life expectancy and then adjusts the ISEW upwards appropriately, although clearly the procedure is not free of controversy.

12.6 Conclusion

We have seen that economists do have a measure of welfare of a country's citizens. It is based upon valuing the flow of output that is produced. That flow can be measured at any of three points in the circular flow of income. This gives us national product, national income and national expenditure, which will all be identical.

The clearest, although not necessarily the best, measure of welfare is national output per head of population. That output should be after allowance has been made for capital depreciation. In recent years attention has been given to attempts to incorporate environmental degradation into the estimates of capital depreciation, but this is fraught with difficulties and as yet there is no agreement about how this should be done. Since governments are always interested in making comparisons of their own country's economic performance with that of other countries, we are unlikely to see in the near future published environmental accounts that will meet with widespread acceptance and agreement.

CHAPTER SUMMARY

1 **The value of output produced in a country in a given year is called gross domestic product (GDP). Adding property income from abroad gives gross national product (GNP).**

2 **Since national product, expenditure and national income are measured at different points of the circular flow of income, they always have the same value.**

3 **GDP is found by summing value-added in each area of activity.**

4 **Subtracting capital depreciation from GNP gives net national product (NNP).**

5 **Resource depletion such as the using up of oil fields is ignored in estimating conventional levels of national income.**

6 **Many pollution costs are ignored in producing national income figures.**

7 **National income figures have only limited value as a measure of a society's level of welfare.**

Questions for discussion

Guidance to the answers for the ***asterisked*** *numbered questions is available to students on the website for the book at* **www.booksites.net/heather**.

1* Distinguish between (a) national and domestic product, (b) gross and net national product, (c) factor cost and market prices.

2 The ignoring of consumer surplus in the calculation of national output is an example of how the figures understate the level of a country's welfare. Ignoring the damage to the earth overstates it. What other factors make the use of national output a poor judge of welfare?

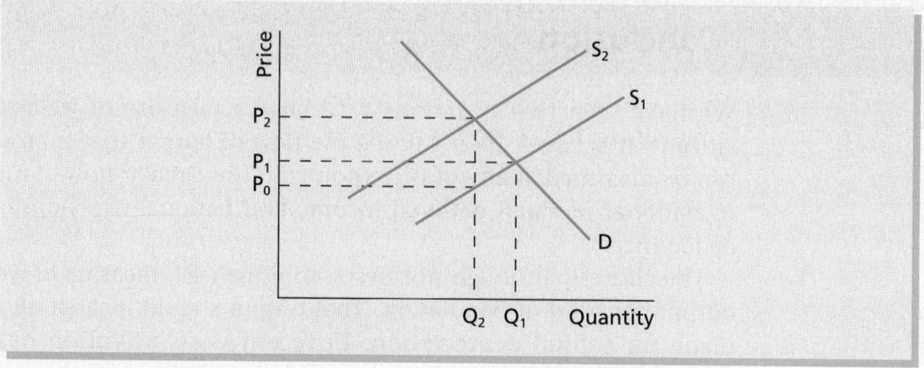

Figure 12.7 Taxing a pollution-creating firm

3* A government imposes a tax on a competitive industry which is polluting the environment. This changes its price output decision as shown in Figure 12.7. According to the national expenditure tables what is the value of the output (a) before the tax (b) after the tax?

4 One way for the government to tackle the problem of ecological damage is to make society aware that it is in its own interest to behave responsibly towards the environment. Why are most economists sceptical about this particular kind of appeal to self-interest to reduce such damage?

5* You are provided with the following information about an economy this year: government current expenditure 200, exports 400, imports 300, GDFI 250, consumers' expenditure 500, net investment 100, net property income 100. Find the level of GDP, GNP, NNP and NDP.

6 Why do economists sometimes refer to pollution as an 'untraded' interdependency? (*Hint*: When firms trade between themselves in the production of intermediate goods, this is a traded interdependency.) What light does this shed on methods of dealing with polluting activity of firms?

7* Reread section 12.4. Suppose an environmental tax was placed on the river polluter. Which measure of valuation of green capital stock depletion would be greater?

8 Using standard national income accounting procedures, which of the following will be allowed for in calculating a country's level of capital depreciation? (a) Wear and tear on a police headquarters, (b) the degradation of a farmer's soil through intensive farming, (c) the cutting down of a forest for making furniture, (d) depreciation of the family car, (e) depreciation of a company car.

9* What problems do you see in using national income data to compare the welfare of citizens of the UK with those of Sweden?

10 Is a zero level of pollution a desirable goal?

Websites

UK National Accounts can be accessed at:

www.statistics.gov.uk/nationalaccounts

One of the best sources of environmental statistics can be found at:

www.environment.detr.gov.uk/des/idek/htm

Notes

1 We said that Figure 12.1 represents a simplified economy. The main simplifications are (a) individual households spend all income received, making no provision for saving; (b) all income is actually received, whereas in reality some income is taken by government in taxation; (c) there is no international trade, i.e. income is spent on domestic production and domestic firms receive no orders from overseas. All these simplifications will be removed in a later chapter.

2 We have assumed here an optimal distribution of income. Recall from earlier chapters, particularly Chapter 4, that the demand curve reflects not only willingness to pay but also ability to pay.

3 The existence of international trade will mean that the circular flow diagram needs to be a little more complex. We make Figure 12.1 more realistic in the next chapter.

4 See Nicholas Crafts (2002) 'UK Real National Income, 1950–1988: Some Grounds for Optimism', *National Institute Economic Review* No. 181, July.

13 Keynesianism and unemployment

Unemployment: *what can the government do?*

CHAPTER OVERVIEW

Millions of people in countries throughout Europe have no job. Many want one but they feel that there is little prospect of finding one. Unemployment is not simply a waste of resources but a human problem of considerable proportions. What can governments do? Is there no way in which government policy could improve the situation?

In this chapter we review
- National income accounts
- Circular flow of income

We introduce
- Keynesian unemployment equilibrium
- Injections and withdrawals
- The multiplier
- The paradox of thrift

13.1 Introduction

The scale of the problem

Unemployment is a serious social problem. It has a dramatic effect upon the living standards and self-esteem not only of the unemployed but of their families too. On a national scale, it is a waste of resources: the opportunity cost of increased output is zero. This, of course, is true of any resource, including unemployed land or capital.

In Chapter 5 we considered the problem of unemployment in particular markets – its micro dimension. In this chapter we concentrate on unemployment at the macro level. An idea of the scale of the problem of unemployed labour can be gained from Figure 13.1 which shows unemployment in Europe as a percentage of the working population. By way of introduction let us note the following.

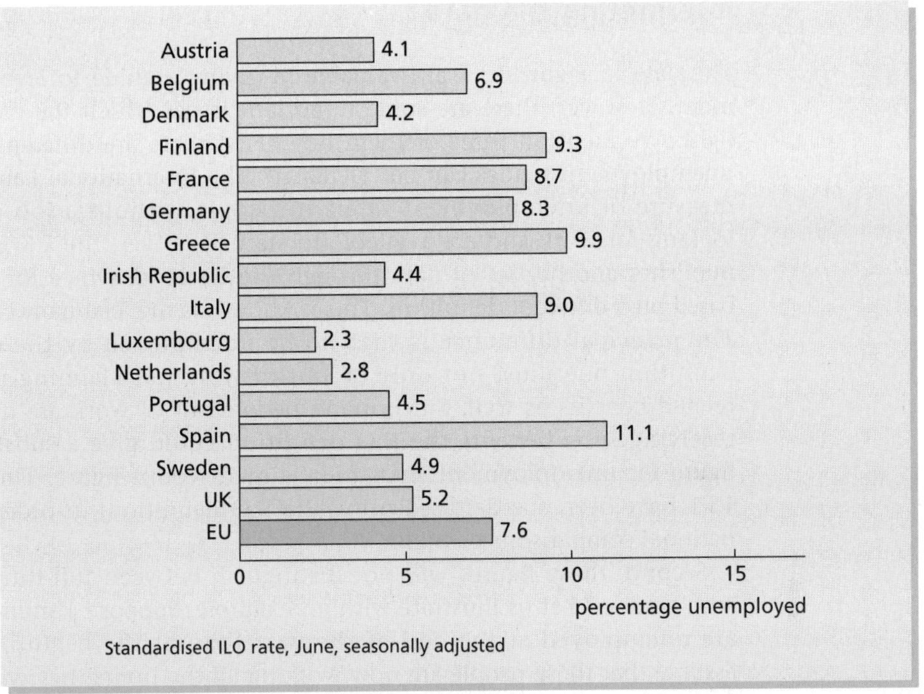

Figure 13.1 **Percentage unemployed for EU economies**
Source: adapted from *Labour Market Trends*

First, unemployment can be very high. For substantial periods over the last 15 years it has been over 3 million, or over 10 per cent of the workforce in the UK. For the EU a figure of around 7.5 per cent may seem acceptable but by the standards of the 1960s it is still very high. Second, the level of employment can vary greatly over time, at least for some parts of the world. In the UK, it was around only 0.5 million in 1973. Third, the position can change very quickly; for example, during a particularly serve recession, in the third quarter of 1992, 382,000 jobs were lost, representing a 1.75 per cent decline in just three months. Next, the problem appears to be worsening over time. Although, as we have said, it can vary greatly, the long-term trend appears to have been upwards over the past 50 years.

Two other things can be seen with reference to Figure 13.1. First, the problem is not unique to just one or two economies. It is a problem for virtually all governments. Second, the *scale* of the problem varies considerably between countries. The problem appears to be relatively small in Luxembourg and the Netherlands, for example, compared with, say, Spain and Greece. For Europe in general, this problem is considerable. In 2002 there were around 18 million people who were unemployed in the EU.

Unemployment problems are not unique to the European economy. Canada, Australia and New Zealand, for example, have all experienced unemployment on a considerable scale during recent years.

Interpreting the data

The data in Figure 13.1 are valuable in giving a guide to levels of unemployment. However, there are some important issues which the data do not highlight. We mention three of them now. First there are different ways in which unemployment figures can be calculated. The International Labour Office (ILO) measure of unemployment refers to people without a job who have been looking for work and are available to start. However, the UK government also publishes another set of data through the National Office for Statistics (NOS) based on a different definition. This is known as the 'claimant count' definition. The principal difference is that, to be unemployed by the claimant count definition one must not only be out of work but claiming unemployment-related benefits as well. Since many people out of work are disqualified from receiving such benefits the ILO definition could give a substantially higher figure for unemployment than the claimant count figure. The data in Figure 13.1 have been standardised using the ILO definition, in order to make international comparisons possible.

Second, these figures will not distinguish between full-time and part-time employment. Let us illustrate with an example. Suppose 1 million fewer people are unemployed at the end of the year than at the beginning. We cannot assume that these people are now working all the hours they wish. It is possible that they have found work for, say 18 hours a week. If they really wanted a 36-hour-week job each one is still 'half-unemployed'. The figures, however, will show them as having been removed from the unemployment register entirely.

One of the reasons why the Netherlands seems to have a relatively low level of unemployment is that many workers are part time. Part-time employment counts for around 33 per cent of all jobs. In Spain the equivalent figure is around 7 per cent.

Third, the unemployment count of Figure 13.1 gives no impression of the *duration* of unemployment, yet it does matter: as you can see from Figure 13.2 many people in Europe have been out of a job for more than a year. 44 per cent of the unemployed in the EU are in this position. This compares with only 6 per cent of those without a job in the USA. The length of time someone is out of the labour market is important. Again, an illustration may help us to see why. Suppose an economy has 2 million people unemployed at the beginning of the year and the same number unemployed at the end. If they are the *same people,* they have been out of the labour market so long that they may find it increasingly difficult to return to it. On the other hand, it may be that most of those out of work at the end of the year are different people from those unemployed at the beginning. This is probably a much less serious situation for the economy in that skills are not being lost. However, one cannot distinguish these two different scenarios simply by considering the unemployment data of Figure 13.1.

Modern economies, then, have a substantial problem in that significant numbers of people are without a job. To say that there is a real problem, however, is not to say that the government is in a position to do much about it. The question we wish to examine is, to what extent *can* a government do anything about it?

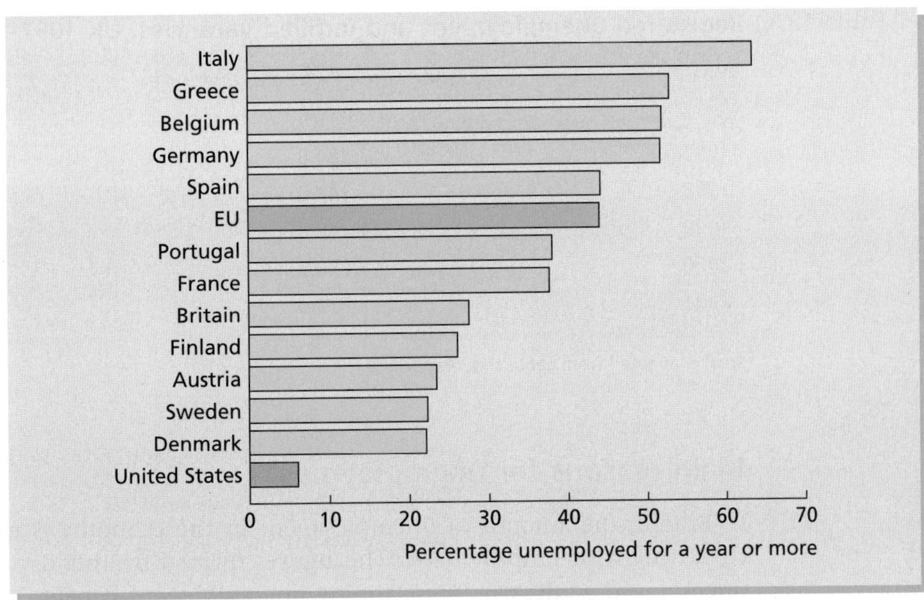

Figure 13.2 **Long-term unemployment in Europe and the USA**
Source: adapted from OECD data

Economists' perspectives on unemployment

Some economists feel that markets, left to themselves, deal with almost all problems far better than any government attempt at intervention. Only a few problems, of the kind we have examined in earlier chapters, will require government control. Other economists are more 'interventionist' in their outlook. One issue which divides economists is the question of whether unemployment is one of those conditions best left to cure itself. If we use a medical metaphor, some economists feel that the 'patient', the economy, needs to be as healthy as possible and governments should undertake policies to promote health, that is, the free working of markets. If a healthy economy is thereby achieved, the unemployment problem will be overcome without direct interference by government. If government does interfere, there will be unforeseen side-effects. Other economists, while recognising that side-effects are a danger, simply do not believe that the unemployment problem will correct itself, or at least that the correction process is unacceptably slow.

There is a view, then, that markets can do many things but that they cannot be relied upon to bring about full employment at a reasonable speed. Government involvement is required. This is a view that was expressed most forcefully by John Maynard Keynes. Those who share this basic outlook, while not in agreement about everything, are known as Keynesians. In this chapter we examine the Keynesian view. We shall see how it can be argued that a market system can give rise to lasting unemployment, and that governments can intervene, helping to eliminate it. An alternative view, critical of the Keynesian position, will be considered in a later chapter.

see pp. 330–9

Table 13.1 Registered unemployment and unfilled vacancies, UK 1997–2001

Year	*Claimant count unemployment (000s)*	*Job vacancies (000s)*
1997	1,584.5	283.3
1998	1,347.8	295.8
1999	1,248.1	314.2
2000	1,088.5	359.1
2001	970.0	394.9

Source: adapted from *Labour Market Trends*

Main reasons for unemployment

In Britain, the amount of unemployment in the economy is measured by the Department of Employment. The figures quoted by this department are for unemployed adults who are claiming unemployment benefit. Why do millions of people find themselves in this position? Several reasons can be found.

First, there is *frictional* unemployment. Markets do not work instantaneously. Some people may leave one job and not take up another for a period of weeks. Meanwhile they claim benefits as unemployed people.

Table 13.1 shows the registered unemployed in the UK over a five-year period when unemployment was falling. As you can see, registered unemployment fell significantly. However, many employers had job vacancies which they could not fill, and that number grew during the period. The vacancies column gives an idea of the *trend* of vacancies but not the true *level*. Only around one-third of vacancies are advertised through job centres. Much of the explanation for job vacancies existing at the same time that there is unemployment is frictional. There is a mismatch between the kinds of job vacancy and the kinds of skill possessed by the unemployed. The vacancies may be for computer programmers and the unemployed may be coal miners. To some extent there is also a regional mismatch. Jobs can exist in one part of the country, the unemployed can be in a different place. You will recall that we considered this problem in Chapter 5.

Second, there is *seasonal* unemployment. Many find work in the summer in tourist areas but are unemployed in the winter months. A proportion of those employed in the construction industry are out of a job if the weather is severe in the winter.

see pp. 138–61

A third category is *structural* unemployment. If demand for the output of an industry falls rapidly, labour inputs are no longer required. A fall in product demand causes unemployment in that industry. The decline in the demand for coal which caused much unemployment amongst miners is a problem we mentioned in Chapter 7. Some of the problems of regional unemployment which we examined in Chapter 5 are structural in origin.

see pp. 93–114

Fourth there is *voluntary* unemployment. Some are unemployed because they do not wish to work at the wage rate being offered to them but would prefer to do nothing and live on state benefits. Much controversy surrounds the question of the extent of this kind of unemployment. It is an issue to which we return in Chapter 16.

see pp. 349–55

There is a fifth kind of unemployment upon which we shall focus in this chapter, namely *demand-deficient* unemployment. By this we mean that people can be unemployed because the volume of demand for goods and services in the whole economy, what we refer to as aggregate demand, is simply not high enough for all those seeking a job to be able to find one. It is important to understand that it is not the lack of demand in one particular area of economic activity that is the problem, but the lack of demand in the economy as a whole. If the demand for output is, in some sense, too low, the demand for labour, which is a demand derived from the demand for output, will also be low. Under these circumstances, government policies will be needed to stimulate demand for output. That is the concept that forms the heart of this chapter. It is a controversial concept. Some economists, those whose views are in essence Keynesian, accept the proposition that governments must manipulate the volume of demand for aggregate output. Others, whom we might call *classical economists*, believe that government attempts to deal with the problem of such unemployment through 'demand management' are worse than useless: it is to give a patient a medicine with unpleasant side-effects when he would recover naturally and unaided. Much of this chapter follows the logic of the Keynesian argument and explains how demand might be manipulated, although we will indicate why the classical economists dissent from these views. In later chapters we shall develop the classical view more fully.

13.2 Equilibrium output in Keynesian thinking

Planned and actual demand

see pp. 253–9

You recall from Chapter 12 that national expenditure is always of the same value as national output. Whatever is produced, there is an expenditure on it by someone or some organisation. However, not all that expenditure is necessarily intended. If a car manufacturer produces a car, it is included in the national output table. Suppose nobody wanted to buy the car and it remained unsold? In the national expenditure account the car appears as a stock item. In essence, then, it is regarded as an item that the firm itself has purchased as part of its stock for selling later. The firm may not have *intended* to 'purchase' the car for holding as stock; it may have wanted to sell it. Actual output was not equal to *planned* expenditure. However, actual output was equal to actual expenditure. Now, what is true of the company's car production can be true of an economy's output. The national income accounts will always show that actual national output equals actual national expenditure. But what happens in an economy if *plans* to purchase output, *planned* expenditure, is not equal to the actual output produced?

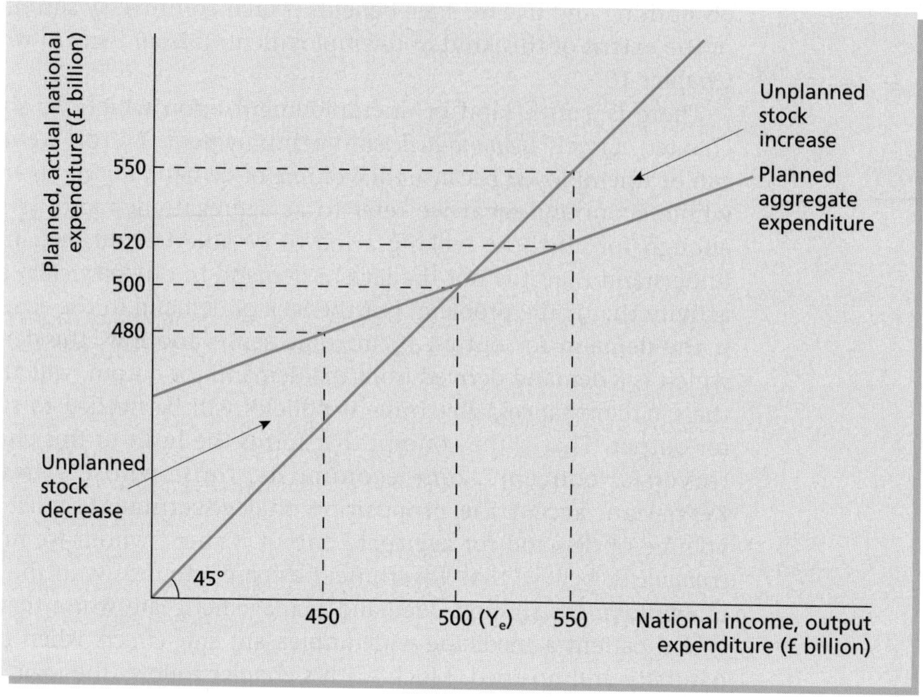

Figure 13.3 **Equilibrium national output**

We can examine this question by referring to Figure 13.3. Consider first the curve labelled planned aggregate expenditure. Plans to purchase output come from consumers, firms (as demand for investment goods), governments, and foreigners who wish to buy British goods (export demand). To the extent that part of the demand for output is met by import demand, planned expenditure on British goods and services is reduced by the amount of planned import demand. The higher national income is, the higher will be plans to purchase output. This is shown in Figure 13.3. The figure illustrates the aggregate of planned expenditure at all possible levels of national income.

Notice that this relationship is shown such that even at a low income there is some expenditure. Some forms of government spending take place whatever the level of income even if it means borrowing. Similarly individuals must spend on basic needs whatever their income, either by borrowing or by 'dissaving', that is running down assets that they previously acquired. Such planned spending which is independent of the level of income we call 'autonomous expenditure'. The expenditure which economic agents are induced to make as income rises we refer to as 'induced' expenditure.

Now consider the line in Figure 13.3 drawn at 45 degrees. It will have the same value on the horizontal axis as on the vertical axis. This is because it is intended to show that the value of national output must equal the value of actual expenditure. So, for example at a national income of £550 billion, *actual* national expenditure must also be £550 billion. However, we have seen that for an economy to be in equilibrium, planned expenditure must equal actual output. Is there any value of national output at which plans to spend will be the same as real output? You can see from the diagram that there is only one such level, and that is £500 billion. At this level of output, plans to purchase are equal to the amount of output being produced. This is the equilibrium level of output, Y_e. The economy is in equilibrium because the amount people wish to purchase equals the amount firms wish to produce.

Stable equilibrium

see pp. 41–3

Before we see the significance of this for unemployment there is one other point of great importance. Y_e is not only an equilibrium level of output, it is also a stable equilibrium. In Chapter 2 we defined equilibrium as a state of rest, and stability as a condition such that movements away from equilibrium were self-correcting. We can see the same principle at work here in a different context. Suppose national output were to rise from £500 billion to £550 billion. Planned expenditure is now £520 billion (see Figure 13.3 again) and actual expenditure is £550 billion. So £30 billion more output is being produced than economic agents wish to buy. Firms' unplanned stocks will be rising since there is an unplanned stock increase of £30 billion. How will firms respond? They will cut back on output to avoid creating further unwanted stock. The result is that national output will fall. Only at a national output of £500 billion will this problem disappear.

Equilibrium and unemployment

We have now established that, given the relationship between income and expenditure, there is a unique level of equilibrium national output to which the economy will tend. The Keynesian argument is that the equilibrium level of national income is by no means certain to be a level at which there is full employment of labour. In terms of the opportunity cost curve we studied in see pp. 8–9 Chapter 1, the economy could be at equilibrium inside the curve. There is nothing in the nature of the market system which will see to it that the economy tends quickly towards a full employment level of output – it could be stuck at Y_e (the equilibrium level of national income) for a substantial period. We con- see pp. 144–6 sidered this possibility in Chapter 7 in the context of the oil industry.

High unemployment can be seen as an excess supply of labour, but if there is an excess labour supply, one might expect the price of labour services, that is wage rates, to fall. This labour market adjustment might continue until all see pp. 97–9 who want a job have one, as discussed in Chapter 5. However, Keynesian economists believe that labour markets do not quickly respond in this way. This leads them to the conclusion that the economy can suffer from demand-deficient unemployment which requires government intervention. The form that that intervention might take is something we shall consider shortly. Before that, however, we can use and extend the above analysis to see why changes in people's attitudes to savings and consumption expenditure can create difficulties for employment prospects.

13.3 The paradox of thrift

Injections and withdrawals

see pp. 11–13

A country with a high level of savings is one with some real advantages. As we saw in Chapter 1, if a country refrains from consumption (saves) it can invest, raising consumption in future years. So a high savings ratio makes funds available to firms for investment purposes. This increases national income in future years. However, in the Keynesian view, a high level of savings can, given certain conditions, damage a country's economic well-being and worsen a country's unemployment problem. Let us develop our analysis of the economy in order to expose this apparent contradiction, or paradox.

see pp. 250–3

In Figure 13.4 we return to the circular flow of income diagram from Chapter 12. We said there that firms will need to produce sufficient output to meet the flow of consumers' expenditure. In fact, firms must produce more than sufficient to satisfy consumption demand. There are other demands made upon their output, as we saw in Chapter 12 when examining the national income accounts. There are demands upon firms from government – government expenditure (G) – from firms wanting to purchase investment goods (I), and from foreigners in the form of export demand (X). These expenditures are in addition to those of households. They are shown in Figure 13.4 as injections into the circular flow of income. Output must be sufficient to meet all these demands.

On the other hand, not all the income that households receive from firms is spent on demands from firms for their output. Some of that income leaks out of

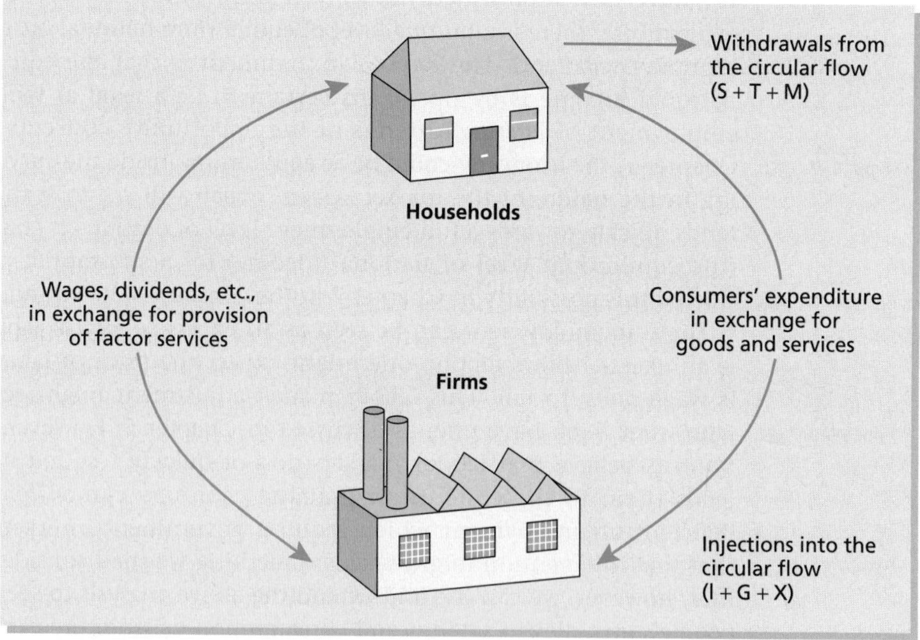

Figure 13.4 **Injections into and withdrawals from the circular flow of income**

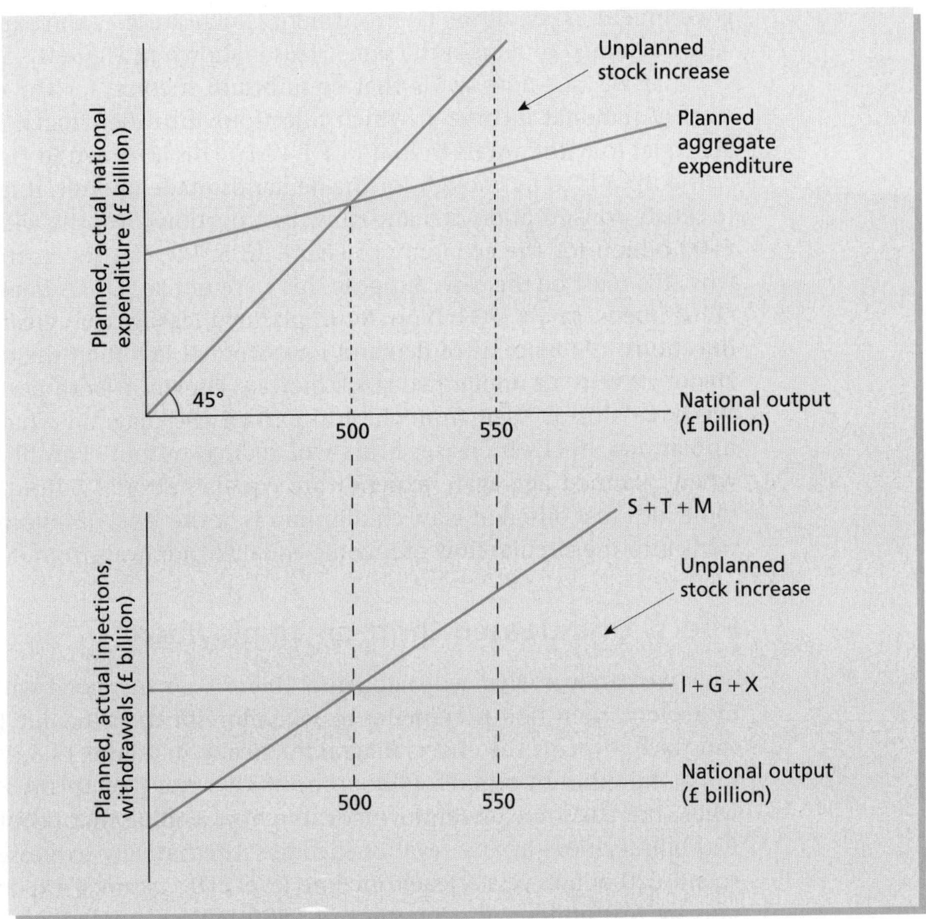

Figure 13.5 Injections and withdrawals: equilibrium national income

the circular flow. What income do households receive which is not spent on current output from firms? What part of their income is withdrawn from the circular flow? One such leakage is savings (S): people choose not to spend all their income. Another is taxation (T) taken by the government, and yet another is import demand (M). To the extent that people use their income to buy imports, they are purchasing goods and services, but it is not domestically produced output. Savings, taxes and imports, then, constitute the leakages, or withdrawals from the circular flow of income. To the extent that households do not use their income for consumption purposes, it reduces the amount of output which firms must produce if aggregate demand is to be satisfied.

Now these injections into and withdrawals from the circular flow of income are represented in Figure 13.5. Look first at withdrawals from the circular flow. As national income increases, people save more, pay more taxes and buy more imports. This gives the positively sloped relationship S + T + M. What about injections? For simplicity we will assume that injections into the circular flow of income are autonomous. In other words, whatever the level of national income, government expenditure, G, investment expenditure, I, and export expenditure, X, are assumed to remain the same. This is shown in Figure 13.5 as I + G + X.

What we can now see is that equilibrium income for the economy is that level of national income at which injections into the circular flow (I + G + X) are equal to withdrawals from it (S + T + M). This is shown in Figure 13.5.

If output is to be enough for the demands made upon it, it must be sufficient to satisfy consumption demand plus the injections, less the withdrawals. This is £500 billion for the economy of Figure 13.5. We can see in the following way why this must be the case. Suppose this were not so. Let us imagine that national income is, say, £550 billion. Since planned leakages are greater than planned injections, the amount of demand for output is less than the output produced. Hence there is an unplanned stock increase shown in both parts of Figure 13.5. We have already seen from the top part of the diagram what happens when unplanned stocks increase: firms will reduce output. Equilibrium is restored where planned aggregate expenditure equals national output. Expressing the same idea in a different way, equilibrium is at the level of output at which injections into the circular flow of income equal withdrawals from it.

Effects of increased thrift on employment

Now we can ask what will happen if there is an increased willingness to save by society, such that they prefer to save more of their income than before. We can trace through the effects diagrammatically in Figure 13.6. We start with an initial equilibrium of £500 billion and we assume that this is a level of output where there is some unemployment. We now assume that people decide to save £20 billion more at any level of income. Alternatively expressed, they plan to spend £20 billion less at each income level. The planned expenditure function falls by £20 billion. At an output of £500 billion, unplanned stock levels rise. Firms respond by reducing output, causing workers to be unemployed. Only when output has fallen to £450 billion is equilibrium restored.

The same effects can be seen on the lower part of the diagram. Since the lower part shows leakages including savings, increased thrift is shown as an upward shift in the withdrawals function from S + T + M (1) to S + T + M (2). Again, one can see the resulting unplanned stock increase, and the fall in national income to its new lower equilibrium of £450 billion.

Under these circumstances increased thrift has reduced aggregate demand, lowered equilibrium output and increased unemployment. One thinks of saving as a good thing to do, and for the individual who does, so it is. He may want a pension or some insurance against losing his job. It can also have advantages for society at large, as we have already seen. However, under certain circumstances, its effects on society can be harmful. Output falls, unemployment rises.

Sometimes increased thrift appears at exactly the wrong time for an economy. If an economy is at full employment, higher aggregate demand can create inflation, and increased willingness to save can reduce inflationary pressure. Suppose, though, that for some reason unemployment is high or rising, the *fear of more unemployment* can cause those who have a job to increase their savings. This will reduce aggregate demand, thereby compounding the problem. We

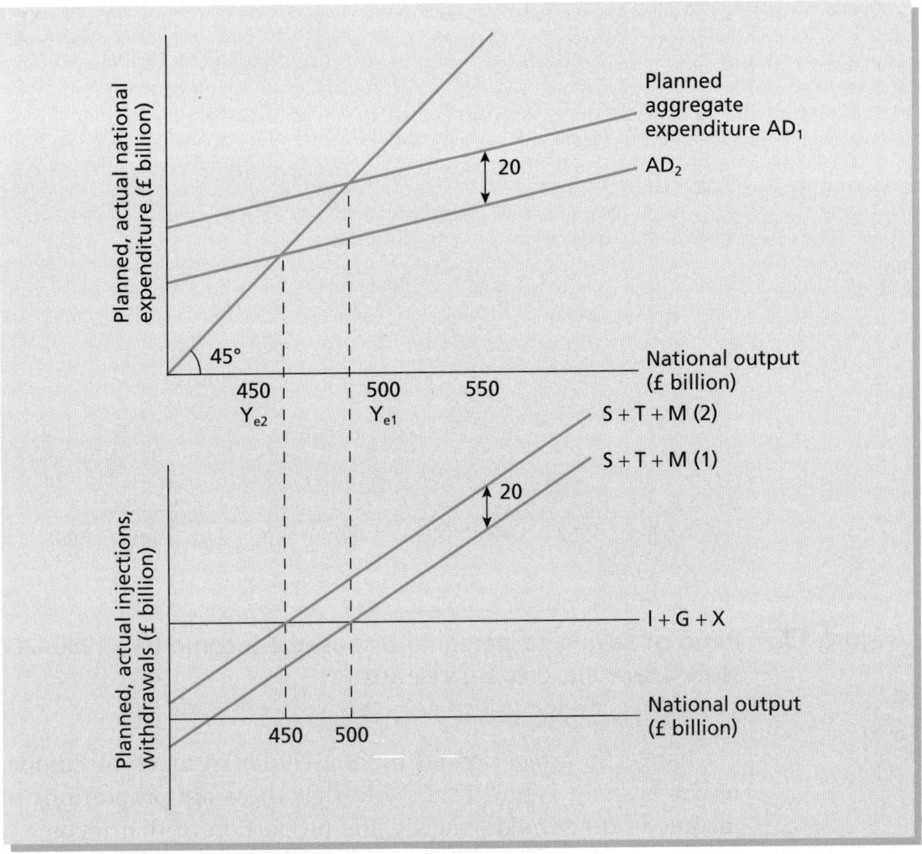

Figure 13.6 **Effects of an increase in thrift by society**

have previously referred to the UK's unemployment problem of the early 1990s, which followed a boom in the mid to late 1980s. Observe in Figure 13.7 how this was mirrored in the rising savings ratio (and thus falling consumption demand) of the recession. The chart shows personal income net of tax, that is personal disposable income minus consumer spending, measured as a percentage of income. Observe the sharp rise in the savings ratio in the UK during the period in which the economy moved into recession and unemployment was rising.

Effects of increased thrift on savings

A particularly surprising result of increased thrift in the circumstances described is its effect on the volume of savings. The volume may not increase at all. In Figure 13.6 households took a decision to increase savings, but the aggregate effect was to reduce output and therefore income. They may now be saving a higher proportion of their income but they have less income. They may therefore not have increased the *volume* of savings at all. It is this phenomenon that gives rise to the expression 'the paradox of thrift'. Intentions by a nation to save more may not result in increased saving at all.

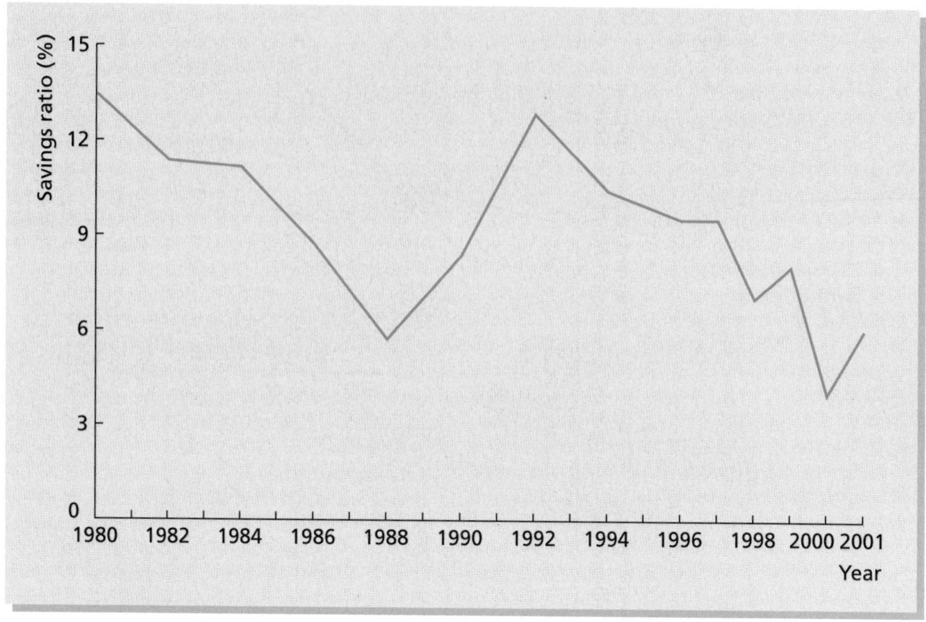

Figure 13.7 **Ratio of saving to personal disposable income UK, 1980–2001**
Source: adapted from OECD and NIESR data

Changes in *actual* savings by households in much of Europe can be seen for recent years in Figure 13.8. Note that these are proportions of the disposable income of households, that is, the proportion of that income left after government taxes. As you can see, over a ten-year period straddling the turn of the century savings ratios declined for the great majority of EU countries.

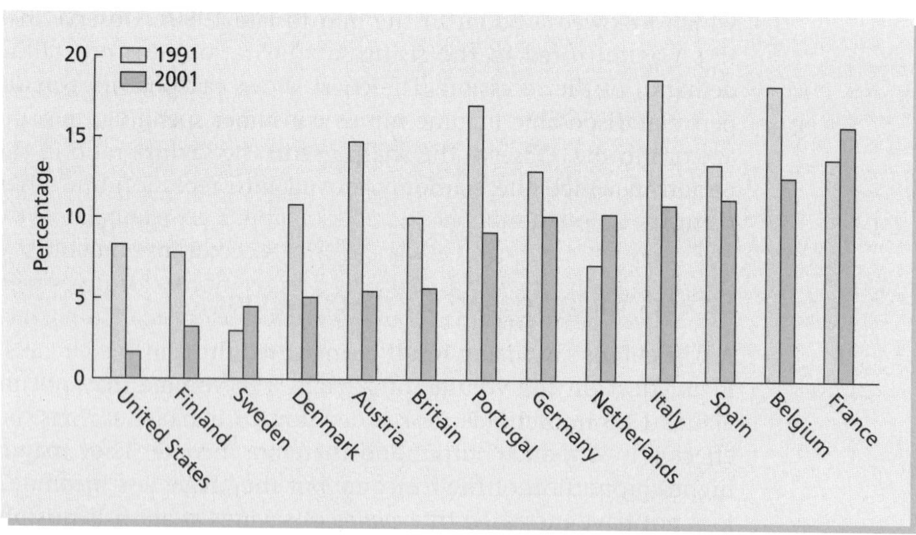

Figure 13.8 **Household saving as a proportion of disposable income**
Source: adapted from OECD data

13.4 Government action on demand-deficient unemployment

As with other EU countries British gross domestic product (GDP) has clearly been less than full employment GDP at times. The Keynesian analysis suggests that some unemployment is a result of demand deficiency. We can now think through what the government can do about it and what its effects on the economy might be.

Possible remedies for demand-deficiency unemployment

Any measure to stimulate aggregate demand can be considered as a possibility for raising output and therefore for reducing demand-deficient unemployment. Referring back to Figure 13.5, anything that shifts the planned expenditure function upwards can be used to achieve the desired effect. We can say this another way. Looking at the lower part of the diagram, the government can attempt either to lower the withdrawals function or to raise the injections function.

We shall list some possible ways of raising the planned expenditure function. Whether these measures equate to a lowering of the withdrawal function or a raising of the injections function in the lower section of the diagram is left for you to consider for yourself.

- *Consumption* can be increased. This might be done by cutting taxes. Cuts might be made to direct tax – the tax on people's income – or to indirect tax, the tax on items of expenditure. The main form of indirect taxation is value added tax (VAT), but there are others such as the taxes on petrol and cigarettes. Consumption can also be increased by lowering interest rates. Some forms of expenditure are particularly sensitive to such a change. Large items of consumer expenditure, such as cars and household goods, are often bought on credit. An alternative means of changing consumption is interest rates. Lowering interest rates has the effect of making such goods cheaper to purchase on credit.[1]
- *Investment* can be increased. This can be private or state investment. The government can increase its own spending. Expenditures on hospital buildings, roads, school buildings and police stations are examples of this. Alternatively, the government can encourage private sector investment. Lower interest rates will make it cheaper for firms to borrow money for investment. Alternatively, see pp. 104–9 it might offer subsidies for investment, as we saw in Chapter 5. Either way, the attempt can be made to boost expenditure.
- *Government current expenditure* can be increased. The government might, for example, employ more nurses or teachers, although such a policy might prove difficult to reverse if the economy were subsequently to be fully employed. Again, the effect is to boost aggregate expenditure.
- If government can *boost export demand*, this will also raise national output.
- Aggregate demand can be increased by *reducing imports*. Since any part of consumers' income spent on the purchase of imports reduces the amount spent

see pp. 413–62

on domestically produced goods and services, switching demand away from imports can raise aggregate demand and therefore the level of employment. As we shall see in Chapters 19 and 20, though, there is no way in which this can be done which is not controversial, especially within the EU since member states have a commitment to free trade within the Union. Reducing imports by, for example, imposing taxes on imports is therefore likely to give rise to a retaliatory policy by the country whose export industries are affected by a fall in export demand. That retaliation will then affect the first country's exports and employment.

Measuring the size of increase in expenditure: the multiplier

An important consideration for a government wishing to increase aggregate demand for the purpose of reducing unemployment is the appropriate *extent* of the demand increase. One reason that this is important is that a given boost to demand will increase expenditure by more than the original increase. In other words national output will rise by a multiple of any increase in demand. There is a 'multiplier' effect on output. To understand why this is so we shall examine Figure 13.9. This is the circular flow of income diagram which was encountered earlier (Figure 13.4).

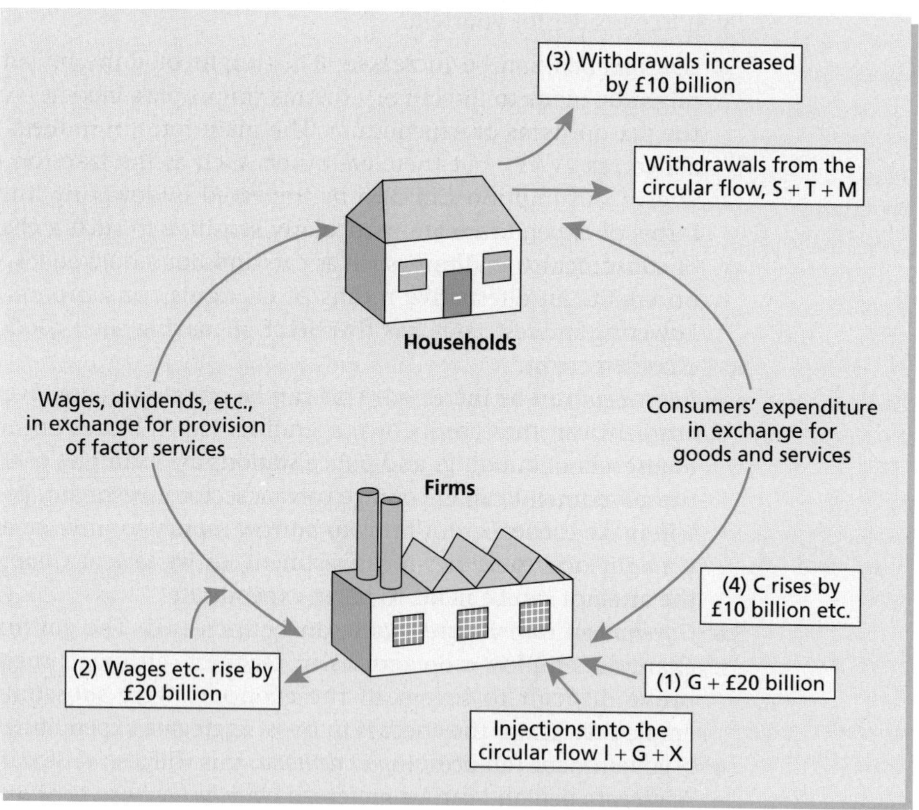

Figure 13.9 **Injection of £20 billion into the circular flow of income**

Table 13.2 Effects on national output of an increase in government spending of £20 billion

Period	*Increase in national output (£ billion)*	*Increase in planned consumption (£ billion)*	*Increase in planned withdrawals (S + T + M) (£ billion)*
1	20	10	10
2	10	5	5
3	5	2.5	2.5
4	2.5	1.25	1.25
⋮	⋮	⋮	⋮
n	40	20	20

Let us assume that this economy has an 'unemployment equilibrium': planned injections are equal to planned withdrawals. Expressing the same idea differently, planned demand is equal to the available output. However, there is a significant level of unemployment which the government wishes to eliminate by increasing aggregate demand. Let us assume that the attempt to do this is through increasing government investment in hospitals, roads and schools to the extent of £20 billion. We must now think through the effects on the economy using Figure 13.9 to do so.

Since an additional £20 billion of output is being demanded by government, construction companies and other firms will increase output by £20 billion. This will raise household incomes by £20 billion, since some people will be employed and receive wages, and others who own shares in the companies will receive increased dividends from the profits.

see pp. 253–9

Remember from Chapter 12 that national output must be identically equal to national income. What will households do with the £20 billion of income that they receive? Some will be taxed away from them; some they will choose to save; some they will spend on imported goods. Let us suppose that 20 per cent goes in income tax, 20 per cent on imports and 10 per cent on increased saving. The other 50 per cent or £10 billion will be spent, further increasing the demand for output by firms.

In the next period, firms will increase output by £10 billion to meet this increased demand. That output represents household incomes, half of which will be withdrawn from the circular flow as taxes, savings and imports. This leaves £5 billion to be spent, and so on.

The process is summarised in Table 13.2 which shows that there will eventually be an increase in national output of twice the original increase in government spending. This is because part of the increase in national income is spent on further consumption. What is true of increase in government spending will be true of decreases too: decreases in government spending will reduce output and therefore incomes causing a multiple reduction in output.

What is the size of this multiplier effect? In the economy illustrated in Table 13.2 the multiplier is 2: a change in government spending led to a change in output of twice that amount. However, the multiplier will be different for different economies; indeed it may be different for the same economy at different times. We can, however, establish a general principle: the multiplier $k = 1/w$ where w is the proportion of any increase in household income not spent but withdrawn from the circular flow. The term w is usually called the marginal propensity to withdraw. In this case, since half of any additional income received by households is withdrawn from the circular flow, the multiplier, $k = 1/0.5 = 2$. In an economy where withdrawals from the circular flow are smaller, the multiplier is higher.

Suppose tax is only 10 per cent of income. Suppose, furthermore, that we save only 5 per cent of any additional income we receive and that 10 per cent of any increase in income is spent on imports. The multiplier would then be:

$$k = \frac{1}{0.1 + 0.05 + 0.1} = \frac{1}{0.25} = 4$$

A formal proof of this general multiplier relationship is given in Appendix 5.

Using the multiplier effect for reducing unemployment

In principle, then, unemployment in an economy can be controlled by changes in government expenditure. The government *can* do something by adding to aggregate demand where it is too low. One way in which it can do this is by increasing its expenditure. However, it will need to have an idea of the size of the multiplier. It will also need to be aware of the extent to which increases in output lead to an increase in the demand for labour.

see pp. 93–114

We can extend our analysis to the problem of regional unemployment that we considered in Chapter 5. If unemployment is high in one part of the country, increased regional expenditure on roads, hospitals and so on can raise income in that part of the country through the multiplier effect. The size of the multiplier will again be determined by w, the propensity to withdraw spending from the circular flow. Again, this will be dependent upon the tax rate, willingness to save out of increased income and willingness to 'import' not only from abroad but from other areas of the country too. The extent to which Scottish output will rise if government increases spending in Scotland is determined partly by whether Scots spend their additional income on cars manufactured in the Midlands.

13.5 Problems in controlling unemployment

Some economists do not believe that Keynesian management of aggregate demand is necessary or desirable. Now we consider three great problems for governments who *do* believe that such control is beneficial.

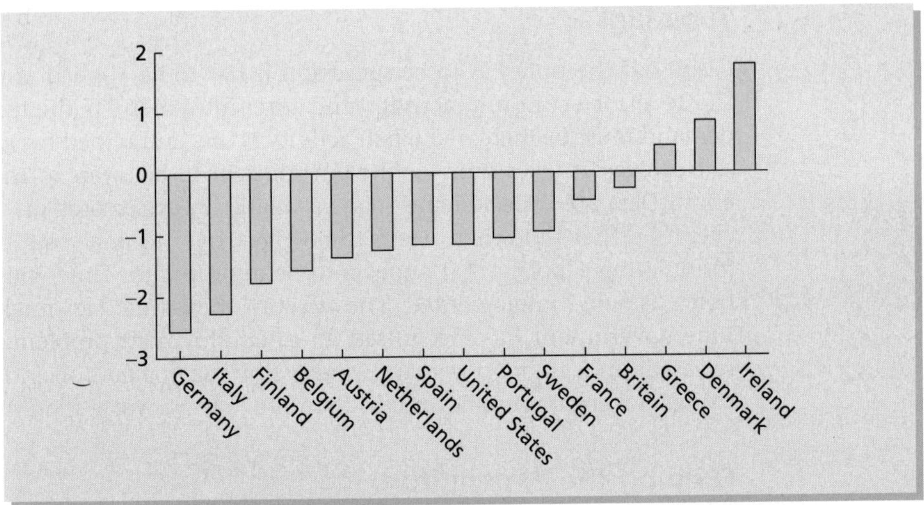

Figure 13.10 **OECD estimates of output gaps in 2002**
Adapted from: OECD, *Economic Outlook*, 2003

Estimating output gaps

A significant problem is knowing the extent to which an economy's output is less than that which gives full employment. Creating too much demand will drive up prices and create inflation. Thus an estimate must be made of the amount of output that represents full employment but is consistent with a stable price level. The difference between this estimate and the actual output of the economy is called the output gap.

This gap can be negative – the economy is producing too little output to give full employment – or positive. A positive output gaps suggests too much demand and the threat of inflation. OECD estimates of European output gaps are given in Figure 13.10. Demand is thought to be too low in most countries but rather too high in a few, notably Ireland.

The problem occurs with estimating the output gap. What level of output represents full employment? We can look at an economy and see what annual increase in output has been achieved over a long period. In the UK, for example, this has been around 2.25 per cent. If we assume that this is what is achievable over the coming years we have an estimate of the output level that is possible. However, this requires an assumption that may be invalid. For example, the arrival of rapid technological change in recent years, particularly in the USA, has led some to argue that potential output is growing much faster than the previous trend would suggest. This gives an estimate for the output gap that is too small. The economy is capable of being run at a higher level of output and a lower level of unemployment than the output gap data suggests.

Not everyone is convinced about the US 'productivity miracle'. However, it does show how difficult it can be to calculate output gaps.

Time lags

Clearly, if the policy is to be successful it has to be applied at the right time. If the level of economic activity and unemployment is fluctuating, aggregate demand must be increased when activity is low and reined back when it is high.

However, it takes time for the government to be aware of the economic situation. Data are collected and made available weeks or perhaps months after the event. Further time then needs to be given over to analysing the situation and formulating a policy that appears to be appropriate. Time will then pass while policy is being implemented. The effect of these time lags might be that by the time government has recognised an unemployment problem, analysed it and released funds to boost demand, a recession may be ending and demand may be rising. Government policy might then prove to be worse than useless.

Funding the expenditure

Suppose a government decides to stimulate demand by increasing government spending. Unless, at the time it takes the decision, it is receiving more in taxes than it is spending, it will create a deficit on its own account that it must fund. It will have to borrow. The extent of this borrowing requirement is called the public sector borrowing requirement, PSBR or 'cash requirement', the PSCR. If the government spends more than it receives in taxes, the PSBR is positive. If it spends less than it receives, the PSBR is negative. A negative PSBR is referred to as a PSDR, the public sector debt repayment. Part of the government's debts that have accumulated over the years can be repaid if the PSBR in any given year is negative.

Part of the logic of Keynesian demand management policy is that, during a recession when unemployment is high there should be a PSBR. On the other hand, when there is a high level of economic activity, there should be no need for a PSBR at all.

If government increases its spending during a recession, how will the increase be funded? Some of it will be funded by increased government income raised by the increase in economic activity. Let us illustrate this by reference to Table 13.3. Government spending, G, was assumed to increase by £20 billion. Output rose, through the multiplier by £40 billion. Remember, though, that government was assumed to receive taxes of 20 per cent of national income. So 20 per cent of the

Table 13.3 Effects on the PSBR of an increase in government spending of £20 billion

	(£ billion)
Initial increase in government spending	20
Eventual increase in national output	40
Eventual increase in planned consumption	20
Eventual increase in planned withdrawals	20
Eventual increase in taxation: 20% of increase in national output	8
Eventual change in PSBR	12

Table 13.4 Treasury forecasts of the UK economy

	Actual 2001	*Forecast 2002*	*Forecast 2003*	*Forecast 2004*
Annual growth in output at constant market prices				
Gross Domestic Product (GDP)	2.25%	2 to 2.5%	3% to 3.5%	2.5% to 3%
GDP at market prices (£bn)	989	1,036–1,041	1,094–1,104	1,149–1,166
Annual growth in expenditure components of GDP at constant market prices				
Domestic demand, of which:	2.75%	2.75% to 3.25%	3% to 3.5%	2.5% to 3%
Household consumption	3.75%	3% to 3.5%	2.25% to 2.75%	1.75% to 2.25%
General government consumption	2.75%	3.25%	3.25%	3.25%
Fixed investment	0.25%	1.5 to 2%	5.75% to 6.25%	4.25% to 4.75%
Change in inventories	–0.25%	0%	0%	0%
Exports	1%	–1.5% to –1%	7.75% to 8.25%	6.5% to 7%
Imports	2.75%	1% to 1.5%	6.5% to 7%	6% to 6.5%
Inflation				
RPIX (Q4)[1]	2.%	2.25%	2.5%	2.5%

[1] RPIX is a measure of inflation which is explained in Chapter 15

Source: adapted from HM Treasury, 'Red Book'

increased national income, or £8 billion, is received in extra tax. Thus the increase in G is £20 billion, and the increase in T is £8 billion. The PSBR will rise by only £12 billion.

In reality, the position for a government will probably be better than this. A significant part of G goes on unemployment benefit. If unemployment is reduced, this aspect of G will also fall.[2] Nevertheless, a significant rise in the PSBR will be inevitable if government wishes to increase expenditure when aggregate demand is low.

Not all of the increase in expenditure during a recession is the result of deliberate government policy. To some extent it is involuntary. A recession increases unemployment and so increases government expenditure on unemployment benefit. This aspect of the economy works as a 'built-in stabiliser'. A fall in private aggregate demand is automatically partly offset by an increase in government demand. There is a tendency for the size of the recession to be limited without government action. The stabilisation of aggregate demand is, to some extent, built into the structure of the economy.

Whatever the state of the economy, governments have a limited control over economic events so that forecasting its income and expenditure is fraught with difficulties. Although it can set tax *rates* it cannot know accurately what this will bring in. This depends upon what is produced. Table 13.4 shows the UK government's forecast of the economy made in 2002. By estimating the changes in the components of expenditure it estimates national output and therefore national income. This enables it to estimate its expected income. However, estimates of household expenditure, firm's investment plans and the volume of exports and imports are also subject to error. Government income is not completely certain, therefore.

Similarly it does not have complete control over its expenditure. It makes plans to spend on health, education etc. but other areas of expenditure are even more difficult to control. As we said earlier, for example, if unemployment is unexpectedly high it not only reduces government income but also increases expenditure on unemployment benefit etc.

Over much of the first decade of the new century the UK government hopes for steady growth and no significant recession. Yet its expenditure plans are such that it expects to spend more than it receives. It will therefore be forced to borrow. This means paying interest to those who lend and taxpayers will have to fund these interest payments. For reasons we have explained, these interest payments tend to be greater in recessions when government borrowing is greater.

13.6 Two fallacies exposed

If you have followed the argument so far you will be in a position to understand why some commonly held views about unemployment are untrue. We shall look at two of them.

'Industries must be protected to safeguard jobs'

There are always pressure groups that have their own interests which they try to persuade governments to protect. The arguments used often centre upon the concern to protect jobs. If subsidies on agricultural products are removed, unemployment amongst farm labourers will rise. If the country stops selling arms to unstable foreign governments, jobs in the defence industry will go. This kind of argument ought not to sound impressive if you have followed this chapter. That the level of unemployment in a particular industry can increase is correct. That the level of unemployment in the economy will rise is much less likely because the level of employment in the economy is determined by the volume of *aggregate* demand. If expenditure is *switched*, employment will simply switch also. There may be a temporary rise in unemployment of, say, agricultural workers following an end to subsidies, but in time it will be absorbed by increases in the demand for other products and services as governments will not reduce total demand but simply change its direction, spending more on, say, health care and less on agricultural subsidies.

'If each person worked less, more people could work'

Millions of people in Europe have no job. Millions of others seem to work excessively long hours and have little time for leisure. A seemingly simple solution is at hand – jobsharing. Some could work fewer hours and others would then be able to work. The French government is at present legislating to enforce such a policy. Almost certainly it will fail. For every difficult problem there is a simple, straightforward, wrong answer.

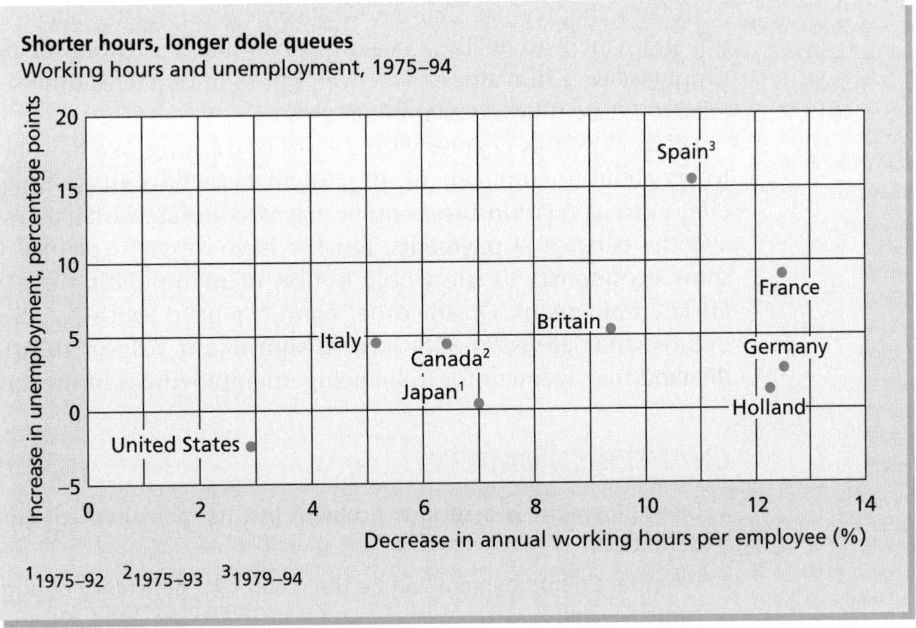

Figure 13.11 Relationship between unemployment and working hours
Source: © *The Economist*, 25 November 1995

To employ two part-timers rather than one full-timer is considerably more expensive. Two people have to be trained. Two lots of paperwork regarding their employment have to be kept. If costs to the firm are higher, they will employ fewer people and produce less output. As we saw in Chapter 12, less output means less income and a lower demand for goods and services, leading to lower employment demand. The volume of labour demand in the economy is not fixed. Jobsharing will reduce aggregate labour demand. Empirical evidence supports this. Look at Figure 13.11. It is clearly not true that those countries that have most reduced annual working hours per employee have found lower levels of unemployment. Indeed, the exact opposite is the case. Longer working hours per employee tends to mean *less* unemployment.

13.7 Conclusion

If unemployment is high, can the government do anything about it? Keynesian economists certainly think that it can. Unemployment can be an indication of a shortage of demand in the economy. The reason for this state of affairs continuing is that markets, especially labour markets, do not adjust quickly. Governments should not therefore wait for markets to clear. They should act. Governments, Keynesians believe, can act to influence aggregate demand and hence unemployment. There are problems and costs involved but, to return to our medical analogy, if the patient is seriously ill, the medicine must be administered and the costs accepted.

In later chapters we shall see why some economists believe an economy with unemployment to be like a person who is sick, for whom the best remedy is not simply to leave him alone to recover, but to improve his fitness, so that his resistance to future illness is that much greater.

Let us close this chapter with a word of warning. We have not said all there is to say about unemployment. In particular, we have not yet given much consideration to its relationship to other macroeconomic variables, especially inflation and the balance of payments. Neither have we yet explained the objections of some economists to the whole notion of manipulating aggregate demand to affect employment. On the other hand, we have seen why some economists do believe that governments have a significant responsibility for short-term demand management for influencing unemployment in the modern economy.

CHAPTER SUMMARY

1. **Unemployment is a serious problem but its measurement creates problems of definition.**
2. **Whether unemployment can be the result of a deficiency of aggregate demand is controversial.**
3. **Keynesians believe that the above is possible because equilibrium for an economy is where planned demand equals actual output. This may not be full employment output.**
4. **An autonomous increase in planned savings may make unemployment worse in the Keynesian view.**
5. **Government can manipulate the volume of planned aggregate demand to try to reduce employment.**
6. **An increase in autonomous demand leads to a multiplied increase in output, the size of this multiplier effect depending upon marginal withdrawals from the circular flow.**
7. **Problems of aggregate demand management include estimating output gaps, time lags and the effects of an increase in the PSBR.**

Questions for discussion

Guidance to the answers for the ***asterisked*** *numbered questions is available to students on the website for the book at* **www.booksites.net/heather**.

1* According to Figure 13.3, what is the level of autonomous demand in the economy? What is the level of induced demand if Y is £600 billion? What is the multiplier?

2 Explain how 'equilibrium' is restored to the economy of Figure 13.3 if national output were to fall to £450 billion.

3* Suppose there is substantial unemployment in the economy which government plans to reduce by increasing aggregate demand. What do you believe to be the relative benefits of raising aggregate demand via changes in consumption, investment, government spending, exports and imports?

4 Which of the proposals for increasing aggregate demand mentioned in Question 3 raise the injections function? Which lower the withdrawals function?

5* Suppose the government were to redistribute income towards equality, raising direct taxes on higher income groups to pay for increased benefits for lower income groups. What is such a policy likely to do to:

(a) the planned expenditure function?
(b) the level of unemployment?

6 The text suggests that the main determinant of consumption (and saving) is income. However, there are other factors influencing the level of domestic consumption. What do you think they are? How significant might they be for the level of employment?

7* How can my decision to save more result in my saving less?

8 How much does it matter if a government has a large PSBR?

9* Which of the following are injections and which withdrawals for the UK economy? (a) A UK student goes on a ski holiday to Sweden. (b) A UK defence company sells a fighter plane to Israel. (c) A purchase of an anthrax vaccine from the USA by the UK government. (d) The UK government purchases a new hospital from a UK builder.

10 To what extent is the present British government Keynesian in its attempts to control unemployment?

Websites

There are many websites containing data on the whole economy that have some data on unemployment including the OECD website at:

www.oecd.org/.

For information on UK employment data the most useful source is information in *Labour Market Trends*. The economic version can be found at:

www.statistics.gov.uk/onlineproducts/

Notes

1 Changes in interest rates also affect the distribution of income. One sometimes gets the impression from the press that lowering interest rates improves the welfare of everyone. In fact, one significant part of its effect is to redistribute income between savers and borrowers. Lower interest rates make it cheaper to borrow, but pensioners relying on interest from their savings will be worse off if interest rates fall.

2 One estimate is that the government could create one million extra jobs by boosting its expenditure by £17 billion. However, about £10 billion would be returned to the Treasury in the form of savings on social security expenditure and increases in income tax, etc. See M. Kitson, J. Michie and H. Sutherland 'The fiscal and distributional implications of job generation', *Cambridge Journal of Economics*, vol. 21, no. 1, January 1997.

14 Investment

Saving for the future: *how much should we invest?*

CHAPTER OVERVIEW

By comparison with some of its European neighbours, Britain is not a particularly rich country. Average income is higher in, for example, France and Germany, whereas in the early post-war years this was not the case. A commonly cited reason for the change is that Britain no longer invests enough. Is it true that some European nations invest more than others? What might countries that invest less do about the problem?

In this chapter we review the following concepts:

- Opportunity cost
- Keynesian equilibrium

We introduce

- Rate of interest
- Investment analysis
- Human capital

14.1 Introduction

During our studies of microeconomics we were often concerned with the concept of opportunity cost. Any action undertaken means that the next best alternative is forgone. The opportunity cost of your trip to the bowling alley last night is not only that you cannot spend that money on something else but that perhaps you are late reading this chapter. If firm A produces output, it uses land, labour and capital which are then not available for the production of something else. The forgone output is the opportunity cost of firm A's output. For an economy, the opportunity cost of investment can be seen as the current consumption forgone. Land, labour and capital devoted to buildings and machinery for next year's consumption cannot produce current output that we could consume now.

see pp. 8–13

In Chapter 1 we introduced these ideas in terms of an opportunity cost curve, or production possibility curve. This was in the context of an East European

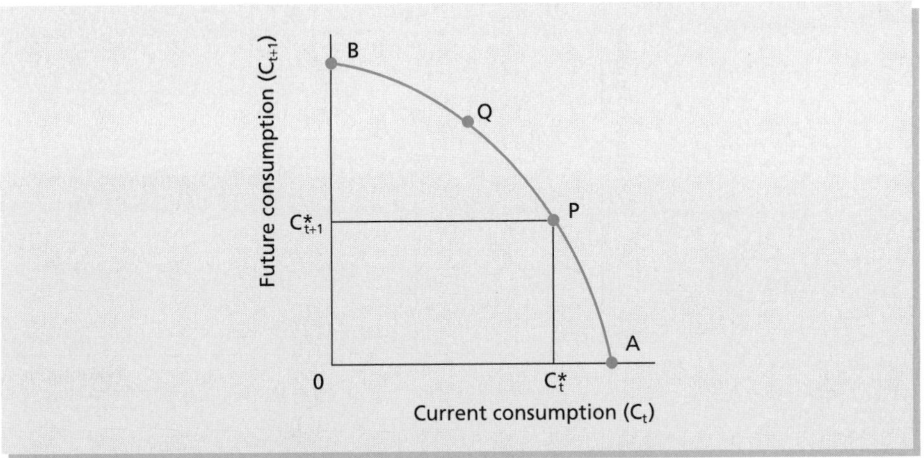

Figure 14.1 **Opportunity cost curve: current and future consumption**

economy, but the principles hold for any society. In Figure 14.1 an economy is represented by an opportunity cost curve AB. This society has full employment and is at point P. It is thus enjoying OC^*_t of current output, whereas it could enjoy OA current output. However, it is choosing to forgo consumption of $A–C^*_t$ in order to invest. This investment will produce consumption in the next period of OC^*_{t+1}. In other words, investment for future consumption involves an opportunity cost in terms of current consumption. Now many people believe that Britain should be at, say, Q. This means forgoing more current consumption, investing more, raising future consumption and thus standards of living. Are they correct, or are these things better left to be decided by market forces?

14.2 The market for investment goods

see p. 275

What determines whether an economy, instead of being at P, is at, say, Q with a greater volume of resources committed to investment? This is a matter of some controversy. As we saw in Chapter 13, Keynesian economists say that there is nothing in the nature of the system even to suggest that an economy will be in equilibrium on the opportunity cost curve. In Keynesian equilibrium, aggregate output (Y) will be sufficient to meet all planned demands upon it. You will recall that these demands are consumption (C), investment (I), government current demand (G) and export demand (X) minus import demand (M). Alternatively, expressed equilibrium output, Y_e, is where planned injections into the circular flow (government, investment and export demand) are equal to planned withdrawals from the circular flow (savings, taxes and imports). This may not be at full employment output, as Figure 14.2 indicates, since full employment Y may be greater than Y_e.

Governments choosing to move the economy towards full employment can in principle do so by raising any item of autonomous demand, including

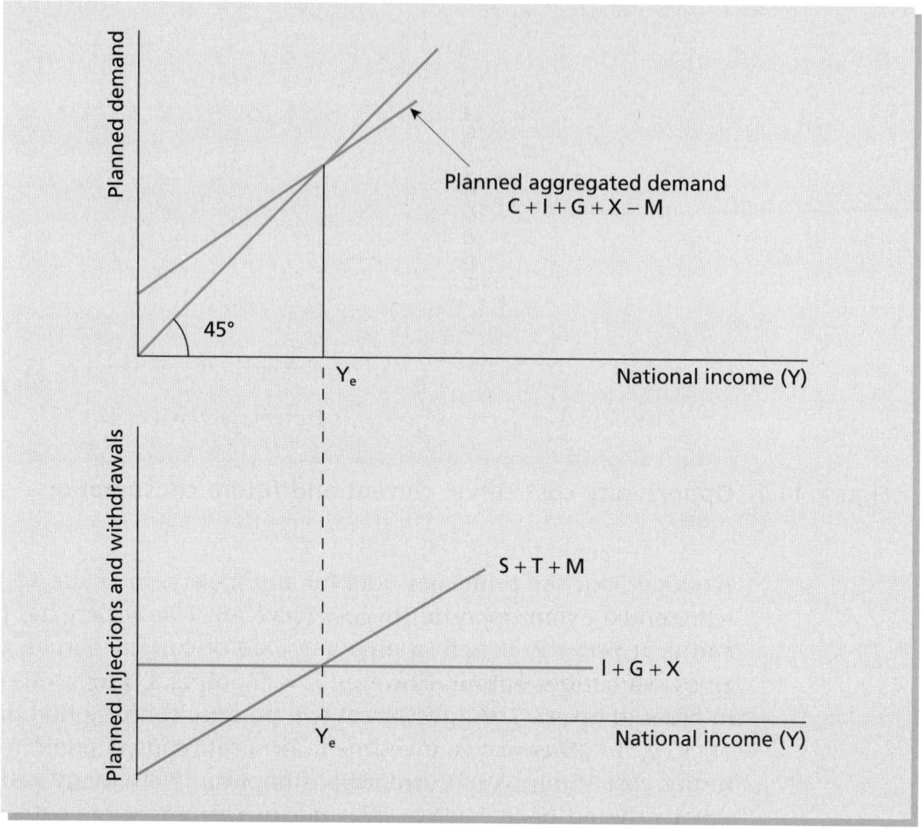

Figure 14.2 Keynesian macroeconomic equilibrium

investment. This will, through the multiplier effect, help to decide where on the opportunity cost curve of Figure 14.1 the economy is located. Notice that in this simple Keynesian model investment is autonomous, that is, it is independent of the level of income.

see pp. 96–9

By comparison the classical view, which we shall be developing in the next few chapters, is that any unemployment constitutes only a short-term problem and that markets will always tend over time to push the economy onto the opportunity cost curve frontier where there is full employment. After all, unemployment means an excess supply of labour services. Given a free labour market, as we saw in Chapter 5, the price of labour services, wage rates, will fall and equilibrium, including full employment, will be restored. The classical criticism of Keynesianism goes further than that. Not only do market forces ensure full employment of labour in the long run but markets also bring about an optimum volume of investment. The volume of investment will be optimally determined without government intervention. The mechanism that ensures that this happens is interest rates. We can use supply and demand analysis to see how it happens.

Consider Figure 14.3, which can be regarded as a market for investment funds where interest rates are the price of using those funds. It is institutions such as

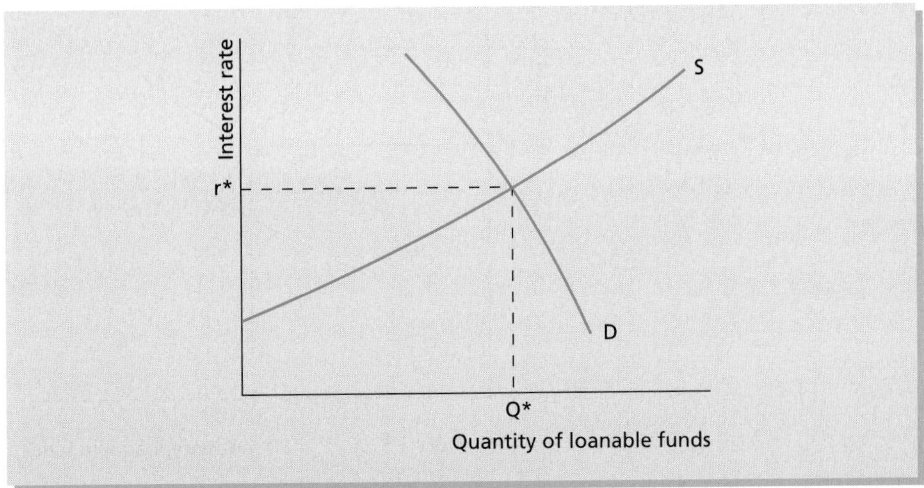

Figure 14.3 **Equilibrium in the market for loanable funds**

banks which operate the market, taking funds from savers and making them available to borrowers. The higher the interest rate, the more willing people will be to save since consumption has a higher opportunity cost. To illustrate the point, suppose that the economy has no inflation and that interest rates are 5 per cent. You have £100 to spend. Spending £100 today costs you something in that you could have bought something for £105 in a year's time. But suppose now interest rates are 10 per cent. You are now choosing between £100 of goods now or £110-worth next year. Higher interest rates have increased the opportunity cost of current consumption. Hence the upwards sloping savings function (S).

The lower the interest rate, the cheaper it is for firms to borrow for investment purposes and so the greater is the quantity of funds demanded. This is shown by the demand curve (D). We shall examine this demand curve in more detail shortly. Therefore, if interest rates are allowed to find their own level, they will be established at r*, a level where the supply and demand for loanable funds are in equilibrium. The volume of investment will thus be optimal and society will obtain the best possible level of welfare from its limited resources.

Let us use the diagram of Figure 14.4 and see how markets adjust in classical equilibrium with respect to investment when society's preferences alter. People have preferences between current and future consumption expressed by the supply and demand curves for loanable funds. Suppose society is now inclined to be more thrifty. People wish, on average, to have more future consumption, and they are prepared to sacrifice current consumption to make this possible. In terms of Figure 14.4 the supply curve for loanable funds shifts to the right, from S_1 to S_2: people are more willing to save than before at each level of interest rate. Banks have more funds available to lend. However, at the present interest rate, r*, there is an excess quantity of these funds supplied. To encourage the use of these funds, the banks will lower the interest rate. The price of these funds now finds an equilibrium at r_1^*. Firms are encouraged to invest more. The quantity of

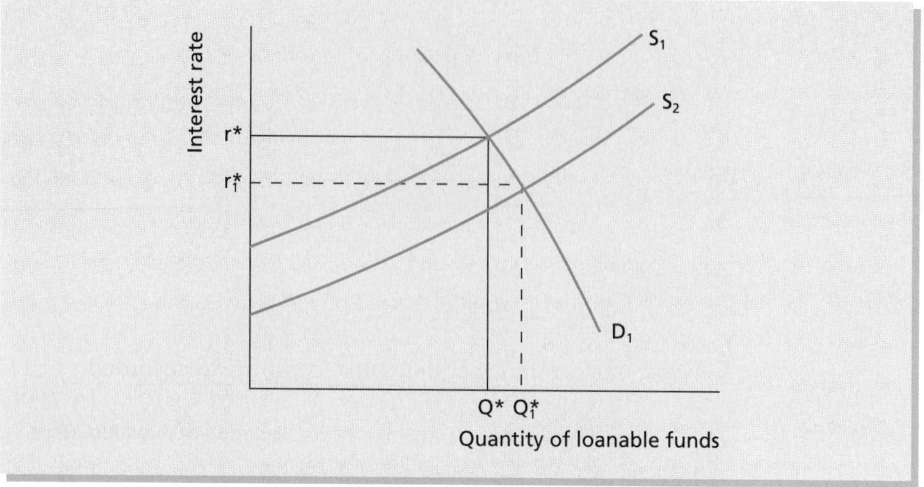

Figure 14.4 **Increased willingness to save and its effect on interest rates**

loanable funds for investment rises from Q* to Q_1^*. Firms use these funds to bid resources away from current consumption. More resources are committed to investment because that is what people want. Again the mechanism is relative prices. This time the key relative price is the rate of interest.

In this view, since society gets the volume of investment that it wants, Britain cannot be investing too little. It may invest less than other countries but that is because its citizens have a greater preference for current consumption, which it has expressed through markets.

Few economists believe that markets work as perfectly as the above suggests, but the model provides a framework for analysing problems of alleged investment inadequacies in Britain that we shall look at later. Before we do that, however, we need to develop our understanding of what investment is and what problems are encountered in measuring its extent.

14.3 The meaning of investment

Investment is often referred to as gross domestic fixed capital formation (GDFCF), an excellent term for picking out its key features.

see pp. 257–9

- *Gross*. During the year some capital wears out and needs replacing. This is called replacement investment. Some investment is new, in the sense that it increases the size of the nation's capital stock. Gross investment includes both replacement investment and additions to the capital stock. You can gain from Table 14.1 an idea of the extent of Britain's investment. We have chosen one particular year, 2001, from the national income accounts that we met in Chapter 12, Britain's GNP by expenditure. We can see that gross domestic capital formation represented about 18 per cent of gross national product (GNP) at that time. How much was that investment simply replacing

Table 14.1 **Investment in Britain, 2001 (£m)**

	Value at current (2001) prices	*Approximate percentage of GDP*
Gross fixed capital formation	162,607	18
Less capital consumption	111,275	12–13
Net capital formation	51,332	5

Source: adapted from ONS (2002) 'Blue Book'

worn out capital? Capital consumption was recorded as £111,275 million, so net investment was only about 5 per cent of GNP, in 2001. Of course these percentages will vary somewhat from year to year. You can see how much for yourself by looking up the data in the national income accounts and undertaking similar calculations on other years' figures.

- *Domestic*. Some investment by British firms is undertaken in other countries, and some investment in this country is made by foreign firms. For example, Japanese car manufacturers have factories in Britain. The figures above refer to investment in Britain, not investment by British firms.
- *Fixed*. Firms 'invest' in stocks of their own products, sometimes intentionally to meet unforeseen changes in demand, sometimes unintentionally when demand falls suddenly and they are left with unsold, unplanned stock. These stock items will not be included in GDFCF since this figure includes only the purchase of capital items such as machinery and buildings.
- *Capital formation*. Investment involves the *formation* of capital. Investment represents not the stock of capital in an economy, but *changes* to that stock. Note that investment is done by firms and governments, not by individuals. What is often referred to as financial investment, such as the purchase of shares, is really saving. The only kind of investment that is made by individuals is the purchase of new housing. The purchase of cars or even washing machines could, in principle, be seen as investment. After all it represents the acquisition of assets that will produce a flow of benefits over several years. However, for statistical purposes these items are regarded as consumer durables, and we assume that the whole value of the product is consumed during one year. One obvious advantage of this unreal assumption is that it avoids the need to work out the extent to which wear and tear on washing machines, and so on, has reduced the value of the nation's capital stock.

14.4 Extent and direction of UK investment

Extent of UK investment

Table 14.1 gave us an idea of the extent of investment in the British economy for one year. Let us look at the proportion of GDP represented by investment in

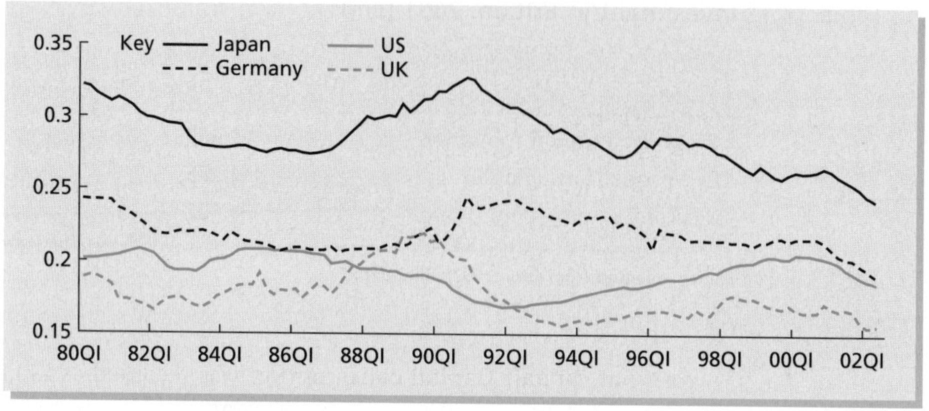

Figure 14.5 **Nominal gross domestic fixed capital formation (% of GDP)**

Source: *National Institute Economic Review*, October 2002, p. 14

Britain over a longer period and compare it with other countries. Figure 14.5 gives a clear indication of the relatively low volume of investment in Britain compared with some other advanced countries. However, you should bear in mind when you look at the figures that this is not investment volumes, but investment as a proportion of output. In absolute terms, UK investment performance is worse than it appears in that the UK has a lower level of national output than many other advanced countries. Many commentators feel that Britain should, in terms of Figure 14.1 be at, say, Q rather than at P. As we have already argued, Britain could be at P because British people have chosen to be current-consumption-orientated. It could also be that the market mechanism is not working well. This is a point to which we shall return.

However, there is a far from perfect correlation between the volume of investment and growth in GDP, which suggests that there are other important factors to consider. The most obvious one is the efficiency with which capital resources are used. As we saw in Table 1.2, some East European economies at the end of the 1980s had much higher ratios of investment to GDP, yet they had substantially lower living standards than that of Britain.

see p. 7

Direction of UK investment

There are also some interesting developments in recent years with respect to the direction of investment. Table 14.2 enables us to see some of the most important of these. During the 1980s and 1990s the relative importance of public sector investment fell significantly. This fall reflected successive governments' desire to reduce government spending, and the shifting of assets out of public into private ownership via the privatisation programme. However, during the early 1990s the greater effect of the recession on private sector spending reversed this trend. By the turn of the century the economic outlook improved, so private sector investment recovered, whilst government determination to control its PSBR has depressed government investment expenditure. In the early years of the twenty-first century government investment as a proportion of total

Table 14.2 UK gross domestic fixed capital formation (GDFCF) at constant (1995) prices, £m

Year	Business investment	General government	Public corporations		Private sector		Total
			NHS trusts	Transfer costs of non-produced assets	Dwellings	Transfer costs of non-produced assets	
	NPEL	DLWF	DFTI	DLWH	DFEA	DLWI	NPQT
1997	93,147	9,712	1,266	288	20,824	6,199	131,436
1998	110,242	9,815	1,366	363	20,967	5,507	148,260
1999	111,951	10,153	1,296	–1	20,258	5,486	149,143
2000	113,973	10,548	1,488	18	20,560	5,399	151,986
2001	115,040	10,862	1,635	–16	19,218	5,700	152,439
2002[1]	104,310	12,834	1,228	–64	21,060	6,192	145,552

[1] First half, annualised

Source: *Economic Trends*, December 2002, © Crown copyright

investment was substantially less than 25 years earlier. By 2002 government expenditure was beginning to increase substantially.

Having seen some of the features of British investment, we now consider the factors affecting such investment. Concentrating on private investment, we begin with the relationship between private investment decisions and the rate of interest.

14.5 Investment decisions and the rate of interest

Making investment decisions

Suppose that we are a company director trying to decide whether a project is worthwhile as an investment. How might we go about making a decision? There will be an initial capital cost (C) but, because of the investment, we expect to receive a flow of income from the sale of the product that the investment will produce. This income will arrive over a period of years until the capital is worn out.

There will be much uncertainty about this cash flow. In particular, there is uncertainty about how much output will be bought, what price we can charge for it and about all the other costs such as the wage bill and the tax liability. We must do the best we can, though, and produce our best estimate of this potential income. It might look like this:

Year	0	1	2	3	4
Cash flow	–£31,700	£10,000	£10,000	£10,000	£10,000

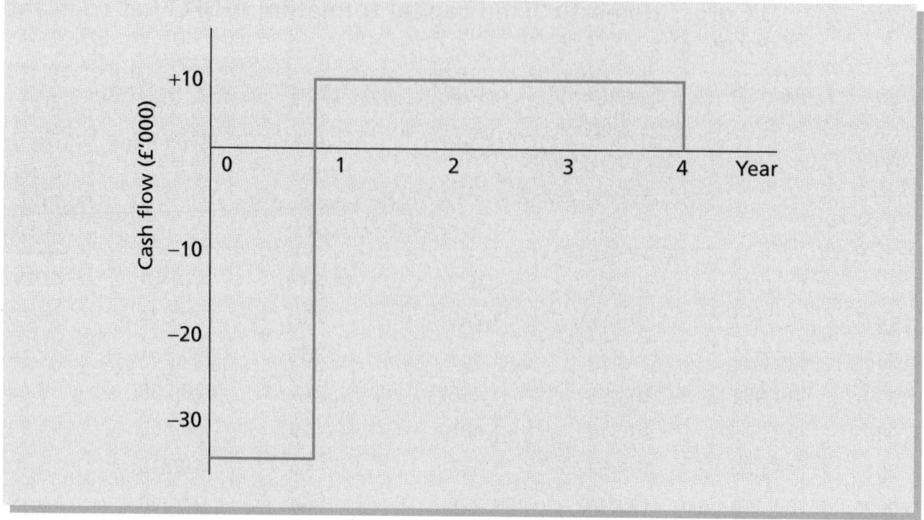

Figure 14.6 Cash flow profile of an investment project

This shows the initial outlay, C, as a minus, since we shall be paying out to purchase the capital. Then we show the 'cash flow' as positive amounts since this represents the income we expect to receive. The cash flow will be the income from the sale of the product less costs of labour, materials and so on. The machinery might be worth something as scrap at the end of its useful life. If so, we would add that to the cash flow in the last year. Here we will assume for simplicity that the scrap value is nil. You can plot this information on a diagram to give what is referred to as a cash flow profile (Figure 14.6).

Let us decide now if the project is worthwhile. To keep things simple, let us assume that (a) we can be quite certain that we have got our numbers right, (b) there will be no inflation over the period. These are huge assumptions but at least they keep the size of the problem manageable.

Can we say that our project costs £31,700 but that it will get back more (£40,000) so it must be worth doing? No, because money earned in the future is worth less to us than if we had it now. If we had it now, we could put it in a bank and it would earn interest. If we have to wait for a year (or more) to obtain the cash flow, we will lose the opportunity of earning this interest. So we need some way of adjusting the numbers to allow for that.

The way this is done is to 'discount' the cash flow. For example, take the £10,000 earned in year 1. We ask, what amount of money do we need now to be able to invest it at a given interest rate in order to turn it into £10,000 in a year's time? We discount the £10,000 using the formula $A\frac{1}{1+r}$, where A is the cash flow and r is the interest rate per annum.

Suppose r is 10 per cent, then in our example we get

$$\text{£}10{,}000 \times \frac{1}{1 + (0.1)} = \frac{10{,}000}{1.01} = \text{£}9{,}090$$

That is, if we had £9,090 now we could put it in a bank at 10 per cent interest and it would be worth £10,000 in a year's time. So the 'present value' of £10,000 in a year's time is, assuming a 10 per cent interest rate, only £9,090. To put it another way, we would be indifferent between £9,090 now and £10,000 in a year's time since the £9,090 now is capable of producing £10,000 a year from now.

What of the £10,000 income for which we have to wait until year 2? Clearly, it is worth even less to us now since we would need to invest less at 10 per cent for two years in order for it to be worth £10,000 by that time. The formula would be

$$A_2\frac{1}{(1+r)} \times \frac{1}{(1+r)} \quad \text{or} \quad A_2\frac{1}{(1+r)^2}$$

where A_2 = cash flow in year 2. This gives £8,260, i.e. we need £8,260 now to invest at 10 per cent for two years to make £10,000 then.

What is the present value of the whole cash flow? The formula we use is:

$$A_1\frac{1}{1+r} + A_2\frac{1}{(1+r)^2} + A_3\frac{1}{(1+r)^3} + \ldots + A_n\frac{1}{(1+r)^n}$$

In our example, the discounted cash flows are

Year	0	1	2	3	4
Cash flow	–£10,000	£9,090	£8,264	£7,513	£6,830

What is the present value of the entire cash flow? If we add up all the discounted cash flows from year 1 we get the gross present value (GPV) which, with slight rounding, becomes £31,700.

We can now decide if our project is worthwhile. We are going to borrow £31,700 and invest in a project with an expected return of, in present value terms, £31,700. Clearly, it is a very marginal project. The difference between the capital cost, C, and the discounted value of the cash flow, GPV, is called the net present value, NPV. Hence NPV = GPV – C. If NPV is positive the project is worthwhile. If NPV is negative it is not. This approach to the investment decision is referred to as the NPV method.

We could look at our investment problem in a different way. We could ask, what is the rate of return implied in our project? This rate is called the internal rate of return (IRR) and can be found by calculating the interest rate that would just discount the cash flows back to the size of the initial outlay. Formally:

$$\textbf{IRR} = \text{the rate, } r\text{, such that} \quad \sum_{k=1}^{n} A_k\frac{1}{(1+r)^k} - C = 0$$

In our example we know that it is 10 per cent. We could then ask ourselves whether it is worth investing in a project which gives us a 10 per cent return when it costs us 10 per cent to borrow the funds. Again, this is a marginal project. If the IRR exceeds the cost of borrowing, then the project is worthwhile. If IRR is less, it is not worth investing in the project. Notice that in the kind of project we have considered the IRR and NPV methods are equivalent.

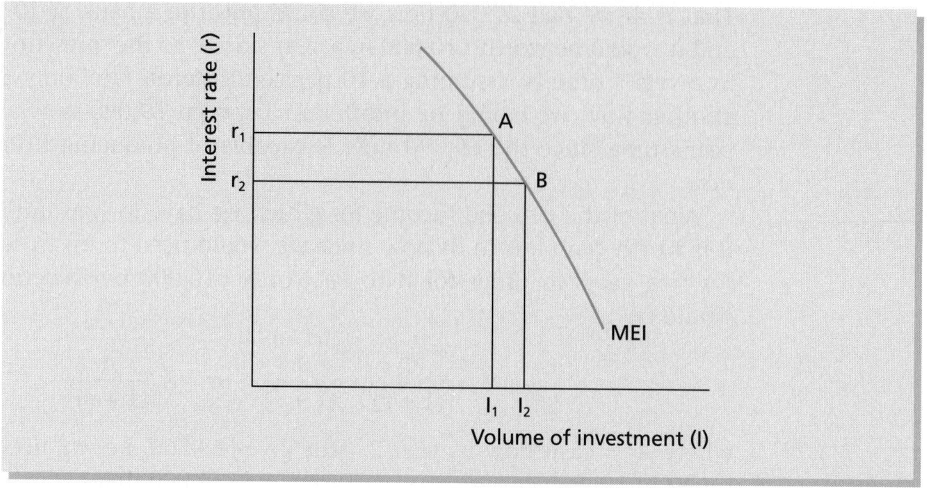

Figure 14.7 **Interest rates and the demand for investment**

Investment decisions and interest rates

You should now be able to see that a lower interest rate implies more investment, as more projects become worthwhile. Consider Figure 14.7 which shows what is called a marginal efficiency of investment (MEI) schedule. In essence, it is a demand curve for investment, showing the relationship between the price of investment finds (r) and the quantity of investment demanded, all other things being equal. The MEI curve ranks all projects according to their IRR. Only a few investment opportunities will achieve a very high IRR. However, the lower the IRR, the more projects there are which will yield at least that rate.

If interest rates are at r_1 in Figure 14.7, all projects are worthwhile down to the marginal one at point A, so I_1 investment is undertaken. If interest rates fall to r_2, the project at r_1 is no longer marginal and investment expands to I_2 with the marginal project at B. The lower the interest rate, the more projects are worthwhile for firms and the higher the volume of investment. A fall in interest rates from r_1 to r_2 would increase the quantity of investment from I_1 to I_2.

We can now see more clearly the reason for the downwards sloping demand curve for loanable funds which we drew in Figure 14.3. Lower interest rates mean that a higher quantity of investment will be undertaken. If more investment is undertaken, more loanable funds will be demanded to make the investment possible. The market mechanism, then, should see to it that we get the right volume of investment. It should also see to it that these investment goods are used efficiently. Assuming that firms wish to maximise profits, they will choose only those projects where consumers value the output highly enough to cover the opportunity costs of the resources used. We shall examine some evidence shortly and see whether this seems to work in practice.

Just like any other demand schedule, the 'price' of investment funds is not the only factor affecting demand. We consider some other possible factors in section 14.6.

see pp. 309–13

Table 14.3 **Short-term interest rates in selected countries**

	USA	*Canada*	*Japan*	*Euro area*	*UK*	*USA*
1999	5.3	4.9	0.2	3.0	5.5	5.6
2000	6.5	5.8	0.3	4.4	6.1	6.0
2001	3.7	3.7	0.1	4.3	5.0	5.0
2002	1.8	2.7	0.1	3.4	4.0	4.5
2003	1.8	3.4	0.1	3.0	4.0	3.7
2004	2.2	4.2	0.2	3.4	4.5	4.0
2005–2008	3.8	5.1	0.8	4.6	4.8	4.9

Adapted from: National Institute Economic Review, October 2002, p. 10

Real or money rates of interest?

So far we have referred simply to interest rates. However, we need to distinguish between nominal rates of interest and real rates. The nominal rate of interest is the one quoted in the market at any given time. The real interest rate is the nominal rate minus the inflation rate. Let us see why we need to make this distinction. You will remember earlier in the chapter that you had £100 which you could either spend or save. Suppose you choose to save it and leave it in the bank for a year at a nominal interest rate of 10 per cent. In one year your £100 has become £110. Suppose, though, inflation is at 10 per cent. The real rate of interest is zero in that the £110 now buys only the same amount of output as the £100 would have bought the year before. Saving for future consumption has in this case not increased the amount you can consume. When people make savings decisions, they may not be willing to forgo current consumption unless it enables greater future consumption. This requires positive real interest rates. In other words, the nominal rate must exceed the rate of inflation. The analysis in this chapter focuses on real interest rates.

Table 14.3 should now help us to understand why investment levels tend to be lower in the UK than in many other countries including much of Europe. Because interest rates have tended to be higher in the UK, marginal investment projects which are not worthwhile in Britain are worthwhile in, for example other European economies. Part of the explanation for the higher UK interest rates we have already considered: it is possible that the UK is more consumption orientated. However, there are other factors to consider, some to do with international currency matters, which we look at in Chapter 20.

see pp. 434–62

Investment analysis in action: the Channel Tunnel

The private sector sometimes undertakes enormous investment projects, and interest rates are a crucial consideration. The biggest private sector investment project ever undertaken in Britain is the Channel Tunnel link between Dover and Calais, being run by a company called Eurotunnel. Eurotunnel contracted the building of the tunnel to a British and French building consortium known

Table 14.4 **Rates of return to Eurotunnel shareholders under various assumptions**

	Approximate IRR (%)	*Year of first dividend*
Eurotunnel base case	15.0	1994
Assumption A	11.9	2003
Assumption B	10.5	2006
Assumption C	9.1	2008

as Transmanche Link. Since the government did not provide any of the funds, Eurotunnel had to raise the finance for the project from a large number of banks plus it had to float some shares.

There were arguments for government funds to be put into the project, but the prime minister (Margaret Thatcher) believed in the power of the market. If the project was worthwhile, funds would be made available. Subsequently, the present government has agreed to invest funds along with the private sector in a modern rail link between London and Dover.

What did the cash flow profile for the Channel Tunnel project look like in 1987 when the decision to invest was made? Eurotunnel estimated the capital costs from the start of building until completion at around £4.7 billion. It estimated that the tunnel would open in the summer of 1993. The cash flows would be determined by many factors, the main ones being the size of passenger and freight traffic from 1993 onwards, the expected proportion of that traffic that could be won in the face of competition, especially from the cross-channel ferries, and the price that could be charged. The price would also depend upon competition. Eurotunnel might be able to offer a superior journey, perhaps a faster or more comfortable one, and therefore ask a higher price. Alternatively, if the journey were similar they could match or undercut the ferries' price, but clearly the severity of the expected competition would be a consideration.

There are enormous problems in estimating the return on an investment of this length and size. Table 14.4 gives some idea of the problem by looking at what happens if some key assumptions are changed. The IRR is the expected rate of return to shareholders investing in the project in the public share offering of 1987 using various assumption as explained.

What are the assumptions on which the table is based? The Eurotunnel base case is the sort of return projected before construction work began. Since 15 per cent is well above the interest rate at the time and above the interest rate likely to obtain in the future, it would have been an attractive project to undertake if the assumptions on which the forecast was made had proved correct. The other estimates are not Eurotunnel's, but are based on the same kind of model. Assumption A is that Eurotunnel faces competition from a rival tunnel from 2022, capital costs have been understated by 12.5 per cent and the tunnel opens one year late, but all other factors are the same as the base case.

Assumption B is that assumption A is correct except that the rate of passenger growth traffic is half that which Eurotunnel originally estimated.

Assumption C is that assumption B is correct except that Eurotunnel only gains half the expected share of the car and coach market.

Clearly, the more pessimistic the assumptions, the lower the IRR. The lower the IRR, the less worthwhile the project is to the potential investor in Eurotunnel and those contributing to the project's finance.

In the event, cost and time overruns occurred and a 12.5 per cent cost overrun was optimistic. The capital cost was in excess of £10 billion. The tunnel became fully operational during 1994. The greatest uncertainty is now whether the revenue will ever be sufficient to make a profit. Eurotunnel itself believes that its original figures now look likely to be a significant underestimate and that the revenue into the next century will cover the significant cost overruns. Clearly, it requires some years from the tunnel's opening before some reliable forecasts can be made of its likely revenue. The early data are not encouraging. For example, Eurostar, the train carrying passengers through the tunnel between London, Paris and Brussels, is operating to about 35 per cent of its expected level.

One can see, then, just how uncertain the returns are on large investment projects, and that interest rates are a crucial factor, whatever the size of the investment.

Some empirical evidence

Does empirical evidence support the argument we have been developing concerning the relationship between investment and interest rates? Does a lower interest rate produce more investment? An article by W. Easton[1] in the *Bank of England Quarterly Bulletin* suggests that it does. Table 14.5 shows the Bank of

Table 14.5 Bank model simulation: all interest rates +1% point (exchange rate fixed) (percentage differences from base, except where stated, after specified)

	1	*4*	*8*	*12*
GDP (output measure)	–	−0.4	−0.7	−0.9
Domestic demand	−0.1	−0.7	−1.1	−1.4
Consumers' expenditure	−0.1	−0.6	−0.9	−1.2
excluding durables	−0.1	−3.5	−4.5	−3.6
Investment	−0.1	−1.3	−2.2	−2.8
excluding private residential	−0.9	−3.2	−3.1	−4.1
GDP deflator	–	−0.1	−0.2	−0.5
Retail price index	0.4	0.3	0.2	–
Average earnings	–	–	−0.1	−0.4
Current account (£ billion)[a]	–	0.6	1.5	2.0
Unemployment ('000)	–	12	35	58
Effective exchange rate	–	–	–	–

[a] Quoted effects are over the year to the specified quarter

Source: *Bank of England Quarterly Bulletin*, May 1990

Table 14.6 **Average annual investment growth: some international comparisons**

	1967–79		*1985–94*		*1995–2000*	
	GDFCF	*GDP*	*GDFCF*	*GDP*	*GDFCF*	*GDP*
EU countries						
UK	1.5	2.4	1.9	2.2	2.9	2.2
France	3.6	4.1	2.5	2.1	3.5	2.5
Germany	2.7	3.7	3.3	2.8	1.0	1.8
Non-EU countries						
Japan	7.7	6.5	4.8	3.3	–1.5	0.8
USA	4.6	2.9	2.9	2.6	8.0	3.2
Canada	4.9	4.9	4.1	2.5	3.9	2.9

Source: adapted from OECD, EIU

England's estimates of the effects of a 1 per cent rise in interest rates on a number of key variables, including investment. A rise in interest rates produces a fall in the volume of investment. The evidence is, however, that some of the strength of the relationship is between residential investment and interest rates. The evidence is not so strong if one concentrates on private investment *net* of residential investment, as Table 14.5 shows.

What is particularly interesting is that earlier studies did *not* find much support for the relationship between interest rates and investment. Easton argues that this might be explained by the deregulation of financial markets in the late 1980s. The relationship may have looked less real when governments regulated the availability of finance as well as its price. Now there is virtually no attempt to control the availability of finance except through its price, which is to say, interest rates.

Is there any evidence that higher investment levels do lead to higher growth rates of GDP? Table 14.6 suggests that there is. Earlier in the chapter we looked at *levels* of investment in various countries. Here we look at *changes* in investment levels and changes in the level of GDP. Notice that those countries with the highest growth rates of investment are those with the fastest GDP growth. Countries such as Japan which experienced deep recession during the 1990s saw both GNP growth and GDFCF growth fall. Conversely, the USA, whose economy boomed during the latter part of the 1990s, saw increasing growth rates in both GDP and GDFCF.

Notice, though, that for the UK higher rates of GDFCF growth have *not* translated into higher GDP growth.

This evidence for the UK strongly suggests that it is not simply the case that the UK is more orientated to current consumption than most other countries. If this were true, one would still expect that if investment growth is faster, then output growth will be correspondingly higher. This has not been so. It suggests that there are question marks against the efficiency with which UK investment is used.

14.6 Investment and other factors

We have argued that there is a relationship between investment and interest rates. We have also seen that higher investment levels are correlated with higher growth rates. Why is the evidence that there is not a better fit? The answer is that other things influence the business community. We briefly consider some of them.

Business expectations

Business confidence about the future will affect the size of the cash flows predicted from an investment project. The higher the level of confidence, the further to the right the demand curve for investment, the MEI schedule, will be. Is there any way in which we can measure such a nebulous thing as the level of confidence? One way is to ask businesses about their future investment plans. The Confederation of British Industry (CBI) does this quarterly. The results are published in *Economic Trends*. How good a guide is the survey to actual business investment decisions? *Economic Trends* measures planned investment against the volume of investment in plant and machinery that had actually been undertaken a year later. The surveys show a good but far from perfect fit, so investment plans do have some value in predicting what is going to happen to investment volumes in the near future.

Business confidence is important in two particular respects. First, it can reduce the expected cash flow of a possible investment project. Consider our cash flow profile from section 14.5. We said then that there will be much uncertainty about these numbers. How will a business handle such risk? One way is to make an allowance for it in the cash flow. Suppose, for example, that the company director calculates that there is only a 50 per cent chance of gaining this cash flow and a 50 per cent chance that the company will get nothing. He might then write down for each year the cash flow multiplied by the degree of risk. In this case the cash flow for each year will be £10,000 × 50% = £5,000. The firm can then treat the cash flow as though it were a certain £5,000 per year that it will receive. Clearly, the greater the perceived doubts about the future, the lower the predicted cash flow. The smaller the cash flows, *ceteris paribus* the less the amount of investment.

However, there is a second respect in which lack of certainty about the future can affect investment. The firm is not faced with a simple choice of undertaking the project or forgetting it. An alternative strategy is frequently available: to delay the project in order to see whether the factors creating the uncertainty materialise. If the fears of the business are realised, the project will be shelved altogether.

Profitability

One could argue that profitability should be positively correlated with investment either because profits increase business confidence or because companies

Table 14.7 **International comparisons of company profitability, 2001**[1]

	All companies	Manufacturing companies	Service companies
1 Norway	20.8	6.7	16.6
2 Finland	14.0	18.9	15.9
3 Belgium	11.9[2]	21.0[2]	8.8[2]
4 UK	11.6	3.6	12.9
⋮			
13 Denmark	8.4[2]	12.0[2]	5.4[2]
14 Japan	7.7[2]	n.a.	n.a.
15 USA	6.9	4.4	17.5
16 France	6.7[2]	n.a.	n.a.
17 Germany	6.5	11.8[3]	6.9[3]
19 Netherlands	5.2	12.0	2.1

[1] Rates of return on capital employed
[2] Data is for 2000
[3] Data is for 1999

Source: adapted from *Economic Trends*, October 2002

find that it is cheaper to use past profits for investment purposes than to seek finance elsewhere. So a firm using an IRR calculation to find the value of an investment may use a lower interest rate as its marginal 'cut-off rate' if it has past profits available. It will never regard the appropriate cut-off rate as zero – those funds still have an opportunity cost.

Financial Trends publishes data on company profitability collected from 33 different countries. Table 14.7 shows that the UK ranks fourth on rates of return on capital employed, above nearly all other European countries. However, this disguises wide variations between companies. For example, as the table also shows, rates of return to UK manufacturing companies are very low. It is the service sector that does well.

One might expect, therefore, that investment in UK manufacturing would be much lower than in many other economies and this is indeed so. On the other hand, Figure 14.8 suggests that the relationship of company profitability to investment is weak, at least for the UK over a substantial period.

A number of factors might account for this. We mention two. First, the figures are gross of tax. Investors are more likely to consider returns net of tax. Second, it may be that other factors are more important in determining investment decisions.

Changes in national income

Unlike the simple model with which we began, investment must depend partly on the level of income. If income rises, demand too will rise, so a higher volume of capital will be required to meet that demand. However, it can be argued that investment is also a function of the rate of change of income. The 'accelerator

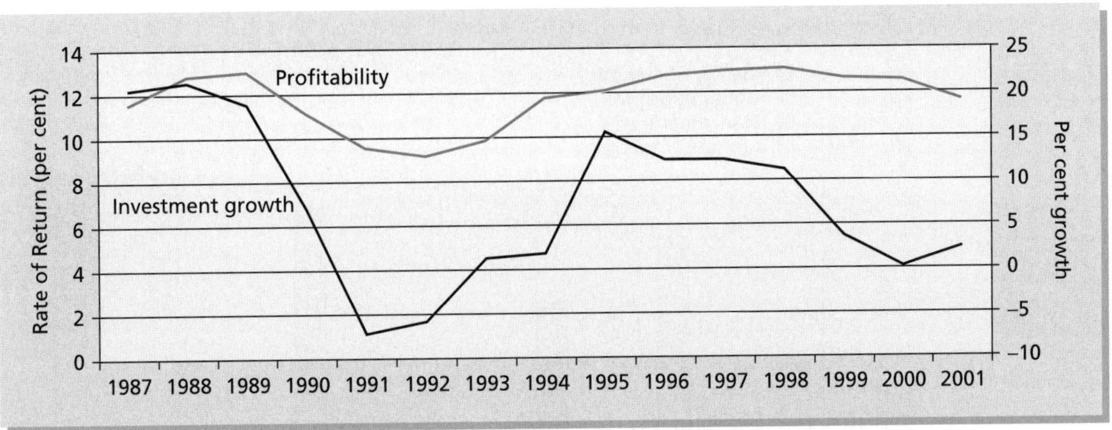

Figure 14.8 UK PNFC[1] profitability and business investment

[1] Private non-financial corporate

Source: *Economic Trends*, October 2002

principle' suggests that firms have a desired stock of capital to meet the volume of demand. Since the value of the capital stock will need to be several times as great as the value of the output produced from it, it follows that small changes in national income can produce relatively large changes in investment. A rise in national income of, say, £100 may mean the need to increase the capital stock by several hundred pounds worth to meet the additional demand. Certainly, investment is the most unstable component in aggregate demand, but attempts to find a close fit between changes in national income and the volume of investment have never been very successful, even if one allows for the inevitable time lags.

Short-termism

One commonly asserted reason why investment in Britain is lower than in many other developed economies is that Britain suffers from short-termism.

Short-termism can take the following form. Companies can be reluctant to invest in projects where the pay-off is some years ahead even if the IRR for the project is high, since the high cost of capital will reduce profits in the short term. They may be reluctant to do this if shareholders, particularly institutional investors, are unwilling to wait and therefore choose to sell the shares of such firms. This will depress the price of those companies' shares and render them liable to takeover. Companies will therefore choose to concentrate on short-term projects. This may have a high cost to the country in that some forms of investment may suffer. One obvious form of investment that would be susceptible is research and development, where the pay-off may be many years ahead. For example, pharmaceutical companies invest millions of pounds. Even if a promising drug is discovered, the period of time before it receives a cash flow from the investment may be 10–20 years. As can be seen from Figure 14.9 Britain's record on research and development expenditure, a form of investment,

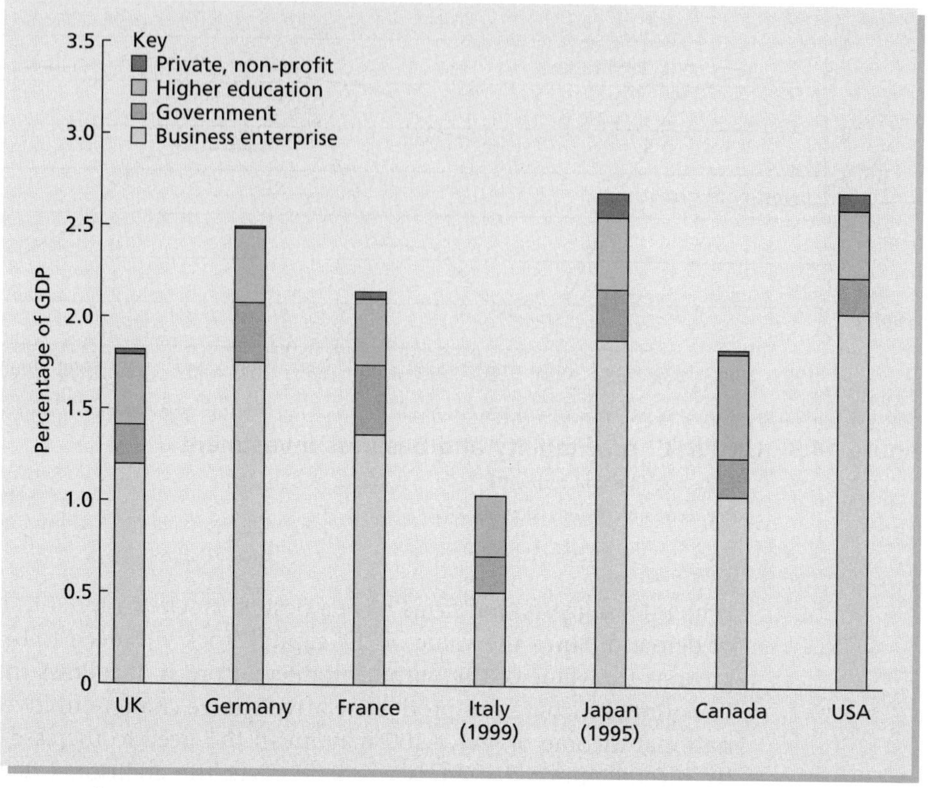

Figure 14.9 **Research and development expenditure in selected countries as a percentage of GDP, 2000**

Source: Economic Trends, August 2002

is not very good by comparison to some other countries. France, Germany, Japan, Canada and the USA all spend more than the UK both in absolute terms and as a proportion of GDP. Arguably, Britain's short-termism is part of the answer for this relatively poor record.

Another form of short-termism may be underinvestment in training. Governments may be reluctant to encourage industry to train its workforce if the rewards of such investment are only going to appear many years later, perhaps after the next general election.

It is, however, possible to argue that short-termism exists only because markets operate in the context of imperfect knowledge. Patrick Foley,[2] for example, argues that the problem is really one of inadequate information. Part of his argument goes as follows. Management may not be short-sighted, it may be that they are reluctant to reveal information beyond the minimum required by law lest they give some advantage to a competitor. A side-effect of this reluctance is that shareholders are denied information. Given their lack of information they may be induced to sell shares in a company that they would have held on to had they been aware of all information, including its long-term prospects. Hence, the difficulty is not that there is a problem of short-termism as such, rather that there is a problem of inadequate information on which investment decisions can be made. Not all economists agree about whether short-termism is a difficulty for the British economy. The difference of viewpoint mainly reflects confidence, or lack of it, in the power of markets to allocate resources effectively.

Successive governments have been committed to the principle that successful economic policy is about making markets work efficiently. Have they succeeded in doing this, and are lower investment levels simply a result of consumer preferences being expressed for more current and less future consumption? There are two ways in which we might think that this is not the case.

First, as we saw in Chapter 13, the UK government has run a PSBR for almost all of its recent history. One way of funding this deficit is by borrowing from its citizens, which it does by issuing debt on which it must pay a competitive interest rate. In doing this it must compete with private firms who wish to use these 'loanable funds' for investment purposes. In terms of Figure 14.3, a PSBR increases the demand curve for loanable funds. If the curve shifts to the right, interest rates will rise, 'crowding out' investment from the private sector. A commitment to a market economy, then, requires a balanced budget, which UK governments have rarely managed to achieve.

Second, to the extent that governments have managed to cut their expenditure in order to move towards a balanced budget, the cuts have tended to be in capital spending – investment – rather than current expenditure – social security etc. The problem here is that government investment expenditure tends to *assist* rather than displace private investment. Road-building, for example, makes industry's transport casts lower and therefore encourages the purchase of plant and machinery. Yet it is these government capital expenditures which are the ones which have tended to suffer in attempts to achieve a balanced budget.

14.7 Weaknesses in the market case?

see pp. 147–50

There is one other area in which we can make out a strong case for saying that the market will not bring about an optimal volume of private investment and might explain why British investment levels are too low. It is an application of ideas we met earlier.

We have seen how the presence of externalities creates a problem for a society leaving its pricing decisions to the market. This is true for investment as well as for pricing. We have seen how there may be external benefits in production that markets ignore. One such example might be investment in education and training. Education and training spending can be seen as a kind of investment in human capital. By increasing people's skills and knowledge one commits resources with an opportunity cost in the hope of a return, over a period of years, of an increase in output. When the value of this output is discounted at an appropriate interest rate, it shows the investment to be worthwhile.

Firms may be unwilling to invest adequately in training their workforce since the people they train may then decide to be employed elsewhere. Society will gain from the training but the firm itself may not do so. Therefore, left to a

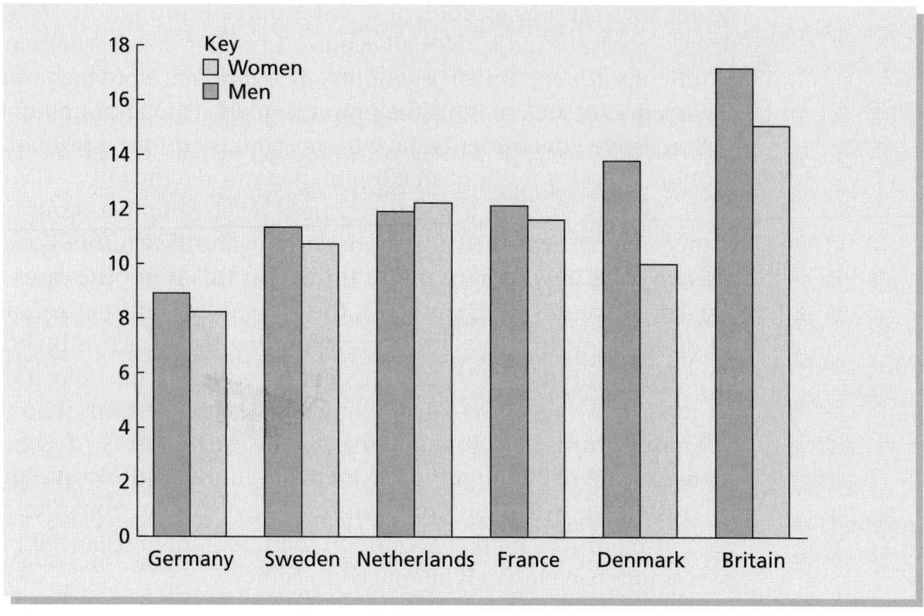

Figure 14.10 **Private real returns to university education 1999–2000**
Source: adapted from OECD data

market the volume of investment in such human capital may be less than optimal. Britain spends much less on education and training than most other advanced nations.

A paper by Leo Doyle[3] of Kleinwort Benson Securities argues that there is a reasonably close positive relationship between investment in education and training and economic welfare: the more a country spends on education and training, the higher its welfare tends to be. This, of course, does not show the direction of causality. Do countries who invest most in education have the highest output? Or is it that countries with the highest GNP can afford large volumes of educational expenditure? A plausible answer is that there is a 'virtuous circle' into which the UK needs to break.[4]

The paper goes on to argue that educational investment should be increased and that if the UK could reach the best attainment level of the OECD, one million people would be removed permanently from the unemployment register. If this were so, it would suggest that such an investment would be very worthwhile. Certainly the UK returns to a university education look impressive. According to the OECD's estimates the annual return to successful students averages 17.3 per cent, substantially more than in other European countries. This can be seen in Figure 14.10. The investment costs are the costs of study plus the opportunity cost of earnings forgone. The cash flow is the post-tax earnings in excess of those earned by school leavers.

However, these are the private gains. The social gains are somewhat lower. This is because the social costs are much higher in that students pay only a fraction of the costs of providing degree courses.

see pp. 270–93

The idea of human capital might also lead us to the view that unemployment is an even worse problem than we saw in Chapter 13. If someone is out of work for a long time, his or her skills are likely to diminish. The value of the human capital thus declines. Not only does unemployment involve an opportunity cost in terms of lost output while the person is unemployed, it may reduce the output that he or she can produce when finally returning to the labour market.

It is easy to see why a government might suffer from short-termism. If the payback to the investment were to be more than five years away, it might feel unwilling to commit such resources through higher taxation. In terms of our investment calculations the NPV must be much higher because cash flows beyond about five years will be ignored – and the government might not win the next election. It can be argued that our election cycle causes governments to be short-termist.

Notice that to the extent that underinvestment in education and training is a problem, it will have an effect on growth and output. It will not show up as a problem in conventional 'investment' statistics such as those shown in Figure 14.5 since these figures refer only to physical investment.

14.8 Conclusion

Does society invest enough? Given that investment uses resources with an opportunity cost, there is clearly an optimal volume of investment for a country to make. Some of that will inevitably be done by governments, since part of that expenditure is in public goods. Whether the volume of private investment can be safely left to the market to decide is a question of some controversy. However, you should be able to see that much of the debate at the macro level about the levels of investment revolves around one's confidence, or lack of it, in the market system that we have been analysing in earlier chapters.

CHAPTER SUMMARY

1. **Investment is the purchase of capital assets either to replace worn out capital or to add to the capital stock.**
2. **Private firms' investment decisions are made on the basis of discounted cash flow decisions.**
3. **In principle, one would expect an inverse relationship between real interest rates and the demand for investment goods.**
4. **The real rate of interest can be seen as being determined in a market for loanable funds.**
5. **Other factors determining private investment decisions are expectations about future profitability and changes in income.**
6. **An important part of society's investment is in human capital.**
7. **Some economists believe that market forces produce too little investment to optimise social welfare.**

Questions for discussion

Guidance to the answers for the ***asterisked*** *numbered questions is available to students on the website for the book at* **www.booksites.net/heather**.

1* Why is it that only the purchase of a *new* house constitutes investment? After all, even if a house is five years old, it will still produce a flow of benefits over a long period.

2 A company has produced the following cash flow profile of a potential investment project. Using NPV (net present value) and assuming that interest rates are 10 per cent, would you recommend that the company goes ahead with the investment? Would it make any difference if interest rates were 15 per cent?

Year 0	Year 1	Year 2	Year 3
–£20,000	£6,000	£12,000	£7,000

3* The project given in question 2 has a rather different cash flow profile from the one given in the text. Which do you think would be more typical and why?

4 Since cash flows are only estimates of incomes that the firm might receive, how could a firm cope with the problem of uncertainty in measuring the cash flow? Consider a major project such as Eurotunnel in particular.

5* What are the main differences for an economy if a government stimulus is in the form of tax cuts rather than increasing government capital spending?

6 Is there so much value to an economy if some of its investment is made in another country? If not, should such outward investment be restricted? Should the government encourage inward investment such as the setting up of Japanese car firms in Britain?

7* Why might the following be seen as examples of investment rather than consumption spending? (a) Subsidising eye tests, (b) hiring more schoolteachers, (c) paying firms to take on trade apprenticeships.

8 What do you see as the major advantages of government being actively involved in the investment decisions of private firms?

9* Does increased investment lead to increased national output or does increased national output lead to increased investment?

10 Should your country spend a higher proportion of its national income on investment?

Websites

Investment and stocks data are given in the UK National Accounts Blue Book and can be accessed at:

www.statistics.gov.uk/statbase/mainmenu.asp

Notes

1 W. W. Easton (1990) 'The Interest Rate Transmission Mechanism in UK and Overseas', *Bank of England Quarterly Bulletin*, Vol. 30, No. 2. We shall use model again in Chapter 20 when we are considering aspects of the international economy.

2 P. Foley (1990) 'Short-termism', *Lloyds Bank Economic Bulletin*, September.

3 L. Doyle (1992) *The Economic Cost of Being Bottom of the Class*, Kleinwort Benson Securities.

4 For an alternative view, arguing that markets are more likely to provide an optimal volume of investment in training than government see 'Training and Jobs: What Works?', *The Economist*, 6 April 1996, pp. 21–3.

15 Inflation, aggregate demand and supply

Beating inflation: *is it really worth it?*

CHAPTER OVERVIEW

Inflation throughout the world is endemic. Prices have risen continually – although at different rates – since the Second World War. European inflation rates are modest and British inflation performance in recent years has been good. In this chapter we ask whether government commitment to its defeat is worth the cost.

In order to do this we review the following concepts:

- Absolute and relative prices
- Investment analysis

We introduce the following concepts:

- Aggregate supply and demand
- Phillips curve
- Rational expectations

15.1 Introduction

Inflation is endemic throughout the world. In virtually all countries, and in virtually every year, movement of the general level of prices is upwards. This has been true over a substantial period. No EU country has succeeded in maintaining a stable price level for any length of time. In the UK the record for much of the past thirty years has been worse than the European average, although its performance in recent years has been considerably better than in the previous fifty years. In most countries, politicians of all major parties insist that tough policies towards the control of inflation are essential. Table 15.1 suggests that the control of inflation has assumed great importance in recent years. In virtually every country the annual increase in the price level has been lower from the mid 1990s onwards than was the case previously. Yet, as we shall see in this chapter, there are costs to be met in bringing inflation under control. Clearly, most governments think that the benefits are great enough to justify those costs. Are they right? We shall discover that virtually all economists agree that there are some benefits in defeating inflation, but there is significant disagreement

Table 15.1 **Inflation: percentage change in consumer prices**

	Ten year averages	
	1984–93	*1994–2003*
Advanced economies	4.2	2.0
United States	3.8	2.4
Japan	1.7	−0.1
Germany	2.4	1.5
United Kingdom	5.0	2.4
Canada	3.9	1.7
Developing countries	48.5	13.7
Regional groups		
Africa	24.3	19.7
Developing Asia	10.2	6.1
Middle East and Turkey	24.2	25.0
Western Hemisphere	184.3	24.7
Countries in transition	72.8	47.0
Heavily indebted poor countries	53.9	27.8

Source: adapted from Eurostat data

about the extent of the costs involved in doing so. However, before we consider what the costs and benefits are we must begin by being clear about what inflation is.

15.2 Inflation: what do we mean?

By inflation we mean a general and persistent rise in the 'average' level of prices. Prices, on average, continue to rise. To put the same thing in a different way, we could say that the value of money is falling. With inflation, a given amount of money income buys less over time. However, we shall need to do better than that. We need to measure more accurately the extent of the change in the price level. The process involves the use of index numbers. Since these are based on the number 100, it makes percentage changes in the price level immediately apparent. The calculation for changes in the price level in Britain is carried out by the Office for National Statistics (ONS) which collects about 130,000 observations on the price changes of around 650 different goods and services from various outlets each month. The data are then grouped into the main areas of consumer expenditure shown in Table 15.2.

We observe the change in price of each good over whatever period we are interested in. In Britain this is done monthly as well as annually. Price changes of those goods on which consumers spend more are more important to consumers, so we attach larger weights to these changes, reflecting that significance. The weights are changed annually to reflect changing patterns of consumer spending.

Table 15.2 Weights in the UK retail price index[1]

Category of expenditure	*Weight*
Alcoholic drinks	68
Catering	52
Clothing and footwear	51
Fares and other travel costs	20
Food	114
Fuel and light	31
Household goods	73
Household services	60
Housing	199
Leisure goods	48
Leisure services	69
Motoring expenditure	141
Personal goods and services	43
Tobacco	31
Sum of weights	1,000

[1] Weights are for 2002

Source: NSO website

The weights column in Table 15.2 can be interpreted in the following way. For every £1,000 of expenditure the average consumer spends £114 on food or 11.4 per cent of his/her income. Hence the weight is 114. Since rather more (£199 out of every £1,000) is consumed by housing costs, this latter receives the appropriate higher weighting.

The process used to establish the price index is as follows. Each change in price of a category of goods is multiplied by its weight. Then we sum these values. Finally we divide that total by the sum of the weights. This gives us the weighted average change in the price level for the particular period.

What would have happened if we had not weighted the price changes? The unweighted average price change would be a slightly different figure in that we would have in effect assumed that all changes in price are of equal importance to consumers. Such an unweighted measure is so unrealistic that it would not be calculated at all.

Some prices rise by more than the average and some by less. Relative prices alter even when there is no overall price change. Suppose in a period of inflation one category of goods rises more slowly than the average. If we were looking at such goods and trying to explain the change using microeconomic analysis, we would be seeking to explain why their price was declining, not why they were rising.

The most commonly quoted measure of inflation in Britain is provided by the retail price index (RPI) produced by the ONS. It is the one we have just calculated. It is frequently called the 'headline rate'. Also published is the 'underlying rate',

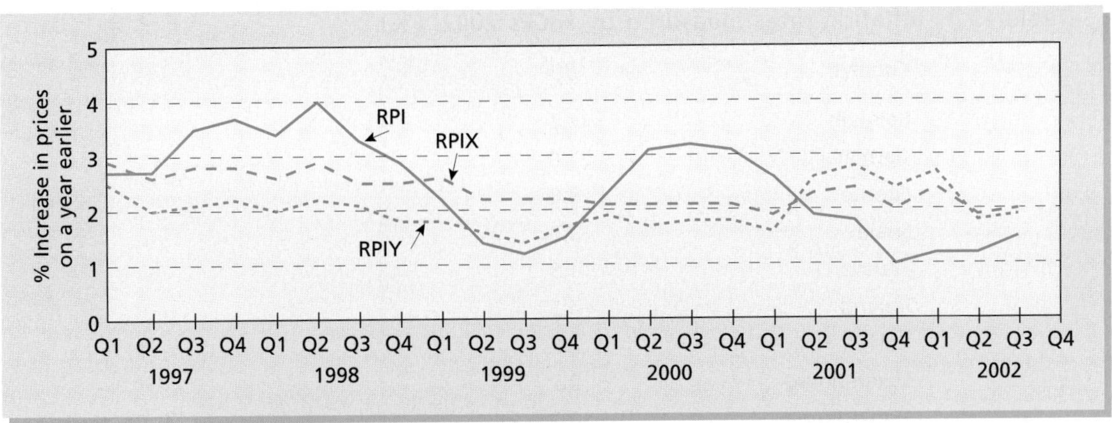

Figure 15.1 Recent UK inflation performance

Source: adapted from ONS data

referred to in Figure 15.1 as RPIX. What is the difference between the two and which is the better measure? The difference is that the underlying rate excludes an item that is quite volatile, namely mortgage interest payments. This is a large item of expenditure for millions of people buying their own homes but is an item that can vary significantly with changes in interest rates in the economy. When interest rates are increasing, the RPI is rising more quickly than the underlying rate, but is falling more quickly when interest rates fall.

There are two main arguments for concentrating on the underlying rate. The first one is that mortgage repayments are not simply a reflection of living costs. People who pay mortgages are acquiring a house, which is an asset. It is a form of saving. The second is that most other countries, including those in the EU, produce a price index that excludes mortgage interest payments. Hence comparisons with other countries are more meaningful if using the underlying rate.

However, it is important to remember that mortgage interest does partly reflect living costs. If one were to produce an RPI from which mortgage repayments are excluded, it would be necessary to put into it some element of housing costs since it is such an important element of a family's expenditure. The government's 'preferred' measure is the underlying rate.

One other measure of UK inflation is given in Figure 15.1. It is referred to as RPIY. This is RPIX from which changes in indirect taxes have been excluded. Sometimes prices rise not because firms' costs of labour, materials, etc. are rising, but because governments increase taxes on goods. In the UK such indirect taxes are heavy on motoring, alcohol and tobacco. Where prices rise as a result of increases in such taxes the price changes are included in the RPI and RPIX measure but excluded from RPIY.

There is one other thing that might well have occurred to you as you studied Table 15.2. The weights are for *average* expenditure. This means that for some groups neither the RPI nor the underlying rate is very realistic. Hence if, for example, student representatives wish to make out a case for more generous grants, they could construct a different index based on average weights for

Table 15.3 Inflation rates measured by HICPs 2002[1] (%)

Country	*HICP*
Belgium	1.2
Germany	1.0
Greece	3.8
Spain	3.5
France	1.8
Ireland	4.5
Italy	2.8
Luxembourg	2.2
Netherlands	3.7
Austria	1.6
Portugal	3.8
Finland	1.4
Denmark	2.5
Sweden	1.2
United Kingdom	1.0
EU15	1.9

[1] Figures are for the year September 2001–September 2002
Source: Eurostat website

student expenditure. This might well show a different change in the cost of living for students as compared with the average household.

Clearly, with so many different measures of inflation, making international comparisons of inflation rates raises difficulties. Since 1996 the European Commission has produced harmonised inflation data. This measure is known as the Harmonised Index of Consumer Prices (HICP). It can differ somewhat from the figures produced by the individual countries. This is inevitable since each country produces its price data in different ways. Let us compare the RPI with HICP.

The HICP includes airfares, university accommodation fees, and foreign students' university tuition fees, unit trust and stockbrokers' charges, all of which are excluded from the RPI. There are also differences in the calculations because the RPI is based on UK household expenditure, whereas HICP includes expenditure by foreign visitors. These and other differences may not make the series hugely different but they are enough to notice, particularly over a long period. Table 15.3 shows a set of inflation figures from the Commission using the common methodology of calculation. Notice that the UK, which is now doing well by the standards of its own recent history, is also now doing very well in EU terms. By the Commission's estimates, some countries overstate inflationary pressures in their economy, especially the Netherlands. Others, including the UK, according to the Commission, understate their degree of inflation.

15.3 The costs of inflation

It is not obvious that inflation is a problem. If money incomes rise as fast as the price level, then living standards are not falling. Indeed, if you recall the logic of national income accounts, it should be clear that a price increase for one person is an income increase for someone else. Nevertheless, there *are* costs to inflation. We shall look briefly at most of them and then concentrate on the most controversial aspect of inflation – its link with unemployment. First, however, we consider other costs of inflation.

Political costs to government

Some commentators have suggested that governments have a vested interest in inflation: the higher that prices rise, the less is the real value of government debt. However, post-war history in Britain tells a different story. The relationship of movements in the price level to general election results suggests that the electorate judges a government very much on its inflation record. In the British election in 1992 the Conservative government was re-elected during a period when growth was negative, unemployment was rising, the balance of payments account was in deficit and interest rates were high (though falling). Nevertheless, the rate of inflation, although positive, was falling. Electorally, then, governments must be wary of inducing inflation as a means of reducing the value of their debt.

It is likely that this aversion of the electorate to inflation will continue. Those on retirement incomes fear that inflation will erode their savings. The proportion of the population that is of retirement age is increasing. It is therefore likely to be politically as well as economically shrewd to place a high priority on the defeat of inflation. There is some economic logic too, as we shall see.

Waste of scarce resources

There are several different ways in which inflation imposes costs on society, in that resources are used up which could have been put to more valuable ends. It could be argued, for example, that much of the time spent by management and unions on the bargaining associated with the annual pay round is a function of a positive rate of inflation. Resources are committed simply to ensure that there is no change in the relative price of labour. The argument needs to be treated with some care. At least part of all this resource usage would be necessary even with zero inflation. The market mechanism still requires some change in relative wage rates over time. It could be argued that some inflation 'oils the wheels' of such changes, in that where market forces dictate a lower equilibrium real wage, unions may find this fact more palatable if they receive a smaller 'increase' rather than, as would be the case with zero inflation, a cut in the nominal wage rate.

An alternative possible resource waste could be working days lost through strikes. The higher the inflation rate, the more frequently labour bargains for

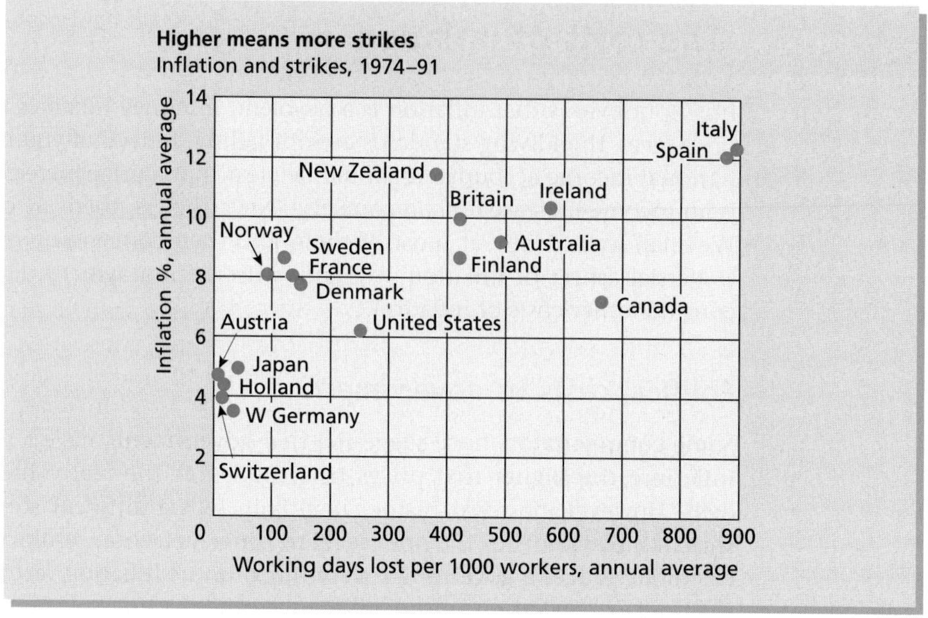

Figure 15.2 **Inflation and strikes, 1974–91**

Source: © *The Economist*, 7 November 1992

increases in nominal wage rates. This increases the danger that the outcome of bargaining will be strike action. Figure 15.2 suggests that there is indeed a positive correlation between inflation rates and working days lost, at least in advanced industrial economies.

However, a waste of resources through inflation is possible not only in the labour market. Resources are also committed, in a society with a permanent inflation rate, to the production of services whose main function is to protect against inflation. For example, speculative purchases of gold are attributable to people's perception that inflation erodes the real value of savings. Resources are then committed to producing a service that would be irrelevant in a society which did not suffer from inflation. This is not to suggest that gold has no intrinsic value, but many purchases of the commodity are not to enjoy its intrinsic worth, but because of its perceived hedge against inflation.

'Menu' costs

During periods of inflation the nominal price of those goods and services whose relative price is not changing still has to be altered. This involves costs. For example, a restaurant owner must go to the expense of altering the prices on the menu. Price lists of many products will need changing. The faster the rate of inflation the worse the problem will be. This problem manifests itself partly through additional resources being committed to the coverage of these 'menu' costs and partly through the reduction in information available. With a stable price level, firms are willing to advertise with the price of the product included in the advertisement. During an inflationary period the high menu costs prevent so much information being available.

'Shoe leather' costs

There is one other cost of inflation. It is a small cost at low inflation rates but probably substantial at the rates which have obtained in, say, Angola, where annual inflation rates in recent years have often been in excess of 100 per cent. Higher inflation tends to mean higher interest rates. Since money in circulation gains no interest, the opportunity cost of holding such money increases. This encourages people to hold less cash and to make more trips to their bank or building society. Such actions impose costs on the individual not only directly – they are sometimes called 'shoe leather' costs – but also indirectly. Banks' and building societies' transactions costs increase if people come often for a little cash rather than fewer times for more.

The above costs are imposed on society during a period of inflation, even if the inflation is correctly anticipated. However, one could argue that economic agents do not correctly anticipate inflation. If this is so, then further costs are imposed on society. It is to these that we now turn.

15.4 Imperfectly anticipated inflation

The costs of imperfectly anticipated inflation are likely to be very much greater than those costs discussed so far. In this section we consider four possible costs of imperfectly anticipated inflation, namely redistributional effects, balance of payments problems, increased uncertainty and the problem of hyperinflation.

Redistributional effects

see p. 305

One problem for an inflationary economy is the capricious way in which it tends to redistribute income. Recall that in Chapter 14 we made a distinction between nominal and real interest rates. Real interest rates are nominal rates minus the rate of inflation. The main reason for the redistributional effect of inflation is that nominal interest rates rarely respond fully to the effects of rising prices. Although there is generally some upward movement of nominal interest rates during an inflationary period, it is rarely sufficient to render real interest rates constant. Therefore when an economy suffers from any more than mild inflationary pressure, income is redistributed from creditors – those who are owed money – to debtors – those who have borrowed. Two illustrations of this process will suffice.

Most people who purchase a house borrow the money from a bank or building society. In reality, they are borrowing from the people who save with these institutions. The institutions themselves are simply intermediaries who make a profit by reducing the transactions costs involved. If inflation is high and interest rates do not rise fully to reflect it, the real value of the mortgage debt falls.

Correspondingly, the real value of the savings of the creditor also falls. Income is therefore redistributed through inflation. The problem is one of imperfectly anticipated inflation: if the creditor had correctly anticipated future events, he or she would have found an inflation-proof method of saving. The problem, then, is a combination of inflation plus imperfect knowledge.

A similar process occurs when inflation reduces the value of the government's debt. Since, with rare exceptions, governments spend more in any year than they receive in taxation, there is a public sector borrowing requirement adding to the national debt. Most of that debt is with its own citizens in the form of national savings, bonds and bills. If interest rates are less than inflation and people are willing to buy government debt because of failing to anticipate inflation correctly, income will be distributed away from private citizens, and possibly companies, towards government.

These redistributional effects can have secondary consequences that may be overlooked. As we have already seen on several occasions, efficient markets require mobility of labour. Unanticipated inflation can reduce that mobility.

A typical contract for professional labour includes a pension entitlement. The size of the pension depends upon the number of years' service with the company and the salary at retirement or at the time the employee leaves the company. Inflation erodes the real value of the salary earned at the time of leaving. In a strongly inflationary economy a person who leaves a firm at, say, 35 to work for another, may discover that at retirement the real value of the pension from the first firm is virtually worthless. This may act as a strong disincentive to change jobs.

see pp. 5–6

Another way of viewing these redistributional problems is to see them as an illustration of the problem mentioned in Chapter 1. Relative price changes can be confused with absolute price changes during inflation. If this happens, then the efficient working of the market system may be adversely affected.

Balance of payments problems

The UK government has frequently argued that inflation control is crucial to retain balance of payments equilibrium. If Britain inflates faster than the rest of the world, import prices become cheaper relative to export prices. Exports fall as foreigners substitute other goods for British ones. Imports rise as domestic consumers switch to cheaper substitute imported goods. The conclusion is that the inflation rate must not be allowed to be greater than that in other countries. This is an argument that many economists would not accept and deserves careful consideration. However, we shall not discuss it further now. It is dealt with in Chapter 20.

see p. 437

Increased uncertainty

see pp. 301–4

Recall what we said in Chapter 14. Investment decisions taken by firms are made by estimating the initial capital cost and the future revenue stream. Then the revenue stream is discounted at an appropriate interest rate to see if the

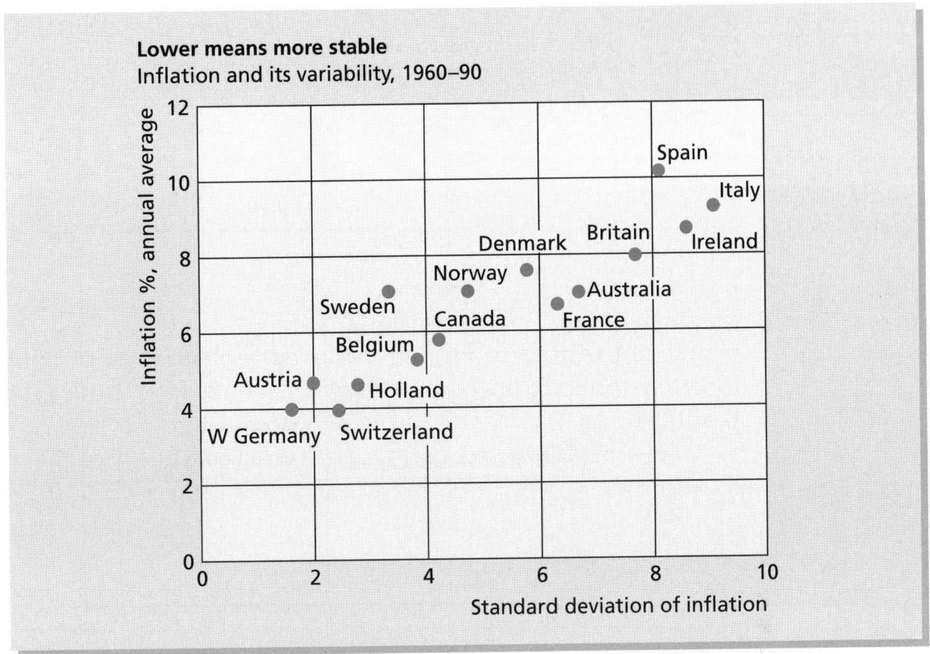

Figure 15.3 Inflation and its variability, 1960–90

Source: © *The Economist*, 7 November 1992

project is worthwhile. We assumed that there was no inflation in the economy. Now suppose there is inflation but future inflation rates are entirely predictable. Any correctly anticipated inflation can easily be built into the investment equation. Thus, we would have

$$\textbf{IRR} = \text{the rate, } r\text{, such that } \sum_{k=1}^{n} A_k \frac{(1+s)^k}{(1+r)^k} - C = 0$$

where A is cash flows, C is capital cost, r is nominal interest rates and s is anticipated inflation. Note that if the nominal interest rate is the same as the inflation rate, the real rate of interest is zero. Assuming that a rise in the price level is not anticipated, it is then a matter of indifference when the cash flows are earned. There is no opportunity cost involved in waiting for the cash flows.

However, unanticipated inflation creates problems. It may reduce the volume of investment because of the increased uncertainty associated with inflation. That is to say, firms are aware that they cannot perfectly anticipate inflation. They may therefore make a greater allowance for risk, reducing the chances that the project will be undertaken. Furthermore, the higher the level of inflation, the greater the likely variation in its rate. This again increases uncertainty and may decrease investment.

Is there any evidence to suggest that this is the case? First, there is evidence that a lower rate of inflation means less variability. Figure 15.3 plots the relationship between the rate of inflation and a measure of its variability for advanced industrial countries. There is clearly a strong positive correlation.

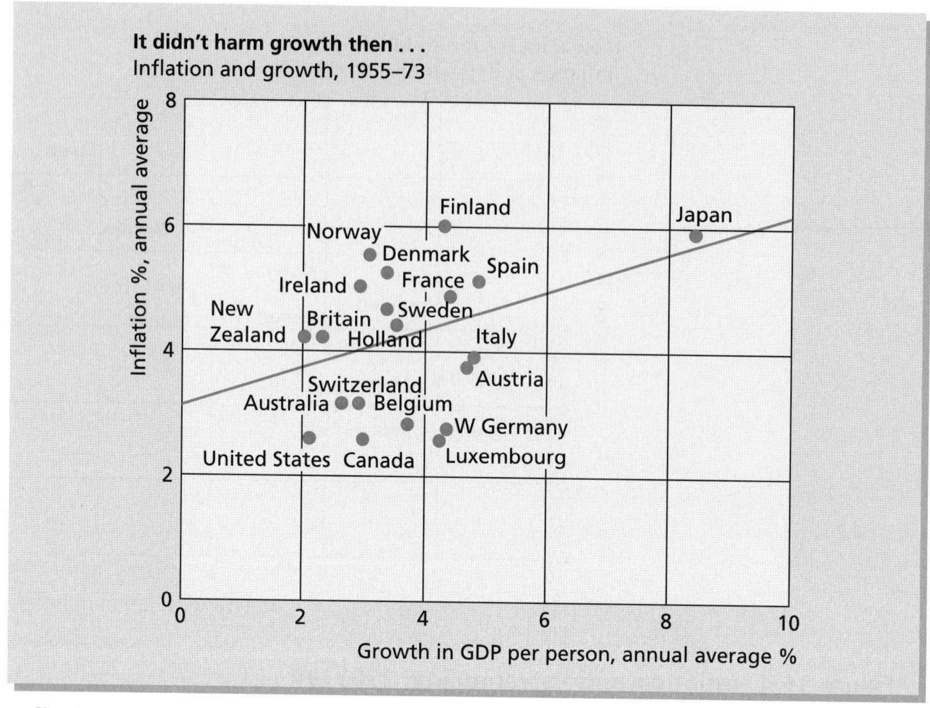

Figure 15.4 **Inflation and growth, 1955–73**

Source: © *The Economist*, 7 November 1992

Does a higher level of inflation lead to less investment? We can measure this correlation indirectly. Since more investment should, *ceteris paribus*, lead to a higher growth rate of gross national product (GNP), we can ask if there is a correlation between inflation and growth.

The evidence here is weak. We can again compare the performances of advanced industrial economies in this respect (see Figures 15.4 and 15.5).

First, consider what happened in the period 1955–73 when inflation was low for most of these countries. If a correlation exists, it is a positive one. That is, countries with higher inflation achieved higher rates of growth. However, if one removes Japan from consideration, there appears to be no correlation at all.

What do we find if we examine the relationship between inflation and gross domestic product (GDP) growth in the period 1974–91? *The Economist* claims that it shows inflation harming growth. As you can see from Figure 15.5, the correlation is again poor. However, it is certainly much improved, though hardly compelling, if one ignores Italy, Spain, Ireland and Switzerland. The reason for ignoring these countries is as follows. Italy, Spain and Ireland began the period with relatively low average incomes per head. They had, therefore, more potential for growth than the others and so had a high growth rate despite having relatively high inflation rates. Switzerland, on the other hand, had the highest income per head and thus had less scope for growth. You must decide for yourself whether the argument for ignoring some countries is convincing.

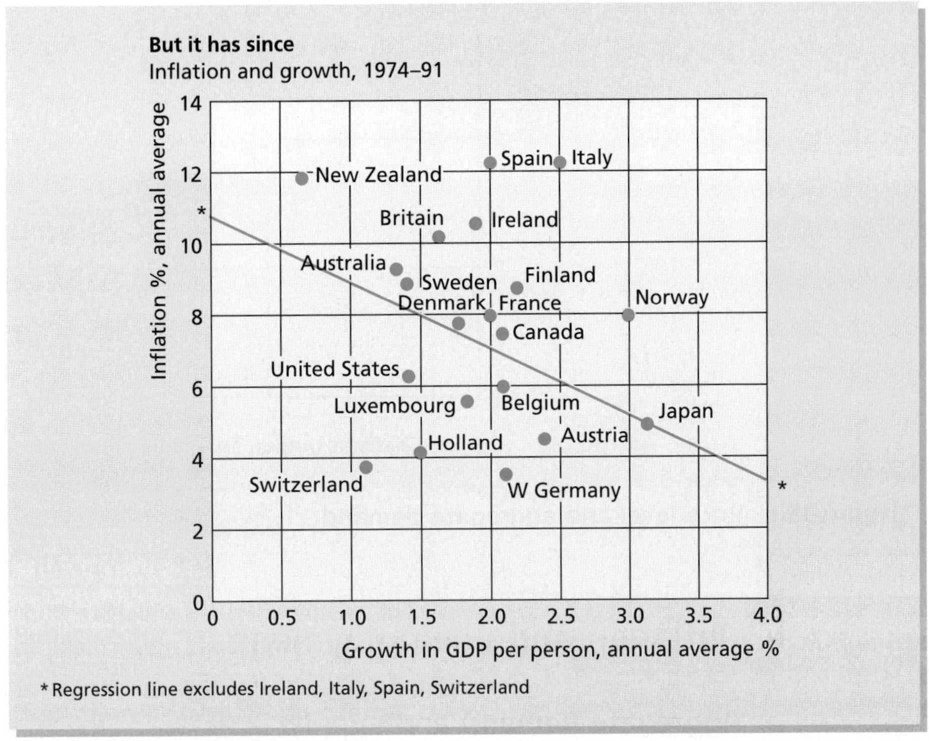

Figure 15.5 **Inflation and growth, 1974–91**

Source: © *The Economist*, 7 November 1992

Does national income in different countries converge over time? If not, it is difficult to argue that, for example, Switzerland has little scope for growth.

Hyperinflation

Some regard any inflation as harmful because it tends to be self-perpetuating. If left unchecked, it produces high rates of inflation known as hyperinflation. Whether this is true is far from certain. What is certain is that if inflation does lead to hyperinflation, an economy will experience enormous problems. The costs of hyperinflation are very high. Perhaps the most valuable function of money is that it acts as a medium of exchange and removes many transaction costs associated with the barter economy. If people lose confidence in money, for example in Germany in the early 1920s when inflation reached several million per cent per week, a market economy cannot function efficiently, if at all. Not even the emerging democracies of Eastern Europe or the economies of Latin America have approached this level of difficulty with inflation.

What we have said so far may cause you to feel that inflation is not painless and that its defeat should be a priority for a government. However, one cannot form a judgement on the matter without examining one more crucial issue. How does inflation affect unemployment? It is to this central question that we now turn.

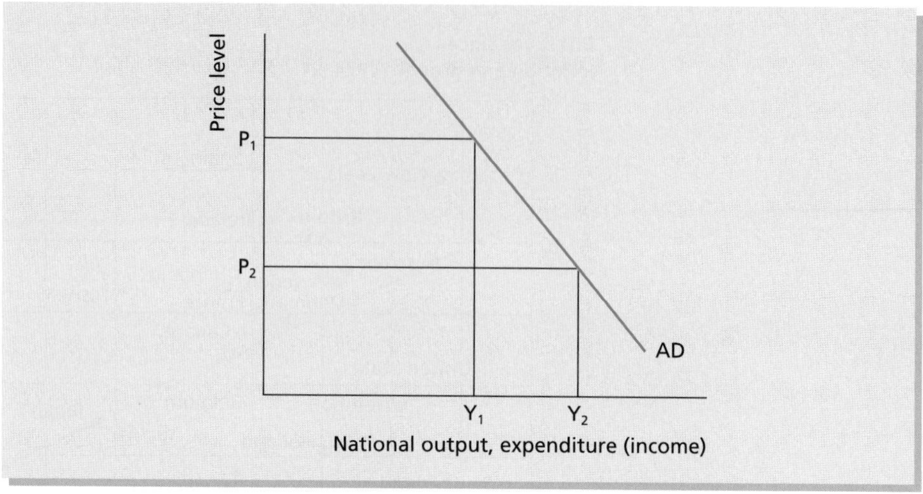

Figure 15.6 **Price level and aggregate demand**

15.5 Inflation and unemployment

Aggregate demand and supply

Demand and supply curves for individual markets show the relationship between the price of a good and the quantity of it demanded and supplied. By now this is familiar to you. Here we will find it useful for understanding the working of the economy at the macro level, if we use aggregate demand and supply curves. In essence this means that we look at the relationship between the price level of all goods and services and the amount of output of all goods and services demanded and supplied. What would these relationships look like? Consider first the aggregate demand curve in Figure 15.6, which shows a greater quantity of goods and services being demanded as the price level falls. Why would this happen?

The answer is that at a lower price level the real value of money will be greater, so people will wish to buy more. Furthermore, it may be that at a lower price level for our goods and services people will switch out of buying imports into buying home-produced output. Thus, for a lower price level, say a decline from P_1 to P_2, the quantity of national output demanded increases from Y_1 to Y_2.

The shape of the aggregate supply curve is much more controversial. We shall consider two possible shapes, the first of which is given in Figure 15.7.

see pp. 283–6

In Chapter 13 we saw the Keynesian view that unemployment can be dealt with via an increase in aggregate demand. We said little about the effect of this increase in demand on the price level. Figure 15.7 will now help us to understand the Keynesian view on the matter. Y_{FE} represents the full employment level of output. Suppose there is much unemployment, since the economy is only producing Y_1 output. There is a deep recession. Aggregate demand is low: at AD_1 the price level is at P_1. Suppose now that aggregate demand is stimulated

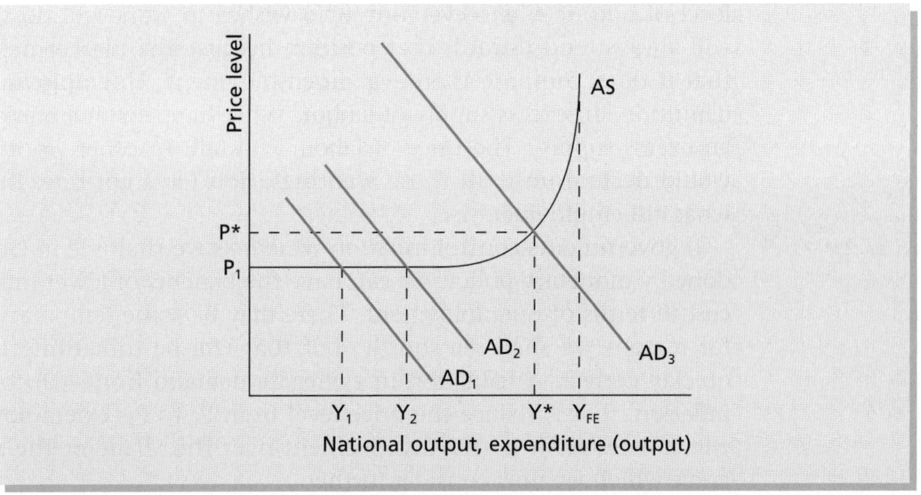

Figure 15.7 **Aggregate demand and a Keynesian aggregate supply curve**

and that it shifts to AD_2. Output increases to Y_2. Firms increase output to meet the increase in demand, yet the price level stays at P_1.

However, there is still unemployment. What happens if government attempts to remove that unemployment via a further stimulus to demand? Suppose it increases demand to AD_3. Output expands to Y*, unemployment falls, but the price level has increased to P*. Moving towards Y_{FE} has generated inflation. Eliminating unemployment altogether would only be possible with substantial inflation. In other words, the aggregate supply curve suggests that there exists a trade-off between inflation and unemployment. Why Keynesians believe this to be so we shall consider shortly.

Another possible shape of the aggregate supply curve is given in Figure 15.8. The vertical aggregate supply curve represents the basis of the classical view.[1] It says that there is a full employment level of output in the economy. That is a

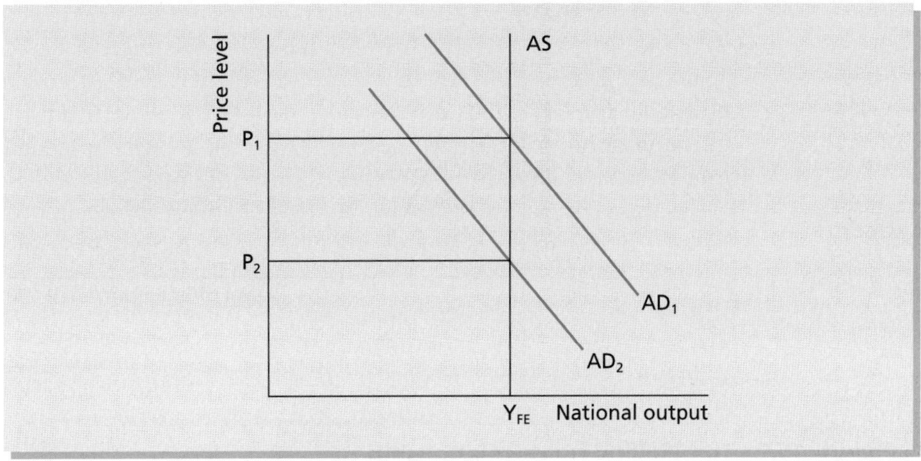

Figure 15.8 **Aggregate demand and a vertical aggregate supply curve**

level of output where everyone who wishes to work will do so. The economy will always tend towards that position because the market mechanism will see that it does. Suppose there was unemployment. Unemployment must be, by definition, an excess supply of labour. What happens in a market where there is an excess supply? The price of labour will fall. In other words, real wage rates would decline until all those wanting a job have got one. In essence, that is what full employment is.

see pp. 394–7

If governments control inflation which, as we shall see in Chapter 18, can be done by monetary policy, we can have the benefits of lower inflation at no great cost in terms of unemployment. There may be some temporary unemployment for reasons we shall see shortly, but that will be something that markets can quickly correct. A reduction in aggregate demand from AD_1 to AD_2 will reduce inflation, that is reduce the price level from P_1 to P_2. Unemployment, however, will not result. It is this disagreement over the shape of the aggregate supply curve which we now consider further.

Developing the Keynesian perspective: the Phillips curve

Support for the Keynesian perspective represented by Figure 15.7 came as the result of empirical observations made by A. W. Phillips. He noted that if one plotted over a period the recorded observations of unemployment and the rate of change of money wages for the British economy, one obtained a picture suggesting a relationship as described by Figure 15.9. Note that this is not a theory, it is a recording of observations. He noted that in years when unemployment was high, the rate of change of money wages was relatively low. The speed at which money wages were changing served as a good proxy for inflation. Not all the observations were exactly on the line, but the line represented a good fit.

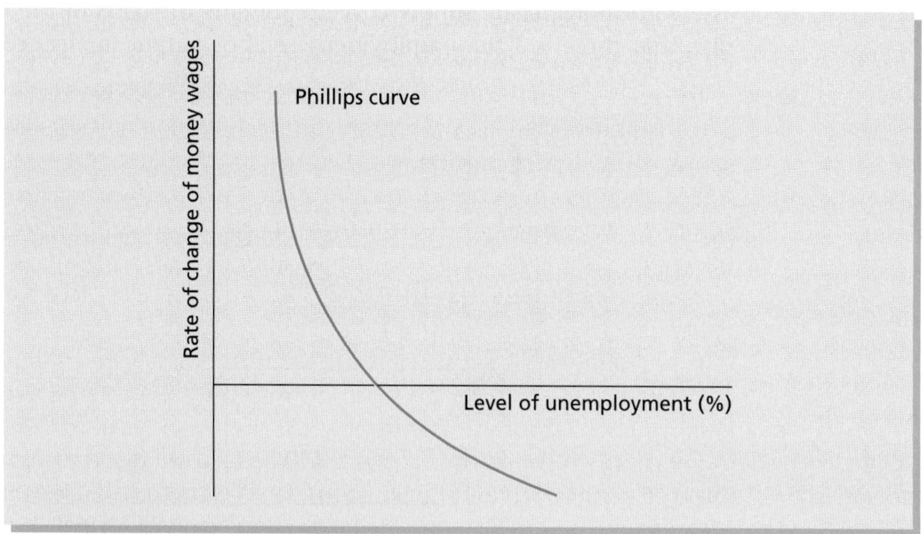

Figure 15.9 The Phillips curve relationship

Now what could give rise to such a relationship? The Phillips argument was as follows. When unemployment is high and there is a pool of labour seeking employment, trade unions' power to gain wage increases is low. If the pool of unemployed labour is smaller, and the labour market tighter, trade unions can negotiate larger increases in money wages.

The next step in the argument is simple. Governments have the power to regulate the volume of aggregate demand in the economy. If they believe the costs of inflation to be high, they can prevent that inflation by tightly controlling aggregate demand. The price they must pay is a higher level of unemployment. If the government feels that the costs of inflation for an economy are low, it can gain the advantages of fuller employment via a higher volume of aggregate demand. The government can assess the costs and benefits of inflation control and act accordingly.

The Phillips curve: a criticism

The Phillips curve was based on observations of the British economy up to 1957. One criticism that can be made is that more recent history has shown it to be out of date. Observations of many years since the 1970s are very far to the right of the original curve. The original curve suggested that with an unemployment level of only 5.5 per cent there would be no change at all in the average level of money wages.[2]

The Keynesians have an interesting response to the criticism. It goes like this. The original Phillips curve was developed during a period of low inflation. Therefore when unions negotiated wage increases, they were using what had been happening to prices in the recent past as a basis for wage claims. Once the rate of inflation starts to rise, unions begin to anticipate what will happen to prices in the coming year, and negotiations proceed on that basis. Higher inflation thus becomes a self-fulfilling prophecy as higher wages chase higher prices in an inflationary spiral. The Phillips curve still holds but expectations of inflation can push the curve to the right.

In recent years this has begun to look plausible. Expectations have been that price inflation will be only around 2–4 per cent per annum and, the curve shows some sign of shifting back inwards to its original position.

The Phillips curve is still useful for the insights it gives. A movement around the curve is referred to as an *activity* shock. A slowdown in economic activity decreases vacancies as firms wish to employ fewer people. At the same time unemployment increases. The opposite effect will take place when the economy expands.

A *structural* shock causes movements in the same direction in both vacancies and unemployment. For example, a worsening in the effectiveness of the process of matching jobs to vacancies shifts the curve outwards.

Figure 15.10 shows the euro area Phillips curve for recent years. It shows evidence of both kinds of shock. From 1980–84 and 1990–94, for example, the vacancy rate declined as the unemployment rate increased over the whole period; however the curve appears to have shifted outwards.

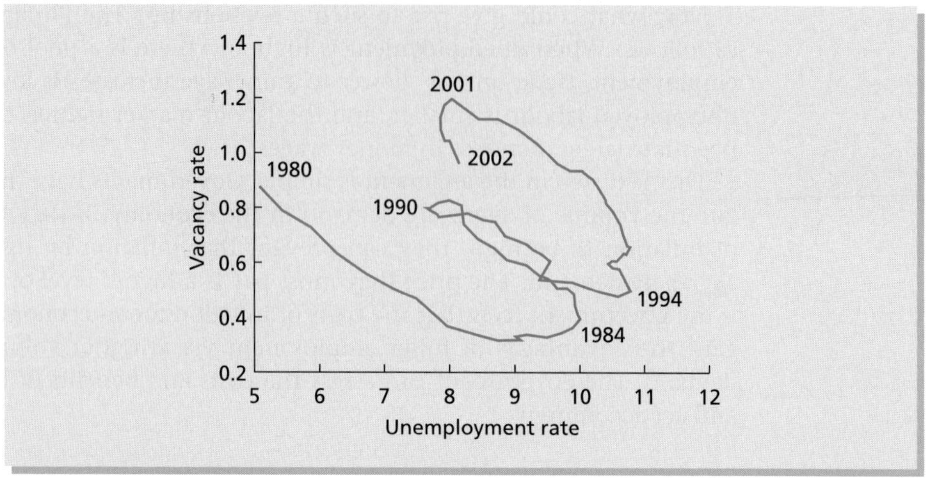

Figure 15.10 Unemployment-vacancy rate relationship in the euro area (in percentage of the labour force)

Note: Vacancy data cover around 64 per cent of the euro area. The 2002 figures include data up to the third quarter

Source: © European Central Bank. Source of original data: *Monthly Bulletin*, December 2002. Data can be obtained free of charge from the European Central Bank via its websites (www.ecb.int) or as hard copy

Two classical perspectives on inflation

Not all Keynesians think alike: there are variations on the Keynesian model, although the Keynesian school of thought can be said to cover those economists whose perspective is that markets do not clear quickly in the way that classical economists believe. Similarly, not all classical thinking is identical, though there is this basic perspective that markets will adjust and do a better job maximising welfare than governments will do by macroeconomic intervention. We now look at two different views of the relationship between inflation and unemployment, both of which are in the classical mould.

The first school of classical thinking is happy to accept the existence of a Phillips curve, but not its policy conclusion. The reason for this is based on what has become known as the 'rational expectations' hypothesis. Remember that the classicals believe that markets clear quickly, resulting in a vertical aggregate supply curve. Does this mean zero unemployment? Not quite. There is a natural rate of unemployment, comprising people who choose not to be working at the going level of real wages. It is voluntary unemployment since markets clear. Anyone who wants a job at the going wage rate for their particular skill can find one. In Figure 15.11 we show that natural rate at an assumed 8 per cent. We can have that at any level of inflation. Remember that in classical thinking unemployment cannot be traded against inflation. To have a lower level of unemployment the government must reduce the natural rate of unemployment. This may be possible, as we shall see in Chapters 16 and 17. How, then, can the Phillips curve be accepted? The argument is an interesting one.

see pp. 341–82

Suppose the economy is at point A in Figure 15.11. There is zero inflation and a natural rate of 8 per cent unemployment. Suppose then that the government,

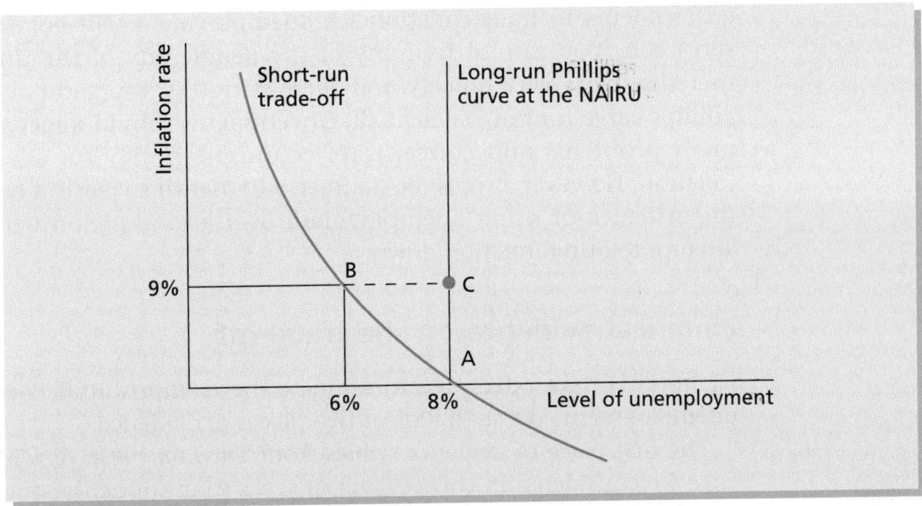

Figure 15.11 Classical view of the Phillips curve

following a Keynesian model, decides that unemployment is too high. It expands aggregate demand, thinking that the cost of a lower unemployment rate of 6 per cent is worth the 9 per cent inflation it will cause. It therefore shifts the economy to point B on the diagram. The problem, according to this school of thinking, is that the economy cannot and will not remain there. What has happened is that some people have been persuaded into employment since they believe that the higher wage rates being paid because of government stimulus to the economy make it worth their while. Soon they will realise that they have been misled. Money wages are higher, real wages are not, since the price level is higher. Once they realise that real wages have not increased they will leave the labour market again and the economy will be at point C. Notice that we now have 9 per cent inflation, with all the costs that that imposes on the economy, and the same level of unemployment as before – the natural rate.

You cannot fool all the people all the time. The government will not be able to keep stimulating the economy and permanently fooling people into thinking that real wages are increasing. Rational expectations suggest that they will incorporate a 9 per cent inflation rate into their thinking. Next time the government may be able to fool people again, but since people have adjusted to thinking in terms of inflation at an annual rate of 9 per cent, it may take an inflation rate of, say, 12 per cent to do it. To get unemployment below 6 per cent it will require, not a positive rate of inflation, but an accelerating rate of inflation. That is why the natural rate of unemployment is sometimes called NAIRU – a non-accelerating inflationary rate of unemployment. In the long run the benefits of zero inflation are available at zero cost. In the short run there is a trade-off between inflation and unemployment.

A second strand of classical thinking takes a different approach. It takes the view that economic agents do not have to wait until inflation figures are announced. They can anticipate changes in the inflation rate from such freely available data as changes in the money supply.[3] On this view any attempt by governments to trade inflation for unemployment will not work even in the short run. You cannot fool any of the people any of the time. Markets will therefore clear very quickly and there is not even a short run trade-off. The Phillips curve is of no value at all. Governments should forget about unemployment problems and concentrate economic policy on the elimination of inflation. However, it must be doubted whether this view can be reconciled with the evidence of rising unemployment over a long period when governments attempt to bring inflation down.

Empirical evidence on the trade-off

Economists have attempted to estimate the relationship between inflation and unemployment. We shall look at two pieces of evidence.

The first piece of evidence comes from *The Economist*. As with previous evidence we considered in this chapter, it seeks to examine the question with reference to the relationship in a large number of advanced industrial countries. Figure 15.12 summarises the position. The data suggest that over the long run there is a positive correlation between inflation and unemployment. Overall, countries with the higher inflation rates tend to have higher unemployment levels, although the relationship is not particularly close.

The Economist therefore argues that it is worth fighting inflation since in the long run it will decrease unemployment and increase national output. The article goes on to argue that if inflation is reduced there will be some short-term

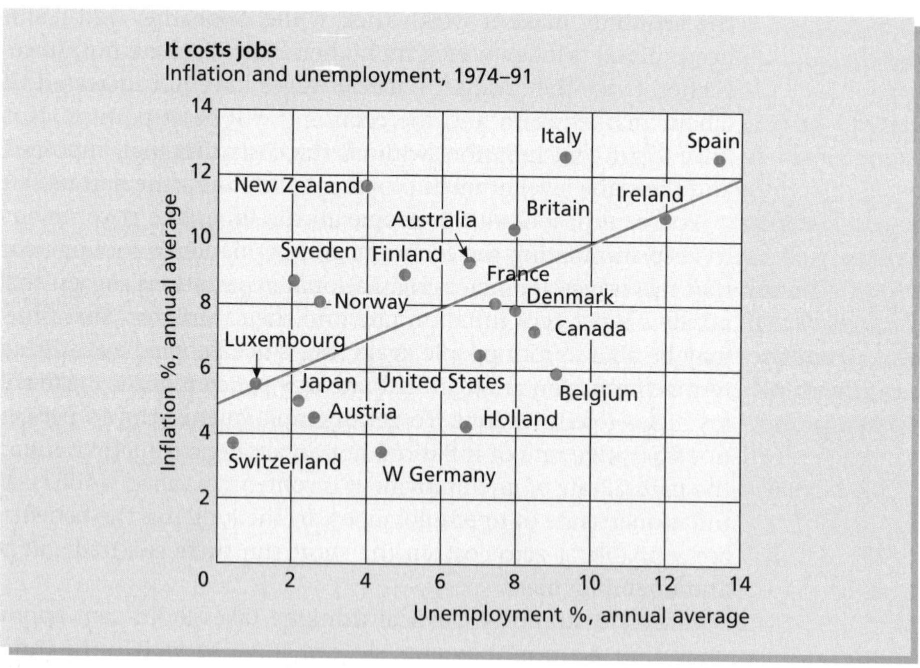

Figure 15.12 Inflation and unemployment

Source: © *The Economist*, 7 November 1992

Table 15.4 **Estimated equilibrium percentage rate of unemployment in the UK**

1969–73	*1974–81*	*1981–86*	*1986–90*	*1991–97*	*1994–98*	*1997–2000*
3.8	7.5	9.5	9.6	8.9	6.9	5.7

Source: S. Nickell (May, 2001) Speech at the Society of Business Economists, www.bankofengland.co.uk

increase in unemployment since, as the Keynesians suggest, labour markets do not adjust quickly. Therefore at the same time that the government seeks to reduce inflation, it should try to undertake policies to reduce the short-term costs involved. We return to this point in the next chapter.

see pp. 346–9

The other piece of evidence comes from the Oxford economist Stephen Nickell. He argues that there is a natural rate of unemployment for the British economy, but this rate has been changing. Applying various statistical techniques to data for the British economy, he argues that this natural rate was rising over time as shown in Table 15.4. He says that there is nothing 'natural' about the natural rate. It can be changed by certain kinds of policy. He therefore prefers the term 'equilibrium rate'.

This natural rate is the one that he argues is consistent with a constant rate of inflation and balanced international trade. Reducing the rate of inflation will require a still higher level of unemployment. Nickell also seeks to consider what factors are responsible for this rising natural rate, but that is something that must wait until the next chapter. During the 1990s others have also attempted to measure the natural rate. The National Institute for Economic and Social Research reckoned it to be 6.8 per cent at the start of the new century.

15.6 Problems with deflation

The history of the past sixty or so years has shown that we live in an inflationary world and that inflation can create problems. Is 'deflation', a general and sustained fall in the price level a problem also? It may not be. For example, in the late nineteenth century in England productivity was rapid and output grew. This increase in aggregate supply depressed the price level with no significantly harmful effects.

On the other hand there are potential dangers with deflation. The Japanese economy from 1997–2003 saw a sharp recession bound up with a period of a sustained fall in the price level. There are three potential dangers of deflation.

First, a falling price level may cause consumers to delay consumption. Prices will be lower tomorrow. A fall in aggregate demand may cause unemployment to grow.

Second, it makes it harder for governments to control the volume of demand. When aggregate demand declines, governments may well deal with the problem partly by cutting interest rates. This makes investment more likely and encourages consumers to borrow in order to spend more. However, it is cuts in real interest rates that are most effective. Real interest rates are the nominal rate of interest minus the inflation rate. Thus nominal interest rates have to be negative when inflation is zero. This is difficult since, if the banks set a negative rate, people would simply hold cash.

Third, deflation increases the real burden of debt. This becomes a particular danger when asset prices such as shares or houses are high. Consumers may then borrow against these assets. If the market for these assets then falls, consumers will feel the need to cut back on their debt levels by saving more. This may cause a fall in demand as we explained when considering the paradox of thrift.

Deflation, then, does not inevitably lead to problems for an economy. However, it is a source of concern when inflation rates get very low.

15.7 Conclusion

Inflation is a general rise in the weighted average price of goods and services. Even if the absolute price level does not rise, relative prices can do so. There are costs imposed on a society that suffers inflation. There is considerable debate as to the costs of government policy to control inflation. Keynesian economists believe the costs to be those associated with the increased unemployment, which they believe is the result of markets failing to clear. Some of the classical school of thought believe that the costs of inflation control are well worth paying in that they are of a short-term nature only. Other classical economists believe that there are not even short-term costs to pay in that markets can clear very fast. The severe, and sometimes lasting, nature of recessions makes this last view difficult to believe. As with other questions, your own view of this debate will be largely determined by the extent of your enthusiasm for the market mechanism and its ability to restore equilibrium speedily.

CHAPTER SUMMARY

1. **Inflation, a sustained rise in the price level, can be measured in various ways depending upon the categories of expenditure included.**
2. **UK inflation rates were once high compared with other European economies but have improved substantially in recent years.**
3. **The costs of inflation are small when the rate of inflation is anticipated, much larger if unanticipated.**
4. **Inflation can be analysed using aggregate demand and supply curves.**
5. **Keynesians believe that there is a trade-off between inflation and unemployment.**
6. **Classical economists believe that in the long run there is no such trade-off.**
7. **Classical economists believe that, whatever the inflation rate, unemployment will tend to adjust towards its 'natural rate'.**

Questions for discussion

Guidance to the answers for the ***asterisked*** *numbered questions is available to students on the website for the book at* **www.booksites.net/heather**.

1* If the market demand curve for some goods shifts to the right, equilibrium price rises. This is evidence of inflation in the economy. Do you agree with this statement? Why or why not?

2 An economy has only three goods in it. During one year good A rises in price by 10 per cent, good B by 20 per cent and the price of good C is unchanged. Consumers spend half their income on good A, 20 per cent of it on good B and the other 30 per cent on good C. Calculate the inflation rate for this economy during the year.

3* How significant will changes in cigarette prices be for the value of the price index over the next ten years?

4 How should an accurate consumer price index reflect a change in government taxation policy which switches from direct to indirect taxes?

5* Why might the way that the RPI is calculated overstate price inflation during a period of recession in the economy? (*Hint*: Compare the ONS selection of goods which form the price index and the selection of a typical shopper looking for the best value goods.)

see pp. 228–9

6 To what extent is the view of the labour market expressed in the Phillips curve relationship consistent with the explanations given in Chapter 11 for the decline in trade union membership?

7* What arguments would Keynesian economists give for rejecting the view that labour markets clear quickly? Are these arguments convincing?

8 We saw that Stephen Nickell expresses the natural rate of unemployment as one consistent with a zero change in inflation. Why does he also express it as one consistent with an international trade balance? (*Hint*: If demand increases does it necessarily lead just to increased prices at home?)

9* To what extent is a low inflation rate the sign of a healthy economy?

10 How convincing do you find the argument that beating inflation has no cost in terms of increased unemployment?

Websites

There are many websites containing data on the whole economy that have some data on inflation, including the OECD website at:

www.oecd.org/

For information on European inflation try Eurostat's website at:

www.europa.eu.int/comm/eurostat

Although only some information is provided free.

Notes

1 We have used the word 'classical' to describe economists whose views are that markets do clear reasonably quickly, and that government intervention to manipulate aggregate demand is therefore not necessary. The process by which markets clear, the speed at which it happens, and the extent to which governments should assist markets to work quickly is a matter of some debate among classical economists. Hence this term embraces a large group of economists who may differ over many things, but they do agree that markets will adjust with a reasonable speed and in this sense have a view quite distinct from Keynesian economists.

2 Phillips' original curve measured unemployment against the rate of change of money wages. Is this the same as measuring unemployment against inflation? The result is similar but not identical. If real output rises then money wages can rise by the same amount without creating inflation. Since output in the UK in real terms has risen on average by about 2.25 per cent per annum, the rate of change of money wages less 2.25 per cent gives a good proxy of inflation.

3 The use of the money supply data to predict inflation rates is dealt with in Chapter 18.

16 Supply side behaviour: taxation

Taxes and benefits: *a just and fair society?*

CHAPTER OVERVIEW

In the past twenty years taxes on high-income earners have been cut in most western economies, in some cases dramatically. Meanwhile, in some countries some at the bottom of the income scale are worse off. The justification for this policy change is to improve the incentive to work, thus raising output in order to improve living standards for all.

In this chapter we examine this argument, reviewing the following concepts:

- Indifference theory
- Supply curve of labour
- Aggregate supply and demand

We introduce the following:

- Income and substitution effects
- Average and marginal tax rates

16.1 Introduction

During the post-war years most western economies experienced a period of unparalleled prosperity. Sustained growth was accompanied by relatively full employment. This was widely attributed to Keynesian macroeconomic policies which emphasised government responsibility in controlling the volume of aggregate demand. Little attention was paid to aggregate supply: the aggregate supply curve was taken as given. A key element in the control of demand was taxation. When demand was thought to be too high, threatening inflation, taxation could be increased. Alternatively, taxation could be lowered if demand was thought to be too low and excessive unemployment was a danger.

During the 1970s such Keynesian policies were increasingly criticised. When the UK Conservative Party returned to power in 1979, it had rejected the Keynesian position. Aggregate demand could look after itself. Markets would see to it that the economy tended towards full employment. The key to successful macroeconomic policy was improving aggregate supply. In essence this meant that policy should be aimed at raising output from a given volume of resources. Ensuing measures included attempts to increase competition in markets where it was felt to be too limited. This covered, for example, pressures in the EU to liberalise air transport (see Chapter 8). Another policy measure was to transfer state industries to the private sector (see Chapter 17). Confidence in markets also resulted in the policy measure on which we now concentrate: reducing the burden of direct taxation in order to stimulate the supply side of the economy. It was believed that lower taxation would stimulate work effort; this would raise output and the economy would grow faster. At the beginning of a new century this view continues to dominate policy making in the UK. It is a view followed but to a lesser extent in a number of European countries.

see pp. 162–82
see pp. 383–409

The rationale for this view raises several important issues. How has the tax system altered as a result of this view? What is the macroeconomic model of the economy implicit in such policies? Is the view that it presents of the labour market correct? Does the evidence suggest that this policy has been successful?

16.2 The tax system in the UK

The nature of the tax system

Our first task is to see what is the burden of taxation that falls on UK citizens who work for their living and how this burden has changed in recent years. Only part of government revenue is from *direct* taxation paid directly to the government out of what is called our factor income. For most people that means tax on income from their labour, a direct tax on wages and salaries. If we own capital, we pay tax on dividends and interest. If we own land, there is a direct tax on the rent received. Similarly, firms pay direct taxes to the government out of the factor income, capital, in the form of a tax on profits.

However, some part of government revenue is received as an *indirect* tax. Indirect taxes do not come directly from our incomes to government. It is only when people spend their incomes that the tax is paid. Value added tax (VAT) is the major but not sole form of indirect tax. When we purchase many goods, a computer for example, 17½ per cent VAT is added to the price received by the supplier; the supplier later passes this extra sum to the government.

Direct tax can be seen from Table 16.1 to be the largest single source of government revenue. Of all direct taxes the two most important are those borne by suppliers of labour: income tax and National Insurance contributions (although a large part of the latter is paid by employers).

Since governments must raise taxes, what is the best way of their doing so? One consideration is the cost of administration. Income taxes are cheap to collect in administrative terms, whereas VAT is expensive. However, there are two other considerations that must weigh heavily when considering how to raise revenue. One is that the tax should be fair: there is an equity consideration. The other is that it should not be such as to discourage people from working, that is, there is an efficiency consideration. The difficulty is that if we believe that taxation

Table 16.1 Main sources of UK government revenue[1]

Source of revenue	*Percentage of total*
Income tax (net of income tax credits)[2]	26.1
National Insurance contributions	15.7
Capital taxes	2.6
Value added tax	15.4
Other indirect taxes	
Petrol duties	5.6
Tobacco duties	1.9
Alcohol duties	1.7
Corporation taxes	
Corporation tax	9.5
Petroleum revenue tax	0.4
National non-domestic rates	4.4
Oil royalties	0.2
Council tax	3.7
Other receipts	12.8
	100.0

[1] Based on 2001/2002 tax year
[2] Gross income tax minus income tax credits.
Source: adapted from HM Treasury data

policy has considerable efficiency effects, we may be faced with a trade-off between efficiency and equity.

Progressive and regressive taxes

Before we examine any possible trade-off between equity and efficiency we have to understand a distinction to be drawn between regressive, proportional and progressive tax systems. A *progressive* tax is one where, as income rises, the proportion of a person's income paid in taxation increases. So higher income earners pay a higher proportion of their income in tax. This is illustrated in Table 16.2, which shows the position of a single man with no dependents paying tax, ignoring National Insurance contributions, to the government in 1978/79. This was the last full year of a Labour government for a long time. Late 1979 brought a change to a Conservative government which was to go on to win a series of general elections in the 1980s and 1990s. The average earnings in 1978/79 were around £4,280 per annum. A man earning £1,040 – about one-quarter of the average wage – could earn £985 without paying income tax, but on each pound earned above that he paid 25 per cent. The proportion of his salary taken by the government in income tax was thus 1.3 per cent, but each additional pound earned would be taxed at 25 per cent. As his income rose, the proportion of it going in tax would also rise. The tax rate on the last pound earned is called the marginal rate. A man earning something near to average earnings, say £5,000 per annum, could have his first £985 free of tax, the next

Table 16.2 Income tax payable by a single person, 1978/79 tax year, UK

Income per annum £	*Average tax rate*[a] %	*Marginal tax rate* %
1,040	1.3	25
2,080	14.5	33
4,000	23.4	33
5,000	25.3	33
15,000	37.8	65
40,000	63.2	83
100,000	75.1	83

[a] Excluding National Insurance contributions

Source: adapted from Budget 'Red Book' data

£750 was taxed at a rate of 25 per cent and the rest at 33 per cent. Therefore, 25.3 per cent of his earnings were taxed away. The very high income earner on £40,000 per annum, that is nearly 10 times average earnings, found the marginal tax rate rising such that the last pounds earned were being taxed at 83 per cent. If he had 'unearned' income, that is income from interest, dividends from shares, or rents on property, the marginal rate was 98 per cent. The steeply rising average tax rate implies a strongly progressive tax, reflecting the view that the rich should bear the heaviest burden.

The incidence of the whole tax system was less progressive than implied in the rate, since part of government revenue is indirect tax. Indirect tax tends, by its very nature, to be less progressive. The rich spend a lower fraction of their income than the poor. A proportional tax is one where, as income rises, the amount of tax paid rises but the proportion of one's income paid in tax stays constant. A regressive system is regarded by most people as very inequitable. It means that as income rises the proportion of an individual's income taken in tax decreases. Notice that the actual amount paid in taxation may still increase in a regressive system.

Now let us examine the situation early in the new century and see how things have changed.

Partly as a result of increasing national prosperity and partly as a consequence of inflation, average money incomes are now much higher. Average earnings for the 1999/2000 tax year are over £20,000 per annum. Table 16.3 shows the income tax position for the tax year 2002/2003. It indicates that several significant changes have taken place since the end of the 1970s. Although the income tax system is still progressive, its degree of progressiveness is markedly more mild. Those on low incomes pay a slightly lower proportion of income in direct tax than in 1979, those on very high incomes pay a far lower proportion than 15 years previously. The highest marginal tax rate has been cut from 83 per cent to 40 per cent. Two other of the system's features are not obvious from the table. One is that the overall burden of direct tax has fallen less than would be indicated by the tables, since National Insurance contributions paid by employees

Table 16.3 Income tax payable by a single person, 2002/2003 tax year, UK

Income per annum £	*Average tax rate*[a] %	*Marginal tax rate*[a] %
4,000	0	0
6,000	2.3	10
10,000	9.6	22
15,000	13.7	22
20,000	15.8	22
30,000	17.9	22
50,000	25.3	40
150,000	35.1	40

[a] Excluding National Insurance contributions

Source: adapted from Budget 'Red Book' data

on average earnings have risen. The other is that government revenue relies somewhat less on direct tax than it used to do, and more on indirect tax. For example, in 1979 the standard rate of VAT was 8 per cent. It is now 17.5 per cent. Since indirect tax is less progressive than direct tax the overall incidence of the tax system is now even less progressive than in 1979. Direct tax cuts have been concentrated, then, on high income earners.

This significant switch is argued by the government to be necessary to preserve incentives to work. Although less equitable, output is stimulated, leading to a higher absolute living standard for all than would otherwise be possible. We shall examine this view in section 16.4. First we consider the assumptions of the underlying macroeconomic model on which these tax changes are based.

Income tax in Europe

Income tax rates tend to be higher in Europe at the top end. Table 16.4 shows the top marginal tax rate in a number of EU countries. The information needs to be treated with care, however. The level of income at which such rates 'cut in'

Table 16.4 Marginal tax rates in selected Western economies

Country	*Top marginal tax (%)*
Denmark	59
France	54
Germany	48.5
Sweden	59[1]
USA	39.6

[1] Swedish national rate is 25% + local taxes of upto 34%

Source: Various national websites

also varies between countries. As you can see, and as you might expect, top marginal tax rates in the USA are relatively low.

16.3 Tax and effects on output

Tax and aggregate demand

One major reason that 'supply-siders' reject the idea of Keynesian equilibrium that we saw in the previous chapter is their view of the labour market. In the Keynesian system the economy can be in equilibrium while significant unemployment of resources exists. One criticism of this view is that if unemployment exists, that must mean, by definition, an excess supply of that resource. If, though, there is an excess supply of, say, labour, the price of labour will fall in the long run to an equilibrium where there is no such excess. In other words, the economy will always adjust towards full employment output.

see pp. 330–40

Let us remind ourselves of the argument that we began to consider in Chapter 15. Figure 16.1(a) is a way of representing the simple Keynesian equilibrium which we saw in the previous chapter. If the economy is at AD_1, cuts in taxation will shift it to AD_2 and output will rise (but the cost is a higher price level) yet there is still some, though less, unemployment. Governments are therefore faced with a trade-off. Reduced unemployment is only possible with a higher price level.

Figure 16.1(b) reminds us of an alternative view. It is labelled in the diagram 'classical' because in essence it represents a market-orientated view of the economy. The classical model argues as follows. Left to themselves, all markets clear and an equilibrium is always found. This, as we saw above, includes labour markets. Thus all resources, including labour, will be productive, given time for the market to adjust. What of the present level of unemployment of labour?

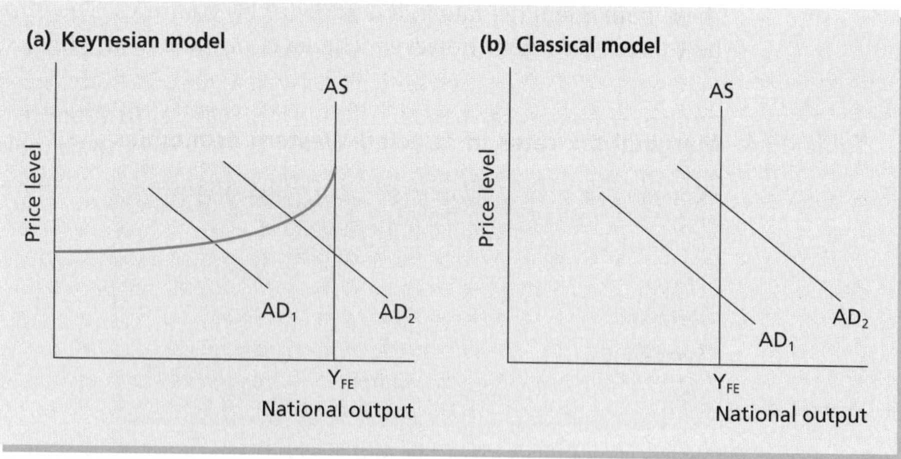

Figure 16.1 **Keynesian and classical equilibrium**

Some people simply choose not to work. For others who do wish to work the problem is only a short-term one. Wage rates are too high for equilibrium in some markets and, given time, the market will take care of the problem. Even then there will always be some friction in the system, which will mean that at any given moment some people are out of a job. This is the 'natural rate of unemployment' which we met in Chapter 15; in Figure 16.1 it is represented as Y_{FE}. In essence this means that there are always impediments to freely adjusting markets such as minimum wage legislation, trade union activity, and social security payments. In the classical view it is part of the government's task to reduce the effect of such impediments so that markets can reach equilibrium quickly and easily.

Markets, then, will tend to adjust to the full employment level of output whatever the price level. Stimulating the economy by lowering taxation must have only one long-run effect. It will raise the price level without changing real output. If the government stimulates aggregate demand as in Figure 16.1(b), money wages will rise. Some people who do not wish to work at the present wage level will think that *real* wages have risen. They will enter the labour market. In time they will discover that given the higher price level, real wages have not changed. They will leave the labour market, and so Y_{FE} is unchanged in the long run. 'Over-full employment' in the short term has been bought at the expense of higher prices. This is the view that we examined in the previous chapter. Here the important point to grasp is that, according to classical thinking, changes in taxation to stimulate aggregate demand cannot work to increase output and decrease unemployment. Stimulating demand will only serve to stir up inflationary pressure.

As we have already seen, equilibrium for an economy must be where planned injections into the circular flow of income, government expenditure (G), investment expenditure (I), and export expenditure (X) are equal to planned withdrawals from the circular flow represented by savings (S), taxes (T) and imports (M). We saw in Chapter 13 how injections are brought to equal withdrawals, in the Keynesian view, by changes in national output. This leads Keynesians to say that equilibrium output is not necessarily full employment output.

We saw in Chapter 14 that classical economists reject this argument because they believe that injections and withdrawals are not brought into equilibrium by changes in output at all. Savings and investment are brought into equilibrium in a market for loanable funds via changes in interest rates. Export and import values tend to equalise through various ways to be looked at in Chapter 20, but often through foreign exchange markets via changes in the value of foreign currency.

Tax and aggregate supply

All this leads to some important conclusions. If markets ensure that S = I and that X = M, it is the government's responsibility to ensure that government expenditure, G, equals government income, T. If the government fails to do this and allows G to be greater than T, aggregate demand will rise. Since the aggregate supply curve is vertical, the effect will not be to raise the equilibrium level of output, but to cause inflation. The government, then, must balance the budget.

However, this simply argues that the government's account should not be in deficit. It does not by itself tell us how any deficit should be corrected: should taxes (T) be increased or spending (G) reduced? In classical thinking, cuts in government expenditure are very much to be preferred to increases in taxation as a way of reducing any public sector borrowing requirement (PSBR).

Why is this? Keynesian thinking is that taxation can be used for manipulating aggregate demand. However, at least in older Keynesian models, the aggregate supply curve is unaffected by tax changes. The classical view is that, by reducing taxes, people will be willing to work harder since they have more incentive if they can keep more of their earnings. This raises potential output in the economy. In other words, income tax cuts will cause the aggregate supply curve to shift to the right. This means that there is value in improving the supply side of the economy rather than simply taking it as given. Therefore, starting from a position of deficit in the PSBR, the preferred classical remedy is to cut G at least until the budget is balanced. Better still would be larger cuts in G. Taxes could then be lowered without creating a deficit in the public finances. Lower income taxes are not the only means of improving the supply side but they are an important means, so a policy of steadily reducing the tax burden over time has become a cherished aim of UK government policy.

If T is to fall over a long period to stimulate aggregate supply, and the budget has to be balanced, G must fall too, either in absolute terms or at least as a proportion of gross domestic product (GDP). This will probably mean, among other things, that in the short term we shall have poorer school buildings, reduced funding for hospitals and unrepaired roads, although to some extent one can compensate for less direct tax by increases in indirect tax and more private expenditure on these things. The cuts in G may not have to be as severe as one might at first think. If a cut in T raises national output, tax revenue will rise also.

see pp. 81–3

Such a policy will also mean making the distribution of income more uneven. We saw in Chapter 4 how that income is now less evenly distributed than it was 10–15 years ago. The motivation behind this policy change should now be clear: it is all part of the supply side revolution.

Supply side tax reforms in other countries

The evidence suggests that the policy of reducing direct taxes, especially on higher income groups, is not a peculiarly British phenomenon. The great majority of western governments have top rates of tax significantly lower than in the mid 1980s. However, as Table 16.5 indicates the overall burden of taxes on labour are not just taxes paid by employees. There are significant burdens on employers. These include national insurance contributions, sickness insurance and pension contributions. Such contributions as a proportion of pay vary significantly. In some countries where income tax is high, taxes on employers are relatively low.

We want to be sure that reducing the tax burden does produce incentives to increase output so that the aggregate supply curve really does shift. Then out of

Table 16.5 **Costs of employing the average worker, 2002**

Country	*Pay (euros)*	*Additional costs[1] (%)*
Denmark	36,300	7
France	33,100	46
Germany	31,500	27
Netherlands	30,300	20
UK	31,300	14

[1] Percentage of pay representing additional costs of employing labour

Source: adapted from Mercer Human Resource Consulting

that increased national income, hospitals, schools, roads and so on can be improved. Whether tax cuts are likely to achieve this is something we now examine.

16.4 The supply of labour: willingness to work

see pp. 75–9

We use indifference curve analysis (see Chapter 4) to build up a picture of how people behave with respect to their willingness to work. Work will result in income being earned, albeit at an opportunity cost, that is leisure must be forgone. You once watched *EastEnders* in the happy thought that it was virtually costless to you. Now as an economist, you have come to realise that although no money changes hands, it can be expensive to watch television. It may be that you could have worked and earned an income during that time.

How much does an hour's leisure cost? Clearly it depends upon the rate per hour that could be earned. All options open to a supplier of labour are described in Figure 16.2 by the budget line. Assuming a wage rate of £5 per hour, the possibilities open to him are 24 hours per day leisure and no income, £120 per day (24 × £5) and no leisure, or some combination of leisure and income described

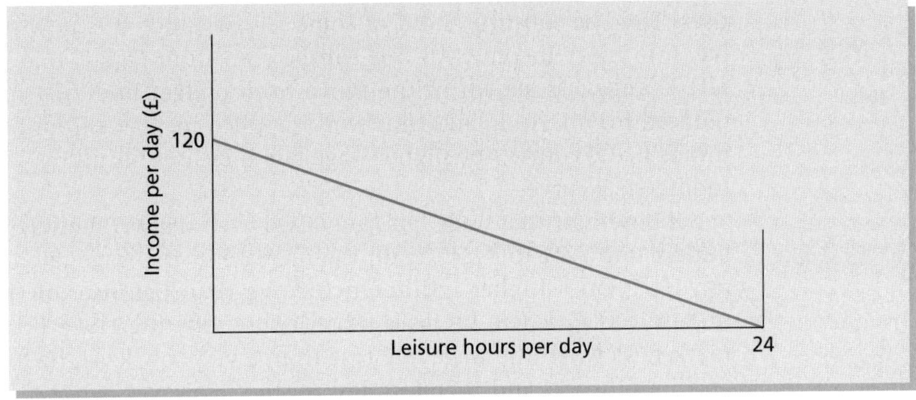

Figure 16.2 **Relative price of leisure and income**

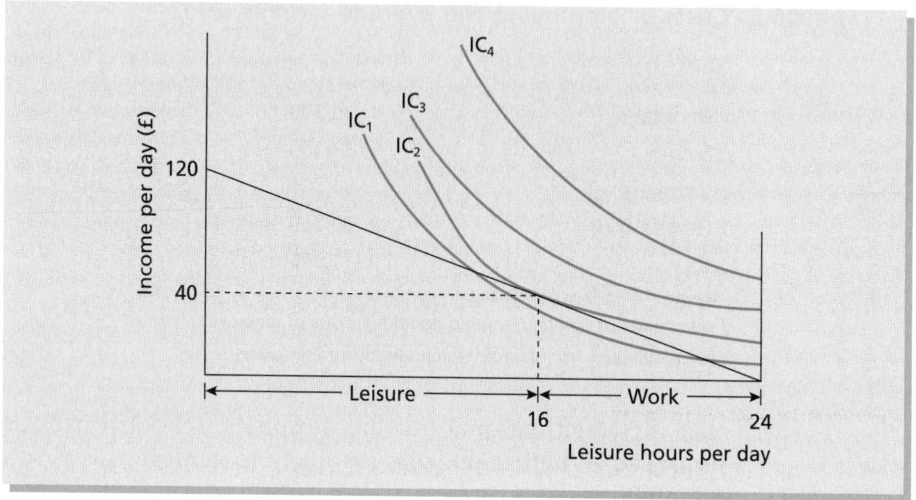

Figure 16.3 Optimising leisure and income

by the budget line. A higher wage rate would imply a steeper budget line with its horizontal intercept still at 24 hours. The combination chosen will depend upon the budget line and personal preferences.

Different people will have different preferences, but it seems reasonable to suggest that for the vast majority there is a diminishing marginal rate of substitution of leisure for income as there is between goods. Therefore we have the familiar shape of the indifference curves in Figure 16.3. This figure also shows the budget line from Figure 16.2 and a labour supplier's preferred combination of income and leisure. He can just reach IC_2 by choosing 16 hours leisure per day and thus 8 hours work per day. This gives him £40 per day income.

If the wage rate is £5 per hour, he supplies 8 hours of labour per day to the market. How much would he supply at other wage rates? We can see this quite easily by changing the budget line from $Y_1$24 to $Y_2$24. Obviously, a steeper budget line implies a higher wage rate. Given the nature of his preferences, something interesting happens. If wage rates are raised from a low level, leisure becomes relatively more expensive. The opportunity cost of watching television rises. Thus he substitutes out of some leisure, since it is now relatively expensive, into more income. All this can be seen from Figure 16.4. When the wage rate changes, as shown in the move from budget line $Y_1$24 to $Y_2$24, leisure is reduced from L_1 to L_2 and thus work supplied increases from 24 minus L_1 to 24 minus L_2. Of course, the higher wage rate increases his utility – he is on a higher indifference curve.

Suppose now that wage rates are raised even higher, shown by the move from budget line $Y_2$24 to $Y_3$24. Again the increase in the wage rate increases his utility. He is on a higher indifference curve than before. Now his best amount of leisure is L_3 where he takes more leisure, offering fewer hours to the labour market. So when the wage rate rose from a very low level, he took more income and more work, and therefore less leisure. However, when the wage rate rose from a higher level to an even higher one, he took more income but less work

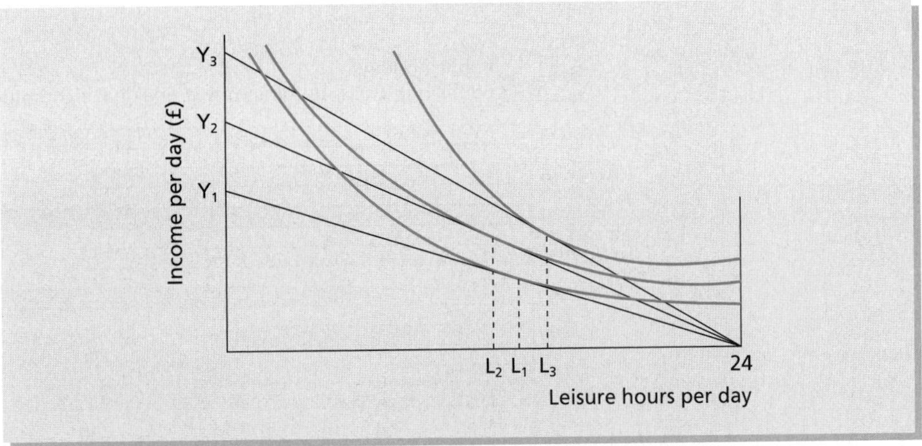

Figure 16.4 Effects of increased wage rates on willingness to work

and more leisure. These effects are shown in Figure 16.5 where we represent his supply curve for labour.

Why does he behave in this way? The answer is that when the wage rate rises there are two effects on his behaviour. The first effect is a 'substitution effect'. Consumers will always substitute out of relatively dear goods into relatively cheap ones when relative prices alter. In this case, leisure has become relatively expensive because of the increase in the wage rate. He will thus tend to reduce his leisure consumption and shift into income as the wage rate increases.

There is also an income effect. The rise in the wage rate makes him better off. It causes his real income to rise. When his income is rising he can buy more other goods and take more leisure also. So these two effects work in opposite directions. When wage rates rise, the substitution effect is encouraging him to work more, but the income effect causes him to work less. These two effects are

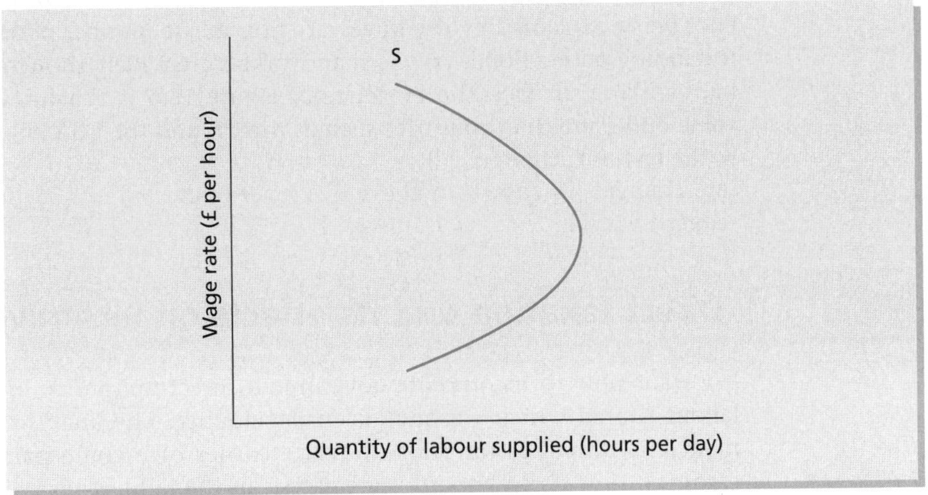

Figure 16.5 A backward-bending supply curve for labour

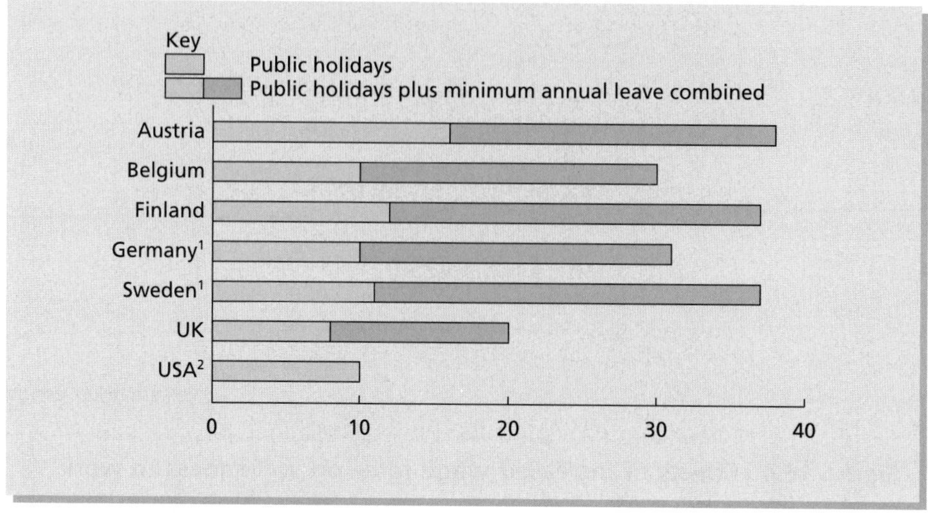

Figure 16.6 Holidays in selected countries

[1] Approximate, as some bank holidays occur less than once per year
[2] No legal minimum annual leave

always present when wage rates rise, but the nature of the diminishing marginal rate of substitution of leisure for income suggests that at lower wage rates the substitution effect will outweigh the income effect. At higher wage rates, however, the income effect will be increasingly likely to be stronger than the substitution effect. This gives us the backwards sloping nature of the supply curve. This theory of labour supply has important implications for policy on direct taxation.

Even if we assume that the vast majority of people have a diminishing marginal rate of substitution of income for leisure, the amount of labour services offered would vary between individuals. Does it vary between countries? The evidence suggests that it does. The average American worker works over 14 per cent more hours during the year than a German worker, much of the difference being explained by the huge variation in the number of days' paid holiday (excluding public holidays). German workers are widely thought to be the most hardworking. In fact, the evidence of Figure 16.6 is that they place a higher value on leisure than countries such as the UK and the USA but are fairly typical of the rest of Europe.

16.5 Direct taxation and its effects on incentives

We want now to incorporate government direct tax policy into the model of labour supply which we have been developing. The analysis of section 16.4 made the unreal assumption that the earner of income paid no tax on his earnings. How do we modify the analysis in the light of taxation policy? Direct taxation will have no effect on the indifference curves – they simply represent

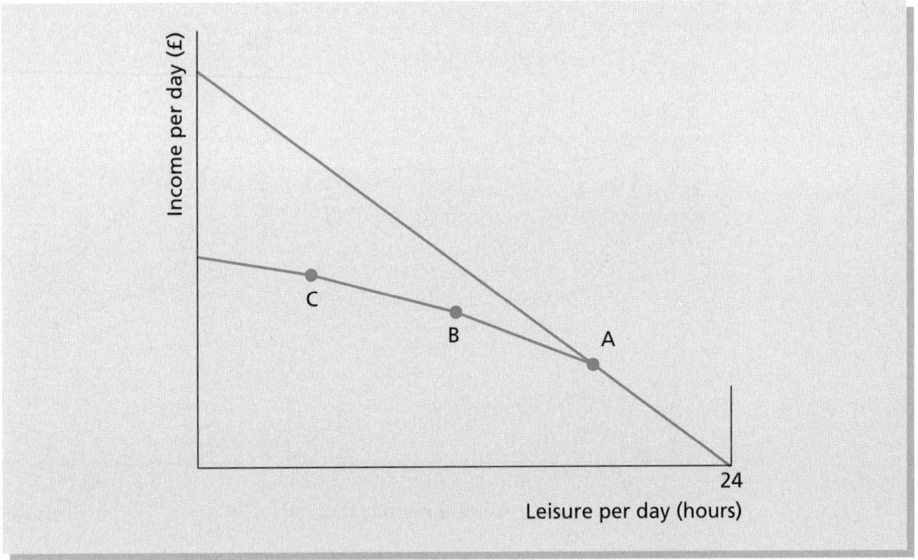

Figure 16.7 Income tax and the relative price of leisure and income

preferences as between income and leisure. It does affect the budget line by altering what is possible. The present tax system in Britain moves the budget line for a supplier of labour as shown in Figure 16.7. For simplicity we ignore National Insurance contributions.

We begin with the familiar straight budget line that assumes no direct tax. How will the introduction of income tax change it? All labour suppliers can earn several thousand pounds per year and pay no tax, so the lowest part of the line remains the same. As income rises above that level, 20 pence in the pound is payable in tax, so possible income is less than it would have been from point A.

The higher the income, the bigger the gap between what one can earn and what one *could have* earned, since tax is paid on every marginal pound earned. The marginal tax rate is higher at some level of income. At point B the slope of the post-tax budget line changes since marginal tax rates are increased to 24 pence in the pound. Finally, at well above average incomes, point C in Figure 16.7, the top rate of tax (40 pence in the pound) applies and the actual budget line becomes still flatter. Government policy has been aimed at pushing the lower budget line up towards the higher one, especially closing the gap at the left-hand end. Remember, the marginal tax rate in 1979 was 83 pence in the pound on earned income. Will the policy increase the supply of labour and thus increase national output and income?

Two things may be said by way of answer. The first, as shown in Figures 16.8(a) and (b), is that it may or may not, depending upon the nature of the labour supplier's leisure preferences. In each of the two diagrams in Figure 16.8 a cut in marginal income tax rates is shown moving the budget line upwards. We choose an extreme example – direct tax is abolished altogether. In each case the cut in tax enables the supplier of labour to reach a higher indifference curve. In each case he has a higher level of income.

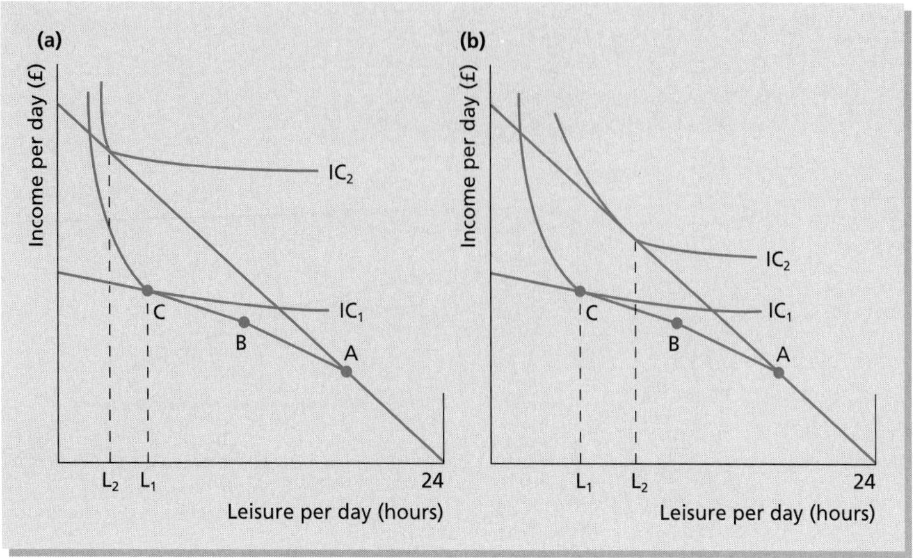

Figure 16.8 Possible effects of income tax on attitude to work

However, note that in case (a) the effect is to cause him to take less leisure, L_1 shifting left to L_2, and therefore to work harder, just as government policy intended that he should. On the other hand, in (b) his response is to take more leisure, moving from L_1 to L_2. The difference in reaction is caused simply by the fact that the income effect for labour supplier (b) is greater than his substitution effect, whereas for labour supplier (a) it is smaller.

We are therefore driven to the conclusion that government policy towards reducing direct taxation is far from certain to succeed. However, there is a second thing that we can say. While cuts in direct tax are not certain to increase output, *the higher the income level the less likely it is to succeed.* We have already shown how indifference analysis has led us to the backwards sloping supply curve for labour, redrawn in Figure 16.9. Cuts in tax rates are in effect increasing the wage rate of the labour supplier. If the wage rate is increased by a tax cut from W_1 to W_2 then more labour is supplied. The increase is from Q_1 to Q_2. If the tax cut applies at higher wage rates, a backwards-bending supply curve is more likely. A rise from W_2 to W_3 decreases labour supply from Q_2 to Q_3.

The conclusion is that concentrating tax cuts at the top end of the income scale may succeed in increasing the labour supply of high earners – but success is less likely than if cuts were made at the other end of the scale. We cannot say, simply from drawing diagrams, at what point the supply curve will bend backwards: that is an empirical matter, and very hard to test. So while theory can tell us that eventually the income effect will outweigh the substitution effect as wage rates rise, it cannot tell us at what wage rate that will occur for most people. Nevertheless, we can say that the higher the income group whose marginal tax rate is being cut, the less likely is the policy to succeed in increasing hours worked.

This argument assumes that, meanwhile, other things remain equal. They may not do so. The Conservative government of the 1980s and 1990s felt that

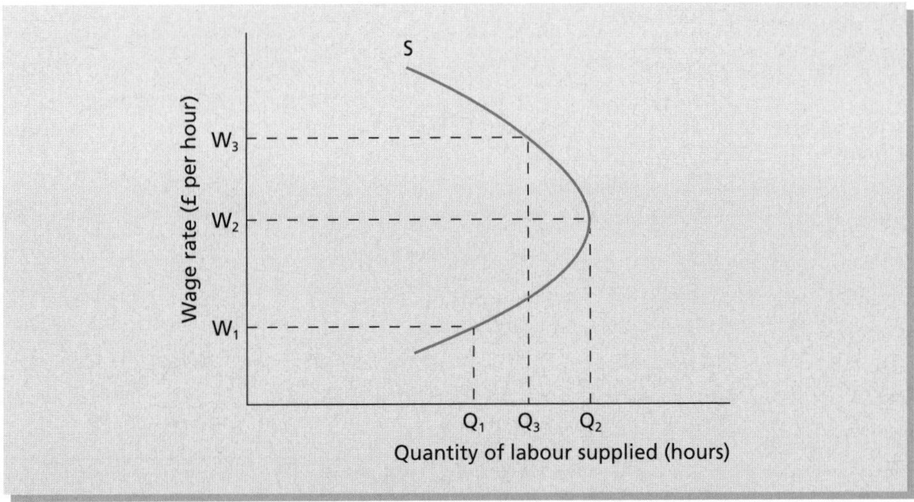

Figure 16.9 **Tax rate changes and willingness to work**

there were other reasons for thinking that cuts in top marginal tax rates might increase labour supply. One consideration is that labour can migrate. High marginal tax rates may encourage high income earners to leave the country and seek employment abroad. Another possibility is that capital might migrate. High marginal tax rates encourage wealth owners to seek offshore tax havens where tax is not payable to the British government. Lower marginal rates of tax may increase government revenue by dissuading people to seek these tax havens.

Those who believe that cuts in marginal tax rates for high income earners *do* encourage people to work harder may take some comfort from Figure 16.7. The country where hours worked is highest is the United States. This is also the country with the highest real wage rates. One cannot make too much of the argument, however: the UK has lower wage rates than Germany but its workers put in longer hours.

16.6 Income support and its effects on incentives

We have so far concentrated on efforts to increase labour supply by changes to taxation policy. We now turn to attempts to increase the supply of labour through changes in income support. Implicit in government policy is the view that some people choose not to work because they would rather be idle and live on state handouts. Of all government expenditure, around one-third goes on social security. These include state pensions, income support, disability benefits and housing benefits. Much of it is 'means tested' so that a decision to work will reduce the amount of benefit received. As Figure 16.10 indicates total spending on social security provision has varied as a proportion of GDP in the UK over recent years but the trend is upwards.

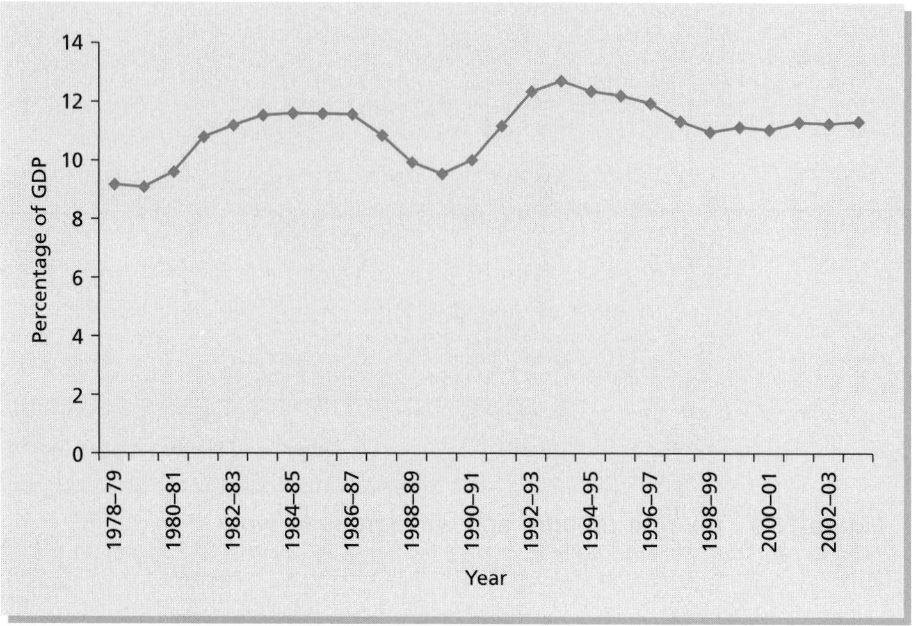

Figure 16.10 **UK social security expenditure, 1979–2004**

Source: adapted from HM Treasury, various years

The argument can easily be seen from Figure 16.11. Given that it is possible to get unemployment-related benefits, the original budget line does not represent the choice of a labour supplier: the bottom part is done away with. However little he chooses to work he can get something from the state, shown as Y_0 in Figure 16.11.

Given his preferences between income and leisure, this man's reaction to income support is to choose 24 hours per day leisure and Y_0 income from the state. Had this not been available he would have chosen Y_1 income and $24 - L_1$

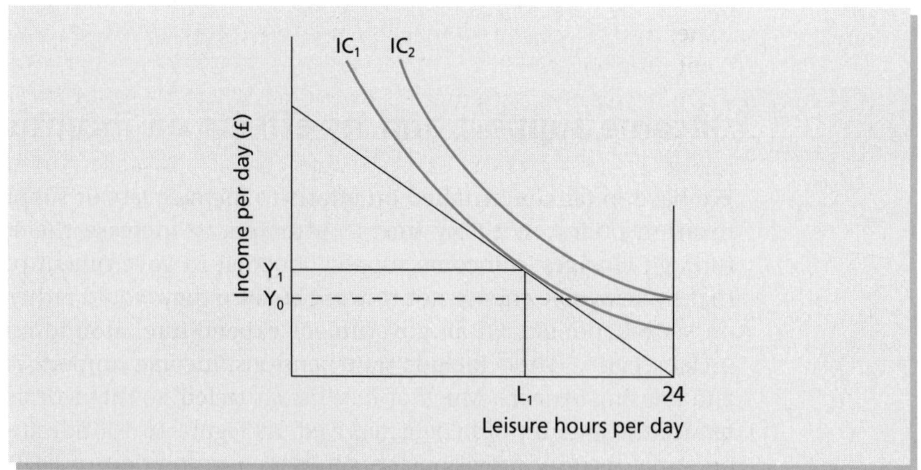

Figure 16.11 **Income support and willingness to work**

labour. The conclusion is that one can reduce the volume of unemployment by getting the idle poor to work. It simply requires a reduction in income support. Politically, the government has not found it easy to reduce many forms of support in money terms. However, the same thing can be achieved in other ways, for example by raising benefits annually by less than the rate of inflation. One significant recent change is that unemployment benefit is being replaced by a jobseeker's allowance, qualification for which is significantly more difficult.

One other thing may create severe disincentive effects. It is the poverty trap. This occurs when an increase in earned income reduces, or produces only a very small increase in, actual income. The person is trapped in poverty. Suppose a previously unemployed person takes a job and earns some income. He may find that he has lost entitlement to family benefits, housing benefit and other state handouts only available to very low income groups. He may then find that his actual income is lower or barely higher for having taken the job. In extreme cases the poverty trap means that it is not simply a question of the additional income from a job not being worth the loss of leisure time: work actually reduces his income. Changes in the operation of the social security system in recent years have reduced this problem, but many disincentives to work remain for the lower income groups. For some low income groups in the UK the effective marginal tax rate can be 97 per cent. Yet for a high income earner it is 40 per cent.

Can it be justified to reduce benefits to such lower income groups to stimulate willingness to work? As so often, an important part of the answer is that much depends upon one's macroeconomic view of the economy. Remember that, from a classical perspective, any unemployment is voluntary since markets, including labour markets, always clear quite quickly. A Keynesian perspective gives a different answer. First, it is possible to be unemployed because there is no job available. There is unemployment equilibrium. Second, cuts in income support will *reduce aggregate demand*. Low income groups spend nearly all their additional income, i.e. they have a marginal propensity to consume of almost one. If the government revenue saved is then given in tax cuts, the recipients of that income will save part of it: they have a lower marginal propensity to consume. Thus aggregate demand will fall, which may exacerbate the unemployment problem.

One interesting attempt to overcome the problem of the poverty trap for many UK families is the Working Families Tax Credit (WFTC). It was introduced in the autumn of 1999 as part of an attempt to make it more profitable for people with families and low incomes to work rather than live on social security payments. The cost of the scheme to the Treasury is about £5bn annually. One element of the credit is the provision of a substantial portion of the cost of childcare. As income rises the size of benefit is reduced.

The WTFC is not without its problems. For some families an increase in gross income of £1,000 per annum means a net gain of around £300 per annum after allowing for income tax, national insurance and the tapered withdrawal of WFTC. This means an effective marginal tax rate of about 70 per cent. In other words a substantial marginal disincentive to work still remains for many households.

16.7 Strands of evidence

Tax rates and the PSBR

Is there any evidence that reductions in the marginal rate of tax on higher income groups have produced improvements in economic welfare? As in so many areas, a difficulty arises in isolating the effect of a particular policy change from all other factors that have an influence. Bearing this in mind one can proceed cautiously in saying that the effects on the PSBR of such reductions are not encouraging. A commonly expressed opinion of supply-siders is the view that income tax cuts have such an effect on incentives that output rises significantly. If output, and therefore incomes, rise significantly, government may increase its income. This is because although it takes a smaller slice of national income, it is a smaller slice of a larger pie.

This can be expressed more formally in terms of what is known as the Laffer curve (Figure 16.12). This shows the claimed effect of government revenue changes in income tax. If income tax rates rise from low levels, 'tax take' increases. However, it rises more slowly as the disincentive of taxation begins to take effect. The disincentive effect is so high at very high marginal rates of tax that government revenue declines. At a 100 per cent income tax rate no one would do anything and government tax revenue would thus be zero. So in principle tax cuts can increase revenue. All other things being equal, this will reduce the PSBR. This assumes that the present tax rate is higher than x in Figure 16.12, x being the optimal tax rate for the purpose of raising revenue.

If the curve accurately reflects reality, it will still not follow that the curve is symmetrical. One of several possible reasons for asymmetry is the Gutmann effect (Figure 16.13). As marginal tax rates are lowered there is another group from whom income tax revenues will be received. These are the people who have been working in the 'black economy'. The black economy refers to those activities earning income which are not declared for income tax purposes. Failure to declare such income is illegal. Those caught risk jail sentences. Many take the risk when the amount they must pay in taxes is high. If marginal tax

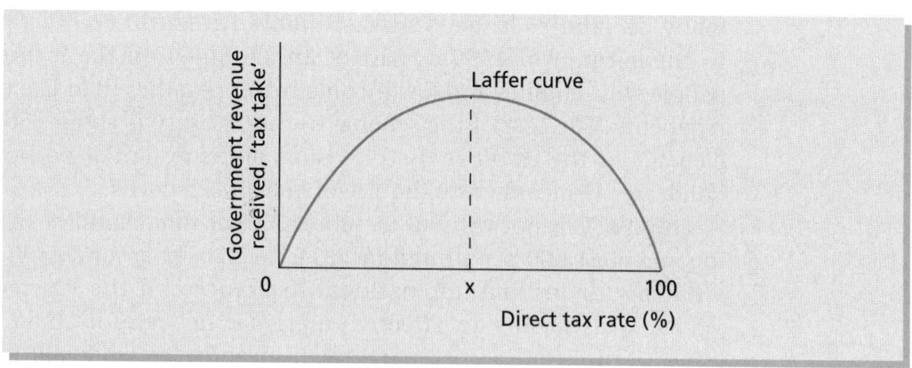

Figure 16.12 **The Laffer curve**

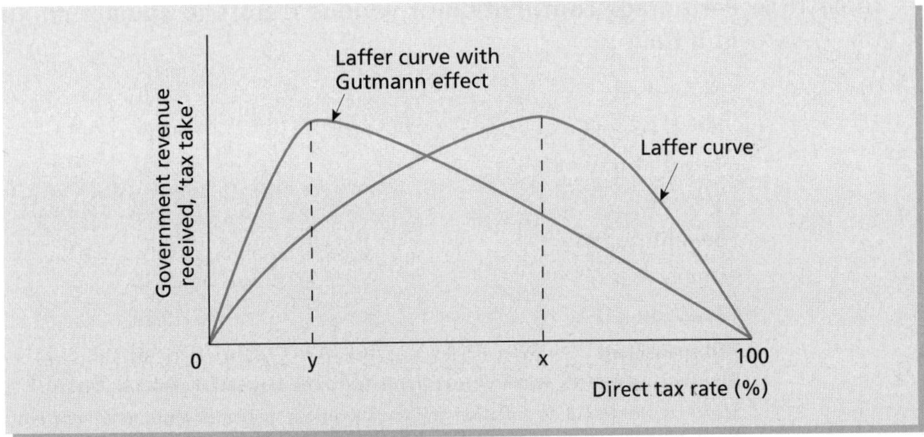

Figure 16.13 The Laffer curve and the Gutmann effect

rates are lowered, some will feel the risk to be no longer worth taking, will declare their income and pay the tax. Thus, as the Laffer curve of Figure 16.13 shows, governments may be able to cut marginal taxes to quite low levels and still increase their tax take as more people are drawn into paying income tax. The optimal tax rate for raising revenue is thus y, where y is significantly lower than x.

Both the British and American governments have begun to be sceptical about the Laffer curve argument. Marginal tax rates have been substantially reduced, but the PSBR is enormous in each country. The American president and the British chancellor have both used tax increases as well as cuts in government expenditure as part of a strategy to hold down the PSBR.

Tax, benefits and the 'natural rate'

see pp. 334–8

A second strand of evidence comes from Stephen Nickell's views on the natural rate of unemployment, which we first considered in Chapter 15. We now look a little more closely at his evidence. He produced some estimates of the contribution of different factors to this unemployment rate. If we focus on the period 1980–87 we can see in Table 16.6 what his estimates were. Since these are difficult to determine, they are estimates that he regarded as 'very rough and ready'.

see pp. 413–33

see p. 274

North Sea oil and terms of trade effects are considered in Chapter 19, but the other four measured factors referred to in the table are of interest now. Mismatch refers essentially to frictional employment referred to in Chapter 13. In particular, it suggests that it is skilled labour that is scarce relative to unskilled labour. 'Unions' refers to the effects of unions in trying to raise wage rates above market wage rates.

Notice in particular the other two factors. The fall in direct tax rates during the 1980s improved the labour market and reduced the natural rate. The sign is negative, but it is a very small number. If these 'rough and ready' estimates are somewhere near correct, the benefit to the economy of cuts in direct taxes was nowhere near as large as the cost of the benefit system in discouraging work

Table 16.6 Percentage contribution of various factors to equilibrium unemployment in Britain

Natural rate	8.70
North Sea oil	−2.86
Terms of trade effects	2.26
Mismatch	2.53
Benefit system	1.12
Unions	1.50
Taxation	−0.20
Unmeasured	1.95

Source: S. Nickell (1990) 'Inflation and the UK labour market', *Oxford Review of Economic Policy*, Vol. 6, No. 4. Reproduced by permission of Oxford University Press

effort. Again, though, it has to be stressed that even if reducing benefits were to improve the working of the labour market, the government might still legitimately choose not to act in this area. It could take the view that the effect on low income groups would be too serious to justify the cuts in benefits.

The pervasiveness of poverty

Critics of UK government social security policy point to studies which show that the poorest members of the community have not shared in increased national income over the past 15–20 years. For example, the Rowntree Report on income and wealth published in 1995 said that the poorest 10 per cent of the population were absolutely poorer in 1991/92 than they were in 1979. Unfortunately, this gives a misleading impression. Whilst some are undoubtedly in that position, many of them are not the same people in 1979 as in 1992. Some of those who were poor in 1979 have got jobs and become much better off. Indeed, this is exactly what government policy is designed to achieve.

One study of the American economy has actually tried to measure this movement out of poverty. The data are for the period 1975–91. During this period the top 20 per cent of families moved from having about seven times that of the bottom 20 per cent to having around eleven times as much. But are we looking at the same people in each case?

Look at Table 16.7. It shows the extent to which people remained in a given quintile of income distribution over that period. Of the poorest 20 per cent of people in 1975 (first quintile), only 5.1 per cent of them were still in that group by 1991. No less than 80.3 per cent had risen to the middle quintile or above. Now consider Table 16.8. The first (lowest) quintile had an average annual income in 1975 of $1,153 at 1993 prices. By 1991 the people who were in that quintile in 1975 had an average income of $26,475 per year at 1993 prices.

Similar studies are now being carried out for the British economy. Between 1991 and 1996 only 58 per cent of adults stayed in a given income quintile. Twenty-one per cent moved down at least one quintile and 22 per cent moved up at least one quintile.

Table 16.7 **Mobility of people between income quintile, USA 1975–91**

Income quintile 1975	*Percentage in each quintile 1991*				
	1st	*2nd*	*3rd*	*4th*	*5th*
5th	0.9	2.8	10.2	23.6	62.5
4th	1.9	9.3	18.8	32.6	37.4
3rd	3.3	19.3	28.3	30.1	19.0
2nd	4.2	23.5	20.3	25.2	26.8
1st	5.1	14.6	21.0	30.3	29.0

Source: Federal Reserve Bank of Dallas, *By Our Own Bootstraps*

Table 16.8 **Increases in incomes by quintiles, USA 1975–91**[a]

Income quintile 1975	*Average income 1975*	*Average income 1991*	*Absolute gain*
5th	45,704	49,678	3,974
4th	22,423	31,292	8,869
3rd	13,030	22,304	9,274
2nd	6,291	28,373	22,082
1st	1,153	26,475	25,322

[a] All figures in US dollars at constant (1993) prices

Source: Federal Reserve Bank of Dallas, *By Our Own Bootstraps*

This is not an argument for saying that nothing should be done to help the poor. It does argue powerfully for a system which enables those on low incomes to increase their income by their own efforts.

16.8 Conclusion

It is never easy for governments to cut taxes. There are always enormous demands made upon the Treasury for state spending. The Conservative administration after 1979 managed some cuts in income tax to encourage the growth of output. The most dramatic cuts in marginal tax rates were at the top end of the income scale, making the distribution of income more uneven. Microeconomic theory does not give great support to this view, suggesting that cuts in tax rates further down the scale are more likely to succeed in encouraging increased output.

Certainly there is no evidence yet that, in the end, lower income groups also benefit from these cuts through increased national output. Some of those on lower incomes are relatively *and* absolutely worse off than they were twenty years ago, although these are probably fairly small in number, if the UK is similar to the United States. There is some evidence that the Conservative government in the 1990s began to accept this. In recent years there have been no further cuts in top rates of tax, and most tax cuts have been concentrated at the lower end of the income scale.

The progressiveness of taxation is an issue that any government has to face. A strongly progressive tax system will tend to give relatively lower average income tax rates but relatively higher marginal ones. This may create disincentives to work but produce a more even distribution of income. On the other hand, a less progressive tax system will give higher average tax rates but lower marginal ones. This may have good incentive effects and therefore helps to raise national output. It does mean, though, that we shall have a more uneven distribution of income, which, depending upon one's perspective, might be regarded as less just.

As far as income support rates are concerned, economic theory would suggest that a cost of establishing an income support scheme is that some will choose to be idle. How serious this problem is cannot be easily ascertained. It is this absence of clear and unambiguous evidence which allows politicians the luxury of not changing their minds.

CHAPTER SUMMARY

1 A tax system can be progressive or regressive depending on whether higher income groups pay a higher or lower proportion of their income in tax.

2 Classical 'supply side' economists believe that governments must balance the budget.

3 Supply side economists also believe that low taxation is essential to give incentives to produce output.

4 Indifference analysis suggests that this is less likely to be true for high income groups where the income effect may outweigh the substitution effect.

5 Indifference analysis suggests that high social security benefits may have disincentive effects on labour suppliers.

6 Economists cannot agree whether a tax and benefit system should concentrate on minimising disincentives or on protecting low income groups.

Questions for discussion

Guidance to the answers for the ***asterisked*** *numbered questions is available to students on the website for the book at* **www.booksites.net/heather**.

1* Consider Table 16.9. It represents two societies with the same average income but with different distributions. Which one is the fairer society?

2 Suppose you were offered an increase in your grant of 10 per cent and all other students on the course also received 10 per cent. As an alternative you were offered a 15 per cent increase but all your colleagues received a 100 per cent increase. Which of these options would you prefer? Why? What does this have to do with the issues discussed in the chapter? (*Hint*: Look at the definition of

Table 16.9 **Hypothetical income distributions (euros)**

	Distribution 1	*Distribution 2*
Barry	60	42
Brenda	20	42
Bill	20	16

Table 16.10 **Hypothetical income taxes and varying annual incomes (euros)**

Income	*Tax paid*
10,000	1,000
20,000	1,500
30,000	3,000
40,000	5,000

Pareto optimality given in Chapter 5, and the distribution of income implicit in direct taxation policy as shown in this chapter.)

3* The UK Conservative administration of the 1980s believed that governments should in all circumstances balance the budget. So in the early 1980s with high unemployment the government chose not to stimulate aggregate demand by tax cuts, but to reduce its deficit by raising taxes. The British Governments of the last twenty years said they believed in a balanced budget in the medium term. What changes in policy does this imply? What do you think might have altered their position from previous administrations?

4 Consider Table 16.10. Is the tax system progressive, regressive or proportional? Check that it is the same throughout the given income range.

5* Suppose you were a poor student buying £30 worth of petrol for your old car. The person at the other pump is a wealthy man putting £30 worth of petrol into his Porsche. The petrol tax must be proportional because you are both paying the same tax. Do you agree?

6 Refer back to Table 16.5. Stephen Nickell sees frictional unemployment as a significant difficulty. Would further reductions in marginal t rates help? Remember that the main mismatch problem is skilled labour shortages. What other policies would help to deal with the problem?

7* What is the best way of determining whether a citizen of the EU is poor?

8 In Chapter 1, we saw that there was no close correlation between the volume of taxation received by a government and growth of GDP. In the light of what you have read in this chapter, do you find this surprising?

9* 'An uneven distribution of income is the sign of a healthy economy.' What do you think the author of this statement means?

10 'It is a curious policy which encourages the rich to work harder by giving them more – and the poor to work harder by giving them less.' How fair is this as an assessment of government taxation policy?

Websites

Up-to-date UK tax data can be found in budget reports that can be accessed at:

www.hm-treasury.gov.uk

Inland revenue statistics can be found at:

www.inlandrevenue.gov.uk/menus/stats.htm

Finally, that well respected body, the Institute of Fiscal Studies has a website with useful analysis of fiscal issues at:

www.ifs.org.uk/

17 Supply side behaviour: privatisation

Privatisation: *a supply side improvement?*

CHAPTER OVERVIEW

Thirty years ago many of the basic goods and services in the UK were provided by the state, including gas, electricity, water and telephone services. The assets which produce this output are now in the private sector where they are being used for private profit. Many other countries are now following this procedure.

Does the public gain or lose from these changes?

In this chapter we review:

- Efficiency
- The public sector borrowing requirement (PSBR)

We introduce

- Efficiency with declining long-run average cost (LRAC)
- Privatisation policy

17.1 Introduction

For over thirty years after the Second World War British economic policy concentrated primarily upon controlling the overall level of economic activity by attempts to manipulate the volume of aggregate demand. This involved increasing government spending and cutting taxes during a downturn in the trade cycle and reversing the policy in the upturn. The supply side was to some extent left to look after itself. In other words, macroeconomic policy was essentially Keynesian in orientation.

The Conservative government from 1979 onwards shifted its emphasis away from the management of aggregate demand towards improving the supply side of the economy. One aspect of this policy we considered in Chapter 16; another that we consider now is the programme of privatisation. It was believed that assets in private hands would in some sense be more productive than in state hands. More output would come from a given volume of resources. Furthermore, areas of economic activity would be opened to market forces.

see pp. 341–64

Table 17.1 Major privatisations since 1979

Year	*Company*	*Revenue (£m)*
1979	BP (part)	276
1981	BP (part)	200
1981	Cable and Wireless (part)	182
1982	Britoil (part)	627
1983	BP (part)	543
1983	Cable and Wireless (part)	263
1984	BT (part)	3,916
1984	Jaguar	297
1985	Britoil (part)	449
1985	Cable and Wireless (part)	900
1986	British Gas	5,600
1987	British Airways	900
1987	Rolls-Royce	1,100
1987	BAA	600
1987	BP (part)	7,200
1988	British Steel	2,400
1989	Water Companies	3,500
1990	Electricity Distribution Companies	5,200
1991	Electricity Generators (part)	3,200
1991	BT (part)	11,100
1994	British Coal	800
1995	Electricity Generators (part)	1,800
1996	Railtrack	1,900
1996	Nuclear Power (British Energy)	2,500

Source: adapted from Financial press, financial statistics

Remember that the supply side view is that macroeconomic policy is primarily concerned with ensuring that markets work properly. In the previous chapter we focused on a resource market – labour. In this chapter we concentrate on markets for goods and services. You should not be surprised if much of this chapter focuses on microeconomic issues: supply side policies are about returning to confidence in markets, rather than upon macroeconomic demand management.

What are the arguments for privatisation? What has happened? What has been the result? The size of the privatisation programme has been remarkable: Table 17.1 gives an indication of the extent of the process with a selection of some of the largest sales. As you can see there have been no substantial sales in the last few years. However, private capital is being brought into air traffic control and the London Underground system. Furthermore, privatisation in many other countries continues at a rapid rate.

From 1990–2001 $1,000 billion worth of assets throughout the world were sold to the private sector, over 40 per cent in Europe. This was mainly in the fifteen countries of the EU but also included in the process were some of the former Eastern European economies that we considered in Chapter 2. The largest programme was in Italy where during that period around $90 billion worth of state assets were disposed of. However, large state transfers have been seen recently in Spain, Germany, France and Portugal among others.

Although the idea of shifting resources out of the state sector is not new, the scale of the procedure in the UK has revolutionised the thinking of many concerning what can be produced within the private sector. Many other areas of economic activity have been considered as possible candidates for privatisation. However, to say that more privatisations are feasible is not to say that they are desirable. It is to the likely major effects of the policy generally rather than the effects upon any one industry in particular that we now turn.

What exactly is privatisation? It is a wide-ranging term. Howard Vane[1] suggests that it covers three areas: (a) denationalisation – selling publicly owned assets to the private sector; (b) contracting-out – franchising to private contractors the production of (state-financed) goods and services previously produced in the public sector; and (c) deregulation – removing various restrictions on competition previously given to statutory monopolies. All three aspects are important, but it is the first that is the focus of our attention here.

Even within this area, namely the sale of publicly owned assets to the private sector, the means of achieving the sale have varied. For example, many industries, such as water and steel, have been sold to members of the public in the form of a public share subscription. In other sales, for example that of the Rover car group which was sold to British Aerospace, there was no opportunity for the public to purchase the assets directly.

Does it matter who owns the assets from which output is produced? If so, why?

17.2 Public ownership of assets: the arguments in favour

Those who see advantages of keeping assets within public ownership will usually express the argument in one or more of the five following ways.

Efficiency

The industries involved are all those where firms have some degree of monopoly power, although in no case is it absolute. Electricity competes with gas. Water has few substitutes, but even here power is not absolute. Where water meters are introduced, quantity demanded falls. Some industries are natural monopolies: that is to say, as output increases in the long run, unit costs of production fall. This means two things. One is that the high level of financing of capital projects may be difficult for private firms. It will require public sector financing to see

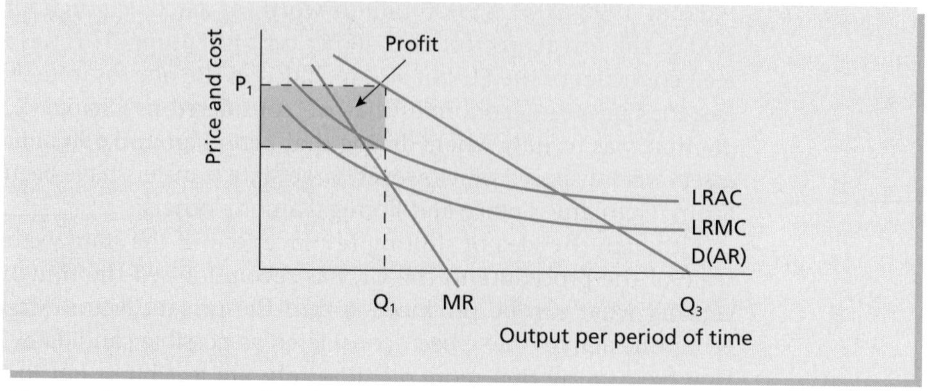

Figure 17.1 Monopoly power and a declining LRAC curve

that adequate investment takes place in such industries. Obvious examples of such industries would include electricity, with huge investment in the national grid, and the water industry.

The other thing that follows from a declining long-run average cost is that consumers will be exploited. Given the cost structure described above, the formation of a monopoly is almost inevitable. Consider Figure 17.1. Since the long-run average cost curve (LRAC) falls we can never expect competition to take place. If there were to be more than one firm, it would pay these firms to merge, increasing output and lowering unit costs.[2]

see pp. 152–4

What price would the monopolist charge? Profit is maximised at Q_1P_1 such that all output is made where addition to cost (LRMC) is less than addition to revenue (MR). The appropriate profit maximising price is clearly the maximum one that consumers are prepared to pay for that output. Now let us ask what would be the output and price that would maximise consumer welfare. Clearly, it would not be Q_3 output and a zero price, even though that would give the greatest output at the lowest price. The reason for rejecting Q_3 output is that the production of output uses resources which have an opportunity cost. The marginal opportunity cost is found in the marginal cost curve. Therefore the socially optimum volume of output is at Q_2 in Figure 17.2 where the additional value to society of the last unit produced is equal to the marginal opportunity cost of the resources used in producing it.

Notice that if Figure 17.2 accurately represents the cost and revenue conditions faced by an industry, the decision to set a socially optimal price will inevitably result in a loss (shown by the shaded area). This must be the case. A falling LRAC implies LRMC below LRAC. Hence LRMC = D, where LRAC is higher than D. Thus total revenue (= output × average revenue) must be less than total cost (= output × average cost). Since no private firm will be willing to operate in a way which means it cannot make a normal profit, state ownership is required if resources are to be allocated optimally. The loss can then be funded out of general taxation. Even if LRMC does not fall continuously, but rises at some level of output, the argument still holds if D intersects LRMC on the downward sloping section of LRMC.

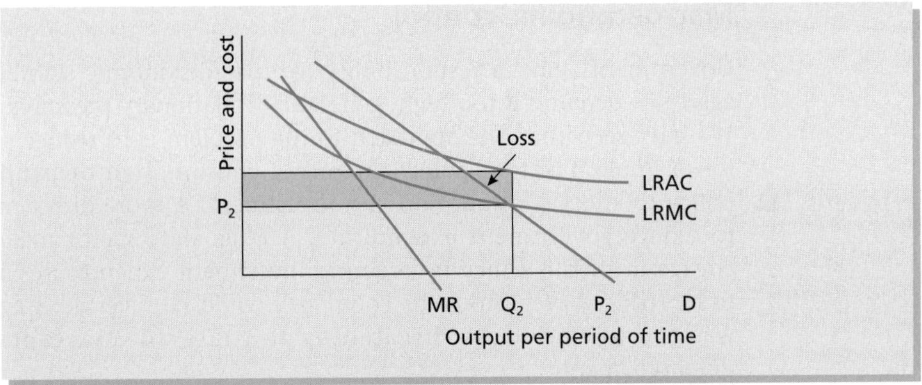

Figure 17.2 Socially optimal price output decisions with declining LRAC

Externalities

To show that MC = D is a socially optimal price/output decision it is necessary to show that long-run marginal private cost (LRMC) is equal to long-run marginal social cost (LMSC). This condition does not always hold. In such circumstances, resources would be better owned by the state sector, which will allow for the external effect that produces this divergence.

Let us illustrate with an example. British Steel, following privatisation, closed the Ravenscraig steel plant in Scotland because it adjudged that revenues from the sale of its steel were less than the incremental costs of production. British Steel took no account of the additional unemployment benefit payable to those unemployed or to those made unemployed through the multiplier effects in Scotland. There is a divergence between social and private cost that a state enterprise could consider but a private producer will not. We have already seen that there is much debate over the speed of resource adjustment that takes place in response to demand changes. However quick it is, there will be some adjustment costs, which will tend to fall at least partly on the state.

see pp. 144–5

Distribution of income

State-produced services such as education and health care can be seen as part of the social wage. Higher income groups contribute more taxation through a progressive tax system, so lower income groups consume more than they pay for. This redistributes income towards equality.

There is no economic distinction between nationalised industries and departments of state in this respect. Therefore, one way of benefiting lower income groups is to produce electricity, gas, water and other basic commodities in the public sector at subsidised prices. State-owned assets can therefore be a means of distributional change. One should bear in mind, however, that subsidies can, in some cases, be largely of benefit to the middle classes. Telephones might be one such example.

Macroeconomic control

Governments have a responsibility for macroeconomic stability. Suppose that aggregate demand is too high, generating inflationary pressures in the economy. We have seen that one approach to the problem is to reduce such demand by, for example, taxation policy to control consumption demand or interest rate policy to affect consumption and investment. A more direct method would be to reduce government expenditure. A large state sector makes it possible to engage in such a policy by ordering investment expenditure in state industries to be reduced or postponed. The policy could be reversed if aggregate demand was too low and was threatening to cause an unacceptable volume of unemployment.

see pp. 261–5

Clearly, the larger the state sector the more potential there is for direct control of the volume of investment and the volume of aggregate demand. Notice that this is a Keynesian view of macroeconomic policy – a point to which we return later in the chapter.

Provision of public goods

see pp. 213–15

A market system cannot provide an optimal volume of public goods. Let us remind ourselves of the meaning of public goods in order to see why.

As we saw in Chapter 10, public goods have several characteristics. One important feature will illustrate the argument that says that the provision of such goods cannot be left to market forces. A public good is one which is consumed equally by all of a country's citizens, or by a group of them. One example we considered was street lighting. If it is provided, the output is not divided between those who wish to consume it. All the citizens consume all of it. Consider Figure 17.3. For a private good, the market demand curve is the horizontal summation of all individual demand curves. The social optimum output (in the absence of market power or externalities) is Q_0. But if the good is a public good the analysis is meaningless. Q_0 output is not divided between the citizens according to individual demand. *All* consume Q_0 streetlighting.

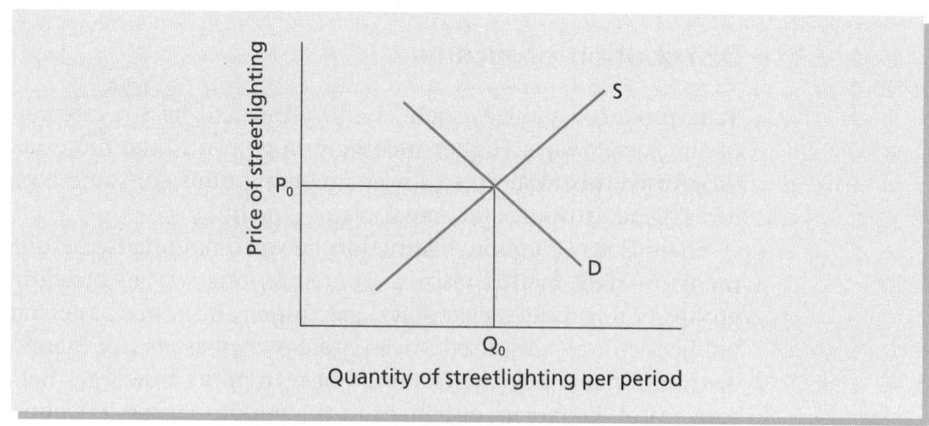

Figure 17.3 The problem of pricing a public good

Certainly, it will be difficult for a government to decide the optimal provision of a public good, but if it is left to the private owners of resources, as we have seen already, the best level of output for society is unlikely to be provided. Government ownership of assets is therefore more likely to maximise economic welfare in this area than is the private ownership of resources.

17.3 Private ownership of assets: counter arguments

Since the late 1970s governments of EU member states have continued to shift resources into the private sector. In the light of what we have said above, on what grounds has is been done? The arguments given above have been almost completely rejected. The exception is t he public goods case. There appears to be no enthusiasm for privatising national defence or street lighting, for example. The other four grounds that we examined are regarded as unacceptable arguments. We shall consider the efficiency arguments in more detail in the next section. Let us first see why the other three arguments have been rejected.

Externalities

Externalities are regarded as irrelevant from the standpoint of resource ownership and the privatisation debate since it is possible to 'internalise' externalities even if resources are in the private sector. Consider the case in Figure 17.4. Assume that industry is tipping effluent into streams and imposing costs on society that it is not bearing itself. The externality has caused a breakdown in the identity between private and social costs. The identity can be restored by imposing a tax on the firm, shifting up the MPC to coincide with the MSC. It does *not* require that the firm's assets be in the public sector. If the external effect were to be an external benefit then an appropriate subsidy can be found, shifting MPC down to coincide with MSC.

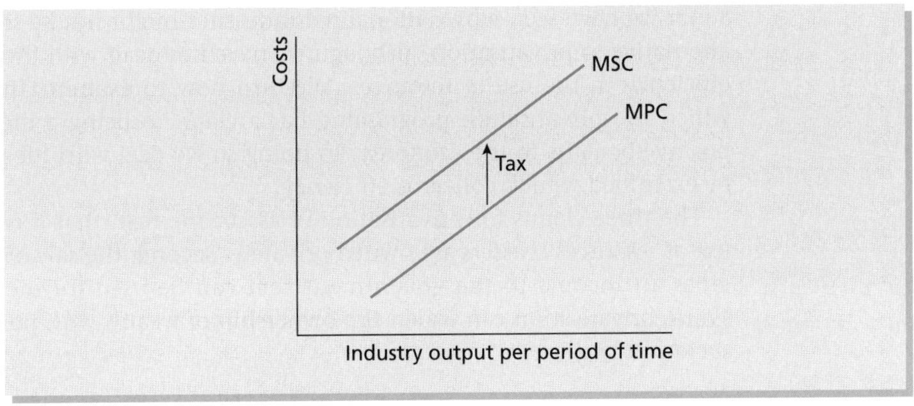

Figure 17.4 **Externalities' private and social costs**

Distribution of income

There are various ways in which income can be redistributed, the most obvious example being a progressive tax system. This is supplemented in Britain by social security payments of various kinds. If income is not thought to be sufficiently evenly distributed, it would be better to increase benefits and make the tax system more progressive. This is because a combination of artificially low prices plus subsidies distorts relative prices and misallocates investment.

The argument, then, is not that income redistribution should not be undertaken. It is that keeping assets in the public sector to keep prices down artificially is an inefficient means of achieving such a redistribution. Nevertheless, as we saw in Chapter 16, supply side economists worry about any policies to redistribute income because of its effects on incentives.

see pp. 341–64

Macroeconomic control

If macroeconomic control of the economy is thought to be appropriate, it can be argued that interfering with individual industries is an unfortunate way of achieving it, for it inevitably misallocates resources. One particularly ineffective attempt to use state assets for macroeconomic control was the effort to control inflation during the Conservative administration of Edward Heath in the early 1970s. Nationalised industry prices were artificially restrained during a period of inflationary pressure in an attempt to break an inflationary spiral. Subsidies to those industries had therefore to be increased. The provision of those subsidies imposed pressures on the PSBR which proved to be inflationary. We explore the link between the PSBR and inflation in Chapter 18. Therefore not only was the policy self-defeating but it also misallocated resources by providing inappropriate relative price signals.

see pp. 394–400

17.4 Claimed benefits of privatisation

So far we have seen why nationalised industries might not be seen as a superior alternative to privatisation, although we have not dealt with the key question of efficiency in the use of resources. We turn now to examine the three areas in which the privatisation programme has a claim to being a means of bringing positive benefits to the economy. In doing so we deal with the argument yet to be examined, which concerns efficiency.

The three claims for privatisation of assets are, first, that it is a *more* efficient use of resources if assets are owned privately. Second, the sale of state assets provides an income to the government that can be used for increasing welfare. Third, privatisation can widen the ownership of wealth with positive benefits to society at large.

Table 17.2 **Record of British Steel Corporation, selected years**

	1980/81	*1983/84*	*1986/87*	*1989/90*	*1992/93*	*1995/96*
Turnover (£m)	2,954	3,358	3,461	5,113	4,303	7,048
Net profit (loss) before tax (£m)	(1,020)	(256)	178	733	(149)	1,102
Productivity (man-hours per tonne)	14.5	7.1	6.2	4.8	4.2	na

Source: adapted from British Steel Corporation, reports and accounts, various years

Benefit 1: efficiency

The efficiency argument for privatisation is based partly on cost efficiency and partly on allocative efficiency. Let us remind ourselves of the distinction. When we talk about cost efficiency, we mean that the firm will produce any given level of output at the lowest possible long-run average cost *for that level of output*. In other words, the firm will be on its cost curve and not above it. Allocative efficiency means producing output in the quantity that reflects society's preferences. It means to produce output where (in the absence of externalities) MC = D.

Privatisation is often argued to improve cost efficiency. Nationalised industries suffer from low morale, so output is lower than it need be. Management has no incentive to reduce waste and improve cost efficiency since it will not be rewarded with increased profits. Only the incentive of improved rewards will lower costs. Privatisation makes that possible.

Does the evidence support this argument? Are private firms more cost efficient than state firms? We have to say that there is no convincing way of demonstrating the matter one way or the other. Any attempt to examine the evidence is likely to prove futile. For example, one way we might try is to compare the pre-privatisation and post-privatisation performance of an industry, say British Steel. Remembering that British Steel was privatised in 1988, consider Table 17.2. What does it tell us about the effects of privatisation? The question is not as easy to answer as we might think.

The productivity figures are impressive. On the other hand, we do not know what would have happened in the absence of privatisation. Perhaps some or even all this improvement would have taken place because of increased competition from abroad and the introduction of better technology. We need to assume that all other factors affecting productivity were held constant.

The profit figures are also impressive at first sight. After all, one can hardly claim that the improvement is due to more consumer exploitation as privatisation approached – that prices were being increased to 'fatten up' the industry prior to the public share offering. Steel is very competitive within Europe. Such a point would have more force in an industry such as water where there are few substitutes and monopoly power is considerable. Nevertheless, the profitability figures still represent difficulties in interpretation. The change in profit levels in recent years certainly reflects the effects of recession as well as the effects of privatisation.

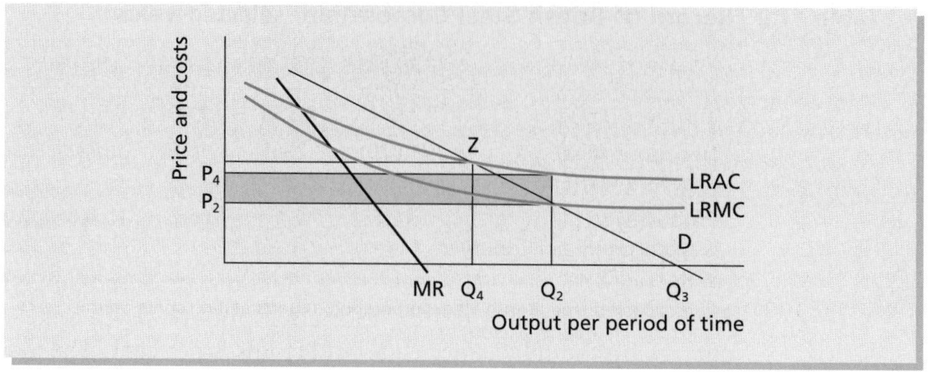

Figure 17.5 **Socially efficient prices and the private sector**

Furthermore, the record over the longer term is made more difficult to interpret as other factors enter consideration. For example, British Steel's record is no longer available. Since 1999 it has become a new company named Corus after a merger with a European steel producer.

To summarise, then, cost efficiency *may* improve with privatisation. There is no certain way of demonstrating it. However, the figures above make a strong prima facie case for saying that privatisation can improve cost efficiency.

We turn now to the important matter of allocative efficiency. Why do some think that this is better achieved if resources are in private hands?

One aspect of this question is access to capital markets. A nationalised concern has to go to government to ask for funds for investment. Whether they will be granted will depend not only on the merits of the case itself but also on the wider considerations of the Treasury – the size of the PSBR, for example. In the private sector, industries such as water and electricity will compete for funds on an equal footing. If consumer demand is strong enough to justify investment, the funds will be forthcoming. The industry no longer has to concern itself with the political problems inherent in state intervention.

An equally important aspect of allocative efficiency is the question of pricing. Advocates of privatisation argue that there is no reason one cannot achieve pricing efficiency in the private sector. Let us examine the argument with reference to Figure 17.5.

There are two points to consider. First, if, as is usual, the LRAC slopes downwards, one can argue that MC = D is not allocatively efficient. The logic of allocative efficiency is that it is the point at which all mutually beneficial trades have taken place. In other words, the assumption is the usual Pareto-optimal idea that all exchanges have taken place where someone's welfare is improved without making anyone else worse off. However, MC = D implies a loss represented by the shaded area.

Since with MC = D losses are made and there is a consequent redistribution of income, it cannot be Pareto-optimal. If, for example, this situation were to describe British Rail, then setting a price where MC = D and subsidising BR means redistributing income from the general taxpayer to railway users. It would be difficult to see how this could be regarded as Pareto-efficient. The best we can do, therefore, is to see that the price/output decision is Q_4, the nearest we can get to MC = D while avoiding losses and a consequent income redistribution.

That leads us to the second point. A price/output of Q_4 P_4 is achievable in the private sector with a suitable price control at P_4. A profit-maximising monopolist operating under a price ceiling of P_4 would choose just that price/output level. This explains why the government has privatised some industries that face little effective competition but has imposed a price control.[3] Let us take two such examples. First consider British Telecom. The company was privatised but had to work under a pricing formula as follows. Each year BT could raise its charges by the retail price index (RPI) less 3 per cent. The view was that technological progress would, over time, move the LRAC downwards so that BT could break even, despite having a falling price level. Subsequently, the formula was tightened, driving prices ever lower. There is now a case for saying that this industry is so competitive that price controls are unnecessary.

Second, look at the example of the water industry. This industry was given a price ceiling of RPI *plus*, the size of the plus varying from one water company to another. The idea of allowing these companies to increase water charges in real terms was to enable them to be sufficiently profitable that they could attract large sums from capital markets. These sums would be needed to engage in major programmes of repairing deteriorating water pipes and so on.

Notice the difficulty involved in deciding whether the policy is successful. Many would argue that water and electricity companies, amongst others, have done far better than break even. Recall that break even means covering all costs including normal profit, that is, they must make a rate of return on capital comparable to other industries with similar risk. Whether their profits are equal to or greater than that is a matter for debate, but it is clearly difficult to obtain an agreed figure as to what contributes a normal profit.

see pp. 204–11

You will recall from Chapter 10 the distinctions we drew between different kinds of efficiency. It would appear that privatisation may lead to an improvement in the efficiency of those industries involved. That said, it would be extremely difficult to demonstrate the fact in any convincing way.

Benefit 2: increased government revenue

One apparent advantage of the privatisation programme is the revenue that it generates. Table 17.1 gives an indication of the revenue received from the largest asset sales and Table 17.3 gives the total amounts received from all UK privatisations in new years. The increase in revenue is more apparent than real. There are three reasons why this is so.

The first reason can be understood if we ask ourselves why anyone is willing to buy these assets from the government. The answer is, of course, because of the expected stream of revenue that will be produced in the form of profits or dividends. As we saw in Chapter 14, the value of the capital will be the discounted value of the expected income stream. Then the government is simply replacing a stream of earnings in the future with a one-off receipt of revenue now. It is not increasing revenue, merely altering the timing of its receipts.

see pp. 301–5

Table 17.3 **UK privatisation receipts (£ billion)**

Year	*Proceeds*	*Year*	*Proceeds*
1979/80	0.4	1991/92	7.9
1980/81	0.2	1992/93	8.2
1981/82	0.5	1993/94	5.5
1982/83	0.5	1994/95	6.3
1983/84	1.1	1995/96	3.0
1984/85	2.1	1996/97	4.2
1985/86	2.7	1997/98	2.5
1986/87	4.5	1998/99	0
1987/88	5.1	1999/00	0
1988/89	7.1	2000/01	0
1989/90	4.2	2001/02	0
1990/91	5.3	2002/03	0

Source: adapted from Treasury statistics

The government may feel that the income generated will enable it to make a better investment. It could use the sales to build more schools or hospitals, for example. Critics have argued that it has in fact been used for tax cuts. This may not necessarily be a valid criticism. The tax cuts may improve the supply side of the economy by increasing output sufficiently to justify the decision to privatise the assets. Whether tax cuts do stimulate the output of the economy in this way is a matter we examined in Chapter 16.

see pp. 341–64

One thing we can say, however, is that since 1979 the public sector's balance sheet has changed significantly. Figure 17.6 records the position. You can see how the value of the public sector's assets as a proportion of GDP has tended to fall. This reflects partly the sale of assets to the private sector. It also reflects government policy to reduce state capital spending. It is easier to cut capital expenditure – road-building, school-building, prisons, etc. – than to cut current spending – pensions, unemployment benefit and so on. It is these two factors, reduced capital spending and the privatisation programme, which account for the decline in public asset values. Taken with the rise in net financial liabilities, mainly outstanding government debt, the public sector balance sheet worsened sharply since the 1990s – although the privatisation process is only one element of the explanation for this.

The second reason that the increased revenue is more apparent than real is that there is a strong case for saying that the assets have been underpriced. The government fixed the price of the shares of each of these companies and offered them to the public and to the institutions. In most cases there was excess demand for the shares and applications were scaled down. Excess demand suggests too low a price. What was the equilibrium price? One idea would be to look at the price at which the shares changed hands on the stock market at the end of the first day of trading. There was often a substantial premium to be

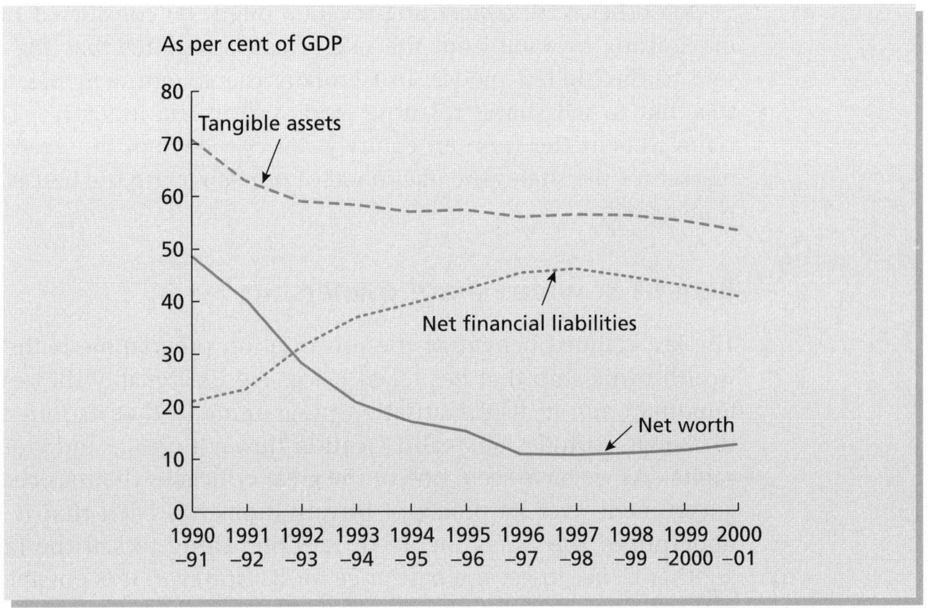

Figure 17.6 Public sector net wealth
Source: NIESR

earned. Premiums in the realm of 30–50 per cent have not been uncommon. Another idea of the extent to which assets have been undervalued can be seen when takeover bids are made for privatised companies. Most of the electricity distributors have been subject to such bids often valuing the company at four or five times its flotation value.

The above criticism has been made of other forms of privatisation also. For example, the Rover group was sold to British Aerospace at an agreed price, but the government did not accept bids from other interested parties. It is quite conceivable that, had it held an auction, the price obtained would have been substantially higher. British Aerospace sold Rover to BMW for a large profit in 1994.

The third reason for thinking that the state's assets could have been sold for more is that there is a basic inconsistency between two of the government's stated aims of the sales. One aim is to get efficiency in the use of resources. Part of this aim means allocative efficiency which, in turn, it can be argued, means that price controls are necessary for reasons given earlier. However, the way to maximise revenue would have been to have no price control. The huge monopoly profits then available to some of these industries would have enabled the government to achieve a much higher price for the sale.

Selling the assets and stipulating no price ceiling for the industry's output is something that should be seriously considered. Remember that monopoly power is a cost when resources are transferred. The new owners would have been prepared to pay a much higher price for industries such as gas and water because they would have been willing to buy the right to the monopoly profits. By preventing the appearance of such profits, revenue from the asset sales could not be maximised.

One other issue concerning revenue might be considered here. The logic of maximising revenue from the sale of assets requires that the assets should be sold to the highest bidder. In Germany the government has tended not to do this, but to sell shares to those employed in the industry.[4] This clearly has a claim to be better from an equity point of view, but by severely restricting the market for the shares the likelihood of not achieving the best price for the assets is increased.

Benefit 3: wider share ownership

The last claimed benefit of the privatisation programme is the wider spread of wealth ownership that has taken place. This is arguably the government's most important aim in its privatisation programme in that its long-term objective is to change attitudes to wealth creation through greater individual ownership of capital. As we have seen, one of the great criticisms that has been levelled at the government over its policy of privatisations has been that it has consistently underpriced the assets involved. It is one thing to sell the family silver; it is another to fail to get the best price for it. However, it is possible for the government to argue that the underpricing of assets to members of the public has been worthwhile. The consequent loss of Exchequer revenue is a small price to pay when set against the benefits obtained by spreading share ownership more than was previously thought possible.

Is this leading to a situation in which people are now buying and selling non-privatised shares, as the government clearly hoped? The evidence suggests that they are not. It is true that in 1987 around 8 per cent of adults in Britain owned shares in at least four companies, whereas in 2000 the figure was around 13 per cent. However, this largely reflects an increase in the number of privatised shares available.

Throughout the 1980s and 1990s there was no discernible effect in slowing the trend towards an increasing proportion of shares being in the hands of the institutions (as we saw in Table 9.2). This steady upward trend over that period was entirely unaffected by privatisation. That said, some individuals who have been encouraged through state asset sales to invest in shares, have taken their share ownership through the unit trusts, and so on, rather than involve themselves directly in the purchase of shares.

17.5 Deregulation

We mentioned earlier in the chapter a key criticism of the privatisation process: monopolies, with their power to misallocate resources, are transferred from the public to the private sector. We saw also that those privatised companies where substantial monopoly power exists have that power curtailed by a price control. A further technique for controlling monopoly power is that of deregulation. Most of the natural monopolies within the public sector have been protected from competition in order to ensure the benefits of economies of scale. This is

Table 17.4 **Welfare effects of deregulation, $US billion, 1990**

Industry	*Consumers*[a]	*Producers*	*Total*	*Additional benefits if deregulation achieves optimality*[a]
Airlines	8.8–14.8	4.9	13.7–19.7	4.9
Railroads	7.2–9.7	3.2	10.4–12.9	0.45
Trucking	15.4	−4.8	10.6	0.0
Telecommunications	0.73–1.6	–	0.73–1.6	11.8
Cable television	0.37–1.3	–	0.37–1.3	0.4–0.8
Brokerage	0.14	−0.14	0.0	0.0
Natural Gas	–	–	–	4.1
Total	32.6–43.0	3.2	35.8–46.2	21.65–22.05

[a] The additional welfare gains are based on assuming regulatory reform actually generates optimal pricing and, where appropriate, optimal service

Source: adapted from C. Winston, 'Economic Deregulation: Days of Reckoning for Microeconomists', *Journal of Economic Literature*, September 1993

still true for some industries. For example, the Post Office, still publicly owned, has a legally determined monopoly power over the delivery of letters (although competition is allowed in parcel deliveries and experimental licences are being given to private companies to compete in some areas). When an industry is privatised it can be deregulated. One illustration of deregulation is allowing companies access to BT's cable network so that BT now has some competition. Another is allowing regional electricity distributors to buy power from whichever source they choose.

Deregulation and privatisation are separate but closely related issues. Deregulation is a way of controlling monopoly power in the private sector and encouraging competition to move price/output decisions in industry closer to the social optimum. Is it effective? The most comprehensive attempt to answer this question is provided by Clifford Winston from his collection of researches into the effects of deregulation on American industry.

The results, for those who believe in the power of deregulation, are encouraging. They suggest that substantial welfare gains can be achieved in the form of lower prices and better services (Table 17.4). Notice that this effect is not simply a transfer of welfare from producers to consumers. There are overall gains. Competition improves efficiency. Notice also that, in some cases, consumers and producers both gain. Cost efficiency is improved by competition. Prices fall but not by as much as costs. Producers increase profits, consumers get lower prices.

The last column in Table 17.4 indicates that, while the process has improved things for society in the United States, prices in those industries do not reflect a welfare optimum. This last column gives an idea of the further benefits available to society if price and output were socially optimal.

The results of the study, then, suggest that deregulation is a powerful way to improve welfare. It is a particularly important means of controlling the monopoly power of privatised industries. All this suggests that the opening up of competition in electricity, gas, telecommunications and elsewhere does have benefits for consumers. Price controls can also be of benefit to consumers. However, there may be a trade-off between these two means of helping the consumer to achieve better value for money from such industries. Firms are attracted into industries in response to profits, but price controls threaten that very profit that would attract new firms to the market. Hence the denial via price controls of some profit to monopolistic industries may slow the arrival of the very competition that deregulation is designed to bring.

17.6 Conclusion

Clearly, the claimed benefits of privatisation are a matter of great debate, but the ramifications go far beyond the UK. The UK was not the first to shift assets out of the state sector, but the scale of the process in this country has captured the imagination of many other governments, so that although some commentators do not expect the process in the UK to continue for much longer, it continues apace in some other countries (see Figure 17.7). Nevertheless, three things might be said with a reasonably high degree of confidence.

First, while the concepts around which the arguments revolve are clear, the empirical evidence does not enable us to resolve the privatisation arguments convincingly. However, the evidence does suggest that, for those monopolies which have been transferred to the private sector, deregulation of the industries

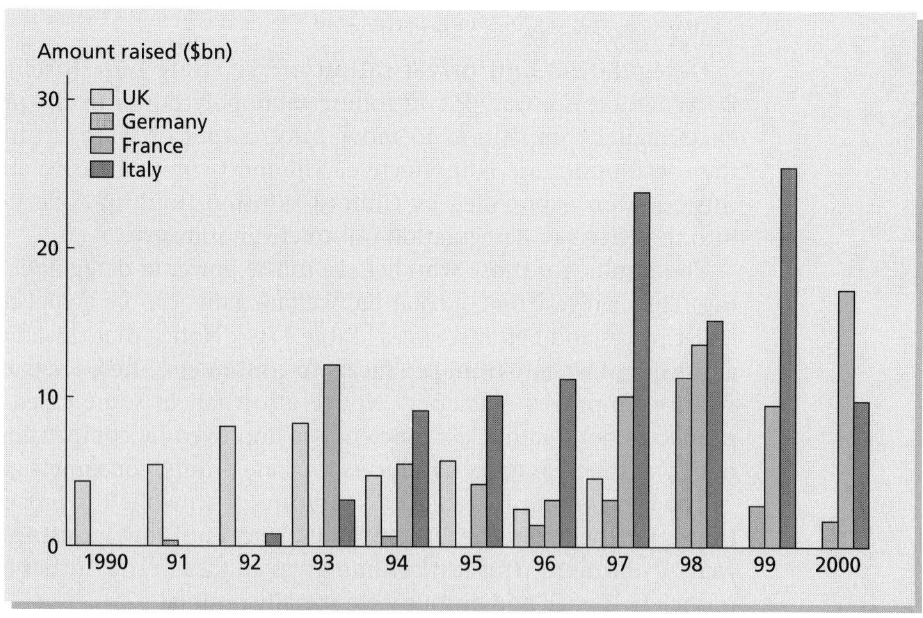

Figure 17.7 Privatisation in UK and selected European countries

Source: 'Slump intervenes in capitalist culture clash', *Financial Times*, 6 November 2002

involved is of some benefit to society. Second, not all privatisations can be judged to have been successful. For example, British Energy, the UK nuclear generator has been close to insolvency in recent years and has relied heavily upon government subsidy. The possibility of re-nationalisation is very real. Indeed this has already effectively happened for one part of the UK rail industry. When the industry was privatised the infrastructure was in the hands of a company called Railtrack and the rolling stock was owned by a number of train operating companies. In 2001 Railtrack was put under administration and the assets are now being run by a non-profit organisation. This effectively means that the UK rail infrastructure has been re-nationalised. Third, the driving force behind the privatisation process was the supply side belief that macroeconomic problems are best dealt with by microeconomic policies designed to make markets work effectively. Your view of macroeconomic policy cannot be divorced from your view of the key microeconomic issue: how effective are markets at allocating resources efficiently?

CHAPTER SUMMARY

1 **A key argument for public ownership of assets is that of allocative efficiency.**

2 **Without subsidies, private natural monopolies will not produce where MC = D, for that would mean a loss.**

3 **Other arguments for nationalisation are based on externalities, the distribution of income, macroeconomic control and public goods.**

4 **Advocates of privatisation believe that privatisation increases cost efficiency and that allocative efficiency can be achieved by such means as price controls.**

5 **Some believe that privatisation brings benefits in terms of increased government revenue and wider share ownership.**

6 **Some evidence suggests that deregulation can improve resource usage.**

Questions for discussion

Guidance to the answers for the ***asterisked*** *numbered questions is available to students on the website for the book at* **www.booksites.net/heather**.

1* Define allocative efficiency. Carefully distinguish between allocative and productive efficiency.

2 If a public sector monopoly faces a downwards sloping demand curve but an upwards sloping LRAC, and sets a socially optimal price/output, will it make losses, break even or make a profit?

3* Refer back to Figure 17.5. Suppose a privatised firm has to operate under a price ceiling of P_4. How much output would it make and what price would it charge?

4 Can you think of ways of testing for the effects of privatisation on an industry's efficiency? What problems do you see with these ideas?

5* To what extent can governments solve their debt problems by public sector asset sales?

6 Until 1994, value added tax (VAT) on domestic fuel in the UK was zero. Now it is 5 per cent. What effect would the introduction of VAT have on domestic fuel prices? Was the decision to impose VAT on domestic fuel the right one?

7* An alternative to price controls as a means to improving efficiency would be to change a firm's cost structure by taxes and subsidies. How would a firm's costs be affected by (a) a per unit tax, (b) a lump sum tax, (c) a per unit subsidy and (d) a lump sum subsidy?

8 How might a government defend itself against the charge that the state's assets were underpriced in a privatisation sale?

9* What problems would occur if a government privatised all education?

10 Do you consider the benefits of the privatisation programmes of the last 25 years to have outweighed the costs?

Websites

Each of the regulations of the natural monopolies has a website. You can look at the Strategic Rail Authority's at:

www.sra.gov.uk

The Office of Gas and Electricity Markets is at:

www.ofgem.gov.uk

The Telecommunications regulator's website is at:

www.oftel.gov.uk

and the Office of Water Services' website can be accessed at:

www.open.gov.uk/ofwat/index.htm

Notes

1 Howard Vane (1992) 'The Thatcher Years: Macroeconomic Policy and Performance of the UK Economy, 1979–1988', *National Westminster Bank Quarterly Review*, May, p. 34.

2 If there were to be several private firms in the market that were prevented from merging to preserve competition, it could be argued that resources would be wasted: the situation would not allow the exploitation of scale economies.

3 There is a frequently unrecognised problem here. If a company such as BT knows that a decrease in costs and an increase in profits will lead to a tightening of its price ceiling, it may come to the conclusion that efforts to reduce costs are rather pointless. Then the policy will no longer be achieving cost efficiency.

4 See Richard Hawkins (1991), 'Privatization in Western Germany, 1957–1990', *National Westminster Bank Quarterly Review*, November, pp. 14–22.

18 Money and banking

Running the economy: *an independent central bank?*

CHAPTER OVERVIEW

The Bank of England is no longer an arm of government. It makes its own independent decisions. Can an independent central bank do for Britain what it appeared to do in Germany for so long – provide economic stability?

In this chapter we review:

- Keynesian equilibrium
- Fiscal policy

We introduce:

- Money market equilibrium
- Monetarism

18.1 Introduction

see pp. 318–22

As we saw in Chapter 15, Britain's inflation record, judged over a long period, has not been particularly good. By comparison with Germany, for example, it has been particularly poor. Indeed it has not looked particularly impressive against the EU's record generally until quite recently. Let us set the inflation record of the UK in recent years in the context of its own history rather than making comparisons with other countries. Figure 18.1 shows UK inflation from 1694 to 2003. What is startlingly obvious is that, despite the improvements of the recent years, post-war Britain's inflation performance has been terrible. In this context it is reasonable to ask whether the relatively low inflation rates of the recent years represent a new era or whether it is just a blip in the post-war inflationary era. In order to answer this question we need to look at the significance of money in a modern economy and how the volume of that money is controlled by government.

It has been suggested that one reason for Britain's poor inflation record over a long period is to be found in the nature of its central bank. In Britain, until recently, the central bank, the Bank of England, was an arm of the government policy. The government decided upon its policy and then instructed the Bank

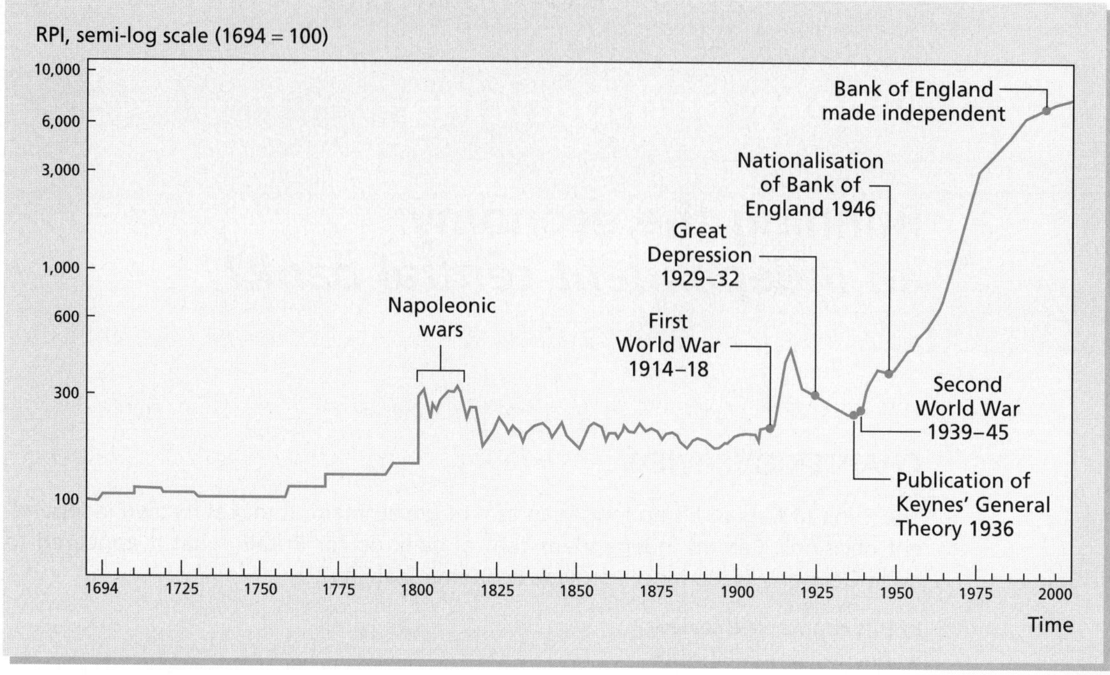

Figure 18.1 Post-war UK inflation in an historical context

of England to carry it out. In Germany, the equivalent organisation, the Bundesbank, had always had a large measure of independence. It was charged with the task of achieving price stability and has to undertake the appropriate policies with respect to the amount of money in circulation in order to achieve it. The state then had to conduct its policy against that background.[1]

In 1997 the nature of the relationship between government and the Bank of England altered. The Chancellor of the Exchequer introduced the most fundamental changes since it was nationalised in 1946.

New legislation gave the Bank the responsibility to set interest rates, and it remains responsible for the overall stability of the financial system. Interest rates have to be set to achieve an inflation target. The target is set out annually in the Budget statement.

The decisions on interest rate policy are now made by a Monetary Policy Committee (MPC), the Governor, two deputies and six others. Decisions are made by a vote of the MPC, each member having one vote. If there is no overall majority the Governor has the casting vote. A representative from the Treasury attends and can join in the discussion but cannot vote.

What brought about such a fundamental change in the relationship of the government to its central bank?

The suspicion is that the British system has a problem in that governments sometimes have a vested interest in inflation. In the short term the government might find that stimulating the economy before an election can induce temporary growth of output. Falls in unemployment, with the associated inflation, will only become apparent after polling day. In the longer term, a further advantage of inflation for government is that the real value of government debt can be reduced over time. This assumes that the inflation rate is greater than interest rates, which has often been the case. In the British system, governments can oblige the central bank to undertake policies to achieve these advantages. With the German system this was impossible. What is it that central banks do? How do their policies affect inflation? The answer is tied up with money and monetary policy.

In this chapter, therefore, we extend our analysis of government macroeconomic policy to include monetary policy. We shall discover that most Keynesian and classical economists are as divided upon this subject as on others we have already examined. Enthusiasm for central bank autonomy depends largely upon the perspective on the monetary issues of macro policy that we shall consider.

There are two aspects to the question of central bank independence. One is whether the Bank of England should be independent. The other aspect is the question of independence of a European central bank given that there is a common currency for a large part of Europe. We shall leave this second aspect until Chapter 20 and restrict our discussion in this chapter mainly to issues raised in a closed economy, that is, one that does not engage in international trade.

see pp. 434–62

First, let us examine how one believes that money enters macroeconomic policy if one has a broadly Keynesian perspective. We can then see how an independent central bank fits into such a macroeconomic framework.

18.2 Keynesian macroeconomic management

see pp. 283–6

When we examined unemployment in Chapter 13 we saw how, in principle, governments can manipulate elements of aggregate demand, which, through the multiplier effect, lead to changes in the level of output. This is important in Keynesian thinking since equilibrium output may not be full employment output.

The manipulation of aggregate demand is achieved primarily by fiscal policy or monetary policy, or more realistically, by some appropriate combination of the two. (In earlier chapters we concentrated on fiscal policy.)

Fiscal policy

In essence, fiscal policy is the use of taxation and/or government expenditure to achieve any of a number of aims. Clearly one aim is to affect the overall level of economic activity. For example, if an increase in output is required, cuts in taxes on consumers can be used to attempt to raise consumption. Alternatively, as we saw in Chapter 13, increased government expenditure can achieve much the same thing. The government sector is sufficiently large to make substantial changes in economic activity through a multiplier effect. In principle, the reverse is also possible. If inflation is a problem, increased taxes and/or decreased government expenditure can reduce aggregate demand. In practice this is more problematic, since either measure is politically sensitive.

see pp. 283–6

Increasing expenditure or decreasing taxes may seem easy politically but they too have problems. The policy may well lead to a deficit in the government's budgetary position and thus oblige the government to borrow. How this public sector borrowing requirement (PSBR) will be financed is an issue to which we return later in the chapter when we come back to the matter of fiscal policy. For the moment, we focus upon monetary policy.

What is money?

The most important feature of money is that it represents a claim on output which you can hold until you are ready to exchange it for goods and services. It thus functions as a medium of exchange that is infinitely more efficient than bartering. In modern society the main form of money is not notes and coins but bank and building society deposits against which you can write cheques. Accordingly, there are two ways of defining money given in Table 18.1. These are perhaps the most important, but there are other definitions also. Wealth can be stored in other ways. For example, we can have a deposit account at a bank against which we cannot write cheques, although it is easy to change it into a liquid form for purchasing items. We can also change shares into liquid form but not so easily and not with such a certain value. Thus there are many definitions of money according to how liquid is the asset which we treat as money.

As you can see from Table 18.1, control of the money supply will need to focus on the ability of the banking system to lend. It is that credit creation that is such a significant factor in determining the amount of money in circulation.

Notice that in the wider definition of the money supply banks create money. Bankers sometimes say that they do not create money, simply make loans. In reality they are the same thing. Suppose Alex has saved £100 from the part-time job at McDonald's, and has deposited it in cash at her bank, let us say Barclays. The £100 is still available to Alex for spending, and is therefore money.

Suppose the bank now feels able to make a loan of £80 to Fennella to get her car repaired. You may feel that the bank has simply lent Fennella some of the money that belongs to Alex. Certainly the bank is performing a function in acting as a middleman: it is bringing together one who wishes to lend and one who wishes to borrow. The exchange is improving the welfare of both or they would not be willing participants in the exchange. But in creating the loan it

Table 18.1 Main definitions of the money supply

Measure	*Includes*
Narrow definition: M_0	Notes and coins in circulation plus operational deposits of commercial banks with the Bank of England
Broad definition: M_4	Notes and coins with the general public and UK private sectors; sterling sight deposits with UK banks; sterling time deposits of the UK private sector with UK banks and building society holdings of the private sector *less* building society holdings of deposits with UK banks

has created money. Fennella has £80 to spend but Alex still has available to her the money she deposited. The bank, in making the loan, has created 'money'. Bank loans are in a real sense money.

If you think about the logic of what the bank is doing you will see that the amount of loans it can create is many times greater than the notes and coins deposited with it. When Fennella writes her cheque to the garage, knowing that her bank, Barclays, has promised to honour it, what happens when the garage presents the cheque to its bank (assume, for simplicity, also Barclays)? The bank will want to keep some of this money in case the garage owner needs it. The rest it will feel able to lend out. The process will continue until the amount of loans is many times greater than Alex's initial £100 cash. It doesn't matter much if the garage owner banks with Lloyds. It simply means that Lloyds rather than Barclays creates the credit. The amount of credit created by the banking system, then, is easily the largest element in a wider definition of the money supply.

The supply of money

Most Keynesian models assume that the supply of money can be determined by the government. Figure 18.2 shows a supply curve for money. If a government wishes to move the supply curve, it can do so through the Bank of England by affecting banks' ability to lend. Suppose it wished to reduce the supply from S_1 to S_2, in Figure 18.2; it could do so in a number of ways. We shall mention three. First, the central bank can insist that the banks have a higher liquidity ratio. That is to say, commercial banks must keep more of their assets in a form easily turned into liquid assets. The extent to which banks can lend will depend upon the volume of their liquid assets. They must retain sufficient liquid assets to meet demands for cash from their customers. The fewer liquid assets they have, the less they will feel able to lend. Clearly if the banks can now lend less, the supply of money is reduced. This is not a method of control that has been used in recent years. Second, the government can sell securities, for example long-term debt, known as bonds. When people buy the bonds, they pay for them with cheques drawn on their banks, thus reducing bank liquidity and hence the money supply. Third, the central bank can insist on special deposits from the commercial banks. The banks are obliged to deposit some of their

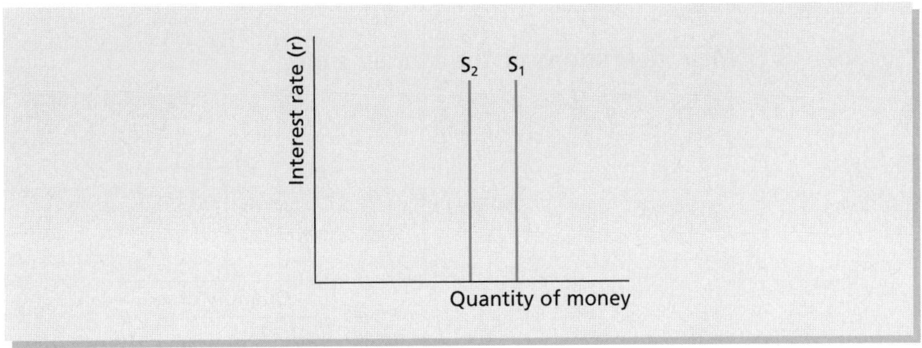

Figure 18.2 **Reducing the supply of money**

funds with the Bank of England. Again the effect is to reduce bank liquidity leading to a reduction in the money supply.

The supply curve of money, then, is in effect a stock of money. It can be M_0, a stock of notes and coins in circulation which the government controls through the Bank of England, since only the Bank is legally empowered to print notes and mint coins. Although the M_4 definition of money gives a far larger amount than M_0, the supply is still, in principle, determined by the government through the Bank of England, since the Bank can effectively control commercial bank lending.

In theory at least, then, the supply of money can be determined by government, working through the Bank of England, the Bank being an instrument of government policy.

Demand for money in Keynesian thinking

What determines the demand for money? To put the question another way, why would people wish to hold their wealth in liquid form rather than in an illiquid form such as shares or government debt such as bonds? There are said to be three motives. First, there is a 'transactions' motive. People wish to hold money so that they can purchase goods and services. Holding all one's wealth as a Goya painting makes buying sausages a difficult business. It can be argued that such a motive is unlikely to be affected by interest rates. If that is so the transactions demand for money (D_t) will be as in Figure 18.3. Alternatively, one could take the view that, as interest rates rise, the opportunity cost of holding one's wealth in the form of money increases, in that a greater amount of interest is forgone. It will certainly be the case that D_t will shift to the right with a rise in income: more money is needed for steak than for sausages.

There is a second motive for holding money: the 'precautionary' demand (D_p). People demand money to be ready to meet unforeseen expenditure, such as an unexpected bill to repair a car. This is probably not interest-rate sensitive either, so we show it on Figure 18.3 as interest inelastic, just as we did for the transactions demand. Again, however, this would shift right as incomes rise. An

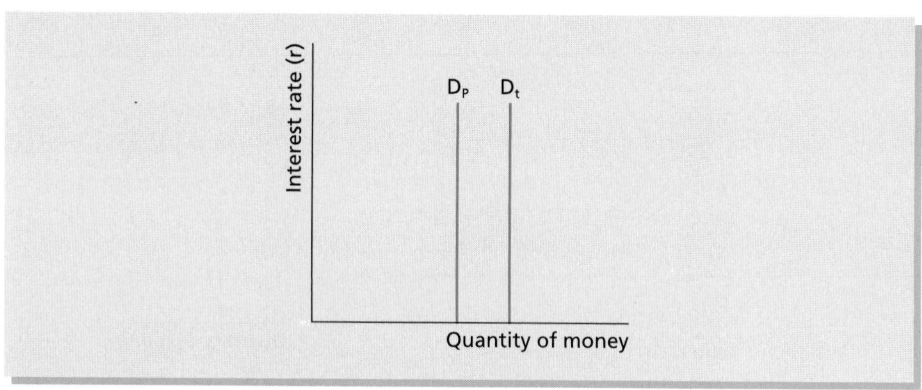

Figure 18.3 **The transactions and precautionary demands for money**

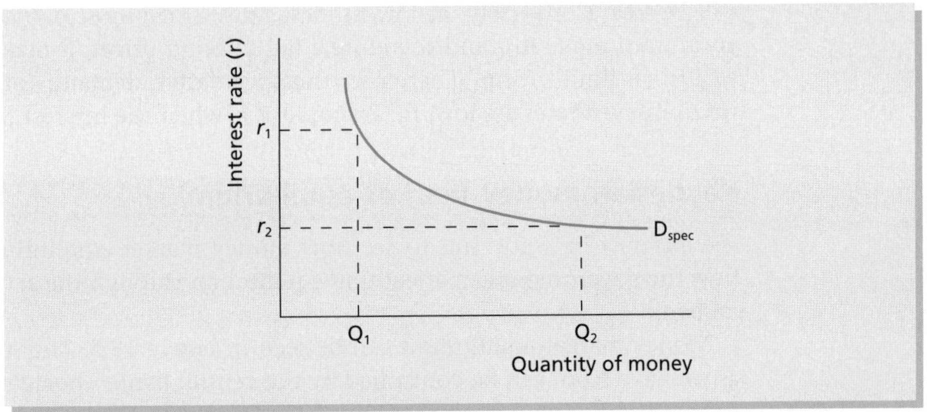

Figure 18.4 The speculative demand for money

unforeseen repair bill for the Mercedes Benz will require more money than one for the Mini.

The third and final motive for holding money, according to Keynesian theory, is the speculative motive. Holding wealth in illiquid form such as shares, antiques or bonds has an advantage in that capital gains can be made if their value appreciates. Wealth in the liquid form of £10 notes under the bed has no such advantage. On the other hand, such illiquid assets have a disadvantage – their value may fall and one may sustain a capital loss. In Keynesian theory, people take this into account when deciding how liquid their assets should be, and that decision is affected by interest rates. Let us see why.

We choose one illiquid asset, the '2.5 per cent consol', to establish the principle here, though what we say about this asset is, in essence, true of all assets. This 2.5 per cent consol is government debt. The holder of this bond is paid £2.50 per annum, representing 2.5 per cent of its face value of £100. The bond is irredeemable, that is the government is never going to pay back the original £100. If one wants to sell it, one has to find someone else willing to buy it. What will the market price be for such a bond? The answer is that it depends upon interest rates. Suppose the present rate of interest is 10 per cent, what is the bond worth? The answer must be about £25. If one paid £25 for the bond and received £2.50 per annum interest, that represents a 10 per cent return on the investment. Since 10 per cent is available at the bank, no one is likely to pay more than £25 for the bond. Suppose interest rates were to be 20 per cent. Clearly no one would pay more than £12.50 for the bond, since that lower bond price would be needed in order that the buyer received a return equal to available returns elsewhere. In general, then, a rise in interest rates will cause a fall in bond prices and vice versa.

Now consider Figure 18.4. Suppose interest rates are high, at r_1. Most people will anticipate that the next move in interest rates will be downwards. They, therefore, expect bond prices to rise in the future. If bond prices are going to rise they will wish to hold their wealth in the form of bonds in order to make a capital gain – so the speculative demand for money (labelled D_{spec} in the figure) will be low. Conversely, at low interest rates, since most people will anticipate an upward move in *r* and therefore a fall in bond prices, it makes sense to hold wealth in liquid form. Therefore, the speculative demand for money is high when interest rates are low, for example at r_2 when the interest rate is at Q_2.

Keynesian money market equilibrium

We are now in a position to see how money market equilibrium is found and how the government can affect that equilibrium through the actions of the central bank.

Money market equilibrium can be seen in Figure 18.5. The supply of money, as we have seen, can be controlled by the central bank. The demand curve, D, is simply the horizontal summation of D_t, D_p and D_{spec} to give the total demand for money, sometimes known as the liquidity preference schedule. Market forces will ensure an equilibrium rate of interest at r_1. If interest rates are at r_2 there is an excess supply of money $Q_1 - Q_2$, that is to say an excess demand for bonds. Hence, bond prices rise and interest rates fall. At r_3 the excess demand for money, $Q_3 - Q_1$, that is the excess supply of bonds, depresses bond prices and raises interest rates.

We now know how, in Keynesian thinking, money market equilibrium is reached. We can easily see how government can manipulate conditions in the money market. It has two options. It can influence the money supply and hence influence interest rates. For example, if it wishes to see lower interest rates, the Bank of England can increase the money supply in ways we have seen, shifting the supply curve of money to the right. Lower interest rates will follow. Unfortunately, this has a problem. One needs to know exactly where the liquidity preference schedule is in order to move the money supply the correct distance rightwards.

As a result, in recent years the alternative option has been favoured. The Bank of England can set the chosen level of interest rates and then supply whatever money is necessary to bring money markets into equilibrium at that rate. As a

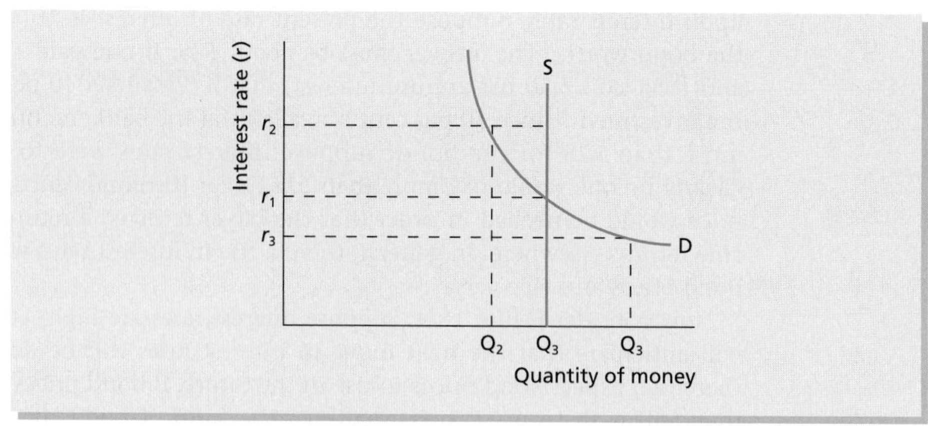

Figure 18.5 **Equilibrium in the money market**

result of this change in policy, announcements of the money supply figures, once seen as measuring the success of government policy in controlling monetary conditions, are now more often seen as indicating the demand for credit from the general public and hence a measure of economic activity.

Now we shall turn to see how the monetary sector, and government control over it, has influences on the real sector. Having done that, we shall see how Keynesian economists would view an independent central bank.

Interrelationships between the real and money sectors

We saw earlier how governments could manipulate the volume of aggregate demand via fiscal policy changes. We can now make two important points about aggregate demand control.

The first point is that an alternative to using fiscal instruments is monetary policy. An upward shift in the aggregate demand function, for example, could be achieved by relaxing monetary conditions and lowering interest rates. Lower interest rates may stimulate investment demand as we considered in Chapter 14. Alternatively, it may raise consumption demand, since lower interest rates reduce the cost of purchasing many consumer durable items such as cars and furniture that are frequently bought on credit. Most Keynesian economists would argue, however, that the extent to which demand is stimulated by lower interest rates is difficult to predict and that fiscal policy is therefore of more value in controlling aggregate demand.

see pp. 301–4

The second point is that the effects of fiscal control cannot be isolated from the monetary sector. There are important interrelationships between the two sectors. We shall illustrate this by looking at what happens if governments choose to stimulate economic activity by fiscal means. Figure 18.6 shows an economy with equilibrium in both the real and monetary sectors. Let us assume that the equilibrium in the real sector is with substantial unemployment. Government thus gives a fiscal stimulus to the economy in an attempt to raise output to full employment output, assumed to be at Y_2. Provided that it knows the value of the multiplier, it can calculate the correct increase in, say,

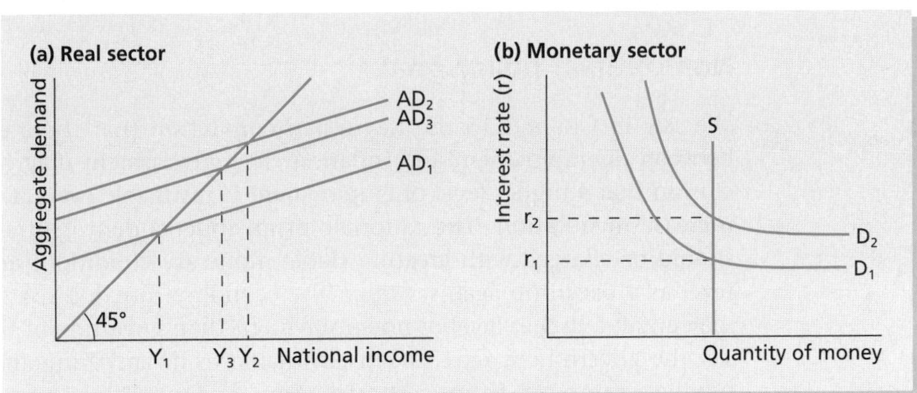

Figure 18.6 **Money and its effect on the real sector**

government expenditure that is required and raise aggregate demand from AD_1 to AD_2, thus moving the economy to a full employment output.

Notice, however, what happens in the monetary sector. As output, and hence income, begins to rise through the multiplier, the transactions and precautionary demand for money increases, shifting money demand from D_1 to D_2. Assuming that the Bank of England does not alter its monetary stance by changing the money supply, interest rates rise. Rising interest rates will choke off some of the expected aggregate demand increase in the real sector. Therefore AD_1 shifts, not to AD_2 as intended, but only to AD_3, leaving the economy with some unemployment at Y_3.

The government will, as a result, be faced with a choice. It can give a larger fiscal stimulus to the economy and accept higher interest rates, or it can operate an accommodating monetary policy. That is, it can get the central bank to allow the money supply to increase sufficiently so as not to increase interest rates.

see pp. 330–3

In all this one must remember what we said in Chapter 15 concerning inflation. The government cannot in reality find a level of Y corresponding to full employment without inflationary pressures in the system. It must choose some optimal mix of inflation and employment.

18.3 Central bank independence in Keynesian economics

We have covered much ground since we first questioned whether the Bank of England should be free from political control by the government, but that ground needed to be covered. We are now in a position to see why many Keynesian economists would be reluctant to allow central bank independence. Many would accept that central bank independence would overcome the problems mentioned at the beginning of the chapter, namely the manipulation of the economy for electoral advantage and government tendency to use inflation to erode the real value of its debt. However, there are five significant potential disadvantages for macroeconomic policy in an independent central bank.

Non-optimal policy goal

see pp. 330–3

We saw in Chapter 15 the Keynesian conviction that there exists a trade-off between unemployment and inflation. The government may come to the conclusion that a higher level of employment is justifiable even at the cost of some increase in inflation. The rationale of an independent central bank is that it should be charged with creating stable monetary conditions and a stable price level as a backdrop against which the economy functions. A stable price level may entail a higher level of unemployment than government thinks is optimal. Yet the government may find itself unable to do anything about it because it has had removed from it the freedom to 'buy' higher employment with increased inflation.

Non-optimal macro policy mix

The government needs both fiscal and monetary policy for macroeconomic control. It has some freedom with respect to the mixture of those policies. For example, as we have just seen, it can stimulate an economy with monetary means, with fiscal means plus an accommodating monetary policy, or with a fiscal policy accepting that monetary conditions will tighten as it does so. At different times it may feel that a different mix is appropriate. An independent central bank reduces government options. A monetary stance is decided by the central bank and thus has to be taken as given. The government will have no power to order the central bank to alter monetary conditions. Government has only fiscal policy as a weapon and may find itself in a position of being unable to operate what it feels is the best mix of fiscal and monetary policy for the economy.

Constrained fiscal policy

So far one might feel that although an independent central bank will mean that government has no power over monetary policy it will at least retain complete freedom over fiscal policy. This is not so. An independent monetary authority will severely curtail fiscal policy also.

Suppose a government, faced with an independent central bank operating a tight monetary stance, decides to give the economy a fiscal stimulus. Unless it is at present running a surplus on its own expenditure it will need to fund the extra debt that will be incurred. If it borrows more, it must borrow from somewhere. In other words, it will increase its public sector borrowing requirement (PSBR). If it approaches the central bank and asks the bank to fund the debt, it may well be refused. The central bank may well feel that this will increase the money supply and thus be inflationary. If the government borrows extra funds from the private sector it will compete with other institutions for loanable funds and, therefore, raise interest rates, mitigating the effects of the fiscal stimulus.

A government cannot even operate an unconstrained fiscal policy, then, if it has to deal with an independent central bank.

Waste of resources

Since government macroeconomic policy is so severely restrained, the government must spend time attempting to guess how the central bank will react to changes in economic policy. Even if it can guess what policy will be adopted, it will be difficult to predict the timing of changes, so that more economic forecasting will be needed. Producing economic forecasts uses scarce resources.

An undemocratic structure

Some regard central bank independence as essentially undemocratic. Such a bank cannot be independent if it is run by executives who are government elected. If they are not elected by government, citizens unhappy with their performance have no opportunity to do anything about it. At least one can vote for a change of government every five years. Obviously it would be possible to make the central bank accountable in some way, but the more accountable it is, the less its independence is guaranteed.

In Chapter 20 we discuss the question of European monetary union where the money supply for EU countries will be determined by the European Central Bank. The Maastricht Treaty, a key agreement among European governments pushing forward such monetary union, states in Article 107:

> Neither the European Central Bank, nor a national central bank, nor any member of their decision-making bodies shall seek or take instructions from any government or any other body. Community institutions and bodies and governments of the member states undertake not to seek to influence the members of decision-making bodies of the European Central Bank or of their national central banks in the performance of their tasks.

It is this degree of independence of a central bank that seems to some commentators unacceptably undemocratic.

The UK government has tried to meet this objection in a number of ways. The inflation target is set by the government, not the Bank. Without prejudice to this objective the Bank is expected to support the government's economic policy, including its objectives for growth and employment. How this can be achieved if there is a trade-off between objectives to be made is not clear. Publication of the Bank's *Inflation Report* each quarter is a statutory requirement. The report has to explain and justify the Bank's analysis of the economy and to explain how its decisions are expected to meet the inflation target and support government economic policy. Finally, in extreme circumstances, if the national interest demands it, the government can with parliamentary approval instruct the Bank on interest rates for a given time.

These safeguards can only go some way to dealing with the objection concerning democracy. There exists a trade-off between independence and accountability.

18.4 An alternative perspective: monetarism

We have already seen that classical economic thinking departs from Keynesian orthodoxy in several respects. It rejects the Keynesian view that there is such a thing as an unemployment equilibrium. In the classical view, markets will always adjust, given time, to full employment output. We have seen, furthermore, that there is no trade-off between unemployment and inflation. The choice for government is between high and perhaps accelerating inflation or zero inflation. The zero inflation option does not involve a cost in terms of increased unemployment, except perhaps temporarily. On the other hand, government is responsible for inflation, which, in the classical view, is basically a monetary phenomenon. This school of thought is often called monetarism and some monetarists are of the classical school. We shall assume, for simplicity,

see pp. 334–6

that the classical view is identical with monetarism. We have already seen some of the ways in which classical thinking can differ over some issues.

We briefly explain the idea behind monetarism and then proceed to show what a difference such a perspective gives to the question of central bank autonomy.

The equation of exchange: a tautology

The monetarist perspective begins with an uncontroversial statement from which it develops an argument that is very controversial. Let us first examine the statement which we shall derive from a simple example.

Four people are on a desert island. They each produce three units of a commodity per year, each unit being worth £1, not for consumption but for exchanging with others. So there is a total of £12 of output or gross domestic product (GDP) in this economy. We found the total by multiplying the number of transactions, T, in the economy by the average price of the goods entering into exchange. In this case, 12 units of output were produced and each one was worth, on average, £1. So GDP equals PT: 12 × £1 = £12.

On this island money is used to make the exchanges possible, but there are only six £1 coins. Will those be enough to enable all the trade to take place? The answer is yes, provided that each coin is used more than once during the course of the year. In fact each coin will have, on average, to be used twice, since 12 exchanges will take place. In other words, the money stock, M, multiplied by the average velocity of its circulation, V, gives us six £1 coins × 2. MV = £12, which must by definition equal the value of the output. Hence MV = PT.

In general this must hold for any economy. Its money stock multiplied by the average velocity of circulation must be equal to the value of national output. This is one form of what is known as the equation of exchange.

The monetarist argument

Since the above is true by definition we can build an argument from it with respect to monetary control. Consider first the size of GDP. In the long run the level of output is going to grow in real terms as improved technology makes greater output possible. In Britain, for example, GDP growth has averaged around 2.5 per cent per annum over a long period. Assuming that real output, T, grows at that rate and we want the price level, P, to be stable, PT will grow by 2.5 per cent or so per year. In the long run the velocity of circulation, V, will, in the monetarist view, be fairly constant, so provided that M is allowed to increase by around 2.5 per cent per annum, it follows that the price level will stay constant.

All that is required is for government to restrict monetary growth in this way and that will ensure a stable price level. When monetary conditions are tightened, temporary periods of unemployment may develop. After all, if banks can lend less and people borrow less, aggregate demand will fall. Nevertheless, see p. 332 for reasons we explained in Chapter 15, any increase in unemployment will soon disappear. In the end, then, inflation reflects government failure, since it is in the hands of government to eliminate inflation through monetary control.

The Conservative government followed the policy implied in the above argument for much of the 1980s. Its policy was embodied in the medium-term financial strategy (MTFS) where the intention was that over time monetary targets of a tighter and tighter nature would be set to squeeze inflation. Controversy has always raged over the extent of the policy's success.

see p. 337

Does the monetarist believe that there will be no unemployment at all if government behaves in this way – that stable prices can be achieved with no unemployment at all? The answer is no, for as you will recall from Chapter 15, the argument is usually expressed in terms of there being a 'natural rate of unemployment' – one in which some do not have a job because of friction in the system, but one in which there is no *demand-deficient* unemployment.

Monetarism and the aggregate demand curve

see pp. 330–7

We can now look back at the classical view of inflation as explained in Chapter 15. We saw there that if aggregate demand rises, then inflation follows. The effects on output were in effect zero, except possibly in the short run. We can now see what might cause AD to shift. The answer, in the classical view, is that it is always a monetary phenomenon.

see pp. 301–5

Let us suppose that government attempts to shift AD outwards via an increase in government spending without accompanying increases in taxation. In other words, the government increases the PSBR. What happens? There are two main possibilities. One is that it will borrow. Since it has to compete for loanable funds, this will tend to push up interest rates. The result will be reduced investment spending as we saw in Chapter 14. The effect of the PSBR has been to raise interest rates, stunt private sector spending and so leave the volume of aggregate demand unaffected. The AD curve had not shifted.

There is some evidence that higher government budget deficits do indeed increase real interest rates. Figure 18.7 shows that there is a positive correlation between the budget deficit as a proportion of GDP and real interest rates. The correlation is far from perfect. One explanation for this is that governments can borrow not only from their own citizens but also from abroad. An increased PSBR in, say, the UK, would make little impact on the demand for loanable funds in a world market which is very large indeed. Nevertheless the relationship does appear to exist.

However, there is a second possible effect of an increase in the PSBR. In order not to raise interest rates the government can borrow funds from the central bank and use this credit to increase its spending. In other words, it increases the money supply. Then AD *does* shift. The shift is a monetary phenomenon.

Let us illustrate with an example. Suppose a government with a zero PSBR then decides to increase health expenditure by taking on an extra nurse. Where will it find the funds to pay her? The first possibility is to borrow the money by issuing government debt. What happens to the money supply? Probably nothing. The nurse receives her pay cheque which she puts into the banking system. However, somewhere else in the banking system somebody else is taking an equal amount of funds out in order to buy the debt which the government is offering for sale. The government has increased the demand for loanable funds

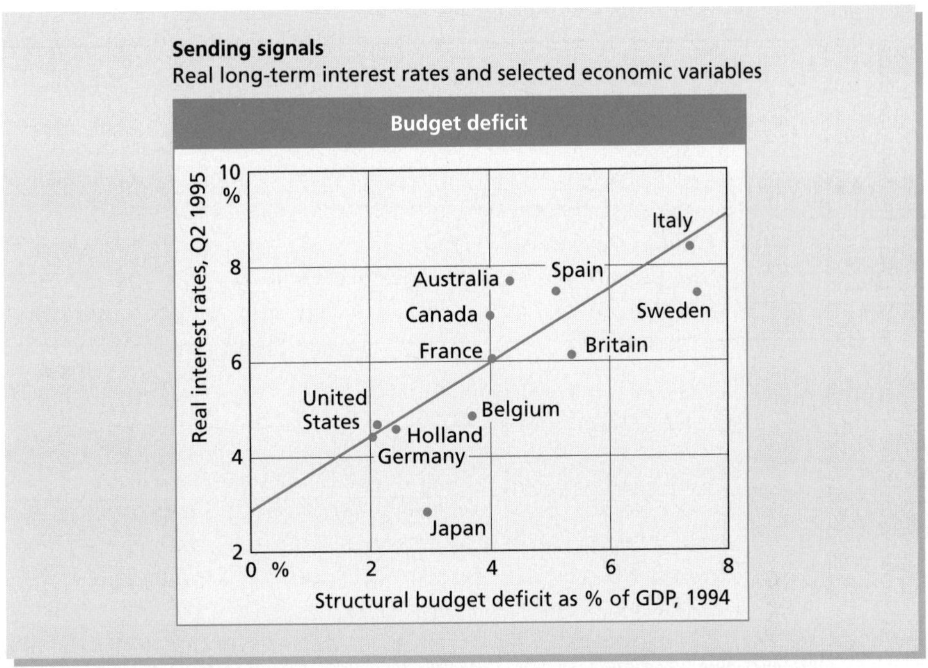

Figure 18.7 Real long-term interest rates and government budget deficits

Source: © *The Economist*, 3 February 1996, based on OECD working paper No. 155

with its potential effect on interest rates but the banking system has no more funds as a result of the increase in government spending.

The second possibility is that government hires the nurse by writing a cheque for her salary, without issuing government debt, instructing the central bank, in effect, to lend it the money. The nurse's cheque appears in the banking system. The bank feels able to make loans against the deposit placed with it, perhaps to enable somebody to buy a car. The effect has been to increase aggregate demand. AD has shifted. This is a monetary phenomenon. Inflationary pressure is the inevitable result.

A monetarist would argue that this second possibility is the fundamental explanation of the UK post-war inflationary boom. It was a legacy of Keynesianism. In an attempt to reduce unemployment, governments ignored the supply side of the economy and concentrated on keeping up a high volume of employment by maintaining high levels of aggregate demand. To do this they financed the demand by running a high PSBR. The PSBR was financed by increases in the money supply. Inflation was the inevitable result.

The velocity of circulation: is it really stable?

The monetarist argument is developed from a tautology. MV = PT is a definition, but the argument developed from it makes some crucial assumptions. That PT is an assumption we have already considered. Another assumption is that increases in M will affect P because V is constant. Is this correct? Is there any evidence to

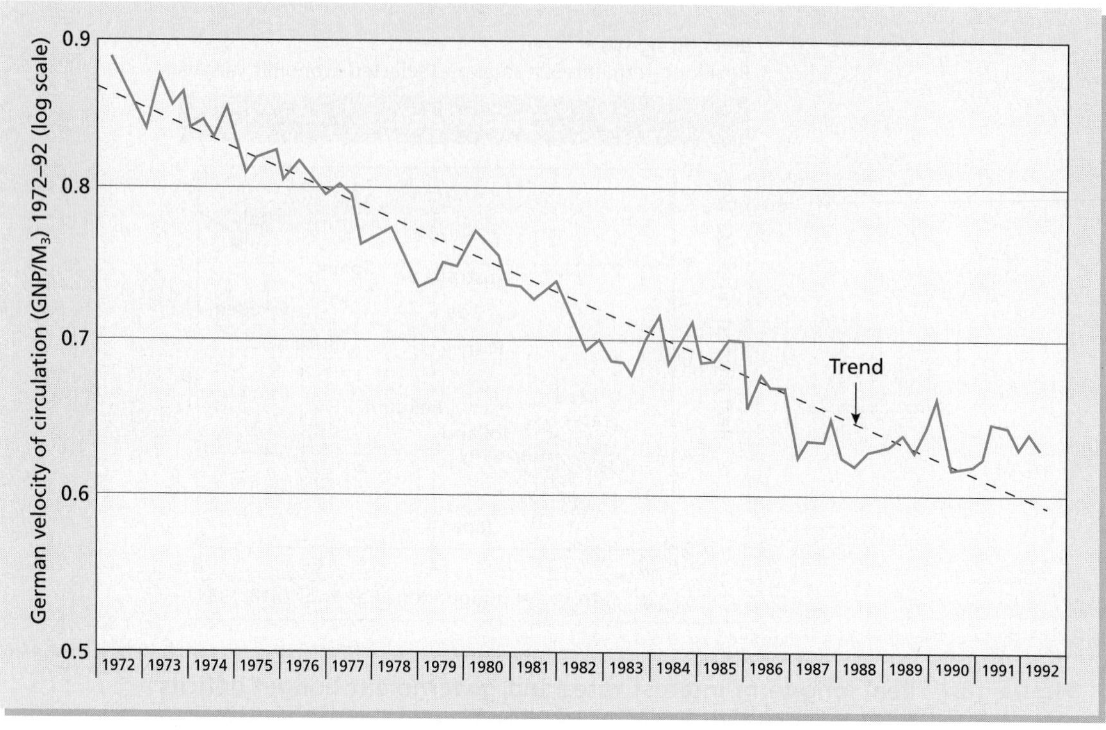

Figure 18.8 German velocity of circulation
Source: J. Scheide, unpublished working paper

suggest that it is so? Perhaps the most impressive empirical support comes from the German economy, where central bank autonomy was regarded as crucial for effective control of the economy until the mark was replaced by the euro.

Figure 18.8 is taken from an unpublished working paper written by Dr Joachim Scheide for the Institut für Weltwirtschaft in Kiel, Germany. It shows the relationship between German GNP and M_3 (a measure of the money supply) over a long time period. Since MV = PT, and since GNP = PT, then $GNP/M_3 = V$, the velocity of circulation.

Notice several points. First, the chosen money supply measure is M_3. In our definitions of the British money supply figures earlier we concentrated on M_0 and M_4. Why, then, is the German data for M_3? What is the difference between M_3 and M_4? Britain used to have a definition of the money supply called M_3 which represented the same measure as the present M_4 with one exception. M_4 includes building society current account deposits which function in the same way as the bank's current account deposits. Since Germany has no such financial bodies, German M_3 is the equivalent of the British M_4 measure.

Next, observe that the trend shows a good fit supporting the monetarist argument, at least for the German economy. For any given period of time the fit may not be very good. For example, there does not appear to be a good fit in the period 1987–92. However, the argument is not that V is stable but that V is stable in the long run. Short-run deviations from the trend are of no consequence.

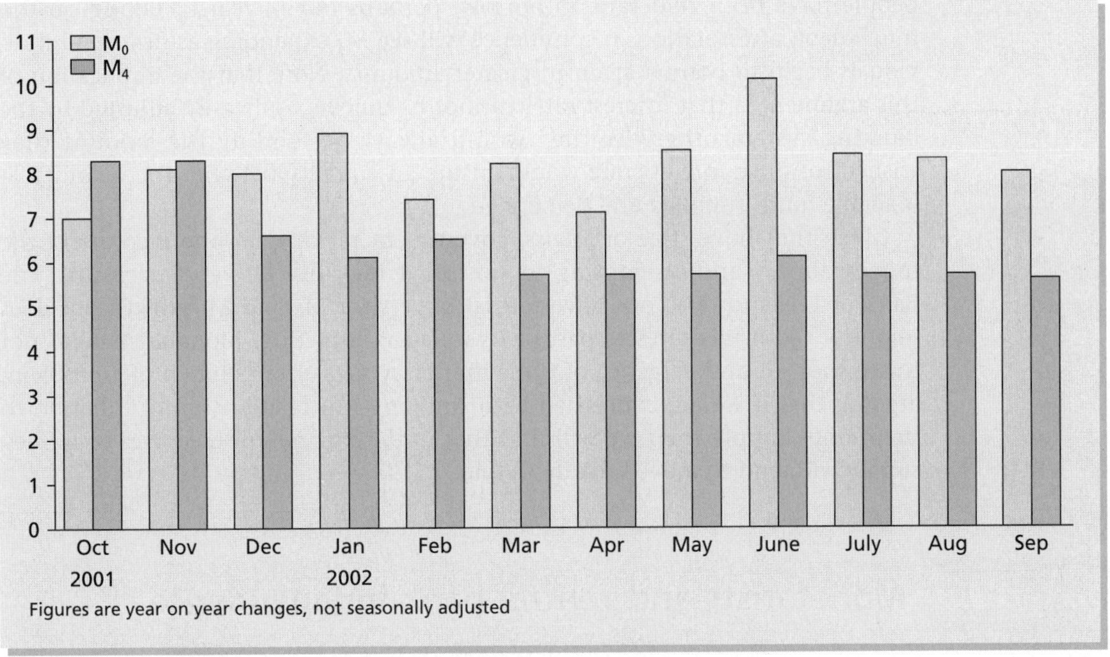

Figure 18.9 Changes in the money supply over twelve months
Source: adapted from Financial statistics, Bank of England

Note, too, that V is not constant. It declines at a rate of about 1 per cent per annum. Does this constitute a problem? The answer is no if it is predictable. The German central bank could control monetary conditions because it could predict reasonably accurately the *trend* in the value of V. You might care to plot the same kind of information for the British economy. Sources such as *Economic Trends* will give you velocity of circulation of both M_0 and M_4 over any time period you choose. If you do this you will see that the relationships appear less stable than for the German economy.

One further problem for monetary control occurs when the size of changes in the money supply varies according to which definition one is using. Consider Figure 18.9 which shows the way in which M_0 and M_4 were changing over a period of one year in the British economy. If the banks' ability to create credit is based ultimately on the amount of cash available to them, why will these two measures of the money supply not always move in parallel? There are various possibilities but two are fairly obvious.

First, if the general public decides to hold more cash, then that cash is not available to the banks, which are therefore unable to make loans against it. In this case M_0 could be rising relatively quickly. However, if the demand for cash were falling and people chose to hold more of their assets in bank accounts rather than as notes and coins in their pockets, M_4 would rise relative to M_0.

Second, even if the amount of notes and coins with the banks were rising, people and firms may not choose to borrow it. In this case M_4 would rise correspondingly slowly compared with M_0. However, if there has been a period when people have been reluctant to borrow, perhaps out of fear of taking on too much debt, a restoration in confidence will see M_4 expanding as firms and individuals begin to borrow again in greater amounts. Note that the implication of this argument is that interest rates cannot be quickly and easily adjusted by the banking system otherwise they would always be lending the amount they wished to, since interest rate would ensure an equality between the quantity of loanable funds supplied and demanded.

Given the above state of affairs, government picking on one measure of the money supply and attempting to control it may not be very successful. The Bank of England does not have formal targets for M_0 and M_4 growth but does 'monitor' both measures as part of its inflation targeting. Monetarists tend not to see short-term divergence of these monetary measures as much of a problem, arguing that if we are concerned with the long-run relationship of inflation to the money supply then we will find that *in the long run* all measures of money supply will tend to move broadly in line.

18.5 Monetarists and central bank independence

It should now be clear that monetarists tend, on the whole, to have some enthusiasm for an independent central bank, and that many of the Keynesian arguments we examined in section 18.3 would be regarded by monetarists as unimpressive. We can express the benefits of a Bank of England free from government interference in three propositions.

Governments do not need discretionary monetary policy

Monetary policy is not a discretionary weapon for ironing out fluctuations in the real sector. Any such fluctuations are best left to the market mechanism. Monetary policy is to be aimed at providing sound money by monetary control. An independent central bank is unlikely to be tempted to manipulate monetary conditions for short-term advantage and can be given unambiguous terms of reference: keep tight control of the money supply and hence inflation.

Fiscal restraint on governments is wholly beneficial

We have seen the Keynesian fears that central bank independence also restricts the degree of fiscal discretion open to governments. To a monetarist, such restrictions are wholly beneficial. Recall what we saw in Chapter 15. In the longer term there can be no unemployment as a result of demand deficiency. There is, therefore, no need for artificial fiscal stimuli to the economy. We saw in Chapter 16 that fiscal policy should be aimed at reducing taxes to improve the supply side of the economy. To make this possible there need to be cuts in public expenditure. The only alternative would be a high PSBR. This would either increase the money supply and be inflationary – a process which an

see pp. 330–6

see pp. 341–64

independent central bank could prevent – or increase interest rates by increasing the demand for loanable funds. This would be a possible route for a government to follow even if it were operating in the context of central bank autonomy, but it would be undesirable in that it would take resources from the private sector and 'crowd out' private sector investment.

From a monetarist perspective, then, reduced room for fiscal discretion would indeed follow from central bank autonomy. However, such an occurrence could only benefit the economy.

Central bank independence reduces economic adjustment costs

Suppose an economy is suffering from inflation and government wishes to reduce it. Monetarists, of course, believe that the appropriate way to do so is by reducing the money supply. Given what we saw in Chapter 15 about expectations on the part of economic agents, there may well be some short-term costs in increased unemployment. This will only be temporary. When economic agents, firms, trade unions and so on realise that the price level is coming down, they will adjust their actions accordingly. Crucial to this procedure is the belief by such agents that if unemployment develops, the government will not lose its nerve and relax monetary policy. It is essential that there is a conviction that this will not happen if the transition costs of increased unemployment are to be temporary.

see pp. 334–6

This is where central bank independence can be so valuable. Economic agents may find it difficult to believe in the determination of governments, particularly near to a general election. They are far more likely to believe in the policy of an independent central bank that does not have the political pressures to bear.

Economic adjustment to lower inflation will thus be faster and less painful, especially in terms of unemployment and lost output.

18.6 How independent is independent?

So far we have assumed that a central bank is either entirely under the government's control or entirely independent. There are, however, degrees of independence. So how independent is independent? One attempt to quantify it is that by Alesina and Grilli (1991, see Table 18.2). They suggest that there are degrees of economic independence in areas such as the determination of interest rates and control over the banking system, and political independence in areas such as the appointment of governors. Tables 18.2(a) and (b) give their attempts to measure the different degrees of independence enjoyed by different European central banks. Note that this study was conducted prior to reforms in the UK.

There are two obvious criticisms that can be made of their classification. The first is that one has to assume that each of the chosen measures is equally important in arriving at a summary measure, whereas in practice this may not

Table 18.2(a) Measures of political independence

Central bank	*1*	*2*	*3*	*4*	*5*	*6*	*7*	*8*	*9*
European Central Bank		*		*	*	*	*	*	6
Germany		*		*	*	*	*	*	6
Netherlands		*		*	*	*	*	*	6
Italy	*	*	*		*				4
Denmark		*					*	*	3
Ireland		*				*		*	3
France		*		*					2
Greece			*					*	2
Spain				*	*				2
Belgium				*					1
Portugal					*				1
UK					*				1

1 Governor not appointed by government
2 Governor appointed for 5+ years
3 Executive not appointed by government
4 Executive appointed for 5+ years
5 No mandatory government representative on executive
6 No government approval of policy decision required
7 Statutory requirement for central bank to pursue price stability
8 Explicit conflicts between central bank and government possible
9 Index of political independence (sum of asterisks in each row)

Table 18.2(b) Measures of economic independence

Central bank	*1*	*2*	*3*	*4*	*5*	*6*	*7*	*8*	*9*
European Central Bank	*	*	*	*	*	*	*	*	8
Germany	*	*	*	*	*	*	*	*	8
Belgium		*	*	*	*	*		*	6
UK	*	*	*	*		*	*		6
Denmark		*			*	*	*		4
France				*	*	*	*		4
Ireland		*	*	*		*			4
Netherlands				*	*	*	*		4
Spain				*	*			*	3
Greece				*		*			2
Portugal				*		*			2
Italy				*					1

1 Government credit from central bank not automatic
2 Government credit from central bank at market interest rate
3 Government credit from central bank for temporary period only
4 Government credit from central bank limited in amount
5 Central bank does not take up unsold government bond issues
6 Discount rate set by central bank
7 No government qualitative controls on commercial bank lending since 1980
8 No government quantitative controls on bank lending since 1980
9 Index of economic independence (sum of asterisks in each row)

Source: A. Alesina and V. U. Grilli (1991) *The European Central Bank: Reshaping Monetary Politics in Europe*, discussion paper no. 563, Centre for Economic Policy Research

be so. The other is that there may be informal links and pressures which formal measures fail to pick up. For example, the German Bundesbank was clearly regarded generally, and in terms of Tables 18.2(a) and (b), as essentially independent. Indeed, Article 3 of the Bundesbankgesetz, or bank statutes, said that the bank was, in the execution of its tasks, independent of orders from the central government. Yet the statutes also said that the Bundesbank must support the general economic policy of the federal government. So when East Germany was incorporated into West Germany the Bonn government allowed an exchange rate of one Ostmark for one Deutschmark for East German citizens. The Bundesbank certainly had no enthusiasm for such a move but was obliged to accept it despite the fact that there were clear monetary implications that it did not like.

Despite the weaknesses of such a system of measurement, the classification in Tables 18.2(a) and (b) does enable us to test whether central bank independence is likely to help macroeconomic policy in the realm of inflation, unemployment and growth. It is to that question that we now turn.

18.7 Central bank independence, prices and growth: some evidence

Using the ideas of independence measurement above, Alesina and Grilli sought to see whether such independence was successful in producing price stability and growth in the major industrialised countries. Figure 18.10 summarises their findings. There is clear evidence of a correlation between central bank autonomy and inflation.

Furthermore, since it is sometimes said that business prefers a stable environment in which to operate, it could be argued that low variability in inflation rates is desirable. Central bank autonomy would appear to give that also. Monetarists would obviously find such evidence encouraging.

What the evidence also shows equally clearly is that autonomy has not led to a high growth rate of output. There appears to be no relationship between central bank independence and high growth rates. This evidence, then, gives no support to the monetarist argument that low inflation can be achieved at no long-run cost in terms of output or unemployment.

The Keynesians might argue that even the evidence regarding price stability does not undermine their position. One might argue that there is a trade-off between inflation and unemployment. Some societies, however, value price stability very highly. One might think of Germany, many of whose senior figures fear a repeat of the appalling hyperinflation of the interwar years. Such societies are willing to see central bank autonomy to produce price stability, even at some cost in terms of growth or unemployment. Other societies, such as Britain, are more tolerant of inflation. To impose central bank autonomy and low inflation on such a society at the cost of higher unemployment would be quite unacceptable. Alas, then, the empirical evidence continues to be inconclusive.

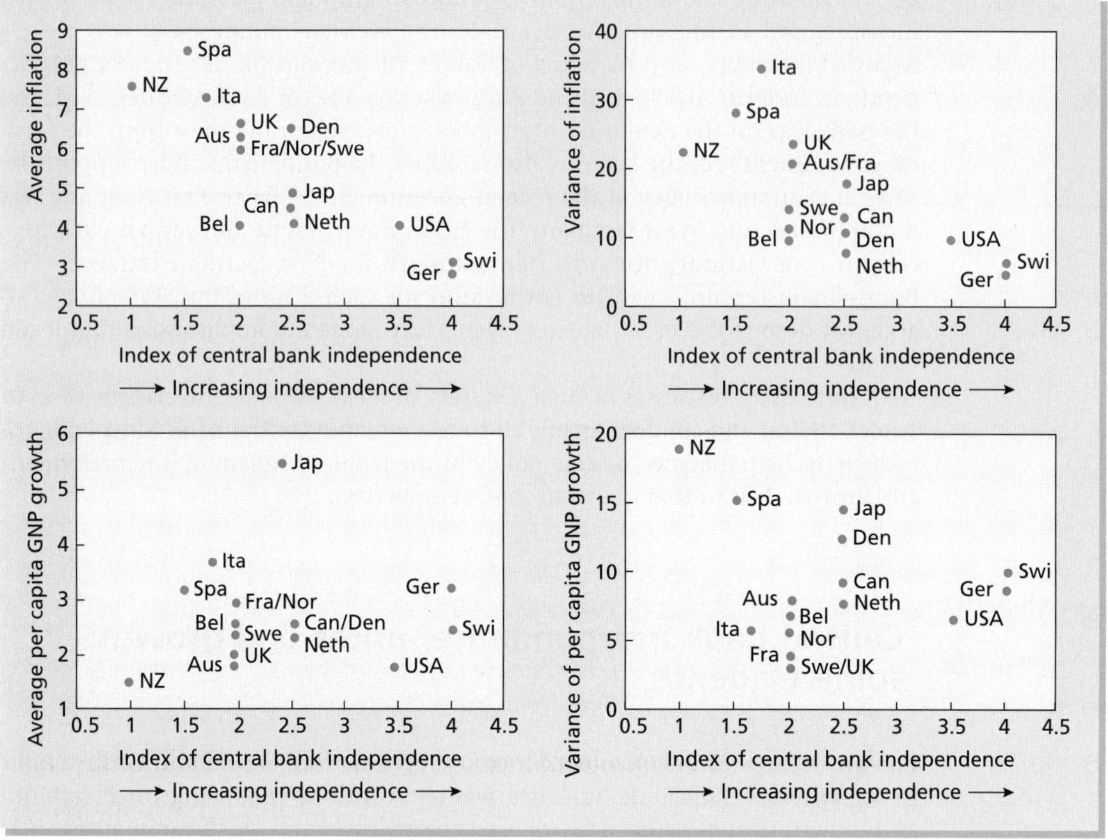

Figure 18.10 **Central bank independence, inflation and growth**

Source: A. Alesina and L. H. Summers (1993) 'Central Bank Independence and Macroeconomic Performance: Some Comparative Evidence', *Journal of Money, Credit and Banking*, Vol. 25, No. 2

18.8 UK Central Bank independence: the early years

How has the independence of the UK Central Bank (the Bank of England) worked in its first few years? We begin to assess the question by considering the inflation target which the government has set.

The inflation target

The current inflation target of the Bank is 2.5 per cent for RPIX and is expected to remain so for some time. If inflation strays by more than 1 per cent either side of the target the MPC chairman must write an open letter to the Chancellor explaining why inflation is adrift, how long the divergence is expected to last and the action taken to bring it back on course.

Clearly whatever action the Bank takes there is a delay before the policy takes effect. This is thought to be about two years before all effects have been worked

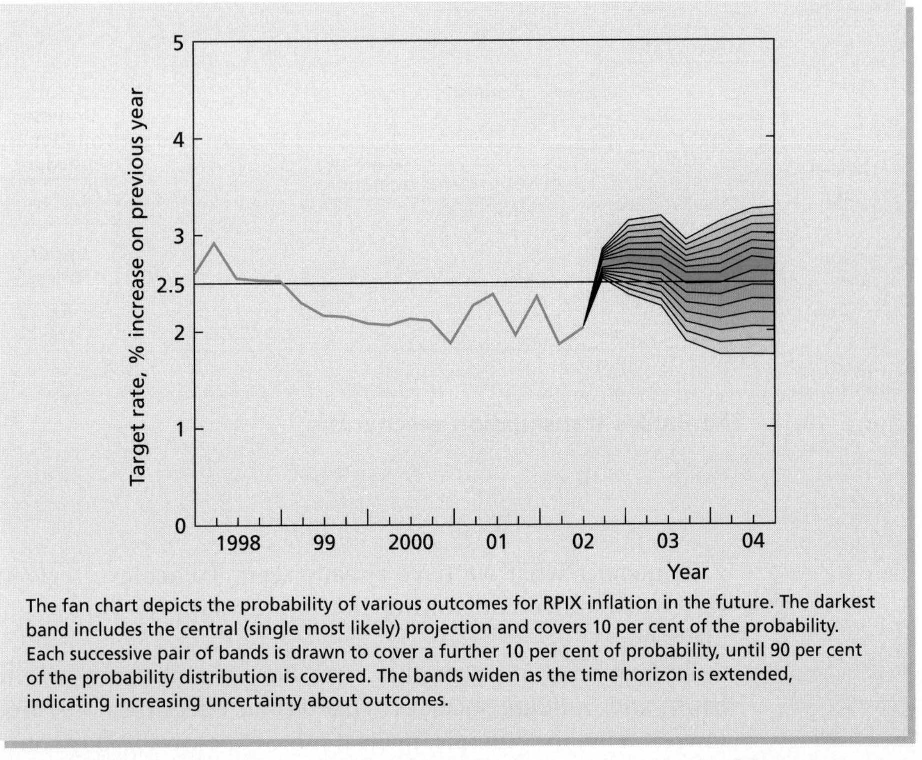

Figure 18.11 **Current RPIX inflation projection based on constant nominal interest rates at 4 per cent**

Source: Bank of England, *Inflation Report*, November 2002

through. The Bank therefore makes forecasts looking to two years ahead. Since there is always a measure of uncertainty about such forecasts a range of outcomes is predicted. Figure 18.11 shows a forecast made during 2002. According to its best estimates the central (most likely) projection was that inflation would move slightly above target for much of the forecast period. The Bank's view of inflation prospects gives a strong idea of the direction of its policy, given its commitment to the inflation target. For example, the projection of Figure 18.11 assumes a constant 4 per cent interest rate. One might therefore expect, unless circumstances change, that interest rates would increase slightly over the period.

The Bank's view of the transmission mechanism

If the Bank is to meet the inflation target it must have a view as to what causes inflation so that it can take the appropriate action. Most members seem to believe that there is no long-run trade-off between inflation and unemployment, so that by keeping inflation to around $2\frac{1}{2}$ per cent it will not jeopardise unemployment. Thus to control inflation requires targeting inflation itself. Figure 18.12 shows the main links between interest rates and inflation.

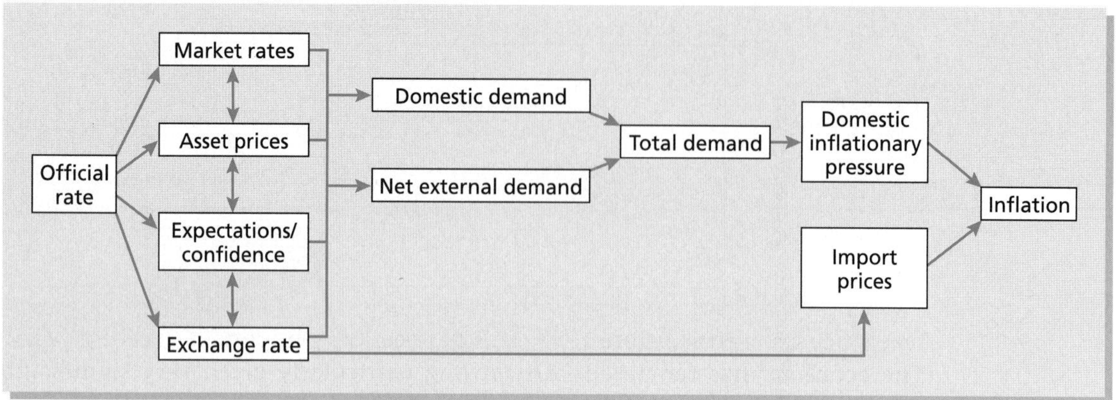

Figure 18.12 **The Bank's transmission mechanism**

Remember what we have already seen. To achieve a given official interest rate will require controlling the money supply. This is not shown on the diagram.

Interest rates affect market rates, for example rates of interest charged by banks and building societies. This has an effect on domestic demand. Higher interest rates, for example, make it more expensive to buy consumer durables on credit, thus reducing demand for these goods. They may also encourage more saving and thus less consumption. Interest rates also affect asset prices such as housing and share prices as we saw in Chapter 2. If higher interest rates produce lower house and share prices, people will feel less wealthy. This will reduce domestic consumption demand. Official rates can also affect confidence in the economy. As we saw in Chapter 11, people's spending patterns are affected by what they believe to be the economic outlook.

As we shall see in Chapter 20, official rates can also affect the external value of sterling. When interest rates rise the value of sterling also tends to rise. This makes our imports cheaper. This may encourage us to buy more imports, reducing domestic demand. Changes in aggregate demand change the degree of inflationary pressure in the economy. If interest rates change the external value of sterling they affect import prices. This affects the costs of firms who rely on imports for raw materials etc. If their costs change, this can feed through into changes in the price level.

The *extent* to which changes in interest rates affect inflation through all these links is not easy to assess. Hence when members of the MPC vote on interest rate changes, it is rarely unanimous. However, these are the major links between interest rates and inflation as seen by the Bank. Remember that it has no direct control over fiscal policy, which remains the responsibility of the Chancellor. However, it has some indirect control. For example, if it believes that the Chancellor is operating too slack a fiscal policy – perhaps by having tax levels too low – and this is creating inflationary pressure, the Bank can offset some of these effects via increases in interest rates.

Assessing MPC performance

Most commentators have applauded the decision to make the Central Bank independent. Most also believe the MPC to have done a good job. Inflation has been consistently close to the target and unemployment has been low compared with its level in the previous 20 years. The MPC has established itself as a body with credibility. Expectations are that the UK will continue as a low-inflation economy. This means that inflation will be lower without the need for higher unemployment to contain it.

There is evidence too that reactions to changes in demand conditions now take place faster than before 1997. This has been very important in recent years. The economy has remained fairly strong particularly given very significant weaknesses in Europe. When EU output and income is low, UK exports to Europe are affected, reducing aggregate demand in the UK and threatening to depress output and increase unemployment. Lowering interest rates quickly has helped to stabilise output levels. All this is not to say that there are no problems. But the problems look more manageable with an independent central bank.

18.9 Conclusion

We began by arguing that views of central bank independence cannot be detached from views about other economic issues. In particular they will be influenced by attitudes towards the suitability of government macroeconomic intervention in the economy and about the trade-off between inflation and unemployment. If one sees macroeconomic intervention as justified and a long-run unemployment/inflation trade-off existing, then central bank independence reduces the scope of government macroeconomic room for manoeuvre and harms economic welfare.

On the other hand, some take the view that macroeconomic intervention, except for control of the money supply, is unnecessary. Markets will bring full employment in the long run. Macroeconomic policy should be aimed at price stability. From that perspective there is much to commend central bank autonomy.

Partly because of the problems of monetarism described in this chapter, the present government does not attempt inflation control solely via the money supply. Instead strategy is determined with reference to expected inflation. This means examining a range of factors such as materials prices, wage pressures, etc. However, a crucial determinant of the inflation forecast is still found in the money supply data.

Our analysis has assumed a closed economy, that is, that there are no significant factors to take into account with respect to the international economy, especially the external value of the currency. Therefore we shall return to the see pp. 434–62 subject of central bank autonomy in Chapter 20 when we have examined the monetary implications of international trade.

CHAPTER SUMMARY

1 **Fiscal policy relates to government taxation and spending; monetary policy to money supply and interest rates.**
2 **Money can be variously defined depending upon the degree of liquidity of an asset.**
3 **Keynesians explain interest rate determination through liquidity preference theory.**
4 **Keynesians believe that monetary policy affects the real sector through interest rates.**
5 **An independent central bank reduces government freedom over macro policy.**
6 **Monetarists believe that inflation is a monetary phenomenon; therefore governments can control inflation via monetary policy.**
7 **The UK operates with a largely independent Central Bank.**

Questions for discussion

Guidance to the answers for the ***asterisked*** *numbered questions is available to students on the website for the book at* **www.booksites.net/heather**.

1* In Erehwon the national output is 100 million pounds. The velocity of circulation is 2. What is the size of the money supply? When the money supply increases by 5 per cent, what will happen to the price level?

2 If a central bank reduces the money supply through selling government debt, does it matter: (a) who purchases the debt? (b) what kind of debt it sells? (c) what it does with income received from its sale?

3* If the money supply is fixed, what would monetarists expect to happen to the price level over time?

4 Given what we saw in Chapter 14 with respect to the influence of interest rates on investment, how much reliance would you place on monetary conditions for influencing the volume of investment?

5* Suppose an economy has a money market as described in Figure 18.5 and therefore an equilibrium interest rate of r_1. In terms of the diagram what would the following be most likely to bring about and therefore what would happen to interest rates? (a) a fall in national income, (b) a decision by the banking sector to reduce the volume of loans made, (c) a rise in the price level, (d) a reduction in government debt.

6 Attempts have been made to resolve empirically the argument that controlling the money supply leads to a stable price level. These have not always been conclusive. Why do you think that is so?

7* In a particular economy all the banks maintain 10 per cent of deposits as cash. One of the banks receives a new deposit of £200. If net withdrawals from the banking system are zero, what will the final increase in deposits be? Now rework your answer, assuming that 20 per cent of deposits are retained as cash. Work out a general formula showing the relationship of cash to deposits.

8 How convincing do you find the attempts to measure the extent of independence central banks have from governments?

9* How, according to Keynesian economists, might an increase in the money supply lead to an increase in GDP? Will this be a real or money increase?

10 Do you think that an independent central bank for Britain is beneficial for the British economy?

Websites

The best website for UK monetary and financial information is the Bank of England's. It is at:

www.bankofengland.co.uk/

Not only does it contain useful statistics but also reports and the text of speeches made in the recent past.

Note

1 The Bundesbank's role in setting interest rates is no more. A European central bank sets interest rates for the whole euro area, including Germany. This will be explained further in Chapter 20.

Part IV

THE INTERNATIONAL ECONOMY

20 **Exchange rates**

19 **Comparative advantage and the balance of payments**

Part III
MACROECONOMICS

Part II
MICROECONOMICS

Part I
INTRODUCTORY CONCEPTS

An understanding of microeconomics and macroeconomics lays the foundation for considering the international economy.

19 Comparative advantage and the balance of payments

Manufacturing trade: *not made in Britain?*

(with Dr Michael Asteris)

CHAPTER OVERVIEW

British homes tend to be full of foreign-produced goods – Japanese television sets, German toasters, Italian washing machines. Many politicians and industrialists believe that Britain's manufacturing sector is in decline and that the country's balance of payments difficulties are a reflection of continued government failure to deal with this problem. The link between manufacturing and the balance of payments is the issue we now consider.

In this chapter we review:

- Opportunity cost
- Efficiency

We introduce:

- Balance of payments
- Law of comparative advantage

19.1 Introduction

Once Britain was known as the workshop of the world because it dominated world trade in industrial goods. However, its share of world manufacturing trade has declined markedly during the past 50 years, while imported manufactured goods have claimed a growing share of the home market. Indeed, since 1983 Britain has been importing annually more manufactured goods than it has been exporting. This imbalance has fuelled fears of British deindustrialisation – the sharp decline in the significance of manufacturing as a proportion of total production.

In this chapter we examine the reasons for the deficit in the UK's manufacturing trade balance and consider its importance. In order to place the issue in context, we begin by looking at the structure of the balance of payments. This will be followed by a review of trends in the manufacturing trade balance and an examination of the law of comparative advantage which determines the quantity of goods exported from and imported into the UK. Thereafter, the focus will be on the extent to which the deterioration in manufacturing trade is a cause for alarm. We will see that much depends on how trends in the balance of payments over the longer term are interpreted and, as with other questions we have examined, how much confidence there is in the power of markets to allocate scarce resources optimally.

19.2 The balance of payments

Basic concepts

The object of the balance of payments accounts is to provide a systematic record, during a specific period of time, of all transactions between residents of the recording country and residents of other nations.

The accounts are analogous to a double-entry bookkeeping system in that every balance of payments transaction involves equal credit and debit items. However, instead of arranging in credit and debit columns which add to the same total, balance of payments entries are listed in the same column but given different signs so that the accounts sum to zero. Hence, in a bookkeeping sense the balance of payments must always balance. In an economic sense, however, balance of payments problems do arise, and the degree to which *individual components* of the accounts are in surplus or deficit can give cause for concern.

Structure of the UK accounts

Table 19.1 presents a summary of the UK balance of payments for the period 1983–2001. It consists of two main sections: the current account and the capital account.

The first part of the current account records all transactions involving current goods and services. Exporting goods or services results in receipts of money from abroad. The receipts are thus regarded as *credit* items and are recorded with a plus sign. Imports, on the other hand, cause outflows of money when the goods or services are paid for. They are therefore viewed as *debit* items and are given a minus sign.

The balance in the trade in goods measures the difference between the value of those goods which are exported and those which are imported. Foodstuffs, raw materials and manufactured goods are included under this heading. It is clear from Table 19.1 that this balance (which was in surplus in the early 1980s) was in deficit in each of the years 1983–2001. Of itself, this run of deficits is of limited significance: the UK has rarely recorded a surplus on the trade in goods since the early nineteenth century. What matters is the *size* of the deficits.

The heading 'trade in services' includes transactions relating to such items as shipping, civil aviation, insurance and banking. The balance is the value of exported services less the value of imported services. The sum of the trade balance and the services balance gives 'trade in goods and services'.

Table 19.1 **UK balance of payments account (£m)**

	1983	*1986*	*1989*	*1992*	*1995*	*1998*	*2001*
Current account (balances)							
Trade in goods	−1,618	−9,617	−24,724	−13,050	−12,023	−21,813	−33,534
Trade in services	3,941	6,505	3,917	5,674	8,481	12,666	11,073
Trade in goods and services	2,323	−3,112	−20,807	−7,376	−3,542	−9,147	−22,461
Investment income	1,205	3,028	74	2,164	2,397	12,568	8,982
Employee compensation	−89	−156	−138	−49	−296	−10	180
Transfers balance	−140	−2,045	−2,620	−4,821	−7,574	−8,225	−7,154
Current balance	3,299	−2,285	−23,491	−10,082	−9,015	−4,184	−20,453
Capital and financial balance	−3,993	−2,206	19,294	6,137	533	473	20,790
Balancing item	694	4,491	4,197	3,945	4,964	4,096	−337

Source: ONS, *United Kingdom Balance of Payments*, 'Pink Book', various editions, © Crown copyright

The heading 'investment income' embraces earnings from overseas branches of domestic companies and income to UK holders of foreign financial assets such as bonds and shares. Of course, there are outflows of such earnings from the UK to foreign asset holders. 'Employee compensation' relates to payment to labour working overseas. What is recorded in Table 19.1 is the balance of all such flows. 'Transfers balance' covers a range of currency flows across the exchanges including government aid and contributions to the EU.

In contrast to the trade in goods, the trade in services and investment income has been in substantial surplus for most of the period since the end of the Napoleonic wars. The transfers balance is always negative. Hence, the size of the current account surplus or deficit is decided by the extent to which the services balance and investment income exceeds or is exceeded by the deficit on the trade in goods plus the transfers deficit.

Turning to the other major section of the balance of payments, the capital and financial balance, this records transactions in UK assets and liabilities. Included under this heading are overseas transactions by banks in the UK and changes in the UK's official reserves. It also includes the purchase and sale of assets in other countries. It may be direct, such as if BP builds an oil rig in Alaska or when a Japanese car company like Toyota builds a car plant in Derbyshire. Alternatively, it might be indirect, for example the purchase by a UK resident of shares in a German engineering company.

In theory, the overall balance of payments – the combined current and capital account – should sum to zero. In practice, since the methods of estimating transactions are neither complete nor precise, there is a need to include a balancing item to reflect the sum of all errors and omissions and thus bring the total of all entries to zero. You can see that this balancing item can be enormous. Often, however, subsequent revisions are made and this will reduce the size of the errors and omissions for earlier years.

Combining the current and capital accounts serves to emphasise that, for a while at least, a country need not worry too much if it has a current account deficit provided that it is able to finance the shortfall by means of capital inflows. A simple analogy may help to explain. Suppose you are a student with a current account at the bank. The bank manager is concerned that you are overdrawn in that your expenditure during the term has been greater than the amount of money in your account makes possible. Although you have spent more than was available in the account in the last term, you might reasonably respond that it should be of little concern to him. After all, (a) he is being paid interest on the overdrawn account and (b) you have a large savings account which can easily fund the deficit on the current account.

The bank manager may accept your explanation, but he is less likely to be so content if he can see that the rate at which you are spending in excess of your income is unsustainable given the limited size of your capital account.

It can be argued that the same is true of a country. The current account deficit is a potential problem if it is large in proportion to overseas assets or if the long-term trend is one which is unsustainable.

Trends in the visible trade balance

Following our examination of the UK's overall balance of payments structure, let us now take a closer look at the visible account items with specific reference to trends in the manufacturing trade balance.

Table 19.2, which provides a commodity analysis of UK visible trade for the years 1991–2001, helps to illuminate the item 'trade in goods' in Table 19.1. The constant deficits for food, beverages and tobacco and basic materials should not occasion any surprise; the UK has long had deficits in these items. In contrast, the credit entry for oil is a relatively recent development. Until North Sea oil came on stream in substantial quantities during the late 1970s, the UK was a major net importer of the fuel. In the space of a few years, however, the UK emerged as a major oil producer. Imports of oil declined and the UK became one of the world's largest exporters of high quality light crude. In 1976 there was a £4.3 billion trade deficit in oil. By 1980 the deficit had been eliminated and in 1985 the UK enjoyed an oil surplus of more than £8 billion.

Figure 19.1 concentrates on these two critical decades, since it was during this time that the UK moved from being a substantial net exporter to a position of being a substantial net importer of manufactured goods. Notice that the balance of payments data of Tables 19.1 and 19.2 are at current prices; Figure 19.1, by contrast, shows the effects of netting out inflation. The picture which then emerges is of an even more dramatic reversal in the fortunes of the manufacturing sector. It is this change from surplus to deficit in the trade balance of both semi-manufactures (such as chemicals and textiles) and finished manufactures, detailed in Table 19.2, which is arguably the most dramatic transformation in the external accounts. The stark nature of the change is highlighted in Figure 19.1, which shows the UK balance of trade in manufactured goods for the period 1970–89 at constant (1985) prices and current prices. In 1970 the surplus on this trade constituted 30 per cent of the average value of exports and imports; as recently as 1980 the proportion was 12 per cent. In 1983, however, the UK had a peacetime deficit in manufactures for the first time since the Industrial Revolution and the shortfall has persisted to varying degrees ever since.

Table 19.2 **Trade on a balance of payments basis: commodity analysis (£m)**

	1991	*1996*	*2001*
Exports			
Food, beverages and tobacco	7,654	11,328	9,754
Basic materials	2,008	2,790	2,622
Oil			
Crude oil	4,370	7,508	10,591
Oil products	2,914	3,420	4,335
Total oil	7,284	10,928	14,926
Coal, gas and electricity	353	650	1,551
Semi-manufactured goods			
Chemicals	13,700	22,166	28,123
Precious stones and silver	2,057	3,609	4,706
Other	13,438	19,533	18,173
Total semi-manufactured goods	29,195	45,308	51,002
Finished manufactured goods			
Motor cars	3,984	8,450	8,261
Other consumer goods	9,183	15,391	14,578
Intermediate goods	20,738	34,320	42,804
Capital goods	16,108	30,542	38,133
Ships and aircraft	5,596	5,536	6,974
Total finished manufactured goods	55,609	94,239	110,750
Commodities and transactions not classified according to kind	1,836	1,953	1,039
Total	103,939	167,196	191,644
Imports			
Food, beverages and tobacco	11,609	17,422	18,785
Basic materials	4,588	6,545	6,461
Oil			
Crude oil	3,763	3,810	4,877
Oil products	2,247	2,308	4,657
Total oil	6,010	6,118	9,534
Coal, gas and electricity	1,613	1,166	1,272
Semi-manufactured goods			
Chemicals	10,599	18,095	23,043
Precious stones and silver	2,070	3,630	5,259
Other	17,722	25,070	25,256
Total semi-manufactured goods	30,391	46,795	53,558
Finished manufactured goods			
Motor cars	5,273	10,978	16,693
Other consumer goods	14,191	20,662	30,340
Intermediate goods	20,742	38,077	43,222
Capital goods	14,324	27,434	35,095
Ships and aircraft	3,505	3,956	8,933
Total finished manufactured goods	58,035	101,107	134,283
Commodities and transactions not classified according to kind	1,916	1,765	1,285
Total	114,162	180,918	225,178

Source: ONS, *United Kingdom Balance of Payments*, 'Pink Book', 2002, © Crown copyright

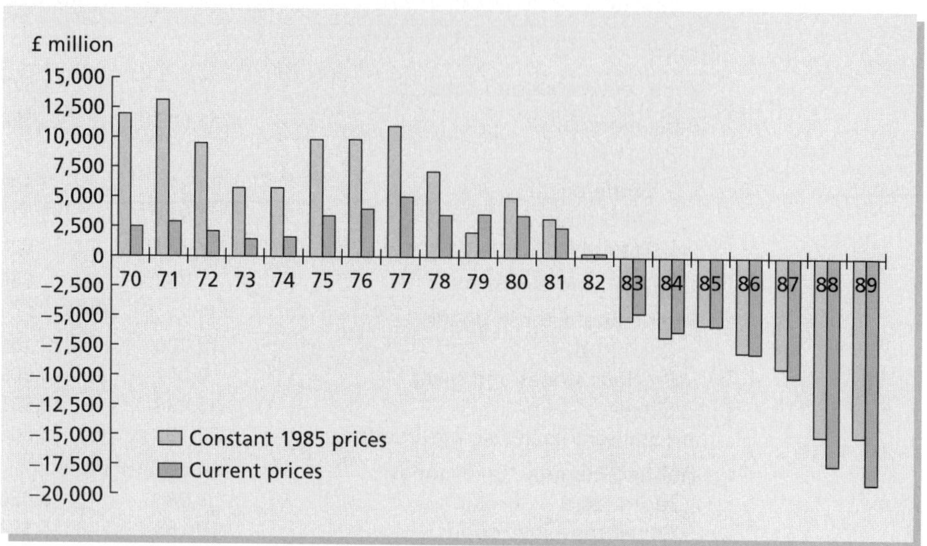

Figure 19.1 **UK balance of trade in manufactured goods, 1970–89**
Source: adapted from ONS, *United Kingdom Balance of Payments*, various editions, 'Pink Book'

Trends in manufacturing output

To a considerable extent the balance of payments statistics that we have examined reflect what has been happening to the performance of the British manufacturing sector. We now consider the main trends in manufacturing industry with particular reference to the period since 1979.

As you can see from Figure 19.2 manufacturing output at constant prices has increased somewhat over the past 20 years, although relatively little since 1991.

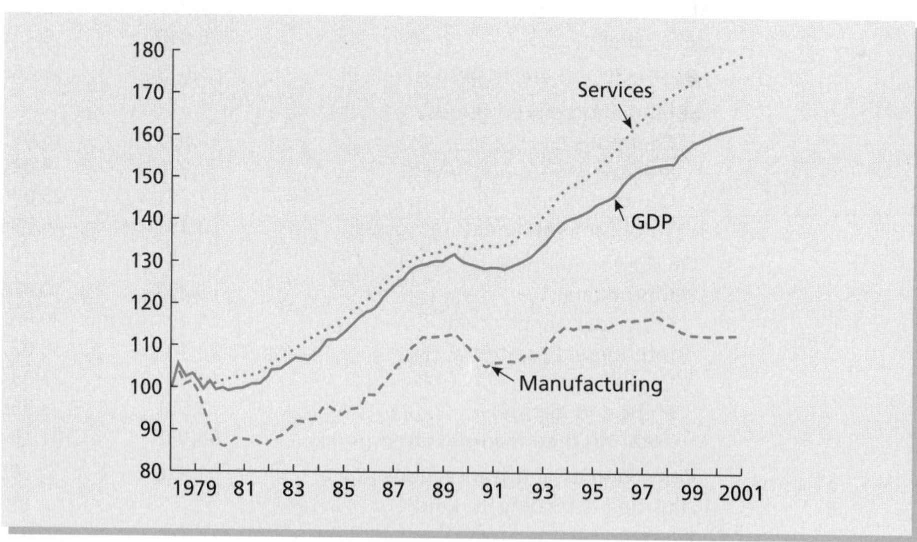

Figure 19.2 **Trends in UK GDP, manufacturing and services**
Source: adapted from NSO data

The recession of the early 1980s caused output to drop substantially. Although it rose quickly during much of the 1980s, the recession of the early 1990s left real output little higher at the turn of the century than in 1989. Furthermore, output has declined sharply as a proportion of GDP manufacturing since the tertiary, or services, sector of the economy has grown quite rapidly.

Figures for individual sectors of the economy as the new century unfolded are given in Table 19.3. Notice that apart from computers and office equipment the high growth areas are *not* in manufacturing.

Table 19.3 UK output growth by industry sector, percentage change on year earlier[a]

	1998	*1999*[b]	*2000*[b]	*2001*[b]	*1999–2001 average*
Computers and office equipment	22.3	7.8	11.7	7.7	9.1
Post and telecoms	8.2	6.5	6.3	7.5	6.8
Financial services	5.6	3.5	4.5	6.2	4.7
Business services	7.9	2.0	4.8	6.4	4.4
Transport services	4.8	2.7	3.6	5.6	4.0
Precision and optical instruments	−3.6	−0.7	5.2	2.4	2.3
Average (GDP growth)	*2.1*	*0.8*	*2.2*	*3.4*	*2.1*
Electricity, gas and water supply	2.1	2.1	1.5	2.2	1.9
Wood and wood products	0.1	−0.9	4.1	2.2	1.8
Solid and nuclear fuels, oil refining	−5.2	−2.3	2.7	4.9	1.8
Hotels and catering	−0.3	−0.2	1.8	3.6	1.7
Distribution and repair	2.4	0.4	1.6	3.1	1.7
Construction	1.6	0.9	2.2	2.0	1.7
Other transport equipment	2.9	1.8	0.9	1.9	1.5
Other electrical engineering	3.5	1.3	1.2	2.1	1.5
Basic metals	−3.7	−0.9	2.4	2.7	1.4
Chemicals	1.6	−0.2	0.7	2.9	1.1
Welfare and recreational services	1.2	0.6	1.0	1.0	0.9
Pulp, paper, printing and publishing	−0.2	−2.0	1.2	3.4	0.9
Mechanical engineering	−0.1	−1.7	1.6	1.5	0.5
Food, drink and tobacco	−1.3	−0.9	−0.2	1.8	0.2
Rubber and plastic products	2.5	−1.6	−0.7	2.5	0.1
Metal products	−1.8	−4.2	1.6	2.4	−0.1
Non-metallic minerals	−2.1	−5.1	−0.6	2.7	−1.0
Agriculture, forestry and fishing	−0.4	−1.5	−0.9	−0.7	−1.0
Textiles and clothing	−8.4	−4.4	1.7	−0.6	−1.1
Motor vehicles and parts	3.7	−10.3	−2.1	6.5	−2.0
Mining and quarrying, incl. oil and gas	2.1	−3.3	−3.7	0.4	−2.2

[a] Ranked by 1999–2001 average
[b] Forecast

Source: Lloyds TSB, *Economic Bulletin*, April 1999

The above should not, however, lead you to imagine that manufacturing output *per worker* has followed a similar pattern. What has in fact happened is that labour productivity, output per person employed, has increased very sharply. Hence manufacturing output is now being produced with considerably fewer people. Over 7 million people worked in the manufacturing sector at the beginning of 1979. By 2002 the number had fallen to well under 4 million, yet aggregate output had risen.

Even so, since we are interested in examining British international trade performance, the above data need to be set in context by asking how the UK's experience compares with that of other countries. The decline in the proportion of output taken by manufacturing is common to most advanced economies, although the extent of the decline is greater in the UK. Productivity too has increased in most countries. To give some idea of the UK's *comparative* performance, manufacturing output has grown over the period in the UK but to a lesser extent than in other major EU countries. However, manufacturing *productivity* performance has been substantially better than in some other economies. Nevertheless, according to the Institute of Economic Affairs,[1] manufacturing output per person is still a little less than in Germany or France, and much lower than in the United States.[2]

19.3 The basis of international trade

In examining whether the UK's deficit in manufacturing trade is of great consequence, it is helpful to understand why countries engage in trade at all. Our judgement about the seriousness of the position will depend much upon our confidence in the market mechanism, hence we need to see how the principles of trade within a country can be extended to trade between countries. The heart of the reason why countries trade is found in the law of comparative advantage.

Understanding comparative advantage

The essence of the *law of comparative advantage* can be understood if we construct a simple model of international trade sufficient for us to understand the great attractions of engaging in trade with other countries.

We assume just two countries, Britain and Germany, whose citizens are interested in the consumption of only two kinds of output, which we shall call manufactures (M) and services (S). There are no government restrictions such as tariff barriers on trade between these countries. We also assume that the markets are competitive in each country. Now let us make some assumptions about the relative abilities of these countries to produce these goods. Table 19.4 tells us that the output of each of these goods in each country requires only labour inputs. Each country has only 40 units of labour.

These units have an opportunity cost. If individuals spend all their time producing services, they cannot produce manufactures. The table shows the assumed amount of labour inputs needed to produce a unit of a given output for each country. In our example, Britain can produce a unit of services for the

Table 19.4 **Assumed relative abilities of Britain and Germany**

	Britain		*Germany*	
	Manufactures (M)	*Services (S)*	*Manufactures (M)*	*Services (S)*
Labour input required per unit of output	4	2	2	2
Possible production level with no international trade	5	10	10	10
Possible total output and consumption without international trade		15M + 20S		

same labour input as Germany but needs twice the labour input to produce a unit of manufactures.

What quantity of manufactures and services can each community enjoy, assuming no international trade? The answer, of course, is that there is a whole series of possibilities, depending upon the proportions of labour devoted to different kinds of production. Table 19.4 shows one possibility among many. It shows the output produced in each country if half of the labour resources are devoted to manufactures and half to services. World output is then 15M + 20S, but since there is no international trade, Britain enjoys the consumption of 5M + 10S and German citizens 10M + 10S.

At first it might be supposed that Germany has nothing to gain from trade with Britain. After all, it is just as effective at producing service output and far better at producing manufactures. However, this supposition would be incorrect. Germany would be willing to trade because the two countries' relative abilities are different. Britain is relatively good at producing services; Germany is relatively good at manufacturing. To produce a unit of service output in Britain requires the sacrifice of half a unit of manufactures. In contrast, for Germany to produce a unit of services requires the sacrifice of a whole unit of manufactures. It would be better, then, for each country to concentrate on producing the good in which it has the comparative advantage, and then to exchange those goods internationally. Let us see how this works out in terms of our example (Table 19.5).

Britain is now producing fewer manufactures but more services, since it is the latter in which Britain has a comparative advantage. With Germany concentrating on the area in which it has a comparative advantage, total output from the two countries can be greater than would be possible without trade. In the case of Table 19.5 we have more manufactures available for consumption but the same volume of services. With different allocations of resources it would be possible for aggregate output to be at a level where services and manufactures are higher than would be possible without trade.

Table 19.6 shows such a possibility. With Germany slightly less specialised, total output with trade is 18M + 22S. This compares with a no trade output

Table 19.5 **Production and consumption with international trade**

	Britain		Germany	
	Manufactures (M)	*Services (S)*	*Manufactures (M)*	*Services (S)*
Labour input required per unit of output	4	2	2	2
Possible production level following an agreement to trade	0	20	20	0
Possible total output and consumption with international trade	20M + 20S			

Table 19.6 **Production and consumption without complete specialisation**

	Britain		Germany	
	Manufactures (M)	*Services (S)*	*Manufactures (M)*	*Services (S)*
Labour input required per unit of output	4	2	2	2
Alternative possible production level following an agreement to trade	0	20	18	2
Alternative possible total output and consumption with international trade	18M + 22S			

of 15M + 20S. Hence international trade can allow consumption patterns which reflect higher living standards than would be possible without such specialisation.

Whether the increased output is in the form of services or manufactures, or both, will be determined by consumer preference expressing itself through markets.

Increasing opportunity cost

Although manufacturing as a proportion of output in Britain has declined over the long term, the sector is still substantial and will continue to be of importance. Why, given what we have seen above, do we produce any manufactured items *at all*? Why do we not produce services and import all manufactures? One of the most important reasons is the principle of increasing opportunity cost.

We assumed in our model of Table 19.4 that, whatever the level of output, the opportunity cost of producing an M in Britain was 2S. However, as we saw

see pp. 8–11

in Chapter 1, this is not likely to be the case. The more output of a good that is being produced, the higher is its opportunity cost. Suppose Britain is producing mainly services and decides to produce even more of them. Marginal resources will have to shift from manufacturing, where they are relatively suited, into services where they are relatively unsuited. The complete specialisation referred to earlier is thus unlikely, but partial specialisation following international trade is inevitable.

The terms of trade

Whatever the increased output made possible by such specialisation, the question now remains as to which country will enjoy the benefits of that output. We are assuming that labour is not required to transport this output between countries. If the transport costs involved in trade were to be more than the potential increase in output, the benefits of international trade might be entirely undone. Let us assume that this is not the case.

The terms on which the countries in our example trade will have to be such as to give both some share of the output gain, otherwise they will not be willing to trade at all. How these terms are established we shall consider further in Chapter 20, but for now the principle can be made clear.

see pp. 435–40

As we have already seen in earlier chapters, the market mechanism brings about an identity between the price of a good and its opportunity cost. Hence in Britain before trade, the price of manufactures would have been 1M : 2S. The price of a manufactured good would have been twice the price of a service item. In Germany manufactures would have been relatively cheap, 1M : 1S, reflecting the lower opportunity cost of manufacturing output.

What happens to price if countries engage in trade? Since manufactures are relatively cheap in Germany the British will buy German manufactures. This will mean that German manufactured prices will increase. This increase in price will encourage some German resource owners to switch production from services to manufactures.

In the meantime, the opposite will happen in Britain. Germans will wish to buy relatively cheap British services. Service output will rise in response to this demand increase. British resource owners will respond by producing more services and fewer manufactures.

Notice that to begin with the relative prices in Britain and Germany were different, but trade moved them towards each other.

Some results of comparative advantage

Two conclusions follow from the law of comparative advantage. The first is that a declining manufacturing sector is not in and of itself a problem. If it reflects increasing specialisation in the production of goods and services in which we have a comparative advantage, the change can be beneficial. The problem occurs when, instead of service output increasing to pay for rising manufactured imports, markets fail to adjust. Resources such as labour may shift out of the sector in decline but remain unemployed for a substantial period. Instead of increased service output there is unemployment and a balance of payments problem.

The second point which emerges is that inefficiency in production is not a barrier to international trade. If we produce less output from a given volume of inputs than is possible, we shall have lower living standards. However, other countries will still wish to trade with us. We do not require an absolute advantage in the production of any commodities, we need only a comparative advantage.

Benefits of free trade

Governments are not always willing to allow the law of comparative advantage to operate. The EU operates a policy of free trade between its members but there are substantial restrictions imposed upon trade between the EU and the rest of the world. Such restrictions reduce welfare. We illustrate the point first with reference to trade between the EU and Eastern Europe.

see pp. 17–20

As we saw in Chapter 1, Eastern Europe is still a very inefficient producer. However, as we have seen in this chapter, free trade will still allow mutually beneficial trade to take place based upon comparative advantage. The EU fears that some of its producers will suffer, at least in the short run, when competition with Eastern Europe is allowed because EU consumers will switch to the relatively cheap imported substitutes. The price gains to consumers, however, will be far greater than the loss to producers.

Empirical evidence of this net gain will be provided in the period 2004–2007 as Eastern European countries, such as Poland, Hungary and Bulgaria, become part of the EU and have no tariff barriers to overcome any more.

We have considered only a tiny part of world trade. The data in Figure 19.3 refer not only to the benefits to the EU and the substantial benefits to Eastern Europe of free trade, but also to the gains of substantial reductions in international trade restrictions as a result of GATT – the General Agreement on Tariffs and Trade. In previous decades GATT encouraged world trade liberalisation. In December 1993, most world governments agreed further mutual reductions in trade barriers. The values given in Figure 19.3 are OECD/World Bank estimates of the increases in output that will obtain by the year 2002 as a result of such an agreement. This shows that there will be 213 billion dollars' worth of extra real output then as a result of the agreement. This is, in all probability, a considerable understatement of the benefits flowing from a further liberalisation of trade. The study calculates only the effects on manufactures, but the GATT round for the first time drew other spheres of activity, notably services, into the arrangement. The law of comparative advantage suggests possible improvements in world output from specialisation in any area of economic activity, not just manufacturing goods. GATT has been superseded by the WTO (World Trade Organization). Another study suggests that the benefits from the liberalisation of service trade will be as large as that for manufactures. Note that almost every part of the world would gain. Any losers could easily be compensated by the gainers. It is sad that although economies can be helped in ways which would bring net benefits to the world as a whole, political considerations result in a

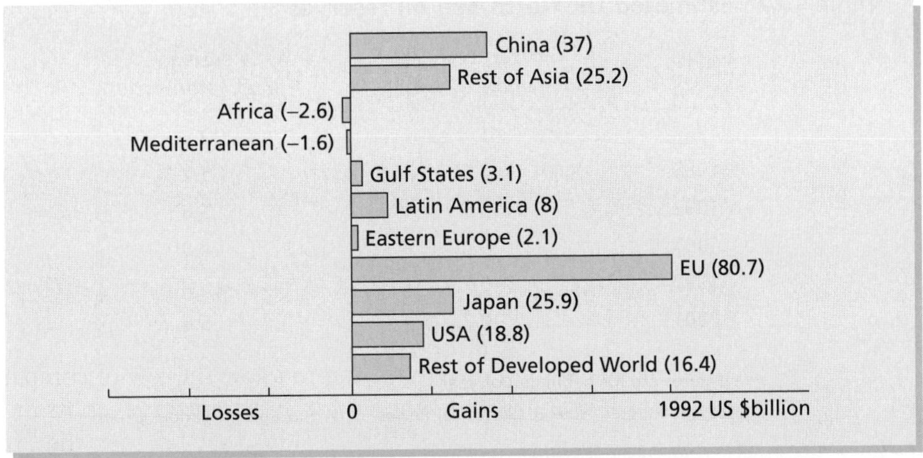

Figure 19.3 Estimated world gains by 2002 from liberalising world trade
Source: adapted from OECD/World Bank data

great reluctance to allow the law of comparative advantage to operate. In 2002 the USA proposed to the WTO the removal of all tariff barriers on industrial goods although even if this were accepted substantial barriers would remain in other sectors, notably agriculture.

Armed with an understanding of the benefits of international trade we can now turn to analyse further the problems of British manufacturing trade.

19.4 How significant is the deficit in manufacturing trade?

That there has been a marked deterioration in Britain's trade balance in manufactures in recent decades is clear. That said, to what extent is this deterioration a cause for concern? Broadly, it is possible to discern two contrasting schools of thought. These can be termed the 'market approach', favoured by successive Conservative administrations, which stresses the self-correcting nature of market forces, and the 'interventionist approach' which argues that urgent action on the part of government and other bodies is required since the market will not restore equilibrium, or at best do it too slowly.

Market approach

We have seen that the law of comparative advantage will enable countries to benefit from engaging in international trade. These advantages are, however, fully realised only under quite restrictive assumptions, essentially optimal resource allocation within a country plus the absence of trade barriers between countries.

Table 19.7 **Estimated UK North Sea oil reserves**

Year[a]	*Proved reserves (billion tonnes)*	*Reserves/ production ratio*
1986	1.7	13.6
1989	0.6	5.2
1992	0.5	5.8
1995	0.6	4.8
1998	0.7	5.2
2001	0.7	5.6

[a] Figures are for beginning of year

Source: adapted from *BP Statistical Review of World Energy*, various issues

The market view is that markets can correct for any misallocation of resources given time. Economies are not always in equilibrium, but they will move towards it if conditions are right.

In the context of the British balance of payments problem with respect to manufacturing trade, industry was once far too protected from international competition. Since the supply side improvements initiated in the early 1980s, markets have become more open and productivity has increased faster than that of many of our competitors. The present requirement is to continue with these reforms, ensuring that the enlarged EU does not impose high tariff barriers against the rest of the world. In short, prices must reflect opportunity costs of production.

Overall, in the judgement of many who favour this approach, markets are already operating increasingly effectively. Let us consider two illustrations of this view, beginning with the effects of North Sea oil.

The long-term decline both in manufacturing as a share of GDP and in the balance of trade in manufactures can be seen, in part at least, as a response to the advent of North Sea oil. The alternative to taking the benefits of oil as an increase in net manufacturing imports would have been either to accumulate huge surpluses on current account and/or to have accepted an even bigger rise in the sterling exchange rate than actually occurred. In the event, manufactures rather than, for example, services took much of the strain of adjusting to a massive change in the balance of trade in oil because the UK's comparative advantage was weakest in this sector and market forces were permitted to take their course.

Table 19.7 shows the decline in the stocks of North Sea oil over recent years as extraction has been at a level higher than the discovery of new fields. Proved reserves of oil are those quantities which geological and engineering information indicates with reasonable certainty can be recovered in the future from known reservoirs, using existing economic and operating conditions.

The reserves/production ratio can be explained as follows. If reserves remaining at the end of a year are divided by that year's production, the result is the length of time that those remaining resources would last if production

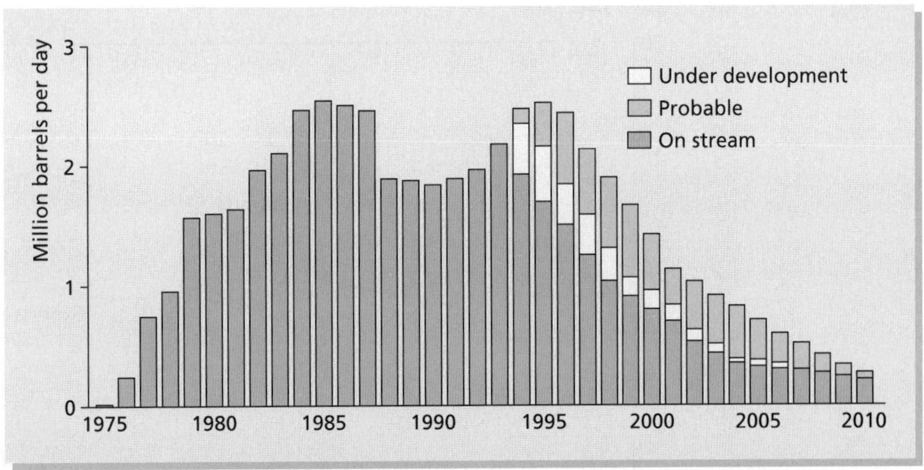

Figure 19.4 **North Sea oil output, actual and potential**

Source: Wood Mackenzie

were to continue at the then current level. So, at the beginning of 2001, at the then level of extraction, the UK had just over five years' supply. In reality, the likely discovery of new fields and improved extraction technology will mean that oil from the UK sector of the North Sea will be available until well beyond that time. However, it will almost certainly be extracted in reduced quantities.

One estimate of UK oil production to the end of this decade is given in Figure 19.4. Oil output is thus expected to fall sharply during this decade.

The decline in North Sea oil output will, according to the market view, automatically be compensated for by an improvement in the non-fuel trade balance, including that for services and manufactures, via a fall in the exchange rate. However, as we shall see in Chapter 20, government policy towards the exchange rate has not always been entirely clear.

see pp. 434–62

A second area in which it is argued that the market mechanism brings automatic corrective forces into play is the area of direct inward investment. The role of foreign investment in rejuvenating British manufacturing could be seen to vindicate a relatively relaxed non-interventionist approach towards the manufacturing trade balance.

The UK is a comparatively open economy. This openness enabled imports of, for example, cars and televisions to replace UK products. However, supply-side reforms in the period since 1979 combined with membership of the EU have made the UK an attractive location for multinational firms, especially those from Japan. Consequently, by the mid 1990s half of EU inward investment was going to the UK, much of it from Japan. That investment has been instrumental in improving the performance of UK manufacturing because Japanese practices have been disseminated throughout industry in general.

In the government's view, the car industry provides an excellent example of how the presence of new Japanese production plants can help to close the gap in Britain's manufacturing trade: motor vehicles were the most important

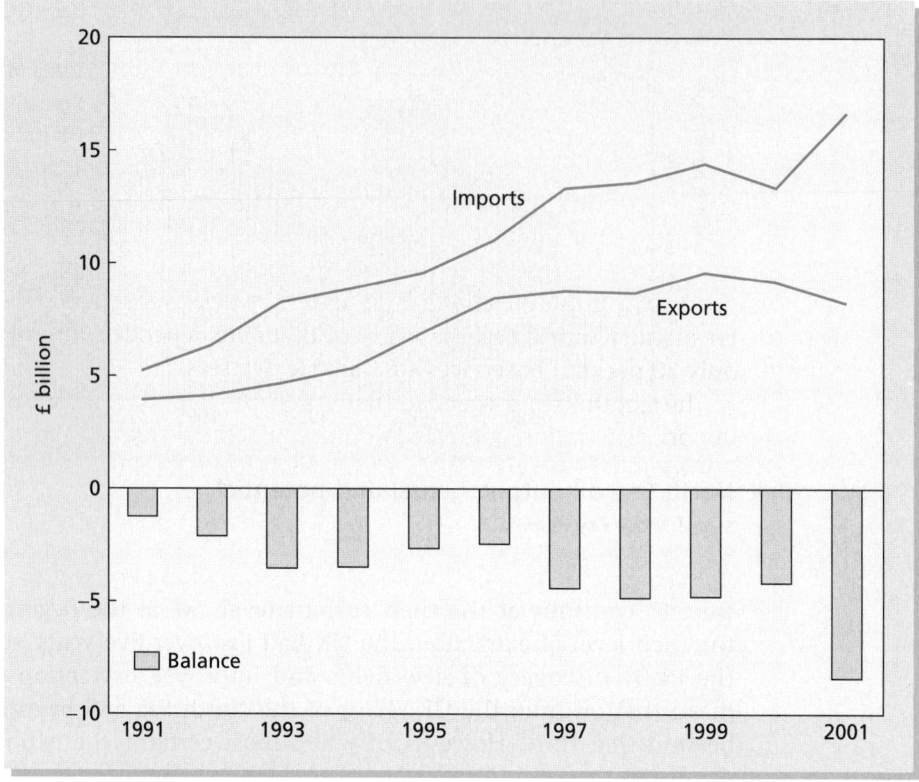

Figure 19.5 **UK Trade in motor cars**

Source: *UK Balance of Payments*, 'Pink Book', 2002

contributor to the growing manufacturing trade deficit of the 1980s. The gap between the value of car exports and car imports was closing in the late 1980s and some estimates were that exports would probably exceed imports by value in the mid-1990s. In the event, these hopes were disappointed. Even so, as Figure 19.5 shows, the value of car exports remains substantial. Much of this can be attributed to Japanese inward investment. Many of the cars manufactured in Britain by Japanese producers are being exported to the rest of the EU. However, two things have worsened the picture into the early years of the new century. First, the rate of growth in the value of imports, which had slowed in the recession of the early 1990s, has been increasing rapidly again. Second, Britain has been getting a lower proportion of EU inward investment including motor products. Some of this decline may reflect uncertainty over the British decision on the euro – an issue we address in Chapter 20.

Interventionist approach

We have considered the view that markets provide the best way of dealing with the problems of British manufacturing. However, we must now consider the alternative view. The interventionist approach is inherently pessimistic. It is epitomised by the House of Lords Select Committee on Overseas Trade which in 1985 published a report on 'the causes and implications of the deficit in the UK's balance of trade in manufactures'. The committee took the view that the decline in manufacturing and in the trade balance in manufactures constituted 'a grave threat to the standard of living and to the political stability of the nation'.

The Committee's report argued that there were two reasons why urgent action was required to revive manufacturing and encourage trade in manufactures. First, because there would not necessarily be a resurgence of manufacturing as North Sea oil diminishes. Second, service industries could not substitute for manufacturing because many of them are dependent on manufacturing and only 20 per cent of services are tradable overseas.

The Committee contended that unless the manufacturing base were enlarged, import penetration combated and manufactured exports encouraged, the country would face adverse effects which would worsen with time, including:

1 A contraction of the manufacturing sector to the point where the successful continuance of it is put at risk.
2 An adverse balance of payments of such magnitude as to require severe deflation of the economy.
3 A stagnant economy and rising inflation driven by a falling exchange rate.

In the light of such dire predictions, their lordships made a number of suggestions as to how the government could improve matters. The proposed measures encompassed the promotion of investment, exports, education, training, and research and development expenditure.

We have already examined the logic of the interventionist case in earlier chapters. Here we comment on the predictions made by the Committee.

Clearly, there has been a long-term contraction of manufacturing in Britain, as we have seen. However, in defence of the market approach, two points can be made. First, UK productivity has risen faster than that of its competitors in the years following the Committee's report. Second, as can be seen from Figure 19.6, the proportion of world trade in manufacturing taken by the UK has remained relatively steady since the early 1980s. In other words, it can be argued that it is the supply side reforms of earlier years that are turning the situation around without the need for resource misallocation through subsidies.

19.5 Conclusion

Which of the two views we have been examining represents the more realistic interpretation of future trends in Britain's manufacturing trade balance? A verdict will inevitably be coloured by the degree of enthusiasm for the market mechanism.

In support of the interventionist view, it can be pointed out that manufacturing accounts for three-fifths of Britains' exports of goods and services by value and earns almost two-thirds of all our foreign currency. It is also an

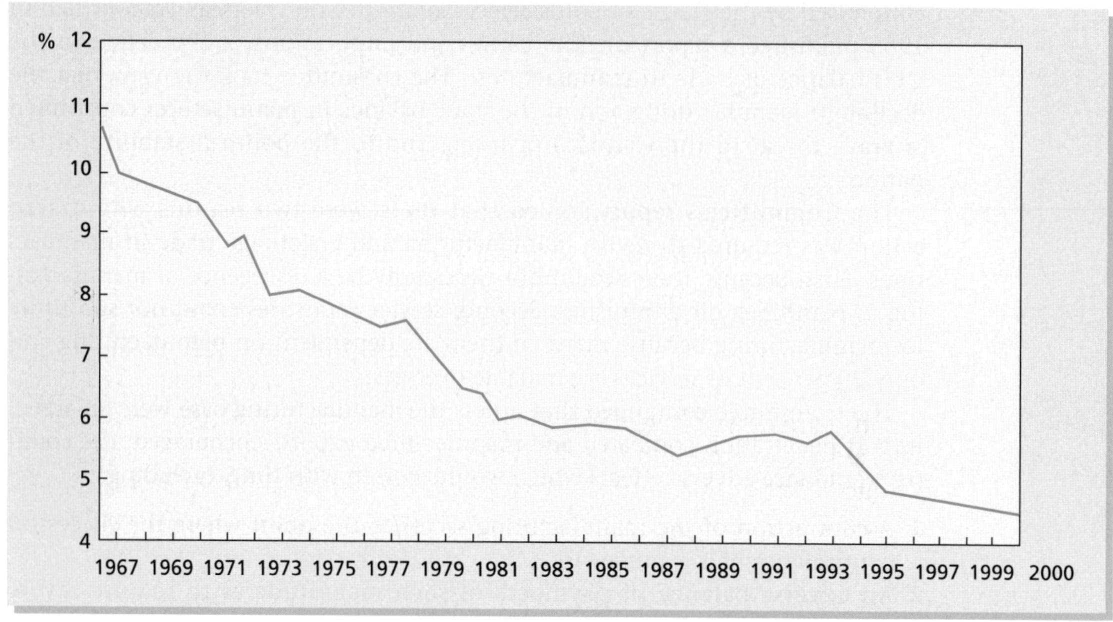

Figure 19.6 **Share of British trade in manufactures, by volume**
Source: adapted from ONS, OECD data

important source of innovation for the economy. Arguably, therefore, the decline in the manufacturing trade balance which, as we noted earlier, has been a remorseless feature of the past four decades is a cause for concern. Simple extrapolation of some historical trends would indicate that the future will be much like the past. The UK will encounter a rapidly deteriorating trade balance in manufactures once it attempts to expand the economy at anything more than a relatively slow pace. In short, this will mean an all too familiar replay of the dismal stop–go cycle which has afflicted the British economy since the Second World War.

Table 19.8 refers specifically to manufacturing unit labour costs of each country. Productivity in the UK has improved over that time. This should, *ceteris*

Table 19.8 **Unit labour costs of manufacturing, selected countries (1995 = 100)**

	USA	*Japan*	*France*	*Germany*	*Denmark*	*Belgium/Luxembourg*	*United Kingdom*	*Euro area*
1997	95.8	95.8	105.0	93.6	107.7	93.9	108.5	101.2
1998	96.2	101.9	107.9	91.1	112.5	93.7	112.4	102.0
1999	95.1	99.2	110.4	90.7	117.2	94.0	112.7	103.2
2000	98.2	93.4	115.4	87.5	121.3	93.6	111.7	104.2
2001	98.8	98.7	120.5	89.0	126.5	96.9	114.3	107.4
2002[a]	97.6	95.3	124.8	90.0	130.8	99.1	118.9	110.2

[a] Second quarter only
Source: adapted from OECD, Eurostat data

paribus, have made the UK more competitive internationally. However, unit labour costs have risen faster over the period than some other economies in the table. The last column enables us to see unit labour costs relative to an average of all its competitors with in the euro area, an important destination for UK exports. This shows that the UK is becoming less competitive, despite its productivity record. One explanation for the trend is the strength of sterling. We return to this point in Chapter 20. But the rise in UK labour costs shown in the second to last column cannot be attributed to this and suggests that difficulties remain in UK labour markets.

There are, however, just a few hopeful signs that the future may not simply be more of the past. The UK is still a powerful magnet for inward manufacturing investment. Much of the output generated by this investment is destined for export. Moreover, UK manufacturing as a whole is better managed than in the past, and wage rate increases do seem to be more closely matched to increases in productivity. Nevertheless, if government had taken a more proactive view of industrial intervention in the past fifteen years, would things have been better?

CHAPTER SUMMARY

1 **The balance of payments current account shows the balance of trade (visible items) plus the balance on invisible items.**

2 **The capital account records monetary transactions; if there is no error in recording, then capital and current account balance will sum to zero.**

3 **The law of comparative advantage says that world output is maximised if each country concentrates on producing those goods in which it has the lowest opportunity cost.**

4 **The relative prices of exports and imports at which a country trades are the terms of trade.**

5 **The proportion of UK GDP accounted for by manufactures has declined and the effects of this can be seen in the balance of trade.**

6 **Economists are divided as to whether the market or government intervention deals best with deindustrialisation and balance of payments problems.**

Questions for discussion

Guidance to the answers for the ***asterisked*** *numbered questions is available to students on the website for the book at* **www.booksites.net/heather**.

1* Distinguish between productivity improvements and increased output levels.

2 'Imports from South-east Asia into Europe should be restricted. Their much lower wages means that the competition is unfair.' Assess this view.

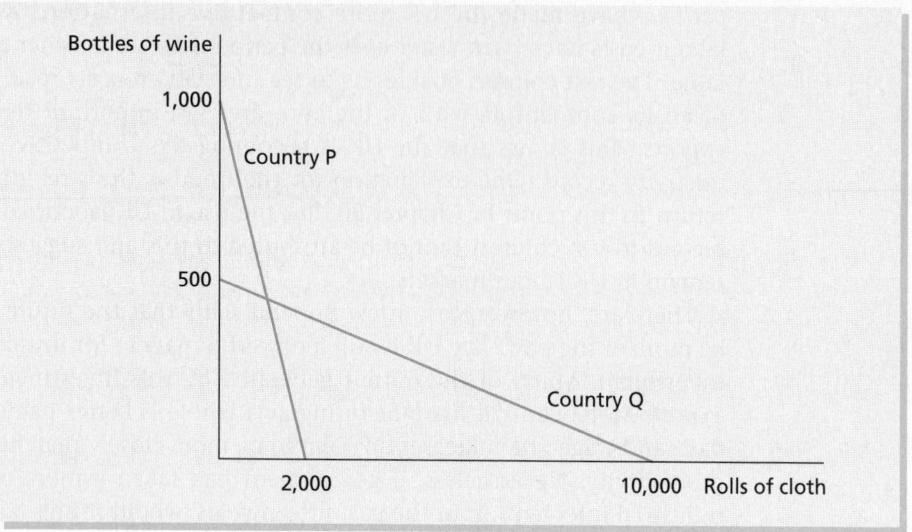

Figure 19.7 **Opportunity cost curves for two countries**

3* What are the effects of large-scale Japanese investment in the UK on (a) manufacturing industry and (b) the balance of payments account? Should such inward investment be encouraged?

4 Why do you think British manufacturing productivity bears better comparison with that of European countries than with the USA?

5* Which of the following would make beneficial trade between two countries impossible? (a) One has a serious balance of payments problem. (b) One country's government subsidises its manufacturing sector. (c) One country has an absolute advantage in the production of all output. (d) Both countries operate a fixed exchange rate. (e) Opportunity cost ratios are different in the two countries. (f) Relative prices before trade are different in the two countries.

6 Does the poor productivity of British manufacturing relative to that of, say, the USA make trade between the two nations more difficult?

7* Figure 19.7 shows the opportunity cost curves of two nations. Say whether each of the following statements is true or false: (a) Country Q has a comparative advantage in cloth. (b) Country P has a comparative advantage in wine. (c) Country Q has an absolute advantage in cloth. (d) These countries can trade profitably with each other. (e) There is nothing in the diagram to suggest that either country will have a balance of payments problem if they engage in trade.

8 If one were to take an interventionist approach, in what ways might government best help manufacturing industry?

9* An economy has a marginal propensity to save of 0.1, a marginal propensity to tax of 0.1 and a marginal propensity to import of 0.2. Suppose now that exports increase by 20 million euros. What happens to (a) national income and (b) the trade balance?

10 To what extent is it a good idea to subsidise manufacturing industry?

Websites

For information on the UK balance of payment figures go to:

www.statistics.gov.uk/onlineproducts/

This enables you to access data from the 'pink book'. There is much information at the European level at:

www.europa.eu.int/comm/eurostat

Notes

1 Institute of Economic Affairs, *Can Deindustrialisation Seriously Damage Your Wealth*?

2 Remember that productivity refers to the amount of output from a given volume of inputs, so a rise in productivity allows the possibility of increased output. However, it may simply lead to more unemployment, in that the same output can be produced from fewer inputs.

20 Exchange rates

Giving up sterling: *too high a price to pay?*

CHAPTER OVERVIEW

Many European countries have given up their own currencies for the euro. Was this sensible? What are the costs and benefits of such a move? Does it make sense for Britain to give up the pound sterling and join such a currency union?

In this chapter we review

- Supply and demand
- Speculation
- Balance of payments

We introduce

- Exchange rate determination
- European monetary union

20.1 Introduction

The post-war economic history of Europe has seen increasing cooperation between many of its member countries. The EU began with agreements on coal and steel in the early 1950s. Later it moved towards the establishment of a community between which there were no tariff barriers, and in which there was cooperation on matters of trade, agriculture and regional matters. Subsequently political institutions of a pan-European nature were established by the EU, and the number of its members was enlarged.

Further integration was achieved with the establishment of an agreement by most EU governments to fix against one another the relative values of their currencies. This process began in 1979 with the establishment of the exchange rate mechanism (ERM). The intention was that by the end of the century this process would have evolved such that some countries would have given up their individual currency and would have replaced it with a common currency. This has now happened. There were 15 countries in the EU when the euro began to circulate. All of them except the UK, Denmark and Sweden are participating. The euro has been legal tender since 2002. Whilst not taking part in the

Table 20.1 **The position of European countries with respect to the euro, 2003**

	In the EU?	*Part of the euro area?*	*Outside the euro but fixing its exchange rate against it?*
Austria	✓	✓	✗
Belgium	✓	✓	✗
Denmark	✓	✗	✓
Finland	✓	✓	✗
France	✓	✓	✗
Germany	✓	✓	✗
Greece	✓	✓	✗
Ireland	✓	✓	✗
Italy	✓	✓	✗
Luxembourg	✓	✓	✗
Netherlands	✓	✓	✗
Norway	✗	✗	✗
Portugal	✓	✓	✗
Spain	✓	✓	✗
Sweden	✓	✗	✗
Switzerland	✗	✗	✗
UK	✓	✗	✗

establishment of the single currency, Denmark has tended to fix the value of its currency to it. The position is summarised in Table 20.1. In this chapter we examine the main economic implications of such a monetary union. We begin by asking what determines the relative values of individual national currencies, with particular emphasis on the balance of payments account. Next, we consider the advantages and problems associated with the kind of fixed exchange rate system and its ultimate development, the single currency. Finally, we consider the particular question of the UK's decision to join or remain outside. During our discussion we shall reconsider the question of an independent central bank, first raised in Chapter 18 in the context of a closed economy.

see pp. 383–409

20.2 Exchange rates and the balance of payments

Supply and demand for foreign currency

Let us begin our examination by considering how the value of a currency such as sterling is decided if the government makes no effort to influence its rate against other currencies. In other words, how is the price of currency determined in a free market? Such a currency is often called a 'floating' currency.

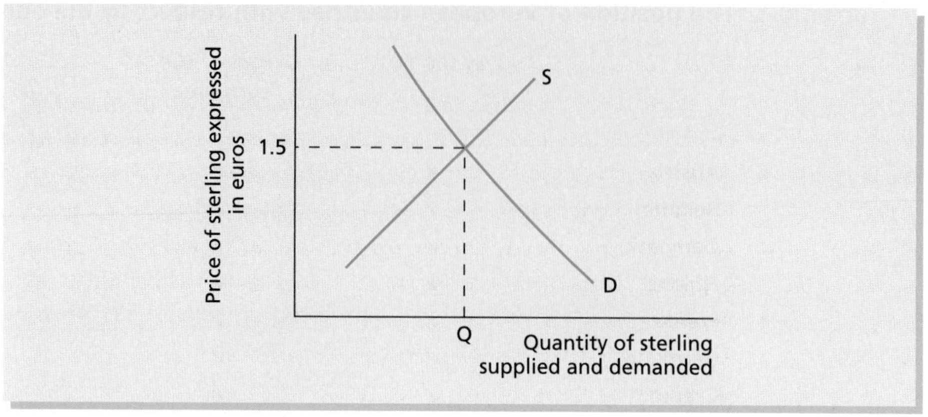

Figure 20.1 **The market for sterling**

When we wish to import goods or services into Britain, the importer must buy the currency of the country from which these items come. If goods are being imported from Germany, the German supplier wishes to have euros, not pounds. The British importer must acquire the appropriate number of euros from the foreign exchange market. He sells pounds and buys euros. This market consists of a large number of traders willing to swap euros for pounds (or vice versa if Germans are buying goods from Britain). At what rate will the foreign exchange market set the price of the two currencies to be exchanged and how is it decided? In essence we have a competitive market with large numbers of buyers and sellers, so we can use supply and demand analysis to determine how this value is established.

Figure 20.1 shows the market for sterling at a given time. Look first at the supply curve. Why does it slope upwards? The higher the price of sterling in terms of euros the more euros are available for a pound. The more euros to the pound, the cheaper it is for Britons to buy German goods. Suppose, for example, the exchange rate is £1 = €2. To buy a German car costing €40,000 will cost a Briton £20,000. If the exchange rate is £1 = €4, the same car would cost the Briton only £10,000. The cheaper German goods are, the more Britons will wish to import. The extent of that willingness will be determined by the price elasticity of demand for German imports. The more German goods that Britons wish to import, the greater the quantity of sterling will be offered in the foreign exchange market in return for euros.

Now examine the demand curve for sterling. The lower the price of sterling the greater the quantity demanded. This is because at a lower price of sterling, Germans find British goods cheaper. At a rate of £1 = €2 a German must spend €2 to acquire a £1 bar of British chocolate. At a rate of £1 = €4 the same chocolate bar will cost the German consumer only half that in euros. The lower price of sterling will, all else being equal, encourage Germans to purchase more sterling. This is just what the demand curve in Figure 20.1 shows. The extent of the increase in the quantity demanded will depend upon the German price elasticity of demand for British goods.

We have considered this principle in terms of the demand for goods and services. It will apply also to the purchase of capital goods, of shares, or to any transaction of an international nature.

Finding an equilibrium value

Just as for any commodity, the equilibrium price of a currency will be the one at which the price of the currency equates quantity demanded with quantity supplied. If a disequilibrium price were to form temporarily, the excess supply or demand would encourage foreign exchange dealers to adjust price back towards equilibrium, assumed in Figure 20.1 to be at €1.5.

In reality the price that is established will be a mid-price between a 'buy' and 'sell' rate. Currency dealers have to cover costs of engaging in the transactions. Therefore the prices at which they will buy currency will differ from the rate at which they will sell it.

Table 20.2 gives some idea of the size of these variations. It shows the rate at which a British individual could expect to pay to buy or sell currency for the purpose of taking a foreign holiday. Suppose Louise wished to go to Italy in the winter of 2003. She changed £1,000 into euros and received 1,420 of them, calculated from the 'bank sells' rate. When she changed her mind and decided not to go, she took her euros back to the bank. She was able to buy £873.30 by exchanging her euros at the 'bank sells' rate of 1,626 euros to the pound. The decision to change her mind was an expensive one. The rate we use to show equilibrium in a diagram such as Figure 20.1 will be the rate midway between the buy and sell rate.

Large companies purchasing considerable volumes of foreign currency can negotiate better deals than those indicated in Table 20.2, since large foreign currency deals involve lower transaction costs. For such companies the spread between the buy and sell rate will be smaller.

These equilibrium values can change quickly – the banks change their tourist rates at least daily, sometimes more often. Sometimes changes can be dramatic enough to make headline news. The reasons for such sudden changes will be considered shortly.

Table 20.2 **Selected main currency rates against sterling, 23 January 2003**

Country	*Currency*	*Bank sells*	*Bank buys*
Germany	Euro	1.42	1.626
Italy	Euro	1.42	1.626
Sweden	Swedish kronor	13.32	15.03
Denmark	Danish kronor	10.69	12.22
USA	US dollar	1.52	1.767
Japan	Yen	182	212
Australia	Australian dollar	2.59	2.96

Equilibrium exchange rates and the balance of payments

There is something that may not be obvious to you from Figure 20.1. One can argue that the equilibrium value we found there is one that will tend to bring an equilibrium to the balance of payments on current account. In other words, it is the one that ensures that the value of exports is equal to the value of imports. Let us try to see why this should be so. It can be expressed in terms of what is known as the purchasing power parity (PPP) theory.

In essence, the theory says that the purchasing power of, say, a pound sterling, that is, what that pound will buy, should be the same as the amount bought by the exchange rate equivalent of its euros in Germany or its dollars in the USA. Suppose the only good bought and sold in Britain and Germany were a McDonald's Big Mac. The fact that the Big Mac is identical wherever it is sold, and is available in most countries of the world, makes it a useful commodity for illustrative purposes. Table 20.3 shows that in Britain in April 2002 the Big Mac cost £1.99 and in the United States $2.49. Then the exchange rate at that time should have been 2.49/1.99 = 1.25. In other words, £1 should have exchanged for $1.25. This would be the PPP exchange rate. Since the actual exchange rate was around $1.45, the pound was somewhat overvalued against the US dollar, according to the Big Mac index, around 16 per cent.

You can check this out from Table 20.3. The pound sterling is overvalued against the dollar by 16 per cent but the euro was undervalued, but only by 5 per cent.

The argument now goes like this. If a country's exchange rate is significantly different from its purchasing power parity, economic forces will push exchange rates back towards the equilibrium rate. If a country's exchange rate is undervalued, its producers have a competitive edge in foreign markets. They will export more. The result is a current account balance of payments surplus for that country. Conversely, an overvalued currency leads to a deficit on the current account. Such a situation cannot continue indefinitely. A surplus or deficit implies an excess supply or demand for the country's currency on the foreign exchange market. The market will then adjust the price back to the PPP equilibrium.

Actual changes over time in the Big Mac index are printed in *The Economist* every so often, or you can find an up-to-date table on their website. Before we leave this aspect of our argument we need to establish that there is a real problem about using the Big Mac index. The PPP argument is based on the relationship between exchange rates and the (weighted) average of all prices in the relevant countries. The Big Mac index is only a guide in so far as the price of the Big Mac is representative of the price level in an economy. Nevertheless, it is an interesting idea that makes exchange rate theory more 'digestible'.

Exchange rates and the capital account

see pp. 414–16

The PPP theory is a long-run concept. A country's balance of payments on current account can be in deficit for some years, as we saw in Chapter 19 with reference to the UK. How is this possible? You will recall that a balance of payments

Table 20.3 ***The Economist*'s Big Mac index**

	Big Mac prices		Implied PPP* of the dollar	Actual dollar exchange rate 23/04/02	Under(–)/over(+) valuation against the dollar, %
	in local currency	in dollars			
United States†	$2.49	2.49	–	–	–
Argentina	Peso 2.50	0.78	1.00	3.13	–68
Australia	A$3.00	1.62	1.20	1.86	–35
Brazil	*Real* 3.06	1.55	1.45	2.34	–38
Britain	£1.99	2.88	1.25‡	1.45‡	+16
Canada	C$3.33	2.12	1.34	1.57	–15
Chile	Peso 1,400	2.16	562	655	–14
China	Yuan 10.50	1.27	4.22	8.28	–49
Czech Rep.	Koruna 56.28	1.66	22.6	34.0	–33
Denmark	DKr24.75	2.96	9.94	8.38	+19
Euro area	€2.67	2.37	0.93§	0.89§	–5
Hong Kong	HK$11.20	1.40	4.50	7.80	–42
Hungary	Forint 459	1.69	184	272	–32
Indonesia	Rupiah 16,000	1.71	6,426	9,430	–32
Israel	Shekel 12.00	2.51	4.82	4.79	+1
Japan	¥262	2.01	105	130	–19
Malaysia	M$5.04	1.33	2.02	3.8	–47
Mexico	Peso 21.90	2.37	8.80	9.28	–5
New Zealand	NZ$3.95	1.77	1.59	2.24	–29
Peru	New Sol 8.50	2.48	3.41	3.43	–1
Philippines	Peso 65.00	1.28	26.1	51.0	–49
Poland	Zloty 5.90	1.46	2.37	4.04	–41
Russia	Rouble 39.00	1.25	15.7	31.2	–50
Singapore	S$3.30	1.81	1.33	1.82	–27
South Africa	Rand 9.70	0.87	3.90	10.9	–64
South Korea	Won 3,100	2.36	1,245	1,304	–5
Sweden	SKr26.00	2.52	10.4	10.3	+1
Switzerland	SFr6.30	3.81	2.53	1.66	+53
Taiwan	NT$70.00	2.01	28.1	34.8	–19
Thailand	Baht 55.00	1.27	22.1	43.3	–49
Turkey	Lira 4,000,000	3.06	1,606,426	1,324,500	+21
Venezuela	Bolivar 2,500	2.92	1,004	857	+17

* Purchasing-power parity: local price divided by price in United States
† Average of New York, Chicago, San Francisco and Atlanta
‡ Dollars per pound
§ Dollars per euro

Source: © *The Economist*, 27 April 2002

deficit is analogous to an individual's running down a savings account. If the account is healthy enough, the individual can 'overspend' for some time by using his/her capital account. In the long run, however, one must live within one's means. Take the illustration further. Overspending can occur by running down assets or by borrowing, or by some combination of the two, so a fall into deficit on the current account will not create a serious problem for a country in the short run, if it has sufficient overseas assets or if foreigners are willing to lend. As we shall see shortly, governments may be able to persuade foreigners to lend by raising interest rates. However, PPP theory suggests that this can only be a short-term solution.

Nevertheless, PPP theory suggests something very important. To the extent that it represents a valid description of reality, governments need not concern themselves with the balance of payments account. The market will adjust the account in the long run towards equilibrium via changes in the exchange rate. In the short run, current account disequilibrium will be dealt with via changes in the capital account.

20.3 The history of the European exchange rate mechanism

Despite the apparent advantages of a 'floating' exchange rate, most governments indulge in attempts to manipulate the external value of their currency in various ways. It may be that a government makes an independent decision to target a value for its exchange rate but is willing to see it deviate from the target if sticking too rigidly to a particular value prevents the realisation of other policy goals. Alternatively, it may take the form of entering into formal agreements with other governments to fix the exchange rate in some way. An example of this latter type of arrangement was the exchange rate mechanism (ERM) of the European monetary system, the forerunner of the euro.

We shall examine the key features of this mechanism and in so doing see why governments often reject the floating system considered above. We shall also see how governments may attempt to fix a rate when market pressures are pushing for a different equilibrium value. So, what advantage accrues from a fixed exchange rate?

The desire to reduce uncertainty

see pp. 420–5

The first reason for a government's attempts to fix an exchange rate is its desire to reduce uncertainty. We saw in Chapter 19 how engaging in international trade can bring benefits in terms of increased consumption of goods and services. For firms engaging in such trade, floating exchange rates can provide considerable uncertainty. Imagine a German firm agreeing to sell a machine to a British company when the exchange rate is £1 = €3. The British company agrees to pay £1,000 (or €3,000) when the machine is made and ready for export from Germany in a year's time. One year later the exchange rate is £1 = €2. If the

Table 20.4 **Proportion of international trade[a] with the EU, selected economies,[b] percentage**

Germany	53.6
Netherlands	64.5
Denmark	67.1
France	62.7
Spain	66.7
Sweden	59.9
UK	49.4

[a] Average of exports and imports [b] Data are for 2000

Source: adapted from national accounts

contract has specified the payment of €3,000, the price of the machine to the British company has risen to £1,500. Alternatively, if the contract specified a price of £1,000, the German company which thought it would receive €3,000 for its machine, will receive only €2,000 when it exchanges the sterling payment in the currency market.

A potential movement in the exchange rate, then, could, if it is large, mean the difference between profit and loss for firms engaging in international trade. One argument behind a fixed exchange system is that more trade will take place than under a floating system because the uncertainty of exchange rate movements is eliminated.

If countries engage in large amounts of trade with one another, the attractions of a fixed exchange rate mechanism are considerable. The members of the EU do trade largely with one another, as Table 20.4 so clearly shows, and share of trade between members is taking an increasing proportion of its total trade. The exchange rate mechanism attempts to fix exchange rates of its participating members against one another but not against other countries. Such a scheme, though it may be desirable, is not essential. Some other trading groups do not fix their exchange rates. The single currency, the euro, is simply an irrevocably fixed exchange rate.

There are, however, objections to governments' intervening in exchange rate determination for this purpose. Two principal objections are that the costs of intervention are too high, and that the goal of reduced uncertainty is not achieved anyhow. Let us examine these two in turn.

The first objection to a fixed exchange system such as the ERM as a means of reducing uncertainty is that it may only be possible to hold an exchange rate at a given level at a very high cost to the economy concerned. An illustration of the argument can be seen with reference to the British experience of ERM. The UK entered the system in 1990 at a rate of £1 = 2.95 Deutschmarks (this was before the German government gave up the mark for the euro). Britain had a balance of payments deficit and there were fears that the rate would need to be lower to restore external balance. However, joining ERM involved a commitment to attempt to fix this rate, at least in the short term. So how can a

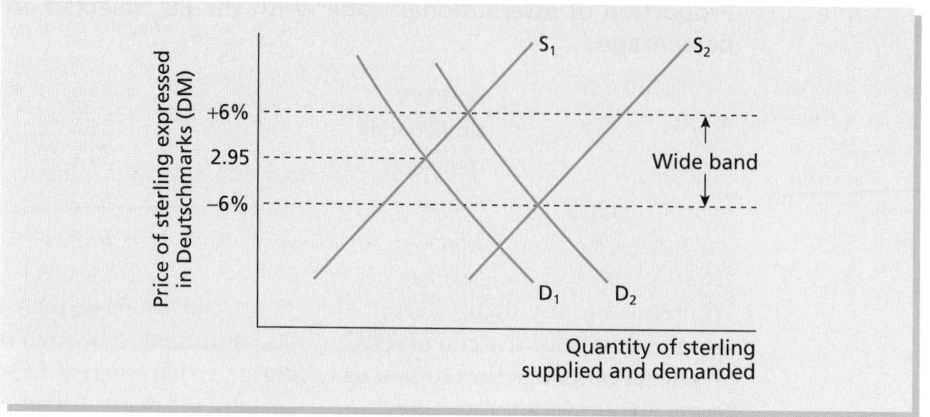

Figure 20.2 **Foreign exchange markets and interest rates during the ERM**

government respond when the market wishes to push the value of sterling down? One key weapon is interest rates.

By raising interest rates sharply, there is an effect on the foreign exchange market (Figure 20.2). S_1D_1 shows the equilibrium price of sterling at entry. The wide band shows the range within which the government agreed to fix the sterling exchange rates. Strictly speaking, this meant a band of not more than 6 per cent higher than the next strongest currency, nor 6 per cent less than the next weakest currency. There was also a 'narrow band' of ±2.25 per cent that most countries in the system operated until August 1993, but the government felt that, at least initially, it would need the greater flexibility given by the wider 6 per cent. Fairly soon after entry, however, a worsening balance of payments position led to sales of sterling. This position is depicted by a movement of the supply curve from S_1 to S_2. The equilibrium value of sterling would then have been below the permitted range. The government's response was to keep interest rates higher than it wanted. Why did that help to keep the value of sterling up?

Imagine that you wish to save some of your funds and you wish to get the best return on those funds. You will look around for some opportunity of a high interest rate. Suppose, further, that you are a German saver. You might consider putting your savings into a UK bank or another UK institution if the interest rate offered were attractive enough. You must weigh up the costs of such a decision, especially the costs we considered in Table 20.2 and the potential problem that, if exchange rates do alter, your original capital might fall in value. However, you will, all things being equal, be more tempted to put your savings in the UK if the UK interest rate differential is increased. What happened to UK interest rates during its membership of ERM? During the early days of its membership they fell. Indeed, many commentators believed that they needed to fall faster and lower, but that the need to keep the demand for sterling high prevented this from happening. This is illustrated in Figure 20.2. Interest rates were higher than would otherwise have been necessary to shift demand from D_1 to D_2. Interest rates, therefore, protected the value of the pound.

The cost of such protection can be high. Britain had a very high level of unemployment at the time. Raising interest rates reduced aggregate demand and compounded the problem. In other words, defending an exchange rate can involve a level of interest rates inappropriate for a country's internal balance, imposing significant costs upon the economy. After leaving the ERM, the external value of sterling fell but interest rates were much lower. This stimulated demand and unemployment fell.

France, on the other hand, continued to stay in the ERM and undertook policies to keep the franc strong against the Deutschmark, especially in terms of its willingness to use high interest rates. Thus, while unemployment in the UK has been falling since the end of 1992, it has continued to be high in France.

The second objection to a fixed exchange system such as ERM is that it can be argued that such a system does not reduce uncertainty very much at all. Sometimes currencies are clearly at a disequilibrium rate. Governments formally agree to alter the level at which the currency is fixed. This can be upwards (a revaluation) or downwards (a devaluation). In practice, the ERM almost always involved the governments of weaker currencies devaluing, rather than those with strong currencies revaluing. Furthermore, to the extent that exchange rates are fixed, interest rates will need to vary. This means that in large part the uncertainty is simply transferred from exchange rate variations to interest rate changes.

Even without the increase in the number of interest rate changes, it could be argued that the possibility of larger, infrequent exchange rate adjustments involves no less uncertainty. They cause as much uncertainty as smaller more frequent adjustments where markets are free to alter exchange rates without government intervention. If this is the case, a fixed exchange system can impose more costs on an economy than benefits.

The desire to reduce speculation

see pp. 41–3

A further motive for fixing an exchange rate is the desire to reduce speculation. Recall that when in Chapter 2 we considered supply and demand curves in relation to the stock market, we saw that speculation in shares could cause changes in prices. We saw too that such speculative forces could either stabilise or destabilise a share price. The same argument can be applied to currency dealing. A currency can change in value not because of its underlying balance of payments position but because of speculative pressures.

All transactions in currency markets are speculative to some extent. A trader may buy raw materials from abroad and stockpile them because he thinks this country's currency will fall. He is speculating even though he is engaging in trade. However, the volume of transactions in the foreign exchange markets is hugely greater than that required for the payment of goods and services.

The turnover in currencies is a huge revenue earner for Britain. However, turnover in sterling makes the UK economy particularly susceptible to speculative pressures.

When governments agree to fix exchange rates between themselves, they commit themselves not only to use interest rate policy to defend these values

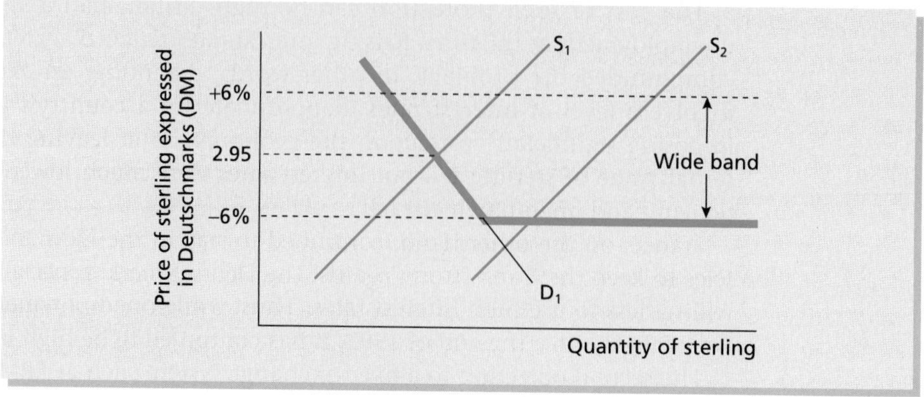

Figure 20.3 **Using reserves as an anti-speculative device during the ERM**

but to use their reserves of currency to fight speculative pressures. Figure 20.3 depicts what this involves. We can use the diagram to see how speculation forced the UK to leave the ERM. In 1992 it was widely believed that sterling was overvalued. Speculators believed it would have to be devalued. If they were correct, profits could be made by selling sterling when its value was high and buying it back after devaluation had made it cheaper. Speculation moved the supply curve from S_1 to S_2. Since the government was committed to a minimum rate of around DM2.78 to the pound sterling, it was forced to act. We have seen that interest rates are a possible weapon. Government dealings in the foreign exchange market are another. The government used its reserves of foreign currency plus borrowings of foreign currency from overseas central banks, notably Germany, to prevent a fall in the sterling exchange rate below its 'floor'. In Britain's case, the floor was 6 per cent below its central rate.

In effect, the government's action changed the demand curve for sterling to that depicted by the thick line in Figure 20.3. If sterling reached its floor of DM2.78 it had to demand whatever sterling was necessary to stabilise the rate at that level. At that exchange rate the demand for sterling must be infinitely elastic.

The reason for government failure and departure from ERM is plain: the government did not have sufficiently large reserves of currency on which to call. Speculative pressures were too great. This was not an isolated event. During the summer of 1993 speculative pressures on several ERM currencies, notably the French franc, forced a major rethink on its members. Bands for most currencies in the system were widened to ±15 per cent, in effect devaluing some currencies. Unfortunately, to the extent that bands are widened, the advantages of a fixed system are lost.

It is not always the case that speculative pressure will be irresistible, particularly in the short run. Speculative pressure on the franc was successfully resisted throughout the mid 1990s. Nevertheless, not everyone is convinced that it makes sense to fix exchange rates in order to avoid speculative pressures on currencies.

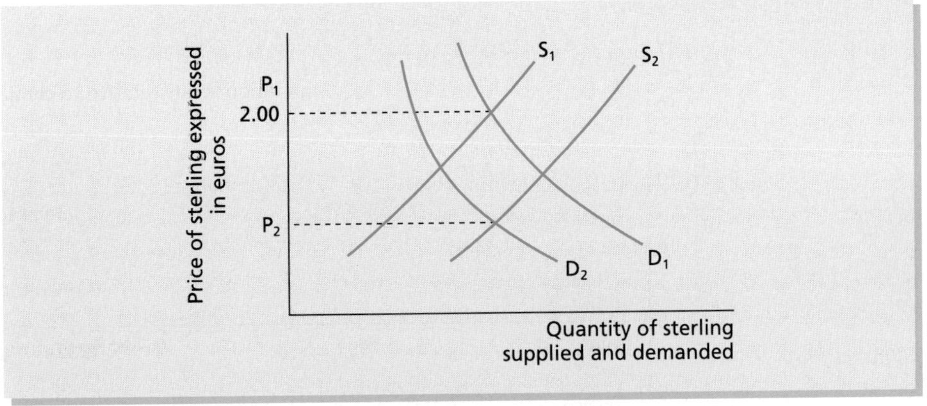

Figure 20.4 **The balance of payments and a floating currency**

Once a single currency is established speculation is clearly impossible against the now defunct individual currencies. However, speculation against the new currency is entirely possible and the euro continues to change in value against other currencies.

The desire to defeat inflation

see pp. 318–40

Sometimes governments believe that fixed exchange rates are an anti-inflationary weapon. In Chapter 15 we considered the extent to which inflation constitutes a problem, concentrating primarily upon the question of the economy's internal balance, especially the relationship of inflation to unemployment. Now we can extend our thinking to the international economy. In particular we shall consider three possible opinions of a link between a fixed exchange rate system and the level of inflation.

The first opinion takes a relaxed view of inflation, saying that there is an adequate mechanism for ensuring that a higher inflation rate in, say, the UK, does not lead to a long-run balance of payments problem. That mechanism is the exchange rate. Figure 20.4 shows the process. We begin with the market for sterling showing an exchange rate of £1 = €2 (P_1). If the UK inflation rate is faster than in the euro area, then, over time, British people will increase their demand for foreign currency to purchase the now relatively cheaper euro area imports. To purchase this foreign exchange, the supply of sterling increases: S_1 shifts to S_2. Since Europeans are switching out of relatively expensive British goods, they supply the foreign exchange market with fewer euros, reducing demand for sterling. The effect is to make the euro more expensive and sterling cheaper, with a new equilibrium at P_2. The result is to make British exports competitive again, thus stimulating British exports and choking off the demand for imports. By this view, the British balance of payments problem that we examined in Chapter 19 is attributable to an overvalued currency. This can be either because of a *formal* fixed exchange rate preventing the floating mechanism operating, or an *informal* one where, for some time, the government

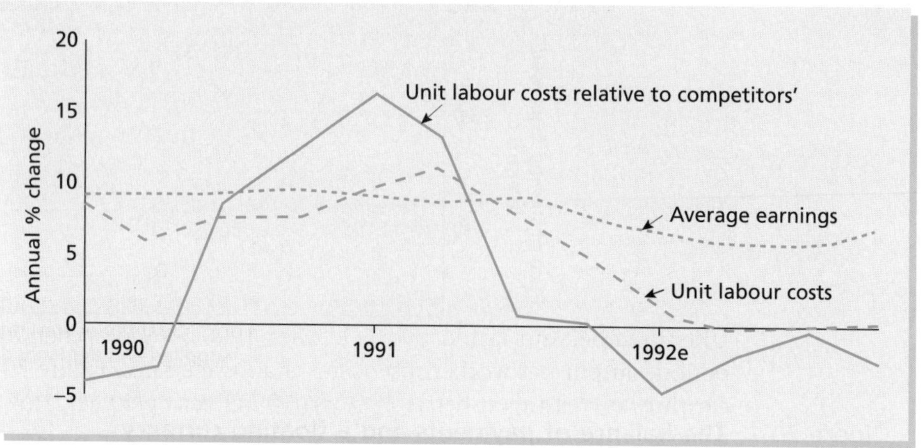

Figure 20.5 **British competitiveness during ERM membership**

Source: Lloyds Bank Economic Bulletin, March 1992

informally fixes the pound at an overvalued rate with excessively high interest rates.[1]

However, there is an objection to this view. It says that the above reasoning is specious. Solving a balance of payments problem via a depreciating exchange rate will not work because the process is self-defeating. Higher import prices feed through into a higher price level. This causes increased wage demands leading to an inflationary spiral and further downward pressure on the exchange rate. It will also not work because of expectations. Once an economy has a reputation for solving its inflation problem by allowing the depreciation of its currency, foreigners will be unwilling to hold it. This creates a further downward pressure on the currency. As a result a fixed exchange rate is preferable.

An alternative way to express the argument is to say that currencies susceptible to periodic depreciation will require high interest rates to compensate for the added risk of holding them. Such risk premiums will impose costs on the domestic economy, notably in discouraging investment.

see p. 305

The UK has had consistently to hold its interest rate levels above Germany's in order to give its currency-holders a risk premium. You can see this clearly from Table 14.3. (You will remember that we considered interest rates there when we examined the question of investment.)

Let us now examine a second view about the relationship between inflation and fixed exchange rates. It says that a fixed exchange rate mechanism can help to defeat inflation by tying a country's inflation rate to the inflation rate of the country to whose currency it is fixed.

We illustrate the argument with respect to Britain's fixed exchange rate during the ERM. If Britain inflates faster than, say, Germany while in the ERM, the temporary effect is, as described in Figure 20.5, a downward pressure on the exchange rate. Since the ERM commits us to a fixed sterling exchange rate, policy measures will be forced on the government to prevent that inflation continuing. These measures can include a number of possibilities discussed in earlier chapters.

When trade unions ask for wage increases, and exchange rates are flexible, employers are inclined to give in to such wage demands. Although the increases add to wage costs, employers believe that they will not price them out of export markets, since higher prices simply result in a fall in the exchange rate.

A fixed exchange system, however, is an announcement to firms by government that inflationary wage increases will not be validated by a fall in the exchange rate. In this way an ERM-type system can stiffen the resolve of employers to resist inflationary wage demands.

During the period of nearly two years in which the UK was a member of the ERM, there was indeed a substantial effect on the wage bargaining process. The UK's membership lasted from October 1990 to September 1992. During that period, output per worker rose faster than wage rates. Figure 20.5 shows average earnings increasing at between 5 and 10 per cent per year. However, unit labour costs improved substantially, because output per worker was rising even faster. Figure 20.5 also shows that unit labour costs in the UK improved relative to its competitors during the period of ERM membership. However, over the period of the 1980s and early 1990s as a whole, unit labour costs worsened by comparison with some major competitors. What is open to debate is whether the ERM was responsible for the improvement or whether it was the effect of rising unemployment – a situation that could have been created outside the ERM.

There is a third view held by some monetarists, about the relationship between inflation and exchange rates. It suggests that if governments fix the money supply and we have a fixed exchange rate, balance of payments equilibrium will result in the long run. Let us see how the argument goes.

see pp. 394–7

Assume a fixed money supply and a balance of payments deficit. A deficit implies that there is a reduction in the money supply circulating in the domestic economy as some part of that money supply leaves the country for the foreign exchange market. Recall from Chapter 18 that, given monetarist assumptions, a decline in the money supply (M) will cause a fall in the price level (P). As the price level falls, imports become dearer, exports become cheaper. As a result, balance of payments equilibrium is restored. Fixing the money supply, then, not only achieves long-run internal balance in the monetarist view, but it achieves external balance also.[2]

In the late 1980s an important part of British economic policy was to make sterling shadow the value of the Deutschmark, even though sterling was not then a member of the ERM. The motive was essentially monetarist. Control of the domestic money supply was proving difficult. Control of the external value of sterling was not simple either – it implied high interest rates at times, since it was interest rates that were used to maintain sterling's parity. On the other hand, one could readily see whether the aim was being achieved. In essence, then, targeting the exchange rate was an indirect way of controlling the money supply.

Whatever the desirability or otherwise of the ERM, its main purpose for most countries was to provide a stepping stone towards a fully fledged monetary union between some of its members. It is to the costs and benefits of such monetary union that we now turn.

20.4 The establishment of European monetary union

Some members of the EU have, as we see, now established monetary union. A few others, including the UK, are sceptical. This is the matter we shall now examine, identifying three areas of potential economic benefit and three areas of potential economic cost of such a monetary union.

Potential benefit 1: eliminating transaction costs

The most obvious benefit of monetary union is the elimination of costs involved in transacting business with different currencies. We saw in Table 20.2 that there are substantial costs for tourists changing currency areas. There are considerable costs for businesses also, which monetary union eliminates. An alternative way of making the same point would be to say that it frees up considerable resources currently engaged in exchanging currencies, enabling those resources to produce output that would have a greater value to society. The European Commission estimates that the saving of resources amounts to about 0.4 per cent of GDP.

Potential benefit 2: increased economic efficiency

see pp. 420–5

When, in Chapter 19, we examined the basis for international trade we saw the law of comparative advantage operate under restrictive conditions. The presence, for example, of import taxes, or any indirect tax, distorts the relationship between price and opportunity cost. Thus the logic of Europe's Single Market is that trade barriers by way of import taxes should be removed. The absence of such barriers has been a feature of intra-EU trade for some years. Other barriers to trade remain: indirect tax rates are, for example, still not harmonised. The most important indirect tax is value added tax (VAT). If VAT rates vary significantly between different member countries, consumers will tend to buy where VAT is lower. Of course, if VAT differences are small then the problem will be correspondingly small since few will think it worth the costs of travel to neighbouring countries to make their purchases. Variations in VAT rates between countries continue to be substantial.

A further step to removing distortions in trade is the adoption of a single currency. The absence of monetary union creates distortion by discouraging producers from engaging in international trade. As we have seen, this can be because of the uncertainty inherent in free exchange rates. Even fixed exchange rates cannot eliminate this fear since the fixing is not irrevocable. The pound sterling, the peseta and the lira, among others, were devalued while in the system. Discouragement to trade can also happen because of the transactions costs to which we referred above.

It can be argued, therefore, that without a monetary union, resources move too much towards sectors isolated from international competition and away from goods such as manufactures that are relatively easily traded. Eliminating exchange rates would not make it possible for all goods and services to enter into international trade. Not many people will fly from Paris to Milan for a hair-cut. However, the removal of separate currencies should increase the ease of trading in some products.

Potential benefit 3: removal of a balance of payments constraint

We have already seen what a concern to an economy the balance of payments account can be. An economy can have an unemployment problem that suggests an expansionist macroeconomic policy but a balance of payments deficit that makes governments fear to stimulate demand for fear of worsening the deficit. Some portion of rising demand will leak into imports, while a reduction in demand will be reflected in a reduced quantity of imports.

Figure 20.6 illustrates an import schedule. It shows imports as a function of national income. The ratio of imports to income is called the *average propensity to import*. On the other hand, the change in imports associated with a change in income is called the *marginal propensity to import*. It shows the extent to which increased prosperity is reflected in increased imports.

This relationship is not necessarily proportional because, during boom periods, short-term domestic supply constraints may cause a particularly sharp increase in imports. Yet even during a period of high unemployment, national income may grow, causing import demand to rise. This creates balance of payments problems.

Monetary union appears to eliminate this problem entirely. There would be no balance of payments accounts for countries with a common currency. Talk of balance of payments deficit with, say, Germany would be as meaningless as talk of a deficit between Hampshire and Surrey. A great constraint upon government policy would be removed through entry into monetary union.

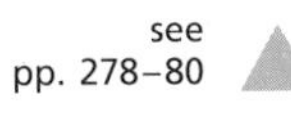
see pp. 278–80

While there is some truth in this assertion, things are not quite so straightforward, as we can see from Figure 20.7. You will recall from Chapter 13 that, in equilibrium, injections into the circular flow of income will be equal to

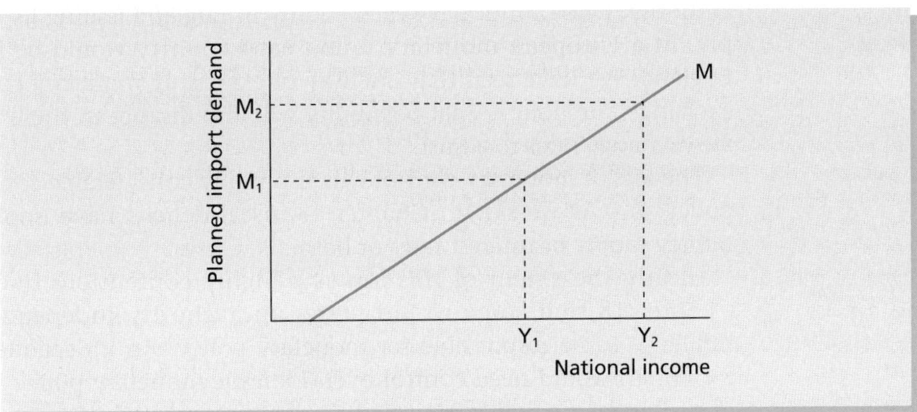

Figure 20.6 **Imports as a function of income**

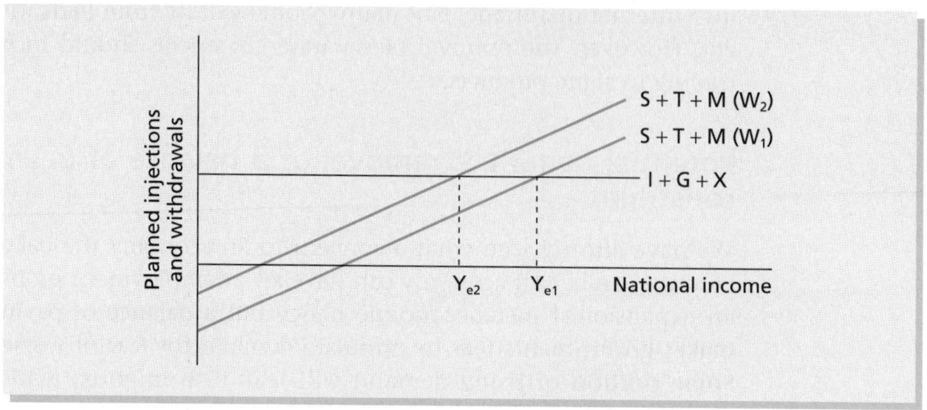

Figure 20.7 **Effects of an increase in autonomous import demand**

withdrawals from it: S + T + M = I + G + X. This is plotted in Figure 20.7. Suppose now a country's citizens show an increased preference for imports. We assume that the increase in import demand is not a function of increased income in this case, simply a change in tastes. The additional leakage out of the circular flow shifts the withdrawals function upwards from W_1 to W_2 in Figure 20.7. The reduction in aggregate demand lowers income through a multiplier effect from Y_{e1} to Y_{e2}.

So an absence of balance of payments data will not mean that the problem does not exist; it will simply appear in a different form. Since a correction cannot be made by an exchange rate adjustment, the problem will surface as a regional problem. National income will be too low in such areas. This is well recognised in Europe. As we saw in Chapter 5, there is much concentration on regional issues because of closer European integration.

see pp. 109–11

Potential cost 1: loss of monetary sovereignty

The most obvious cost of monetary union is that each country which joins it must concede its sovereignty over monetary policy to a central monetary authority. One cannot have each county in England issuing its own money supply. In a European monetary union each country would be like a county in England. We have seen that one way of exercising monetary control is through exchange rate policy. That possibility will also disappear: there will be no separate exchange rates to adjust.

see p. 393

The loss of monetary control will also imply considerable constraints on fiscal policy too. As we saw in Chapter 18, fiscal deficits have implications for the money supply or interest rates or both.

see pp. 383–409

Clearly the extent of this loss is a highly contentious one. We argued in Chapter 18 that some would prefer an authority independent of political influence to be responsible for monetary policy. An independent central bank for Britain would need control over domestic monetary policy and the conduct of exchange rate policy. However, in a monetary union there cannot be a British central bank at all. It must be a European one.

see pp. 383–409

Loss of monetary sovereignty is a real cost, then. As we saw in Chapter 18, it depends upon one's views with respect to macroeconomic policy-making as to whether it matters very much.

Potential cost 2: short-term adjustment costs

If a strong economy is to form a monetary union with a weaker one, there will be difficulties for the weaker one. If the weaker country's budgetary position is weak, in that there is a high PSBR or large national debt, its monetary growth is likely to be excessive. On the other hand, if interest rates are much higher, currency flows will be high, as we saw earlier in the chapter. This, too, will have implications for the money supply. But if its monetary growth is excessive, it is likely to have a problem with inflation. If there are inflationary pressures in the weaker economy, it cannot adjust inside the monetary union via exchange rate depreciation. Therefore countries that wish to achieve monetary union will need to see their economies converging in terms of the key macroeconomic variables.

In the light of these factors the only countries that qualified for entry into full monetary union are those that, European heads of government agreed, met the following convergence criteria.

1 *Inflation performance.* Inflation had to be not more than 1.5 per cent above the average of the 'best' three countries' performance.
2 *Government debt.* The national debt had to be not more than 60 per cent of GDP.[3]
3 *Government borrowing.* The PSBR had to be not more than 3 per cent of GDP.
4 *Exchange rates.* A country had to have been in the ERM and its exchange rate should have stayed within the normal fluctuation margins of the ERM for a minimum of two years.
5 *Interest rates.* Interest rates, the rate on long-term government debt, had to be not more than 2 per cent above the 'best' three countries' performance.

The countries involved in monetary union met with considerable success in adjusting their economies to meet the criteria. Figure 20.8 shows how much lower inflation was as the date for union approached. Note that not only was inflation lower but variations between member countries were also smaller.

There was also a significant reduction in government borrowing over the same period. Figure 20.9 shows how the EU average PSBR fell from well over 4 per cent of GDP in 1991 to an average of well under 2 per cent by 1998.

A picture of similar considerable achievement can be seen in Figure 20.10 with respect to interest rates with a decline from an average around 11 per cent in 1991 to around 5 per cent in 1998. Again, the variation between members is also much less. One reason for the performance with respect to interest rates was the success with inflation. Since inflation was lower, nominal interest rates would inevitably decline if real interest rates were to stay constant. In fact real interest rates also declined over the period. There was one very peculiar absentee from the list of qualifications for membership of monetary union. No reference was made to unemployment. Whatever a country's level of unemployment it would not be excluded from joining EMU. In fact unemployment rose during

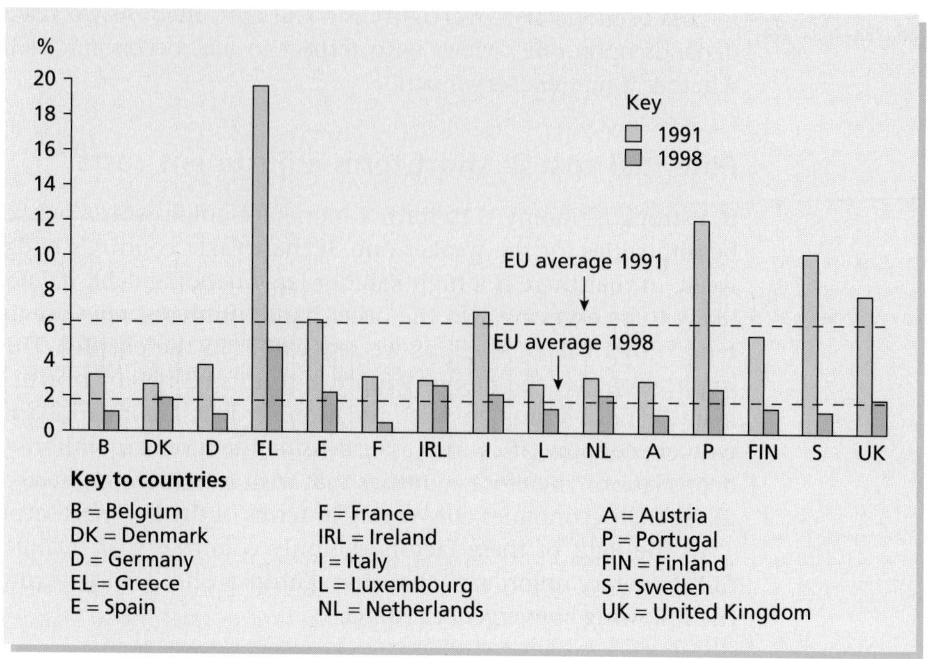

Figure 20.8 Inflation rates in the EU

Source: adapted from Eurostat data

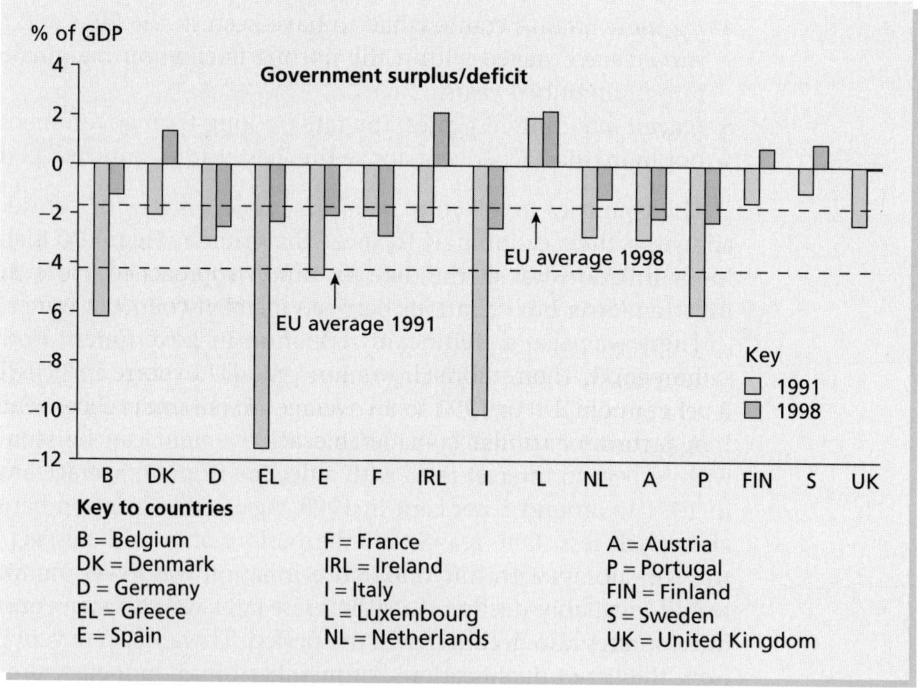

Figure 20.9 EU governments' budgetary positions

Source: adapted from Eurostat data

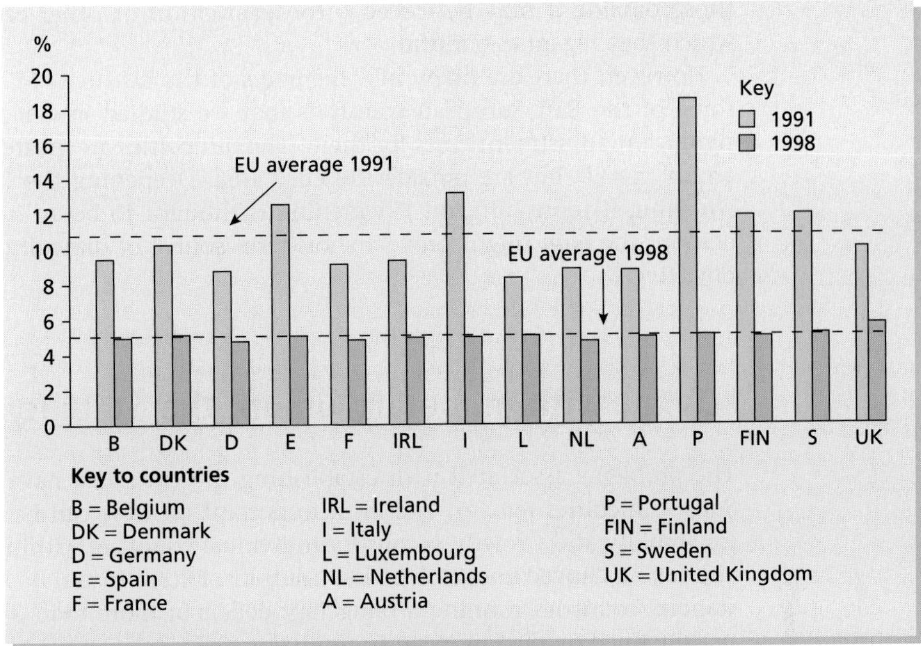

Figure 20.10 **Nominal long-term interest rates in the EU**

Source: adapted from Eurostat data

Table 20.5 **Unemployment in the European Union, percentage**

1991–96	1997	1998	1999	2000	2001	2002	2003[a]
10.2	10.1	8.5	8.7	7.9	7.4	7.5	7.5

[a] Forecast

Source: adapted from Eurostat data

the period to transition. This also is hardly surprising. The sharp cuts in aggregate demand which were the result of cutting budget deficits were always likely to cause unemployment to increase. Table 20.5 shows a very high level of unemployment in the early 1990s. Yet these figures continue to be substantial.

Inevitably, then, monetary union produced short-term costs, notably in the level of unemployment. It will be some time before it becomes clear whether the long-term benefits justify the price paid.

Potential cost 3: deepening hinders widening

Since the formation in 1958 of the original 'common market' with six members, the EU has expanded in number. The disparities now in terms of economic development are greater than they were, which makes a closer union harder. Now that there is a large and powerful area of monetary union, the non-euro members could be disadvantaged. For example, inward investment into the EU from Japan or the United States may be drawn to the currency area for fear that those outside it may be forced into devaluation or other economic policies which they regard as harmful.

However, there are many new members of the EU (from May 2004), notably some of the East European countries that we studied in Chapter 1. There are significant adjustment costs for them. The difficulties are greater still while they are in the EU but are outside the euro area. Deepening the Union will make widening it more difficult. If widening is thought to be an important consideration, the euro might prove a short-term source of difficulty in meeting that objective.

20.5 Living with monetary union: the Stability Pact

The problems associated with establishing the euro area have not gone away. Some difficulties remain. The most important of these can be seen in the Pact for Stability and Growth. It calls for individual countries within the euro area to aim for a balanced budget or to be in surplus. Except in certain specified circumstances, countries running a budgetary deficit of more than 3 per cent can be heavily fined by the European Commission.

The rationale for the Pact

The Pact was originally proposed by Germany but agreed by all euro area governments. It was felt necessary to determine that countries continued to operate with a measure of fiscal prudence. Let us suppose that the government of one member runs a substantial deficit. It can do so by borrowing. This is possible by the issuing of a substantial quantity of its bonds. Those who hold that country's bonds may now fear that they may not be repaid, or at least, paid under less favourable circumstances. They will therefore sell those bonds, increasing their supply and depressing their price. Banks holding a lot of these bonds find that the value of their assets has been eroded substantially. Depositors might now fear for the safety of their deposits and withdraw funds, threatening the banks with collapse.

The ECB will now come under pressure to buy the bonds of the government that is in trouble. This is partly to prevent a collapse in that country but partly to prevent it spreading to other counties in the Union. Thus the weak countries' actions may threaten the strong.

The problem, then, is that the citizens of the strong countries being run prudently are bailing out the citizens of the weak. The weaker economies are tempted to be free riders at the expense of the strong. It is to eliminate this 'public good' problem that the Pact was established.

Problems with the Pact

In practice the Pact created pressures that were not anticipated. Recession and considerable unemployment has been a fact of life in Europe for many years.

During a recession tax receipts fall and government expenditure rises. The result is budget deficits. The Keynesian remedy is to accept this situation and indeed possibly to enlarge the deficit as a countercyclical device. The Pact prevents this remedy. Ironically, it was Germany that first found their budget deficit breaching the 3 per cent limit, although other countries struggled also. Arguably, therefore, the Stability Pact does more harm than good.

All this suggests that there are continuing costs in being part of a single currency area. However, it does not necessarily follow that the costs outweigh the benefits.

20.6 The UK and monetary union

Should the UK be part of European Monetary Union? We have already seen the potential costs and benefits of such a union in general terms but there are four matters to which the UK in particular must give attention in making an assessment. Note that although there are significant political issues, we concentrate here only upon economic considerations.

UK convergence costs

If the UK were to adopt the single currency it would need to meet the convergence criteria we have already considered. In fact it already meets the criteria with respect to interest rates, inflation and government budgetary position. The one ground on which it does not qualify is the exchange rate condition.

Given the entry criteria sterling should stay in a fixed relation to the euro for a period of two years. This is a constraint on economic policy. For example, the Bank of England has to set interest rates, as we saw in Chapter 18, to achieve an internal goal, an inflation rate of around $2^{1}/_{2}$ per cent. As we have seen in this chapter, interest rates are a key weapon to control the external value of sterling. It is not inconceivable that the appropriate rate of interest for achieving internal balance is inappropriate for keeping the value of sterling in a fixed relationship to the euro.

A far more serious problem, however, occurs if the UK enters monetary union at the 'wrong' exchange rate. For example, the current value of sterling (at least according to Table 20.3) is too high against the euro. This would make UK producers uncompetitive with the rest of the euro area with a potential for unemployment in the foreseeable future.

UK balance of payments difficulties

As we have seen, balance of payments difficulties can remain for a country even if it is part of a currency union. An excess of imports over exports has the same effect on output and employment, but with no possibility of a correction through exchange rate adjustment.

The UK has an exceptionally high tendency to devote rises in national income to imports, especially to manufactured imports. Referring back to Figure 20.6,

Table 20.6 **Employer's benefit costs[a] as % of base pay[b]**

Italy	43
France	46
Belgium	41
Greece	38
Spain	37
Portugal	32
Finland	27
Germany	27
Austria	26
Ireland	20
Netherlands	21
UK	14
Luxembourg	19

[a] Includes social security, mandatory benefits and voluntary benefits [b] Figures are for 2002

Source: Mercer Human Resource Consulting

when national income moves from Y_1 to Y_2, the increase in imports from M_1 to M_2 is considerable. In other words, the UK income elasticity of demand for imports is higher than that of many other countries. The potential for a fall in national income is therefore considerable. In terms of Figure 20.7 for any given increase in imports the movement from $Y._1$ to $Y._2$ could be large.

Although, faced with this problem, the UK could not devolve its currency two other things could provide an alternative solution to the problem. One is an active regional policy by Europe. However, it can be argued that the slowness of decision making in granting regional aid would make this an unattractive solution.

The alternative solution would be flexible labour markets. If unemployment appears and wage rates are flexible enough equilibrium employment can be restored through the process described in Chapter 5. However, the signs within the euro area do not look good. The evidence suggests rather inflexible labour markets. First, employers have high costs to meet in addition to the wages they pay. Table 20.6 shows, for example, that in Italy social security costs etc. add another 54 per cent to wage costs. In the UK, by comparison, the figure is 19 per cent. The fear then is that Britain would be committing itself to a monetary union with no possibility of exchange rate adjustment but no other efficient adjustment mechanism either. Something of that labour inflexibility can also be seen in Table 20.5. Unemployment in Europe has been around 10 per cent for a decade.

The UK trade cycle

All Western European economies are subject to trade cycles. Although the long-term trend for growth is upward, actual growth rates fluctuate around the trend

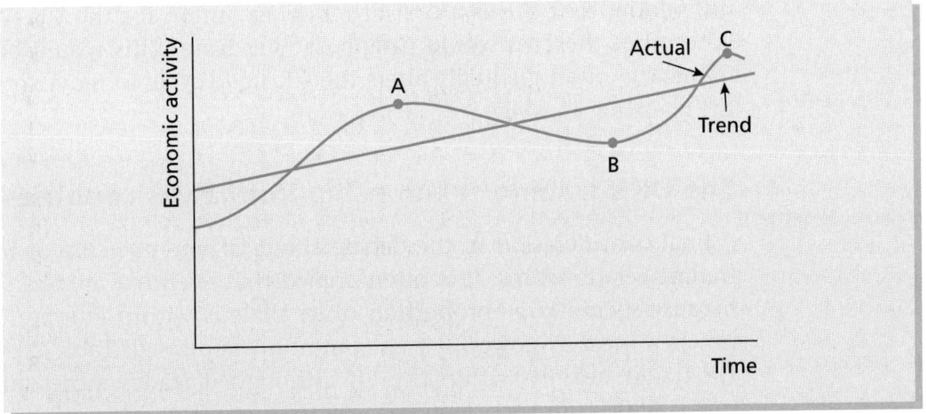

Figure 20.11 **Economic activity and trade cycles**

as shown in Figure 20.11. Governments attempt to limit the size of the fluctuations from trend. At a time represented by, say, point A in the diagram the fear of inflation engendered by high output and full employment causes governments to raise interest rates and/or tighten fiscal policy. At a point in the trade cycle such as point B the reverse government policy tends to apply in order to prevent falling output and rising unemployment. Inside a monetary union with one central bank one interest rate is set for the whole region. It will be relatively high at points A and C and relatively low at point B.

There is concern, however, that the UK trade cycle does not synchronise with that of the rest of Europe. We can use Figure 20.12 to show what that means. Monetary policy for Europe will be inappropriate for the UK, so that, for example, when European interest rates are high at point A they will need to be low for the UK which is at point D. This difference in appropriate interest rates will be impossible inside a monetary union. The problem cannot be overcome by differing fiscal policies. We have already seen that a single central bank setting a common interest rate imposes severe restrictions on fiscal freedom. There is

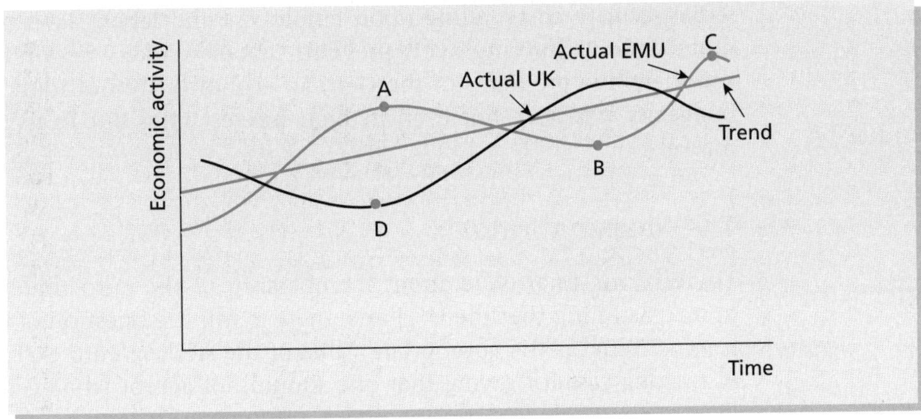

Figure 20.12 **UK and European trade cycles**

little doubt that this is a cost of monetary union for the UK. What is less clear is whether the cost would disappear over time. This would be the case if full monetary union gradually alters the UK trade cycle to move in step with that of the countries in EMU.

The UK's trading relationship with EMU countries

A final consideration in the debate about UK membership of EMU concerns its trading relationships. It is often argued that eventual membership is inevitable because such a large proportion of its trade is within Europe. This argument is nowhere near as powerful as is commonly supposed. Table 20.4 shows that the UK trades heavily within the EU although it trades more outside than other major EMU countries. However, the important consideration is the proportion of UK *output* which is traded within the EU. This figure is around 10 per cent. In other words 90 per cent of UK output is *not* traded within the EU. On this ground there is no convincing reason for saying that monetary union is essential for the UK.

The UK and the Stability Pact

Given what we have already seen about the Stability and Growth Pact, some see this as a further argument for the UK to remain outside the euro area. The Pact can be seen as a further harmful constraint upon UK economic policy. Others, particularly those of a monetarist persuasion do not see this as a difficulty. There are two reasons for this more optimistic view.

First, sound economic policy would require the government to follow the constraint of the Pact in any case. If one believes that a balanced budget is at all times essential, the Pact is of no significance. The appropriate policy is to balance the budget and to leave markets, especially labour markets, to bring about full employment equilibrium.

The second consideration is closely linked to this. The problem of high unemployment in Europe, one can argue, is not that of governments aiming for a balanced budget. Rather it is inflexible European labour markets. The high social security costs falling upon employers and labour laws making dismissal more difficult for employers prevents labour markets responding flexibly. On this view, the problems of the German economy are not found primarily in its budgetary position, nor even in high interest rates but in its inflexible labour markets.

The 'docking' rate

There is one final issue about membership of the euro that we briefly touch upon. Assuming that the UK joins, there is still the question of the *rate* at which it joins. What is the appropriate value of the sterling/euro exchange rate? There is a strong case for saying that one should not accept whatever rate happens to exist at the time. PPP is a long-term argument. The rate existing at the time of entry may not be one that reflects long-run equilibrium.

As with some other matters pertaining to the euro, there are contrasting views about the seriousness of this problem. There is an argument that sees the problem as of little consequence. Most studies suggest that the PPP rate of the pound sterling to the euro is around 1.35–1.40. For the period that the euro has been in existence sterling has been closer to 1.6. But as we saw earlier in the chapter, markets will gradually adjust that rate. So the foreign exchange market can be left to establish such a rate in the period before entry. A more pessimistic view sees little evidence that markets can be relied upon unaided to give an appropriate exchange rate. It would require a lowering of interest rates in the UK to drive the value of sterling downwards. However, the interest rate needed to achieve that level is one that may not be appropriate to achieve internal balance for the economy. On this view the docking rate provides a further difficulty for euro membership.

20.7 Conclusion

It is impossible for a country such as the UK to isolate itself from international trade. The law of comparative advantage leaves us in no doubt that the UK would be far poorer without such trade. However, there is great debate about how it conducts policy towards trade in general and its exchange rate in particular. In this chapter we have concentrated on exchange rate policy. What are the major options available to the UK?

At present, the UK is not part of any exchange rate mechanism, although it is committed to free trade in Europe as part of the Single European Market. It could remain so, either allowing its exchange rate to float or attempting to tie it informally to the euro.

Alternatively it could abandon sterling altogether for the euro. It is extremely difficult to compare the costs and benefits of such a decision, although it has enormous implications, social, political and economic.

One way to view the economic advantages and disadvantages to the UK of rejoining the ERM is to ask whether the EU is an 'optimal currency area'. This is an area of countries where factors of production are mobile, wages and prices adjust easily to changes in demand and supply, and where the countries concerned already have substantial trading links with one another. Under these circumstances the net benefits of a single currency will almost certainly be positive. In the absence of these conditions countries may be better off outside such a union in order to retain some exchange rate flexibility. Unfortunately it is difficult to be precise about the extent to which the above conditions must be fulfilled for the benefits of joining to outweigh the costs.

CHAPTER SUMMARY

1. **The external value of a currency is determined by its supply and demand.**
2. **Purchasing power parity theory suggests that a currency's value tends towards a level such that balance of payments disequilibrium will be corrected.**

3 **Some economists believe that government intervention in currency markets can reduce business uncertainty, speculation and inflation.**

4 **A monetary union has both costs and benefits for its members.**

5 **Countries that have formed European monetary union paid substantial costs in that convergence criteria were severe.**

6 **It is difficult to assess whether the costs of monetary union outweigh the benefits.**

Questions for discussion

Guidance to the answers for the ***asterisked*** *numbered questions is available to students on the website for the book at* **www.booksites.net/heather.**

1* A country is suffering from a balance of payments deficit. The external value of its currency then falls. Would the government prefer that export demand was elastic, inelastic or unitary? Would the government prefer that import demand was elastic, inelastic or unitary?

2 In the chapter we showed how the British government might use reserves as an anti-speculative device. We did it by describing a market for sterling in euro terms and assumed that the speculative pressure came from the sale of sterling. Sketch the same process by constructing a diagram showing the market for euros in sterling terms.

3* Consider Figure 20.13, which shows the market for euros in sterling terms. Which of the following would tend to shift the demand curve to the right? (a) An decrease in UK incomes, (b) an increase in EU interest rates, (c) an increase in the European price level, (d) an increase in the UK price level.

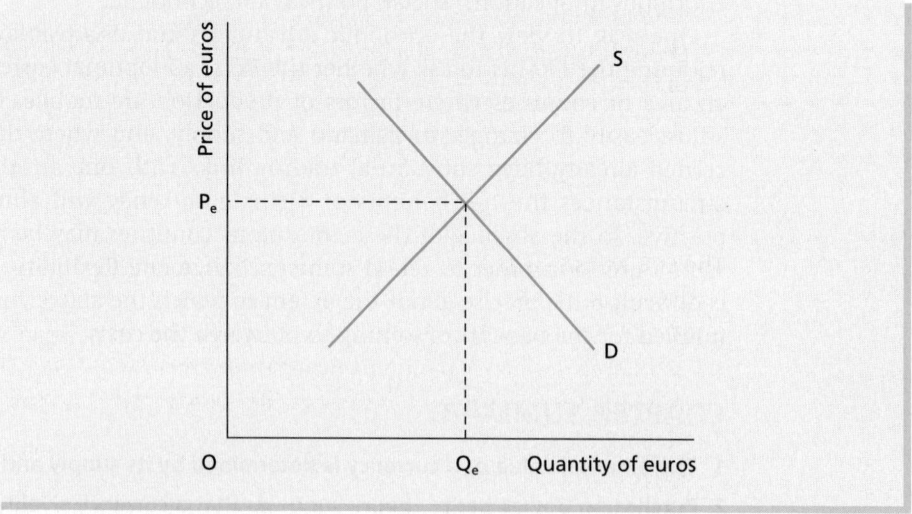

Figure 20.13 **The market for euros**

Table 20.7 **Bank model simulation: all interest rates +1% point**

	Exchange rate, fixed				*Exchange rate, free*
	1	*4*	*8*	*12*	*12*
Retail price index	0.4	0.3	0.2	–	−0.7
Current account (£ billion)	–	0.6	1.5	2.0	1.9

Percentage differences from base, except where stated, after specified quarter

Source: *Bank of England Quarterly Bulletin*, Vol. 30, No. 2, 1990

4 We considered in Chapter 14 the Bank of England model's figure for the effect of an interest rate increase of 1 per cent on the economy. The figures quoted were assuming that exchange rates were fixed. Table 20.7 reproduces some data from the model but also estimates interest rate effects assuming exchange rates are free to float. Comment on the different predicted effects under floating exchange rates.

5* How impressive do you find the argument that joining the euro would eliminate the balance of payments constraint on UK economic policy?

6 As we saw in the chapter, the nature of the ERM altered in the summer of 1993. To relieve speculative pressure on European currencies there was a substantial widening of the bands within which currencies were permitted to fluctuate. Was this decision in the interest of the ERM?

7* An economy operates with a fixed exchange rate. Why would a balance of payments deficit tend to put downward pressure on its domestic price level?

8 The former Eastern European economies that are members of the EU from May 2004 are committed to joining the euro at some stage in the future. What problems do you foresee with this?

9* For countries within the EU much of their trade is with other European partners. Much the same thing can be said of other trading blocs. To what extent is this a good thing?

10 Should sterling float, be in the ERM or be abandoned for a European currency union?

Websites

The ECB website is at:

www.ecb.int/

It contains information about the ECB and also a wealth of other information about the euro area. Economic data for the euro area can also be found at:

www.europa.eu.int/comm/economy-finance/indicators_en.htm

The Economist's website is at:

www.economist.com/

You can find information about the Big Mac index and much more, but it is a subscription site.

Notes

1 As we have seen before, the assumption is that markets adjust easily, quickly and correctly to eliminate disequilibrium.

2 Of course, a fixed exchange rate without a fixed money supply can be inflationary. Suppose sterling is tending to appreciate. The government prevents the rise of the pound by selling sterling. This, in and of itself, increases the money supply. There are more pounds in circulation. To prevent the effects of increased money supply, this will have to be 'sterilised'. The government will have to sell government debt to the value of its foreign exchange dealings, thereby preventing an increase in the supply of money.

3 National debt and the PSBR are not the same thing. The PSBR is a flow: it represents the difference between government expenditure and government income in a given year. The national debt is a stock: it represents the stock of all government debt accumulated over many years.

AFTERWORD

An overview of the economic system

If you have read through the previous 20 chapters of this book you have thought about a large number of topics of interest to economists and gained some insight into how economists analyse these issues. However, you have done much more. You have covered, at least to some extent, all of the major topics in an introductory economics course and can use the understanding you have gained to talk through any topic of interest to economists. Here we draw the strands of your knowledge together.

We began in Chapter 1 by examining the problem of scarcity. Output has an opportunity cost. In a competitive market system the scarcity problem is dealt with by a price mechanism. The price of any output reflects the opportunity cost of the resources committed to its production. We saw in Chapter 2 how supply and demand analysis helps us understand how the prices of many outputs are determined.

We then focused on demand. Why do consumers behave in the way they do? Chapters 3 and 4 gave insights into consumer behaviour. Then we turned to supply. Since willingness to supply is crucially determined by costs, Chapter 5 examined the relationship of output to cost in both the short and long run. In the short run, costs are determined by the law of diminishing returns. In the long run, economies and diseconomies of scale explain costs.

An understanding of consumer behaviour and production costs enabled us to understand in more detail how prices are determined. In perfectly competitive markets, where supply and demand analysis is most useful, firms have no control over prices. They accept the ruling market price and make decisions about output. They maximise profits at an output at which marginal cost is equal to marginal revenue. However, competition sees to it that in the long run they make only a normal profit. In other words they just cover opportunity costs. So firms are willing to remain in the industry if consumer demand remains at that level. This was the focus of Chapter 6.

In Chapters 7 and 8 we examined price determination in other markets. In monopolistic competition firms produce where marginal cost is equal to marginal revenue. They make only a normal profit in long-run equilibrium because entry barriers are low. However, the use of society's resources by such industries may not be ideal. Price does not reflect marginal opportunity cost. In monopolistic industries entry barriers enable incumbent firms to make profits in excess of normal as well as enabling them to produce an output at which price does not reflect marginal opportunity cost. In oligopolistic industries where entry barriers are also high, we have price and non-price competition among the few. As we explained in Chapter 9, where entry barriers are substantial, firms may not seek to maximise profits. They may not be obliged to if there are effective limits to the extent of competition.

An understanding of pricing behaviour enabled us in Chapter 10 further to explore aspects of efficiency and market failure. Businesses frequently think about cost efficiency but an equal concern of economists is allocative efficiency, since this concept enables us to examine whether scarce resources are used optimally.

The price mechanism helps us to understand how markets determine the price of output. It also aids us in understanding of input prices. Chapter 11 gave insights into the pricing of one key resource, that of labour. As with output markets prices may or may not be allocatively efficient.

Chapter 12 developed a key microeconomic issue of external costs and market failure but also introduced the macro economy. How do we measure the national output of an economy in the course of the year? Understanding National Income accounts prepared us for grappling with the question of 'full employment output' in Chapter 13. Can markets be safely left to bring about a level of output that uses all society's resources and causes us to operate close to the opportunity cost curve? Keynesian economists believe that they cannot and so governments must manipulate the volume of aggregate demand. In this chapter we also considered what this means for the government's budgetary position.

In the longer term the opportunity cost curve will shift outwards. One way of bringing this about is by society's forgoing current consumption in order to invest. Investment was accordingly the subject of Chapter 14. We showed how, in principle, the market can give an optimal volume of investment, in particular by considering the effect of interest rates on investment. As in other areas of the economy, however, it is possible to argue that markets fail to deliver optimality.

In Chapter 15 we considered inflation. We saw how it can be measured. However, we also examined the causes of inflation, concentrating especially on the controversy between Keynesian and classical economists over the relationship between inflation and unemployment. To Keynesians there is a trade-off but to classicals, if the trade-off exists at all, it is only in the short run.

Classical scholars worry that high levels of taxation cause disincentive effects in the production of goods and services. Accordingly Chapter 16 considered the distribution of income and the effects of the tax system on aggregate supply. Chapter 17 also focused on supply. Classical economists believe that markets optimise the use of scarce resources. So the chapter considered one aspect of this, the privatisation programme. Transferring resources from the state to the private sector can have effects at both the micro level of the economy in terms of allocative efficiency and at the macro level in terms of its effect on the government's finances.

Chapter 18 returned to the Keynesian/Classical controversy. This time we examined monetary policy and explained in more detail the determination of the money supply and interest rates. We did this in the context of the UK's central bank, the Bank of England.

The final two chapters, 19 and 20 concentrated on the international economy. In Chapter 19 we examined a balance of payments account. We also explained the law of comparative advantage that underlies international trade. We also thought about the extent to which markets can be left to achieve balance of payments equilibrium. Finally, the focus of Chapter 20 was the foreign exchange market and its role in facilitating international trade and payments.

By the end of the book, therefore, you have examined how a modern market economy functions at both the micro and macro level. You should feel in a position now to think through your own view not only upon the topics we used to illustrate these principles but upon a host of questions that we did not directly tackle. You have developed a set of techniques for analysing economic problems. I hope you find them valuable to your thinking for many years to come.

APPENDIX 1

Guide to sources of information

Many students of economics spend so much of their study time reading the course textbooks that they do not find time to consult other sources of information. This is understandable. It is also unfortunate. Data in textbooks inevitably become dated, so it is good to supplement the texts with information which is being constantly updated. There is a vast amount of such material.

The purpose of this appendix is to provide a list of the major sources of data and information which you will find useful at an introductory level in addition to the websites given at the end of each chapter. The list is not comprehensive; it simply points you to those sources which are most widely used and most readily available. These publications will be available at university and college libraries and at larger public libraries also. You can buy your own copies of some titles fairly cheaply. Some publications are free; others are quite expensive.

Annual Abstract of Statistics

This publication covers a wide range of social and economic variables. The data are generally annual observations. It is published once a year.

Bank of England Quarterly Bulletin

The data in this quarterly publication cover mainly financial and monetary topics. The *Bulletin* also contains some good articles, not all of which are strictly limited to money and banking matters.

Economic Briefing

Available at four-monthly intervals and produced by HM Treasury, this publication is designed and written with students in mind. The coverage of material is limited.

Economic Review

Published five times per year, this publication is aimed at students of economics.

Economic Surveys

Annual publications by the OECD on individual countries. They provide invaluable updated data and reports on all major countries.

Economic Trends

This is a very valuable publication from the Central Statistical Office. It is published monthly and is therefore very up to date. A good range of data is published as well as some excellent articles on current economic issues.

Economics and Business Education

Formerly published under the title *Economics*, this is published three times a year by the Economics Association. Each issue contains just a few, but quite substantial articles, some of which are on economic topics, some on the teaching of economics and business.

The Economist

A weekly publication, *The Economist* is widely available and is read throughout the business world. It covers a wide range of stories on economics and political matters. A comprehensive source of economic news and analysis from all parts of the world.

Finance and Development

This is published quarterly by the International Monetary Fund and the World Bank; each edition contains about ten articles on international issues. Particularly valuable for Third World issues.

Labour Market Trends

A monthly publication with up-to-date statistics on labour market matters. Contains some international data also and relevant articles of interest.

Lloyds Bank Economic Bulletin

This is published, free, bi-monthly. It takes one topic of current economic interest and examines it in a way which is usually comprehensible for a first-year student. There is also a brief update on the international financial outlook.

National Income and Expenditure

This is known as the 'Blue Book'. It is published in September of each year, giving data on a wide range of economic topics, not only for the previous year, but for the last ten. It is very useful.

New Economy

A quarterly publication containing lively articles of current economic interest giving a generally 'left of centre' perspective.

OECD Economic Outlook

This is published twice yearly. It provides data on a range of basic topics across all OECD countries.

Social Trends

An annual publication covering much social data. If you are interested in wealth, income and its distribution, or in household spending patterns, it is very useful.

If you require data which you cannot find, the Government Statistical Service may well be able to help. It produces annually a publication called *Government*

Statistics: A Brief Guide to Sources which will probably enable you to find any published government statistics you need. Failing that, consult the more comprehensive, but less frequently published, *Guide to Official Statistics*, which any reference library will hold.

APPENDIX 2

Sources of information on share prices

Markets work best in the presence of adequate information. If you are thinking of investing in some equities, what information is available for you so that you can make a rational decision? One source of information is company accounts. In order to have a full listing on the Stock Exchange, a company must produce fully audited accounts twice a year. This can be a valuable source of information about a company's prospects but an analysis of company accounts is beyond the scope of this appendix.

Another valuable source is the financial pages of the *Financial Times* which, among many other things, give information about each company's shares at the close of share trading on the previous day. It would be worth buying a copy so that you can see the information in print for yourself. If you are interested in a UK company, turn to the section of the *FT* called 'Companies and markets'; if you want information on a leading company in another country, look at the section 'World Stock Markets'. Near the back you will find 'London Share Service'. Pick a company, perhaps one you know well like Marks & Spencer. You will need to know what general sector it is under – electricity, transport, chemicals, or whatever. ICI, for example, is listed under 'chemicals'; Marks & Spencer under 'general retailers'. Provided you have not picked a Monday edition, you will find the following information.

Column 1

This gives the name of the company and sometimes a technical note about anything to which the *Financial Times* wishes to draw your attention.

Columns 2 and 3

Column 2 gives the price at the end of trading on the previous day. This is the mid-price. We saw earlier that there is a spread of prices between what one can buy the stock for and a lower price at which one can sell. So a closing mid-price of, say, 210 pence might represent a closing bid price of 213 pence and an offer price of 207 pence. Column 3 gives the change in the mid-price on the previous day's close.

The change can be quite substantial even in that short time. Demand may have shifted in response to some news which significantly affects the prospects of the stock. Possibly, it is simply that shares have gone ex dividend, that is, the people buying have just missed this year's dividend and will have to wait for the next one. Hence demand will have fallen suddenly.

Columns 4 and 5

These tell you the highest and the lowest price at which your chosen share has traded in the past year or so. You can now look at the current price to see if this is near the top of its traded range, indicating that the market thinks the company is doing well, or it may be near the bottom, an indicator that market expectations for the company are not good. You can also see how volatile the market has been in the past year or so. You may be surprised at how much the value of your shares can rise and fall in a year.

Column 6

Column 6 is the column headed 'vol '000s'. This shows the number of shares that changed hands on that day.

Column 7

This is the gross yield of the share, calculated as the dividend before tax paid multiplied by 100 and divided by the share price. Thus, if your chosen share had a 5 pence gross dividend payment and the share price was £1, the gross yield is $(5p \times 100)/100p = 5$.

Remember what we said about risk. If the company is thought to be secure and relatively risk-free, the share price will be higher and the gross yield lower. Higher yields usually indicate riskier shares.

Column 8

This is the P/E, or price/earnings, ratio. The earnings of the company in the last year, net of taxation, are taken and expressed as a proportion of the share price. So if the company above had a net earnings per share of 25 pence and its share price was still 100 pence then its P/E ratio would be 100/25 = 4. Clearly, therefore, all other things being equal, a high P/E ratio indicates a share highly valued by financial investors.

In the Monday edition of the *FT*, some of the above information is missing but several additional pieces are provided, the most important of which are as follows:

Column 3

The column headed 'WK % ch'nge' gives the change in the mid-price of the share not in pence but in percentage terms over the previous week's trading. Political or economic events can make these changes substantial.

Column 4

This column, headed 'Div', gives the dividend paid in pence per share during the last year assuming tax deducted at the standard rate. Some companies may not have been in a position to pay a dividend at all if their profits have been low or non-existent. Sometimes a company will pay a dividend out of reserves if it is confident that trading has been difficult but will pick up again soon.

Column 5

The proportion of net (after-tax) profits paid out in dividends can vary greatly between companies. So one might like to know how comfortably the company can afford to pay that level of dividend. The 'cover' tells us how many times the dividend is covered by its net profits. So a cover of 2.7 says that its net profits would have paid out a dividend of 2.7 times as much if it had distributed all its net profits. All other things being equal, it is clearly good if a company's dividend is well covered. The company is then giving a return to shareholders and still retaining funds for future use.

Column 6

Column 6 is the column headed 'Market cap £m'. This shows the stock market's valuation of the whole company at the close of dealings at the end of that week. It is simply the number of shares issued multiplied by the market price of each share. It therefore shows the value placed by the market on the whole company. This value is often substantially different from the valuation of the company's assets as shown in the company balance sheet.

The other Monday columns refer to the timing of dividend pay-out by each company, the amount of dividend paid and a City line number. If you ring it, up-to-the-minute information can be provided on that particular share, although the cost of the call is not cheap.

The *Financial Times* also provides indications of the 'average' level of prices of shares. There are several different averages. The most commonly quoted one is the *Financial Times* Stock Exchange (FTSE) index of the leading 100 companies, called the 'Footsie'. It is a weighted average value of all the leading 100 companies' share prices. Unlike most indices, it is based on the number of 1,000 – the base at the end of 1983. It reached 6,000 in August 1998. It fall below 4,000 during 2002. On most days, the Footsie will only change by a small number, but unexpected changes in economic conditions might cause it to rise or fall by 100 points, or even more.

If your television has Ceefax or Teletext, you can find what is happening to the Footsie every minute. Share prices for many companies are adjusted and given every hour or two. For fuller up-to-the-minute information you can go into a share shop and see current prices of all companies changing even more rapidly. There are also various websites where you can find this information.

What we have now looked at are only some of the main features of the British equity market. Information is available in the *Financial Times* and on Ceefax and Teletext, on the change in other indices for other countries, the best known of which are the Dow Jones index in New York, the Nikkei in Tokyo and the Hang Seng in Hong Kong. There are also measures now of movements in the average of leading European stocks, as the British equities market is seen more and more in the context of Europe as a whole.

APPENDIX 3

Measuring the distribution of income: the Gini coefficient

It is possible to measure the unevenness of any distribution of income by the use of a *Gini coefficient*. The simplest formula for this is:

$$G = \frac{1}{N}\sum_{i=1}^{N} a(N - 2i + 1)$$

where N is the number of income groups and a is the proportion of total income received by a given group.

We illustrate its use by an example. Let us divide the population into five equal-sized groups (quintile groups – this is the form in which UK data are usually presented). Let us assume that income is perfectly evenly distributed. Here, $N = 5$, $a = 20$ (*for every group*) and i takes values from 1 to 5.

$$G = \frac{1}{N}\sum_{i=1}^{N} a(N - 2i + 1)$$

$$G = \frac{1}{5}\{20(5 - 2 + 1) + 20(5 - 4 + 1) + 20(5 - 6 + 1) + 20(5 - 8 + 1) + 20(5 - 10 + 1)\}$$

$$G = \frac{1}{5}(80 + 40 + 0 - 40 - 80) = 0$$

So $G = 0$. That is, income distribution is completely even across the groups. G is the area bounded by the line of absolute equality and the Lorenz curve, expressed as a proportion of the whole triangle under the line of absolute equality. The line for the above figures follows the line of absolute equality. For any income data the value of G must be between 0 and 100. Those values closer to 0 indicate a more even spread of income; those nearer to 100 more uneven. A value of 0 indicates absolute equality; a value of 100 indicates absolute inequality. The Gini coefficient enables us to compare different income distributions even if two Lorenz curves cross as in Figure A3.1, in that we are comparing the appropriate areas in each case.

The simple formula given above assumes that all households within a given group have the same (equivalised) income. *Economic Trends* uses a rather more sophisticated form of calculation in which this assumption is dropped. The

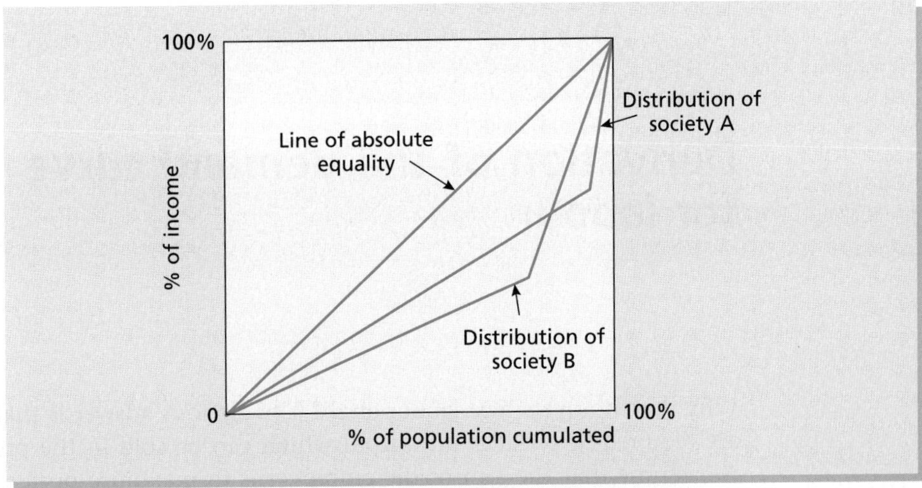

Figure A3.1 **Using a Gini coefficient to compare income distributions**

values for the Gini coefficient are then given as follows. For 1979, equivalised original income has a value of 44; disposable income is 27. For 2000/01 the respective values are 51 and 35. Income is less evenly distributed in 2000/01 than in 1979.

APPENDIX 4

Derivation of the demand curve for labour

Why do employers hire labour at all? The obvious answer is that labour services are required to produce an output which can be sold in the product market. If we assume that the aim of the employer is to maximise profits, the labour will only be demanded if the output can be sold at a profit which is at least 'normal'. We often say that labour is a 'derived' demand: the demand for labour is derived from the demand for the output which that labour produces.

Let us now consider the relationship between costs and revenue in order to determine the quantity of labour that a firm will demand. The concept of profit maximisation focuses the analysis on marginal revenue and marginal cost, as we first saw in Chapter 6.

see pp. 121–5

Recall that marginal revenue is the change in total revenue owing to the sale of one more unit of output. In the context of labour demand, the relevant concept is marginal revenue product. This is the amount of output produced by the last (marginal) employee multiplied by the marginal revenue received when that output is sold. In other words, we are discovering the value to the employer of the output which the additional worker produces. So the employer's decision about labour employment is determined partly in the product market, where the price of the output is set. However, it is also determined partly by the productivity of the marginal employee, and the more employees are taken on, the less will be produced by the marginal unit of labour. You may remember why this is so from Chapter 5.

see pp. 100–3

In the short run, the law of diminishing returns will set in as the employer expands his workforce. That is, beyond some point, if an additional person is employed, he/she raises output, but by a smaller amount than the previously employed person. We showed that to be the case in Chapter 5 also.

Now let us assume for simplicity that the price of the output is fixed as far as the employer is concerned (that is, there is perfect competition in the product market, so that price equals marginal revenue). Then, beyond some point, as the firm employs additional labour, and the amount of additional output declines, what is happening to the value of that additional output? With marginal revenue constant, marginal revenue product must decrease as more labour is taken on.

The marginal cost we will assume to be equal to the wage that the employer must pay. So the employer will take on labour up to the point where the declining marginal product equals the wage rate. This is the amount of employment where the marginal cost to the employer is equal to the value of the marginal output. It therefore represents his profit-maximising level of employment. Should the wage rate alter, the employer will alter the quantity of labour demanded. The marginal revenue product curve becomes the demand curve for labour, sloping from top left to bottom right as for most demand curves.

This derivation is based on simplifying assumptions. However, the conclusion about the shape of the demand curve for labour holds when the main assumptions are relaxed.

APPENDIX 5

Determination of the multiplier

see pp. 283–6

This appendix demonstrates formally the determination of the multiplier introduced in Chapter 13.

Assume a closed economy (no international trade) and no government sector. Thus in equilibrium $Y = C + I$ where:

Y = aggregate output/income/expenditure
C = planned consumption
I = planned investment

i.e. output must be sufficient to meet demands from consumers and firms' plans to invest.

Assume, further, that planned investment is autonomous, that is independent of the level of income, and that consumption is some proportion of income, c. Then:

$$C = cY$$

Hence:

$$Y = cY + I$$

$$Y(1 - c) = I$$

$$\frac{Y}{I} = \frac{1}{1 - c}$$

If this is true for levels of national income then it will be true for changes also, i.e.:

$$\frac{\Delta Y}{\Delta I} = \frac{1}{1 - c}$$

Now $c + s = 1$, where s is the proportion of income that consumers wish to save (all income is saved or spent). Hence:

$$\frac{\Delta Y}{\Delta I} = \frac{1}{s}$$

In an open economy with a government sector, saving is not the only withdrawal from the circular flow of income. People pay a proportion of their additional income in taxes, t, and spend a proportion of their additional income on imports, m. Then:

$$\frac{\Delta Y}{\Delta I} = \frac{1}{s + t + m} \quad \text{or} \quad \frac{1}{w}$$

where *w* is the propensity to withdraw from the circular flow. This is the multiplier. In terms of our example in Table 13.3:

$$\frac{40}{20} = \frac{1}{0.5} = 2$$

Glossary

The purpose of this glossary is to provide you with concise definitions of the main terms that you will meet in your study of economics. Most of these terms are used at some point in this book but a number of terms not used elsewhere in the book are also defined here, since you may meet them in other reading.

Abnormal profit: The level of profit which is in excess of the income required to prevent a firm from switching its resources to an alternative use. It is also known as *supernormal* profit.

Absolute advantage: A country has an absolute advantage if it can produce a commodity using fewer resources than other countries. See also **Comparative advantage**.

Accelerator principle: The principle that the level of aggregate investment is determined by the rate at which national income is changing.

Ad valorem tax: A tax imposed on a good or service which is a proportion of its price rather than an absolute amount.

Adverse selection: The problem an insuring organisation has that those who choose to insure will tend to be in a high risk category.

Aggregate demand: The sum of all expenditures in the economy. This will be expenditure by consumers, plus investment, plus government expenditure, plus expenditure on exports, less expenditure on imports. The term may refer to intended demand or actual demand.

Aggregate supply: The total amount of all outputs which firms will wish to supply at different possible price levels.

Aggregate supply curve: A graphical construction showing the amount of planned total output at different possible price levels.

Allocative efficiency: Refers to a situation in which the output of each good in an economy is at a level which reflects the preference of consumers. Marginal social cost of production will equal marginal social benefit.

Appreciation: See **Depreciation**.

Arbitrage: The purchase of goods, services, currencies or commodities at a price less than the price prevailing elsewhere and their subsequent resale in the higher priced market.

Automatic stabilisers: Features of an economic system which automatically counter the tendency of the business cycle. For example, when aggregate demand expands and inflation begins to occur, the proportion of income taken in tax rises without the need of a government policy change, automatically dampening demand.

Autonomous demand: Demand which does not depend upon the level of income. For example, if a consumer has a zero income he/she will still spend either by running down assets or by borrowing. See also **Induced demand**.

Average cost: See **Average total cost**.

Average cost pricing: See **Full cost pricing**.

Average fixed cost: The fixed cost per unit of output, found by taking the total fixed cost and dividing by the number of units of output produced. It is a short-run concept since there are no fixed costs in the long run.

Average physical product: This is a short-run concept. It is the amount of output produced per unit of labour, found by taking the total output (product) produced and dividing by the number of units of labour employed.

Average product: See **Average physical product**.

Average propensity to consume: The proportion of total household income used for consumption expenditure. It is calculated as total consumption divided by total household income.

Average revenue: Revenue per unit of output, calculated as total revenue received for selling a product or service divided by the number of units produced.

Average tax rate: The ratio of taxes to income, calculated as total income divided by total taxes paid.

Average total cost: Cost per unit of production, calculated as total cost of producing a given level of output divided by the number of units produced. This is sometimes called *unit cost*.

Average variable cost: A short-run concept since all costs are variable in the long run. It is the variable cost per unit of production, and calculated as the total variable cost of producing a given level of output divided by the number of units produced.

Balanced budget: A situation in which the government's income from taxes etc. during a given time period exactly matches its expenditure.

Balance of payments: The record of a country's transactions with the rest of the world, consisting of a current account recording flows of currency from goods and services purchased or sold abroad, and a capital account recording flows of currency from the purchase and sales of financial assets.

Balance of trade: One part of the balance of payments account. It is the difference between the value of **visible exports** and the value of **visible imports** in a given period.

Bank of England: The name given to the British central bank. It takes responsibility for supervising monetary activity in Britain. It advises the government on interest rates and implements government policy in this area.

Barriers to entry: The obstacles which new firms have to overcome to start up in an industry and compete with existing firms.

Black economy: Illegal economic activity which is not officially recorded, usually because the participants wish to avoid paying taxes on the income received from such activity.

Black market: A situation which arises when governments attempt to keep the price of a good below its market equilibrium. Goods are then traded unofficially at relatively high prices. This unofficial market is called a black market.

Bonds: Debt issued by governments or companies in order to raise long-term finance. Holders of the debt receive a fixed amount of interest annually. Government bonds are known as gilts – they are gilt-edged in that there is virtually no risk of government default.

Bridlington Rules: British trades union agreements restricting attempts by one union to persuade workers to switch membership from another union.

Budget line: A graphical representation of the constraint placed upon a household's ability to consume. This constraint exists because of the household's limited income and because of the prices of the goods that it wishes to buy.

Bundesbank: The name given to the German central bank which supervised monetary activity and took decisions on monetary control and interest rates on behalf of the German economy until the mark was replaced by the euro. See also **Central bank**.

Business cycle: This describes the fluctuations in economic activity. Economies often go through periods of relatively high growth and high employment (booms) followed by periods of low or negative growth and high unemployment (slumps or recessions).

Capital: The stock of plant, machinery, buildings and equipment held by a firm, individual or government. They are sometimes referred to as fixed capital to distinguish them from stocks of materials, work in progress and finished goods which are called working capital.

Capital account: See **Balance of payments**.

Capitalism: A form of economic organisation in which the means of production are owned privately rather than by the state. The owners are then free to allocate these resources in whatever way they choose.

Cartel: A group of sellers who agree to act jointly in order to gain monopoly profits. It usually takes the form of agreed output restrictions in order to boost price. See also **OPEC**.

Cash flow: The stream of earnings which a company enjoys or expects to enjoy over time from a given investment.

Central bank: The bankers' bank. Almost always an official institution that acts also as the government's bank. It supervises the monetary activity of an economy and usually has responsibility for monetary control and interest rates. See also **Bank of England** and **Bundesbank**.

***Ceteris paribus*:** 'All other things remaining equal'. It is an assumption that allows us to focus on and explain the behaviour of certain key variables in response to a change in just one or two others.

Change in demand: The result of a change in a variable, other than the price of the good itself, affecting plans to purchase a particular good. It is shown diagrammatically as a shift of the whole demand curve either towards the origin (decrease in demand) or away from the origin (increase in demand).

Change in quantity demanded: A change in the amount of a good that consumers wish to purchase as a result of a change in its price, all other things remaining equal. It is shown diagrammatically by a movement along a demand curve: either upwards (a decrease in quantity demanded) or downwards (an increase in quantity demanded).

Change in quantity supplied: A change in the amount of a good that suppliers will wish to bring to the market as a result of a change in the good's price, all other things remaining equal. It is shown diagrammatically by a movement along a supply curve: either upwards (an increase in quantity supplied) or downwards (a decrease in quantity supplied).

Change in supply: The result of a change in a variable, other than the price of the good itself, affecting plans to supply a particular good. It is shown diagrammatically as a shift in the whole supply curve either upwards to the left (a decrease in supply) or downwards to the right (an increase in supply).

Classical economics: A school of thought which believes that free markets best allocate scarce resources and that free markets will also ensure full employment of such resources. Modern developments in elaborating these concepts are sometimes called neoclassical economics. See also **Neoclassical economics**.

Closed economy: An economy in which there is no foreign trade sector, that is there are neither exports nor imports.

Closed shop: A situation in which only those belonging to a trade union can be employed in a particular firm. Employment in the firm is closed to any non-union worker.

Cohesion fund: A fund established by the countries of the European Union and used to give financial support to relatively poor areas and countries in order to limit the differences in income levels between rich and poor areas.

Competition commission: The body responsible for seeing that UK industries remain competitive. See Monopolies and Mergers Commission.

Comparative advantage: A country has a comparative advantage in the production of a good if it has a lower opportunity cost in producing the good than other countries. A country may have an absolute disadvantage in all commodities but still enjoy a comparative advantage in one good. See also **Absolute advantage**.

Complements: Two goods are complements if their cross-price elasticity of demand is positive. So if a fall in the price of petrol increases the quantity of cars demanded, *ceteris paribus*, then we can say that cars and petrol are complements.

Concentration: A measure of the extent to which market power resides in the hands of a few suppliers. The proportion of an industry's output in the hands of the largest, say, four firms is the four-firm concentration ratio.

Concentration ratio: See **Concentration**.

Constant prices: The effect of inflation has been removed. Data are given at constant prices when they are shown as if the purchasing power of money had remained constant.

Consumer durables: Products bought by households and whose benefits are expected to last over a number of years. They include washing machines, furniture and carpets.

Consumers' expenditure: The purchase of new goods and services by households.

Consumer sovereignty: The idea that consumers dictate the pattern of resource allocation by their decisions to purchase. Producers respond to consumers' expenditure plans by increasing output where demand is rising and reducing it where demand is falling.

Consumer surplus: The value of consumption of goods and services to consumers in excess of the price they have to pay to acquire them.

Consumption function: The relationship between the amount that households plan to consume and their real disposable income.

Consumption goods: Products bought by households, the benefits of which are used up in a short time. Examples are food and washing powder.

Contestability: The contestability of a market is a measure of the ease with which new firms can enter and leave it, usually expressed in terms of the cost of entry and exit. A perfectly contestable market is one in which entry and exit are both costless.

Convergence criteria: The conditions that each country of the European Union has to meet if it wishes to enter into a common currency agreement. The criteria relate to exchange rate stability, inflation performance and government debt burden.

Cost efficiency: This is achieved when a firm produces a given level of output at the minimum cost possible given the state of technology and input prices.

Cross elasticity of demand: This measures the responsiveness of the demand for one good when the price of another changes, *ceteris paribus*. It is the proportionate change in quantity of good A demanded divided by the proportionate change in the price of good B.

Crowding out: The reduction in private sector expenditure, especially investment, which occurs as a result of the expansion of public sector expenditure.

Current account: See **Balance of payments**.

Customs union: An arrangement among a group of countries whereby there are no trade restrictions between them and where there is an agreed common external trade barrier restricting the import of goods from outside the group.

Cyclical unemployment: Unemployment of resources, especially labour, that results from a fall in aggregate demand as a result of the operation of the business cycle. See also **Business cycle**.

Deflation: A fall in the general level of prices. Alternatively expressed, it is a rise in the value of money.

Deflationary gap: A shortfall in the volume of aggregate demand which would be necessary to secure a full employment level of national output (income).

Deindustrialisation: The term used to refer to the process by which the proportion of national output accounted for by the manufacturing sector has declined in recent years. This process has taken place in many advanced nations but has been especially noticeable in Britain.

Demand curve: A graphical representation of the relationship which exists at any one time between plans to purchase a good or service and its price, *ceteris paribus*.

Demand-deficient unemployment: The unemployment of resources, especially labour, which results from an insufficient level of aggregate demand in the economy.

Demand management: The manipulation by government of the level of economic activity in order to achieve desired objectives such as a stable price level or full employment.

Depreciation: A fall in the value of an asset. It may refer to the decline in value of a country's physical capital stock as a result of wear and tear on machinery etc. It can also refer to the fall in the value of a country's currency relative to the currency of other countries under a floating exchange rate system. A rise in the value of the country's currency is referred to as its appreciation. See also **Devaluation**.

Deregulation: The opening of an industry to market forces by removing state controls and regulations.

Devaluation: The decline in the external value of a country's currency which occurs under a fixed exchange rate system if the government declares that a new, lower external value of the currency will now be fixed.

Diminishing returns: This is a short-run concept. As more of a variable factor is added to a given quantity of the fixed factor, beyond some point the extra output produced by a small addition of the variable factor will, *ceteris paribus*, get smaller.

Direct taxation: A tax imposed directly upon any factor income. Examples are income tax and profits tax.

Diseconomies of scale: As output is increased in the long run, beyond some point unit costs may rise. Those factors which may cause such a rise, such as the bureaucracy of large firms, are called diseconomies of scale.

Disposable income: The level of income available to households after the deduction of income tax and National Insurance contributions.

Distribution of income: The way in which the level of a country's total household income is distributed among its citizens.

Dividends: The payment received by shareholders from the profits made by firms.

Dumping: The procedure of selling goods in foreign markets at less than their cost of manufacture.

Economic rent: The income earned by a factor of production in excess of its transfer earnings. Alternatively expressed, the income earned over and above the amount required to cover the factor's opportunity cost. See also **Transfer earnings**.

Economies of scale: Those factors which cause average cost of production to fall as output is increased in the long run.

Efficiency: Efficiency is achieved when resources are being used in an optimal way. There are several aspects to efficiency; principally they are technical, cost and allocative efficiency. See also **Technical efficiency**, **Cost efficiency**, **Allocative efficiency**.

Elasticity of demand: See **Own-price elasticity of demand** and **Cross elasticity of demand**.

Elasticity of supply: The extent to which suppliers' plans to supply output to the market are sensitive to changes in the price of the commodity, *ceteris paribus*. Defined as proportionate change in quantity supplied divided by the proportionate change in the price which caused it.

Entry barriers: See **Barriers to entry**.

Equation of exchange: The volume of money (M) multiplied by the average number of times that a unit of that money changes hands in the course of the year (V) must, by definition, equal the price level (P) multiplied by the real volume of output (Q). $MV = PQ$ where PQ is gross domestic product. Also known as the *Fisher equation*.

Equilibrium: A state of rest. A state where there is no internal force for change. For example, in the market for a product, if quantity supplied is equal to quantity demanded we have an equilibrium price.

Equities: Ordinary shares in companies.

Equity: In economics equity refers to the distribution of income. Most economists believe that there is no objective way of determining what is a just distribution.

European Central Bank: The European Bank responsible for monetary control and interest rates within the euro zone.

Exchange rate: The price of a country's currency expressed in terms of other currencies.

Exchange rate mechanism (ERM): A system in which each member state of the European Union can agree to limit the extent of its currency fluctuations against other members' currencies within the mechanism. Most countries of the EU are members of the ERM.

Excludability: A feature of most goods which enables suppliers to exclude people from the benefit of consumption unless they pay for those benefits. One feature of public goods such as streetlighting is their non-excludability.

External economies of scale: The lowering of firms' long-run average cost curves as a result of the expansion of an industry's output. Internal economies of scale are a function of a firm's output, shown by a movement down along its unit cost curve. External economies are a function of an industry's output, shown by the downward shift of each firm's unit cost curve.

Externalities: The costs or benefits accruing to parties external to an exchange. These, in the absence of government policy, will not be reflected in market prices.

Factor cost: Valuation in terms of the payments made to factors of production for services rendered in producing output. GNP at factor cost is the value of output net of indirect taxes and subsidies. Such taxes and subsidies distort the relationship between market prices and the factor costs of producing the output. See also **Factors of production**.

Factors of production: The resources used to produce output, sometimes referred to as inputs into the production process.

Final goods: Goods sold to consumers. Goods sold to other firms are called *intermediate goods*.

Fiscal policy: Government policy which involves changes in either the level of its expenditure or the level of its income. Sometimes called *budgetary policy*.

Fisher equation: See **Equation of exchange**.

Fixed capital: See **Capital**.

Fixed costs: A short-run concept. Those costs which do not vary when output changes.

Fixed exchange rate: The external value of a country's currency is set at a predetermined level by government and is held at that fixed rate by interest rate policy and/or by government buying and selling of currency.

Foreign exchange market: Where dealers engage in the buying and selling of international currencies.

Foreign reserves: Stocks of gold and convertible currency held by central banks.

Free good: A good whose price is zero because at current levels of consumption the opportunity cost of its production is zero; for example, air.

Free-rider: Someone who chooses not to offer to purchase a public good because he/she thinks that his/her decision will not reduce the amount of it available for his/her consumption. See also **Public goods**.

Free trade: International exchange of goods and services unconstrained by such restrictions as tariffs or quotas.

Frictional unemployment: Unemployment of labour arising from a mismatch between the kinds of job which are in demand and the kinds of labour service being offered for sale.

Full cost pricing: The setting of price by firms arrived at by calculating the average cost of production including all overhead costs then adding on a percentage amount for profit.

GATT: General Agreement on Tariffs and Trade. An organisation supported by most governments, which sought to reduce, by negotiation, tariff and quota restrictions on international trade. It has now been replaced by the World Trade Organization.

GDFCF: Gross domestic fixed capital formation. The value of the expenditure on plant, machinery and equipment during the course of the year without making allowance for the reduction in the value of the existing capital stock.

Gilts: See **Bonds**.

Gross domestic expenditure: Expenditure on all the output produced within the borders of the economy within a year before allowance for the depreciation of the capital stock. Subtracting depreciation gives net domestic expenditure.

Gross domestic income: The value of all incomes earned within the borders of the economy within a year, before the deduction of depreciation of the capital stock. Subtracting depreciation gives net domestic income.

Gross domestic product: The value of all the output produced within the borders of the economy within a year before allowance for the depreciation of capital stock. Subtracting depreciation gives net domestic product.

Gross national expenditure: Gross domestic expenditure plus net property income from abroad. See also **Gross domestic product** and **Net property income from abroad**.

Gross national income: Gross domestic income plus net property income from abroad. See also **Gross domestic income** and **Net property income from abroad**.

Gross national product: Gross domestic product plus net property income from abroad. See also **Gross domestic product** and **Net property income from abroad**.

Gross present value: See **Net present value**.

Growth and stability pact: An agreement between countries in the euro zone to limit the size of government budget deficits.

Gutmann effect: That increase in tax revenues as a result of a cut in direct tax rates which occurs because people no longer feel that it is worth the risk of not declaring taxable earnings.

Human capital: The stock of skill, knowledge and experience in people as a result of having invested in their training and education.

Imports: Goods and services produced abroad but purchased by this country.

Income distribution: See **Distribution of income**.

Income effect: When a price change causes a change in the consumption of a good, part of that consumption change is due to a relative price change (the substitution effect). However, part of the consumption change has been brought about by the resulting change in real income. That part of the consumption change which has resulted from the real income change we call the income effect. See also **Substitution effect**.

Income elasticity of demand: The responsiveness of quantity demanded to changes in real income, *ceteris paribus*. Defined as proportionate change in quantity demanded divided by the proportionate change in real income which caused it.

Indifference curve: The locus of points on a graph showing all of the combinations of goods which yield a consumer the same level of utility.

Indirect tax: A tax not imposed directly upon factor incomes but on goods or services which consumers purchase. Value added tax is an example.

Induced demand: The change in aggregate demand brought about by a change in the level of national income.

Infant industry: An industry in the early stages of its development, often given government assistance until it has matured sufficiently to withstand foreign competition without such help.

Inferior good: A good the consumption of which declines as consumer real income increases. Its income elasticity of demand is negative.

Inflation: A rise in an index of retail prices. Alternatively, it can be defined as a fall in the purchasing power of money.

Inflationary gap: The extent to which planned aggregate demand exceeds national output at the full employment level of income.

Injections: Expenditures on output other than those arising from households. They are government, investment and export expenditures.

Insider trading: Dealing in shares on the basis of information not available to the public.

Interest: Payment to capital owners for the opportunity to use such capital resources now rather than in the future.

Intermediate goods: See **Final goods**.

Internal rate of return: The rate at which a cash flow will need to be discounted to reduce its value to that which equals the project's capital cost.

Inventories: Stocks of goods.

Investment: Expenditure on plant, machinery and building and new housing, in order to produce goods and services for future consumption. Additions to the capital stock, whether replacing worn out stock or net additions to it.

Invisible trade: Exports and imports of services such as shipping insurance and banking services.

Isocost curve: A graphical construction showing all the combinations of resources that firms can just afford to purchase for a given level of expenditure.

Isoquant: The locus of points on a graph showing all the combinations of resources that are just capable of producing a given level of output.

J-curve: A possible reaction of a country's balance of trade to a fall in the value of its currency. The trade balance worsens at first then improves giving the shape of a J if the trade balance is plotted against time.

Keynesian economics: The economics of those who follow the ideas of John Maynard Keynes who rejected the classical view that markets would always adjust to eliminate unemployment. In the Keynesian view, unemployment equilibrium is a possibility.

Kinked demand: A demand curve which some economists believe to be that which faces oligopolists. Demand is relatively elastic above the existing price and relatively inelastic below it.

Laffer curve: A graphical construction showing the relationship between tax rates and revenue raised by taxation.

Law of comparative advantage: This states that a country will tend to specialise in the production of goods in which it has a comparative advantage, exporting some of those goods in order to finance the imports of goods in which it has a comparative disadvantage. See also **Comparative advantage**.

Leakages: See **Withdrawals**.

Liquidity preference: The desire to hold wealth in a form easily converted to cash.

Long run: The period of time in which firms can vary the level of all factors of production employed.

Lorenz curve: A graphical construction showing the distribution of income between households.

Macroeconomics: The branch of economics which studies economy-wide aggregate data such as national output or unemployment.

Marginal cost pricing: The setting of price by equating marginal cost with the quantity demanded.

Marginal physical product: The change in the number of units of total output arising from the addition of one unit of labour input, all other input levels remaining constant.

Marginal private cost: The extra cost borne by a firm if it increases its own output by one unit. In the absence of externalities it will be equal to marginal social cost. See also **Marginal social cost**.

Marginal propensity to consume: The proportion of any change in household income spent on goods and services. Calculated as change in consumption divided by change income.

Marginal propensity to save: The proportion of any change in household income not spent on goods and services but saved. Calculated as change in saving divided by change in income.

Marginal propensity to withdraw: The proportion of any change in household income not spent on domestic consumption. Consumers do not spend all of their additional in income, since some of that increase is taxed, some saved and some spent on imports.

Marginal revenue: The change in total revenue received by a firm as a result of a one unit change in its output.

Marginal social cost: The cost to society which results when a firm increases its output by one unit. The marginal social cost equals the marginal private cost plus any marginal external cost or less any marginal external benefit. See also **Marginal private cost** and **External cost**.

Marginal tax rate: The proportion of any additional income earned which is taken in taxation by government.

Marginal utility: The change in total satisfaction arising from a one unit increase in the consumption of a good, the consumption of all other goods remaining equal.

Market: Any arrangement which makes possible the buying and selling of goods, services or inputs.

Market clearing price: The price at which the quantity that consumers wish to purchase is equal to the quantity that suppliers wish to sell.

Market economy: An economy in which resources are privately owned and allocated by prices which are free to change in response to changes in supply and/or demand.

Menu costs: One of the costs to society of inflation. It refers to the costs of needing to adjust menus, price lists, etc. more frequently in times of inflation since absolute prices are rising even if relative prices stay constant.

Merger: The amalgamation of two (or more) firms into a single organisation.

Merit goods: Goods which the government believes are not provided in optimal quantities by the market because of inadequate consumer information or because of an uneven distribution of income. An example would be education.

Microeconomics: The branch of economics which studies individual markets rather than broad aggregate data.

Minimum efficient scale: The smallest level of output that will enable a firm to minimise its long-run average cost of production.

Mixed economy: An economy in which some resources are privately owned and respond to market signals but other resources are owned by the state.

Models: Simplified representations of the economy, or a part of it, enabling clearer understanding and predictions of future behaviour.

Monetarism: The view that macroeconomic problems such as growth and unemployment are best corrected by markets and that inflation is caused solely by excessive growth of the money supply.

Monetary Policy Committee (MPC): The name of the group at the Bank of England that decides upon interest rates.

Monetary union: A situation in which two or more countries' governments agree to the circulation of a common currency.

Money: That which is generally accepted as a means of exchanging goods and services and as a means of settling debt.

Money supply: The amount of money in circulation at any one time. There are various definitions depending upon how liquid an asset needs to be to be called money.

Monopolies and Mergers Commission: A government body which examined (a) the implications of proposed mergers and takeovers and (b) any industries referred to it where there are potential monopoly abuses. It is now called the Competition Commission.

Monopolistic competition: A market structure which comprises many firms producing a similar but differentiated product and in which there are no significant barriers to the entry of new firms.

Monopoly: A market structure where one firm produces all of the industry's output.

Monopsony: A market structure in which there is only one buyer.

Moral hazard: The situation in which an insuring organisation finds itself, where the insured has now less financial incentive to behave cautiously.

Multiplier: The relationship between a change in autonomous demand and the resulting change in real national income. If a rise in autonomous demand of £1 causes national income to increase by £3, the multiplier is 3.

National debt: The total amount owed by the government, to either UK or foreign citizens and institutions. The PSBR in any one year is the extent to which the national debt has changed. See also **Public sector borrowing requirement**.

Natural monopoly: A market structure where economies of scale are present over such a large level of output that total costs of production of the industry would be minimised if there were only one firm.

Natural rate of unemployment: The level of unemployment of labour that exists because some choose not to work at the present wage rate.

Neoclassical economics: Developments from the classical school of economics. Macro-economic questions can be resolved by examining markets at the micro level and aggregating such behaviour so as to predict macro variables.

Net domestic expenditure: See **Gross domestic expenditure**.

Net domestic income: See **Gross domestic income**.

Net domestic product: See **Gross domestic product**.

Net national expenditure: Gross national expenditure less depreciation. See also **Gross national expenditure**.

Net national income: Gross national income less depreciation. See also **Gross national income**.

Net national product: Gross national product less depreciation. See also **Gross national product**.

Net present value (NPV): The future stream of earnings from a project is discounted to give its present worth. This is its gross present value, GPV. GPV less the capital cost gives NPV.

Net property income from abroad: The inflow from overseas of profits, dividends and interest paid on capital owned abroad less the outflow of profits, dividends and interest paid on capital located in this country but owned by foreign individuals or organisations.

Nominal interest rate: The rate of interest which takes no account of the inflation rate.

Non-accelerating inflation rate of unemployment (NAIRU): The level of unemployment which is consistent with a stable price level.

Non-renewable resources: Resources which, once used up, cannot be replaced. Examples would be oil and natural gas stocks.

Non-rival goods: Goods for which consumers are not rivals for their consumption. For example, if one person watches the weather forecast, it does not prevent others from watching it also. See also **Public goods**.

Normal profit: The income to a firm which is just sufficient to cover the opportunity cost of its resources. In other words it is just enough income to make the firm willing to keep its resources in their present use.

Normative economics: The branch of economics dealing with value judgements. See also **Value judgement**.

Office of Fair Trading: A government body responsible for monitoring and investigating trading activities and for identifying potential monopoly power abuse, which it can then refer to the Monopolies and Mergers Commission for more detailed investigation.

Oligopoly: A market structure in which there are only a few large suppliers of a product and usually substantial entry barriers.

OPEC: The Organization of Petroleum Exporting Countries. A group of major oil-exporting countries organised as a cartel, which seeks to operate a system of voluntary quotas to restrict oil supply and hence influence oil prices. See also **Cartel**.

Open economy: An economy in which there is a foreign trade sector, i.e. there are exports and imports.

Open market operations: Purchase or sale of securities by a central bank in order to increase or reduce the money supply.

Opportunity cost: The cost of meeting a want expressed in terms of the output of the next most desired alternative which has to be forgone.

Opportunity cost curve: A graphical representation of the alternative possible combinations of output available to a society at any one time assuming productive efficiency and full employment. Also called a *production possibility curve/frontier.*

Output effect: When the price of a resource falls, firms will use more of that resource and less of the relatively expensive one(s). This is the substitution effect. However, the lower costs attributable to the fall in the resource price will cause output to increase. This increased output is called the output effect of the change in the resource price.

Own-price elasticity of demand: The sensitivity of demand for a good to changes in its price. Calculated as proportionate change in quantity of good A demanded divided by the proportionate change in price of good A.

Paradox of thrift: This describes the situation in which household decisions to save do not lead to more actual savings. Decisions to save more lower consumption. This reduces output, and therefore income. The resultant lower income level means that actual savings have not risen, even though households intended to save more.

Paradox of value: Some relatively trivial goods, such as diamonds, exchange for a much higher price than more fundamentally important goods, such as bread.

Pareto optimality: A Pareto-optimal state is one in which it is not possible to improve the welfare of one person without making someone else worse off. A Pareto-optimal improvement is therefore one which makes at least one person better off without making anyone worse off.

Peak-use pricing: Pricing output to reflect changes in demand at certain periods of time such that prices are highest at times of peak demand. Industries using such pricing include electricity, rail travel and telecommunications.

Perfect competition: A theoretical market structure in which there are many firms each of which is too small to influence price and where there are no barriers to exit or entry. Such firms are price-takers in that they must take the price given by the market rather than set their own price.

Phillips curve: A graph showing the relationship between the level of unemployment and the rate of change of money wages (a proxy for inflation).

Planned economy: An economy in which resources are owned by the state and where production decisions are taken on the basis of state planning rather than by a market mechanism.

Positive economics: The branch of economics dealing with statements that are verifiable with reference to evidence rather than with statements that involve value judgements.

Potential output: The level of output that an economy will achieve when it is on its opportunity cost curve.

Poverty line: An arbitrarily defined level of income below which it is felt that people are impoverished, often being unable to take a part in society.

Poverty trap: A situation in which a rise in a person's earned income makes him/her no better off, or even worse off, since the rise triggers a withdrawal of some state income support.

Precautionary demand for money: The desire to hold wealth in a liquid form in order to meet unanticipated expenditures.

Price discrimination: The practice of charging different customers different prices for the same good, made possible by the fact that different customers can be segregated into different markets and have differing elasticities of demand.

Price elasticity of demand: See **Own price elasticity of demand.**

Price-taker: See **Perfect competition.**

Private cost: The cost borne by a firm in producing output. In the absence of externalities it will be equal to social cost. See also **Social cost.**

Privatisation: The process by which state-owned resources are transferred into private ownership.

Production possibility curve: See **Opportunity cost curve.**

Productivity: The output of a good or service per unit of input, usually labour.

Profit: The difference between the revenue received by a firm for selling its output and the cost of producing the output.

Profit maximisation: An assumption of some models of firm behaviour. A firm has a single aim: to produce a price and output which enable it to make the greatest possible profit.

Progressive tax: A tax whereby, as income rises, the proportion of that income paid to the government in taxation rises, i.e. the average tax rate rises as income rises. See **Average tax rate.**

Proportional tax: A tax whereby, as income rises, the proportion of that income paid to the government in taxation stays the same, i.e. the average tax rate does not change as income changes. See **Average tax rate.**

Public goods: Those goods which are non-rival and non-excludable and which are consumed equally by all. If all these features are present it is a pure public good. If one or more but not all are present they are impure public goods. See also **Non-rival goods** and **Excludability.**

Public sector borrowing requirement (PSBR): The amount that the government must borrow in order to finance a deficit when its expenditure is greater than its income.

Public sector debt repayment (PSDR): The extent to which government income exceeds government expenditure. This surplus is the extent to which it can reduce its debt.

Public sector net cash requirement: The new name for the **Public sector borrowing requirement.**

Purchasing power: The amount of goods and services which a given sum of money will buy.

Purchasing power parity theory: The view that two countries' exchange rates are in equilibrium when the domestic purchasing power in each country is equivalent at that exchange rate. If £1 = DM2 and this represents an equilibrium value, then £1 will buy in Britain the same goods that DM2 will purchase in Germany.

Quantity theory of money: A theory based on the equation of exchange. In the long run V, the velocity of circulation will be constant. Hence if changes in Q, real output, can be predicted, an increase in the money supply at the rate at which Q changes will give a constant price level, P. See also **Equation of exchange.**

Quota: A restriction on the number of units of a good which the government will allow to be imported or exported in a given time period.

Rational expectations: A hypothesis that economic agents utilise and assess available data to make rational forecasts of the effects of economic policy changes.

Real interest rate: The nominal money rate of interest minus the inflation rate. It shows the percentage increase in the purchasing power of a sum of money in one year's time for the lender.

Real output: The value of goods and services produced expressed in money whose purchasing power is constant. Inflation over some time period will therefore not by itself suggest that there has been any change in real output.

Real wage rate: The nominal money wage rate deflated by a suitable price index to show the purchasing power of a given wage rate.

Recession: A period of time during which the economy's real output is declining.

Regressive tax: A tax whereby, as income rises, the proportion of that income paid to the government in taxation falls, i.e. the average tax rate falls as income rises.

Relative price: The price of a good expressed in terms of other goods rather than in terms of money.

Resources: See **Factors of production**.

Retail price index (RPI): An important measure of inflation, the retail price index is an index of prices of a representative basket of goods purchased by consumers.

Savings: Income not used for consuming goods and services in the current time period.

Savings ratio: The proportion of consumers' real income devoted to savings. Calculated as total savings divided by total income. See also **Savings**.

Say's law: 'Supply creates its own demand'. The argument is that since output generates the same quantity of income, there can never be a shortage of effective demand for output.

Shoe leather costs: Part of the costs to society associated with inflation. Higher inflation means higher money interest rates encouraging people to hold less cash. They therefore make more trips to banks etc., imposing transaction costs on society.

Shut-down point: The price at which a firm will shut down its operations in the short run because it thereby makes less of a loss than if it continued to produce. This occurs when price is at minimum average variable cost.

Social cost: The cost to society of producing a given volume of output. It is equal to private cost plus any external cost or benefit. See also **Private cost** and **External cost**.

Specific tax: A tax denominated as a particular money amount rather than as a percentage of the commodity's price. See also **Ad valorem tax**.

Speculation: The purchase or sale of a commodity, currency, share, etc., in anticipation of a change in its price.

Speculative demand for money: The desire to hold wealth in a liquid form as part of a decision to profit from expected changes in financial capital assets such as bonds.

Sticky prices: Prices which do not respond quickly and easily to changes in production costs.

Structural budget deficit: The government's budget deficit which would obtain given current fiscal policy if the economy were operating at the level of full employment which is consistent with a stable price level. In other words, it ignores that part of the deficit due to an economy being in recession.

Structural unemployment: Unemployment resulting from changes in the structure of the economy, such as a major fall in demand for an important industry's output.

Subsidies: A payment by government designed to reduce the production cost to a firm of a particular product.

Substitute: A good whose demand increases when the price of another good increases, since consumers regard the two goods as performing a similar function for them. The cross elasticity of demand for the two goods is positive. See also **Cross elasticity of demand**.

Substitution effect: That part of the change in the consumption of a good following a relative price change not caused by the resulting change in real income. See also **Income effect**.

Supernormal profit: See **Abnormal profit**.

Supply curve: A graphical representation of the relationship which exists at any one time between plans to offer a good or service for sale and its price, *ceteris paribus*.

Takeover: The acquisition by company A of a controlling proportion of the shares of company B. If the board of company B resists such an attempt, it is referred to as a hostile takeover bid.

Tariff: A tax on imported goods or services.

Technical efficiency: This is achieved when a firm produces a given level of output such that it cannot do so using less of one resource without using more of another.

Terms of trade: A measurement of the prices of exports relative to the price of imports. Take the index of export prices and divide by the index of import prices, then multiply by 100. If export prices increase relative to import prices then the terms of trade move in our favour. If export prices decrease relative to import prices then the terms of trade move against us.

Thrift: See **Paradox of thrift**.

Total physical product: This is a short-run concept, calculated as the total amount of output produced by a given volume of labour input, holding constant the level of other inputs. The amount is expressed in units of output rather than value.

Total utility: See **Utility**.

Trade cycle: See **Business cycle**.

Trade union: An organisation of workers which, acting as an entity, seeks to secure wage levels and conditions of employment which could not be achieved by workers bargaining individually.

Transaction costs: Those costs which arise as a result of the exchange process, such as time spent negotiating prices and checking that agreements have been adhered to.

Transactions demand for money: The desire to hold wealth in liquid form so as to make possible the purchase of goods and services in the current time period.

Transfer earnings: The minimum payment to a factor of production needed to keep it in its present use, that is an earning which reflects that factor's opportunity cost.

Transfer payment: Income received as a result of income redistribution rather than as a reward for output produced. An example would be student grants.

Transmission mechanism: The process by which changes in the monetary sector of the economy affect the real sector in terms of output changes and alterations to the price level.

Underwriting: The agreement of an organisation such as a merchant bank or insurance company to take on risks in return for an insurance premium, for example guaranteeing that a new share issue will be fully subscribed.

Unit cost: See **Average total cost**.

Unit trusts: Organisations which buy shares on behalf of many small financial investors enabling the transaction costs of purchase and sale to be reduced and spreading the risk of shareholding.

Utility: The ability of a good or service to satisfy wants.

Valuation ratio: The market value of a company (as determined by the current price of its shares multiplied by the number of shares issued) divided by the book value of its assets as recorded in its balance sheet.

Value-added: The value of an industry's sales less the purchase of domestic intermediate goods, less the value of imports.

Value added tax (VAT): A tax on the value added by an industry or firm, expressed as a percentage. It is an example of an ad valorem tax. See also **Value-added** and **Ad valorem tax**.

Value in exchange: The total amount received by a firm or industry from the sale of a commodity. Alternatively viewed, it is the total expenditure by consumers on the commodity.

Value in use: Value in exchange plus consumer surplus. See also **Value in exchange** and **Consumer surplus**.

Variable costs: Those costs which change as a firm's output changes. In the short run they are the costs which are not fixed. In the long run, since no costs are fixed, all costs are variable.

Velocity of circulation: The average number of times that a unit of the money stock changes hands in a year. See also **Equation of exchange**.

Visible trade: Exports and imports of physical goods. The difference in value of such exports and imports is known as the visible trade balance.

Wealth: The stock of assets owned less liabilities owed.

Wealth effect: The change in aggregate demand as a result of a change in consumers' wealth. For example, a fall in house prices makes many people feel less wealthy. They may therefore be less willing to purchase goods and services as a result of feeling poorer.

Withdrawals: That part of households' incomes not spent on domestically produced output. This will be savings, taxes and import expenditures.

Working capital: See **Capital**.

World Trade Organization: See **General Agreement on Tariffs and Trade (GATT)**.

Index

Note: Single page numbers in **bold** indicate glossary definitions. Other bold pages indicate chapters. Countries, organisations and firms mentioned only *once* are *generally* omitted